Readings in Western Civilization

℧ **Vere dignum**

University of Chicago Readings in Western Civilization
John W. Boyer and Julius Kirshner, General Editors

University of Chicago
Readings in Western Civilization

John W. Boyer and Julius Kirshner, General Editors

4
Medieval
Europe

Edited by Julius Kirshner
and Karl F. Morrison

The University of Chicago Press

Chicago and London

Eric Cochrane, 1928–1985

ἀθάνατος μνήμη
Immortal memory

Julius Kirshner is professor of history at the University of Chicago and an editor of the *Journal of Modern History*.

Karl F. Morrison is the Lessing Professor of History and Poetics at Rutgers University. From 1965 to 1984, he was professor of history at the University of Chicago.

The University of Chicago Press, Chicago 60637
The University of Chicago Press, Ltd., London
© 1986 by The University of Chicago
All rights reserved. Published 1986
Printed in the United States of America
97 96 95 94 93   654

Library of Congress Cataloging-in-Publication Data
Main entry under title:

University of Chicago readings in Western civilization.

   Includes bibliographies and indexes.
   Contents: — v. 4. Medieval Europe / edited by
Julius Kirshner and Karl F. Morrison.
   1. Civilization, Occidental—History—Sources.
2. Europe—Civilization—Sources.   I. Boyer, John W.
II. Kirshner, Julius.   III. Title: Readings in
Western Civilization.
CB245.U64   1986   909'.09821   85-16328
ISBN 0-226-06934-6 (v. 1)
ISBN 0-226-06935-4 (pbk. : v. 1)

ISBN 0-226-06942-7 (v. 4)
ISBN 0-226-06943-5 (pbk. : v. 4)

Contents

Series Editors' Foreword

This series is the result of almost four decades of teaching the History of Western Civilization course at the College of the University of Chicago. The course was founded in its present form in the late 1940s by a group of young historians at Chicago, including William H. McNeill, Christian Mackauer, and Sylvia Thrupp, and has been sustained during the past twenty-five years by the distinguished teaching of Eric Cochrane, Hanna H. Gray, Charles M. Gray, and Karl J. Weintraub. In the beginning it served as a counterpoint to the antihistorical and positivistic thrust of the general education curriculum in the social sciences in the Hutchins College. Western Civilization has since been incorporated as a year-long course into different parts of the College program, from the first to the last year. It now forms part of the general intercivilizational requirement for sophomores and juniors. It is still taught, as it has been almost constantly since its inception, in discussion groups ranging from twenty to thirty students.

Although both the readings and the instructors of the course have changed over the years, its purpose has remained the same. It seeks not to provide students with morsels of Western culture, nor to nourish their moral and aesthetic sensitivities, and much less to attract recruits for the history profession. Its purpose instead is to raise a whole set of complex conceptual questions regarding the nature of time and change and the intended and unintended consequences of human action and consciousness. Students in this course learn to analyze past events and ideas by rigorously examining a variety of texts. This is in contrast to parallel courses in the social sciences, which teach students to deploy synchronic and quantitative techniques in analyzing society, usually without reference to historical context or process.

Ours is a history course that aims not at imparting relevant facts or exotic ideas but at providing students with the critical tools by which to analyze texts produced in the distant or near past. It also serves a related purpose: to familiarize students with major epochs of that Western historical tradition to which most of them, albeit at times unknowingly, are heirs.

The major curricular vehicle of the course is the *Readings in Western Civilization*, a nine-volume series of primary sources in translation, beginning with Periclean Athens and concluding with Europe in the twentieth century. The series is not meant to be a comprehensive survey of Western history. Rather, in each volume, we provide a large number of documents on specific themes in the belief that depth, not breadth, is the surest antidote to superficiality. The very extensiveness of the documentation in each volume allows for a variety of approaches to the same theme. At the same time the concentrated focus of individual volumes makes it possible for them to serve as source readings in more advanced and specialized courses.

Many people contributed to the publication of these volumes. The enthusiastic collaboration and labors of the members of the Western Civilization staff made it possible for these *Readings* to be published. We thank Barbara Boyer for providing superb editorial direction to the project and Mary Van Steenbergh for her dedication in creating beautifully text-edited manuscripts. Steven Wheatley's advice in procuring funding for this project was invaluable. Members of the University of Chicago Press have given their unstinting support and guidance. We also appreciate the confidence and support accorded by Donald N. Levine, the Dean of the College at the University of Chicago. Above all, we are deeply grateful for the extraordinary dedication, energy, and erudition which our colleague and current chairperson of the course, Eric Cochrane, has contributed to the *Readings in Western Civilization*.

We are grateful to the National Endowment for the Humanities for providing generous funding for the preparation and publication of the volumes.

John W. Boyer and Julius Kirshner

General Introduction

The documents in this collection range in date from the sixth to the fourteenth centuries. With one exception, they derive from the areas now known as the British Isles, France, Germany, and Italy (including the special category of papal documents). The collection has been designed for use in a general course on the history of Western civilization. Consequently, it has a wider scope than a collection intended for a specialized course, say, in the history of the Church, of philosophy, or of constitutions. Moreover, the subject is Latin Christendom, excluding Byzantium and Islam. The editors have sought to elucidate some pivotal subjects, rather than to portray the immense panorama of nearly a millennium in European history. In their choice of topics and in their principles of selection and exclusion, they have conformed with the objectives of the series in which this volume appears.

Since one object of the series is to enlarge the range of materials for classroom discussion, the editors have decided that there was no need to duplicate here many texts that are already available elsewhere.

Though they differ from each other in emphasis and approach, the editors of the present volume share some points of view that have guided their work, and that may distinguish this collection from others in the series. It is as well to state them at the outset. They believe that it is possible, within broad outlines, to identify a complex narrative pattern in the history of Europe between the sixth and the fourteenth centuries. The chronological poles of this period are (a) the beginning of social reconstruction after the political disintegration of the Roman Empire, and (b) the decay of the order that began to emerge in the sixth century and reached its fullest development in the thirteenth century. The dissolution of the fourteenth century was followed by another period of reconstitution, extending from the sixteenth to the nineteenth centuries, which is the subject of succeeding volumes in the series. If a family, institution, or society is to survive a catastrophe, it has to regroup and reform itself. In that sense, catastrophe integrates as well as disrupts. It brings forth such life as there may be in the ashes. Thus, the editors see a recurrent pattern of disintegration and reconstitution, requiring centuries to complete, revealed in these documents.

The editors have been guided also by a second assumption: namely, that European culture is defined by its inner stresses and disharmonies, as well as by its points of concord. The movements of reconstitution actually crystallize groups and institutions that are poised in continuous struggle. Thus, the inner stresses that brought about the disintegration of the thirteenth and fourteenth centuries were present almost from the beginning, in the sixth century. The difference was that, in the thirteenth and fourteenth centuries, the crystallization of antagonisms reached such a magnitude that the entire social fabric had to be transformed.

Finally, we have assumed that the inner stresses of European society in the period under review owed much to Christian militance. The confrontation of the world's hatred, the admonition to triumph over the world by converting it, so dominant in the Gospel, was taken up and institutionalized in monasticism, and, from monasticism, it penetrated the whole of European culture. It appeared most clearly in the long and intricate process called the conversion of Europe, which had an extension, after the fifteenth century, in the spread of Christian missions to every continent, often in the characteristic guise of imperialism. Christian militance in the period covered by this volume was all the more intense because Latin Christendom itself was beset by encircling enemies, first by pagans in Europe, and later by Islam. The Crusades expressed collective aggressiveness against this hostile encirclement.

The editors believe that many lines of inquiry lead from these three assumptions, and that the following documents indicate some of their principal directions.

Conforming with the general intent of this series, the editors have attempted to provide an array of topics and documents that will serve a variety of needs. In the course on the history of Western civilization at the University of Chicago, for which the present volume has been prepared, experimentation with different topics and documents is the rule. Thus, they submit this collection, not as a closed and complete course of study, but as materials that can be used in very different contexts.

For background and guidance concerning specific topics, the following highly selective list of books can be recommended.

Select Bibliography

General Works

R. R. Bolgar. *The Classical Heritage and Its Beneficiaries from the Caro-lingian Age to the End of the Renaissance*. New York: Harper, 1964.

Robert Folz. *The Concept of Empire in Western Europe from the Fifth to the Fourteenth Century*. Trans. Sheila Ann Ogilvie. New York: Harper, 1969.

Jean Leclercq et al. *The Spirituality of the Middle Ages*. New York: Sea-bury, 1982. (*The History of Christian Spirituality*, vol. 2.)

John H. Mundy. *Europe in the High Middle Ages, 1150–1309*. London: Longman, 1973.

N. J. G. Pounds. *An Historical Geography of Europe, 450 B.C.–A.D. 1300*. Cambridge: Cambridge University Press, 1973.

R. W. Southern. *The Making of the Middle Ages*. New Haven: Yale, 1953.

Joseph R. Strayer. *On the Medieval Origins of the Modern State*. Prince-ton: Princeton University Press, 1970.

Brian Tierney. *Religion, Law, and the Growth of Constitutional Thought, 1150–1650*. New York: Cambridge University Press, 1982.

Religion and Empire

Rosamond McKitterick. *The Frankish Kingdoms under the Carolingians, 751–989*. London: Longman, 1983.

Lucien Musset. *The Germanic Invasions: The Making of Europe, A.D. 400–600*. Trans. Edward and Columba James. University Park, Pa.: Pennsylvania State University Press, 1975.

The Investiture Conflict

Karl F. Morrison. *Tradition and Authority in the Western Church, ca. 300–1140*. Princeton: Princeton University Press, 1969.

Gerd Tellenbach. *Church, State and Christian Society at the Time of the Investiture Conflict*. Trans. R. F. Bennett. New York: Harper, 1970.

Twelfth-Century Renaissance

Robert L. Benson and Giles Constable, eds. *Renaissance and Renewal in the Twelfth Century*. Cambridge, Mass.: Harvard University Press, 1982.

Charles Homer Haskins. *The Renaissance of the Twelfth Century*. Cambridge, Mass.: Harvard University Press, 1927.

Papal Monarchy and Its Critics

Robert Ian Moore. *Origins of European Dissent*. London: Allen Lane, 1977.
Albert C. Shannon. *The Popes and Heresy in the Thirteenth Century*. Villanova, Pa.: Augustinian Press, 1949.

Storm over the Papacy

Malcolm Lambert. *Medieval Heresy: Popular Movements from Bogomil to Hus*. London: Edward Arnold, 1977.
Heiko A. Oberman. *The Harvest of Medieval Theology*, 2d ed. Grand Rapids: Eerdmans, 1967.

1
Foundations and Developments

The texts in this section concern two moments in the general story of the post-Roman reconstitution of Europe. The first is the earliest stages, the formation of "the first Europe"; the second is the period when the contours of Europe, having been formed, were drawn with increasing clarity. In the first period (between the sixth and the tenth centuries), monastic institutions played a primary role. The monastery was the beneficiary and the depository of what was left of Roman culture. Monasticism was driven by a burning vigilance and zeal for the conversion of non-Christian peoples inside and outside the former Roman territories, and this fervor to overcome the world by converting it became a major impulse of cultural reconstruction. Monasticism preserved the language, and some books, ideals, and political institutions of the late Antique world. By its work of Christianization, it intruded itself as an alien element in a Germanic world, but it also introduced two fateful patterns: the pattern of a new political order, which proved basic to the reconstitution of Europe, and the countervailing pattern of stresses within that order, stresses that insured the repetition of a cycle of collapse and renewal.

In the first subtopic of this section, particular focus is on monasticism's role in exchanges between England and the Continent. A long series of intermittent, random encounters accelerated in time and contributed to the formation of the Carolingian Empire, "the first Europe." However, the forces of coalescence also imparted to the new institutions characteristic frictions that quickly brought them down. A new recovery, from a higher level, began.

In the second and third subtopics of this section, the reconstitution has been accomplished. The texts included here derive from the eleventh, twelfth, and thirteenth centuries, and they concern the substrata of social cohesion. Later texts in this volume portray the glittering heights of imperial and papal diplomacy. Here, a picture emerges of frictions among classes and regions, complex and intricate tensions, at the level of agricultural and commercial production, society's base.

Religion and Empire

The following texts elucidate the slow, unplanned reconstitution of Europe by people who were pursuing quite diverse goals. The main actors are kings and monks; the goal that united them was the conversion of Europe to Christianity.

The period covered by these texts is ca. 590–900. They derive from Frankish Gaul, Anglo-Saxon England, the Rhine valley, Italy, and a network of distant areas into which western Europeans found their ways. Ironically, each contribution to cultural unity, from near or far, carried with it its own disintegrative tension.

Pope Gregory I (590–604) was the last of the four great Latin Fathers. (The others were Ambrose, Augustine of Hippo, and Jerome.) Born into the highest circles of the Roman aristocracy and launched on a conventional career in politics, he experienced a sudden conversion to the monastic life. Withstanding barbarian invaders of Italy and negotiating with the Byzantine emperors, who still claimed dominance over Rome, Gregory yet had time and energy to promote the work of conversion by sending Augustine, later archbishop of Canterbury, to preach to the Anglo-Saxons, and to attend to the spiritual vigor of the Church. One of Gregory of Tours' clergy was present at the consecration of Gregory I as pope, and took back to the distant city of Tours an account of his character and of the events leading up to his election. In the portion of his *Dialogues* reproduced below (document 1), Gregory looked back to his spiritual forefather, Saint Benedict of Nursia (ca. 480–ca. 547), founder of the Benedictine order of monks, and of its great center, the monastery of Monte Cassino. The text reveals the fiery ardor of monasticism, and also the conflicts that existed within monasticism itself.

The Venerable Bede (672/73–735) was born in Northumbria, and his parents presented him as an oblate, at the age of seven, to the monastery of Saint Peter, at Wearmouth. Benedict Biscop (ca. 628–689/90), the founder of Saint Peter's, was still abbot at that time, and he became Bede's patron. Benedict himself made five journeys to Rome, and took great pains to enrich his monastery with the best that he could find on the Continent or in England of books and objects of art, as well as of spiritual discipline. Before 685, Benedict sent Bede to his new foundation, the monastery of Saint Paul, at Jarrow, not far from Wearmouth, and it appears that, with two minor exceptions, Bede spent his entire life in one or the other of these monasteries. And yet, the extraordinary breadth of his early education is evident in the many works that he wrote as a man. He wrote on numerous technical subjects, such as orthography and the reckoning of time; he wrote scriptural commentaries; and, above all, he wrote his *History of the English Church and People*. Though his physical movements were restricted to a small area, the network of his communications was large. It extended to the royal court of Northumbria, to many monasteries, and to Rome, where letters were transcribed for inclusion in his *History*. His influence was also extensive. As a writer, he achieved a standing almost equivalent with that of the early Church Fathers. As a teacher, he guided the formation of Archbishop Egbert of York, who, in turn, taught Alcuin, one of the framers of the Carolingian Renaissance. The excerpt below (document 2) comes from one of Bede's more intimate works, the *Lives of the Abbots of Wearmouth and Jarrow* (completed about 725). Writing about his own monastic home, and his own friends, Bede yet portrays the divergence in a monastery between ideal and reality.

Adamnan (ca. 628–704) belonged to the Celtic wing of Christianity, so mistrusted and despised by Bede. Born in Ireland, he became abbot of Iona (679). In Northumbria, he personally rejected Celtic practices that monks obedient to Rome had condemned, but he was unable to impose Roman practices on his own monastery. He made extensive travels in an attempt to win adherence to Roman norms. His major writing is a biography of Saint Columba (about 521–597), the great Irish missionary who founded Iona. His transcription of the monk Arculf's account of travels through the Near East (document 3) illustrates the contact with alien societies and cultures that was sustained in the seventh century, a vestige of the ecumenical character of the Roman Empire. It is to be compared with Aetheria's account of her travels, late in the fourth century, excerpts from which appear in volume 3 of this series.

Einhard (about 770–840), in his *Life of Charlemagne* (document 4), represents the culmination of the cultural reconstitution that had begun two centuries earlier. The friend and advisor of Charlemagne, Einhard memorialized this fleeting moment of glory in the *Life*, one of the earliest biographies of a layman written in postclassical Europe. Einhard himself was a gifted artist, as well as a writer, politician, and landed magnate. Steeped in the nostalgia for the Christian Roman Empire that was characteristic of the Carolingian Renaissance, Einhard portrayed the greatness of his hero in terms borrowed from Suetonius's *Life of Augustus*. He unfolded the vast scope of the Frankish world, extending as far afield as Byzantium, Baghdad, Jerusalem, and North Africa. But the shadows were already deepening. Einhard wrote his biography under Charlemagne's son and successor, Louis the Pious (814–840), even as the order that had begun to decay under Charlemagne irreparably crumbled under the double impact of civil war and foreign attacks.

The *Capitulare de villis* (807) (document 5) is an inventory of royal estates, commanded by Charlemagne. It belongs to a kind of legislation, the capitularies, or decrees, made up of separate chapters (*capitula*), some of which may be very full and detailed, and others of which may be only a few key words. It is not known whether the *Capitulare de villis*, concerning royal estates as it does, represents a typical state of affairs. It is not even known whether this, or any other capitulary, was enforced, or was enforceable, by local officials.

Regino was abbot of the monastery of Prüm (from 892 to 899), which he may have seen burned by the Vikings in 882. After his abbacy, he moved to the former home of Gregory of Tours and, much later, of Alcuin, the monastery of Saint Martin of Tours, and, finally, to the monastery of Saint Maximin, in Trier, where he died (915). His history (document 6) is a major source of information about the Carolingian Empire in the late ninth century, and especially about the fragmentation of its remnants after the death of the Emperor Charles the Fat (888). Lamenting the decadence of collective life and fearing total ruin, Regino praised the sterner virtues, in which his kings were conspicuously lacking. His historical writings, his literary style, his work on music theory, and his own compilation of liturgical antiphons and responses demonstrate that the learning and the desire for learning that characterized the Carolingian Renaissance were still ardent. But the tantalizing gulf between desire and fulfilment is evident in Regino's sense of steady retreat before the disintegrative forces of the Vikings and of chronic internal dissent.

---

1. Gregory I's Account of Benedict's Life (ca. 600)

How a Broken Cleaning-Vessel Was Repaired

When he had already abandoned the study of literature and decided to look for a solitary retreat, he was followed only by his nurse, who loved him dearly. After reaching a place called Affile, where many fine people were living together in a spirit of love, they stayed at the church of the blessed

From *Gregory the Great's Dialogues*, bk. 2, *Saint Benedict*, translated by Myra L. Uhlfelder, Library of Liberal Arts Series (Indianapolis: Bobbs-Merrill, 1967), pp. 4–11, 44–49. © 1967 by Bobbs-Merrill, Inc., a subsidiary of ITT.

apostle, Peter. Then his nurse asked the neighboring women to lend her a vessel for cleaning wheat. She carelessly left it on a table, so that it fell and was broken into two parts. When she came back soon afterwards, she burst into tears at finding the vessel broken. Now since Benedict was a pious and devoted youth, he was touched by his nurse's sadness when he saw her weeping. He therefore took both parts of the broken vessel and was in tears himself as he knelt in prayer. When he stood up, he found the vessel beside him in such good condition that no traces of the break could be detected. He lost no time in gently comforting his nurse, and gave her back whole the vessel which he had taken away broken. This incident became known to everyone in the place, and was regarded with such awe that the inhabitants of Affile hung the vessel at the entrance of the church to show everyone, then and in the future, with what great holiness the young Benedict had begun his religious life. That vessel has been there before the eyes of all for many years, and even until these times of the Lombards it has hung above the door of the church.

But Benedict had a greater desire to endure the evils of the world than to receive its praises. He preferred to be worn out in toiling for God rather than lifted up by acclaim granted in this life. He therefore escaped secretly from his nurse and went in search of a retreat in the desolate spot named Subiaco, about forty miles from Rome. From this place, cold, clear water is poured out, and the copious supply is first gathered together there in a large lake, but finally drawn off in a stream. While he was on his way there, he met a monk named Romanus, who asked him where he was going. After learning of Benedict's desire, Romanus kept his secret and helped him by giving him a monk's habit and by serving his needs as well as he could. The man of God, then, arrived at this place, confined himself in a very narrow cave, and for three years remained undiscovered by anyone except the monk Romanus. The latter lived close by in a monastery under the rule of the abbot Deodatus. But he piously stole some time from his abbot, and on certain days he would deliver to Benedict whatever bread he could take away from his own ration.

There was no path to this cave from Romanus's monastery because a high cliff towered above it. Romanus used to tie the bread to a long rope and lower it from the cliff. He also put a little bell on the rope so that the man of God might know from the ringing of the bell when Romanus was supplying him with bread and might come out to take it. But the Devil begrudged the loving act of one man and the refreshment provided for the other. Therefore one day as he saw the bread being lowered, he threw a stone and broke the bell. Nevertheless, Romanus continued to serve Benedict's needs properly. But almighty God wished Romanus to rest from his toil and desired also to display Benedict's life to men as an example, that it might shine brightly like a light set upon a candlestick,[1] to glow for all who live in the house of God.

Now some distance away there lived a certain priest, who had prepared his festal meal for Easter. The Lord saw fit to appear to him in a vision and to say: "You are preparing a luxurious banquet for yourself while my servant there is tortured by hunger." At once the priest got up, and on Easter Day he took the foods which he had prepared for himself and made his way toward the place. He looked for the man of God in the steep places of the mountains, in the hollows of the valleys, in the ditches of the earth, and he found him hiding in the cave. When they had sat down together after praying and blessing the almighty Lord, they talked about spiritual matters. Then the priest said, "Well now, let us eat, for today is Easter." Benedict answered, "I know that it is Easter, because I have been granted the blessing of seeing you." In fact Benedict was so far removed from men that he did not know that Easter fell on that very day. But the venerable priest stated again, "This day really is the Easter festival of our Lord's resurrection. It is not at all appropriate for you to fast, because I was sent especially to share equally with you the gifts of almighty God." Therefore they blessed God and ate. And so when they had had their fill of both food and conversation, the priest returned to his church.

At the same time, some shepherds, too, came upon Benedict hiding in the cave. When they saw him among the bushes dressed in hides, they thought that he was some beast. But after they found out that he was a servant of God, many of them were converted from their bestial natures to the grace of piety. In this way his name became known to all throughout the neighboring regions. From that time he began to be visited by many men who gave him the food of the body and took back, in turn, the spiritual sustenance of life which they had received from his lips.

How Benedict Overcame the Temptation of the Flesh

One day while he was alone, the Tempter was present. A small dark bird, commonly called a blackbird, began to flutter about his face and to press upon him so persistently that he could have caught it if he had wished. But when Benedict had made the sign of the cross, the bird went away. After it had left, however, a greater temptation of the flesh than he had ever experienced overtook the holy man. For the evil spirit brought back before his mind's eye a certain woman whom he had once seen. So intensely did the Tempter inflame his mind by the sight of that woman that he could hardly control his passion. He was overcome by sensuality, and almost considered

---

1. Matt. 5:15.

abandoning his solitary retreat. Then suddenly God graciously looked upon him and he returned to himself. Since he saw that thickets of nettles and thorn bushes were growing nearby, he stripped off his garment and flung himself naked upon those stinging thorns and the burning nettles. He rolled about there for a long time, and came out with his whole body wounded by them. So through the wounds of the skin he drew out from his body the wound of the mind by changing his lust to pain. Although he burned painfully on the outside, he had put out the forbidden flame within. He conquered sin, then, by transforming the fire. From that time on, as he later used to tell his disciples, he had such control over temptation of the flesh that he never again experienced a sensation like that. Later many began to abandon the world and to come eagerly to be instructed by him. Free as he was from the weakness of temptation, he became an appropriate teacher of virtues. That is the meaning of Moses' precept that Levites should serve from the age of twenty-five and above, and that they should be guardians of the vessels from their fiftieth year.[2]

Peter. I already have a glimmering of what you have told me. But please explain this point more fully.

Gregory. Obviously, Peter, the temptation of the flesh burns hot in youth. But from the fiftieth year, the heat of the body begins to cool. The sacred vessels are the hearts of the faithful. When those chosen are still subject to temptation, they must be subordinate and serve, and be worn out by obedient toil. But when the heat of temptation has withdrawn at an age when the mind is tranquil, they are guardians of the vessels because they become the teachers of souls.

Peter. I admit that I like what you say. But since you have begun your account, please continue to tell about the life of that righteous man.

How a Glass Vessel Was Broken by the Sign of the Cross

When temptation withdrew then, the man of God, like cultivated land with the thorns dug out, bore fruit more abundantly from his crop of virtues. And so through the report about his remarkable way of life, his name became famous. Now not far off was a monastic community whose abbot had died. The whole group of those monks went to the venerable Benedict and earnestly begged him to be their leader. He refused for a long time because he foresaw that his way of life could never be compatible with theirs. But finally he was won over by their entreaties and gave his consent. Since Benedict enforced the discipline of the Rule, no one was allowed as before to stray lawlessly to right or left from the path of the monastic life. There-

2. Num. 8:24–26.

fore the brothers under his guidance raged like madmen and first began to blame themselves for demanding him as their head; for it was true that their crookedness was at odds with his complete uprightness. They observed that forbidden acts were not permitted under his administration, and they felt resentment at giving up their customary practices. It was hard for them to have to think new thoughts with minds set in an old track. Now since the life of the good is always a burden to those of evil character, they began to devise some means to kill him; and when they had formed their plot, they mixed the wine with poison. According to the custom of the monastery, as Benedict was at table they presented the glass vessel with that deadly drink for his blessing. When he had stretched out his hand and made the sign of the cross, the vessel was shattered although it was being held at a distance. In fact, it was broken to pieces just as if he had cast a stone rather than the sign of the cross against it. The man of God understood at once that it had contained the drink of death, which could not endure the sign of life. He stood up immediately, calm in appearance and self-possessed, and said to the assembly of brothers: "O brothers, may almighty God have mercy upon you. Why did you wish to commit such an act against me? Surely I told you before that your ways would not be in harmony with mine. Go and look for an abbot like yourselves, for after this you cannot keep me." Then he returned to the place of his beloved solitude, and lived alone with himself within the sight of the One who looks down from above.

Peter. I do not understand very clearly the meaning of "lived with himself."

Gregory. If the holy man had been willing to keep a tight rein on the monks who were all conspiring against him and were far removed from his way of life, perhaps he would have lost his customary forcefulness and his calm restraint, and would have let his mind's eye fall from the light of contemplation. Then, as a result of wearing himself out by correcting them constantly, he would care less about his own affairs. Perhaps he would abandon himself without finding them. For whenever we are led too far outside ourselves through the motion of thought, we *are* ourselves but we are not *with* ourselves since we lose sight of ourselves and stray over other paths. Or do we say that that man was with himself who went away to a distant region, used up the portion which he had received, attached himself to one of the citizens of that region, and fed the swine, which he saw eating husks while he was starving himself? But after a while when he began to reflect about the good things which he had lost, it is written about him: "But when he came to himself, he said, 'How many of my father's hired servants have bread enough and to spare'."[3] If he was with himself then, from where did he return to himself?

3. Luke 15:17.

I would therefore say that this venerable man lived with himself because he was always under his own supervision, always beholding himself before the eyes of the Creator, always examining himself. He did not let his mind's eye wander outside himself.

Peter. What is the meaning, then, of what was written about the apostle Peter, when he had been led from the prison by the angel? "And Peter came to himself, and said, 'Now I am sure that the Lord has sent his angel and rescued me from the hand of Herod and from all that the Jewish people were expecting'."[4]

Gregory. The explanation, Peter, is that we are drawn outside ourselves in two ways. Either we fall beneath ourselves through the downward course of thought, or we are raised above ourselves by the grace of contemplation. So he who fed the swine fell beneath himself through the waywardness of the mind and through impurity. The man, however, whom the angel freed and carried off in a state of ecstasy was outside himself, of course, but above. Both returned to themselves, therefore, since the one recovered himself after wandering astray; the other returned from the height of contemplation to his former state of ordinary human understanding. The venerable Benedict, then, lived with himself in that solitude while he guarded himself within the confines of thought. For whenever his fervent contemplation carried him upward, he undoubtedly left himself below.

Peter. I like what you say. But please tell me whether he should have abandoned the brothers once he had taken them in his charge.

Gregory. In my opinion, Peter, an assembly of evil men should be patiently endured only when there are some good ones among them who may be helped. For when fruitful results from the good are wholly lacking, one's toil for the wicked is sometimes pointless, especially if there are tasks close at hand which can produce better fruit for God. For whose protection, then, should the holy man have stayed when he realized that all without exception were persecuting him?

I must also mention that often when good men consider their efforts fruitless, they move to toil in another place where they may produce fruit. That explains the conduct of the illustrious preacher, who yearned to be released from the flesh and to be with Christ, for whom "To live is Christ, and to die is gain,"[5] who not only longed himself for the contests of suffering, but aroused others, too, to endure them. When he had been persecuted at Damascus, in an effort to escape he looked for a wall, a rope, and a basket; and he allowed himself to be let down secretly.[6] We surely would not say that Paul was afraid of death, for he himself bears witness that he eagerly desired it in his love for Jesus. But since he saw that he had heavy

4. Acts 12:11.   5. Phil. 1:21.
6. Acts 9:25; 2 Cor. 11:32–33.

toil and little fruit in that place, he saved himself for fruitful labor elsewhere. For the brave soldier of God was unwilling to be kept in confinement, and looked for a field of combat. Just so in the case of Benedict too,
as you will quickly find out if you are willing to listen. The unteachable
monks whom he abandoned there were fewer than those whom he aroused
elsewhere from the death of the soul.

Peter. Both logic and your evidence prove your point. But please return
to your orderly account of the great father's life.

Gregory. In this same solitary spot the holy man was gaining greater
miraculous powers and was visited by more signs from heaven. Many persons were therefore gathered together by him there for the service of almighty God. And so, with the help of the almighty Lord Jesus Christ, he
built twelve monasteries there, appointed abbots, and assigned twelve
monks to each one. He kept a few monks with himself, those for whom it
would be best, in his judgment, to continue their training in his presence.
Also at that time devout nobles began to flock to him from Rome, and to
give him their sons to be reared for the service of almighty God. Then, too,
Euthicius entrusted to him his son Maurus, and Tertullus, a patrician, his
son Placidus, both of them promising youths. Since Maurus, the younger,
was a boy of outstanding character, he began to be the master's helper; and
Placidus, while still a child, was quite mature.

About the Way That the World Was Gathered Up before Benedict's Eyes and about the Soul of Germanus, Bishop of Capua

On another occasion Benedict received one of his customary visits from
the deacon Servandus, abbot of the monastery which had been built in the
region of Campania by the former patrician Liberius. Since Servandus too
was filled with knowledge of spiritual matters, he used to come to discuss
them with Benedict so that both of them might have a foretaste of the heavenly joy which they could not yet attain in all its perfection. When the hour
came for rest, Benedict settled in the upper part of the tower and the deacon Servandus in the lower, from which a passageway led straight up to the
top. In front of this tower was a spacious room in which the disciples of
both men were resting. While the monks were still asleep, Benedict was
keeping his vigil before the hour of the nightly prayer. As he stood by the
window praying to almighty God, at a still unseasonable hour of the night
he suddenly looked and saw that a light, shed from above, had scattered all
the shades of night. In fact, that light which had flashed out in the darkness
was so radiant that it surpassed the day in brightness. A miracle followed
this vision. As Benedict himself afterwards related, the whole world, as
though gathered up under a single ray of the sun, was brought before his

eyes. While Benedict fixed his gaze intently upon the brilliantly flashing light, he saw the soul of Germanus, Bishop of Capua, being carried to heaven by angels in a fiery globe. Then, since he wished to have a witness of such a great miracle, he loudly called the deacon Servandus several times. Servandus was disturbed by Benedict's extraordinary shouting, and so he went up, looked intently, and saw a small trace of the light. As he stood dumbfounded at this great miracle, Benedict told him in order what had happened. Then Benedict immediately ordered the pious Theoprobus in Cassino to send a messenger to Capua that very night to find out and report about Bishop Germanus. The command was carried out, and the messenger learned that Bishop Germanus had already died. By close questioning, he discovered that the death had occurred at the very instant when Benedict noticed the ascent.

Peter. What a remarkable, astonishing incident! But since I have never had an experience like the one you describe, when the whole world was gathered together and brought before his eyes as though beneath a single ray of the sun, I cannot conceive of it. How can the whole world become visible to a single man?

Gregory. Hold fast to what I tell you, Peter. To a soul that beholds the Creator, all creation is narrow in compass. For when a man views the Creator's light, no matter how little of it, all creation becomes small in his eyes. By the light of the inmost vision, the inner recesses of his mind are opened up and so expanded in God that they are above the universe. In fact, the soul of the beholder rises even above itself. When it is caught up above itself in God's light, it is made ampler within. As it looks down from its height, it grasps the smallness of what it could not take in in its lowly state. Therefore as Benedict gazed at the fiery globe, he saw angels, too, returning to heaven. He could undoubtedly have seen these visions only in God's light. Why is it strange, then, if he saw the world gathered before him when he was outside the world, raised up in the light of the soul? To say that the world was gathered together before his eyes does not mean that heaven and earth shrank, but that the mind of the beholder was expanded so that he could easily see everything below God since he himself was caught up in God. In that light which gleamed for the outer eyes, then, there was an inner light of the heart. When this carried the soul of the beholder to the upper regions, it revealed to him how narrow in compass everything below really was.

Peter. I think that I have profited from not understanding your words since you made your explanation so much fuller because I was slow-witted. But now that you have made your point perfectly clear, please go on with your account.

That Benedict Had Written a Rule for Monks

Gregory. I should like to tell many other stories about this venerable abbot, Peter. But I am purposely omitting some incidents because I am hurrying along to tell about the achievements of other saints. However, I want you to realize that in addition to the many miracles which made him famous, he also distinguished himself by his teaching. He wrote a *Rule* for monks, a work outstanding in good judgment and clearly expressed. Whoever may wish to have a fuller understanding of his character and his life can find all the acts of his administration in this *Book of the Rule*. For that saint was incapable of teaching a way of life that he did not practice.

How the Prophecy of His Death Was Reported to the Brothers

The year that he was to depart from this life, he announced the day of his most holy death to some of the disciples with him and to others who lived far off. He ordered the monks with him to keep his words a secret, and he pointed out to the others what kind of sign they would receive when his soul departed from his body. Six days before his death, he ordered his sepulchre to be opened. Then, soon afterward, he caught a fever and began to be exhausted by the fierce burning. His weakness increased day by day, and on the sixth day he had his disciples carry him into the chapel. There he fortified himself against death by receiving the Lord's body and blood. As he supported his weak limbs with the help of his disciples, he stood with hands raised to heaven and drew his last breath while praying. On that day, the very same vision appeared to two monks, one who was from his monastery and the other from quite far away. In it they saw a road, strewn with carpets and flashing with many lamps, which led straight eastward from his cell to heaven. Above this road stood a man radiant in appearance and dressed in a stately robe. When he asked whose road this was, they confessed that they did not know, and he told them, "This is the road by which Benedict, beloved by the Lord, is ascending to heaven." Then just as the disciples present saw the holy man's death, so those absent became aware of it from the sign which had been foretold to them. He was buried in the chapel of the blessed John the Baptist, which he had built after destroying the altar of Apollo.

How a Madwoman Was Restored to Health in His Cave

In the cave at Subiaco where he once lived, he still performs dazzling miracles when the faithful beg him to do so. The incident which I am about to relate happened recently. There was a woman, stricken in mind, who had completely lost her reason and was wandering day and night over mountains, valleys, forests, and plains. She rested only where exhaustion had forced her to stop. One day as she wandered aimlessly, she came to the cave of the blessed Benedict and, without knowing what she was doing, entered and stayed there. In the morning when she left, her reason was as sound as if she had never been mad. And in addition, for the rest of her life, she kept the sanity which had been restored to her.

Peter. How may we explain the fact that often when the martyrs too offer their protection, they grant greater favors through their relics than through their own bodies, and produce more impressive wonders in a place where their remains do not lie?

Gregory. Where the remains of the holy martyrs lie, Peter, there is no doubt that they have the power to display many signs, as indeed they do; and they reveal countless wonders to those who seek them with pure heart. But since weak spirits may doubt whether they are present to hear prayers where it is known the remains of their bodies do not lie, greater signs must be shown where the weak may be unsure of their presence. Those whose hearts are firmly fixed in God earn greater merit of faith by their conviction that the saints hear their supplications even though they are absent in body. That is why Truth Itself, to increase the faith of His disciples, said, "If I do not go away, the Counselor will not come to you." Since it is certain that the Counselor, the Spirit, always proceeds from the Father and the Son, why does the Son say that he will withdraw in order that He may come who never withdraws from the Son? Because when the disciples saw the Lord in the flesh with the eyes of the flesh, they yearned always to do so. Therefore it was right for them to be told, "If I do not go away, the Counselor will not come to you." [7] In plain words this statement meant, "If I do not withdraw my body, I cannot show the love of the Spirit. Unless you stop seeing me in the flesh, you will never learn to love me in spirit."

Peter. I like what you say.

Gregory. Now we must stop speaking for a while and let silence restore our powers of speech for telling the miracles of others.

7. John 16:7.

2. Bede, *The Lives of the Abbots* (ca. 650–690)

Beginneth the Life of the Holy Abbots of the Monastery in Wearmouth and Jarrow, Benedict, Ceolfrid, Eosterwine, Sigfrid, and Hwaetbert

Set in Order by Bede, Priest and Monk of the Said Monastery

1. Biscop[1] surnamed Benedict, a devout servant of Christ, being favoured of heavenly grace, built a monastery in honour of the most blessed Peter, chief of the apostles, by the mouth of the river Wear, on the north side, Egfrid the venerable and right godly king of that nation aiding him with a grant of land; and amid innumerable travails of journeyings or sicknesses Biscop diligently ruled the said monastery for 16 years with that same devotion wherewith he did build it. And that I may use the words of the blessed pope Gregory,[2] where he extolleth the life of an abbot that had Biscop's surname: "He was a man of venerable life, Benedict in grace and in name, having the heart of a man of ripe age even from the time of his boyhood, for in the ways of his life he was beyond his years and gave not his heart to any pleasure." He was come of noble lineage among the English, but being no less noble of mind he was lifted up to be deserving of the company of angels for evermore. In brief, when he was thane to king Oswy and received of his hand a gift of land suitable to his degree, being at the time about 25 years of age, he disdained the perishable possession that he might obtain one that was eternal; he despised earthly warfare with its reward that decayeth, that in warfare for the true King he might be vouchsafed to have a kingdom without end in the heavenly city; he forsook home, kinsfolk and country for Christ's sake and the Gospel's, that he might receive an hundredfold and have everlasting life; he refused to be in the bonds of carnal wedlock, in order that in the glory of virginity he might follow the Lamb without spot in the kingdom of heaven; he would not beget mortal children by carnal generation, being foreordained of Christ to bring up for Him by spiritual instruction sons to be immortal in the heavenly life.

2. So, leaving his native land he went to Rome,[3] and set himself also to visit and worship in the body the places where are the bodies of the blessed

From *Lives of the Abbots*, bk. 1, chaps. 1–6, 9–13, and bk. 2, chap. 14, in *Opera Historica*, translated by J. E. King, Loeb Classical Library (Cambridge, Mass.: Harvard University Press, 1930), pp. 393–407, 413–27. © 1930 by Harvard University Press. Some footnotes deleted. Reprinted by permission of the publisher.

1. An unusual name, which comes, however, in a genealogy of the kings of Lindsey. He is also called Biscop Baducing.
2. At the beginning of Book II of the *Dialogi*.
3. With Wilfrid in 653.

apostles, with love of which he had ever been kindled; and by and by having returned home he never ceased diligently to love, honour, and proclaim
to all whom he might those rules of ecclesiastical life which he saw at
Rome. At which time Alchfrid, son of the aforesaid king Oswy, being also
himself minded to visit Rome for the purpose of worshipping at the churches
of the blessed apostles, took Biscop for his companion in the same journey.
But when his father recalled him from his purpose in the said journey and
caused him to remain in his own country and kingdom, none the less
Biscop, being a young man of virtuous nature, forthwith finished the journey which was begun, and hastened with great speed to return to Rome in
the days of pope Vitalian of blessed memory, whom we named before;[4] and
on this, as also on the visit he made before, having enjoyed abundantly the
delights of wholesome learning, he departed thence after a few months and
came to the island of Lérins,[5] where he joined the company of monks, received the tonsure, and having the mark of the vow of a monk he kept the
rule of discipline with all due care; but after being for two years trained in
the learning that belongeth to monastical conversation, he was once more
overcome of the love he bore toward blessed Peter, the chief of the apostles,
and determined once again to visit the city hallowed of his body.

3. And not long after, by the coming of a merchant vessel he had his
wish.[6] Now at that time Egbert, king of Kent, had sent from Britain a man
named Wighard[7] who had been chosen for the office of bishop, and had
been well instructed in all ecclesiastical usage by the Roman scholars of the
blessed pope Gregory in Kent; and Egbert desired to have him ordained
bishop at Rome, so that having a prelate of his own nation and tongue,[8] he
and all the people under him might be the more perfectly instructed whether
in the words or mysteries of the faith: insomuch as they would receive these
things, not through an interpreter, but by the lips and hand withal of a man
that was of their own kin and tribe. But when he came to Rome, this
Wighard, with all his company that came with him, died of a disease that
fell upon them, before he could receive pontifical rank. Whereupon the
apostolical pope, unwilling that this godly embassy of the faithful should
fail of its due fruit by reason of the death of the ambassadors, took counsel
and chose one of his own men, whom he might send to Britain for archbishop, to wit Theodore, a man learned in secular no less than in ecclesiastical philosophy, and that in both languages, Greek that is and Latin,

4. This must have been added by an annotator, for the *Ecclesiastical History* was written
after this treatise. Vitalian's date is 657–72.

5. In a group of islands off Cannes.   6. The third visit.

7. *Eccl. Hist.* iii. 29.

8. This seems to imply that the Roman priests had not learnt, or only imperfectly learnt,
the native language.

and he gave him for colleague and counsellor a man of no less stoutness of heart and wisdom, the abbot Hadrian: and because he saw that the venerable Benedict would be a prudent, diligent, devout and notable man, he entrusted unto him the bishop whom he had ordained, and all his company, bidding him give up the pilgrimage which he had undertaken for Christ's sake, and in regard of a higher advantage return to his countrymen, bringing the teacher of truth they had earnestly required, to the which teacher he might become interpreter as well as guide, both on the way thither and when he was teaching therein. Benedict did as he was bidden: they came to Kent,[9] and were very gladly received: Theodore ascended the episcopal throne: Benedict took upon him the governance of the monastery of blessed Peter the apostle, whereof the aforementioned Hadrian was presently made abbot.

4. The which monastery when Benedict had ruled for two years, he hastened to make his third[10] journey to Rome: which he carried out with his accustomable success, and brought back many books of all subjects of divine learning, which had been either bought at a price, or been given him freely of his friends. And when on his way home he was come to Vienne, he there recovered of the friends to whom he had entrusted them the books that he had bought. Whereupon having entered into Britain he was minded to go to Cenwalh king of the West Saxons, of whose friendship he had before had benefit, and received help of his service. But at that same time, Cenwalh being cut off by untimely death, Benedict at length turned his steps to his own people and the land wherein he was born, and came to the court of Egfrid, king of the Transhumbrian region; unto him he rehearsed all the things he had done since the time that he left home in his youth; he openly shewed the zeal for religion which was kindled in him; he discovered to him all the precepts of ecclesiastical and monastical usage which he had learned at Rome or anywhere about, displaying all the divine volumes and the precious relics of the blessed apostles or martyrs of Christ, which he had brought with him; and he found such grace and favour in the eyes of the king that he forthwith bestowed upon him, out of his own estate, seventy hides of land, and bade him build a monastery there in honour of the chief pastor of the Church. The which was built, as I also mentioned in the preface, at the mouth of the river Wear toward the north, in the 674th year from the Lord's incarnation, in the second indiction, and in the 4th year of the rule of king Egfrid.

5. And when not more than a year had passed after the foundation of the monastery, Benedict crossed the ocean to France, where he required, pro-

9. 669.
10. Actually the fourth, but the third from Britain.

cured, and brought away masons to build him a church of stone, after the Roman fashion which he always loved. And in this work, out of the affection he had for the blessed Peter in whose honour he wrought it, he shewed such zeal that within the course of one year from the time the foundations were laid, the roof was put on, and men might see the solemnities of mass celebrated therein. Further, when the work was drawing nigh to completion, he sent messengers to France, which should bring over makers of glass (a sort of craftsman till that time unknown in Britain) to glaze the windows of the church, its side-chapels and clerestory. And so it was done, and they came: and not only did they finish the work that was required of them, but also caused the English people thereby to understand and learn this manner of craft: the which without doubt was worthily meet for the fastening in of church lamps, and for the manifold employments to which vessels are put. Moreover, this devout buyer, because he could not find them at home, took care to fetch from oversea all manner of things, to wit sacred vessels and vestments that were suitable to the ministry of the altar and the church.

6. Further, to the intent he might obtain for his church from the boundaries of Rome those ornaments also and writings which could not be found even in France, this diligent steward made a fourth[11] journey thither (after he had well ordered his monastery according to the rule), and when he had brought it to an end, he returned laden with a more abundant gain of spiritual merchandise than before. First, because he brought home a vast number of books of every kind: Secondly, because he procured a plentiful grace of the relics of the blessed apostles and martyrs of Christ to be profitable to many English churches: Thirdly, because he introduced into his monastery the order of chanting, singing, and ministering in church according to the manner of the Roman usage, having indeed asked and obtained of pope Agatho[12] leave to bring to the English in Britain a Roman teacher for his monastery, to wit John, archchanter of the church of the blessed apostle Peter and abbot of the monastery of the blessed Martin. The which John coming thither, not only by the word of his lips delivered what he had learned at Rome to his scholars of ecclesiastical things, but also left good store of writings which are still preserved for the sake of his memory in the library of the said monastery. Fourthly, Benedict brought a worthy gift, namely, a letter of privilege from the venerable pope Agatho, which he obtained with the leave and consent of king Egfrid,[13] and at his desire and request, whereby the monastery built by him was rendered wholly safe and secure continually from all assault from without. Fifthly, he brought home

11. The fourth from Britain.   12. Became pope 678.
13. In view probably of the controversies with Wilfrid.

sacred pictures to adorn the church of the blessed apostle Peter built by him, namely, the similitude of the blessed mother of God and ever Virgin Mary, and also of the 12 apostles, with the which he might compass the central vault of the said church by means of a board running along from wall to wall; similitudes of the Gospel story for the adornment of the south wall of the church; similitudes of the visions in the Revelation of the blessed John for the ornament of the north wall in like manner, in order that all men which entered the church, even if they might not read, should either look (whatsoever way they turned) upon the gracious countenance of Christ and His saints, though it were but in a picture; or might call to mind a more lively sense of the blessing of the Lord's incarnation, or having, as it were before their eyes, the peril of the last judgment might remember more closely to examine themselves.

9. But now that thus much hath been given as foretaste touching the life of the venerable Eosterwine, let us return to the course of our story. No long time after Benedict had appointed him abbot over the monastery of the blessed apostle Peter, and Ceolfrid abbot over the monastery of blessed Paul, he hastened from Britain to Rome for the fifth time, and returned enriched as always with a countless number of gifts of advantage to the churches, namely, a great store indeed of sacred books, yet with the wealth, as before, of no lesser a present of sacred pictures. For at this time also he brought with him paintings of the Lord's history, with the which he might compass about the whole church of the blessed mother of God, built by him within the greater monastery;[14] he also displayed, for the adorning of the monastery and church of the blessed apostle Paul, paintings shewing the agreement of the Old and New Testaments, most cunningly ordered: for example, a picture of Isaac carrying the wood on which he was to be slain, was joined (in the next space answerable above) to one of the Lord carrying the cross on which He likewise was to suffer. He also set together the Son of Man lifted up on the cross with the serpent lifted up by Moses in the wilderness. Amongst other things he also brought home two palls all of silk of exceeding goodly workmanship, with the which he afterward purchased from king Aldfrid and his counsellors (for Egfrid after his return he found had now been killed) three hides of land south of the river Wear, near the mouth.

10. But in the midst of the gladness that he brought in his coming, he found sorrowful tidings at home: to wit, that the venerable priest Eosterwine (whom at the point to go away he had appointed abbot), as well as no small number of the brethren committed to his charge, had already departed this world of a pestilence which was everywhere raging. Yet was

14. Wearmouth.

there comfort too, because he found that Sigfrid the deacon, a man as meek as he was reverend, had been by and by appointed in the room of Eosterwine out of the said monastery, being chosen thereto both of the brethren as well as of his fellow-abbot Ceolfrid. He was a man well instructed in the knowledge of the Scriptures, adorned with excellent virtues, endowed with a wonderful gift of abstinence, albeit he was grievously hampered in safeguarding the powers of his mind with bodily sickness, being sore troubled to keep the innocency of his heart by reason of a noisome and incurable malady of the lungs.

11. And not long after, Benedict also himself began to be distressed with an attack of sickness. For in order that the virtue of patience might be added to give proof beside of their great zeal for religion, the mercy of God caused them both to be cast into bed of a temporal malady; to the end that after sickness had been conquered of death, He might refresh them with the abiding rest of heavenly peace and light. For both Sigfrid, chastened (as I have said) with the long trouble of his inward parts, drew to his end, and Benedict was so weakened during three years with the ailment of a creeping palsy, that he was utterly dead in all the lower part of his body, the upper parts alone (without life in which a man may not remain alive) being preserved for the exercise of the virtue of patience; and both of them endeavoured in the midst of their pain to give continual thanks to their Maker, and to be ever occupied with the praise of God and the encouragement of their brethren. Benedict set himself to strengthen the brethren, that ofttimes came unto him, in the observance of the rule which he had given them: "For ye are not to think," quoth he, "that of my own heart without direction I have set forth the ordinances that I have appointed for you. For all the things I have found most excellent in 17 monasteries, whereunto I came in the travel to and fro of my long and often journeyings, I committed to memory and conveyed to you to keep and profit therefrom." The glorious library of a very great store of books which he had brought with him from Rome (and which in regard of instruction in the Church could not be spared) he commanded to be diligently kept whole and complete, and not marred by neglect, nor broken up and scattered. Moreover, this charge he was constantly wont to repeat to the said brethren, namely, that in the choice of an abbot none of them should think that family kindred should be sought for rather than uprightness of life and doctrine. "And I tell you of a truth," quoth he, "that comparing the two evils, I deem it far more tolerable that all this place where I have built the monastery should be made a wilderness for ever, if God so will, than that my brother after the flesh, whom we know to be walking not in the way of truth, should follow me in the governance thereof as abbot. Therefore, my brethren, be ye always very careful never to choose a father for the sake of his family, nor one

from any place outside. But in accordance with the rule of our sometime
abbot, the great Benedict, and in accordance with the decrees of our letter
of privilege, look ye out with common consent in the assembly of your
congregation the man which, by reason of his good life and wise doctrine,
shall be shewn better fitted and more worthy than others for the fulfilment
of such a ministry, and whomsoever ye shall all with one accord upon loving enquiry judge and choose to be the best: then summon the bishop, and
require him to confirm this man with the accustomed blessing to be your
abbot. For they," he said, "which beget carnal sons by carnal process must
needs seek carnal and earthly heirs for a carnal and earthly inheritance; but
they which beget spiritual sons by the spiritual seed of the word, must in all
things be spiritual in their doings. Let them then reckon him as the eldest
son among their spiritual children, who is thus endowed with more abundant spiritual grace, just as earthly parents are wont to acknowledge their
firstborn son as the chief of their offspring, and to consider him to be preferred before the rest, when they divide their inheritance."

12. Nor must I forebear to tell how ofttimes the venerable abbot Benedict in order to abate the weariness of the long nights, when he could not
sleep by reason of his grievous malady, would call a reader and have him
read to him the story of Job's patience, or some other passage of Scripture,
whereby in his sickness he might be comforted and be exalted with a more
lively hope to things above out of the depth wherein he was brought down.
And because he could in no wise rise to pray, nor without difficulty give
utterance or lift up his voice to fulfil the course of the regular psalmody,
this wise man, taught of his love of religion, accustomed himself, at the
several hours of the daily and nightly prayers, to summon unto him some of
the brethren which should sing the appointed psalms antiphonally, that so
he himself singing with them so far as he might, should by their aid fulfil
what he could not accomplish of himself.

13. But when the two abbots, worn out by long-continued sickness, perceived that they were nigh unto death, and would not be fit to rule the monastery (for so sore lay their bodily sickness upon them, perfecting in them
the power of Christ), that one day, when each desired to see and speak with
the other, before departing this life, Sigfrid was carried on a stretcher
to the chamber where Benedict too was himself laid upon his pallet, and
their attendants placing them side by side, their heads were set on the same
pillow (a lamentable sight), and albeit their faces were close together they
had not strength to bring them near to kiss each other; yet even this they
brought to pass with the help of the brethren. Then Benedict, after wholesome counsel held with Sigfrid and all the brethren, summoned abbot
Ceolfrid whom he had set over the monastery of the blessed apostle Paul,

being his kinsman [15] not in the bond of the flesh so much as in fellowship of virtue; and all the rest agreeing and deeming it most expedient, he appointed him father over both monasteries; for he judged it best in every way for the maintenance of the peace, unity and agreement of the two places that they should continually have one father and governor; oftentimes recounting the example of the kingdom of Israel, which could not ever be driven from its boundaries by foreign nations, and remained without hurt, so long as it was ruled by one and the same leader from its own nation; but when afterward on account of its former sins the people became enemies to one another and were parted asunder with contention, it gradually perished and fell to ruin from its former stability. He likewise bade them unceasingly remember the Gospel precept,[16] which says that "every kingdom divided against itself shall be brought to desolation."

Book 2

14. So when after these things two months had gone by, in the first place Sigfrid the venerable abbot, beloved of God, was brought into the refreshment of eternal rest through the fire and water of temporal tribulation, and entered into his home in the kingdom of heaven, paying unto the Lord in sacrifices of continual praise the vows he had promised with often parting of clean lips; and when 4 more months were passed, Benedict, the conqueror over sin and glorious worker of righteousness, being conquered of bodily weakness came to his end. "The night falls chilly with winter blasts"; but for that holy man is soon to rise the day of everlasting happiness, peace and light. The brethren assemble at the church, and sleeplessly pass the dark hours in prayers and psalms: lightening the burden of their father's departure with the unceasing melody of praise to God. Other abide in the chamber, where Benedict, sick in body but strong in mind, was looking for his passage from death and his entry into life. All that night, as was the custom to be done other nights too, the Gospel is read aloud of a priest to comfort his pain; as the hour of his departure is at hand, the sacrament of the Lord's body and blood is given him for his voyage provision; and so this holy soul, searched and tried with the slow flames of profitable chastisement, leaveth the furnace of earth in the flesh, and flieth in deliverance to the glory of heavenly bliss. And to his departure in great triumph, which might not be let or hindered in any way of evil spirits, witness is borne also by the psalm which at that time was being sung for him. For

15. So that Benedict, Eosterwine, and Ceolfrid were all related to one another and of noble birth.

16. Matt. 12:25.

the brethren, hurrying together to the church at nightfall, sang through the psalter, and had at that time reached the 82nd psalm which has for its title "Lord, who shall be like unto Thee?" of the which psalm is the whole meaning, that the enemies of the name of Christ, whether they be carnal or ghostly, do strive to break up and destroy always the Church of Christ and always every faithful soul; but contrariwise they themselves shall be confounded and dismayed and perish everlastingly, their strength being weakened of the Lord, to Whom there is none like, Who only is the highest over all the earth. Whence it was rightly understood to be disposed from heaven that such psalm should be said in the hour when his soul was leaving his body, against whom, the Lord being his helper, no enemy might prevail. In the 16th year after he had founded the monastery, this confessor fell asleep in the Lord, on the 12th day of January, and was buried in the church of the blessed apostle Peter; so that after death his body lay not far from the relics and the altar of him whom, while he was in the flesh, he ever loved, and who opened for him the door of entry into the kingdom of heaven. For 16 years, as we have said, he ruled the monastery; the first 8 of himself without appointment of a second abbot beside; the last 8 with the venerable and holy Eosterwine, Sigfrid and Ceolfrid to aid him with the title, authority, and office of abbot; the first during 4 years, the second during 3 years and the last during one.

3. Adamnan, *Arculf's Narrative about the Holy Places* (ca. 700)

Book 1

The Situation of Jerusalem, the Gates of the City, the Yearly Market, the Site of the Temple, the Oratory of the Saracens, the Great Houses

As to the situation of Jerusalem, we shall now write a few of the details that the sainted Arculf dictated to me, Adamnan; but what is found in the books of others as to the position of that city, we shall pass over. In the great circuit of its walls, Arculf counted eighty-four towers and twice three gates, which are placed in the following order in the circuit of the city: the Gate of David, on the west side of Mount Sion, is reckoned first; second, the Gate of the Place of the Fuller; third, the Gate of St. Stephen; fourth, the Gate of Benjamin; fifth, a portlet, that is a little gate, by which is the descent by steps to the Valley of Josaphat; sixth, the Gate Thecuitis.

This then is the order round the intervals between those gates and tow-

From Adamnan, *Arculf's Narrative about the Holy Places*, translated by James Rose Macpherson (London, 1889).

ers: from the above-mentioned gate of David it turns towards the northern part of the circuit, and thence towards the east. But although six gates are counted in the walls, yet of those the entries of three gates are more commonly frequented; one to the west, another to the north, a third to the east; while that part of the walls with its interposed towers, which extends from the above-mentioned Gate of David across the northern brow of Mount Sion (which overhangs the city from the south), as far as the face of that mountain which looks eastwards, where the rock is precipitous, is proved to have no gates.

But this too, it seems to me, should not be passed over, which the sainted Arculf, formerly spoken of, told us as to the honour of that city in Christ: On the fifteenth day of the month of September yearly, an almost countless multitude of various nations is in the habit of gathering from all sides to Jerusalem for the purposes of commerce by mutual sale and purchase. Whence it necessarily happens that crowds of various nations stay in that hospitable city for some days, while the very great number of their camels and horses and asses, not to speak of mules and oxen, for their varied baggage, strews the streets of the city here and there with the abominations of their excrements: the smell of which brings no ordinary nuisance to the citizens and even makes walking difficult. Wonderful to say, on the night after the above-mentioned day of departure with the various beasts of burden of the crowds, an immense abundance of rain falls from the clouds on that city, which washes all the abominable filths from the streets, and cleanses it from the uncleannesses. For the very situation of Jerusalem, beginning from the northern brow of Mount Sion, has been so disposed by its Founder, God, on a lofty declivity, sloping down to the lower ground of the northern and eastern walls, that that overabundance of rain cannot settle at all in the streets, like stagnant water, but rushes down, like rivers, from the higher to the lower ground: and further this inundation of the very waters of heaven, flowing through the eastern gates, and bearing with it all the filthy abominations, enters the Valley of Josaphat and swells the torrent of Cedron: and after having thus baptized Jerusalem, this overabundance of rain always ceases. Hence therefore we must in no negligent manner note in what honour this chosen and glorious city is held in the sight of the Eternal Sire, Who does not permit it to remain longer filthy, but because of the honour of His Only Begotten cleanses it so quickly, since it has within the circuit of its walls the honoured sites of His sacred Cross and Resurrection.

But in that renowned place where once the Temple had been magnificently constructed, placed in the neighbourhood of the wall from the east, the Saracens now frequent a four-sided house of prayer, which they have built rudely, constructing it by raising boards and great beams on some remains of ruins: this house can, it is said, hold three thousand men at once.

Arculf, when we asked him about the dwellings of that city, answered: "I remember that I both saw and visited many buildings of that city, and that I very often observed a good many great houses of stone through the whole of the large city, surrounded by walls, formed with marvellous skill." But all these we must now, I think, pass over, with the exception of the structure of those buildings which have been marvellously built in the Holy Places, those namely of the Cross and the Resurrection: as to these we asked Arculf very carefully, especially as to the Sepulchre of the Lord and the Church constructed over it, the form of which Arculf himself depicted for me on a tablet covered with wax.

The Site of the Altar of Abraham

Between these two churches lies that illustrious place where the patriarch Abraham built an altar, laid on it the pile of wood, and seized the drawn sword to offer in sacrifice his own son, Isaac: where is now a wooden table of considerable size on which the alms of the poor are offered by the people. This also the sainted Arculf added, as I enquired of him more diligently: Between the Anastasis, that is the round church we have often mentioned above, and the Basilica of Constantine, lies a small square extending to the Church of Golgotha, where lamps burn always by day and night.

The Recess Situated between the Church of Calvary and the Basilica of Constantine, in Which Are Kept the Cup of the Lord and the Sponge from Which, as He Hung on the Tree, He Drank Vinegar and Wine

Between that Basilica of Golgotha and the Martyrium there is a recess (exedra) in which is the Cup of the Lord, which He blessed and gave with His own hand to the Apostles in the supper on the day before He suffered, as He and they sat at meat with one another; the cup is of silver, holding the measure of a French quart, and has two little handles placed on it, one on each side. In this cup also is the sponge which those who were crucifying the Lord filled with vinegar and, putting it on hyssop, offered to His mouth. From the same cup, as is said, the Lord drank after His Resurrection, as He sat at meat with the apostles. The sainted Arculf saw it and touched it with his own hand, and kissed it through the opening of the perforated cover of the case within which it is concealed: indeed, the whole people of the city resort greatly to this cup with immense veneration.

The Spear of the Soldier with Which He Pierced the Side of the Lord

Arculf also saw that spear of the soldier with which he smote through the side of the Lord as He hung on the Cross. The spear is fixed in a wooden cross in the portico of the Basilica of Constantine, its shaft being broken into two parts: and this also the whole city of Jerusalem resorts to, kisses, and venerates.

The Place of the Ascension of the Lord and the Church Built on It

On the whole Mount of Olivet there seems to be no spot higher than that from which the Lord is said to have ascended into the heavens, where there stands a great round church, having in its circuit three vaulted porticoes covered over above. The interior of the church, without roof or vault, lies open to heaven under the open air, having in its eastern side an altar protected under a narrow covering. So that in this way the interior has no vault, in order that from the place where the Divine footprints are last seen, when the Lord was carried up into heaven in a cloud, the way may be always open and free to the eyes of those who pray towards heaven.

For when this basilica, of which I have now made slight mention, was building, that place of the footprints of the Lord, as we find written elsewhere, could not be enclosed under the covering with the rest of the buildings. Whatever was applied, the unaccustomed earth, refusing to receive anything human, cast back into the face of those who brought it. And, moreover, the mark of the dust that was trodden by the Lord is so lasting that the impression of the footsteps may be perceived; and although the faith of such as gather daily at the spot snatches away some of what was trodden by the Lord, yet the area perceives no loss, and the ground still retains that same appearance of being marked by the impress of footsteps.

Further, as the sainted Arculf, who carefully visited this spot, relates, a brass hollow cylinder of large circumference, flattened on the top, has been placed here, its height being shown by measurement to reach one's neck. In the centre of it is an opening of some size, through which the uncovered marks of the feet of the Lord are plainly and clearly seen from above, impressed in the dust. In that cylinder there is, in the western side, as it were, a door; so that any entering by it can easily approach the place of the sacred dust, and through the open hole in the wheel may take up in their outstretched hands some particles of the sacred dust.

Thus the narrative of our Arculf as to the footprints of the Lord quite accords with the writings of others—to the effect that they could not be covered in any way, whether by the roof of the house or by any special lower and closer covering; so that they can always be seen by all that enter, and the marks of the feet of the Lord can be clearly seen depicted in the dust of that place. For these footprints of the Lord are lighted by the brightness of an immense lamp hanging on pulleys above that cylinder in the church, and burning day and night.

Further in the western side of the round church we have mentioned above, twice four windows have been formed high up with glazed shutters, and in these windows there burn as many lamps placed opposite them, within and close to them. These lamps hang in chains, and are so placed that each lamp may hang neither higher nor lower, but may be seen, as it were, fixed to its own window, opposite and close to which it is specially seen. The brightness of these lamps is so great that, as their light is copiously poured through the glass from the summit of the Mountain of Olivet, not only is the part of the mountain nearest the round basilica to the west illuminated, but also the lofty path which rises by steps up to the city of Jerusalem from the Valley of Josaphat, is clearly illuminated in a wonderful manner, even on dark nights; while the greater part of the city that lies nearest at hand on the opposite side is similarly illuminated by the same brightness. The effect of this brilliant and admirable coruscation of the eight great lamps shining by night from the holy mountain and from the site of the Lord's ascension, as Arculf related, is to pour into the hearts of the believing onlookers a greater eagerness of the Divine love, and to strike the mind with a certain fear along with vast inward compunction.

This also Arculf related to me about the same round church: That on the anniversary of the Lord's Ascension, at mid-day, after the solemnities of the Mass have been celebrated in that basilica, a most violent tempest of wind comes on regularly every year, so that no one can stand or sit in that church or in the neighbouring places, but all lie prostrate in prayer with their faces in the ground until that terrible tempest has passed.

The result of this terrific blast is that that part of the house cannot be vaulted over; so that above the spot where the footsteps of the Lord are impressed and are clearly shown, within the opening in the centre of the above-named cylinder, the way always appears open to heaven. For the blast of the above-mentioned wind destroyed, in accordance with the Divine will, whatever materials had been gathered for preparing a vault above it, if any human art made the attempt.

This account of this dreadful storm was given to us by the sainted Arculf, who was himself present in that Church of Mount Olivet at the very hour of the day of the Lord's Ascension when that fierce storm arose.

A drawing of this round church is shown below, however unworthily it may have been drawn; while the form of the brass cylinder is also shown placed in the middle of the church.

This also we learned from the narrative of the sainted Arculf: That in that round church, besides the usual light of the eight lamps mentioned above as shining within the church by night, there are usually added on the night of the Lord's Ascension almost innumerable other lamps, which by their terrible and admirable brightness, poured abundantly through the glass of the windows, not only illuminate the Mount of Olivet, but make it seem to be wholly on fire; while the whole city and the places in the neighbourhood are also lit up.

Book 2

The Rock Situated beyond the Wall, upon Which the Water, in Which He Was First Washed after His Birth, Was Poured

Here I think I must briefly mention the rock lying beyond the wall, upon which the water of the first bathing of the Lord's body after His birth, was poured from the top of the wall out of the vessel into which it had been put. This water of the sacred bath, poured from the wall, found a receptacle in a rock lying below, which had been hollowed out by nature like a trench: and this water has been constantly replenished from that day to our own time during the course of many ages, so that the cavity is shown full of the purest water with any loss or diminution, our Saviour miraculously bringing this about from the day of His nativity, of which the prophet sings: "Who brought water out of the rock;" [1] and the Apostle Paul, "Now that Rock was Christ," [2] who, contrary to nature, brought water or a stream out of the hardest rock in the desert to console His thirsting people. Such is the power of God and the wisdom of God, who brought out water also from that rock of Bethlehem and keeps its cavity always full of water: this our Arculf inspected with his own eyes, and he washed his face in it.

The Valley of Mambre, and the Sepulchre of the Four Patriarchs

To the east of Hebron is a field with a double cave, looking towards Mambre, which Abraham bought from Ephron the Hittite, for a possession of a double sepulchre.

In the valley of this field the sainted Arculf visited the site of the Sepulchre of Arba, that is, of the four patriarchs, Abraham, and Isaac, and Jacob, and Adam, the first man, whose feet are not, as is customary in other parts of the world, turned towards the east in burial, but are turned to the south, and their heads to the north. The site of these sepulchres is surrounded by a low rectangular wall. Adam, the first created, to whom, when he sinned, immediately after the sin was committed, God the Creator said: "Dust thou art, and to the dust thou shalt return," is separated somewhat from the other three, next the northern side of the rectangular stone rampart, buried not in a stone sepulchre cut out in the rock above ground, as other honoured men of his seed lie, but buried in the ground, covered with earth, and himself, dust, turned into dust, rests waiting the resurrection

1. Isa. 48:21.   2. 1 Cor. 10:4.

with all his seed. And thus in that sepulchre is fulfilled the divine sentence uttered to him as to himself.

And after the example of the Sepulchre of the first parent, the other three Patriarchs also rest in sleep covered with common dust, their four Sepulchres having placed above them small monuments, cut out and hewn from single stones, in the form of a basilica, and formed according to the measure of the length and the breadth of each Sepulchre. The three adjoining Sepulchres of Abraham and Isaac and Jacob are protected by three hard white stones, placed over them, formed according to the shape of which we have now written, as has been said above; while Adam's Sepulchre is also protected by a stone placed over it, but of darker colour and poorer workmanship. Arculf saw also the poorer and smaller monuments of the three women, namely Sara, and Rebecca, and Lia, buried in the earth. The sepulchral field of those patriarchs is found to be one furlong from the wall of that most ancient Hebron, towards the east. This Hebron, it is said, was founded before all the cities, not only of Palestine, but also preceded in its foundation all the cities of Egypt, although it has now been so miserably destroyed.

Thus far let it suffice to have written as to the Sepulchres of the Patriarchs.

Nazareth and Its Churches

The city of Nazareth, as Arculf who stayed in it relates, is situated on a mountain. It is, like Capharnaum, unwalled, yet it has large houses built of stone, and also two very large churches. One of these, in the middle of the city, is built upon two vaults, on the spot where there once stood the house in which our Lord the Saviour was brought up. Among the mounds below this church, which, as has been said, is supported upon two mounds and intervening arches, there is a very clear spring, frequented by all the citizens, who draw water from it, and from the same spring water is raised in vessels to the church above by means of wheels. The other church is reputed to be built on the site of the house in which the Archangel Gabriel came and addressed the Blessed Mary, whom he found there alone at that hour. This information as to Nazareth we have obtained from the sainted Arculf, who stayed there two nights and as many days, but was prevented from staying longer in it, as he was compelled to hasten onwards by a soldier of Christ, well acquainted with sites, a Burgundian living a solitary life, Peter by name, who thence returned circuitously to that solitary place where he had formerly stayed.

Mount Tabor

Mount Tabor is in Galilee, three miles from the Lake of Cinnereth, marvellously round on every side, looking from its northern side over the lake we have just named. It is very grassy and flowery, having an ample plain on its pleasant summit, and is surrounded by a very large wood. In the middle of this level surface is a great monastery of monks, with a large number of their cells. For its summit is not drawn up to a narrow peak, but is spread over a level surface of twenty-four furlongs in length, while its height is thirty furlongs.

On this higher plain are also three very celebrated churches of no small construction, according to the number of those tabernacles of which Peter spoke to the Lord on that holy mountain, while he rejoiced in the heavenly vision, but yet was terrified by it, saying: "It is good that we should be here; if Thou wilt, let us make here three tabernacles, one for Thee and one for Moses and one for Elias." The buildings of the monasteries and the three churches mentioned above, with the cells of the monks, are all surrounded by a stone wall. There the sainted Arculf spent one night on the top of that holy mountain, for Peter, the Burgundian Christian, who was his guide in those places, would not allow him to stay in one hospice longer, but hurried him on.

It should here be noted that the name of that famous mountain ought to be written in Greek with Θ and long ω, Θαβὼρ, and in Latin with the aspirate Thabor, the letter o being long. The proper orthography of the word is found in Greek books.

Alexandria, and the River Nile and Its Crocodiles

That great city, which was once the metropolis of Egypt, was formerly called in Hebrew No. It is a very populous city, deriving its name of Alexandria, a name known and famous among all nations, from its founder Alexander, the king of Macedonia, from whom it received both the magnitude of a city and its name. As to its situation, Arculf gave us an account, which differs in no way from what we have learned in the course of our previous reading.

Going down from Jerusalem and beginning his voyage at Joppa, he had a journey of forty days to Alexandria, of which Nahum the prophet speaks briefly, when he says: "Water round about it, whose riches are the sea, waters are its walls."[3] For on the south it is surrounded by the mouths of the river Nile, while on the north, as the outline of its position clearly shows, it

3. Nah. 3:8, of No.

is situated upon the Nile and the sea, so that on this side and on that it is surrounded by water. The city lies like an enclosure between Egypt and the Great Sea, without a [natural] haven, difficult to approach from without. Its port is more difficult than others, in form like the human body, more capacious at the head and the roads, but narrower in the straits, in which it receives the movements of the sea and ships, by which some aids to breathing are given to the port. When one has escaped the narrows and mouths of the port, a stretch of sea is spread out before one, far and wide, like the form of the rest of the body. On the right side of the port there is a small island, on which is a very high tower, which the Greeks and the Latins have in common called, from its use, Pharus, because it is seen by voyagers at a great distance, in order that, before they approach the port, they may, specially during the night, recognise the proximity of land by the light of the flames, that they may not be deceived by the darkness and fall upon rocks or fail to recognise the boundaries of the entrance. Men are accordingly employed there by whom torches and other masses of wood which have been collected are set on fire to serve as a guide to the land, showing the narrow entrance of the straits, the bosom of the waves, and the windings of the entrance, lest the slender keel should graze the rocks and in the very entrance strike upon the rocks that are hidden by the waves. Accordingly a ship ought to be somewhat deflected from the straight course, to prevent its running into danger from striking on hidden stones. For the approach in the port is narrower on the right side, but the port is wider on the left. Round the island also, beams of immense size have been regularly laid down, to prevent the foundations of the island from yielding to the constant collision of the rising sea, and being loosened by the injury. So that the middle channel, among rugged rocks and broken masses of earth, is beyond doubt always unquiet, and it is dangerous for ships to enter through the roughness of the passage.

The port extends in size over thirty furlongs, and it is quite safe even in the greatest storms, as the above-mentioned straits and the obstacle of the island repel the waves of the sea, the bosom of the port being so defended by them as to be removed from the reach of tempests and at peace from breakers by which the entrance is made rough. Nor are the safety and the size of the port undeservedly so great, since there must be borne into it whatever is needful for the use of the whole city. For the needs of the innumerable population of those districts give rise to much commerce for the use of the whole city, and the district is very fruitful, and, besides abounding in all other gifts and trades of the earth, it supplies corn for the whole world, and other necessary merchandise. The region is beyond doubt wanting in rain, but the irrigation of the Nile supplies spontaneous showers, so that the fields are tempered at once by the rain of heaven and by the fruitfulness of the earth; and the situation is thus convenient both for sailors and for husbandmen. These sail, those sow; these are borne round on their voyages, those till the land, sowing without need of ploughing, travelling without waggons. You see a country intersected by watercourses, and houses throughout the land raised as it were upon walls, on the banks of the navigable rivers, standing on the edge of each bank of the river Nile. The river is navigable, they say, up to the city of Elephanti; a ship is prevented from proceeding further by the cataracts, that is, flowing hills of water, not from want of depth, but from the fall of the whole river and the downward rush of the waters.

The narrative of the sainted Arculf about the situation of Alexandria and the Nile is proved not to differ from what we have learned from our reading in the books of others. We have, indeed, abbreviated some excerpts from these writings and inserted them in this description, as to the havenlessness of this city or the difficulty of its haven, as to the island and the tower built on it, as to the terminal position of Alexandria between the sea and the mouths of the river Nile, etc. Hence it happens beyond doubt that the site of the city, which is as it were choked between these two limits, extends from west to east very far along a narrow stretch of ground, as the narrative of Arculf shows; he relates that he began to enter the city at the third hour of the day in the month of October, and on account of the length of the city could hardly reach the other end of its length before evening. It is surrounded by a long circuit of walls, fortified by frequent towers, constructed along the margin of the river and the curving shore of the sea.

Further, as one coming from Egypt enters the city of Alexandria, one meets on the north side a large church, in which Mark the Evangelist is buried; his sepulchre is shown before the altar in the eastern end of this four-sided church, and a monument of him has been built above it of marble.

So much, then, about Alexandria, which, as we have said above, was called No before it was so much enlarged by Alexander the Great, and which, as we further said above, adjoins what is called the Canopean mouth of the river Nile, separating Asia from Egypt and also Lybia. On account of the inundation of Egypt by the river Nile, they construct raised mounds along its banks, which, if they should be broken by the negligence of the watchmen or by too great an irruption of water, by no means irrigate the flooded fields, but spoil them and lay them waste. On this account a considerable number of the inhabitants of the plains of Egypt, according to the narrative of the sainted Arculf, who often sailed over that river in Egypt, live above the water in houses supported on transverse beams.

Arculf relates that crocodiles live in the river Nile, quadrupeds of no great size, very voracious, and so strong that one of them, if it can find a horse or an ass or an ox eating grass on the river bank, suddenly rushes out and attacks it, or even seizing one foot of the animal with its jaws, drags it under the water, and completely devours the entire animal.

Book 3

The City of Constantinople

Arculf, who has been mentioned so often, on his return from Alexandria, stayed for some days in the island of Crete, and sailed thence to Constantinople, where he spent some months. This city is, beyond doubt, the metropolis of the Roman Empire. It is surrounded by the waves of the sea except on the north; the sea breaking out from the Great Sea for forty miles, while from the wall of Constantinople it still further stretches sixty miles up to the mouths of the river Danube. This imperial city is surrounded by no small circuit of walls, twelve miles in length; it is a promontory by the sea-side, having, like Alexandria or Carthage, walls built along the sea coast, additionally strengthened by frequent towers, after the fashion of Tyre; within the city walls it has numerous houses, very many of which are of marvellous size; these are of stone, and are built after the fashion of the dwelling-houses of Rome.

The Church in Which the Cross of the Lord Is Preserved

But we must not be silent as to that most celebrated round church in that city, built of stone and of marvellous size. According to the narrative of the sainted Arculf, who visited it for no short time, it rises from the bottom of its foundations in three walls, being built in triple form to a great height, and it is finished in a very round simple crowning vault of great beauty. This is supported on great arches, with a wide space between each of the above-mentioned walls, suited and convenient either for dwelling or for praying to God in. In the northern part of the interior of the house is shown a very large and very beautiful ambry, in which is kept a wooden chest, which is similarly covered over with wooden work: in which is shut up that wooden Cross of Salvation on which our Saviour hung for the salvation of the human race. This notable chest, as the sainted Arculf relates, is raised with its treasure of such preciousness upon a golden altar, on three consecutive days after the lapse of a year. This altar also is in the same round church, being two cubits long and one broad. On three successive days only throughout the year is the Lord's Cross raised and placed on the altar, that is, on [the day of] the Supper of the Lord, when the Emperor and the armies enter the church and, approaching the altar, after that sacred chest has been opened, kiss the Cross of Salvation.

First of all the Emperor of the world kisses it with bent face, then one going up after another in the order of rank or age, all kiss the Cross with honour. Then on the next day, that is, on the sixth day of the week before Easter, the Queen, the matrons, and all the women of the people, approach it in the above-mentioned order and kiss it with all reverence. On the third day, that is, on [the day of] the Paschal Sabbath, the bishop and all the clergy after him approach in order, with fear and trembling and all honour, kissing the Cross of Victory, which is placed in its chest. When these sacred and joyful kissings of the Sacred Cross are finished, that venerable chest is closed, and with its honoured treasure is borne back to its ambry.

But this also should be carefully noted that there are not two but three short pieces of wood in the Cross, that is, the cross-beam and the long one which is cut and divided into two equal parts; while from these threefold venerated beams when the chest is opened, there arises an odour of a wonderful fragrance, as if all sorts of flowers had been collected in it, wonderfully full of sweetness, satiating and gladdening all in the open space before the inner walls of that church, who stand still as they enter at that moment; for from the knots of those threefold beams a sweet-smelling liquid distills, like pressed-out oil, which causes all men of whatever race, who have assembled and enter the church, to perceive the above-mentioned fragrance of so great sweetness. This liquid is such that if even a little drop of it be laid on the sick, they easily recover their health, whatever be the trouble or disease they have been afflicted with.

But as to these let this suffice.

St. George the Confessor

Arculf, the sainted man, who gave us all these details as to the Cross of the Lord, which he saw with his own eyes and kissed, gave us also an account of a Confessor named George, which he learned in the city of Constantinople from some well-informed citizens, who were accustomed to narrate it in this form:

In a house in the city of Diospolis there stands the marble column of George the Confessor, to which, during a time of persecution, he was bound while he was scourged, and on which his likeness is impressed; he was, however, loosed from his chains and lived for many years after the scourging. It happened one day that a hard-hearted and unbelieving fellow, mounted on horseback, having entered that house and seen the marble column, asked those who were there, "Whose is this likeness engraved on the marble column?" They reply, "This is the likeness of George the Confessor, who was bound to this column and scourged." On hearing this, that most rough fellow, greatly enraged at the insensible object, and instigated by the devil, struck with his lance at the likeness of the sainted Confessor. The lance of that assailant penetrating the mass in a marvellous manner, as if it were a ball of snow, perforated the exterior of that stone column, and its iron point sticking fast was retained in the interior and could not be drawn out by any means. Its shaft, however, striking the marble likeness of the sainted Confessor, was broken on the outside. The horse also of that wretched fellow, on which he was mounted, fell dead under him at that moment on the pavement of the house. The wretched man himself too, falling to the ground at the same time, put out his hands to the marble column, and his fingers, entering it as if it were flour or clay, stuck fast impressed in that column. On seeing this, the miserable man, who could not draw back the ten fingers of his two hands, as they stuck fast together in the marble likeness of the sainted Confessor, invokes in penitence the name of the Eternal God and of His Confessor, and prays with tears to be released from that bond. The merciful God, who does not wish the death of a sinner but that he may be converted and live, accepted his tearful penitence, and not only released him from that present visible bond of marble, but also mercifully set him free from the invisible bonds of sin, saved by faith.

Hence it is clearly shown in what honour George has been held with God, whom he confessed amid tortures, since his bust, which, in the course of nature, is impenetrable, was made penetrable by penitence, which also made the equally impenetrating lance of his adversary penetrating, and made the weak fingers of that fellow, which in the same course of nature were impenetrating, powerfully penetrating, which at first were so fastened in the marble that even that hard man could not draw them back, but which, when in the same moment he was so terrified and thus softened into penitence, he drew back by the pity of God. Marvellous to say, the marks of his twice five fingers appear down to the present day inserted up to the roots in the marble column; and the sainted Arculf inserted in their place his own ten fingers, which similarly entered up to the roots. Further, the blood of that fellow's horse, the haunch of which, as it fell dead on the pavement, was broken in two, cannot be washed out or removed by any means, but that horse's blood remains indelible on the pavement of the house down to our times.

4. Einhard, *The Life of Charlemagne* (ca. 750–814)

But there are still other reasons, neither unwarrantable nor insufficient, in my opinion, that urge me to write on this subject, namely, the care that

From *The Life of Charlemagne by Einhard*, translated by Samuel Eper Turner (Ann Arbor: University of Michigan Press, 1960), pp. 15–18, 23–28, 40–67.

King Charles bestowed upon me in my childhood, and my constant friendship with himself and his children after I took up my abode at court. In this way he strongly endeared me to himself, and made me greatly his debtor as well in death as in life, so that were I, unmindful of the benefits conferred upon me, to keep silence concerning the most glorious and illustrious deeds of a man who claims so much at my hands, and suffer his life to lack due eulogy and written memorial, as if he had never lived, I should deservedly appear ungrateful, and be so considered, albeit my powers are feeble, scanty, next to nothing indeed, and not at all adapted to write and set forth a life that would tax the eloquence of a Tully.

I submit the book. It contains the history of a very great and distinguished man; but there is nothing in it to wonder at besides his deeds, except the fact that I, who am a barbarian, and very little versed in the Roman language, seem to suppose myself capable of writing gracefully and respectably in Latin, and to carry my presumption so far as to disdain the sentiment that Cicero is said in the first book of the "Tusculan Disputations" to have expressed when speaking of the Latin authors. His words are: "It is an outrageous abuse both of time and literature for a man to commit his thoughts to writing without having the ability either to arrange them or elucidate them, or attract readers by some charm of style." This dictum of the famous orator might have deterred me from writing if I had not made up my mind that it was better to risk the opinions of the world, and put my little talents for composition to the test, than to slight the memory of so great a man for the sake of sparing myself.

The Life of the Emperor Charles

1. The Merovingian family, from which the Franks used to choose their kings, is commonly said to have lasted until the time of Childeric, who was deposed, shaved, and thrust into the cloister by command of the Roman Pontiff Stephen. But although, to all outward appearance, it ended with him, it had long since been devoid of vital strength, and conspicuous only from bearing the empty epithet royal; the real power and authority in the kingdom lay in the hands of the chief officer of the court, the so-called Mayor of the Palace, and he was at the head of affairs. There was nothing left the King to do but to be content with his name of King, his flowing hair, and long beard, to sit on his throne and play the ruler, to give ear to the ambassadors that came from all quarters, and to dismiss them, as if on his own responsibility, in words that were, in fact, suggested to him, or even imposed upon him. He had nothing that he could call his own beyond this vain title of King and the precarious support allowed by the Mayor of the Palace in his discretion, except a single country seat, that brought him but

a very small income. There was a dwelling house upon this, and a small number of servants attached to it, sufficient to perform the necessary offices. When he had to go abroad, he used to ride in a cart, drawn by a yoke of oxen, driven, peasant-fashion, by a ploughman; he rode in this way to the palace and to the general assembly of the people, that met once a year for the welfare of the kingdom, and he returned him in like manner. The Mayor of the Palace took charge of the government and of everything that had to be planned or executed at home or abroad.

2. At the time of Childeric's deposition, Pepin, the father of King Charles, held this office of Mayor of the Palace, one might almost say, by hereditary right; for Pepin's father, Charles, had received it at the hands of his father, Pepin, and filled it with distinction. It was this Charles that crushed the tyrants who claimed to rule the whole Frank land as their own, and that utterly routed the Saracens, when they attempted the conquest of Gaul, in two great battles—one in Aquitania, near the town of Poitiers, and the other on the River Berre, near Narbonne—and compelled them to return to Spain. This honor was usually conferred by the people only upon men eminent from their illustrious birth and ample wealth. For some years, ostensibly under King Childeric, Pepin, the father of King Charles, shared the duties inherited from his father and grandfather most amicably with his brother, Carloman. The latter, then, for reasons unknown, renounced the heavy cares of an earthly crown and retired to Rome. Here he exchanged his worldly garb for a cowl, and built a monastery on Mt. Oreste, near the Church of St. Sylvester, where he enjoyed for several years the seclusion that he desired, in company with certain others who had the same object in view. But so many distinguished Franks made the pilgrimage to Rome to fulfill their vows, and insisted upon paying their respects to him, as their former lord, on the way, that the repose which he so much loved was broken by these frequent visits, and he was driven to change his abode. Accordingly, when he found that his plans were frustrated by his many visitors, he abandoned the mountain, and withdrew to the Monastery of St. Benedict, on Monte Cassino, in the province of Samnium, and passed the rest of his days there in the exercises of religion.

3. Pepin, however, was raised, by decree of the Roman Pontiff, from the rank of Mayor of the Palace to that of King, and ruled alone over the Franks for fifteen years or more. He died of dropsy, in Paris, at the close of the Aquitanian war, which he had waged with William, Duke of Aquitania, for nine successive years, and left two sons, Charles and Carloman, upon whom, by the grace of God, the succession devolved.

The Franks, in a general assembly of the people, made them both kings, on condition that they should divide the whole kingdom equally between them, Charles to take and rule the part that had belonged to their father,

Pepin, and Carloman the part which their uncle, Carloman, had governed. The conditions were accepted, and each entered into possession of the share of the kingdom that fell to him by this arrangement; but peace was only maintained between them with the greatest difficulty, because many of Carloman's party kept trying to disturb their good understanding, and there were some even who plotted to involve them in a war with each other. The event, however, showed the danger to have been rather imaginary than real, for at Carloman's death his widow fled to Italy with her sons and her principal adherents, and without reason, despite her husband's brother, put herself and her children under the protection of Desiderius, King of the Lombards. Carloman had succumbed to disease after ruling two years in common with his brother, and at his death Charles was unanimously elected King of the Franks.

4. It would be folly, I think, to write a word concerning Charles' birth and infancy, or even his boyhood, for nothing has ever been written on the subject, and there is no one alive now who can give information of it. Accordingly, I have determined to pass that by as unknown, and to proceed at once to treat of his character, his deeds, and such other facts of his life as are worth telling and setting forth, and shall first give an account of his deeds at home and abroad, then of his character and pursuits, and lastly of his administration and death, omitting nothing worth knowing or necessary to know.

5. His first undertaking in a military way was the Aquitanian war, begun by his father, but not brought to a close; and because he thought that it could be readily carried through, he took it up while his brother was yet alive, calling upon him to render aid. The campaign once opened, he conducted it with the greatest vigor, notwithstanding his brother withheld the assistance that he had promised, and did not desist or shrink from his self-imposed task until, by his patience and firmness, he had completely gained his ends. He compelled Hunold, who had attempted to seize Aquitania after Waifar's death, and renew the war then almost concluded, to abandon Aquitania and flee to Gascony. Even here he gave him no rest, but crossed the River Garonne, built the castle of Fronsac, and sent ambassadors to Lupus, Duke of Gascony, to demand the surrender of the fugitive, threatening to take him by force unless he were promptly given up to him. Thereupon Lupus chose the wiser course, and not only gave Hunold up, but submitted himself, with the province which he ruled, to the King.

9. In the midst of this vigorous and almost uninterrupted struggle with the Saxons, he covered the frontier by garrisons at the proper points, and marched over the Pyrenees into Spain at the head of all the forces that he could muster. All the towns and castles that he attacked surrendered, and up to the time of his homeward march he sustained no loss whatever; but on

his return through the Pyrenees he had cause to rue the treachery of the Gascons. That region is well adapted for ambushes by reason of the thick forests that cover it; and as the army was advancing in the long line of march necessitated by the narrowness of the road, the Gascons, who lay in ambush on the top of a very high mountain, attacked the rear of the baggage train and the rear guard in charge of it, and hurled them down to the very bottom of the valley. In the struggle that ensued, they cut them off to a man; they then plundered the baggage, and dispersed with all speed in every direction under cover of approaching night. The lightness of their armor and the nature of the battleground stood the Gascons in good stead on this occasion, whereas the Franks fought at a disadvantage in every respect, because of the weight of their armor and the unevenness of the ground. Eggihard, the King's steward; Anselm, Count Palatine; and Roland, Governor of the March of Brittany, with very many others, fell in this engagement. This ill turn could not be avenged for the nonce, because the enemy scattered so widely after carrying out their plan that not the least clue could be had to their whereabouts.

15. Such are the wars, most skilfully planned and successfully fought, which this most powerful king waged during the forty-seven years of his reign. He so largely increased the Frank kingdom, which was already great and strong when he received it at his father's hands, that more than double its former territory was added to it. The authority of the Franks was formerly confined to that part of Gaul included between the Rhine and the Loire, the Ocean and the Balearic Sea; to that part of Germany which is inhabited by the so-called Eastern Franks, and is bounded by Saxony and the Danube, the Rhine and the Saale—this stream separates the Thuringians from the Sorabians; and to the country of the Alemanni and Bavarians. By the wars above mentioned he first made tributary Aquitania, Gascony, and the whole of the region of the Pyrenees as far as the River Ebro, which rises in the land of the Navarrese, flows through the most fertile districts of Spain, and empties into the Balearic Sea, beneath the walls of the city of Tortosa. He next reduced and made tributary all Italy from Aosta to Lower Calabria, where the boundary line runs between the Beneventans and the Greeks, a territory more than a thousand miles long; then Saxony, which constitutes no small part of Germany, and is reckoned to be twice as wide as the country inhabited by the Franks, while about equal to it in length; in addition, both Pannonias, Dacia beyond the Danube, and Istria, Liburnia, and Dalmatia, except the cities on the coast, which he left to the Greek Emperor for friendship's sake, and because of the treaty that he had made with him. In fine, he vanquished and made tributary all the wild and barbarous tribes dwelling in Germany between the Rhine and the Vistula, the Ocean and the Danube, all of which speak very much the same language,

but differ widely from one another in customs and dress. The chief among them are the Welatabians, the Sorabians, the Abodriti, and the Bohemians, and he had to make war upon these; but the rest, by far the larger number, submitted to him of their own accord.

16. He added to the glory of his reign by gaining the good will of several kings and nations; so close, indeed, was the alliance that he contracted with Alfonso, King of Galicia and Asturias, that the latter, when sending letters or ambassadors to Charles, invariably styled himself his man. His munificence won the kings of the Scots also to pay such deference to his wishes that they never gave him any other title than lord, or themselves than subjects and slaves: there are letters from them extant in which these feelings in his regard are expressed. His relations with Aaron, King of the Persians, who ruled over almost the whole of the East, India excepted, were so friendly that this prince preferred his favor to that of all the kings and potentates of the earth, and considered that to him alone marks of honor and munificence were due. Accordingly, when the ambassadors sent by Charles to visit the most holy sepulchre and place of resurrection of our Lord and Savior presented themselves before him with gifts, and made known their master's wishes, he not only granted what was asked, but gave possession of that holy and blessed spot. When they returned, he dispatched his ambassadors with them, and sent magnificent gifts, besides stuffs, perfumes, and other rich products of the Eastern lands. A few years before this, Charles had asked him for an elephant, and he sent the only one that he had. The Emperors of Constantinople, Nicephorus, Michael, and Leo, made advances to Charles, and sought friendship and alliance with him by several embassies; and even when the Greeks suspected him of designing to wrest the empire from them, because of his assumption of the title Emperor, they made a close alliance with him, that he might have no cause of offense. In fact, the power of the Franks was always viewed by the Greeks and Romans with a jealous eye, whence the Greek proverb "Have the Frank for your friend, but not for your neighbor."

17. This King, who showed himself so great in extending his empire and subduing foreign nations, and was constantly occupied with plans to that end, undertook also very many works calculated to adorn and benefit his kingdom, and brought several of them to completion. Among these, the most deserving of mention are the basilica of the Holy Mother of God at Aix-la-Chapelle, built in the most admirable manner, and a bridge over the Rhine at Mayence, half a mile long, the breadth of the river at this point. This bridge was destroyed by fire the year before Charles died, but, owing to his death so soon after, could not be repaired, although he had intended to rebuild it in stone. He began two palaces of beautiful workmanship— one near his manor called Ingelheim, not far from Mayence; the other at

Nimeguen, on the Waal, the stream that washes the south side of the island of the Batavians. But, above all, sacred edifices were the object of his care throughout his whole kingdom; and whenever he found them falling to ruin from age, he commanded the priests and fathers who had charge of them to repair them, and made sure by commissioners that his instructions were obeyed. He also fitted out a fleet for the war with the Northmen; the vessels required for this purpose were built on the rivers that flow from Gaul and Germany into the Northern Ocean. Moreover, since the Northmen continually overran and laid waste the Gallic and German coasts, he caused watch and ward to be kept in all the harbors, and at the mouths of rivers large enough to admit the entrance of vessels, to prevent the enemy from disembarking; and in the South, in Narbonensis and Septimania, and along the whole coast of Italy as far as Rome, he took the same precautions against the Moors, who had recently begun their piratical practices. Hence, Italy suffered no great harm in his time at the hands of the Moors, nor Gaul and Germany from the Northmen, save that the Moors got possession of the Etruscan town of Civita Vecchia by treachery, and sacked it, and the Northmen harried some of the islands in Frisia off the German coast.

18. Thus did Charles defend and increase as well as beautify his kingdom, as is well known; and here let me express my admiration of his great qualities and his extraordinary constancy alike in good and evil fortune. I will now forthwith proceed to give the details of his private and family life.

After his father's death, while sharing the kingdom with his brother, he bore his unfriendliness and jealousy most patiently, and, to the wonder of all, could not be provoked to be angry with him. Later he married a daughter of Desiderius, King of the Lombards, at the instance of his mother; but he repudiated her at the end of a year for some reason unknown, and married Hildegard, a woman of high birth, of Suabian origin. He had three sons by her—Charles, Pepin, and Louis—and as many daughters—Hruodrud, Bertha, and Gisela. He had three other daughters besides these—Theoderada, Hiltrud, and Ruodhaid—two by his third wife, Fastrada, a woman of East Frankish (that is to say, of German) origin, and the third by a concubine, whose name for the moment escapes me. At the death of Fastrada, he married Liutgard, an Alemannic woman, who bore him no children. After her death he had three concubines—Gersuinda, a Saxon, by whom he had Adaltrud; Regina, who was the mother of Drogo and Hugh; and Ethelind, by whom he had Theodoric. Charles' mother, Berthrada, passed her old age with him in great honor; he entertained the greatest veneration for her; and there was never any disagreement between them except when he divorced the daughter of King Desiderius, whom he had married to please her. She died soon after Hildegard, after living to see three grandsons and as many granddaughters in her son's house, and he buried her with great pomp in the Basilica of St. Denis, where his father lay. He had an only sister, Gisela, who had consecrated herself to a religious life from girlhood, and he cherished as much affection for her as for his mother. She also died a few years before him in the nunnery where she had passed her life.

19. The plan that he adopted for his children's education was, first of all, to have both boys and girls instructed in the liberal arts, to which he also turned his own attention. As soon as their years admitted, in accordance with the custom of the Franks, the boys had to learn horsemanship, and to practice war and the chase, and the girls to familiarize themselves with cloth-making, and to handle distaff and spindle, that they might not grow indolent through idleness, and he fostered in them every virtuous sentiment. He only lost three of all his children before his death, two sons and one daughter, Charles, who was the eldest, Pepin, whom he had made King of Italy, and Hruodrud, his oldest daughter, whom he had betrothed to Constantine, Emperor of the Greeks. Pepin left one son, named Bernard, and five daughters, Adelaide, Atula, Guntrada, Berthaid, and Theoderada. The King gave a striking proof of his fatherly affection at the time of Pepin's death: he appointed the grandson to succeed Pepin, and had the grand-daughters brought up with his own daughters. When his sons and his daughter died, he was not so calm as might have been expected from his remarkably strong mind, for his affections were no less strong, and moved him to tears. Again, when he was told of the death of Hadrian, the Roman Pontiff, whom he had loved most of all his friends, he wept as much as if he had lost a brother, or a very dear son. He was by nature most ready to contract friendships, and not only made friends easily, but clung to them persistently, and cherished most fondly those with whom he had formed such ties. He was so careful of the training of his sons and daughters that he never took his meals without them when he was at home, and never made a journey without them; his sons would ride at his side, and his daughters follow him, while a number of his bodyguard, detailed for their protection, brought up the rear. Strange to say, although they were very handsome women, and he loved them very dearly, he was never willing to marry any of them to a man of their own nation or to a foreigner, but kept them all at home until his death, saying that he could not dispense with their society. Hence, though otherwise happy, he experienced the malignity of fortune as far as they were concerned; yet he concealed his knowledge of the rumors current in regard to them, and of the suspicions entertained of their honor.

20. By one of his concubines he had a son, handsome in face, but hunchbacked, named Pepin, whom I omitted to mention in the list of his children. When Charles was at war with the Huns, and was wintering in

Bavaria, this Pepin shammed sickness, and plotted against his father in company with some of the leading Franks, who seduced him with vain promises of the royal authority. When his deceit was discovered, and the conspirators were punished, his head was shaved, and he was suffered, in accordance with his wishes, to devote himself to a religious life in the monastery of Prüm. A formidable conspiracy against Charles had previously been set on foot in Germany, but all the traitors were banished, some of them without mutilation, others after their eyes had been put out. Three of them only lost their lives; they drew their swords and resisted arrest, and, after killing several men, were cut down, because they could not be otherwise overpowered. It is supposed that the cruelty of Queen Fastrada was the primary cause of these plots, and they were both due to Charles' apparent acquiescence in his wife's cruel conduct, and deviation from the usual kindness and gentleness of his disposition. All the rest of his life he was regarded by everyone with the utmost love and affection, so much so that not the least accusation of unjust rigor was ever made against him.

21. He liked foreigners, and was at great pains to take them under his protection. There were often so many of them, both in the palace and the kingdom, that they might reasonably have been considered a nuisance; but he, with his broad humanity, was very little disturbed by such annoyances, because he felt himself compensated for these great inconveniences by the praises of his generosity and the reward of high renown.

22. Charles was large and strong, and of lofty stature, though not disproportionately tall (his height is well known to have been seven times the length of his foot); the upper part of his head was round, his eyes very large and animated, nose a little long, hair fair, and face laughing and merry. Thus his appearance was always stately and dignified, whether he was standing or sitting; although his neck was thick and somewhat short; and his belly rather prominent; but the symmetry of the rest of his body concealed these defects. His gait was firm, his whole carriage manly, and his voice clear, but not so strong as his size led one to expect. His health was excellent, except during the four years preceding his death, when he was subject to frequent fevers; at the last he even limped a little with one foot. Even in those years he consulted rather his own inclinations than the advice of physicians, who were almost hateful to him, because they wanted him to give up roasts, to which he was accustomed, and to eat boiled meat instead. In accordance with the national custom, he took frequent exercise on horseback and in the chase, accomplishments in which scarcely any people in the world can equal the Franks. He enjoyed the exhalations from natural warm springs, and often practiced swimming, in which he was such an adept that none could surpass him; and hence it was that he built his palace at Aix-la-Chapelle, and lived there constantly during his latter years until

his death. He used not only to invite his sons to his bath, but his nobles and friends, and now and then a troop of his retinue or bodyguard, so that a hundred or more persons sometimes bathed with him.

23. He used to wear the national, that is to say, the Frank, dress—next his skin a linen shirt and linen breeches, and above these a tunic fringed with silk; while hose fastened by bands covered his lower limbs, and shoes his feet, and he protected his shoulders and chest in winter by a close-fitting coat of otter or marten skins. Over all he flung a blue cloak, and he always had a sword girt about him, usually one with a gold or silver hilt and belt; he sometimes carried a jeweled sword, but only on great feastdays or at the reception of ambassadors from foreign nations. He despised foreign costumes, however handsome, and never allowed himself to be robed in them, except twice in Rome, when he donned the Roman tunic, chlamys, and shoes; the first time at the request of Pope Hadrian, the second to gratify Leo, Hadrian's successor. On great feastdays he made use of embroidered clothes and shoes bedecked with precious stones, his cloak was fastened by a golden buckle, and he appeared crowned with a diadem of gold and gems, but on other days his dress varied little from the common dress of the people.

24. Charles was temperate in eating, and particularly so in drinking, for he abominated drunkenness in anybody, much more in himself and those of his household; but he could not easily abstain from food, and often complained that fasts injured his health. He very rarely gave entertainments, only on great feastdays, and then to large numbers of people. His meals ordinarily consisted of four courses, not counting the roast, which his huntsmen used to bring in on the spit; he was more fond of this than of any other dish. While at table, he listened to reading or music. The subjects of the readings were the stories and deeds of olden time: he was fond, too, of St. Augustine's books, and especially of the one entitled "The City of God." He was so moderate in the use of wine and all sorts of drink that he rarely allowed himself more than three cups in the course of a meal. In summer, after the midday meal, he would eat some fruit, drain a single cup, put off his clothes and shoes, just as he did for the night, and rest for two or three hours. He was in the habit of awaking and rising from bed four or five times during the night. While he was dressing and putting on his shoes, he not only gave audience to his friends, but if the Count of the Palace told him of any suit in which his judgment was necessary, he had the parties brought before him forthwith, took cognizance of the case, and gave his decision, just as if he were sitting on the judgment seat. This was not the only business that he transacted at this time, but he performed any duty of the day whatever, whether he had to attend to the matter himself, or to give commands concerning it to his officers.

25. Charles had the gift of ready and fluent speech, and could express whatever he had to say with the utmost clearness. He was not satisfied with command of his native language merely, but gave attention to the study of foreign ones, and in particular was such a master of Latin that he could speak it as well as his native tongue; but he could understand Greek better than he could speak it. He was so eloquent, indeed, that he might have passed for a teacher of eloquence. He most zealously cultivated the liberal arts, held those who taught them in great esteem, and conferred great honors upon them. He took lessons in grammar of the deacon Peter of Pisa, at that time an aged man. Another deacon, Albin of Britain, surnamed Alcuin, a man of Saxon extraction, who was the greatest scholar of the day, was his teacher in other branches of learning. The King spent much time and labor with him studying rhetoric, dialectics, and especially astronomy; he learned to reckon, and used to investigate the motions of the heavenly bodies most curiously, with an intelligent scrutiny. He also tried to write, and used to keep tablets and blanks in bed under his pillow, that at leisure hours he might accustom his hand to form the letters; however, as he did not begin his efforts in due season, but late in life, they met with ill success.

26. He cherished with the greatest fervor and devotion the principles of the Christian religion, which had been instilled into him from infancy. Hence it was that he built the beautiful basilica at Aix-la-Chapelle, which he adorned with gold and silver and lamps, and with rails and doors of solid brass. He had the columns and marbles for this structure brought from Rome and Ravenna, for he could not find such as were suitable elsewhere. He was a constant worshipper at this church as long as his health permitted, going morning and evening, even after nightfall, besides attending mass; and he took care that all the services there conducted should be administered with the utmost possible propriety, very often warning the sextons not to let any improper or unclean thing be brought into the building or remain in it. He provided it with a great number of sacred vessels of gold and silver and with such a quantity of clerical robes that not even the doorkeepers who fill the humblest office in the church were obliged to wear their everyday clothes when in the exercise of their duties. He was at great pains to improve the church reading and psalmody, for he was well skilled in both, although he neither read in public nor sang, except in a low tone and with others.

27. He was very forward in succoring the poor, and in that gratuitous generosity which the Greeks call alms, so much so that he not only made a point of giving in his own country and his own kingdom, but when he discovered that there were Christians living in poverty in Syria, Egypt, and Africa, at Jerusalem, Alexandria, and Carthage, he had compassion on

their wants, and used to send money over the seas to them. The reason that he zealously strove to make friends with the kings beyond seas was that he might get help and relief to the Christians living under their rule. He cherished the Church of St. Peter the Apostle at Rome above all other holy and sacred places, and heaped its treasury with a vast wealth of gold, silver, and precious stones. He sent great and countless gifts to the popes, and throughout his whole reign the wish that he had nearest at heart was to re-establish the ancient authority of the city of Rome under his care and by his influence, and to defend and protect the Church of St. Peter, and to beautify and enrich it out of his own store above all other churches. Although he held it in such veneration, he only repaired to Rome to pay his vows and make his supplications four times during the whole forty-seven years that he reigned.

28. When he made his last journey thither, he had also other ends in view. The Romans had inflicted many injuries upon the Pontiff Leo, tearing out his eyes and cutting out his tongue, so that he had been compelled to call upon the King for help. Charles accordingly went to Rome, to set in order the affairs of the Church, which were in great confusion, and passed the whole winter there. It was then that he received the titles of Emperor and Augustus, to which he at first had such an aversion that he declared that he would not have set foot in the Church the day that they were conferred, although it was a great feast-day, if he could have foreseen the design of the Pope. He bore very patiently with the jealousy which the Roman emperors showed upon his assuming these titles, for they took this step very ill; and by dint of frequent embassies and letters, in which he addressed them as brothers, he made their haughtiness yield to his magnanimity, a quality in which he was unquestionably much their superior.

29. It was after he had received the imperial name that, finding the laws of his people very defective (the Franks have two sets of laws, very different in many particulars), he determined to add what was wanting, to reconcile the discrepancies, and to correct what was vicious and wrongly cited in them. However, he went no further in this matter than to supplement the laws by a few capitularies, and those imperfect ones; but he caused the unwritten laws of all the tribes that came under his rule to be compiled and reduced to writing. He also had the old rude songs that celebrate the deeds and wars of the ancient kings written out for transmission to posterity. He began a grammar of his native language. He gave the months names in his own tongue, in place of the Latin and barbarous names by which they were formerly known among the Franks. He likewise designated the winds by twelve appropriate names; there were hardly more than four distinctive ones in use before. He called January, Wintarmanoth; February, Hornung; March, Lentzinmanoth; April, Ostarmanoth; May, Winnemanoth; June,

Brachmanoth; July, Heuvimanoth; August, Aranmanoth; September, Witu-
manoth; October, Windumemanoth; November, Herbistmanoth; December,
Heilagmanoth. He styled the winds as follows; Subsolanus, Ostroniwint;
Eurus, Ostsundroni; Euroauster, Sundostroni; Auster, Sundroni; Austro-
Africus, Sundwestroni; Africus, Westsundroni; Zephyrus, Westroni; Cau-
rus, Westnordroni; Circius, Nordwestroni; Septentrio, Nordroni; Aquilo,
Nordostroni; Vulturnus, Ostnordroni.

30. Toward the close of his life, when he was broken by ill-health and
old age, he summoned Louis, King of Aquitania, his only surviving son by
Hildegard, and gathered together all the chief men of the whole kingdom of
the Franks in a solemn assembly. He appointed Louis, with their unanimous consent, to rule with himself over the whole kingdom, and constituted him heir to the imperial name; then, placing the diadem upon his son's
head, he bade him be proclaimed Emperor and Augustus. This step was
hailed by all present with great favor, for it really seemed as if God had
prompted him to it for the kingdom's good; it increased the King's dignity,
and struck no little terror into foreign nations. After sending his son back
to Aquitania, although weak from age he set out to hunt, as usual, near his
palace at Aix-la-Chapelle, and passed the rest of the autumn in the chase,
returning thither about the first of November. While wintering there, he
was seized, in the month of January, with a high fever, and took to his bed.
As soon as he was taken sick, he prescribed for himself abstinence from
food, as he always used to do in case of fever, thinking that the disease
could be driven off, or at least mitigated, by fasting. Besides the fever, he
suffered from a pain in the side, which the Greeks call pleurisy; but he still
persisted in fasting, and in keeping up his strength only by draughts taken
at very long intervals. He died January twenty-eighth, the seventh day from
the time that he took to his bed, at nine o'clock in the morning, after partaking of the holy communion, in the seventy-second year of his age and the
forty-seventh of his reign.

31. His body was washed and cared for in the usual manner, and was
then carried to the church, and interred amid the greatest lamentations of
all the people. There was some question at first where to lay him, because
in his lifetime he had given no directions as to his burial; but at length all
agreed that he could nowhere be more honorably entombed than in the very
basilica that he had built in the town at his own expense, for love of God
and our Lord Jesus Christ, and in honor of the Holy and Eternal Virgin,
His Mother. He was buried there the same day that he died, and a gilded
arch was erected above his tomb with his image and an inscription. The
words of the inscription were as follows: "In this tomb lies the body of
Charles, the Great and Orthodox Emperor, who gloriously extended the
kingdom of the Franks, and reigned prosperously for forty-seven years. He

died at more than seventy years of age, in the year of our Lord 814, the 7th Indiction, on the 28th day of January."

32. Very many omens had portended his approaching end, a fact that he had recognized as well as others. Eclipses both of the sun and moon were very frequent during the last three years of his life, and a black spot was visible on the sun for the space of seven days. The gallery between the basilica and the palace, which he had built at great pains and labor, fell in sudden ruin to the ground on the day of the Ascension of our Lord. The wooden bridge over the Rhine at Mayence, which he had caused to be constructed with admirable skill, at the cost of ten years' hard work, so that it seemed as if it might last forever, was so completely consumed in three hours by an accidental fire that not a single splinter of it was left, except what was under water. Moreover, one day in his last campaign into Saxony against Godfred, King of the Danes, Charles himself saw a ball of fire fall suddenly from the heavens with a great light, just as he was leaving camp before sunrise to set out on the march. It rushed across the clear sky from right to left, and everybody was wondering what was the meaning of the sign, when the horse which he was riding gave a sudden plunge, head foremost, and fell, and threw him to the ground so heavily that his cloak buckle was broken and his sword belt shattered; and after his servants had hastened to him and relieved him of his arms, he could not rise without their assistance. He happened to have a javelin in his hand when he was thrown, and this was struck from his grasp with such force that it was found lying at a distance of twenty feet or more from the spot. Again, the palace at Aix-la-Chapelle frequently trembled, the roofs of whatever buildings he tarried in kept up a continual crackling noise, the basilica in which he was afterwards buried was struck by lightning, and the gilded ball that adorned the pinnacle of the roof was shattered by the thunderbolt and hurled upon the bishop's house adjoining. In this same basilica, on the margin of the cornice that ran around the interior, between the upper and lower tiers of arches, a legend was inscribed in red letters, stating who was the builder of the temple, the last words of which were *Karolus Princeps*. The year that he died it was remarked by some, a few months before his decease, that the letters of the word *Princeps* were so effaced as to be no longer decipherable. But Charles despised, or affected to despise, all these omens, as having no reference whatever to him.

33. It had been his intention to make a will, that he might give some share in the inheritance to his daughters and the children of his concubines; but it was begun too late and could not be finished. Three years before his death, however, he made a division of his treasures, money, clothes, and other movable goods in the presence of his friends and servants, and called them to witness it, that their voices might insure the ratification of the dis-

position thus made. He had a summary drawn up of his wishes regarding this distribution of his property, the terms and text of which are as follows:

"In the name of the Lord God, the Almighty Father, Son, and Holy Ghost. This is the inventory and division dictated by the most glorious and most pious Lord Charles, Emperor Augustus, in the 811th year of the Incarnation of our Lord Jesus Christ, in the 43rd year of his reign in France and 37th in Italy, the 11th of his empire, and the 4th Indiction, which considerations of piety and prudence have determined him, and the favor of God enabled him, to make of his treasures and money ascertained this day to be in his treasure chamber. In this division he is especially desirous to provide not only that the largess of alms which Christians usually make of their possessions shall be made for himself in due course and order out of his wealth, but also that his heirs shall be free from all doubt, and know clearly what belongs to them, and be able to share their property by suitable partition without litigation or strife. With this intention and to this end he has first divided all his substance and movable goods ascertained to be in his treasure chamber on the day aforesaid in gold, silver, precious stones, and royal ornaments into three lots, and has subdivided and set off two of the said lots into twenty-one parts, keeping the third entire. The first two lots have been thus subdivided into twenty-one parts because there are in his kingdom twenty-one recognized metropolitan cities, and in order that each archbishopric may receive by way of alms, at the hands of his heirs and friends, one of the said parts, and that the archbishop who shall then administer its affairs shall take the part given to it, and share the same with his suffragans in such manner that one third shall go to the Church, and the remaining two thirds be divided among the suffragans. The twenty-one parts into which the first two lots are to be distributed, according to the number of recognized metropolitan cities, have been set apart one from another, and each has been put aside by itself in a box labeled with the name of the city for which it is destined. The names of the cities to which this alms or largess is to be sent are as follows: Rome, Ravenna, Milan, Friuli, Grado, Cologne, Mayence, Salzburg, Treves, Sens, Besançon, Lyons, Rouen, Rheims, Arles, Vienne, Moutiers-en-Tarantaise, Embrun, Bordeaux, Tours, and Bourges. The third lot, which he wishes to be kept entire, is to be bestowed as follows: While the first two lots are to be divided into the parts aforesaid, and set aside under seal, the third lot shall be employed for the owner's daily needs, as property which he shall be under no obligation to part with in order to fulfill any vow, and this as long as he shall be in the flesh, or consider it necessary for his use. But upon his death, or voluntary renunciation of the affairs of this world, this said lot shall be divided into four parts, and one thereof shall be added to the aforesaid twenty-one parts; the second shall be assigned to his sons and daughters, and to the sons and daughters of his sons, to be distributed among them in just and equal partition; the third, in accordance with the custom common among Christians, shall be devoted to the poor; and the fourth shall go to the support of the men servants and maid servants on duty in the palace. It is his wish that to this said third lot of the whole amount, which consists, as well as the rest, of gold and silver, shall be added all the vessels and utensils of brass, iron, and other metals, together with the arms, clothing, and other movable goods, costly and cheap, adapted to divers uses, as hangings, coverlets, carpets, woolen stuffs, leathern articles, pack-saddles, and whatsoever shall be found in his treasure chamber and wardrobe at that time, in order that thus the parts of the said lot may be augmented, and the alms distributed reach more persons. He ordains that his chapel—that is to say, its church property, as well that which he has provided and collected as that which came to him by inheritance from his father—shall remain entire, and not be dissevered by any partition whatever. If, however, any vessels, books, or other articles be found therein which are certainly known not to have been given by him to the said chapel, whoever wants them shall have them on paying their value at a fair estimation. He likewise commands that the books which he has collected in his library in great numbers shall be sold for fair prices to such as want them, and the money received therefrom given to the poor. It is well known that among his other property and treasures are three silver tables, and one very large and massive golden one. He directs and commands that the square silver table, upon which there is a representation of the city of Constantinople, shall be sent to the Basilica of St. Peter the Apostle at Rome, with the other gifts destined therefor; that the round one, adorned with a delineation of the city of Rome, shall be given to the Episcopal Church at Ravenna; that the third, which far surpasses the other two in weight and in beauty of workmanship, and is made in three circles, showing the plan of the whole universe, drawn with skill and delicacy, shall go, together with the golden table, fourthly above mentioned, to increase that lot which is to be devoted to his heirs and to alms.

This deed, and the dispositions thereof, he has made and appointed in the presence of the bishops, abbots, and counts able to be present, whose names are hereto subscribed: Bishops—Hildebald, Ricolf, Arno, Wolfar, Bernoin, Laidrad, John, Theodulf, Jesse, Heito, Waltgaud. Abbots—Fredugis, Adalung, Angilbert, Irmino. Counts—Walacho, Meginher, Otulf, Stephen, Unruoch, Burchard, Meginhard, Hatto, Rihwin, Edo, Ercangar, Gerold, Bero, Hildiger, Rocculf."

Charles' son Louis, who by the grace of God succeeded him, after examining this summary, took pains to fulfill all its conditions most religiously as soon as possible after his father's death.

5. Articles from the *Capitulare de Villis* (807)

12. That each steward shall make an annual statement of all our income: an account of our lands cultivated by the oxen which our ploughmen drive and of our lands which the tenants of farms ought to plough; an account of the pigs, of the rents, of the obligations and fines; of the game taken in our forests without our permission; of the various compositions; of the mills, of the forest, of the fields, of the bridges, and ships: of the free-men and the hundreds who are under obligations to our treasury; of markets, vineyards, and those who owe wine to us; of the hay, fire-wood, torches, planks, and other kinds of lumber; of the waste-lands; of the fruits of the trees, of the nut trees, larger and smaller; of the grafted trees of all kinds; of the gardens; of the turnips; of the fish-ponds; of the hides, skins, and horns; of the honey, wax; of the fat, tallow and soap; of the mulberry wine, cooked wine, mead, vinegar, beer, wine new and old; of the new grain and the old; of the hens and eggs; of the geese; the number of fishermen, smiths [workers in metal], sword-makers, and shoe-makers; of the bins and boxes; of the turners and saddlers; of the forges and mines, that is iron and other mines; of the lead mines; of the tributaries; of the colts and fillies; they shall make all these known to us, set forth separately and in order, at Christmas, in order that we may know what and how much of each thing we have.

22. In each of our estates our stewards are to have as many cowhouses, piggeries, sheep-folds, stables for goats, as possible, and they ought never to be without these. And let them have in addition cows furnished by our serfs for performing their service, so that the cow-houses and plows shall be in no way weakened by the service on our demesne. And when they have to provide meat, let them have steers lame, but healthy, and cows and horses which are not mangy, or other beasts which are not diseased and, as we have said, our cow-houses and plows are not to be weakened for this.

34. They must provide with the greatest care, that whatever is prepared or made with the hands, that is, lard, smoked meat, salt meat, partially salted meat, wine, vinegar, mulberry wine, cooked wine, *garns*, mustard, cheese, butter, malt, beer, mead, honey, wax, flour, all should be prepared and made with the greatest cleanliness.

40. That each steward on each of our domains shall always have, for the sake of ornament, swans, peacocks, pheasants, ducks, pigeons, partridges, turtle-doves.

42. That in each of our estates, the chambers shall be provided with

From *Translations and Reprints from the Original Sources of European History*, vol. 2, sec. 2 (Philadelphia: University of Pennsylvania Press, 1900).

counterpanes, cushions, pillows, bed-clothes, coverings for the tables and benches; vessels of brass, lead, iron and wood; andirons, chains, pot-hooks, adzes, axes, augers, cutlasses and all other kinds of tools, so that it shall never be necessary to go elsewhere for them, or to borrow them. And the weapons, which are carried against the enemy, shall be well cared for, so as to keep them in good condition; and when they are brought back they shall be placed in the chamber.

43. For our women's work they are to give at the proper time, as has been ordered, the materials, that is the linen, wool, woad, vermillion, madder, wool-combs, teasels, soap, grease, vessels and the other objects which are necessary.

44. Of the food-products other than meat, two-thirds shall be sent each year for our own use, that is of the vegetables, fish, cheese, butter, honey, mustard, vinegar, millet, panic, dried and green herbs, radishes, and in addition of the wax, soap and other small products; and they shall tell us how much is left by a statement, as we have said above; and they shall not neglect this as in the past; because from those two-thirds, we wish to know how much remains.

45. That each steward shall have in his district good workmen, namely, blacksmiths, gold-smiths, silver-smiths, shoemakers, turners, carpenters, sword-makers, fishermen, foilers, soap-makers, men who know how to make beer, cider, perry, and all the other kinds of beverages, bakers to make pastry for our table, net-makers who know how to make nets for hunting, fishing and fowling, and the others who are too numerous to be designated.

6. Regino of Prüm, *On the Breakdown of the Carolingian Empire* (ca. 910)

<u>888</u>

In the year of the incarnation of the Lord 888, on the twelfth of January, Emperor Charles, the third of this name and dignity, died and was buried in the monastery of Reichenau.[1] He was a most Christian prince, feared God,

From Regino of Prüm, *Chronica*, in *Quellen zur Karolingischen Reichsgeschichte, III Freiherr vom Stein Gedächtnisausgabe VII*, edited by Reinhold Rau (Darmstadt: Wissenschaftliche Buchgesellschaft, 1975), pp. 278–96. Translated for this volume by Constantin Fasolt.

1. Charles III, "the Fat," born 839, died 888. Youngest of the three sons of Louis II, "the German," grandson of Louis the Pious, and great-grandson of Charlemagne. On the death of his father in 876, he became king of Alemannia, one of the three parts into which the East-Frankish kingdom of Louis II was divided. In 881 he was crowned emperor, and in 882 was

wholeheartedly observed his mandates, obeyed ecclesiastical sanctions with great devotion, was generous with alms, unceasingly gave himself to prayer and the singing of psalms, was indefatigably intent on praising God, and entrusted all of his hopes and plans to divine dispensation. This is why everything happily turned out for the best for him. In fact, he had no trouble at all in taking possession of all of the kingdoms of the Franks in a short time and without conflict or opposition, even though his predecessors had not acquired them without much effort and bloodshed. That towards the end of his life he was divested of his dignities and deprived of all his goods was, we believe, a temptation designed not only to purify him but, more important, to prove his excellence. For it is reported that he bore his ill fortune with great patience, keeping his vows to offer thanks in adversity as well as in prosperity. Therefore he either has already received, or is without any doubt going to receive, the crown of life, which God promised to those who love him.

Lacking a legitimate heir after his death, the kingdoms which had obeyed his command dissolved their union and broke into parts. Without waiting any longer for their natural lord, each of them decided to elect a king for itself from within the kingdom. This caused great wars, not because the Franks were lacking princes who were noble, strong, and wise enough to rule the kingdoms, but because they were so equally matched in their generosity, dignity, and power that the discord increased, because no one excelled so much above the others that they would have deigned to submit to his lordship. Frankland could have produced many princes well suited to handle the helm of the kingdom if fortune had not armed them to destroy each other in their striving for excellence.

A part of the Italian people thus appointed Berengar the son of Everhard, who held the duchy of the Friulians, as their king, and another decided to raise Wido, the son of Lanbert, Duke of the Spoletans, to the same royal dignity.[2] So much destruction arose on both sides from this discord, and so much human blood was shed, that, in agreement with the word of

---

lucky enough to inherit his brother Louis III's possessions, who had already inherited the share of the third brother, Carloman. He was elected king of the West-Frankish kingdom in 885 and thus managed to unite the entire Carolingian realm one last time. An East-Frankish assembly deposed him in 887 because of his failure to contain the Normans, and elected Arnulf of Carinthia as his successor.

2. It is worth noting that the new kings mentioned here came from important East-Frankish families, and were thus not as indigenous to the parts into which the Carolingian Empire broke as Regino claims. The duchy of Spoleto and the march of Friuli were two of the four most important political units in Italy. The others were Tuscany and the papal state. Berengar, marquis of Friuli, a grandson of Louis the Pious through his mother, had long been allied with the East-Frankish kings. As Regino points out, Berengar was defeated by his rival Wido, duke of Spoleto, who was crowned emperor in 894, but died two years later. Berengar became a vassal of Arnulf in order to gain assistance in his endeavor to prevent Wido from

the Lord, the "kingdom divided against itself" would almost have incurred the woe of desolation.[3] In the end, Wido won and expelled Berengar from the kingdom. Berengar therefore approached King Arnulf and demanded protection against his enemy.[4] What Arnulf did, however, and how he entered the Italian kingdom twice with his army, will be recounted in the proper place.[5]

The people of the Gauls, meanwhile, assembled, and all alike, with the consent of Arnulf, advised and wanted to make Duke Odo their king.[6] He was the son of Robert, whom we have mentioned before, a vigorous man, more handsome, tall, strong, and wise than others. He ruled the commonwealth manfully and became an indefatigable defender against the unremitting depredations by the Northmen.

At the same time Rudolf, the son of Conrad and nephew of the abbot Hugo, whom we also mentioned above, occupied the province between the Iura and the Pennine Alps, and in St. Maurice, having brought in certain leading men and some priests, placed a crown on his head and ordered that he should be called king.[7] Then he sent legates through Lothar's entire kingdom and with his suggestions and promises beguiled the minds of the bishops and noblemen to favor him. When this was announced to Arnulf,

---

taking charge of his home territory, the march of Friuli. After the death of Wido's son Lanbert, he succeeded in becoming king of Italy in 898, and was crowned emperor in 915. Much criticized because of his failure to control Hungarian and Saracen raids on Italy, and his willingness to bargain with the Hungarians, he died in 924.

3. Cf. Matt. 12.25.

4. Arnulf of Carinthia, born ca. 850, died 899. Illegitimate son of Carloman, and thus great-great-grandson of Charlemagne, became duke of Carinthia on his father's death in 880, and was elected king of the East-Frankish realm in 887 because of his proven abilities as a military leader. Having consolidated his power by the victory over the Northmen on 1 November 891 on the Dyle which is described by Regino in the present selection, he entered Italy twice, in 894 and 895, to battle with Wido of Spoleto, and was crowned emperor after Wido's death in 896. His son Louis IV, the Child (893–911), was the last Carolingian ruler over the East-Frankish realm.

5. He does so under the years 894 and 896, which are not included in this selection.

6. Odo I, Eudes in French, born ca. 860, died 898, count of Paris. He excelled by his defense of Paris against the Northmen in 885–86 and later by a victory won over them in 888. He was the first ruler of the West-Frankish kingdom to come from the family which, under the name of Capetians, ruled France without interruption for the centuries after 987. The Carolingian candidate for the throne, Charles, "the Simple," was born in 879 and thus was too young to rule in 888. Odo, too, placed himself under Arnulf's protection in 888, before going to Reims to be crowned king. In 893 Charles III was set up as a counter-king. Odo negotiated with him in 897, and designated him for the succession, so that Carolingian rule was restored again.

7. Rudolf I of Burgundy came from an influential family. His father, Count Conrad of Auxerre, had united the dioceses of Geneva, Lausanne, and Sion in his hand, creating a Trans-Jurane duchy and the basis for a new Burgundian kingdom. Having taken control of this area in 888, and having been made king, Rudolf attempted to revive the Lotharingian kingdom. He conquered Alsace and Lorraine, but surrendered them to Arnulf in October 888 in

he at once attacked him with an army. Rudolf escaped by narrow paths and sought protection for his life in the most secure places among the cliffs.[8] For the rest of Arnulf's life, he and Zwentibold, his son, persecuted this Rudolf, but they could not harm him because, as has just been said, the inaccessibility of these regions, which only wild goats can penetrate at many points, completely prevented the closed ranks of his pursuers from entering.[9]

In the same year, the Northmen, who were besieging the city of the Parisians, did something so extraordinary that it has never been heard of before, whether in our own or in the preceding age. For when they realized that the city could not be taken, they began to exert all of their strength and all of their cleverness to try and leave the city behind, sail their fleet with all of their troops up the Seine, enter the Yonne, and thus be free to penetrate the borders of Burgundy. But because the citizens of Paris did what they could to prohibit them from going upstream, they dragged their ships for more than two miles overland and, having in this way avoided any danger, set them afloat on the waters of the Seine again. Soon after, they left the Seine and, sailing with all speed up the Yonne, as they had planned, put in at Sens. There they set up camp, blockaded the city by a siege for six straight months, and ruined almost the whole of Burgundy with robbery, murder, and fire. But because the citizens of Sens fought back vigorously, and because God protected them, they could in no way capture Sens, although they tried to do so many times in the sweat of their labor with all of their skills and siege-engines.

In the midst of the difficulties imposed by the siege, Everhardus, the metropolitan of that place, a man resplendent with saintliness and wisdom, was freed from the shackles of his body and crossed over to his celestial homeland. Waltarius, the nephew of Bishop Waltarius of Orleans, was raised to his chair, but he was far inferior to his predecessor in morals, religion, and dedication to philosophy.

889

In the year of the incarnation of the Lord 889, the Hungarians, a most ferocious people, more cruel than any wild animal, and so unheard of in previ-

---

return for recognition of his royal title in Burgundy. In 894 Arnulf went back on his word and tried to subdue Rudolf, but failed. Even though he made his son Zwentibold king of Burgundy and Lorraine in 895, Rudolf maintained his rule and passed the kingdom on to his son Rudolf II in 912.

8. Regino is referring to Rudolf I's Trans-Jurane Kingdom of Burgundy in what is nowadays Eastern Switzerland.

9. Zwentibold, illegitimate son of King Arnulf, born ca. 870, died 900. Arnulf had him made king of Lorraine in 895 and entrusted the battle with Rudolf of Burgundy to him.

ous centuries that not even their name was known, marched out of the Scythian realms and out of the immense swamps created by the floods of the Don. Before we follow the cruel deeds of this people with our pen, however, it may not be superfluous if, relying on the words of the historians, we point out a few things about the topography of Scythia and the customs of the Scythians.[10]

Scythia, they say, stretching out in the East, is bordered by the Black Sea on one side, by the Ripheian mountains on the other, and by Asia and the river Ithasis in its back.[11] Its extent in length and width is considerable. Because they cultivate the land only very rarely, the people who live there have no borders among themselves. They have no houses or roofs or settlements since they constantly pasture their cattle and their smaller animals and are used to roam untilled and uninhabited country. Women and children they take along in carts, which they also use as houses by covering them with hides for protection against rain and cold. Theft is the greatest crime for them. What, indeed, would be left in those woods for people who have no house to protect them, but only their animals, their cattle and their food, if it were permitted to steal? Gold and silver they do not desire in the same degree as other mortals. They hunt and fish, and feed on milk and honey. The uses of wool and clothes are unknown to them, and although they are afflicted by constant colds, they wear only the hides of wild animals and rodents. Thrice they attempted to conquer Asia, but themselves they always remained either untouched or unconquered by foreign powers. They have become famous for the excellence of their women no less than of their men, since the men founded the Parthian and Bactrian kingdoms, and their women the kingdom of the Amazones, so that for those who consider the deeds of the men and the women it is altogether impossible to decide which of the two sexes is the more distinguished

10. As Regino points out himself, the following information is copied from other historians. They are Justinus and Paul the Deacon. Justinus was a Roman historian of the second or third century A.D. who compiled an abridgement of the first universal history of antiquity written by one Pompeius Trogus at the time of Augustus. Justinus was therefore dealing with the Scythians of ancient history. This Indo-European nomadic people was generally thought to inhabit the area between the Don and the Danube, but probably came from further east. What Justinus has to say about them in the passages copied by Regino (Justinus 2.2–3 and 41.2–3) has nothing to do with the Hungarians who invaded Europe during the early Middle Ages, except that both groups were nomads.

Paul the Deacon, born ca. 720, died after 787, was a Lombard monk of noble descent who played an important role as a historian at the court of Charlemagne. The information copied by Regino is taken from his *History of the Lombards* 1.1, where Paul, repeating Germanic lore, describes the causes which led Germanic tribes to leave Scandinavia in antiquity. Regino is thus again attributing information to the Hungarians which is not related to them at all.

11. The Ithasis, or Itz, is a little river in Germany. The Phasis, today called Rioni, in the Caucasus is really meant. Regino repeated an error in his copy of Justinus.

among them. They drove Darius, the king of the Persians, in shameful flight from Scythia and slaughtered Cyrus with his entire army. In the same way they destroyed Alexander the Great's Duke Sopyrion with all his troops. They only heard of Roman arms, but never experienced them. They are rugged workers and fighters and have immensely strong bodies. But they abound in such multitudes of people that their hereditary soil is insufficient to nourish them.[12] This is because the further the regions of the North are removed from the heat of the sun and the more they are frozen by cold snow, the healthier they are for human bodies and the more suitable for propagation, just as, on the other hand, all southern regions always abound in as many more illnesses, and are so much the less suitable for bringing forth human beings, as they are closer to the heat of the sun. This is the reason why such multitudes of people are born under the North Star, so that it is quite proper to refer to this entire region from the Don all the way to sunset by the one general name "Germany," even though individual places within it also have their own names.[13] Since Germany is so populous, large groups of captives are often carried away and sold for money to southern peoples. Many tribes have also left this region of their own accord, because it produces so many human beings that it can hardly nourish them. They mostly have troubled the adjacent parts of Europe, but they have reached Asia as well. The destroyed cities in all of Illyricum and Gaul prove it everywhere, and especially those in unfortunate Italy, which has experienced the savagery of almost all of these tribes.

The Hungarian people, then,[14] were driven out of these regions and away from their own home by a neighboring people, the Pechenegs, because the Pechenegs surpassed them in numbers and bravery and because, as we have explained, their inherited lands were insufficient to accommodate their swelling numbers.[15] Having thus been put to flight by the violence of the Pechenegs, the Hungarians bade their homeland farewell and set out to seek for countries which they might inhabit and where they might establish settlements. First, they roamed the deserts of the Pannonians and the Avars and sought their daily food by hunting and fishing. Then, by frequent and destructive inroads, they broke through the borders of the Carinthians, Moravians, and Bulgarians, killed a few by the sword and many

---

12. At this point in his description, Regino is beginning to copy Paul the Deacon, *History of the Lombards* 1.1.

13. Playing on the proximity of "Germany" to "germination."

14. At this point Regino resumes with his own account.

15. The Pechenegs were Turkic nomads of unknown geographic origin who inhabited the region between the Volga and the Ural Mountains in the eighth and ninth centuries. Pressed by the Khazars on their eastern flank, they moved into the Southern Ukraine, and thus forced the Hungarians living there to look for land and booty further west.

thousands with arrows, which they shoot so skillfully from their bows of horn that it is almost impossible to protect oneself from their blows.

To be sure, they do not know how to give battle in formation at close quarters or how to conquer besieged cities. They fight by charging with their horses or by retreating, often even simulating flight, nor can they fight for long. They would indeed be unendurable if their determination and perseverance were as intense as their onslaught. Most of the time they abandon the battle at the very height of fighting and soon afterwards turn from flight to fight again, so that just when one really believes victory is won, the real test is still to come.

Their kind of combat is so much the more dangerous as other people are less used to it. The only difference between their attacks and those of the Bretons is that the latter use spears and the former arrows. They do not live like human beings, but like wild animals, seeing that, as rumor has it, they feed on raw meat, drink blood, cut into pieces the hearts of the human beings whom they capture and swallow them like medicine, are not softened by any compassion, and have no stomach for piety. They cut their hair down to the skin with an iron instrument.

They ride their horses all the time. They are in the habit of walking, standing, thinking, and conversing on them. They teach their children and slaves very diligently how to ride and shoot with bow and arrow. They are overweening, factious, dishonest, and licentious, as is to be expected from people who attribute the same fierceness to women as to men. They allow themselves no rest in stirring up turbulence abroad or at home, are taciturn by nature, and more readily inclined to act than to speak.[16]

Not only the regions already mentioned, then, but also the greatest part of the kingdom of Italy were devastated by the cruelty of this most abominable people.

In the same year the Northmen left Sens and returned to Paris with all their troops. Since the citizens of Paris prevented them from moving further downriver, they set up camp once again and attacked the city with all their might, but still could not prevail over the assistance rendered by God. A few days later, they again went up the Seine with their fleet, entered the Marne, burned down Troyes, and pillaged the entire region up to Verdun and Toul.[17]

In those days Liutbert, bishop of Mainz, was raised above human affairs. With the consent of Duke Boppo of the Thuringians and King Arnulf, Sunzo was elected as his successor. He was religious and simple, adequately taught in sacred letters, had from infancy been reared in the monastery of Fulda under the rule of the abbot, and had become a monk.

16. This paragraph is copied from Justinus's description of the Parthians, Book 41.2–3.
17. Troyes is on the Seine, Verdun on the Meuse, and Toul on the Moselle.

890

In the year of the incarnation of the Lord 890, King Arnulf handed the duchy of the Bohemians to Zwentibold, the king of the Moravian Slavs.[18] The Bohemians had heretofore had a prince of their own kindred and tribe and had maintained the fealty they had promised to the kings of the Franks without violating their agreement. Arnulf did this because, even before he was raised to the summit of the realm, he had already been joined with Zwentibold in intimate friendship. In point of fact, Zwentibold lifted the son, whom Arnulf had received from a mistress, out of the sacred font and had him called by his own name, Zwentibold.[19] The elevation of Zwentibold, however, provided a considerable stimulus for discords and defection. For the Bohemians, on the one hand, abandoned the fealty they had kept for so long, and Zwentibold, on the other, believing he had gained much strength by the addition of another kingdom, puffed out with conceit and pride, rebelled against Arnulf. When Arnulf learned of this, he invaded the kingdom of the Moravians with an army and leveled everything he found outside the towns to the ground. In the end, when even the remaining fruit-trees were being cut out with their roots, Zwentibold asked for peace and somewhat belatedly, having given his son in surety, obtained it.

At the same time, the Northmen left the Marne and returned to Paris again. Because the bridge completely prohibited their descent downriver, they set up camp for a third time and once again began to attack the said city. But the citizens, who had been hardened by their constant labors in defense and watchfulness, and who had become quite practiced in the unremitting warfare, fought back so courageously that the Northmen gave up, and, sweating a lot, dragged their ships overland. Thus they returned to the riverbed and moved their fleet to Brittany. They besieged a certain castle in the area of Coutances which is called St.-Lô. Since they cut off all access to the water fountain, the inhabitants dried up with thirst and an agreement of surrender was arranged, stipulating that the Northmen might take everything away, but would leave them alive. When the inhabitants emerged

18. Zwentibold I, or Svatopluk I, ruled the Moravian Slavs from 870 to his death in 894. The Moravians had benefited from the defeats inflicted by Charlemagne on the Avars, and managed to establish a sizeable realm under Rastislav about the middle of the ninth century. In order to further Moravian independence from the Franks, Rastislav encouraged connections with the Byzantine Empire. His nephew Svatopluk I surrendered Rastislav to King Louis II of the East-Frankish kingdom in 870, and submitted himself in 874. As is here described, he later rebelled against Arnulf. After Svatopluk's death in 894, his sons recognized Arnulf's authority. In 906, the Moravian state was destroyed by the Hungarians, whom Arnulf had originally called in to help suppress Moravian rebels.

19. See above, n. 9.

from their fortified place, this treacherous tribe violated their trust and the promises that had been given and slaughtered them all without thinking twice. Among the people they killed was the bishop of Coutances.

At that time there was a violent disagreement between Alanus and Vidicheil, dukes of Brittany, concerning the division of their realm.[20] When the heathen found the Bretons so deeply split and divided, not geographically so much as in spirit, they confidently attacked them. Since the Bretons each fought their own war, rather than a single war of all in common, and because they refused to assist each other, as if the victory of one of them would not have redounded to the advantage of all of them, they were badly harmed by the enemy. Everywhere they retreated and all of their possessions were plundered up to the river Blavet. Then they understood for the first time how much damage they were doing to themselves by their discord, and how much it served to increase the strength of their enemies. They reassured each other by intermediaries, determined the time and place for an attack, and planned a war with combined forces. Then, out of a desire to increase the glory of his name, Vidicheil, who was the younger of the two dukes, joined battle without waiting for Alanus and his companions, killed many thousand enemies, and forced the rest to seek shelter in some village. When, however, he thoughtlessly pursued them further than was necessary, he was killed by them, unaware that it is good to gain victory, but not good to extend one's victory further than is warranted, because it is dangerous to lose hope. After this happened, Alanus united all of Brittany and vowed to give a tenth of all of his belongings to God and St. Peter in Rome, should he be able to overcome the enemies with the help of God's power. When all of the Bretons undertook the same vow, he attacked, and when the battle was joined he routed the enemy so bloodily that barely forty out of fifteen thousand men returned to the fleet.[21]

When at that time Bishop Willibert, a most saintly man and very knowledgeable in divine and human affairs, was withdrawn from the light of this world, the venerable Herimann was elected by the people and the clergy to take charge of the church of Cologne. Around the same time Salomon, bishop of the church of Constance, also departed from the world. The other Salomon who at that time held the abbacy of St. Gall and was well known not only for his nobility but also for the virtues of prudence and wisdom, succeeded him. He is recognized to be the third bishop of Constance with this name.

20. Alan, count of Vannes from 877 to his death in 907, and Vidicheil, count of Rennes from 877–890.

21. These, like other numbers in this text, are as unreliable as is notoriously the case with medieval chroniclers.

891

In the year of the incarnation of the Lord 891, the Northmen, badly weakened by two successive defeats in Brittany, moved their fleet to the kingdom of Lothar, put up a camp and engaged in plunder. King Arnulf sent an army against them, ordered tents to be put up near the Meuse, and the enemies to be prevented from crossing the river. But before the army was assembled at the appointed place near the fortified settlement of Maastricht, the Northmen, keeping upstream, crossed the Meuse near Liège, left the army of their enemies behind, and dispersed in the forests and swamps in the vicinity of the palace of Aix-la-Chapelle. Whomever they encountered, they killed. They also captured a great many carts and vehicles in which provisions were being transported to the army. When rumors of these events reached the army, which was almost fully gathered on the day of the nativity of St. John the Baptist,[22] complete stupefaction, rather than merely terror, seized the minds of all. The leaders convoked an assembly at which they discussed not so much the danger as the question what to do now, uncertain, as they were, whether the enemies would enter the land of the Ripuarians and aim for Cologne, or make their move through Prüm and march towards Trèves, or at the very least cross the Meuse and hurry towards their fleet out of fear of the host assembled to defeat them. Night came and dissolved the assembly. When on the following day dawn sent forth the first rays of its light, all of them took up their arms and marched downriver, banners raised and ready for battle. When they had crossed a river called Geule, their lines stopped in formation. So as to avoid tiring the entire army in vain, they then came to the conclusion that every one of the leaders should dispatch twelve of his men, who should be combined to form a team and track down the enemies. While they were still discussing this, scouts of the Northmen suddenly appeared. The whole host pursued them helter-skelter without even having consulted with its leaders and in some village stumbled on units of foot-soldiers who were massed together and thus easily repelled their scattered attackers and forced them to retreat. Then, as is their custom, the Northmen rattled their quivers, raised their shouts to heaven, and joined battle. When the horsemen of the Northmen heard the shouting, they, too, rushed to the attack as quickly as they could. As the battle grew more bitter, the sins of the army of Christians made them turn their backs. Bishop Sunzo of Mainz and Count Arnulf[23] were killed in this battle, as were countless noblemen. Having completed their victory, the Northmen entered the camp which was filled with all kinds of

22. June 24.
23. Count Arnulf of Lorraine, not to be confused with King Arnulf.

riches. They butchered whom they had captured in battle and, weighed down with booty, returned to their fleet. This massacre occurred on the 26th of June.

While this was going on, King Arnulf, restraining the insolence of the Slavs, stayed near the borders of Bavaria. When the slaughter of his people and the victory of the enemies were announced to him, he was at first extremely saddened by the loss of his faithful men, and moaned his grief that the Franks, who had not been defeated before, had now shown their backs to their adversaries. Then, pondering in his bold breast the shamefulness of the affair, and set on fire by the thought of the enemy, he quickly gathered an army in the eastern kingdoms, crossed the Rhine, and put up camp on the banks of the Meuse. After a few days the Northmen, elated by the outcome of the previous encounter, set out for plunder with all of their force. The king moved against them with troops ready for battle. The Northmen, seeing the ranks approaching on the banks of the river which is called Dyle, fortified their position with a pile of wood and earth, as is their custom, and taunted the troops with guffaws and abuses, repeatedly insulting and ridiculing them by reminding them of the Geule, their shameful flight, and the slaughter that had been performed on them. Soon they were to suffer something similar. His bile rising, the king ordered the army to dismount and to fight the enemy on foot. As soon as he had said this, the men jumped from their horses, shouted encouragements, broke into the enemies' stronghold and, because God in heaven gave them strength, struck them dead with their swords and prostrated them on the ground. Hardly one man was left from their countless host who could report the dire news to the fleet. Having thus brought the matter to a happy conclusion, Arnulf returned to the Bavarians.

In the same year the venerable abbot Hatho, who had up to this point been father to many monks in the monastery of Reichenau, was consecrated metropolitan of the church of Mainz.

892

In the year of the incarnation of the Lord 892, in the month of February, the Northmen who had remained near their ships crossed the Meuse, invaded the district of the Ripuarians, and, swallowing up everything with their congenital cruelty, arrived in Bonn. Leaving from there, they seized a village called Lannesdorf. A Christian army met them there, but did nothing worthy of being considered manful. When night came, the Northmen left the village. Because they were afraid of the enemy's onslaught, they did not dare to venture onto the flat land and the fields, but constantly kept to the forest instead, left the army behind and to their left, and moved their troops as quickly as they could to the monastery of Prüm. The abbot and the congregation of his brethren barely managed to escape as they were just about to break into the monastery. The Northmen entered the monastery, devastated everything, killed some of the monks, slaughtered most of the servants, and took the rest captive. Leaving from there, they entered the Ardennes where they attacked and quickly conquered a fortification which had only recently been constructed on some high mountain, where countless people had sought security. They killed all of them, returned with vast booty to their fleet, loaded their ships, and sailed with all of their troops back to the lands beyond the sea.

Rural Society

Western civilization at the turn of the tenth century was fundamentally a rural society. Almost everyone lived directly from the land, with small-scale rural cultivators constituting the greater part of the population. Most people lived in villages, isolated hamlets, and scattered farmsteads. Rulers, clergy, warriors, merchant venturers, and town craftsmen also spent the greater part of their lives in rural society. However, modern research has permanently shattered the myth that this was a homogeneous society. There were, for example, a variety of personal statuses in France, including a nobility of Carolingian dukes and counts; viscounts, castellans, nonnoble freemen, rustic knights, knights serving as armed retainers or mercenaries, free peasants, peasants at various levels of dependent tenure, shepherds, woodsmen, peddlers, servants, and vagabonds. In England the meaning of lordship varied throughout the Middle Ages. It could refer to the status of a modest knight as well as of a great baron, or to the status of an abbot as well as of a bishop. The lines between one status and another were often blurred, and it was possible for the same person, in different roles, to possess several correspondingly different statuses.

Further, the period from the late tenth century onward was marked by social and economic transformations spurred by an increase in population and in land under cultivation. Widely different regional variations took shape. To be sure, a new relationship between nobility and knighthood evolved during this period. Originally the nobility stemmed from blood and kinship. Wealth in the form of land was a source of prestige—and many nobles had extensive landholdings—but many who were not noble had equivalent landed wealth and also enjoyed high status.

Knighthood conferred honor, and most nobles were knights, but they shared this status with men of peasant status with meager resources. As the costs of equipping and attending a knight soared, the gulf dividing those who could afford the costs of warfare and those who could not widened. In the twelfth century, knights without sufficient resources began to tumble into the upper ranks of the peasantry. At the same time, the nobility resorted to money payments to avoid knightly service to the crown. Once open to many, the profession of knighthood thus became limited to an aristocracy of wealth and leisure supported by income from land which the knights did not work themselves.

The myth of homogeneity has also been attacked from the viewpoint of political order. Nobles, knights, peasants—all were subject to a bewildering body of social and economic customs often designated as the "feudal system," a designation first used by Adam Smith, in his *Wealth of Nations* (1776). But men and women of the Middle Ages, it must be emphasized, were unaware that their society was feudal or constituted a feudal system. The cultural and legal categories which they used referred to changing local customs encompassing ties of dependency, land tenure, vassalage, and the fief. This is well illustrated in the selection from the Norman *Summa de legibus* (document 7), a compilation of customs undertaken by an anonymous lawyer before 1258. Such compilations were drawn up nearly everywhere in thirteenth-century Europe in response to a perceived need to codify custom and practice for the purpose of legal regulation. However, they described local patterns of political relationships, and, generally, were private works that might or might not be applied by justices in their courts.

The central relationship between the nobles and knights and the peasants was the exploitation of personal dependence. Considerable light is shed upon this relationship in the following selections. The description of personal statuses in English rural society at the time of Edward the Confessor (1042–66) distinguishes three categories of peasants, who all enjoyed liberty, but who were, however, dependent upon a lord (document 8). A document of 1279 describes the services owed by peasants attached to the manor of Alwalton (document 13). The gradual development of the rural economy, the rights and privileges of the lord, and the ways in which villagers participated in commercial activity are illustrated by the customals of the monks of Saint Aubin of Angers (1080–82) and the village of Chapelaude in the region of Berri (1150) (documents 9–10). Although a lord's power to exploit their labor and persons remained extensive, his power over his dependents varied widely from time to time and place to place (documents 11–12).

7. Lords, Vassals, and Tenants in the Norman *Summa de legibus* (before 1258)

On the Duke

1. The duke of Normandy or the prince is the one who holds the lordship [*principatum*] over the entire duchy. This dignity the lord king of France holds together with the other honors to which, with the aid of the Lord, he has been raised. From this it pertains to him to preserve the peace of the land, to correct the people by the rod of justice, and by the measure of equity to end private disputes. Therefore, he should through the justiciars subject to him see to it that the people under his authority rejoice in the rule of justice and the tranquillity of peace. He should search out, capture, and keep in strong prisons, until they have received the wages of their crimes, robbers, thieves, arsonists, murderers, the violent deflowerers of virgins, rapers of women, committers of mayhem and other public disturbers, and others held in public infamy, who may cause damage to life or limb.

Concerning Liege Homage

1. The duke of Normandy ought to have liege homage or the loyalty of all the men of his entire province. From this they are bound to him against all men, who may live or die, to offer the assistance of their own body in counsel and in aid, and to show themselves to him inoffensive in all things, and in nothing to take the side of his adversaries.

2. He also is obligated to rule, protect, defend, and treat them according to the rights, customs, and laws of the land.

On Fealty

1. All those living in the province are bound to do and to maintain fealty to the duke. For this they are bound to show themselves inoffensive and faithful to him in all things, and not to procure anything against his interests, nor to give counsel or aid to his manifest enemies. Whoever may be discovered to have violated this by evident cause should be reputed notorious traitors of the prince, and all their possessions shall forever remain to the prince, if for this they are convicted and condemned. For all men in Normandy are bound to observe fealty to the prince. Therefore, no one ought to receive homage or fealty from anyone else unless reserving higher

From *The History of Feudalism*, translated by David Herlihy (New York: Harper and Row, 1970), pp. 177–87.

fealty to the prince. This is also to be explicitly stated in receiving their fealty.

2. Between other lords and their vassals, faith ought so to be maintained that neither one of them ought to call for corporal violence or for violent blows against the person of another party. If any of them should be accused of this in court and convicted, he is bound altogether to lose his fief for violating the faith he was obligated to observe.

3. If this act should be discovered in a lord, homage should revert to his superior and dues should no longer be given, excepting what is owed the prince.

4. If, however, a vassal should be shown guilty of this, he shall be deprived of his land and right, which shall remain to the lord. It is of course understood that they will be clearly convicted of this in court, as the custom of Normandy requires.

Concerning the Army

1. Service in the army is to be done with arms for the benefit of the prince as it has been customary in fiefs and in towns. This service is for forty days in defense of the land and for the prince's need, when he sets forth in any expedition; those who hold fiefs or live in towns delegated for this service ought to and are bound to perform it. For all knight's fees [fiefs of a knight] instituted for the service of the duchy must fulfill this service; counties and baronies also, as well as all towns having a commune.

2. Knight's fees in the counties and baronies which were not established for the service of the duchy do not owe service in the army, but only to the lords to whom they are subjected, excepting, however, the general levy of the prince [retrobanium], to which all who are capable of bearing arms are bound to come without any excuse.

3. The general levy is said to occur when the duke of Normandy, in order to repel an attack of the enemy in any expedition, goes through Normandy and orders that all who are capable of wielding arms should arm themselves for his help, no matter in what sort of arms they may be found, in order to repel the enemy. However, after forty days are completed in the service of the prince, if the need of the prince should demand it, they shall remain in his service at the expense of the prince, as reason should require.

4. No one who owes this service may by any manner excuse himself from service in the army of the prince, unless by the evident impairment of his own body, and then he is bound to send a substitute who can perform for him the service which he owes.

5. At times the name of military aid is given to that monetary payment which the prince of Normandy allows his barons and knights to collect

from their [subvassals] who hold from them a knight's fee or from their tenants on a knight's fee, if his barons and knights have served more than forty days. And they were not otherwise able to demand from their tenants a greater aid than that which was conceded to them by the prince of the Normans.

6. Concerning the fiefs which pertain to the duchy, if anyone should deny that any land or fief is of this sort, inquiry ought to be made through the prince or his bailiffs concerning the truth of the matter without any exception; since the service of these fiefs belongs to the duke, in any diminution of a fief not providing due service the duke may suffer damage. If it is decided that it is a knight's fee, the one holding it is bound to do that service to the prince according to the size of his possession. And this is to be understood not only concerning the fiefs of the prince, but also the fiefs of the barons which pertain to the duchy.

7. It is to be noted also that the barons hold certain fiefs assigned to the service of the duke; they were established before these baronies were granted. These types of fiefs must fulfill service with the barons; whoever does this service fulfills it at the prince's will.

8. The barons ought not to have from the other fiefs, which were not established for the service of the duchy, more than the aid conceded by the prince, as has been said. If perchance they have fiefs so constituted so that one or two, three, or four or more of them ought to provide the service of a single knight for the duke, each of them according to its size should perform and pay a portion of the service, as the barons and the knights may assign to them. Nevertheless, each of them shall be bound to relief and aid for the service of their lords. For although fiefs of this sort are considered as a single unit in regard to the duke's service, nonetheless they are many in relation to the homage owed their lord, and each of them in this respect retains the dignity of a single fief.

9. From all this it is evident that not without reason at the time of English rule it was customary in Normandy that all men holding a knight's fee were bound to possess a horse and armor and that, when they reached the age of twenty-one, they were bound to be enlisted among the knights, so that they would be found ready and prepared at the command of the prince or of their lords.

On Tenures

1. Concerning tenures the following is to be done.

The tenure is the manner by which tenements are held from their lords.

2. Certain tenures are held through homage, others through parage, others through burgage, and others through alms.

3. Fiefs held through homage are those in which the observance of faith between the lord and his vassal is expressly promised, reserving the higher faith due to the duke of Normandy. This is received from the lord with his hands outstretched and the hands of the one making the homage placed between them; this is explained more fully in the following chapter.

4. Fiefs are held through parage when a brother or a relative receives a part of the inheritances of his ancestors, which he holds from an older relative. The older relative is in turn responsible for all the individual obligations which the portions of the fief require and which are due to its principal lords. This is made clear below.

5. By burgage are held allods and tenures established in cities which have the customs of burgesses.

6. In alms are held lands given in charity to churches.

7. Besides these, in different parts of Normandy exist fiefs held by bordage, when a cottage is given to anyone for the performance of servile labors and mean services. This holding cannot be sold or given or pledged by the one who received it in inheritance under this sort of tenure, and he does not do homage.

8. There are also held certain free tenements without homage or parage in lay fief. This situation results from an agreement made between certain persons. For example, if a person holds a fief paying twenty shillings a year, and gives half of it to a third party, that third party holds it from him and not from [the lord who] holds homage over it. The third party shall perform no homage as the total fief is considered to be held by a single homage from the lord. This kind of tenure is called voluntary, since it results from the wishes of the ones giving and receiving it and not from the necessity of inheritance.

9. It is also to be noted that certain tenures are of monetary payments, as when someone holds a rent assigned to him while the land remains to the one who holds it.

Certain tenures are of land, such as when one holds of another the fief of the land of another.

Certain tenures are of an office, such as when one holds a certain office from another, for example, holding a warren or a privilege in forests, in markets, or in other places, or holding a sergeancy, or a fine or anything else, which are held from the lords without the possession of lands.

On Homage

1. Now homage is to be considered. Homage is the promise of keeping faith, offering no obstruction in just and necessary things but rather providing counsel and aid. It is performed by extending and joining the hands and

placing them within the hands of the one receiving homage, with these words: "I become your vassal to bear for you faith against all others, reserving only the fealty owed to the duke of Normandy."

2. It is to be noted that a certain type of homage concerns a fief, another type faith and service, and another type the preservation of the peace.

3. Homage concerning a fief is performed in the manner described above.

4. Homage concerning faith and service is performed when one person receives another as his vassal who is to keep faith to him and to give him service of his own body, to fight for him if necessary, and to do other service of this sort. And if, in return for this, he gives him a pension, this shall not pass on to his heirs unless it is explicitly stated by a condition made between them. Also, if the one serving should perchance succumb while fighting for the other, the pension shall revert to the lord. It is to be understood that he shall hold for his entire life that fief which was conferred upon him by his lord, for whom, upon entering a fight, he succumbed on the field.

And this type of homage is done in the manner described above, with, however, these added words: "Reserving faith to all my other lords."

5. A homage is also sometimes performed for preserving the peace; it is called homage of payment [*paga*], because it was performed as a pledge of peace between certain persons, such as when one person pursues another for any criminal act and peace is agreed on between them, so that the one who prosecuted does homage to the other for conserving that peace. This sort of homage is received as a pledge agreed upon.

And this type of homage is performed in the manner described above with, however, these words stated and heard: "Saving the faith of all my other lords and especially for preserving the peace."

6. In homage it is also implied that the vassal be a guarantor to the lords. For the vassal is bound to provide security for his lord in any court if he should be prosecuted for personal injury and shall appear before a justice at the assigned time. He should extend to the lord a sum equal to the rent he owes him for one year, from his movables, pledges to be paid, debts, and loans.

7. The lord has the right of judgment over all the fiefs which are held from him, whether they are held indirectly or directly.

For certain fiefs are held directly of the lords, as are those which a man holds from his lord, with no other person between them.

Those fiefs are held indirectly when some person comes between the lord and the tenant. And by this manner, all descendants hold fiefs through an older relative, and all tenants hold fiefs under a vassal who is bound by homage to the lord.

8. No one can do justice upon the fief of another unless it is held from him.

9. It should also be noted that no one may sell or pledge the land which he holds of the lord through homage without the special consent of the lord. In regard to a third part or less, many have been accustomed to sell or pledge land, since enough land remained for them in fief through which they were able to fulfill and pay fully to their lords all rights, services, jurisdictions, and offices.

On Tenure by Parage

1. Tenure by parage occurs when the one holding and the one from whom the property is held happen to be equals, by reason of relationship, in the portions of the inheritance deriving from their ancestors. And by this manner those born later hold from those born before up to the sixth degree of kinship; in that degree they are obligated to do fealty to the one born earlier; in the seventh degree of kinship he shall be held to do homage and to hold by homage what was formerly held by parage.

2. The one born earlier may exercise justice over those born later for the dues and services which pertain to the lord of the fief. He cannot exercise justice for other reasons, saving only in three cases, that is, for injury caused to his person or to his first-born or to his wife.

On Tenure by Burgage

1. Concerning tenures by burgage it is to be understood that they can be sold and purchased, just as movable property, without the consent of the lord, and the fees from them ought to be paid according to the custom of the towns.

2. It is also to be noted that the sales of these tenures cannot be revoked by heirs or relatives.

3. It is also to be noted that widows have a half of the sales of this sort of tenure made in their lifetime by their husbands, [which they may claim] from the heirs of their husbands after their husbands' death.

4. Note also that sisters in holdings of this type receive an equal portion with brothers.

5. Note also that holdings of this sort do not provide the usual reliefs or aids in Normandy.

6. Many things held by burgage tenure are also held through homage; this, however, is not done by the customs of the towns, but through an agreement among their possessors. And although the agreement among them ought to be observed, nonetheless, as far as pertains to others, it

ought to be considered as tenure by burgage, and it shall retain all the conditions of burgage tenure unless an express condition made in the contract was clearly opposed.

Concerning Tenure by Alms

1. Those who hold lands given in full charity to God and those serving God are said to hold by alms. In this situation the donors retain nothing whatsoever for themselves or their heirs, unless only a right of patronage, and [the recipients] hold from them by alms as from patrons.

2. No one may grant from any land which does not belong to him. Therefore, it is to be noted that neither the duke nor the baron nor anyone, if his men should grant from the lands which they hold from him, may for this reason suffer any injury and, in spite of the grant, the lord shall exercise justice in the lands granted and shall claim his rights.

And it is also to be noted that since the duke has justice and rights of his lordship in the lands of all his subjects, he alone can make the alms free or pure [frankalmoign].

3. Many lands have been granted which are held by the peasants possessing them as a lay fief and not by alms; that which laymen hold in them as their own retains the condition of a lay fief. But when peasants are known to hold lands which were given in alms, those things are alms and are to be held in the manner of alms.

4. That which in the manner of alms or as alms has been possessed peacefully without interruption for a space of thirty years is clearly subject to the jurisdiction of the ecclesiastical court. And if a dispute arises concerning this, it ought to be settled in the court of the duke by an inquisition. For since the jurisdiction of fiefs is known to pertain to the duke of Normandy, disputes arising over them, concerning their manner of tenure, ought to be settled in the duke's court.

Concerning Reliefs

1. After the above, it is to be noted that the lords of fiefs ought to have reliefs for the lands which are held from them in homage at the passing or the death of those from whom they have the homage.

2. However, men in Normandy may retire in two ways: they may enter religion and renounce all worldly possessions, in which case the inheritance passes to their heirs, and relief and a new homage issues from the heir; or they give the fief to others, retaining nothing in it, whether by a sale or something of the sort, in which case relief and new homage follows. Therefore, it is clear that relief is implicit in homage. For wherever relief is

paid, it is necessary that there should also be homage. But the opposite need not be true. For there are many fiefs in various parts of Normandy such as immunities, franchises, and many other offices, which are not subjected to relief; although they require homage, nevertheless they do not pay relief.

3. It is to be known that in fiefs through the whole of Normandy relief is generally defined: in knight's fiefs, fifteen pounds; in baronies, one hundred pounds; and in acres of land under cultivation, the relief is twelve pennies per acre. It is, however, to be understood that a household pays a relief of three shillings, and by this, it frees the first acre of the entire tenement even if there is not a full acre.

4. It is to be known that in various parts of Normandy according to the various customs of taking relief in them, lands which publicly are not subject to cultivation are subject to a variety of reliefs. These lands are to pay relief according to the various traditions observed since antiquity, such as in mills and ovens which are held of themselves without any tenements.

However, mills which have banal rights attached, if they are held of themselves without any fief, customarily pay sixty shillings in relief. If, however, the mills are held together with a knight's fief, to which a sergeancy or a *vavassoria* or other free fiefs pertain, in the payment of the fief's relief, the relief of the mill is also satisfied.

5. Other possessions preserve other customs concerning relief, such as forests and wooded land which have never been subjected to cultivation; many of these in various parts of Normandy customarily pay relief in union with other holdings.

6. Concerning wooded lands which in Normandy are called dead lands, relief in many places is paid at the rate of six pennies per acre.

7. It is to be noted that at the death of the person who holds in homage from a lord, relief is paid by the heir who succeeds him; and with his passing, in making new homage for the same, the fief is released by the lord.

8. Aid in relief is owed when the lord dies and the heir of this same lord who held the fief secures its release from the chief lord. The aid given ought to be one-half of the value of the relief of the fief held. Therefore, it is to be generally known that all fiefs which owe relief also owe aid in relief at the death of the lord of those tenants. This aid is due to the heirs of the lords, and thus they help them and are bound to help them in releasing their fief from the superior lord.

9. Therefore, it should be noted that certain fiefs are held directly from the prince, and others indirectly. The former are those which are called tenancies-in-chief, such as counties and baronies, and knight's fiefs and free sergeancies and other fiefs which are held in chief and are not subjected to any knight's fief.

To the lords of this sort of fief are owed the three principal aids of Normandy.

Fiefs held indirectly are those which descend from the tenancies-in-chief and are subjected to them, such as servile *vavassorie*, which are held in return for carrying services or for a male horse, and other fiefs which are held according to acres from the chief lord.

10. It is to be noted that for the voluntary retirement of the lord, unless it should be done for the profession of religion, through which he is unable to return to any earthly possession, aid in relief is not owed. Thus, aid is not required when one sells his land or grants it to his son or to an heir, who then does homage to the chief lord and pays relief. The vassals of the fief shall not be bound to pay aid in fief for this, since their lord is not retiring forever, even though to the world he is reputed entirely dead.

Concerning the Chief Aids

1. After the above, now the chief aids of Normandy are to be considered. They are called the chief aids because they are to be rendered to the chief lords.

2. The chief aids of Normandy are three: the first when the first-born son of the lord is elevated to the order of knighthood; the second, when the first-born daughter of the lord is to be married; the third, when the body of the lord is to be ransomed from prison when he is captured in a war of the duke of Normandy.

3. Aids of this sort are in certain fiefs equal to one-half the relief. And in other fiefs, to a third part of the relief.

Vavassorie in some fiefs are accustomed to pay ten shillings in aid. For since a diversity of aids is accustomed to follow a diversity of lords, the customs preserved since antiquity concerning the payment of aids are scrupulously to be observed.

4. It is to be known that if any tenancy-in-chief should be distributed into portions among relatives, each of the sharers in his portion ought to be considered as chief lord and ought to receive payment of the chief aids.

5. It is also to be noted that subtenants are not bound to pay aid to the chief lord, but they are bound to help the intermediate lord to pay his aid to the chief lord. And such aid is called subaid [*subauxilium*] and ought to be one-half the chief aid.

8. Personal Status in England at the Time of Edward the Confessor (ca. 1050)

. . . The right of the *geneat* varies according to what is established in the manor. In some he pays a rent, and delivers each year a pig for the pasture, rides and performs a carting service and provides means of transport, works and shelters his lord, harvests and scythes, makes parks for deer and looks after the places where deer can be got, builds the lord's house and its enclosure, conducts strangers to the village, pays the church taxes and alms, guards his lord, looks after his horses and carries messages far and near according to orders.

The right of the *kotsetla* varies according to the custom of the manor. In some he must work for his lord every Monday throughout the year, and three days a week at harvest time. He does not pay for the land. He must have five acres or more if that is the custom of the manor; and if it is less, it is too little, for his labour is heavy. He must give St. Peter's penny at Ascensiontide like every free man must and he must perform also the services on the demesne of his lord if he receives an order to do so, mounting guard by the sea, labouring on the enclosures of the king's deer and other things belonging to his station. He must pay church taxes at Martinmas.

The exactions of the *gebur* vary, here heavy, elsewhere light. In certain manors the custom is that he performs weekly labour on two days throughout the year and three days from Candlemas to Easter. If he performs cartage service he does not have to work while his horse is out. At Michaelmas he must pay six pennies in dues, at Martinmas 23 *setiers* of barley and two hens, at Easter a lamb or two pennies. He must in his turn sleep in the lord's sheepfold from Martinmas until Easter. From the beginning of ploughing until Martinmas he must plough an acre each week, and must take the seed himself to the manorial barn. He must also plough three acres in labour service and two on the pasture. . . . He must also plough three acres for his labour service, sowing them from his own barn; he must pay St. Peter's penny. Each pair of *gebur* must keep a hunting dog and each *gebur* must give six loaves to the manorial swineherd when he takes the herd to be fattened.

On the land where this custom applies the tenant must receive two oxen, a cow, six sheep and seven sown acres. When he has performed all the duties which fall upon him, he must be given the tools which he has need of

From Georges Duby, *Rural Economy and Country Life in the Medieval West*, translated by Cynthia Postan (Columbia, S.C.: University of South Carolina Press, 1968), pp. 443–44. © 1968 by Edward Arnold, Ltd. Reprinted by permission of the University of South Carolina Press and Edward Arnold, Ltd.

for his labour and the utensils for his household. At his death, the lord may enter into possession of what he leaves.

The law of the manor is fixed on each manor; in one place, as I have said, it is heavier, elsewhere it is lighter, for the customs are not the same in all manors. In some, the *gebur* must pay a rent in honey, elsewhere in food, elsewhere in beer. . . .

9. Customal of the Monks of Saint Aubin, Angers (1080–82)

The men of Méron will have pasture at Lanthon for their animals, save for their sheep and goats, from Michaelmas until St. Aubin's Day, up till the time the bushes bear fruit and foliage. From St. Aubin's Day until Michaelmas, the woodland pasture shall be forbidden to all beasts belonging to villeins. Throughout the year, if any animal enters the wood to save itself and if the shepherd can show that he had no hand in knowingly directing it into the woods, he shall not pay a fine for this. . . .

. . . Tolls shall not be paid for what is carried on the neck, save for feathers, wax, lard, beehives and foreign and costly goods. For feathers, a denier; for a table or a honeycomb, a halfpenny; for a hive, a halfpenny; for more than six sous of lard, a halfpenny; for a ham with its lard, a denier; for a bed with bedding one denier; for a wedding outfit, four deniers; for an unshod horse or mare, one denier; if it is shod, two deniers; for an ox, an ass, or a pig, a halfpenny; for three sheep or three goats, one denier; for one load of wool, one denier.

If several men have loaded an ass with different kinds of merchandise, they shall owe toll for the ass, save if it is foreign or costly merchandise. For other things, the toll shall be paid according to its value. . . .

. . . For anything that a man of Méron shall bring in from outside for his own food, whether it be the fruit of his labour or goods that he has purchased, either bread, wine, meat, hay or any other thing, so long as he does not sell it, he shall not pay toll; if he sells anything here, he shall pay toll on the day on which he sells it.

. . . If shepherds or others take secretly in the vineyards fruit or grapes to eat and take home, but not to make wine, or if they steal as much as three sheaves, or take them from one field to another to steal them, and

From Georges Duby, *Rural Economy and Country Life in the Medieval West*, translated by Cynthia Postan (Columbia, S.C.: University of South Carolina Press, 1968), p. 410. © 1968 by Edward Arnold, Ltd. Reprinted by permission of the University of South Carolina Press and Edward Arnold, Ltd.

these things shall be found by their owner and taken back as his, this shall not be judged as larceny.

Similarly, little things, like a knife, an arrow, a bow, a shield, or an ass's traces. If such things, or others as small, are stolen, we prescribe that it shall not be judged as larceny.

If a villein of Méron removes his animals to a place outside the manor, and if he brings them back within a year and a day, he shall not pay toll. But if he hands these animals over to another man to be fattened, he shall pay toll the day when they return. Then he shall pay toll according to the increase.

If a villein wishes to sell the skins of his animals, such as catskins, lambskins or other similar skins, he shall pay no toll, unless, in buying and selling he shall act as a merchant.

10. Customal of the Village of Chapelaude (ca. 1150)

8. . . . [The prior] will have credit in the village for bread, meat and other merchandises up to fourteen days. For wine which is sold he shall have credit for the fourteen days following the sale of the wine.

9. If a man of importance is lodging with the monks, and if there is no meat to be found in the village, the sergeants shall take pigs and chickens, and on the judgment of two or three men, the prior shall pay the price to those to whom they belong at the end of fourteen days.

10. Whenever he shall so wish, the prior shall sell his wine under privilege (*ban*), save at fairtimes. No inhabitant of the village shall then be allowed to sell his, so long as there shall remain anything to sell of the monks' wine, save if he has put it up to auction before the *ban*. But at fairtime whoever wishes may sell, from one Sunday to the next, even if there is a *ban*; after this Sunday, no one, save those who shall have begun to sell the wine put up for auction before the *ban*. If anyone does otherwise and dares to violate the *ban*, he shall pay sixty sous. The monks shall not sell wine under the *ban* dearer than any other.

11. No one shall dare to increase or decrease the size of the measure of wine or grain which the prior has established. If he does so, he shall pay a fine and the measure of the wrong size shall be broken. If he wishes to make a second one and hold it as customary, he shall pay sixty sous.

From Georges Duby, *Rural Economy and Country Life in the Medieval West*, translated by Cynthia Postan (Columbia, S.C.: University of South Carolina Press, 1968), pp. 412–13. © 1968 by Edward Arnold, Ltd. Reprinted by permission of the University of South Carolina Press and Edward Arnold, Ltd.

12. If anyone sells bread, wine or meat, to a traveller more dearly than to his neighbor, and is convicted of doing so, he shall first of all indemnify the man he shall have cheated, and then shall pay a fine according to his condition. If it is habitual, as mentioned before.

13. If anyone dares to raise the sale price of wine, such as has been fixed, he must not do so and shall be liable to a fine.

14. If the bakers, save at the fairs, make loaves for sale smaller than they ought to be in relation to the price of wheat, either they shall lose the loaves or else they shall pay a fine.

15. If anyone, living between the four crosses, bakes bread elsewhere than in the oven of St. Denis, and this is proved, he shall first pay the charge for baking, and then a fine.

16. If anyone has a damper and habitually bakes his bread below it, the damper shall be broken and he shall pay a fine.

17. Similarly, if it is proved that someone has ground grain elsewhere than in the saint's mill, he shall pay the right of multure and a fine.

18. It is laid down that every inhabitant of la Chapelle who shall expose wine to sell shall give the monks one *setier* per cask.

19. If anyone kills an ox or a pig for sale, he shall give one pennyworth of pork, two of beef.

20. If anyone exports from the village wine on an ass or in a cart to trade, he shall pay a halfpenny per ass, and four deniers per cart.

21. The prior shall impose in the village, with the council of monks and the sergeants, a currency which shall be useful to him and to the burgesses and which shall be accepted around la Chapelle, at Huriel, at St. Desire and other neighbouring places. . . .

29. It shall be added that no one, either villager or stranger, may seize a pledge inside the crosses without having carried a complaint before the prior or the provost; if he does so, he shall pay a fine and give back the pledge that he has seized, unless he can prove that he was ignorant of the prohibition. But he may seize a pledge if a promise of payment has been made in the village; nevertheless, he shall not carry the pledge outside the village, he shall not provoke a brawl with the debtor if the latter takes back the pledge and he shall not seize the pledge a second time. He shall first carry a complaint to the prior who shall enquire into his right and that of the other party.

11. Exchange of Female Serfs (1144)

Louis, by the grace of God, king of France and Acquitaine, to all and for ever. We make known to all, present and future, that we have granted to the church of St. Peter at Chartres, Havissa daughter of Renaud de Dambron, wife of Gilon Lemaire, mayor of Germignonville, who was ours in servile status, and we have given her to be owned in person and perpetually, with all the fruit of her womb. The abbot and the monks of the said church have given us in exchange another woman of their *familia*, with the approval of Pierre Lemaire and Renaux de Rebrechien. . . .

From Georges Duby, *Rural Economy and Country Life in the Medieval West*, translated by Cynthia Postan (Columbia, S.C.: University of South Carolina Press, 1968), p. 444. © 1968 by Edward Arnold, Ltd. Reprinted by permission of the University of South Carolina Press and Edward Arnold, Ltd.

12. A Master Renounces His Rights (1228)

Peter Boterel, to William, by the grace of God bishop of Norwich, to Goscelin, archdeacon, and to Earl Conan, his lord, greeting. Know ye that for the souls of my father, my mother, my ancestors, and for my own soul, I have given to the church of St. Melaine at Rennes, Godwin, reeve of Nettlestead (Suffolk), and his heirs, with all that they hold of me. I have given it in perpetual alms, free and quit of all service, exaction and custom and released from all charge towards me, that he may leave my authority except for the service of the King and the Earl. I grant that the said Godwin and his heirs continue to enjoy in my village of Nettlestead the same rights in the commons that they held previously, in the woods, plains, pastures, waters, roads, paths and in all places. Furthermore, I give to the same church 12 acres of my demesne . . . quit and free of everything due to me and to the King and Earl. And if Godwin or one of his heirs is guilty of default for the service which he owes me, he shall be judged for this by the monks in the court of the said church. The same Godwin and his heirs shall not be forced by me or my bailiffs to go to the Hundred or the Shire, but after having paid the customary tax they may remain in peace. Furthermore I desire the said Church to hold this gift from me and my heirs, freely and in peace, for ever. The witnesses are: Maxilde, my wife, who joins me in this gift and agrees to it; Adam, the priest of the village . . . Godric of the fountain, William, son of Lifrum . . . and the whole village of Nettlestead.

From D. C. Douglas, *The Social Structure of Medieval East Anglia* (Oxford: Clarendon Press, 1927).

13. The Manor of Alwalton (1279)

The abbot of Peterborough holds the manor of Alwalton and vill from the lord king directly; which manor and vill with its appurtenances the lord Edward, formerly king of England gave to the said abbot and convent of that place in free, pure, and perpetual alms. And the court of the said manor with its garden contains one-half an acre. And to the whole of the said vill of Alwalton belong 5 hides and a half and 1 virgate of land and a half; of which each hide contains 5 virgates of land and each virgate contains 25 acres. Of these hides the said abbot has in demesne 1 hide and a half of land and half a virgate, which contain as above. Likewise he has there 8 acres of meadow. Also he has there 3 water mills. Likewise he has there a common fish pond with a fish-weir on the bank of the Nene, which begins at Wildlake and extends to the mill of Newton and contains in length 2 leagues. Likewise he has there a ferry with a boat.

Free Tenants. Thomas le Boteler holds a messuage with a court yard which contains 1 rood, and 3 acres of land, by charter, paying thence yearly to the said abbot 14s.

Likewise the rector of the church of Alwalton holds 1 virgate of land with its appurtenances, with which the said church was anciently endowed. Likewise the said rector has a holding the tenant of which holds 1 rood of ground by paying to the said rector yearly 1d.

And the abbot of Peterborough is patron of the church.

Villeins. Hugh Miller holds 1 virgate of land in villeinage by paying thence to the said abbot 3s. 1d. Likewise the same Hugh works through the whole year except 1 week at Christmas, 1 week at Easter, and 1 at Whitsuntide, that is in each week 3 days, each day with 1 man, and in autumn each day with 2 men, performing the said works at the will of the said abbot as in plowing and other work. Likewise he gives 1 bushel of wheat for benseed and 18 sheaves of oats for foddercorn. Likewise he gives 3 hens and 1 cock yearly and 5 eggs at Easter. Likewise he does carrying to Peterborough and to Jakele and no where else, at the will of the said abbot. Likewise if he sells a brood mare in his court yard for 10s. or more, he shall give to the said abbot 4d., and if for less he shall give nothing to the aforesaid. He gives also merchet[1] and heriot, and is tallaged at the feast of

From *Translations and Reprints of Original Sources of European History*, vol. 3, secs. 4–7 (Philadelphia: University of Pennsylvania Press, 1900).

1. Merchet, from Latin *maritagium*, was a payment collected by the lord of the manor, usually from the father of a girl of villein status on her marriage, but also frequently from widows remarrying, and even from men on their marriage. The payment of merchet was one of the most constant tests of villenage. See Maitland Sel. Pl. in *Manorial Courts*, Publications of Selden Soc. II, 94.

St. Michael, at the will of the said abbot. There are also there 17 other villeins, viz. John of Ganesoupe, Robert son of Walter, Ralph son of the reeve, Emma at Pertre, William son of Reginald, Thomas son of Gunnilda, Eda widow of Ralph, Ralph Reeve, William Reeve, William son of William Reeve, Thomas Flegg, Henry Abbot, William Hereward, Serle son of William Reeve, Walter Palmer, William Abbot, Henry Serle; each of whom holds 1 virgate of land in villenage, paying and doing in all things, each for himself, to the said abbot yearly just as the said Hugh Miller. There are also 5 other villeins, viz. Simon Mariot, Robert of Hastone, Thomas Smith, John Mustard, and William Carter, each of whom holds half a virgate of land by paying and doing in all things half of the whole service which Hugh Miller pays and does.

Cotters. Henry, son of the miller, holds a cottage with a croft which contains 1 rood, paying thence yearly to the said abbot 2s. Likewise he works for 3 days in carrying hay and in other works at the will of the said abbot, each day with 1 man and in autumn 1 day in cutting grain with 1 man.

Likewise Ralph Miller holds a cottage with a croft which contains a rood, paying to the said abbot 2s.; and he works just as the said Henry.

Likewise William Arnold holds a cottage with a croft which contains half a rood, paying to the abbot 2d.; and he works just as the said Henry.

Likewise Hugh Day holds a cottage with a croft which contains 1 rood, paying to the abbot 8d.; and he works just as the said Henry.

Likewise Sara, widow of Matthew Miller, holds a cottage and a croft which contains half a rood, paying to the said abbot 4d.; and she works just as the said Henry.

Likewise Sara, widow of William Miller, holds a cottage and a croft which contains half a rood, paying to the abbot 4d.; and she works just as the said Henry.

Likewise William Kendale holds a cottage and a croft which contains 1 rood, paying to the abbot 8d.; and he works just as the said Henry.[2]

Likewise William Drake holds a cottage with a croft which contains half a rood, paying to the abbot 6d.; and he works just as the said Henry.

There are there also 6 other cotters, viz. William Drake Jr., Amycia the widow, Alice the widow, Robert son of Eda, William Pepper, William Coleman, each of whom holds a cottage with a croft which contains half a rood, paying and doing in all things, each for himself, just as the said William Drake.

2. Here ten other cotters are named, their holdings, varying from a half rood to an acre, specified, and their payments and services indicated.

Likewise William Russel holds a cottage with a croft which contains half a rood, paying to the abbot 8d.; and he works in all things just as the said Henry Miller.

There are moreover there 5 other cotters, viz. Walter Pestel, Ralph Shepherd, Henry Abbot, Matilda Tut, Jordan Mustard, each of whom holds a cottage with a croft which contains half a rood, paying thence and doing in all things to the said abbot just as the said William Russel.

Likewise Beatrice of Hampton holds a cottage and a croft which contains 1 rood, paying to the abbot 12d.; and she works in all things just as the said Henry.

Likewise Hugh Miller holds 3 acres of land, paying to the abbot 42d.

Likewise Thomas, son of Richard, holds a cottage with a croft which contains half a rood, and 3 acres of land, paying to the abbot 4s.; and he works just as the said Henry.

Likewise Ralph Reeve holds a cottage with a croft which contains 1 rood, and 1 acre of land, paying to the abbot 2s.; and he works just as the said Henry.

Likewise each of the said cottagers, except the widows, gives yearly after Christmas a penny which is called a head-penny.

Towns

By the early Middle Ages many of the urban centers of the Roman Empire outside Italy had vanished or had shrunk to small towns or agrarian settlements encircled with walls constructed from the ruins of abandoned buildings. This was especially true of northern Europe. Once a beautiful Roman city and an episcopal center, Paris had become a fortified island in the Seine River, whose fortifications were built with the stones and bricks of the circus, ruined villas, and baths. The invasions of the ninth century dealt a blow daunting to these remnants of urban civilization. The old Roman towns and new monastic centers in England, Gaul, and the Danubian basin unable to withstand the invaders had become tiny fortified agrarian sites or garrison points. But, in time, another great reversal took place. These wretched settlements, in turn, became pre-urban nuclei, from which developed many leading medieval towns. The term for these nuclei varied—burg, borough, bury, castellum, chateau, and castello—but all referred to a fortified settlement.

Although agrarian settlements, topographical continuity, and fortification played an important role in providing necessities, building materials, and protection to the town's inhabitants, these factors alone cannot explain the development of the medieval town. More than anything else it was the revival of trade that stimulated the advance of urban life from the eleventh century onward. Trading settlements or suburbs of itinerant merchants often clustered around the burg. Eventually fortifications were constructed to protect the population of the suburbs, which in many instances began to overshadow in numbers and in power the armed garrisons and episcopal officers inside the walled core of the burg. The grant of a market to the archbishop of Hamburg in 965 reminds us that a bishop was often the town's chief administrative officer (document 14). With the general increase in both population and long-distance trade and industry, this pattern of urbanization might repeat itself every twenty or fifty or hundred years. In other instances new towns arose on sites that were neither fortified nor ecclesiastical centers. This happened in Flanders, Brabant, and northern France, where towns like Bruges and Ypres arose on sites that were conducive to commerce and manufacture. Whatever its origins, the commercial character of the medieval town stood in marked contrast to the Roman municipality. In northern Europe, where the nobles shunned both trade and towns, the cleavage between town and rural society was deep.

Roman cities in Italy and parts of southern France fared better than their northern counterparts. Some like Aquileia were destroyed, but most like Naples, Milan, Pavia, and Marseille survived. In Italy urban development was more a matter of the regrowth inside and new growth outside the Roman walls. Towns flourished by virtue of their maritime position and their trading connections with the Levant. New towns, of course, were founded, the most famous being Venice, situated in the mud flats off the coast of the Venetian plain. Originally, Florence had been a bridge center on the Arno River. A salient characteristic of the Italian town was that in addition to the craftsmen, merchants, laborers, governmental officials, ecclesiastics, and other inhabitants, the nobles continued to live there as they had in Roman times. Another characteristic was the interdependency between the urban center and surrounding countryside, called *contado*, where many townsmen had villas and estates.

Medieval towns were miniature in comparison to the great metropolises of the Ancient world. In 1300 northern Italy was the most urbanized region in Europe, with a large number of towns ranging in population from 10,000 to 30,000 inhabitants. Venice boasted a population of 90,000 in 1338, while Florence was bursting with about 100,000 souls in the 1330s. The county of Flanders, with Ghent, Bruges, and Ypres, was the most heavily urbanized region in northern Europe. The population of Paris, northern Europe's greatest city, rose to about 80,000 in 1328. The artisans and laborers who worked in these towns were typically recruited from both the free and unfree peasantry of the surrounding countryside. In Italy many merchants originally hailed from the nobility, while in the north many merchants seem to have been the younger sons of knights and wealthy farmers.

Whatever their origins, medieval townsmen were united in seeking personal liberty, security, and autonomy in managing their own commercial, political, fiscal, and judicial affairs. In return for agreeing to supply their lords with badly needed revenue, townsmen throughout Europe had obtained charters containing the privileges they sought (document 15). Regulations for the governance of towns (documents 16 and 18) as well as for artisan and merchant guilds (document 17) were drawn up. It would be a mistake to view medieval towns as peaceful havens of commercial rationality. Towns were rife with destructive conflict between social groups and between powerful urban families. A unique institution, the office of the podestà, was developed in Italy to preserve the peace and enforce the law. Initially an imperial official, the podestà became elective after the Peace of Constance (1183). At first, the podestà was elected from the town's own citizens, but gradually foreign nobles were preferred to fellow citizens because they stood above local conflicts. The podestà was a salaried official, who normally held office for a year (and could be called to account after the expiration of his term in office), and who brought with him a retinue of notaries, jurists, and squires. Manuals were composed by jurists and notaries to instruct those who wished to serve as podestà on how to conduct themselves. Composed in the 1240s, John of Viterbo's manual, *On the Government of Cities*, was the most celebrated example of this genre (document 19).

---

14. Grant of a Market to the Archbishop of Hamburg (965)

In the name of the undivided Trinity. Otto by the favor of God emperor, Augustus. If we grant the requests of clergymen and liberally endow the places which are dedicated to the worship of God, we believe that it will undoubtedly assist in securing for us the eternal reward. Therefore, let all know that for the love of God we have granted the petition of Adaldagus, the reverend archbishop of Hamburg, and have given him permission to establish a market in the place called Bremen. In connection with the market we grant him jurisdiction, tolls, a mint, and all other things connected

From Oliver J. Thatcher and Edgar H. McNeal, *A Source Book for Medieval History* (New York: Charles Scribner's Sons, 1933), p. 580.

therewith to which our royal treasury would have a right. We also take
under our special protection all the merchants who live in that place, and
grant them the same protection and rights as those merchants have who live
in other royal cities. And no one shall have any jurisdiction there except the
aforesaid archbishop and those to whom he may delegate it. Signed with
our hand and sealed with our ring.

15. Customs of Saint-Omer (ca. 1100)

Customs of the Guild (ca. 1080)

1. If any merchant residing in our town or in the "suburb" [1] refuses to enter
our guild, he will get no help from us at all if, on his way elsewhere, he is
attacked, loses his belongings, or is challenged to a duel. [2]

2. If someone who does not belong to the guild bids a certain price for
some merchandise like clothes, belts, or anything like that, and someone
who does belong to the guild appears on the scene, the merchant will buy
the merchandise for which he had bid, even against his will.

3. If, on the other hand, someone who does belong to the guild has bid a
certain price for some merchandise, [3] and it has nothing to do with food and
is worth 5 shillings or more, and someone else who belongs to the guild
appears on the scene, the latter shall have a portion of that merchandise if
he wishes. If the one who did the bidding should deny the newcomer his
portion and can be convicted of having denied him the portion by the testimony of two guild members before the doyen, [4] he shall pay two shillings in
compensation.

4. When the time for the drinking-feast [5] is approaching, the law is that

From Georges Espinas, *Revue du Nord* 29 (1947). Translated for this volume by Constantin Fasolt.

1. Because §27 seems to indicate that every member of the guild resided within city walls,
suburbium here probably does not have the usual meaning of "suburb." More likely it refers
to a merchants' quarter that was separate from the settlement existing prior to the arrival of
the merchants but was still enclosed by city walls. Already before 1071 the merchants' quarter
of St. Omer had been enlarged from a size of, at most, 8 to perhaps 25 hectares to accommodate their growing numbers.

2. The merchants of St. Omer had exemption from duels confirmed in the charter granted
to them by Count William I in 1127.

3. The term is *mercatus*, which usually means "market," but may also refer to what is
sold at markets. The term for merchandise in the previous paragraph is *wara*, i.e., "ware."

4. *Decanus*. As will become more apparent below, the doyens are the governing officials
of the guild.

5. *Potatio*, i.e., drinking party. The ancient pagan associations from which guilds descended had regularly followed the practice of gathering for social and religious ceremonies in
which the consumption of alcoholic beverages played a crucial part.

the doyens summon the members of the guild to their chapter-meeting on the day before the feast. There they command the guild members to come in peace to their seats at the ninth hour[6] and to keep peace with each other concerning both old and recent deeds.

5. It has been established, moreover, that if someone brings along someone else to drink, like a son, a nephew, or an attendant, he shall give 12 pennies for everyone. We exclude the masters[7] from this rule.

6. But if someone comes to the feast who does not belong to the guild and is caught drinking there in secret, he shall give 5 shillings or instantly purchase membership in the guild. We except clerics, knights, and foreign merchants from this rule.[8]

7. If someone brings clogs or wooden shoes into the guildhall, he shall give half an ounce of silver, that is 10 pennies.[9]

8. If someone insults the doyens, he shall give two ounces of silver.

9. If someone insults anyone else and two people have heard it, he shall give half an ounce.

10. If someone hits anyone with a fist, a loaf of bread, or a stone, since no other weapons are available, he shall give two ounces.

11. If someone rises up in anger from his seat against another, he shall give one ounce.

12. If someone begins to shout or stands up after the bell has been heard, he shall give half an ounce.

13. If someone carries a cup filled with drink out of the guildhall without permission, he shall give half an ounce.

14. If someone has not come to the chapter when prime is striking,[10] he shall give 12 pennies. Someone who leaves it without permission, and without having been forced by illness, will give 12 pennies.

15. For every insult in deed or word that is committed during the two days of the feast one must answer to the doyens, and no other judge. For that is how it was decided at the time of Castellan Wulfric Rabel, and how jurisdiction in such matters was divided between Wulfric and the burghers.[11]

16. It is established that the doyens will procure the wine and what is necessary for the guild, as long as they are reimbursed for the purchases.

6. That is, between about 2 and 3 P.M.

7. *Magistri.* The meaning of the term is doubtful.

8. Perhaps the exception suggests that none of these groups were eligible to join the guild.

9. The purpose was to prevent the shoes from being used for fighting, not an unknown occurrence at such feasts.

10. That is, between about 5 and 6 A.M.

11. Wulfric Rabel's time in office as Castellan of St. Omer, from 1072 to 1083, establishes the earliest possible date for this document.

17. During our feast, the gate-keepers who are serving at the gates while the burghers[12] are at the feast or the chapter, will each receive one lot;[13] each butler, one lot per night; each usher, one lot.

18. If a member of the guild is ill and his neighbors know it for a fact, he shall receive one lot each night.

19. If someone is away from the region, his wife shall have one lot each night.

20. But if he is on his honeymoon,[14] the guild is not answerable for his wine to anyone.

21. All of the priests present at vespers shall each have one lot every night; "all," because we belong to different parishes.[15]

22. The guardian[16] of Saint-Omer who sounds prime, whereby we are united for our chapter, and who furnishes the relics for us, one lot each night.

23. Four sureties are taken for the reason that, so long as one of them is alive, he can stand in for the total for which all of them pledged themselves. But when the debtor has died, all sureties are free.[17]

24. If someone purchases membership in the guild, whether he is young or old, he shall pay two pennies to the notary[18] and also two pennies to the doyens before he is entered in the charter.

25. On the two days, the doyens and their notary have the right to eat before prime in the chambers of the guildhall at common expense, and to have as much wine as they like.[19] If that is impossible because they are occupied with some business, each doyen shall have half a measure after the chapter at his lodging and the notary one lot, instead of their drinking at matins[20] before the chapter meets. Each night, when everything has been justly ordered and distributed, each doyen shall have one measure at his lodging, and the notary half a measure.

26. If someone wants to enter the gates[21] with his arms, the arms shall

12. Note that "burgher" is here used almost interchangeably with "member of the guild." The gate-keepers, *custodes portarum portas servantes*, are either the men who guard the gates of the guildhall, or those who protect the gates of the town.

13. The lot is a measure of liquids, in this case of wine.

14. *In nuptiis*. The translation is uncertain.

15. In 1100 St. Omer was already large enough to have six different churches. Vespers begin about 4 or 5 P.M.

16. *Custos*.

17. This paragraph is mutilated.

18. The town notary had originally been appointed by the count of Flanders, but the following paragraph seems to suggest that this notary was appointed by the guild.

19. *Vinum tantum*: transcription and translation are doubtful.

20. That is, sometime after 3 but certainly before 6 A.M.

21. Since all arms are prohibited in the guildhall, these are obviously the gates of the town.

be detained by the gate-keepers until he leaves again, or until his host or someone else he knows testifies that he keeps the peace.

27. When the feast is finished and all expenses have been paid, and something is left over, it shall be given to the common utility for streets, gates, or the fortification of the town.

28. In the end we urge all our successors in Christ to have mercy on the poor and the lepers.

Customs of the Town (1127)

I, William, by God's grace Count of the Flemings, not wishing to oppose the petition of the burghers of Saint-Omer, especially because they gladly accepted my petition concerning the consulate of Flanders and always behaved more honorably and faithfully towards me than the other Flemings, concede the underwritten laws or customs in perpetuity to them and order them to remain permanently valid.[1]

1. First of all, I shall make peace with every one of them, maintain and defend them without malice like my own men, and agree to have the right judgment of the aldermen enforced against anyone, myself included. I also

1. William I Clito, count of Flanders (1127–28) was the son of Robert II Curthose, duke of Normandy (1087–1106), and grandson of William the Conqueror. He had lost Normandy to his uncle King Henry I of England (1100–1135) in 1106 and had unsuccessfully tried to take it back from him by starting a rebellion in 1123. In 1127 he was thus still looking for a suitable fief. When Charles the Good, count of Flanders since 1119, was murdered in Bruges on 2 March 1127 without leaving an heir behind, King Louis VI of France (1108–37) saw an opportunity to strengthen his hand in that wealthy county and supported the candidacy of William Clito. Clito was in fact elected count of Flanders by an assembly of Flemish barons. The Flemish towns, however, had not participated in the election and threatened to withhold allegiance to the new count if their rights were not recognized. Since William could not have done without their support, he agreed to their conditions in April and issued generous privileges to the towns of Bruges, Ghent, St. Omer, and others. The present document is the only one that remains. Given its origin in Clito's attempt to curry favor with the townsmen of St. Omer, it probably reflects their wishes rather closely, perhaps even those of most Flemish towns, although its form is that of a privilege condescendingly granted by a feudal lord in response to a petition of his feudal subjects. William Clito hardly intended to let the towns get away with a permanent increase in their liberties. When a few months later his position in Flanders seemed to have become strong enough, he showed his hand, and the towns rebelled against him in order to maintain their newly won rights. Their power and the ambitions of additional pretenders to the county were too much for the unlucky man. He was killed in July 1128 and succeeded by Thierry of Alsace (1128–68). Thierry avoided William's mistake by granting a charter to its citizens in 1128 which, although technically new so as not to appear to confirm a measure taken by Thierry's defeated predecessor, is virtually identical with the one given here. It did become the lasting constitutional basis for the relationship between the count and the town.

grant to the aldermen liberties as extensive as any which other aldermen in my land may have.[2]

2. If a burgher of Saint-Omer has lent his money to someone, and the borrower has of his own free will entered the agreement before qualified men who own heritable real estate in his town,[3] and the borrower does not pay the debt on the appointed day, he or his goods shall be detained until he has returned everything. If he refuses to pay up, or denies the agreement but is refuted by the testimony of two aldermen or two sworn witnesses, he shall be detained until he has paid the debt.

3. If someone has been sued in canon law[4] by someone, he shall not leave the town of Saint-Omer[5] to seek justice elsewhere. What is right shall be determined by the judgment of clerics and aldermen in St. Omer instead, before the bishop, his archdeacon, or his priest. Nor does he have to answer someone except for three reasons, namely breaking into a church or its vestibule, wounding a cleric, or overpowering and violating a woman. If the complaint regards other matters, it shall be settled before the judges and my provost.[6] For this is what was established before Count Charles and Bishop John.[7]

4. I also grant to them the liberty which they enjoyed at the time of my predecessors, namely that they need never do military service[8] outside

2. *Scabini*, here translated as "aldermen," were originally the members of the count's court adjudicating lawsuits in the town. They were probably still appointed by the count at this time, but as the document shows they were now largely independent of him and had turned into the town's supreme magistrates.

3. According to established practice in St. Omer, loans had to be witnessed in order to be valid. The terminology here used to describe the preferred witnesses, *legitimi homines et in villa sua hereditarii*, distinguishes them from mere residents in town, such as those mentioned in §5, by their possession of real estate which is, moreover, owned in full heredity, that is without any feudal restrictions burdening it. This reflects the trend among increasingly sedentary merchants to invest in real estate, in addition to long-distance trade, and also the origins of that kind of urban aristocracy which is later called the bourgeoisie.

4. *De iure christianitatis.*

5. *Villa Sancti Audomari.*

6. *Coram iudicibus et preposito meo*, apparently judicial representatives of the count responsible for this particular kind of case.

7. The three main authorities with which the citizens of St. Omer were liable to conflict were the count of Flanders, who controlled secular jurisdiction, the bishop of Thérouanne, who controlled spiritual jurisdiction, and the abbot of the famous Benedictine monastery St. Bertin, which had originally owned all of the land in the area, including the territory of nearby St. Omer, and which retained considerable vestiges of its former power. This paragraph reflects a settlement reached by Count Charles the Good and Bishop John of Thérouanne that defined the extent of their jurisdiction and the citizens' right not to need to go to Thérouanne in the specified cases.

8. *Expeditio.*

their own land, except if a hostile army invades Flanders. Then they must defend me and my land.

5. I completely release all of those who have their guild, are its members, and reside within the limits of their town from paying tolls[9] at the ports of Dixmuiden and Gravelines. I also release them from paying *sewerp*[10] throughout Flanders. At Bapaume I establish the same toll for them as is paid by the people of Arras.

6. No one who has travelled to the Emperor's land on business shall be forced by my men to pay the *hansa*.[11]

7. If at any time I should manage to conquer any land in addition to Flanders, or if peace between me and my uncle, King Henry of England,[12] should be agreed upon, I shall have them entered in the agreement as free from all tolls and customs in that conquered land or in the entire Kingdom of England.

8. If anyone raises a complaint against them in any market of Flanders, they shall, without a duel, undergo judgment by the aldermen about every complaint. From duels, however, they shall henceforth be exempt.

9. I exempt all of those who live within the walls of Saint-Omer, and those who are going to live there in future, from *cavagium*, that is, the poll-tax, and from the rights of the advocate.[13]

10. The money which was taken from them after the death of Count Charles, and which is still being held for them because of their faithfulness towards me, I shall have returned to them within a year, or else I shall permit them to obtain justice through a judgment of the aldermen.[14]

9. *Teloneum* is a proportionate tax levied on the sale and purchase, and sometimes the transport, of goods.

10. The etymology of *sewerp* suggests that it refers to the property right of a feudal lord, in this case the count, in jetsam washed onto his land from shipwrecks, but it may also mean his right to anything at all found on his lands without the owner being known.

11. *Hansa* is a sort of protection money for safety in traveling, payable at certain points on the roads to and from markets, as well as at the markets themselves, to the local merchants in return for the right to participate in the market. Flanders was a French fief, but closely connected to the empire by geographical proximity and feudal as well as mercantile interests.

12. King Henry I of England, ruled from 1100 to 1135. The reason for the enmity between William Clito and Henry I has been indicated above, n. 1.

13. Note that this paragraph mentions rights granted to all residents of St. Omer, and not only to those who are members of the guild, as in the preceding four paragraphs. The advocate was the official who exercised jurisdiction for the abbey of St. Bertin. In 1056 Count Baldwin V (1036–69) had sharply curtailed the area under the advocate's control in favor of the burghers of St. Omer. It may therefore be that this paragraph merely refers to the abolition of annual payments which they had been obliged to make to the advocate since that time in return for their freedom from his jurisdiction. What precisely the rights of the advocate were, however, is impossible to say.

14. This paragraph seems to refer to a specific incident of the kind which the count promises to prevent from occurring in the future in §13.

11. They have, furthermore, asked the King of France and Raoul of Péronnes to be free from all tolls, crossing, and passing dues wherever in their land they may go.[15] I, too, wish them to be so free.

12. I order their commune[16] to continue as they have sworn it, will not permit it to be dissolved by anyone, and grant to them everything that is right, and right justice, as best it exists in my land, that is, in Flanders.

13. And just as I wish the better and freer burghers of Flanders to be freed from all customs henceforth, so shall I demand no scot and tallage[17] from them, and make no petition for their money.

14. My mint in Saint-Omer, from which I have annually derived 30 pounds, and whatever I ought to have in it, I order to be used to repair their losses and maintain their guild. The burghers, however, shall keep the coinage stable and good throughout my life, which will redound to the advantage of their town.[18]

15. The guards who are on duty every night throughout the year, watching over the castle of Saint-Omer, who are accustomed unjustly and violently to exact a loaf of bread and one or two pennies at Christmas from every house in this town, namely in Saint-Omer and Saint Bertin,[19] or who have taken money pledged to the poor instead, beyond their fief and livelihood,[20] which of old has been allotted them in oats, cheeses, and sheepskins, shall not dare to exact anything at all henceforth beyond their fief and livelihood.

16. Whoever travels to Nieuwerleeden, wherever he may have come from, shall have licence to go to Saint-Omer with his goods in whichever ship he chooses.

17. Should I come to an agreement with Count Stephen of Boulogne,[21] I shall include their liberty from toll and *sewerp* at Wissant and throughout his land in the settlement.

18. I allow them to use the pasture found near St. Omer in the forest

15. *Traversum* and *passagium*, payable for the use of bridges, ferries, and roads.

16. *Communio*, that is the sworn association of the burghers which formed the backbone of the municipal movement.

17. *Tallage* and *scot* are regularly collected feudal taxes on individuals and communities. The vague term "customs" is designed to cover any other such payments as may have been traditionally levied.

18. William Clito's extraordinary surrender of the count's mint to the burghers of St. Omer was no longer included in Thierry of Alsace's reissue of the charter in 1128.

19. The monastery of St. Bertin needs to be mentioned specially because it is not formally part of the town of St. Omer.

20. *Feodum et prebenda*.

21. Stephen of Boulogne, better known as Stephen of Blois, was Henry I's favorite nephew and thus involved in the enmities between William Clito and the king of England. But note that he appears among the witnesses of this charter.

called Lo, in the fens,[22] the meadows, the heath,[23] and the fallow,[24] excepting the land of the Lazars,[25] as was the case at the time of Count Robert the Bearded.[26]

19. I also wish the houses which are in the ministry of the advocate of Saint-Bertin[27] to be free from all customs, except that every one of those which are inhabited shall give 12 pennies on Saint Michael's day, 12 pennies in bread dues and 12 pennies in beer dues.[28] The empty ones however shall not give anything.

20. If any foreigner attacks a burgher of Saint-Omer and inflicts insult or injury on him or violently robs him, avoids arrest, and gets away with his transgression, and afterwards he is summoned by the Castellan[29] or his wife, or by his standard-bearer, and refuses or neglects to appear within three days to do satisfaction, the community of the citizens shall avenge their brother's injury. If, as a result of taking vengeance, a house is demolished or burned, or if anyone is wounded or killed, the avenger shall not be held liable in his body or his goods, nor shall he come to experience, or stand in fear of, my displeasure in this respect. But if the person who committed the injury is immediately arrested, he shall be promptly judged according to the laws and customs of the town and punished according to the magnitude of his deed, which is to say that he shall give an eye for an eye, a tooth for a tooth, and a head for a head.

21. Whoever perturbs or molests a burgher of Saint-Omer because of the death of Eustache of Steenvorde shall be considered guilty of treason and the death of Count Charles, since whatever has been done in this affair was done out of faithfulness to me, and I want to reconcile them with his relatives and establish peace among them, as I have sworn and given my faith.[30]

22. *Paludes.*   23. *Bruera.*

24. *Hongrecoltra.*

25. A leper colony. Cf. *Customs of the Guild*, §28.

26. The lands here mentioned, which had originally belonged to St. Bertin, were to the southeast of St. Omer, as the names "Les Bruyères," "De Hongrecoultre," and the "Forest of Loo" still attest. Since there is no Count Robert the Bearded, this may refer either to Count Robert I the Frisian (1072–92), or, more likely, to Baldwin IV the Bearded (988–1036).

27. The "ministry of the advocate" is probably not an office but an area within the limits of St. Omer itself, where the advocate of St. Bertin may have retained specific rights until 1127, in spite of the reduction of his power in the middle of the eleventh century.

28. *Brotban* and *byrban*, feudal dues, in other places often levied on grain and wine, rather than beer.

29. The castellans were vassals of the count who controlled his castle and functioned as his highest representatives in town. By this time they may have held their fiefs in a manner approaching the hereditary.

30. Eustache of Steenvorde had been a participant in the assassination of Count Charles the Good. He was killed in St. Omer on 7 April 1127 and burned with the house in which he had sought refuge, just a week before this charter was issued.

To maintain this commune and to observe the aforesaid customs and conventions was faithfully promised and confirmed with an oath by:

Louis, King of the French
William, Count of Flanders
Raoul of Péronnes [Count of Vermandois]
Hugh of Candavena [Count of Saint Pol]
Hosto, the Castellan [of Saint-Omer]
William, his brother
Robert of Béthune
William, his son
Anselm of Hesdin
Stephen, Count of Boulogne
Manasses, Count of Guînes
Walter of Lillers
Baldwin of Ghent
Hiwanus, his brother
Roger, Castellan of Lille
Robert, his son
Razo of Gavere
Daniel of Dendermonde
Elias of Sensen
Henry of Bourbourg
Eustachius the Advocate
Arnulf, his son
The Castellan of Ghent
Gervase
Peter, the Standard-bearer
Stephen of Seningham

This privilege was confirmed and solemnly ratified and commended by Count William's and the said barons' faiths and oaths in the year of the incarnation of the Lord 1127, on Thursday, April 14, the day of Saint Tiburtius and Saint Valerian.

16. Customs of Lorris (1155)

1. Every one who has a house in the parish of Lorris shall pay as *cens* sixpence only for his house, and for each acre of land that he possesses in the parish.[1]

From F. A. Ogg, *A Source Book in Medieval History* (New York: American Book Company, 1907), pp. 328–30.

1. This trifling payment of sixpence a year was made in recognition of the lordship of the king, the grantor of the charter. Aside from it, the burgher had full rights over his land.

2. No inhabitant of the parish of Lorris shall be required to pay a toll or any other tax on his provisions; and let him not be made to pay any measurage fee on the grain which he has raised by his own labor.[2]

3. No burgher shall go on an expedition, on foot or on horseback, from which he cannot return the same day to his home if he desires.[3]

4. No burgher shall pay toll on the road to Étampes, to Orleans, to Milly (which is in the Gâtinais), or to Melun.[4]

5. No one who has property in the parish of Lorris shall forfeit it for any offense whatsoever, unless the offense shall have been committed against us or any of our *hôtes*.[5]

6. No person while on his way to the fairs and markets of Lorris, or returning, shall be arrested or disturbed, unless he shall have committed an offense on the same day.[6]

9. No one, neither we nor any other, shall exact from the burghers of Lorris any tallage, tax, or subsidy.[7]

12. If a man shall have had a quarrel with another, but without breaking into a fortified house, and if the parties shall have reached an agreement without bringing a suit before the provost, no fine shall be due to us or our provost on account of the affair.[8]

2. The burghers, who were often engaged in agriculture as well as commerce, are to be exempt from tolls on commodities bought for their own sustenance and from the ordinary fees due the lord for each measure of grain harvested.

3. The object of this provision is to restrict the amount of military service due the king. The burghers of small places like Lorris were farmers and traders who made poor soldiers and who were ordinarily exempted from service by their lords. The provision for Lorris practically amounted to an exemption, for such service as was permissible under chapter 3 of the charter was not worth much.

4. The Gâtinais was the region in which Lorris was situated. Étampes, Milly, and Melun all lay to the north of Lorris, in the direction of Paris. Orleans lay to the west. The king's object in granting the burghers the right to carry goods to the towns specified without payment of tolls was to encourage commercial intercourse.

5. This protects the landed property of the burghers against the crown and crown officials. Fine or imprisonment, not confiscation of land, was the penalty for crime. *Hôtes* denotes persons receiving land from the king and under his direct protection.

6. This provision is intended to attract merchants to Lorris by placing them under the king's protection and assuring them that they would not be molested on account of old offenses.

7. This chapter safeguards the personal property of the burghers, as chapter 5 safeguards their land. Arbitrary imposts are forbidden and any of the inhabitants who as serfs had been paying arbitrary tallage are relieved of the burden. The nominal *cens* (chap. 1) was to be the only regular payment due the king.

8. An agreement outside of court was allowable in all cases except when there was a serious breach of the public peace. The provost was the chief officer of the town. He was appointed by the crown and was charged chiefly with the administration of justice and the collection of revenues. All suits of the burghers were tried in his court. They had no active part in their own government, as was generally true of the franchise towns.

15. No inhabitant of Lorris is to render us the obligation of *corvée*, except twice a year, when our wine is to be carried to Orleans, and not elsewhere.[9]

16. No one shall be detained in prison if he can furnish surety that he will present himself for judgment.

17. Any burgher who wishes to sell his property shall have the privilege of doing so; and, having received the price of the sale, he shall have the right to go from the town freely and without molestation, if he so desires, unless he has committed some offense in it.

18. Any one who shall dwell a year and a day in the parish of Lorris, without any claim having pursued him there, and without having refused to lay his case before us or our provost, shall abide there freely and without molestation.[10]

35. We ordain that every time there shall be a change of provosts in the town the new provost shall take an oath faithfully to observe these regulations; and the same thing shall be done by new sergeants[11] every time that they are installed.

9. Another part of the charter specifies that only those burghers who owned horses and carts were expected to render the king even this service.

10. This clause, which is very common in the town charters of the twelfth century (especially in the case of towns on the royal domain) is intended to attract serfs from other regions and so to build up population. As a rule the towns were places of refuge from seignorial oppression, and the present charter undertakes to limit the time within which the lord might recover his serf who had fled to Lorris to a year and a day—except in cases where the serf should refuse to recognize the jurisdiction of the provost's court in the matter of the lord's claim.

11. The sergeants were deputies of the provost, somewhat on the order of town constables.

17. Regulations of the Shearers Guild of Arras (1236)

Here is the Shearers' Charter, on which they were first founded.

This is the first ordinance of the shearers, who were founded in the name of the Fraternity of God and St. Julien, with the agreement and consent of those who were at the time mayor and aldermen [officers of the guild].

1. Whoever would engage in the trade of a shearer shall be in the Confraternity of St. Julien, and shall pay all the dues, and observe the decrees made by the brethren.

2. That is to say: first, that whoever is a master shearer shall pay 14 solidi to the Fraternity. And there may not be more than one master shearer

From Thomas C. Mendenhall, Basil D. Henning, A. S. Foord, eds., *Ideas and Institutions in European History, 800–1715* (New York: Holt, Rinehart and Winston, 1964), pp. 88–90. © 1964 by Holt, Rinehart and Winston. Reprinted by permission of CBS College Publishing.

working in a house. And he shall be a master shearer all the year, and have arms for the need of the town.

3. And a journeyman shall pay 5 solidi to the Fraternity.

4. And whoever wishes to learn the trade shall be the son of a burgess or he shall live in the town for a year and a day; and he shall serve three years to learn this trade.

5. And he shall give to his master 3 muids [approx. 52 liters of grain] for his bed and board; and he ought to bring the first muid to his master at the beginning of his apprenticeship, and another muid a year from that day, and a third muid at the beginning of the third year.

6. And no one may be a master of this trade of shearer if he has not lived a year and a day in the town, in order that it may be known whether or not he comes from a good place. . . .

8. And if masters, or journeymen, or apprentices, stay in the town to do their work they owe 40 solidi, if they have done this without the permission of the aldermen of Arras.

9. And whoever does work on Saturday afternoon, or on the Eve of the Feast of Our Lady, or after Vespers on the Eve of the Feast of St. Julien, and completes the day by working, shall pay, if he be a master, 12 denarii, and if he be a journeyman, 6 denarii. And whoever works in the four days of Christmas, or in the eight days of Easter, or in the eight days of Pentecost, owes 5 solidi. . . .

11. And an apprentice owes to the Fraternity for his apprenticeship 5 solidi.

12. And whoever puts the cloth of another in pledge shall pay 10 solidi to the Fraternity, and he shall not work at the trade for a year and a day.

13. And whoever does work in defiance of the mayor and aldermen shall pay 5 solidi.

14. And if a master flee outside the town with another's cloth and a journeyman aids him to flee, if he does not tell the mayor and aldermen, the master shall pay 20 solidi to the Fraternity and the journeyman 10 solidi: and they shall not work at the trade for a year and a day. . . .

16. And those who are fed at the expense of the city shall be put to work first. And he who slights them for strangers owes 5 solidi: but if the stranger be put to work he cannot be removed as long as the master wishes to keep him. . . . And when a master does not work hard he pays 5 solidi, and a journeyman 2 solidi. . . .

18. And after the half year the mayor and aldermen shall fix such wages as he ought to have.

19. And whatever journeyman shall carry off from his master, or from his fellow man, or from a burgess of the town, anything for which complaint is made, shall pay 5 solidi.

20. And whoever maligns the mayor and aldermen, that is while on the business of the Fraternity, shall pay 5 solidi. . . .

22. And no one who is not a shearer may be a master, in order that the work may be done in the best way, and no draper may cut cloth in his house, if it be not his own work, except he be a shearer, because drapers cannot be masters.

23. And if a draper or a merchant has work to do in his house, he may take such workmen as he wishes into his house, so long as the work be done in his house. And he who infringes this shall give 5 solidi to the Fraternity. . . .

25. And each master ought to have his arms when he is summoned. And if he has not he should pay 20 solidi.

26-30. [Other regulations concerning defense.]

31. And whatever brother has finished cloth in his house and does not inform the mayor and aldermen, and it be found in his house, whatever he may say, shall forfeit 10 solidi to the Fraternity.

32. And if a master does not give a journeyman such wage as is his due, then he shall pay 5 solidi.

33. And he who overlooks the forfeits of this Fraternity, if he does not wish to pay them when the mayor and aldermen summon him either for the army or the district, then he owes 10 solidi, and he shall not work at the trade until he has paid. Every forfeit of 5 solidi, and the fines which the mayor and aldermen command, shall be written down. All the fincs of the Fraternity ought to go for the purchase of arms and for the needs of the Fraternity.

34. And whatever brother of this Fraternity shall betray his confrère for others shall not work at the trade for a year and a day.

35. And whatever brother of this Fraternity perjures himself shall not work at the trade for forty days. And if he does so he shall pay 10 solidi if he be a master, but if he be a journeyman let him pay 5 solidi.

36. And should a master of this Fraternity die and leave a male heir he may learn the trade anywhere there is no apprentice.

37. And no apprentice shall cut to the selvage for half a year, and this is to obtain good work. And no master or journeyman may cut by himself because no one can measure cloth well alone. And whoever infringes this rule shall pay 5 solidi to the Fraternity for each offense.

38. Any brother whatsoever who lays hands on, or does wrong to, the mayor and aldermen of this Fraternity, as long as they work for the city and the Fraternity, shall not work at his trade in the city for a year and a day. And if he should do so, let him be banished from the town for a year and a day, saving the appeal to Monseigneur the King and his Castellan.

39. And the brethren of this Fraternity, and the mayor and aldermen

shall not forbid any brother to give law and do right and justice to all when it is demanded of them, or when some one claims from them. And he who infringes this shall not have the help of the aldermen at all.

18. Statutes of Volterra (1244)

On the Election of the Consuls and the Podestà and How They Are to Be Summoned

If the person elected consul is not in the city of Volterra, the consuls or the podestà should send for him, and they may take whatever steps are necessary to do this. This holds true for the podestà elect also. And whosoever may be named consul will be asked by the consuls or the podestà whether he will accept the office, and if he rejects it or refuses to swear to the consuls or the podestà that he will accept the consulship, the consuls or the podestà will then summon another to be consul instead. And they shall do this within three days of the refusal. But he who accepts the consulship, or promises that he will accept it, that man shall be consul. And he who serves as consul for a term will not be eligible again for the office for three years. Likewise, he who is podestà for a term shall not serve again as podestà until three years have passed.

On the Election of Officials for the Commune of Volterra

The new consuls or the podestà are bound to choose one good man who will choose two better and more suitable men whom he may know; and these will swear to choose for the commune, in good faith, six councillors, a treasurer, a notary, overseers, a treasurer of the customs house, and messengers, all good and true men.

On Not Changing the Constitution for a Year

No chapter of this constitution shall be changed for a whole year unless by certain constitutional experts who shall be chosen for this purpose, and these alone may change the constitution for the coming year. And we say that no emendation may be placed in the laws of the commune of Volterra save by these designated experts. These men shall be called before the full assembly of citizens or before the council where the advisors of the commune sit together with the consuls of the merchants and the lords of the

From John H. Mundy and Peter Riesenberg, *The Medieval Town* (Princeton, N. J.: D. Van Nostrand Co., 1958), pp. 154–57.

district, or the majority of these, and where also there are 100 men of the town. And, when the experts are questioned, they should be questioned by the person who swore in good faith to choose them. And if any one of the consuls, or the podestà or any other person of this city or its territory should do otherwise, or cause the contrary to be done, he shall be fined 100 pounds; and the person who writes any illegal constitution will be fined 25 pounds and will lose his office for ten years. Moreover, when the consuls or the podestà believe that the constitution should be emended or changed for the following year, they should summon the constitutional experts three months before the expiration of their office.

With Regard to Anyone Making a Conspiracy against the Commune

Should anyone order or make any organization or conspiracy or sworn association against the well-being of the commune of Volterra, he shall pay a fine of 50 pounds; and whoever writes this agreement will pay a fine of 100 shillings unless this should be done by the word of the consuls or the podestà with the consent of all or the majority of them and of the consuls of the merchants.

Oath of the Citizens of Volterra

In the name of the Lord, amen. I, N, swear on the holy gospels of God to observe and fulfill and never violate by fraud each and every order which the consuls or podestà of Volterra should have me obey, during the term of their office, for the honor of the commune. Likewise, the advice which the consuls or the podestà may ask of me I shall give to the best of my ability, and in all honesty. Likewise, the confidence or secrets which may be made to me by the consuls or the podestà or by some other person in the name of the commune of Volterra, these trusts I shall hold and not violate save with the consent of the consuls or the podestà, lest he who trusted me be injured.

Likewise, if I should hear the great bell sound once the call to assembly I shall come to the public meeting without arms and I shall remain in good faith until the end of the meeting, should there be one, and I shall not leave except by permission of the consuls or the podestà or their designated representative. Likewise, if I should hear the two great bells sounding the call to assembly I shall appear at the designated place armed, and shall not leave save by the express wish of the consuls or the podestà or their delegates. Likewise, if the said consuls or podestà should ask me, or if one of them should ask me for my tower or any other fortified place, I shall give it to them for their purposes, and I shall not take it back or attempt to take it back against their will. Likewise, I swear to help maintain the salt monopoly. And all this I swear to do and observe in good faith without deceit throughout the tenure of the consuls and the podestà. And let this document stand unaltered, and let nothing be added to it.

19. John of Viterbo, *On the Government of Cities* (1240s)

On the Meaning of the City (*Civitas*)

A city is said to exist for the liberty of its citizens, or the immunity of its inhabitants, as it is called in the case of a fortified place; for the walls of the city are built that they might be of assistance to the inhabitants. This noun *civitas* is syncopated and thus its meaning comes from the three syllables which *civitas* contains in itself, that is—*ci*, and *vi*, and *tas*—ci, that is, *citra*—vi, that is, *vim*—tas, that is *habitas*; hence *civitas*, that is, you live without force. One resides there without force, since the governor of the city ("because we cannot be equal to the more powerful")[1] will protect the humbler men so that they will not suffer injuries inflicted by more powerful men.[2] Likewise, "it is not right for anyone to be oppressed by the power of his adversary; for if this situation exists, it reflects the envy of the governor of the province."[3] Likewise, since a man's house is his most secure refuge and place of safety, no one ought to drag him from there against his will, nor is anyone in the city to be constrained by violent fear. Likewise, there is truly an immunity, because the inhabitants of the city are made immune and are protected by the walls and towers of the city from hostile forces.

On the Creation of Cities

Cities were created or founded for a particular end. I do not speak of the holy, celestial city of Jerusalem, which is called the great city, the city of our Lord, whose explanation I leave to theologians and prophets, as it is not up to me to turn my attention to heaven. But I speak of cities of this age which are founded so that anyone may keep his possessions, and his guardianship of his belongings will not be troubled. In this respect Tullius says: "The man who shall govern the commonwealth must, however, make it his first duty that everyone shall keep what belongs to him and that private citizens not be publicly deprived of their possessions. . . ."[4]

From G. Salvemini, ed., *Johannis Viterbiensis Liber de regimine civitatum*, in *Bibliotheca iuridica medii aevi*, III (Bologna, 1901), pp. 218–19, 228, 233, 260. Translated for this volume by Julius Kirshner.

1. *Dig.* 4. 7. 1.   2. *Dig.* 1. 18. 6.
3. *Dig.* 1. 16. 9.   4. Cicero, *De Off.* II. 73.

The Oath of the Podestà

In truth, the oath of the podestà is customarily administered by a judge in the following manner. "You Lord B shall swear on the Holy Bible that you hold in your hands, to administer the affairs and business of this city relevant to your office, and to rule, unite, govern, maintain, and preserve this city and its *contado* and district and all men and each man, little as well as great, foot soldiers as well as cavalrymen; and to maintain and protect their rights [*iura*] and to preserve and to assure observance of the laws and enactments for minors as well as adults and especially for little children, orphans, widows, and for other unhappy people, and for everybody else who shall come to petition or answer charges under your jurisdiction and that of your judges. Likewise to defend, preserve, and maintain the churches, sacred places, hospitals, and other venerated places, roads, travelers, and merchants; and to guard inviolately the enactments of this city on which you are swearing with a sound and unsullied conscience, preserving exceptions, if some things have been made exceptions, and without hatred, love, guile, friendship, fraud, favors, and all deceit according to our sound and pure common understanding, from the next coming Kalends of January for one year and the whole day of the Kalends of January." Having said these things let him who has administered the oath say, "Just as I have administered so you Lord B shall swear; and you promise to respect the commune of Florence with good faith and without fraud, guile and without any kind of deceit; thus may God and this Holy Bible help you"; and afterwards the judges, the notaries, the chamberlains, the knights of the podestà, and even the esquires take oaths of confirmation.

The Speech of the New Podestà

"We ask the chivalry and the people and all other good folk who are here in this assembly and generally all the commons of the city that for your own honor we ought to be heard up to the end of our speech. And we pray and cry out our thanks to the high God, Our Lord, and to the Glorious Virgin the Madonna Saint Mary, his blessed Mother, and to the saint who is patron of this city, that he through his most holy mercy and piety permit and grant to us to say and to effect whatever may be in his most holy honor and pleasure, be it to the honor of us and our company and of all our court, or be it to the honor, praise, peace, concord and grandeur, and good state of the commune of this city and of its friends."

On Consultation with the Council

Indeed, on those matters which are grave and dangerous or pertain to the essential interests of the city, the podestà ought to confer with the council after it has been assembled and do so again and again should the seriousness of the situation demand it. "In the multitude of counselors there is safety." (Prov. 11:14). Then, certainly, the podestà may act with the knowledge and advice of the city's council. . . . If, however, the gravity of the situation requires yet greater counsel, other wiser citizens elected by the entire citizenry should be summoned to give it, that is, representatives of the judges and lawyers, consuls of merchants and bankers, priors of the guilds; and representatives of all others who have knowledge of the issue, shall be summoned so that the gravity of the situation may be known to all in positions of responsibility, and so that there may be no excuses afterwards on the grounds that the issue was of no importance. All shall approve matters that touch all and let the consensus of all determine the future of all.

2
The Investiture Conflict

The Investiture Conflict formally began in 1075, when Pope Gregory VII (1073–85) excommunicated Henry IV (1056–1106), the German king. It formally ended in 1123, when the First Lateran Council approved a formal agreement that Pope Calixtus II (1119–24) and the Emperor Henry V (1098–1125) had made a few months earlier (1122). In the meantime, separate spheres of the conflict had arisen in France and England, but Germany remained the focus of greatest intensity. Like other great conflicts, it began slowly, with a number of apparently unrelated skirmishes, before sustained battle was actually joined. Like other conflicts, its implications ran far beyond its central issue, which, in the case of the Investiture Conflict, was whether laypersons (kings or other secular princes) could confer the symbols and the substance of spiritual office on clergy. Finally, again like so many great controversies, it stirred up issues that continued to fester long after formal settlement had been reached.

Long after the Concordat of Worms, Europeans continued to feel stresses in four areas opened by the Investiture Controversy. The first of those areas lay between Church government and secular government. Some argued that the Church was a branch of secular administration, since the king was the head of the Church. Others held that the Church was a state within the state, an enclave of privilege within the secular community and protected by the secular government, but immune from many liabilities that rested on other subjects. Still others contended that the Church, headed by the pope, was a superior government encompassing all other governments, and that popes could install and depose kings.

The second area of stress lay between "territorial" or "national" churches and the bishop of Rome. This area was characterized by a dispute between those who believed that the Church was a representative, or constitutional, order, and those who considered it a monarchy. What check, if any, did the Church as a whole have over the pope? Could local assemblies of bishops, or general councils, acting in the name of the whole Church, judge and depose wicked popes and install new ones? These were some vital questions that arose in the course of dispute.

A third area of stress existed within the Roman church itself, between the pope and the cardinals. The *Papal Election Decree* (1059) (document 21) was an early sign of the growing power of the College of Cardinals. Soon it was asked whether papal authority had been conferred on the pope alone, as an absolute head, or on the pope and cardinals as a standing commission that represented, and was accountable to, the Roman church and, beyond it, to the whole body of the faithful.

Finally, a last area of tension was opened within kingdoms (here, specifically, within the German kingdom) between the king and the politically articulate community. Constitutional issues arose comparable with those in the Church. It was debated whether the king were accountable only to God, or whether there were orders and institutions in society that he represented and that could call him to account.

The documents in this section, ranging from 1059 to 1122, elucidate the slow beginning of the Investiture Controversy, its issues, and its anticlimactic formal settlement.

A few words about two of the texts may be in order.

The Life of Henry IV (document 20) is an anonymous work written at an indeterminate time and place. It was certainly composed after the emperor's death (1106), and by a person close to him. Before its discovery and publication early in the sixteenth century, the Investiture Conflict was known chiefly from texts by popes and their sympathizers. The *Life of Henry IV* disclosed a reverent appraisal of Pope Gregory VII's great adversary, an appraisal that had important results for the development of Reformation ideologies.

Ivo of Chartres (ca. 1040–1116) was educated in Paris and (like Anselm of Canterbury, below, p. 172) at the monastery of Bec under Lanfranc. In 1090, he became bishop of Chartres, only to be imprisoned two years later for obstructing King Philip I's efforts to abandon his wife and remarry. He had towering importance for his systematization of canon law. His extensive correspondence (about 288 letters are preserved) illuminates many aspects of ecclesiastical, political, and cultural life in his day. His exchange of letters with Archbishop Ioscerannus of Lyon (1111/1112) (document 29) followed a dramatic turn of events in the Investiture Conflict. In 1112, Pope Paschal II had ceded the right of investiture to the Emperor Henry V, thus abandoning everything for which his predecessors had fought for forty years. The pope acted under duress, and he repudiated his cession almost immediately. However, the event raised a number of important questions: (1) whether the pope could err in matters of faith; (2) whether a council were competent to judge an apparently erroneous pope; and (3) whether lay investiture were, after all, legitimate. In his exchange with Ioscerannus, Ivo considered the proposition whether lay investiture were a heresy (as the Gregorian reformers had held), or a matter of administrative regulation that the pope could allow, if it were not a cause of scandal to the faithful and if it did not infringe prior rights.

20. *The Life of the Emperor Henry IV* (1056–1106)

1. "Oh, that my head were waters and mine eyes a fountain of tears," [1] so that I might lament, might lament not the destruction of a captured city, [2] not the captivity of the base populace, not the loss of my own property, but the death of the august Emperor Henry, who was my hope and my only comfort, [3] nay more (to say nothing of myself), the death of him who was the glory of Rome, the splendor of the Empire, the light of the world! [4] Henceforth will life be joyous to me? Will there be a day or an hour without tears? Or shall I be able with you, most cherished friend, to speak of him without weeping? [5] Behold, as I write what unbearable grief has dictated, the tears fall, [6] the letters are wet with my weeping, and the eye washes away what the hand writes.

But you may protest my unrestrained grief and counsel me to hold back my weeping, lest perhaps it become known to those who rejoice at the Emperor's death. You counsel me rightly, I confess. But I cannot command myself not to grieve, [7] I cannot contain myself from mourning. Although they may whet their furor upon me, although they may long to tear me limb from limb, [8] grief knows no fear, grief feels no pains inflicted.

Nor do I alone lament his death. Rome bemoans it; all the Roman Empire bewails it; rich and poor in common (except the waylayers of his power and life) weep because of it. Nor is this a cause of private grief for me; a sense of duty forces me to lament this public calamity. For when he retired from the stage, justice left his lands, [9] peace departed, and deception crept into the place of good faith. The chorus of those praising God was hushed,

From *Imperial Lives and Letters of the Eleventh Century*, translated by T. E. Mommsen and Karl F. Morrison (New York: Columbia University Press, 1962), pp. 101–37. © 1962 by Columbia University Press. Reprinted by permission of the publisher.

1. Jer. 9:1.   2. Cf. *Aeneid* II, 643.
3. Cf. Ps. 70:5; Heb. 6:18; Col. 4:11; Wipo, *Sequentia Paschalis*, Bresslau ed., p. 65.
4. Cf. Prov. 20:27; John 5:35; 2 Pet. 1:19.
5. Sulpicius Severus, Letter 2 to the Deacon Aurelius on the death of St. Martin.
6. Ibid.   7. Ibid.
8. Ibid.   9. Cf. Virgil, *Georgics* II, 474.

the solemnity of the Divine Office fell silent, "the voice of rejoicing and salvation" is no longer heard in the "tabernacles of the righteous," [10] since he who solemnly ordained all these things is no longer reached [by them]. The monasteries have lost their patron, the cloisters their father. Now, indeed, that he is dead, and no longer to be seen, one comes to realize what emoluments, what honors he conferred upon them. And thus, a true reason for grief is at hand for all cloisters, for at his entombment their glory was entombed.

Woe, O Mainz, what great splendor have you forfeited, you who lost such a cultivator of the arts for the rebuilding of your minster, once in ruins! [11] If he had survived to put the last touch to the work of your minster which he had begun, it would indeed contend with that famous minster at Speier, which he began from the very foundation [12] and brought to completion throughout with wondrous massiveness and sculptured work, to such a point that this work is worthy of praise and admiration above all the works of the kings of old. It is difficult to believe how he adorned this minster with gold, silver, precious stones, and silk vestments unless one has the opportunity to see it. [13]

Your reason for grieving, O ye poor, is indeed the greatest, for you have been made poor now alone, when you have lost him who comforted your poverty. He fed you, he washed you with his own hands, he covered your nakedness. [14] Lazarus lay not before his door, but before his table; he looked not for crumbs, [15] but for regal delicacies. At this table, he did not shrink from the corruption and stench of the ulcerous man, [16] although the minister of his table [steward] contracted his nostrils into a wrinkle or stopped them up against the stinkard. [17] In his chamber lay the blind, the halt, and those consumed with divers illnesses. From these, he himself removed their foot-coverings; [18] to these he gave places to sleep; these, he covered, rising [from his bed] at night. [19] Nor did he shrink even from the touch of one whom illness had forced to soil the bed.

The poor preceded his entourage; they accompanied it; they followed it.

10. Ps. 118:15.

11. It burned in 1081, according to Marianus Scotus.

12. It was actually begun by Conrad II in 1030 and completed by Henry IV at the end of his reign. See Otto of Freising, *Deeds of the Emperor Frederick*, I, x: "This church, as is seen today, he [Henry IV] himself constructed with wondrous and artful work."

13. Cf. Sallust, *Catiline* 13, 1.

14. Cf. Sulpicius Severus, *Life of St. Martin*, chap. 2.

15. Luke 16:20 ff.

16. Cf. Sulpicius, *Life of St. Martin*, chap. 18.

17. Cf. Ps. 22:24.

18. Sulpicius, *Life of St. Martin*, chap. 2.

19. Cf. Joshua 3:1.

Although he had commended the care of them to his intimates, he himself, nonetheless, cared for them as though they had been commended to no one. But everywhere throughout his manors, he set aside sustenance for the poor; and he wished to know personally their number and when they died, so that he could both care for the memory of the deceased and be sure that another had been substituted in his place.[20] Whenever the barrenness of a year inflicted a famine [upon the people], he undertook to feed many thousands, truly mindful of the word of the Lord, commanding: "Make to yourselves friends of the mammon of unrighteousness, that when ye fail, they may receive you into the everlasting tabernacle."[21]

With what grief do we think the poor are afflicted, when they consider that they have had, but no longer have now these good things which we have enumerated, and much more than we have enumerated. For who devotes this humanitarian care to them? Who serves more fully in these offices of mercy, in which Henry the Emperor served? O man, marked out with the praise of pious duty and humility! He commanded the world; the poor, him. The world ministered to him; he, to the poor.

These things about that goodness of mercy toward the poor, which he loved much and which he could not conceal from men, we have spoken of first, not in accord with the worth of [his] deed, but in accord with the capacity of [our] mind; for who could know what he did [secretly] with God alone as witness? About the other virtues for which he was renowned, indeed, we shall make few remarks, for we are in no position to tell everything.

Let no one wonder if I mingle the happy deeds of his life with the lament of his death, since it is the wont of those who grieve, when they lament a dead friend, to recount his whole life and habits to the increase of their grief.[22] And so I rejoice to write about him; I rejoice to indulge [my] grief[23] and to weep for the dead, who, while he lived, was my joy.

Now he acted the part of a commander; now, that of a common soldier[24] thus showing forth in the one that office which he had to bear, and in the other, humility. He was so acute of mind and of such great discernment that, while the princes hesitated to make a decision in the case of a legal matter which had to be resolved, or in dealing with the affairs of state, he swiftly loosed the knot and set forth clearly what was the more equitable, what the more useful, drawing this, as it were, from the secret place of wisdom itself. He gave attention to the words of others; he himself spoke few; nor did he burst forth to be the first to make a decision, but awaited that of others. He perceived the workings of the mind of him upon whose

20. Livy II, 7, 6.
21. Luke 16:9.
22. Cf. Lucan X, 178.
23. *Aeneid* II, 776.
24. Sallust, *Catiline* 60.

face he fixed the sharpness of his eyes; and he saw as though with lynxlike eyes, whether he carried toward him hate or love in his heart. Nor is it unpraiseworthy that in a throng of the foremost men he seemed to stand out above the rest and taller than he actually was and that he presented a certain awesome splendor in his countenance with which he struck back the gaze of onlookers as though with lightning, while, on the other hand, among the members of his household and in a small number of companions he appeared placid of countenance and equal [in stature] to the others.

Not only did the powerful of his Empire fear him, but his repute terrified both the kings of the East and those of the West, so much that they became tributaries before they were conquered. The king of Greece himself, to dissemble his fear, earnestly sought his friendship and with gifts came before him whom he feared as a potential enemy, lest he become an [actual] enemy. The golden altar tablet in Speier bears witness to this, admirable as much because of the novelty of its art as because of the weight of metal. The king of Greece sent that tablet when he learned that the good pleasure and zealous concern of the Emperor was hot toward the Speier minster, a noble gift most worthy both of him who sent it and of him to whom it was sent. But also the king of Africa added greatly to his fisc since he feared greatly the power of the Emperor.

He oppressed the oppressors of the paupers; he gave despoilers to the spoil;[25] he beat back those who were abusive of him and rose up against his power, to such a degree that even today traces of his royal vengeance are seen among their posterity. After he had done this, he provided both for the state of his own affairs in the present and for the affairs of the Empire in the future, to the end that those men might learn not to disturb peace nor to vex the Empire with arms.

Here I would break off my pen; for we have come to factions, to deceptions, and to crimes, of which to write true things is a danger, to write false, a crime. "Here the wolf threatens, there the hound."[26] What, therefore, shall I do? "Shall I speak, or be silent?"[27] My hand begins and falters, writes and rejects, notes and erases, so much that I almost do not know what I will.[28] But it is foul to leave mutilated something begun and to have painted the head without the members. I shall persevere, therefore, as I began,[29] steadfast and secure in the fact that as your trustworthiness has been completely proven to me,[30] so you will reveal these writings to no one; or if perchance they go abroad, that you will not reveal the author.

25. Cf. Jer. 17:8.

26. Horace, *Satires* II, 2, 64.

27. Cf. *Aeneid* III, 39.

28. Ovid, *Metamorphoses* IX, 522 ff.

29. Sallust, *Jugurtha* 102, 9.

30. Cf. Ovid, *Ex Ponto* II, 7, 82; Sallust, *Catiline* 20, 2; Sulpicius, *Life of St. Martin*, chap. 5.

2. When Emperor Henry whom we discuss here, still a boy, succeeded in the kingship his father, the most glorious Emperor Henry III (for while he was still a boy his father yielded to nature),[31] war did not disturb the peace; trumpet calls did not break the quiet;[32] rapine was not rampant; fidelity did not speak falsely—since the kingdom yet held to its former state. Justice was still full of its own vigor; power[33] was still full of its own right. Agnes, the most serene Empress, a woman of manly disposition, sustained greatly this happy state of the kingdom, she who together with her son with equal right governed the commonwealth. But since immature age inspires too little fear, and while awe languishes, audacity increases, the boyish years of the King excited in many the spirit of crime. Therefore, everyone strove to become equal to the one greater than him, or even greater, and the might of many increased through crime;[34] nor was there any fear of the law, which had little authority under the young boy-king.

And so that they could do everything with more license, they first robbed of her child the mother[35] whose mature wisdom and grave habits they feared, pleading that it was dishonorable for the kingdom to be administered by a woman (although one may read of many queens who administered kingdoms with manly wisdom). But after the boy-king, once drawn away from the bosom of his mother, came into the hands of the princes to be raised,[36] whatever they prescribed for him to do, he did like the boy he was. Whomever they wished, he exalted; whomever they wished, he set down; so that they may rightly be said not to have ministered (*ministrasse*) to their king so much as to have given orders (*imperasse*) to him. When they dealt with the affairs of the kingdom, they took counsel not so much for the affairs of the kingdom as for their own; and in everything they did, it was their primary concern to put their own advantage above everything else.

This was certainly the greatest perfidy, that they left to his own devices in his boyish acts him who ought to have been kept, so to speak, under seal, in order thus to elicit from him what they strove to obtain.[37]

But when he passed into that measure of age and mind in which he could discern what was honorable, what shameful, what useful, and what was not,[38] he reconsidered what he had done while led by the suggestions of the princes and condemned many things which he had done. And, having become his own judge, he changed those of his acts which were to be changed. He also prohibited wars, violence, and rapine; he strove to recall peace and justice, which had been expelled, to restore neglected laws, and

---

31. 1056. Sallust, *Jugurtha* 14, 15.   32. Cf. Lucan IV, 395.
33. The Gelasian "potestas" of the regal office.
34. Sallust, *Jugurtha* 14, 7; *Catiline* 39, 1.
35. 1062.   36. Cf. *Aeneid* VII, 484.
37. See Gregory VII, *Register* I, 29a.   38. Horace, *Epist.* I, 2, 3.

to check the license of crime. Those accustomed to crime whom he could not coerce by edict, he corrected, more mildly, indeed, than the wrong demanded by the stricture of the law and the legal prerogative of the Curia. Those men called this not justice, but injury; and they who had cast law aside disdained to be bound by law, just as they who were racing through every impiety,[39] disdained to suffer the reins, and they gave their attention to plans by which they might either kill him or deprive him of his office, not remembering that they owed peace to their citizens, justice to the kingdom, fidelity to the King.

3. Therefore the Saxons, a hard people, harsh in wars, as rashly inclined to arms as bold, making for themselves a claim to pre-eminent acclamation by having undertaken the furious raid, suddenly rushed upon the King with arms.[40] The King considered it dangerous to engage in conflict with a few against innumerable armed men and escaped with difficulty;[41] he preferred life to praise, safety to the changes of fortune. When the Saxons thus saw that their undertaking had not answered to their desires—O inhuman mind, O shameful vengeance!—they disinterred the bones of the son of the King[42] (for he had not yet been made Emperor). The King, aroused by these two most heavy wrongs, led an army against that people, fought, and was victorious.[43] He was victorious, I say, over the armed host set up against him, not against the stubborn resistance which had been built up. For although he conquered those gathered in battle, put the conquered to flight, followed hard on the fugitives; although he laid waste their goods, destroyed their fortifications, and did everything which is to the victor's taste—for all that, they could not be forced to surrender. After he had departed thence and had, in a short time, restrengthened his army, he moved against them a second time. Since they mistrusted their own forces, most gravely shaken as they were in the earlier war, they decided on what was the next best thing to safety—to give themselves up. They hoped that the King would be content with surrender alone and would grant his pardon easily. But the outcome was far different from what they had hoped. For the King sent those who had been sentenced to exile into other lands where, under close confinement, they awaited the edict of release.

From this exile, some slipped away in flight; others were released by their guards through bribery. When they had returned to their country and their homes, they bound themselves together in a new conspiracy [pledged]

39. Cf. Lucan V, 312.   40. 1073.
41. From the Harzburg, 1073.
42. At the Harzburg, 1074. The body of Henry's brother, Conrad, also buried at the Harzburg, was likewise disinterred.
43. The Battle of the Unstrut, 1075.

that they were ready to die before being cast down again in surrender. But their conspiracy became even stronger, for some Lombards, Franks, Bavarians, and Swabians adhered to them after exchanging the faithful assurance[44] that they would batter the King with wars on every hand.

They saw, however, that the King would be touched by wars, not cast down; vexed, not conquered; indeed, his strength until that time was unassailable. In order to extenuate his resources, they fabricated and wrote up criminal charges against him mixing true things with false—the worst and most foul which hate and spiteful malice could devise and which, if I were to put them down, would make me ill in writing and you, in reading them. Thus they accused him before the Roman pontiff, Gregory, saying that it was not seemly that so profligate a man, known more by crime than by title, should rule, most of all since Rome had not conferred the regal dignity upon him; that it was necessary that her right in setting up kings be returned to Rome; and that the Pope and Rome, according to the counsel of the princes, should provide a king whose life and wisdom would be congruent with so great an honor.

The Pope, deluded by this act of stealth and, at the same time, urged on by the honor of creating a king, which they had thrust upon him in a spirit of deception, bound the King with the ban and commanded the bishops and the other princes of the kingdom to withdraw themselves from communion with the excommunicated King: [He announced] that he would go very soon into the German regions, where one might deal with ecclesiastical affairs, and most especially with the problems of the kingship. Nay, he even added this: he absolved all who had vowed fealty to the King of their oath, so that this absolution might force against him those whom the obligation of fealty held.[45] This deed displeased many—if one may be displeased with what the Pope does—and they asserted that what had been done was done as ineffectually as illicitly. But I should not dare to present their assertions, lest I seem to rebut with them the act of the Pope.

Soon most of the bishops, those whom love as much as those whom fear had drawn to the side of the King, fearing for their office, withdrew their assistance from him. This also the greater part of the great nobles did. Then, indeed, seeing that his cause was set in the narrows,[46] the King conceived a plan as secret as astute and seized upon a sudden and unexpected journey to meet the Pope. And with one deed he did two—namely, he both received the loosing of the ban and cut off at mid-point a conference of the Pope with his adversaries which he had suspected. As for the criminal

---

44. In 1076, after Henry's excommunication. Sallust, *Catiline* 44, 3.
45. This did not occur until 1080.   46. Livy XXVI, 17, 5.

charges placed upon him, he answered little, since he averred that it was not for him to answer the accusation of his enemies, even though it were true.[47]

What did it profit you to have done this, to the end that he might be bound with the ban, when loosed from the ban he is free to use mightily his might? What did it profit you to have accused him with fabricated crimes, when he should have scattered your accusation with easy response, as the wind [scatters] the dust? Nay more, what madness armed you against your king and the ruler of the world? Your conspiratorial malignity profited nothing, accomplished nothing.

Whom the hand of God had established in kingship, yours could not cast down. Where was the fidelity which you vowed to him?[48] Wherefore were you forgetful of the benefices which he conferred upon you with regal liberality? Use sane counsel, not rage, to the purpose that you repent you of the undertaking, lest perchance coming upon you more strongly, he may conquer you[49] and crush you with his feet, and lest that vengeance rage which may show to future ages what the royal hand can do. At least, you, O bishops, see "lest ye perish from the just way";[50] see lest you transgress your promises of fidelity. Otherwise, you yourselves know what will overtake you.

4. When the King returned from the Pope, having received a benediction in place of a malediction, he found Duke Rudolf created king over him. After the news of his return had been heard, he [Rudolf] fled into Saxony, prepared for flight rather than for battle, pushed aside rather than conquered. It is easy to receive a kingdom, difficult to guard it. But let no one be amazed that a man trained and vigorous in martial affairs now had fled, since the more just and the victorious cause[51] often sends brave men into fear and flight. O avarice, that worst of plagues, which turns athwart good habits and often drags the very virtues into vices![52] This Rudolf, an excellent duke, a man of great authority and praise through the whole kingdom, tenacious of the true and the right, brave in arms,[53] and, finally, proven in every kind of virtue—he, I say, conquered by avarice which conquers all else, and become the supplanter of his lord, gave fidelity second place to an uncertain honor. There were those, indeed, who said that he had been spurred on by the Pope[54] and that a man of such great virtue had never yielded to avarice more than to counsel. As their proof, they mentioned the following fact: when, after the absolution of the King, Rudolf

---

47. Canossa, 1077.
49. Cf. Luke 11:22.
51. Lucan I, 1, 8.
53. Lucan V, 345.

48. Ovid, *Heroides* II, 31.
50. Ps. 2:12.
52. Sallust, *Catiline* 10, 4; 11, 1.
54. Cf. Sallust, *Catiline*, 48, 8.

usurped the royal office, the Pope kept silent, in accord with the sentence of the comic poet: "Who keeps silent gives acclaim enough." [55]

And so, after Rudolf had withdrawn—whose head, if he had been apprehended, the avenging sword would, with good reason, have turned around [56]—the king invaded Bavaria and Swabia and inflicted devastation upon those who had banded together in the conspiracy against him; he shattered their fortification. And yet, he did not avenge himself in measure of the substance of the wrong done to him, but knowing how to use the bridle in vengeance, he held the reins of revenge far below the measure of the wrong.

But Rudolf, to compensate for the shame of flight with a deed of valor, besieged the city of Würzburg, where the fight was waged, however, with deceit more than with valor. For after the King had called together an army to cast forth the enemy, [57] and a battle line of the two sides had been drawn up, and the foremost men in the ranks were joining battle among themselves, certain horsemen of the royal side who placed themselves beside the King, like dependents [acting] in good faith, suddenly turned their weapons upon him, having been bribed for this purpose. But since his body was protected by bronze [armor], they inflicted a bruise, not a wound. Woe, most wretched men, for whom a price was the cause both of crime and of destruction, whom both crime and vengeance enveloped on one and the same spot; for so many avenging right hands fell upon them in frenzy that they preserved not even the form of human corpses. There is a tumult; a clamor is raised; [58] word is spread that the King has been killed; the army, terrified at this word, flees, the enemy follows. And since, except for a few, the horsemen found safety in their horses, a pitiable fate befell the foot soldiers alone. [59] Thus, the more criminal the nature of the victory, the less its glory. [60]

So the enemy returned into Saxony after the city [Würzburg] had been taken and a garrison stationed there. [61] What profit, O reprobate [Rudolf], did you get, either from the random slaughter of a fleeing mob or from the lucky capture of a city, when you were not master of the city long and of the kingdom never? For the King, after a short time, returned with an army and retook the city which had been snatched away; for those to whom the prov-

---

55. Terence, *Eunuchus* III, 2, 23.
56. The figure is that of the falling head. Cf. Lucan VIII, 673.
57. 1086.   58. *Aeneid* II, 313.
59. Cf. Lucan IV, 769 f.   60. Cf. Ovid, *Metamorphoses* VII, 333.
61. The author seems to have confused the battle with Rudolf at Mellrichstadt (1077–78) with the Battle of Bleichfeld (1086). Rudolf besieged Würzburg in 1077; Herman of Salm, in 1086.

ince of guarding the city had been handed over had fled from the city.[62] Afterwards, he entered Saxony on several occasions with an army[63] and retired either as victor or with things at a standstill.[64] But on his last return, he was victorious in a victory as noteworthy as happy, and a great proof was given to the world that no one might rise up against his lord. For Rudolf, with his right hand cut off, provided an example of the most worthy vindication of treachery, he who did not fear to violate the fealty sworn to his king. And as though other wounds were not sufficient for death, a penalty was inflicted upon that member [with which the vow was made], that the guilt might be known through the penalty.[65]

But something else noteworthy happened in this victory—namely, that the victorious army, as well as the conquered, fled. Indeed, divine clemency ordained this from above, so that after the ruin of the head [Rudolf] the impiety of slaughter on both sides might be prevented through flight on both sides.

But the harsh people was not warned by the loss suffered or by the sign shown; but rather, to conquer through obstinacy which it could not conquer through fighting, it constituted Herman[66] its new king.

He likewise perished in a strange way. For when the Saxons drove him away from their land (whatever it was in him that displeased them)[67] he returned into his native land[68] bearing the empty name of king.[69] Then, he betook himself to Herman, the bishop of Trier,[70] whom, too, the inexpugnable strength of his fortifications had driven to the rash venture of declaring against the king. How great was the power of the king, who had to be fed not from his own resources, but from those of others! One day, when he was on a journey, he thought that, as a prank, they should rush as seeming enemies upon the castle to which they were going and test how much boldness, how much valor, lay in the spirits of the defenders. How amazing was the way, how unlooked-for, in which he discovered how what was going to happen [that is, death, the inevitable] might be! When they tore into the gate, which was found without bars and without a guard, some who were within seized arms against the attackers in a manly way, whereas others weakly sought shelters. But a woman who had gone into the tower, woman in sex, not in spirit, cast a millstone down upon the King's head. And so he died at a womanly hand, that his death might be the more igno-

---

62. Sallust, *Catiline* 46, 4.

63. 1079, 1080, and 1087–89 on frequent occasions.

64. Cf. Sallust, *Catiline* 39, 4.

65. 1080, in a battle on the Elster River.   66. 1081.

67. They had turned to Ekbert, margrave of Meissen.

68. Lorraine.   69. 1088. Cf. Lucan V, 389.

70. Egilbert was then archbishop of Trier. Herman of Metz, who seems to be meant here, was subsequently expelled from his see.

minious. But to whitewash this dishonor, they transferred by agreement the deed of the woman to the person of a man.[71]

5. After the two kings had met this fate, there was long hesitation in the creation of kings, and the fear [produced by] the past disaster stretched into the future as well.[72] Finally cupidity was victorious and drove Ekbert the margrave with a bold hand to strive for the kingship.[73] In death, indeed, he learned too late what one can be taught from the losses of another.

There was a city in Saxony which turned to his [Henry's] side, since it saw the fortune of the King going in a favorable course, taking for granted its security both because of the strength of its position and because of the royal succor. The Saxon nobles bore this with poor grace and invested the city with a siege.[74] But Margrave Ekbert, who had become swollen with the hope of becoming master of the royal power, went with greater zeal than anyone else to that siege in order to adapt himself to the end which he strove to attain. After he had sent a multitude of men ahead, he himself followed with a few.[75]

A hidden path led him through a certain grove after he had turned off from the public road not perchance to fall among enemies—for who is so powerful he lacks an enemy or who does not fear hostile ambushes? How hidden are your judgments, O God, and with what wondrous order do you hide what you are going to do and reveal what you have hidden.[76] Already the noonday heat of the sun burned the horses and those seated on the horses, and, as it happened, the heat of the day kindled thirst. So heavy a sleep, moreover, stole upon the weary men that they hung their necks drooping in sleep, and the horses, not turned with their bits, took free rein. Not very far in the recess of the forest, they saw a solitary mill,[77] where they turned aside and gave themselves to sleep. Meanwhile, the miller was sent to bring drink from the village for those athirst.

While he was hastening with a goatskin bag set on his shoulders, he met on his way some shield-bearers going to the afore-mentioned siege who were secretly vassals of the King although they belonged to the opposing side. He was questioned by them, whence he came, whither he went, why he hurried so out of breath; and, not knowing how to conceal what he knew, he revealed the identity of his guest and the reason for his trip.

These men, stunned with fear, or rather with joy, discussed among

---

71. 1088.   72. Cf. Lucan II, 333.

73. Actually, Ekbert was elected while Herman was still alive.

74. No other source tells of this siege, though in 1088 Ekbert besieged Quedlinburg, which was held by the Abbess Adelheid, half-sister of Henry IV. The chronicler Bernold says that Ekbert was slain in ambush through the craft of Adelheid. (*MGH SS.*, V, 450.).

75. 1090.   76. Cf. Rom. 11:33.

77. Apparently near the Selke River.

themselves what they should do—what danger, on the other hand, what reward, what valor, what praise, what mark of fidelity would be in it if they should smite so great an enemy of the King. [They argued] that this opportunity had not been brought before them for nothing, that very great valor was proved through very great hazards. Thus they stirred up the spirits of each other and hurried with horses spurred to the mill; they arrived there in desire before they had with horses.

The fight, once begun, was long and doubtful of outcome, since the combatants were equals in valor and number. The one side [the partisans of Henry] fought for praise; the other, for life.[78] The fortune of the King finally was victorious, and the fiercest enemy, slain not in the battle line, but in a mill, fell ignominiously.[79] You are happy, indeed, and have always a great name, O mill,[80] to which men are attracted not so much by the turning which is your purpose as by your fame, you who tell about this battle while grinding and grind while telling.

Thus this assembly of nobles [at the siege] was put into confusion; it cleared the battlefield; and so withdrew from the siege without having achieved their aim.[81]

And so the affairs of the King were advanced daily into a higher and happier state. Those of his adversaries, however, turned downward, and all of their undertakings ended with a shameful outcome.

6. When, therefore, they saw that they had no success, either in arms or in the election of kings, they armed themselves again with calumnies and accused him before the Pope, besides other things, of many and impious deeds.[82] They asserted that often he had been exiled from the royal office because of his crime; that he had slain the most Christian kings whom they themselves had created, not without the authority of the Pope; that he had usurped the royal office through bloodshed; that he had laid everything waste with fire, pillage, and the sword; and that he had exercised his tyranny against the Church and the kingdom in every way.

On their accusation, the Pope again bound him with the ban, as they proposed. But this ban was not considered to be of great weight, in that it was seen to be not an act of reason, but of whim; not of love, but of hate.

The King, however, perceiving that the Pope was inclined to strip him of the kingship, and that he would not be content with any [act of] obedience from him other than his renunciation of the kingship, was forced to relapse from obedience into rebellion, from humility into swollen pride, and readied

---

78. Cf. Sallust, *Jugurtha* 94, 5.

79. Cf. *De unitate ecclesiae conservanda* II, 35: "Afterwards he was slain in a wretched manner, discovered in some hut, not to say what is truer, in a mill."

80. Lucan VII, 139; Horace, *Carmina* III, 9, 7.

81. Sallust, *Jugurtha* 58, 7.   82. 1080.

himself to do to the Pope what the Pope intended to be done to him. Cease, I pray, O glorious King, cease from this attempt to cast down the ecclesiastical head from his summit, to make yourself a criminal by recompensing injury. To suffer injury is the part of felicity; to render it, that of crime.

And so the King sought reasons and opportunities to cast him out. And it was found that he had occupied the Roman See, which he had rejected once before and which, therefore, he should have rejected [at the time of his election], since he had willfully aspired to it while he was archdeacon and his lord was still living.[83] Whether these things are true or false can be discovered with too little accuracy. Some averred it; others said that it was a fabrication. For each party, Rome entered into the argument: the one argued that Rome, the mistress of the world, would never countenance such an impiety; the others, that this handmaid of cupidity [Rome] would easily let any impiety pass, for a price. As for me, however, the matter must be left unsettled, since I cannot defend, nor do I dare to affirm, uncertain things.

Therefore, the King went to Rome with an army, crushing whatever stood in his way.[84] He subdued the cities: those which were proud, he pressed hard; the lofty, he bent low; he scattered factions.

At his approach, Rome, who ought to have prepared honors for him, was persuaded to ready arms, as though the Punic Hannibal had crossed the Alps;[85] and she shut her gates to her king as though to an enemy. Whence, the King, stirred by just indignation, cut off the city by a siege, as the state of affairs demanded.[86] Men were sent out all about to destroy castles, to devastate villages, to pillage goods; and he caused harm to the province without, since Rome had shut herself within. Without, there was war; within, fear.[87] On every side, war machines lept forth; here, the battering ram struck the wall; there, a soldier prepared to climb a ladder. On the other side, those who were in the city hurled shafts, stones, stakes burned on the end [hardened in fire],[88] and fire; sometimes they came out and entered close combat.[89] On each side, the fight was carried on bravely; their good cause made these [the Henricans] bold; their peril made the others so.

One day,[90] when each army, weary from the fighting and the summer heat,[91] had given themselves up to sleep about midday, and, as fortune wished, no look-out kept watch, one of the shield-bearers went alone to the

---

83. These charges had already been presented by Henry and his bishops at Worms in 1076.

84. 1081.   85. Cf. Lucan I, 304 f.

86. 1081–84. Sallust, *Jugurtha* 35, 5.   87. II Corinthians 7:5.

88. *Aeneid* VII, 524.   89. Cf. Sallust, *Jugurtha*, chaps. 57, 60.

90. June 3, 1083.

91. Cf. Sulpicius, *Life of St. Martin*, chap. 3.

wall to gather stakes. He saw that the wall and ramparts were unoccupied, and with his pricked and attentive ears he also discovered that no one was near within the walls. Assisted by confidence of mind and lightness of body, he worked his way up with hands and feet, until finally he touched the summit of the wall.[92] Then, indeed, when he cast his eyes around and saw no one, set between hope and fear,[93] he signaled to his comrades by every movement of his body, and scarcely did he keep himself from shouting when they gave attention too slowly to his signals. Hastening with arms and ladders which they had snatched up, and going over the wall more swiftly, as they say, than can be told, they slew, captured, put to flight those who had come too late to the defense of the captured city.[94]

The King disdained to enter by way of the gate which now had been thrown open, for at that point every man in the ranks to the rear would have been slowed by the ones marching in front of him and every man to the fore would have been shoved on by the pressure of those behind. But to avenge the rash shutting [of the gates], he ordered that the wall be broken and that they lay open an entrance for him so wide that the whole army drawn up side by side and shoulder to shoulder could sweep in at the same time.

Then, certainly, death was everywhere; everywhere, mourning.[95] Rome trembled while the height of her towers was battered and fell.[96] The Pope fled,[97] and he who had pushed everyone into peril deserted all in peril. At last, Rome contritely repented her of her presumption, and she who could have deserved earlier to be honored by the King with gifts now, in the presence of the King, obtained with difficulty, and with a great deal of money, the privilege not to be wholly destroyed.

Shortly, when everything had been quieted, the King presented in public the reason why he had come; he reported what criminal treatment he had received at the hands of the Pope; and after many had confessed that this

92. Cf. Sallust, *Jugurtha*, chaps. 93, 94.

93. *Aeneid* I, 218.

94. In Gregory's November synod, 1083, the following report was made: "But the persecution of this same Henry precluded three Lenten Synods. Once he approached St. Paul [St. Paul's without the Walls]; twice, St. Peter's; and finally, after much blood was shed, he took the walls of Porticus [the Leonine City] not so much through the bravery of his men, as through the negligence of the citizens. Indeed, the Roman mob (that is, the more copious part of the city), wearied by the two-year's war, was laboring under keen hunger, since they were not allowed to go out to neighboring towns or camps, nor did Henry's sworn men wish to go to the city for trade. Many also had left the city, driven away by hunger. And at length as their interest in the war declined, the others prosecuted it with increasingly less zeal, and without any qualms, they neglected their guard posts as much as they pleased."

95. *Aeneid* II, 369.

96. The destruction of the walls of the Leonine city.

97. Actually Gregory VII took refuge in the Castel Sant' Angelo until the Norman forces under Robert Guiscard forced Henry's retreat from Rome (1084).

had indeed happened so, he designated Pope Clement for the election of all.[98] After he had been consecrated Emperor with the common approval of all and made patrician by him [Clement], he confined himself in Rome for some time,[99] to remold everything into solid concord.

7. We must not pass by a story which the account of reliable persons spread into the German regions and which Rome herself averred.

The Emperor was accustomed to frequent a certain oratory to pray, and he let no day pass without going there. He had chosen for himself, however, a familiar place in that same oratory for prayer, a place where he might spend his time the more intently, the more secretly, in prayer.[100]

A certain man of impious mind observed this habit of his. And, whether urged on by his own or by the wickedness of another, he placed a great stone on a beam in position to strike from above the head of the Emperor; and, by removing from the paneled ceiling a tablet which looked directly down on the head of the Emperor, he opened a hole to send the weight through. He tested this arrangement very often, using a slackened rope so that the stone would not go awry in falling. After everything had been tested sufficiently, this servant of guile scaled up one night and watched from above until the Emperor stood to pray in his customary place. Then, that man, greedy for the destruction of another, but ignorant of his own, hurled the weight against the head of the Emperor.[101] The unhappy man, himself a weight, fell together with his weight, but the Emperor was not harmed, for he had moved slightly from his place. The affair became known swiftly through all of Rome,[102] and the common mob (*plebs*), which cannot be quieted easily once it has been aroused, in a frenzy, and against the will of the Emperor, pulled the half-living body[103] over rocks and stones and rent it asunder.[104] But everyone, attributing the affair to a miraculous sign, not to an accident, became the more devotedly subject to the Emperor in the bonds of fidelity and of their feelings. And the hostile plot not only confirmed in loyalty those already faithful to him, but also made many loyal who had been his enemies; and so, he [the would-be assassin] who strove to do harm actually did good.

Finally, when everything in Rome was set in order and a garrison had been established in the City,[105] lest she alter her state of fidelity, the Em-

---

98. Wibert of Ravenna had already been elected as Clement III in 1080 at Brixen. The election was repeated in 1084, and Wibert was consecrated.

99. For one month.

100. Cf. Sulpicius, *Life of St. Martin*, chap. 10.

101. Ibid., chap. 5.   102. Cf. 1 Macc. 7:3.

103. Cf. Ovid, *Fasti* II, 838.   104. Cf. Jude 14:6.

105. The garrison consisted of 300 German knights under the command of Udalrich of Godesheim (1083).

peror, functioning in the height of his new dignity, went back into the German kingdom. But no fortune lasts long; for those whom the Emperor had established as a garrison in Rome were seized with sickness which both the place and the season produced—for it was summer—and died without even one survivor.[106] Then, when the yoke of the garrison had been removed, Rome, made mistress of her own decisions, reverted to type;[107] and, after she had taken up arms again against the Emperor and had expelled the Pope [Clement],[108] she constituted another; for that earlier Gregory had departed from life. When this was revealed to the Emperor, he set out again with an army against Rome. But when he came into Italy, he was met by envoys from Rome who bore a pact of peace, and [at the same time] a report reached him of a hostile enterprise at his back. Thus he returned to Germany[109] and left behind in Italy his son Conrad, who at that time was already the heir-designate of the kingdom,[110] assigning to him the task of working against Mathilda—that grasping woman who was laying claim to almost all of Italy—and taking out of the hand of a woman that kingdom which would be his in the future.

What may enemies do when children themselves rise up against their parents? Or whence may one assure himself of security when he is not safe from him whom he begat? Let marriages now cease; let no one hope for an heir: your heir will be your enemy, for not only does he rob you of your house and lands, but he also makes haste to rob you of your life.

The son of the Emperor, who as we have said, was left by his father in Italy, and left for a definite reason, as we have also told, was won over by the persuasions of Mathilda—for whom may not womanly guile corrupt or deceive?—and joined his father's enemies. He set the crown upon his own head,[111] usurped the royal office, profaned right, confounded order, fought against nature, and sought the blood of his father, since he would not have been able to reign save by the blood of his father.

When a running report brought this news to the enemies of the Emperor, they were exultant, they applauded, they sang, they praised the deed of the son, [and they praised] especially the woman who was the chief mover of the deed.[112] They sent envoys straightway to thrust a spur into the spirit of the new king and to add oil to the fire,[113] to vow perpetual fidelity and mate-

106. One account says that "scarcely thirty" survived. (*MGH SS.*, V, 438.)

107. Terence, *Adelphi* I, 1, 46.

108. Wibert was expelled during the summer of 1085, but returned shortly after. He was expelled again in 1089 and returned again in 1091.

109. He remained in Italy until 1097; when Conrad rebelled in 1093, he stayed in northern Italy.

110. Conrad was consecrated as king in 1087.

111. He was crowned king of Italy by Anselm, archbishop of Milan, in 1093 at Monza.

112. Cf. *Aeneid* I, 364.   113. Horace, *Satires* II, 3, 321.

rial assistance for their own interests (but actually against them), although long ago they had covenanted never to obey the son or the father.

The Emperor, on the other hand, however much he grieved inwardly at this report, outwardly maintained himself, nonetheless, in his grave demeanor and lamented, not his own, but his son's fortune. When, however, he could not recall him from his undertaking, he sought not so much to avenge his own injury as through vengeance to remove a model of wrongdoing. And so he turned his thoughts toward disinheriting his son and to advancing his [Conrad's] brother Henry, still a boy, into the royal office.[114] Therefore, after the Emperor had held many assemblies with the great nobles, he stated his complaints against his son Conrad: namely, that he had joined the enemies of the royal office and usurped the royal office and that he strove to deprive his father not only of the royal office, but also of life. He said that the wrong done to him ought to be considered a wrong done to the state, or if this were not to cause concern to anyone, at least they should serve the cause of the state so as to avoid the danger that anyone would become king through force and crime;[115] or rather, that they should transfer the election which the elder son had rightly lost to his younger son. Many raised objections against this, relying more on ingenuity than on the just and the true; many, however, were in favor of the public good and were in accord with the decision and the desire of the Emperor. Finally, all came together on one decision and gave their approval with harmonious good will.

First, the invader [Conrad] was adjudged by decree of the Curia, and then the Emperor constituted his younger son heir to the kingdom.[116] Lest he also go into the path of his brother,[117] he [Henry IV] received from him a solemn vow,[118] specifically that he would never intrude himself either into the royal power or into the lands of his father while he [the father] was living, except, perchance, by his consent. Already then, there was muttering and fear that there would be intestine war in the future between the two brothers and that a great disaster was in store for the kingdom. But He who dispenses all removed this fear with the death of the elder son[119] and gave an opportunity for the kingdom to return into single harmony.

When these things had been transacted thus, the enemies of the Emperor who had found themselves so often deprived of a head, not having anyone else to whom they might adhere, were rendered more agreeable by treaty and converted, which was the very best thing, wars into peace and castles into [bastions of] domestic security.

114. 1097.
115. Sallust, *Jugurtha* 14, 7.
116. 1098, at Mainz.
117. Cf. Matt. 10:5.
118. Repeated in 1099 during the coronation of Henry V at Aachen.
119. 1101.

8. Therefore, so that there might be peace and tranquillity everywhere, when the magnates had been called together to the Curia,[120] he [Henry IV] had the peace strengthened throughout the whole kingdom under an oath, and, to bridle the evils which came into being before that time, he decreed grave punishments against transgressors [of the decree]. Indeed, the decree of peace profited the miserable and the poor as much as it harmed the perverse and the powerful, for to those [the poor] it brought resources; to these [the powerful] want and hunger.[121] For as regards those who had squandered their goods on soldiers so that encompassed by a large force of knights they might advance in the world and might far outstrip others with their force of armed men—when the license to do robbery was taken from them (so it may be said of them in time of peace), they toiled in poverty; hunger possessed their storehouses. He who lately was borne on a frothing steed now began to be content even with a rustic draft horse. He who lately sought no robe other than one which glowed, tinted with reddish purple, said that he had done well if now he had a robe which nature had tinted with her own color. Gold rejoiced that it was no longer trampled in the mire, when want forced the use of iron spurs. Finally, whatever vanity, whatever superfluity corrupt fashions had brought in, Mistress Penury destroyed it all. Securely, the sailor passed hamlets situated on river banks, for which the loot of captured ships used to afford sustenance, while now the chief of the hamlet hungered. A wondrous fact and no less amusing: while others avenged their injuries with injuries, the Emperor avenged his with peace.

When, however, the lords with their followers had been restrained for some years by this law, distressed because they were not allowed to practice their wickedness with freedom, they set in motion again muttering against the Emperor; they sowed again a dark rumor[122] about his deeds.

Of what, I ask, has he been guilty? Without doubt, it was this: that he forbade crimes, that he recalled peace and justice, that the highwayman did not beset the road, that the forest did not conceal his ambushes, that the merchant and boatmen might go their way freely, that the robber hungered since robbery was forbidden.

Why, I pray, does it please you to live in no way other than from robbery? Return to the fields those whom you have assigned from the field to arms; balance the number of your followers with which you scattered foolishly in order to have more men-at-arms; and then your barns and storehouses will abound with all good things. And no longer will it be nec-

---

120. Mainz, 1103.   121. Sallust, *Historia* II, 96, 6.
122. Cf. Lucan VII, 2.

essary to take things not one's own, when everyone can subsist abundantly on his own.

Under such conditions the Emperor would not be charged with a crime, nor war be promoted in the kingdom; under such conditions you would have [the wherewithal] to satisfy the body, and you would save your souls as well, which is most felicitous. But I waste my time; I ask the ass to play the lyre: [123] bad customs grown usual are never removed or, if so, with difficulty.

9. Therefore, those accustomed to rapine turned their minds again to the promotion of wars in order to find occasion for recovering their habitual way of life. They sought again to find a rival for the Emperor; to this end they thought his son most suitable. [124]

And so to find a place for the suggestion—these were the first allurements of deception—they frequently took him along with them on hunts. [125] They baited him with lures of feasts; with jests they launched into the sundering of his spirit and dragged him along with them to the doing of many things which youth inspires. Finally, as is the case among youths, they were bound together with a certain bond of comradeship, so that they even plighted their fidelity and gave the right hand in common secrets. When, therefore, they thought that he, ensnared as he was with much craft, could be caught, one day among other things, as though in an aside, they brought his father into mention. They were amazed [they said] that he could suffer so harsh a father, that he was no different from a slave. His father was an old man and incapable of managing the reins of the kingdom; and if he put off the assumption of the kingship until his [father's] death, beyond all doubt another would snatch it from him ahead of time. Because of the envy and hatred which existed toward his father, he would have many supporters; indeed, he would transfer the good wishes of all to himself if he made no delay in taking over the government of the kingdom which he had received, most of all since long ago both the Church had cast away his father, excommunicate, and the great nobles of the kingdom had rejected him. And finally, they said that that which he had imprudently vowed should not be observed, but rather that he would at last have sanctified himself if he made void the vow vowed to an excommunicate.

Since the father, on his side, suspected no evil from his son, he approved his familiarity with the greater men of the kingdom, hoping that just as they had become united in affection in the present so they would after-

123. Cf. St. Jerome to Marcellus 27, 1.

124. The leaders in this conspiracy as named by the chronicler Ekkehard of Aura were Diotpald, margrave of the Nordgau; Bernger, count of Sulzbach; and Otto, count of Hapsburg.

125. 1104.

wards bear him asssistance the more faithfully and efficaciously in obtaining the kingship.

What more? Suddenly enticed and drawn away by lust, as youth is always seducible, he was lacking neither in desire nor in action for [the fulfillment] of the malignant proposal. Therefore, the son of the Emperor watched for the time when his defection from his father would be of the greatest inconvenience to his father. And when the Emperor was marching with an army against certain rebels among the Saxons, at the very time when the Saxons, through envoys, were pressing for negotiations, his son suddenly deserted him, taking many men away from him.[126] Without doubt he [Henry V] will be deserted by those who had persuaded him to become a deserter.

The Emperor sent envoys[127] after him and recalled him as much with tears as with commands, entreating him not to cause grief to his old father; rather, not to offend the Father of all, not to expose himself to the scorn of men, not to make himself a subject of idle talk for the world. [He urged him], moreover, to be mindful of the bond with which he had obligated himself to him. Those who had suggested such things to him, [he said], were enemies, not friends; waylayers, not advisers in good faith.

He [Henry V] cast all this completely aside and averred that he would have no further dealing with him since he was excommunicate. Thus he pursued his own cause under the guise of the cause of God. Instantly, he rushed through Bavaria, Swabia, and Saxony; he convened the great nobles; he attracted all, as they were "characters desirous of revolution"; and he crept into the regal power as though he had entombed his father. Soon he besieged threateningly the castle of Nürenberg. The disaster sustained there by each side is evidence of how great the valor was with which the battle was joined. But the less hope those besieged had, the greater their spirit; and unless the Emperor, forbearing to punish crime, had ordered the surrender of the castle,[128] he [Henry V] would still labor there with a useless siege if only hunger, which overcomes everything, did not subdue it. Lo, how great the father's pious sense of duty! In return for the deed of his son, he showed the spirit of paternal affection; he paid no heed to the wrong, but to nature; he preferred that the town be given over rather than that it be freed by bringing peril to his son; he preferred to endure his wrongs rather than to avenge them. The townsfolk, therefore, after they had been offered the sort of settlement they wanted, surrendered the town; and after the army was disbanded, the King betook himself to Regensburg,

126. December 1104, from the imperial camp at Fritzlar.

127. 1105. The archbishops of Cologne and Trier, Frederick, duke of Swabia, and Erlung of Würzburg.

128. Not supported by other accounts.

to make it stable for himself and immovable in solidly established good faith, since until that time it had been ambivalently disposed.

As soon as the Emperor learned this—he resided at that moment in the city of Würzburg—he thought that his son could be apprehended either on his journey or in the city; and with so swift and so silent a course did he follow his footsteps that no one had foreknowledge of his journey before a rather considerable band of his men crossed the Danube and rushed up to the city with swiftly driven horses. His son, dumbfounded at so sudden and unexpected a thing, fled from the city.

Why do you flee him whom you ought not to flee; why do you flee your father?[129] He follows you, he does not pursue you; he follows, I say, not as an enemy, but as a father, not to destroy, but to save; he follows to restore to a quiet state the commonwealth thrown into turmoil by you, and to provide for your affairs in the future.

After sending out messengers immediately through Bavaria and Swabia, the King recollected his scattered army, a fact which forced the Emperor to summon an army for himself. Thus the two armies came against each other on the Regen River; here the father, there the son; here devotion, there madness settled down together.

And when the more powerful of each side convened as mediators in such great dissension, those who were from the side of the Emperor were enticed by persuasive words and attracted by many and great promises and thus grew cold in their loyalty toward the Emperor; and unless he had sensed this deceitfulness of his intimates, he would have been left in danger alone, with only a few men.

Therefore, he thought that he had to yield to crime and fortune, and after the fashion of David, he fled lest his son become a parricide.

How wondrously works the grace of God! With how plain a sign[130] does it teach us, if we would be taught, if we would not have a blind heart.

Since the Emperor assumed that his enemies would pursue him in the direction in which he had gone, he turned aside to the Duke of Bohemia, who received him with great honor, although of late in no good way he had abandoned him in the narrows, and he conducted him into Saxony. Although he had dangerous and brave enemies there, he was nevertheless honorably conducted through their midst and by them to the Rhine.

Whence this unless "the hand of the Lord was with him,"[131] and he had an invisible leader who led him safe through shafts, through enemies?[132] You had been warned by this miracle, O son of the Emperor, if you could

---

129. Cf. Eusebius-Rufinus, *Historia ecclesiastica* III, 23.
130. 2 Macc. 14:15.   131. Luke 1:66.
132. *Aeneid* II, 527.

have been warned, to learn to revere your father, not to harry him whom even his enemies revered when he had come into their hands. But you will be warned more harshly, since you are not corrected by this very mild admonition.

When, however, the flight of the Emperor had become known, that event took many men away from him and caused much to be added to the affairs of his son, but to be subtracted from his own affairs.

10. In order to spur on the fortune which favored him, the King straightway scheduled a Curia at Mainz on the birth of the Lord. He invited the great nobles and summoned many so that he could announce to all that he wished to be the master of things. Even the Emperor, when he had summoned those men needful to him [his intimate advisers], was disposed to go to this Curia, for he wished to place in question whether what had been done to him had been done rightly or otherwise. When his adversaries had learned this, they feared both for themselves and for their case if his armed retinue should prove as mighty as his legal grounds.

Thus they suggested this act of deception to the King. [They proposed] that he confess his wrong before his father, having assumed an expression of deepest repentance, and earnestly entreat him for pardon. [He was to say] that he was sorry to have agreed to malignant proposals and that he was ready [to render] full satisfaction if only he found his pardon. And if he could thus find an opportunity for deception, he should use it; if not, however, fraud itself should be held for fidelity, pretense for truth.

When he came to his father,[133] instructed in this artifice, the father believed the words and the tears of his son and fell upon his neck weeping and kissing him, joyful after the example of that father in the Gospel [who learned] that the son who had been dead had revived and that he who had been lost was found.[134] What more? He acquitted his son of punishment as of crime; and to reproach his son with fatherly gentleness was to him to avenge the wrongdoing of his son, as in that comment of the comic poet: "For a great sin of the son, slight punishment is enough for the father."[135]

After these dealings, just as he had deceived his father with feigned repentance, so also he did with counsel. For he suggested to his father, as it had been suggested to him himself, that they both should dismiss so great a host and then go to the Curia with moderate forces, that there was nothing which would offer resistance to him since they had come together in concord, and that everything would be destroyed if they went on with this great force.

This advice (good, indeed, had it not been deceptive) pleased his father,

133. At Coblenz.   134. Luke 15:24.
135. Terence, *Andria* V, 3, 32.

and after the great host had been dismissed, he went with not more than three hundred men to the Curia, accompanied by his son. He turned off for the night to a resting place,[136] and there the father amused himself with his son in a wondrous way through that whole night; he conversed and joked, he embraced and kissed him, eager to make up for what he had lost through the long interruption of this enjoyment, but not knowing that that night of amusement was the last.

It is amazing that fraud ever had so well-ordered a fortune. For on the next day, when they were drawing near to Mainz, there came a man under the guise of a messenger whose task was to say that the Bavarians and the Swabians had come to Mainz with a monstrous host. Then his son suggested to the Emperor that it would not be safe to go into the midst of enemies, unless their dispositions had been fathomed beforehand, and [added] that the audacity of men is unbridled. [He advised] that he should rather turn aside to a castle[137] which was nearby, while he himself convened them, sought out the resolve of their undertaking, and conducted them to him to seek his favor.

The Emperor did as his son suggested; he turned aside to the castle, not discerning the snare of craft which the lovely appearance of lying faith had woven. When, however, the Emperor had entered with a few men, the gate was closed and entrance was denied to his vassals. Then the fraud was revealed: he who had been received as lord was held as captive.

And so after he had posted guards to watch over his father, he returned with this triumph of deceit to the Curia at Mainz and related with great boasting, a though he had done a deed of valor, how ingeniously he had caught his father. Then, indeed, the Curia resounded with applause and gladness, and they ascribed impiety to justice and deceit to virtue. At once he sent an envoy[138] to his father, ordering him, if he wished to save his life, to transmit without delay the cross, the crown, the lance, and the other regalia to him and to transfer into his hand the strongest fortifications he held. Neither did the father delay to do everything which he had been ordered, nor did he consider the Empire more valuable than himself. But it was thought that he had not rendered satisfaction enough in this [matter] unless he himself came also in person and, in the sight of all, renounced the Empire. He came,[139] therefore, not of his own power, but brought forth under arrest. Alone he stood before those who once had stood before him, and not having the liberty of arguing his case in debate, he spoke as the fortune of a captive demands. Asked whether his renunciation of the Empire were voluntary, he answered not what his desire would have, but what

136. Bingen.
138. Wibert of Groitsch.
137. Böckelheim.
139. To Ingelheim.

necessity constrained [him to say]. He said that, indeed, he renounced the Empire not constrained by force, but induced by his own will. Already, [he said], his powers to manage the reins of the royal power had failed him, and he was no longer possessed by fierce desire for it [the power], since from long practice he had learned that it held more trouble than glory. It was time, [he added], for him to set off the honor together with the burden and to provide for his soul. Only, [he warned], his son should be wary lest he do something against him which would be unworthy both for him [Henry V] to do and for him [Henry IV] to suffer.

Both the speech of the Emperor and his fortune moved many to laments and tears;[140] not even nature herself, however, could move his son to pity. And when he fell at the feet of his son, praying that he acknowledge in him at any rate the rights he held through nature [that is, the father-son relationship], he turned neither countenance nor mind to his father,[141] although it was rather he who ought to have fallen prostrate at his father's feet in that, impatient of delay,[142] he had seized ahead of time the kingdom from that very man by whom he had been designated its inheritor. Moreover, he prayed forgiveness from all whom he had ever unjustly injured. But he also prostrated himself at the feet of the apostolic legate,[143] praying and beseeching him to loose him from the ban and to restore him to the communion of the church. Laymen, moved by compassion, gave their forgiveness; but the legate of the Apostolic Lord denied absolution, averring that this was not of his power and that it was necessary for him to look for the grace of absolution from the Pope himself.

What more? After he had renounced the imperial dignity, he departed deprived and retired to a certain manor which his son had allowed him for sustenance. How impotent is the power of the world, how uncertain, how unstable! But that ought not to be called power which cannot bring to pass everything it wishes and which he who attains it can lose.

11. After things had been transacted in this fashion, and the Curia was ended,[144] the King passed through the upper regions and cities of the Rhine, and, as circumstances demanded, he subjected to himself some by grants of benefices, others by inflicting injuries upon them.

When, however, he had entered Alsace, his fortune came to a standstill for some time,[145] as there he engaged in a battle the outcome of which was as unhappy as its inception unwise. For when his followers were loitering about arrogantly in the village of Ruffach, which was powerful by virtue of

140. Lucan IX, 146 f. Cf. Sulpicius Severus, *Ep.* 2.
141. Cf. *Aeneid* II, 741.   142. Lucan VI, 424.
143. Richard, cardinal bishop of Albano.
144. 1106.   145. Lucan VII, 547.

its large body of residents and its weapons, a numerous assembly of burghers stood in the way of wrongdoing; and yet, since wrongdoing exceeded
measure, they could not endure it.

But when the King heard the tumult, he hastened not to prevent wrong-
doing, but to help it on, not to quiet the battle, but to stir it up the more.
This called out the whole village in a tumultuous throng; the irrevocable
mob ran out,[146] the woman with the man, the servant with the master, the
base with the brave; and, as is often the case, injury brought out the true
feeling. The battle was begun, and flight was begun; for when those who
were on the royal side saw the onslaught of the raging crowd and the matter
set in the narrows, they thought that their ruin lay in valor, that safety lay in
flight alone;[147] and those who could saved their lives through flight. O unhappy event, O shame of royal dignity: with the King in flight, the regal
insignia were made the booty of the mob.

Come to your senses at last, good King, come to your senses, and recognize wrath from above in this which has fallen your lot. It is the judgment of the wrath of God that you should flee, who had put your father to
flight, and that you should lose the insignia which you had stolen from your
father.

But afterwards when they [the insignia] had been recovered through a
pact of peace and a grant of pardon, the deep wound of the injury made the
King change his attitude. And when he had gathered a rather large force,[148]
he laid waste the village with fire and looting and raged with indiscriminate
slaughter against the men of this place.

But since he suspected that what fortune alone had dared against him[149]
had resulted from a stratagem of his father, he began to plot new plots of
injuries against him; and in order to obviate any source of hindrance for
himself, he directed his thoughts to a plan by which either to capture
[Henry IV] or to expel him.

And so, he decided that, if it could come about, he would arrest him
[Henry IV] at the Easter services which were to be celebrated for him at
Liége (where he had heard that he [Henry IV] had found fidelity and a refuge for his fortune) and that he would demand satisfaction from the
Bishop[150] who had wronged him by receiving the rival of his honor. And
when the father saw that his son had decided to celebrate Easter at Liége,
he directed a legation to him in this fashion:

"If I asked you, O sweetest son, whether the tradition of men or the

146. Lucan I, 509.   147. Cf. Sallust, *Catiline* 58, 16.
148. Lucan I, 466.   149. Lucan IV, 402 f.
150. Otbert of Liége. Cf. Terence, *Andria* IV, 1, 15.

mandate of God is to be held superior and greater, you would respond, unless you have been led away from truth, that he is like a dumb animal who does not prefer heavenly things to earthly, divine to human.

"Why, therefore, do you listen to those who suggest to you 'Harry your father' more than to the word of God Himself: 'Honor your father'?[151] These men deceive you; they do not instruct you; they do not provide for your honor, but they are envious of it;[152] they knit the snares of treacherous disloyalty under the appearance of fidelity. They cannot attain otherwise the destruction of your honor save through our destruction.

"It may very well have been because of the exigencies of my sins—this is the opinion of my adversaries—that God has cast me down so to rule no longer.[153] Nevertheless, it was not your part to have labored to cast me out and to have snatched away from me prematurely the kingdom which I had prepared for you. Barbarous kingdoms condemn and disavow such an inhuman deed; the very pagans abhor it, and those who do not know God recognize what they should owe to nature in loving men.

"But what wonder if malignant stealth succeeds in deception at the seducible and immature time of life [that is, youth] when evil counsels sometimes bend even old men and a fixed state of mind to evil? My fortune results from the crime of another rather than from yours; for you were in the hands of beguilers, not they in yours. If, however, you add injury [to this], you can no longer be excused, since you know that an injury is a crime once it has been done and that you cannot do one halfway.

"For I have heard that you have decided to celebrate Easter at Liége; there the Bishop received me with fidelity and devotion when there was no one who was mindful of our benefices or who shared our lot. Surely, it is fitting that you respond with royal liberality to the kindnesses he has shown me; and the more faithfully he is proven to have acted toward us, the more certain you will be able to be of his fidelity. Unless perchance he receive you here in his house, he has decided to keep me with him at the Easter festival. But you say that it is worthy and meet for this festival to join rather than to divide us and that you wish, that you strongly desire, me to pass the days of Easter gladness here with you.

"This, indeed, I also would desire altogether if there were not something which I should fear. For I am unable not to fear those who repent of having allowed me to live when my death and life was in their hands. All things are suspect to me; all things are to be feared, most of all in a crowd where it is the more difficult to guard against danger the greater the opportunity for criminal action. It is for this reason that I have retired far from

151. Exod. 20:12.   152. Cf. Sallust, *Jugurtha* 85, 18.
153. 1 Sam. 15:23.

the midst of those who hated me, and I have withdrawn myself into the outermost limits of your kingdom;[154] so that either I might be safe through remoteness of place or if my fortune should demand that I seek human company beyond [the borders] I could the more swiftly leave your kingdom.

"I pray, therefore, that, for the sake of your father, you set the Easter Curia for another place and that you let me abide (although this may not be permitted to an emperor, at least let it be allowed a guest) in the house of him who received me for the sake of humanity, lest it be told either to my ridicule or to your shame that on the feast of the Lord's resurrection it was my fate to be forced to seek uncertain lodgings. If you do what I ask, I shall be most thankful; but if not, I prefer to be a beggar in foreign realms rather than to be held for a laughing-stock[155] in the realms once my own."

The son heard this legation of his father with a deaf ear, nor could he be deflected from his resolve. For this reason, since Easter was now imminent, the father wanted to withdraw; but the Bishop and Duke Henry,[156] who himself had also been invited by the Bishop, kept him from departing. They said that they could not suffer that, cast from the houses of men on so great a festival, he should seek out the forests and the lairs of wild animals[157] and that he had, indeed, been stripped without cause of Empire, but not of the loving service of his friends. If they were permitted to enjoy peace, they added, they desired nothing more than peace; but if, on the other hand, the affair were to be carried on with weapons, weapons would not be far from their hands. Not to be a source of ruin to them, he averred that it would be more advantageous if he withdrew than if he stayed; but finally, he gave them his consent when they insisted more importunately and remained as they demanded.

12. And so a great cavalry force went far before the face of [that is, in advance of] the King and came to a bridge of the river which is called Meuse. [Walrabo], the son of the afore-mentioned Duke [Henry], occupied the bank on the opposite side of the river with a few men, for he had stationed the main body of his armed men in opportune places not far away for ambuscades. To provoke a battle, he now spurred on his horse in a straight course, and now he rode about in circles, asking if an equal number of them dared to engage in battle with him. With no delay, an equal number from the side of the King crossed over to them and joined battle; with varying moves, they now carried the battle forward, now turned to flight. Meanwhile, one man after another secretly crossed the bridge, increased the number of his comrades, and through this breach of the agree-

---

154. Ps. 18:18–19.   155. Terence, *Hecyra* I, 247.
156. Henry of Limburg, duke of Lorraine.
157. Cf. Lucan II, 153; Ovid, *Metamorphoses* I, 592, and VI, 668.

ment on the terms of battle, changed the struggle from one between equals to one between unequals.

When the son of the Duke saw this, he turned his back with his men, not so much to flee as to deceive, not so much to avoid danger by fleeing as to lead those following them into danger. On the other side, when those on the opposite bank saw the flight, they crossed the bridge at full speed and pursued the one fleeing, ignorant of their future lot and of the deception which lay hidden.[158] But after they had come to the place where the ambushes were arranged, men dashed forth from the ambuscades and threw themselves with a great onslaught against the pursuers. The latter were terrified by the unexpected danger and turned back in flight, not being able to use their arms rationally[159] because of their confounding fear.

But of what advantage was it to have turned their breasts and to have lain open their backs to wounds? And so, many were taken, many maimed, many killed; and the blood-stained victor[160] had no bounds to his enormities[161] save that dictated by his own aversion to the deed.

In fact, at the bridge where the fleeing mass was pressed together the impious hand[162] performed the more heinous deeds the less the tightly packed crowd could move. But the river engulfed more by far than the sword consumed;[163] for when the enemy pressed from the back, they cast themselves into the river impelled by fear, and thunderstruck and confused they dashed from death into death. One was yet to see another misfortune there, certainly the greatest one: for the bridge, heavily weighted by the multitude, suddenly collapsed, and the river enveloped men and horses alike. No one had an opportunity to escape; skill in swimming brought advantage to none; for hindered either by the weight of arms or by the press of clinging companions, everyone was drawn into the depths. This evil was the more heinous, as it occurred on the very Day of Preparation [Good Friday], and the magnitude of the heinous deed mounted through the religious awe of the season.

13. After things had passed in this way, the King changed his route and turned toward Cologne. But since it also had denied entrance to him in advance, after passing Easter Sunday in a village which is called Bonn, he returned quickly to Mainz, and, through legates whom he scattered everywhere, he directed a complaint to the nobles in this fashion:

"Even if I had seized the kingdom by usurpation, still I should beat back those resisting our power as much as I were able. Now, however, since I have obeyed your precepts in assuming the office of kingship, has anyone

158. Cf. Josh. 8:14.
159. *Aeneid* II, 314.
160. Lucan V, 758.
161. Lucan I, 334.
162. Sallust, *Jugurtha* 14, 14.
163. Cf. 2 Sam. 18, 8; *Aeneid* II, 600.

dared with impunity in abuse of the public weal to vex the kingdom and us with arms?

"For when we were on the way to Liége, where our Easter Curia was to be held, and had come to the river Meuse, the Bishop of Liége and Duke Henry, in both of whose faith and devotion to service we placed great confidence, secretly set ambuscades for us; and they slaughtered, captured, and put our men to flight, as ours were unprepared for battle. It is as much a cause of shame to tell that this disaster, as great as it was, should have happened there as it is to dismiss it unavenged. Therefore, constrained as I was both by the severity of the outcome and by the pressure of time [that is, by the nearness of Easter], I turned aside to Cologne. When she, quite proudly, refused to receive me, I spent the holy day of Easter as I might in the village of Bonn. To which royal person was such great and degrading abuse ever offered?

"This degrading abuse does not touch me alone; you have been cast into contempt. These usurpers do not wish your decrees to have authority; they want only their own statutes to be firmly established; and finally, they long to be regarded as those upon whom the whole weight of kingship rests. They are ready to destroy the king whom you have constituted in order that none of those things which you have decreed may be given any thought. Therefore, this, my injury, is an injury done to the kingdom rather than to me; for the casting down of one head, even the highest one, is a loss to the kingdom which can be repaired; but to crush the princes under foot is to effect the ruin of the kingdom.

"Will we bear these things with impunity, and will their pride become the more puffed up through our base forbearance? O may we who are called dishonored not also be called unavenged. It is enough to have said a few words; only idle spirits need the spur of prolix exhortation. May the cause serve as incitement more than words.

"Since, therefore, the forces of the commonwealth must be used against such proud enemies, in asking we command, and in commanding we ask of you a campaign [against the enemy] for the assembling of which we ordain the time, the Kalends of July, and the place, the city of Würzburg."

When, therefore, Duke Henry and the people of Cologne, together with the people of Liége, had heard that the King wished to lead an army against them, they readied arms, they assembled troops, they strengthened their cities and girded themselves for resistance with equal will and zeal. They also urged the Emperor with counsels and entreaties to resume the imperial office which he had set aside, convicted not by regular order, but constrained by force and by a death-directed sword.[164] [They said] that they

---

164. Cf. *Aeneid* I, 91.

would fail him neither in arms nor in spirit and that, in a short time, he would have many supporters, since many were much horrified at so unwonted and inhuman an outrage. He resisted their urgent solicitation, basing his position on the following argument: that it was impossible to recover a lost Empire by force of arms, an Empire which he had not been able to hold fast by force of arms when it was in his possession; that he did not regard it so highly that he deemed it worthy to be regained with the destruction of many men; and that it would be happier and safer for him to live as one deprived, although he had been undeservedly deposed. In this way, one side presented its argument and the other gave its in turn; and since they did not cease to insist that he not cast off from himself the good will which surrounded him, he neither consented nor declined entirely, but looking to the future, he kept their headstrong spirits in suspense with indecisive hope.[165]

They therefore fortified first Cologne, which was to bear the first onslaught, with a ditch and towers; they collected military levies, stationed a garrison there, and then awaited their peril with brave spirits. So also they strengthened the other cities which they believed would be invaded, with fortifications, war machines, and the strength of soldiers. But a manifesto was also sped to people everywhere with a severe admonition to the effect that they should be prepared against the army which was about to come upon them in great pride and should defend their fatherland, freedom, and life,[166] nor should they allow either their wives to be given up to the wantonness of corruption or their fields to be distributed among other lords.

Already the King had crossed the Rhine with a strong army, and with a great onslaught he assailed first Cologne, which stood out among the other cities like their head; he thought thus to subject the members to himself more easily after he had trodden down so strong a head. But the results did not, by far, match the expectation; for his men were driven back in a bloody repulse, and with their camps situated at a distance they had to beset the city with a siege.

Rather, however, I should have said that the besiegers were besieged by the besieged; for when the ships which came down the Rhine carrying provisions to the army were intercepted, they labored under oppressive hunger as though fettered by a kind of siege.

Meanwhile, to free the city from the siege, the strength of the whole fatherland came together from all sides. But the Emperor, detesting such impious bloodshed, counseled resolutely against a battle.[167] Why, he asked,

165. Rather, he went to Cologne and supervised its fortification himself. Cf. Ovid, *Metamorphoses* VII, 307.

166. Cf. Sallust, *Catiline*, 58, 11.   167. This is dubious.

did they have so great an ardor for breaking the siege which could not be broken except with a great disaster to their own side? If they devoted their whole concern to seizing the city, which was quite safe by virtue both of the strength of the walls and of the brave soldiery, and very well furnished with every kind of sustenance (with even the Rhine River adding its bene- ficial services since through ships it would afford [the besieged] with what- ever delicacies they desired, despite the besiegers), they would give aid to the hated besieger. Rather, he said, they should permit them [the besiegers] to rage forth to their own ruin and to assail the inexpugnable city, whence they would carry away only wounds and the fallen.[168] They should permit them to devastate [the land] far and wide, since, when the supplies of the countryside were used up, they would begin to hunger; they should permit them to move about pillaging, since horses and men would be worn out by their labor. And, [he concluded], perchance victory would be won for them at slight cost, if only they would be patient for a little while and bide their time, which was all to their advantage.

Thus recalled from open battle by the urging of the Emperor, they merely observed the sallies of the enemy and, by killing[169] here and there those ignorant of the terrain, struck such fear into the enemy that he no longer roamed afield.

Everything, indeed, which the Emperor had predicted came to pass. For as often as they attempted to break open the city gates, to tear through the walls with a battering ram, to cast down the towers with catapults, they bore only wounds and corpses back to the camps, their aim still unattained. Men and horses were exhausted as much by the lack of food as by the enor- mity of their labor, and they lost their strength; for with the fields all about laid waste, they found nothing, but they did not take it upon themselves to go farther because of the enemy lying hidden in ambushes. To these evils sickness also was added, which the stench of the camps, as is usually the case, spread abroad with diseased air. This disease either weakened or killed outright not only common men, but even the princes themselves. Wearied by this kind of adversity in their affairs, they were in doubt as to what they were to do, since though they wished to die, they found no occa- sion for battle; or if they were ready to retreat, they were certain that the enemy would press them from behind; and thus they feared that their army would be scattered in flight.

While they tossed in this tempest of the mind, a report came suddenly and left only serenity where there had been the clouds of such great pertur- bation. For the report was that the Emperor had paid his debt of death.

168. *Aeneid* VII, 574.   169. *Aeneid* II, 384.

At this news, they were first doubtful; but when a messenger[170] had come bearing with orders the last gift of the father to his son—namely, a ring and a sword—such great gladness arose that the voices of those rejoicing could scarcely be stilled.

But there was no less mourning[171] around the bier of the Emperor: the great nobles wailed; the common men lamented; everywhere moaning was heard, everywhere the agony of lament, everywhere the voice of those grieving. At these exequies widows, orphans and finally, the paupers of the whole fatherland came together;[172] they weep that they have been orphaned of their father; they shed tears on the body; they kiss his great hands. With difficulty they were drawn away from embracing the dead body; with difficulty it was made possible to bury it. But they did not desert the tomb;[173] they spent their time there with vigils, tears, and prayers, reciting with weeping, and weeping in reciting them, what works of mercy he had done toward them.[174]

And yet, his death was not to be lamented, since it had been preceded by a good life. He had held to the upright faith and the steadfast hope and also, in his last days, to a bitter contrition of the heart; he also was not ashamed to make public confession of the shameful things which he had committed and ate with all the eagerness of his heart the bread of the Lord's body.

You are happy, O Emperor Henry, who have procured for yourself such guardians, such intercessors, you who now receive in manifold abundance from the hand of the Lord that which you hid secretly in the hands of the poor. You have exchanged a turbulent kingdom for a tranquil; a defective, for an eternal; an earthly, for the celestial. Now at last you reign; now you bear a diadem which neither your heir may snatch from you, nor an enemy envy. Therefore, tears must be contained, if they can be contained. To this, your felicity, is owed dancing, not lamenting; exultation, not wailing; the voices of rejoicing, not of lamentation.

After this outcome of affairs, those who had undertaken war against the royal majesty [Henry V], with their hope dead, lost in spirit and in strength. They did what had to be done in these straits, and whoever could do it, in

170. There were two messengers, Erkenbald, the treasurer of Henry IV, and Burchard, bishop of Münster.

171. *Aeneid* IX, 452.

172. Cf. Sulpicius Severus, *Ep.* 3.

173. According to Otto of Freising (*Deeds of the Emperor Frederick*, I, x), Henry's viscera were buried at Liége, and his body was carried to Speier, where it was buried "in the church of Mary, the Blessed Mother of God and Perpetual Virgin, in royal state beside the emperors, his father and grandfather." Actually this was delayed for some time until Henry V obtained release of his father's excommunication and moved the body from the unconsecrated chapel in Speier where he had first buried it.

174. Cf. Ps. 74:21.

whatever way, by surrender or by the payment of money, returned to the favor of the King.[175]

Lo, then, you have something about the deeds of the Emperor Henry, about his expenditures for the poor, about his fortune, and about his death. Just as all this could not be written by me without tears, so it cannot be read by you without tears.

175. Among them, Otbert, the bishop of Liége, Henry's former protector, who received Henry V as a canon of his cathedral church in 1107.

21. Papal Election Decree (1059)

. . . Supported by the authority of our predecessors and the other holy fathers, we decree and order that:

When the pontiff of this universal Roman church dies the cardinal bishops shall first confer together most diligently concerning the election; next they shall summon the other cardinal clergy; and then the rest of the clergy and the people shall approach to give their assent to the new election, the greatest care being taken lest the evil of venality creep in by any way whatsoever. The most eminent churchmen shall be the leaders in carrying out the election of a pope, the others followers. Certainly this order of election will be found right and lawful if anyone examines the rules and acts of the various fathers and also calls to mind the judgment of our holy predecessor Leo. "No reason permits," he says, "that men should be regarded as bishops who have not been chosen by the clergy or requested by the people or consecrated by the bishops of the province with the approval of the metro- *bishop of important city* politan." But since the apostolic see is superior to all the churches in the world it can have no metropolitan set over it, and so the cardinal bishops who raise the chosen pontiff to the summit of the apostolic dignity undoubtedly act in place of a metropolitan. They shall make their choice from the members of this church if a suitable man is to be found there, but if not they shall take one from another church, saving the honor and reverence due to our beloved son Henry who is now king and who, it is hoped, will in future become emperor with God's grace, according as we have now conceded this to him and to his successors who shall personally obtain this right from the apostolic see.

If, however, the perversity of corrupt and evil men so prevails that a pure, sincere and free election cannot be made in the City, the cardinal bishops, together with the God-fearing clergy and the Catholic laity, even

From Brian Tierney, *The Crisis of Church and State, 1050–1300* (Englewood Cliffs, N.J.: Prentice-Hall, 1964), pp. 42–43. © 1964 by Prentice-Hall, Inc.

though they are few, may have the right and power of electing a pontiff for the apostolic see in any convenient place.

If, after an election has been made, a time of war or the efforts of any malignant men shall make it impossible for the person elected to be enthroned in the apostolic see according to custom, it is clear that, nonetheless, the person elected shall acquire authority to rule the Roman church and to dispose of all its resources as a true pope, for we know that the blessed Gregory acted thus before his consecration. . . .

22. Letter of Gregory VII Proposing a Crusade to Henry IV (1074)

Gregory, bishop, servant of the servants of God, to the glorious King Henry, greeting and apostolic benediction.

If God would grant by some act of his grace that my thoughts might lie open before you, I know beyond a doubt that no person could separate you from my sincere affection. But even as it is, I have entire confidence in his mercy, that it shall one day become clear that I am truly devoted to you. For to this I am directed by the common law of all Christian men; to this the majesty of empire and the mild sway of the Apostolic See impel me; so that if I do not love you as I ought, I am trusting in vain in the mercy of God through the merits of St. Peter.

But, since I desire to labor day and night in the Lord's vineyard, through many dangers even unto death, I will always strive with God's help to preserve a sacred and merited affection not only towards you whom God has placed at the summit of earthly affairs and through whom many may be led either to wander from the path of rectitude or to observe the faith of Christ, but also toward the least among Christians. For he who should try to approach the marriage feast of the king without this wedding garment will suffer a monstrous disgrace. Alas! Those who are daily plotting to sow discord between us pay no attention to these truths, that with these nets prepared at the Devil's prompting they may catch their own advantage and conceal their own vices by which they are madly calling down upon themselves the wrath of God and of St. Peter. I therefore warn and exhort you, my best beloved son, to turn your ear away from them and listen without reserve to those who seek not their own but the things that are of Jesus Christ and who do not set their own honor or profit above righteousness, so that through their counsel you may not forfeit the glory of this life, but may gain with confidence the life that is in Christ Jesus.

From *The Correspondence of Pope Gregory VII*, translated by Ephraim Emerton (New York: Columbia University Press, 1932), pp. 56–58. © 1932 by Columbia University Press. Reprinted by permission of the publisher.

Further, I call to your attention that the Christians beyond the sea, a great part of whom are being destroyed by the heathen with unheard-of slaughter and are daily being slain like so many sheep, have humbly sent to beg me to succor these our brethren in whatever ways I can, that the religion of Christ may not utterly perish in our time—which God forbid! I, therefore, smitten with exceeding grief and led even to long for death—for I would rather stake my life for these than reign over the whole earth and neglect them—have succeeded in arousing certain Christian men so that they are eager to risk their lives for their brethren in defense of the law of Christ and to show forth more clearly than the day the nobility of the sons of God. This summons has been readily accepted by Italians and northerners, by divine inspiration as I believe—nay, as I can absolutely assure you—and already fifty thousand men are preparing, if they can have me for their leader and prelate, to take up arms against the enemies of God and push forward even to the sepulcher of the Lord under his supreme leadership.

I am especially moved toward this undertaking because the Church of Constantinople, differing from us on the doctrine of the Holy Spirit, is seeking the fellowship of the Apostolic See, the Armenians are almost entirely estranged from the Catholic faith and almost all the Easterners are waiting to see how the faith of the Apostle Peter will decide among their divergent views. For it is the call of our time that the word of command shall be fulfilled which our blessed Savior deigned to speak to the prince of the apostles: "I have prayed for thee that thy faith fail not: and when thou art converted, strengthen thy brethren." And because our fathers, in whose footsteps we, though unworthy, desire to walk, often went to those regions for the strengthening of the Catholic faith, we also, aided by the prayers of all Christian men, are under compulsion to go over there for the same faith and for the defense of Christians—provided that the way shall be opened with Christ as our guide—for the way of man is not in his own hand, and the steps of a man are ordered by the Lord.

But, since a great undertaking calls for the aid and counsel of the great, if God shall grant me to begin this, I beg you for your advice and for your help according to your good pleasure. For if it shall please God that I go, I shall leave the Roman Church, under God, in your hands to guard her as a holy mother and to defend her for his honor.

Advise me at the earliest possible moment of your pleasure in this matter and what your divinely inspired judgment may determine. If I did not have better hopes of you than many suppose, these exhortations would be in vain. But since there is perchance no man whom you can completely trust in regard to the sincerity of my affection for you, I leave to the Holy Spirit, which can do all things, to show you in its own way what I ask of you and how great is my devotion to you, and may it in the same way so dispose your heart toward me that the desires of the wicked may come to naught and those of the righteous may increase. These two desires are keeping incessant watch upon us two—though in different ways—and are fighting according to the wishes of those from whom they proceed.

May Almighty God, from whom cometh every good thing, cleanse you from all your sins by the merits and the authority of the blessed Apostles Peter and Paul, and make you to walk in the way of his commandments and lead you into life eternal.

23. *Dictatus Papae* (1075)

1. That the Roman church was founded by the Lord alone.

2. That only the Roman pontiff is by right called "universal."

3. That he alone can depose or reinstate bishops.

4. That his legate—even if of an inferior rank—takes precedence of all bishops in council; and he can give sentence of deposition against them.

5. That the pope can depose absentees.

6. That, among other things, we ought not to stay in the same house with persons excommunicated by him.

7. That it is permitted for him alone, according to the need of the time, to establish new laws, to form peoples into new congregations, to make a canonry into an abbacy, and, on the other hand, to divide a rich episcopacy and unite needy ones.

8. That he alone can use imperial insignia.

9. That only the pope's feet are to be kissed by all princes.

10. That his name only is recited in churches.

11. That this is a unique name in the world.

12. That it is licit for him to depose emperors.

13. That it is licit for him to transfer bishops, under pressure of need, from see to see.

14. That he has the power to ordain a cleric from any church to whatever place he wishes.

15. That a man ordained by him can preside over another church, but not do military service; and that he ought not to receive a higher rank from another bishop.

16. That no synod ought to be called "general" without his authority.

17. That no chapter or book can be held to be canonical without his authority.

From E. Caspar, ed., *Das Register Gregors VII* (Berlin, 1920–23), pp. 202–8. Translated for this volume by Karl F. Morrison.

18. That his sentence ought to be reconsidered by no one, and he alone can reconsider [the judgments] of all.

19. That he ought to be judged by no one.

20. That no one may dare condemn a person appealing to the Apostolic See.

21. That greater cases of any church ought to be referred to her [the Apostolic See].

22. That the Roman church has never erred, nor, by Scripture's testimony, will it ever err.

23. That the Roman pontiff, if he be canonically ordained, indubitably becomes holy through the merits of Blessed Peter, according to the witness of St. Ennodius, Bishop of Pavia, with many holy Fathers concurring, as is contained in decrees of Blessed Symmachus, the Pope.

24. That by his precept and license it is licit for subjects to bring charges.

25. That he can, without a synodal assembly, depose and reinstate bishops.

26. That no one is considered catholic who is not in harmony with the Roman church.

27. That he can absolve subjects of wicked men from fealty.

24. Letter of Gregory VII to Henry IV (1075)

Gregory, bishop, servant of God's servants, to King Henry, greeting and the apostolic benediction—but with the understanding that he obeys the Apostolic See as becomes a Christian king.

Considering and weighing carefully to how strict a judge we must render an account of the stewardship committed to us by St. Peter, prince of the Apostles, we have hesitated to send you the apostolic benediction, since you are reported to be in voluntary communication with men who are under the censure of the Apostolic See and of a synod. If this is true, you yourself know that you cannot receive the favor of God nor the apostolic blessing unless you shall first put away those excommunicated persons and force them to do penance and shall yourself obtain absolution and forgiveness for your sin by due repentance and satisfaction. Wherefore we counsel Your Excellency, if you feel yourself guilty in this matter, to make your confession at once to some pious bishop who, with our sanction, may impose upon you a penance suited to the offense, may absolve you and

From *The Correspondence of Pope Gregory VII*, translated by Ephraim Emerton (New York: Columbia University Press, 1932), pp. 86–91. © 1932 by Columbia University Press. Reprinted by permission of the publisher.

with your consent in writing may be free to send us a true report of the manner of your penance.

We marvel exceedingly that you have sent us so many devoted letters and displayed such humility by the spoken words of your legates, calling yourself a son of our Holy Mother Church and subject to us in the faith, singular in affection, a leader in devotion, commending yourself with every expression of gentleness and reverence, and yet in action showing yourself most bitterly hostile to the canons and apostolic decrees in those duties especially required by loyalty to the Church. Not to mention other cases, the way you have observed your promises in the Milan affair, made through your mother and through bishops, our colleagues, whom we sent to you, and what your intentions were in making them is evident to all. And now, heaping wounds upon wounds, you have handed over the sees of Fermo and Spoleto—if indeed a church may be given over by any human power—to persons entirely unknown to us, whereas it is not lawful to consecrate anyone except after probation and with due knowledge.

It would have been becoming to you, since you confess yourself to be a son of the Church, to give more respectful attention to the master of the Church, that is, to Peter, prince of the Apostles. To him, if you are of the Lord's flock, you have been committed for your pasture, since Christ said to him: "Peter, feed my sheep," and again: "To thee are given the keys of Heaven, and whatsoever thou shalt bind on earth shall be bound in Heaven and whatsoever thou shalt loose on earth shall be loosed in Heaven." Now, while we, unworthy sinner that we are, stand in his place of power, still whatever you send to us, whether in writing or by word of mouth, he himself receives, and while we read what is written or hear the voice of those who speak, he discerns with subtle insight from what spirit the message comes. Wherefore Your Highness should beware lest any defect of will toward the Apostolic See be found in your words or in your messages and should pay due reverence, not to us but to Almighty God, in all matters touching the welfare of the Christian faith and the status of the Church. And this we say although our Lord deigned to declare: "He who heareth you heareth me; and he who despiseth you despiseth me."

We know that one who does not refuse to obey God in those matters in which we have spoken according to the statutes of the holy fathers does not scorn to observe our admonitions even as if he had received them from the lips of the Apostle himself. For if our Lord, out of reverence for the chair of Moses, commanded the Apostles to observe the teaching of the scribes and pharisees who sat thereon, there can be no doubt that the apostolic and gospel teaching, whose seat and foundation is Christ, should be accepted and maintained by those who are chosen to the service of teaching.

At a synod held at Rome during the current year, and over which Divine Providence willed us to preside, several of your subjects being present, we saw that the order of the Christian religion had long been greatly disturbed and its chief and proper function, the redemption of souls, had fallen low and through the wiles of the Devil had been trodden under foot. Startled by this danger and by the manifest ruin of the Lord's flock we returned to the teaching of the holy fathers, declaring no novelties nor any inventions of our own, but holding that the primary and only rule of discipline and the well-trodden way of the saints should again be sought and followed, all wandering paths to be abandoned. For we know that there is no other way of salvation and eternal life for the flock of Christ and their shepherds except that shown by him who said: "I am the door and he who enters by me shall be saved and shall find pasture." This was taught by the Apostles and observed by the holy fathers and we have learned it from the Gospels and from every page of Holy Writ.

This edict [against lay investiture], which some who place the honor of men above that of God call an intolerable burden, we, using the right word, call rather a truth and a light necessary for salvation, and we have given judgment that it is to be heartily accepted and obeyed, not only by you and your subjects but by all princes and peoples who confess and worship Christ—though it is our especial wish and would be especially fitting for you, that you should excel others in devotion to Christ as you are their superior in fame, in station and in valor.

Nevertheless, in order that these demands may not seem to you too burdensome or unfair we have sent you word by your own liegemen not to be troubled by this reform of an evil practice but to send us prudent and pious legates from your own people. If these can show in any reasonable way how we can moderate the decision of the holy fathers [at the Council] saving the honor of the eternal king and without peril to our own soul, we will condescend to hear their counsel. It would in fact have been the fair thing for you, even if you had not been so graciously admonished, to make reasonable inquiry of us in what respect we had offended you or assailed your honor, before you proceeded to violate the apostolic decrees. But how little you cared for our warnings or for doing right was shown by your later actions.

However, since the long-enduring patience of God summons you to improvement, we hope that with increase of understanding your heart and mind may be turned to obey the commands of God. We warn you with a father's love that you accept the rule of Christ, that you consider the peril of preferring your own honor to his, that you do not hamper by your actions the freedom of that Church which he deigned to bind to himself as a bride by a divine union, but, that she may increase as greatly as possible, you will begin to lend to Almighty God and to St. Peter, by whom also your own glory may merit increase, the aid of your valor by faithful devotion.

Now you ought to recognize your special obligation to them for the triumph over your enemies which they have granted you, and while they are making you happy and singularly prosperous, they ought to find your devotion increased by their favor to you. That the fear of God, in whose hand is all the might of kings and emperors, may impress this upon you more than any admonitions of mine, bear in mind what happened to Saul after he had won a victory by command of the prophet, how he boasted of his triumph, scorning the prophet's admonitions, and how he was rebuked by the Lord, and also what favor followed David the king as a reward for his humility in the midst of the tokens of his bravery.

Finally, as to what we have read in your letters and do not mention here we will give you no decided answer until your legates, Radbod, Adalbert and Odescalcus, to whom we entrust this, have returned to us and have more fully reported your decision upon the matters which we commissioned them to discuss with you.

25. Henry IV's Position (1076)

Henry's Letter Condemning Gregory VII (24 January 1076)

Henry, King not by usurpation, but by the pious ordination of God, to Hildebrand, now not Pope, but false monk:

You have deserved such a salutation as this because of the confusion you have wrought; for you left untouched no order of the Church which you could make a sharer of confusion instead of honor, of malediction instead of benediction.

For to discuss a few outstanding points among many: Not only have you dared to touch the rectors of the holy church—the archbishops, the bishops, and the priests, anointed of the Lord as they are—but you have trodden them under foot like slaves who know not what their lord may do. In crushing them you have gained for yourself acclaim from the mouth of the rabble. You have judged that all these know nothing, while you alone know everything. In any case, you have sedulously used this knowledge not for edification, but for destruction, so greatly that we may believe Saint Gregory, whose name you have arrogated to yourself, rightly made this proph-

From *Imperial Lives and Letters of the Eleventh Century*, translated by T. E. Mommsen and Karl F. Morrison (New York: Columbia University Press, 1962), pp. 151–52. © 1962 by Columbia University Press. Reprinted by permission of the publisher.

ecy of you when he said: "From the abundance of his subjects, the mind of the prelate is often exalted, and he thinks that he has more knowledge than anyone else, since he sees that he has more power than anyone else."

And we, indeed, bore with all these abuses, since we were eager to preserve the honor of the Apostolic See. But you construed our humility as fear, and so you were emboldened to rise up even against the royal power itself, granted to us by God. You dared to threaten to take the kingship away from us—as though we had received the kingship from you, as though kingship and empire were in your hand and not in the hand of God.

Our Lord, Jesus Christ, has called us to kingship, but has not called you to the priesthood. For you have risen by these steps: namely, by cunning, which the monastic profession abhors, to money; by money to favor; by favor to the sword. By the sword you have come to the throne of peace, and from the throne of peace you have destroyed the peace. You have armed subjects against their prelates; you who have not been called by God have taught that our bishops who have been called by God are to be spurned; you have usurped for laymen the bishops' ministry over priests, with the result that these laymen depose and condemn the very men whom the laymen themselves received as teachers from the hand of God, through the imposition of the hands of bishops.

You have also touched me, one who, though unworthy, has been anointed to kingship among the anointed. This wrong you have done to me, although as the tradition of the holy Fathers has taught, I am to be judged by God alone and am not to be deposed for any crime unless—may it never happen—I should deviate from the Faith. For the prudence of the holy bishops entrusted the judgment and the deposition even of Julian the Apostate not to themselves, but to God alone. The true pope Saint Peter also exclaims, "Fear God, honor the king." You, however, since you do not fear God, dishonor me, ordained of Him.

Wherefore, when Saint Paul gave no quarter to an angel from heaven if the angel should preach heterodoxy, he did not except you who are now teaching heterodoxy throughout the earth. For he says, "If anyone, either I or an angel from heaven, preach any other gospel unto you than that which we have preached unto you, let him be accursed." Descend, therefore, condemned by this anathema and by the common judgment of all our bishops and of ourself. Relinquish the Apostolic See which you have arrogated. Let another mount the throne of Saint Peter, another who will not cloak violence with religion but who will teach the pure doctrine of Saint Peter.

I, Henry, King by the grace of God, together with all our bishops, say to you: Descend! Descend!

26. Renunciation of Gregory VII by the German Bishops (Synod of Worms, 1076)

Siegfried, archbishop of Mainz, Udo of Trier, William of Utrecht, Herman of Metz, Henry of Liège, Ricbert of Verden, Bido of Toul, Hozeman of Speier, Burchard of Halberstadt, Werner of Strassburg, Burchard of Basel, Otto of Constance, Adalbero of Würzburg, Rupert of Bamberg, Otto of Regensburg, Egilbert of Freising, Ulric of Eichstätt, Frederick of Münster, Eilbert of Minden, Hezilo of Hildesheim, Benno of Osnabrück, Eppo of Naumburg, Imadus of Paderborn, Tiedo of Brandenburg, Burchard of Lausanne, and Bruno of Verona, to Brother Hildebrand:

When you had first usurped the government of the Church, we knew well how, with your accustomed arrogance, you had presumed to enter so illicit and nefarious an undertaking against human and divine law. We thought, nevertheless, that the pernicious beginnings of your administration ought to be left unnoticed in prudent silence. We did this specifically in the hope that such criminal beginnings would be emended and wiped away somewhat by the probity and industry of your later rule. But now, just as the deplorable state of the universal Church cries out and laments, through the increasing wickedness of your actions and decrees, you are woefully and stubbornly in step with your evil beginnings.

Our Lord and Redeemer impressed the goodness of peace and love upon his Faithful as their distinctive character,[1] a fact to which there are more testimonies than can be included in the brevity of a letter. But by way of contrast, you have inflicted wounds with proud cruelty and cruel pride, you are eager for profane innovations,[2] you delight in a great name rather than in a good one, and with unheard-of self-exaltation, like a standard bearer of schism, you distend all the limbs of the Church which before your times led a quiet and tranquil life, according to the admonition of the Apostle.[3] Finally, the flame of discord, which you stirred up through terrible factions in the Roman church, you spread with raging madness through all the churches of Italy, Germany, Gaul, and Spain. For you have taken from the bishops, so far as you could, all that power which is known to have been divinely conferred upon them through the grace of the Holy Spirit, which works mightily in ordinations. Through you all administration of ecclesiastical affairs has been assigned to popular madness. Since some now consider no one a bishop or priest save the man who begs that office of Your

From *Imperial Lives and Letters of the Eleventh Century*, translated by T. E. Mommsen and Karl F. Morrison (New York: Columbia University Press, 1962), pp. 101–37. © 1962 by Columbia University Press. Reprinted by permission of the publisher.

1. John 13:35; 1 John 2:5.   2. 1 Tim. 6:20.
3. 1 Tim. 2:2.

Arrogance with a most unworthy servility, you have shaken into pitiable disorder the whole strength of the apostolic institution and that most comely distribution of the limbs of Christ, which the Doctor of the Gentiles so often commends and teaches.[4] And so through these boastful decrees of yours—and this cannot be said without tears—the name of Christ has all but perished. Who, however, is not struck dumb by the baseness of your arrogant usurpation of new power, power not due you, to the end that you may destroy the rights due the whole brotherhood?[5] For you assert that if any sin of one of our parishioners comes to your notice, even if only by rumor, none of us has any further power to bind or to loose the party involved, for you alone may do it, or one whom you delegate especially for this purpose. Can anyone schooled in sacred learning fail to see how this assertion exceeds all madness?

We have judged that it would be worse than any other evil for us to allow the Church of God to be so gravely jeopardized—nay, rather, almost destroyed—any longer through these and other presumptuous airs of yours. Therefore, it has pleased us to make known to you by the common counsel of all of us something which we have left unsaid until now: that is, the reason why you cannot now be, nor could you ever have been, the head of the Apostolic See.

In the time of the Emperor Henry [III] of good memory, you bound yourself with a solemn oath[6] that for the lifetime of that Emperor and for that of his son, our lord the glorious King who now presides at the summit of affairs, you would neither obtain the papacy yourself nor suffer another to obtain it, insofar as you were able, without the consent and approbation either of the father in his lifetime or of the son in his. And there are many bishops today who were witnesses of this solemn oath, who saw it then with their own eyes and heard it with their own ears. Remember also that in order to remove jealous rivalry when ambition for the papacy tickled some of the cardinals, you obligated yourself with a solemn oath never to assume the papacy both on the plea and on condition that they did the same thing themselves. We have seen in what a holy way you observed each of these solemn vows. Again, when a synod was celebrated in the time of Pope Nicholas [II], in which one hundred twenty-five bishops sat together, it was decided and decreed under anathema that no one would ever become pope except by the election of the cardinals and the approbation of the people, and by the consent and authority of the king. And of this council and decree, you yourself were author, advocate, and subscriber.

---

4. Rom. 12:5; 1 Cor. 12:2.   5. Cf. 1 Pet. 2:17.

6. "Corporali sacramento": an oath (1) on the Blessed Host, or (2) on the Scriptures; (3) on a cross, or (4) on relics.

In addition to this, you have filled the entire Church, as it were, with the stench of the gravest of scandals, rising from your intimacy and cohabitation with another's wife[7] who is more closely integrated into your household than is necessary. In this affair, our sense of decency is affected more than our legal case, although the general complaint is sounded everywhere that all judgments and all decrees are enacted by women in the Apostolic See, and ultimately that the whole orb of the Church is administered by this new senate of women. For no one can complain adequately of the wrongs and the abuse suffered by the bishops, whom you call most undeservedly sons of whores and other names of this sort.

Since your accession was tainted by such great perjuries, since the Church of God is imperiled by so great a tempest arising from abuse born of your innovations, and since you have degraded your life and conduct by such multifarious infamy, we declare that in the future we shall observe no longer the obedience which we have not promised to you. And since none of us, as you have publicly declared, has hitherto been a bishop to you, you also will now be pope to none of us.

7. Mathilda of Tuscany.

27. Letter of Gregory to Bishop Herman of Metz (1081)

Gregory, bishop, servant of the servants of God, to [our] beloved brother in Christ, Herman, bishop of Metz: greeting and apostolic benediction.

We do not doubt that what we have learned about your readiness for labors and for dangers that have had to be suffered in defense of truth is of divine gift. It is the ineffable grace and wondrous clemency of this gift that never permits its elect to wander at all, and never allows them to be utterly ruined or cast down; though they may be shaken in time of persecution, the divine gift, by a certain useful testing, toughens them through their fear. Just as among base men fear dispirits the one man when he sees another shamefully flee, so also among strong men one man who acts more bravely than another, who advances more ardently, inflames the manly heart. We have therefore taken care to commend this to Your Charity with the voice of exhortation so that you may delight in standing among the foremost on the battle line of the Christian religion all the more, as you know beyond doubt that they are the nearest and most worthy to God the Victor.

You have asked that you be helped and fortified, as it were, with our letters against the madness of them who gabble with a wicked tongue that

From *Imperial Lives and Letters of the Eleventh Century*, translated by T. E. Mommsen and Karl F. Morrison (New York: Columbia University Press, 1962), pp. 39–46. © 1962 by Columbia University Press. Reprinted by permission of the publisher.

the authority of the holy and Apostolic See could not excommunicate King Henry, a man, a mocker of Christian law, a destroyer that is of churches and of the Empire, and an author and abetter of heretics; and that it could not absolve anyone from an oath of fidelity to him. This seems to us not entirely necessary, however, since so many very certain testimonies to this fact may be found in the pages of the Holy Scriptures. Nor do we believe that those who impudently detract from and withstand truth, compounding their own damnation, have enforced the brazenness of their defense with these thoughts so much through ignorance as through the hysteria of wretched despair. No wonder; for it is the practice of reprobates, in protecting their wickedness, to undertake defense of men like themselves, since they consider it of no account to incur the destructiveness of falsehood.

For to say a few things about many, who does not know the voice of our Lord and Savior, Jesus Christ, saying in the Gospel, "Thou art Peter, and upon this rock I shall build my Church and the gates of Hell shall not prevail against it, and to you I shall give the keys of the kingdom of heaven; and whatsoever you shall bind on earth shall be bound also in heaven, and whatsoever you shall loose upon earth will be loosed also in heaven." Are kings excepted here, or are they not of the flocks which the Son of God committed to St. Peter? Who, I ask, thinks he has been excluded from the power of Peter in this universal concession of binding and loosing, except perhaps that unhappy man who, unwilling to bear the Lord's yoke, submits himself to the devil's burden and refuses to be in the number of Christ's flock? It profits him very little, for his miserable freedom, to have struck off from his proud neck the power divinely ceded to St. Peter, since the more anyone through arrogance fights against it, the more heavily he bears it in judgment to his own damnation.

This institution of divine will, therefore, this foundation of the Church's dispensation, this privilege principally given and confirmed to St. Peter, prince of the Apostles, by heavenly decree, the holy Fathers have received with great veneration and kept when they called the holy Roman church, "universal mother," both in general councils, and in other writings and in their deeds. And when they accepted her testimonies in confirmation of the faith and in the understanding of sacred religion, as also her judgments, they agreed on this and assented as though with one spirit and one voice: that all greater matters and important business, and also the judgments of all churches, ought to be referred to her as to a mother and head; that they could never be appealed from her; and that no one ought or could reconsider or refute her judgments. *2 Powers*

Wherefore, St. Gelasius, the pope, writing to the Emperor Anastasius, sustained by divine authority, taught him what and how he ought to feel about the principate of the holy and Apostolic See. "Although," he said, "it is right for the necks of the faithful to bend generally before all priests who think rightly about divine matters, how much more must acquiescence be shown to the pontiff of this see, whom Supreme Divinity willed to stand above all priests and, conforming to it, the general piety of the Church has perpetually honored. Wherefore, Your Prudence clearly knows that no one, by any human counsel at all, can ever make himself equal to the privilege and confession of him whom the voice of Christ exalted above all, whom the venerable Church has always confessed and has, in her devotion, as her head." Pope Julius, also, writing to the eastern bishops about the power of this same holy and Apostolic See, says: "It had befitted you, brethren, to speak accurately, and not ironically, in regard to the holy Roman and apostolic church, since even our Lord Jesus Christ having addressed her honorably says: 'Thou art Peter, and upon this rock I shall build my church and the gates of hell shall not prevail against it; and to you I shall give the keys of the kingdom of heaven.' For, by a singular privilege, the power was granted her to open and close the gates of the heavenly kingdom to whomever she wishes." The power of opening and closing heaven has been given her, therefore, and is she not allowed to judge of the earth?

It could not be so. Do you not recall what the most blessed Apostle Paul says: "Do you not know that we shall judge angels? How much more worldly things." St. Gregory the pope also established that kings fell from their office if they presumed to violate decrees of the Apostolic See, writing to a certain Abbot Senator in these words: "But if any king, priest, judge, or secular person knowing this text of our constitution be tempted to go against it, let him lose the dignity of his power and honor, and let him know that, for the iniquity he perpetrated, he stands culpable by divine judgment; and unless he restores whatever he wickedly stole, or, with suitable penance, laments what he has illicitly done, let him be alien to the most holy body and blood of the Lord, our Redeemer, Jesus Christ, and let him fall under severe retribution in the eternal scrutiny."

But if St. Gregory, on all counts a most gentle doctor, decreed that kings who violated his statutes concerning one travelers' inn not only be deposed but also be excommunicated and damned in the eternal scrutiny, who can reprove us for having deposed and excommunicated Henry—a man who not only scorns apostolic judgments, but also tramples his mother the Church under foot in as far as he can, preys most shamelessly on and destroys most cruelly the whole kingdom and churches—unless perchance it be a man like him? We have learned this from the teaching of St. Peter, in a letter on the ordination of Clement, in which he speaks as follows: "If anyone be a friend to those to whom he"—speaking of the same Clement—"does not speak, he is himself one of them who wish to exterminate the Church of God; and, although he seems to be with us in his body, in mind and soul he is against us, and he is a far more evil foe than those who are outside and clearly enemies. For he does hostile acts under the guise of friendships, and scatters and devastates the Church." Note, therefore, most beloved, that, if he imposes such a grave judgment on a man who, by friendship or discourse, associates with those whom the pope opposes for their acts, with how great a punishment he condemns the very man he opposes for his own acts.

But to come back to the subject: is the office invented even by men ignorant of God not subject to that office which the providence of omnipotent God invented to His honor and mercifully bestowed upon the world? Just as His Son is unhesitatingly believed to be God and man, so also He is considered the High Priest, the head of all priests, sitting at the right hand of the Father and always interceding for us. He despised worldly kingship, on account of which the sons of the world vaunt themselves, and came voluntarily to the priesthood of the Cross. Who does not know that kings and dukes had their beginning from those, ignorant of God, who with blind greed and intolerable presumption strove at the agitation of the prince of the world, namely the devil, to dominate their equals, that is men, through pride, rapines, perfidy, murders, and finally by nearly all sorts of crimes. Indeed, when they constrain priests of the Lord to bow down to their footsteps, with whom may they more correctly be compared than with him who is the head over all the sons of pride? Tempting the High Priest Himself, the head of priests, the Son of the Most High, and promising Him all the kingdoms of the earth, he says: "All these I shall give to you if you fall down and adore me."

Who doubts that the priests of Christ are counted fathers and masters of kings and princes and all faithful people? Is it not acknowledged to be pitiable madness if a son strives to subjugate his father to himself—or a disciple, his master—and to subject to his power with iniquitous obligations a man by whom he believes he can be bound and loosed not only on earth, but also in Heaven? As St. Gregory recalls in the letter sent to the Emperor Maurice, the Emperor Constantine the Great, lord of all kings and princes and of almost the whole earth, clearly understood these things in the holy Nicene synod: sitting last after all the bishops, he did not presume to give any sentence of judgment on them, but, calling them gods, he judged that they were not under his jurisdiction, but that he hung on their decision. When he was persuading the aforementioned Emperor Anastasius not to consider as an injury the truth that was imparted to his senses, the previously cited Pope Gelasius went on, saying: "There are indeed two, Emperor Augustus, by which this world is principally ruled, the hallowed authority of pontiffs and the royal power. Between them, the weight of the priests is the heavier, inasmuch as they are to render account even for those same kings in the divine scrutiny." And, after interposing a few things, he said, "Know therefore that in these things you hang on their judgment, and that they are unwilling to be governed according to your will."

Supported therefore by such establishments and by such authorities, many pontiffs have excommunicated—some of them kings, others emperors. For if some special example be required concerning the persons of princes, St. Innocent the pope excommunicated the Emperor Arcadius because he agreed that St. John Chrysostom be expelled from his see. Again, another Roman pontiff deposed a king of the Franks, not indeed because of his iniquities, but because he was not of advantage in such great power, and substituted in his place Pippin, father of the emperor Charlemagne, and absolved all men belonging to the Frankish tribe of the oath of fidelity which they had made to the deposed king. This also holy Church often does by regular authority when it absolves knights of the bond of the oath made to those bishops who have been deposed by apostolic authority from pontifical rank. And St. Ambrose, although a saint, still not universal bishop of the Church, excluded the Emperor Theodosius the Great from the Church, excommunicating him for a wrong which, in the eyes of other bishops, was not so grave. He also in his writings shows that the degree by which gold is more precious than lead is less than that by which the episcopal office is loftier than the royal power. He writes in this fashion toward the beginning of his pastoral book: "The episcopal honor, brethren, and its sublimity can be equated with no comparatives. If you compare it with the splendor of kings and the diadem of princes, they would be as far inferior as if you compared the metallic hue of lead with the splendor of gold; indeed, you may see the necks of kings and princes bowed to the knees of priests, and, having kissed their right hand, they believe that they are strengthened by their prayers." And, after a few things, "You ought to know, brethren, that we have said all these things first to show that there is nothing in this world more excellent than priests, that nothing is found more sublime than bishops."

Your Fraternity ought to have remembered that the power of an exorcist is conceded to be greater—since he is established a spiritual emperor to cast out demons—than what the cause of worldly dominion can bestow on any layman. Surely demons—alas, more's the pity—lord it over all kings and princes of the earth who do not live religiously and in their acts do not fear God as is meet; and they confound them in wretched servitude. For such men do not wish to have command as religious priests do, led by divine love to the honor of God and the utility of souls; but they strive to dominate others so as to display their pride and fulfill the lust of their soul.

Of them, St. Augustine says in his first book on Christian doctrine, "But when someone strives to dominate those who are naturally his equals, that is men, it is indeed unbearable pride." But, furthermore, exorcists, as we have said, have command [*imperium*] from God over demons; how much more, therefore, over them who are subject to demons and the members of demons? If therefore exorcists are so much more exalted than these, how much more yet are priests?

Besides, every Christian king, coming to his end, suppliant and pitiable, requires the work of a priest so that he may evade the prison of Hell, turn from the darkness into the light, and appear in God's judgment absolved of the bonds of sin. But who—not only among priests, but even among laymen—finding himself at the end has implored the help of an earthly king for the salvation of his soul? But what king or emperor, by virtue of the office imposed upon him, can tear any Christian from the devil's power by holy baptism and number him among the sons of God, and fortify him with holy chrism? And, what is of greatest moment in the Christian religion, who among them can with his own mouth make the body and blood of the Lord, and to which of them has been given the power of binding and loosing in heaven and on earth?

From these proofs it is patently inferred by what great power the office of priests excels. Or which of them can ordain any cleric in holy Church? How much less could a king depose him for some wrong? For in ecclesiastical orders, deposition belongs to a higher power than ordaining. Bishops can ordain other bishops, but in no way can they depose them without the authority of the Apostolic See. What smatterer, therefore, can airily doubt that priests take precedence of kings? And if kings are to be judged for their sins by priests, by whom ought they more rightly to be judged than by the Roman pontiff?

To summarize: It is right to understand that any good Christians are kings more appropriately than bad princes. For in seeking God's glory, the former rule themselves rigorously, but, seeking for themselves not what are God's but their own things, the latter tyrannically oppress others as enemies. The first are the body of the true king, Christ; but the others are that of the devil. Good Christians command themselves to this end, that they may rule eternally with the supreme Emperor. But the power of wicked princes does it to the end that they may perish with the prince of darkness, who is king over all the sons of pride.

Indeed, it is far from astonishing that wicked pontiffs concur with an evil king, whom they love and fear because of honors gotten wickedly through him; by ordaining simoniacally anybody who comes along they even sell God at a cheap price. For as the elect are indissolubly united to their head, so also the reprobates are brazenly leagued with him who is the head of malice, especially against the good. To be sure, we should not argue against these men so much as bewail them with tearful laments, so that omnipotent God may snatch them from the snares of Satan, by which they are held captive, and at last lead them, after dangers, to knowledge of truth.

So much for kings and emperors who, thoroughly bloated with worldly glory, rule not for God but for themselves. But since it is our office to allot exhortation to each man according to the order or office in which he is seen to live, we take care, motivated by God, to provide the weapons of humility to emperors and kings so that when their mind finds itself raised on high and is disposed to delight in its singular glory, it may abase itself by these means and it may sense that what gave it happiness is rather to be feared.

Let it therefore diligently perceive how perilous and how fearful is the imperial or royal office in which very few are saved and those who through God's mercy come to salvation are not glorified by the judgment of the Holy Ghost in the Church equally with many paupers. For, from the beginning of the world until these our times, we have not found in the whole of authentic literature seven emperors or kings whose life could be as outstanding in religion and adorned with the virtue of signs as that of the innumerable multitude of them that have despised the world, although we believe that many of them have found the salvation of mercy before omnipotent God. To pass over the Apostles and martyrs, which of the emperors or kings has distinguished himself with miracles to equal Martin, Antony, and Benedict? What emperor or king has raised the dead, purified lepers, or enlightened the blind? Behold, holy Church indeed praises and reveres the Emperor Constantine of pious memory, Theodosius and Honorius, Charles and Louis, lovers of justice, propagators of the Christian religion, and defenders of churches. But it does not declare that they blazed forth with such a great glory of miracles [as the saints]. Moreover, to how many names of kings or emperors has holy Church established that basilicas or altars are to be dedicated, and to the honor of how many of them has it decreed that masses are to be celebrated? Let kings and other princes fear lest, the more they rejoice to have been exalted over men in this life, the more by far they may be laid low beneath the eternal fires. Wherefore, it has been written: "Powerful men powerfully suffer torments." They are to give account to God for as many men as they have subject to their dominion.

But if it is no small labor for one private religious to guard his own soul, how great is the labor incumbent upon princes for many thousands of souls? Further, if the judgment of holy Church strictly binds a sinner for the murder of one man, what will be the case concerning those who give over many thousands to death for the sake of this world's honor? Although they sometimes say "*mea culpa*" with the mouth for killing many men, still they rejoice in the heart for the enlargement of what passes for honor among them; they do not wish that they had not done what they have done; they do not grieve that they have driven their brethren into Tartarus. And since they do not repent with their whole heart and they do not wish to lose what they have gained or held at the cost of human blood, their penitence remains before God without the worthy fruit of penitence. Wherefore, it is indeed to be feared and often recalled to their memory that, as we said before, since the beginning of the world very few kings, in the several kingdoms of the earth, are found to be saints, though the multitude of kings is innumerable. By contrast, in the succession of pontiffs to only one see, namely the Roman, from the time of St. Peter the Apostle, nearly one hundred are counted among the most holy of men. But how could this be, unless the kings of the earth and princes, misled by vainglory, as was said before, prefer their own interests to spiritual matters, while religious pontiffs, on the other hand, despising vainglory, prefer God's interests to fleshly matters. The first readily punish men who offend against them, but in equanimity bear with those who sin against God; the latter quickly forget men who sin against them, but do not lightly pardon those who offend God. The former, thoroughly given over to worldly acts, weigh spiritual concerns lightly; the others, sedulously meditating on heavenly matters, despise those things that are worldly.

All Christians therefore are to be admonished, if they wish to reign with Christ, not to strive to rule with the ambition of worldly power, but rather to have before their eyes what St. Gregory the most holy pope says by way of admonition in his pastoral book: "And so among these things what is to be pursued, what is to be held, except that a man mighty in virtues may be forced to come to government, while one empty of virtues should not be forced to accede." But if men who fear God come under force, with great fear, to the Apostolic See, in which when rightly ordained they are made better men through the merits of St. Peter the Apostle, with how much fear and trembling must one accede to the throne of a kingdom in which even the good and humble, as is known in Saul and David, become worse men? For what we have earlier said about the Apostolic See, although we know it from experience, is thus contained in the decrees of St. Symmachus the pope: "He," that is, St. Peter, "has sent to his successors an everlasting gift of merits with a heritage of innocence." And, after a few things, "For who doubts that he is holy whom the height of so great an office exalts? If good qualities acquired through merit are lacking in him, those suffice which are provided by the earlier tenant of the place. For he either raises brilliant men to these heights or he enlightens those who are raised."

Wherefore, those whom holy Church of her own will calls with deliberate counsel to government or empire, not for transient glory but for the salvation of many, should humbly obey and always beware the witness that St. Gregory bears in the same pastoral book: "Indeed, he becomes like the apostate angel when, though a man, he disdains to be like men. After meritorious humility, Saul thus swelled up in a tumor of pride because of his exalted power. He had been preferred because of humility; because of pride, he was rejected, as the Lord testifies saying: 'When you were but a small child in your eyes, did I not establish you as head among the tribes of Israel?'" And a little further on: "But in an amazing way when he was a small child to himself, he was great to the Lord, but when he seemed great to himself, he was a child to the Lord." And let them vigilantly remember what the Lord says in the Gospel: "I seek not my own glory," and "Whoever wishes to be first among you, let him be the servant of all." Let them always prefer God's honor to their own; let them embrace and guard justice by preserving each man's right for him; let them not go in the counsel of the impious, but with an agreeable heart let them always adhere to the religious. Let them not seek to subdue or subject holy Church to themselves as a handmaiden; but indeed let them fittingly strive to honor her eyes, namely the priests of the Lord, by acknowledging them as masters and fathers. For if we are ordered to honor fleshly fathers and mothers, how much more, spiritual? And if he who curses his fleshly father and mother is to be punished with death, what does the man deserve who curses his spiritual father and mother? Let them not strive, misled by carnal love, to set their son over the flock for which Christ poured out His blood, if they can find one better and more useful to that flock; let them not inflict the greatest damage on holy Church by loving their son more than God. For patently a man is clearly shown not to love God and his neighbor as suits a Christian if he fails to provide as well as he can for the great utility and need of his holy mother, the Church. When this virtue, namely charity, is neglected, whatever good anyone does will lack every fruit of salvation. And so, in humbly doing these things and keeping the love of God and neighbor, as is right, let them trust in the mercy of Him who said, "Learn of me, for I am meek and lowly of heart." If they humbly imitate Him, they will pass from a servile and transitory realm to one that is truly free and eternal.

28. Urban II, *Speech at the Council of Clermont* (27 November 1095)

The Version of Fulcher of Chartres, Including His Description of Conditions in Western Europe at the Time

In the year of our Lord 1095, in the reign of the so-called Emperor Henry in Germany and of King Philip in France, throughout Europe evils of all kinds waxed strong because of vacillating faith. Pope Urban II then ruled in the city of Rome. He was a man admirable in life and habits, who always strove wisely and energetically to raise the status of Holy Church higher and higher. . . .

But the devil, who always desires man's destruction and goes about like a raging lion seeking whom he may devour, stirred up to the confusion of the people a certain rival to Urban, Wibert by name. Incited by the stimulus of pride and supported by the shamelessness of the aforesaid Emperor of the Bavarians, Wibert attempted to usurp the papal office while Urban's predecessor, Gregory, that is Hildebrand, was the legitimate Pope; and he thus caused Gregory himself to be cast out of St. Peter's. So the better people refused to recognize him because he acted thus perversely. After the death of Hildebrand, Urban, lawfully elected, was consecrated by the cardinal bishops, and the greater and holier part of the people submitted in obedience to him. Wibert, however, urged on by the support of the aforesaid Emperor and by the instigation of the Roman citizens, for some time kept Urban a stranger to the Church of St. Peter; but Urban, although he was banished from the Church, went about through the country, reconciling to God the people who had gone somewhat astray. Wibert, however, puffed up by the primacy of the Church, showed himself indulgent to sinners, and exercising the office of pope, although unjustly, amongst his adherents, he denounced as ridiculous the acts of Urban. But in the year in which the Franks first passed through Rome on their way to Jerusalem, Urban obtained the complete papal power everywhere, with the help of a certain most noble matron, Matilda by name, who then had great influence in the Roman state. Wibert was then in Germany. So there were two Popes; and many did not know which to obey, or from which counsel should be taken, or who should remedy the ills of Christianity. Some favored the one; some the other. But it was clear to the intelligence of men that Urban was the better, for he is rightly considered better who controls his passions, just as

From August C. Krey, *The First Crusade: The Accounts of Eye-Witnesses and Participants* (Princeton: Princeton University Press, 1921), pp. 24–30. © 1921 by Princeton University Press.

if they were enemies. Wibert was Archbishop of the city of Ravenna. He was very rich and revelled in honor and wealth. It was a wonder that such riches did not satisfy him. Ought he to be considered by all an exemplar of right living who, himself a lover of pomp, boldly assumes to usurp the sceptre of Almighty God? Truly, this office must not be seized by force, but accepted with fear and humility.

What wonder that the whole world was a prey to disturbance and confusion? For when the Roman Church, which is the source of correction for all Christianity, is troubled by any disorder, the sorrow is communicated from the nerves of the head to the members subject to it, and these suffer sympathetically. This Church, indeed, our mother, as it were, at whose bosom we were nourished, by whose doctrine we were instructed and strengthened, by whose counsel we were admonished, was by this proud Wibert greatly afflicted. For when the head is thus struck, the members at once are sick. If the head be sick, the other members suffer. Since the head was thus sick, pain was engendered in the enfeebled members; for in all parts of Europe peace, goodness, faith, were boldly trampled under foot, within the Church and without, by the high, as well as by the low. It was necessary both that an end be put to these evils, and that, in accordance with the plan suggested by Pope Urban, they turn against the pagans the strength formerly used in prosecuting battles among themselves. . . .

He saw, moreover, the faith of Christendom greatly degraded by all, by the clergy as well as by the laity, and peace totally disregarded; for the princes of the land were incessantly engaged in armed strife, now these, now those quarreling among themselves. He saw the goods of the land stolen from the owners; and many, who were unjustly taken captive and most barbarously cast into foul prisons, he saw ransomed for excessive sums, or tormented there by the three evils, starvation, thirst, and cold, or allowed to perish by unseen death. He also saw holy places violated, monasteries and villas destroyed by fire, and not a little human suffering, both the divine and the human being held in derision.

When he heard, too, that interior parts of Romania were held oppressed by the Turks, and that Christians were subjected to destructive and savage attacks, he was moved by compassionate pity; and prompted by the love of God, he crossed the Alps and came into Gaul. He there called a council at Clermont in Auvergne, which council had been fittingly proclaimed by envoys in all directions. It is estimated that there were three hundred and ten bishops and abbots who bore the crozier. When they were assembled on the day appointed for the council, Urban, in an eloquent address full of sweetness, made known the object of the meeting. With the plaintive voice of the afflicted Church he bewailed in a long discourse the great disturbances which, as has been mentioned above, agitated the world where faith had been undermined. Then as a supplicant, he exhorted all to resume the fullness of their faith, and in good earnest to try diligently to withstand the deceits of the devil, and to raise to its pristine honor the status of Holy Church, now most unmercifully crippled by the wicked.

"Dearest brethren," he said, "I, Urban, invested by the permission of God with the papal tiara, and spiritual ruler over the whole world, have come here in this great crisis to you, servants of God, as a messenger of divine admonition. I wish those whom I have believed good and faithful dispensers of the ministry of God to be found free from shameful dissimulation. For if there be in you any disposition or crookedness contrary to God's law, because you have lost the moderation of reason and justice, I shall earnestly endeavor to correct it at once, with divine assistance. For the Lord has made you stewards over His family, that you provide it with pleasant-tasting meat in season. You will be blessed, indeed, if the Lord shall find you faithful in stewardship. You are also called shepherds; see that you do not the work of hirelings. Be true shepherds and have your crooks always in your hands. Sleep not, but defend everywhere the flock committed to your care. For if through your carelessness or neglect the wolf carries off a sheep, doubtless you will not only lose the reward prepared for you by our Lord, but, after having first been tortured by the strokes of the lictor, you will also be savagely hurled into the abode of the damned. In the words of the Gospel, 'Ye are the salt of the earth'! But, it is asked, 'If ye fail, wherewith shall it be salted?' Oh, what a salting! Indeed, you must strive by the salt of your wisdom to correct this foolish people, over-eager for the pleasures of the world, lest the Lord find them insipid and rank, corrupted by crimes at the time when He wished to speak to them. For if because of your slothful performance of duty He shall discover any worms in them, that is to say any sins, He will in contempt order them to be cast forthwith into the abyss of uncleanness; and because you will be unable to make good to Him such a loss, He will surely banish you, condemned by His judgment, from the presence of His love. But one that salteth ought to be prudent, foresighted, learned, peaceful, watchful, respectable, pious, just, fair-minded, pure. For how can the unlearned make others learned, the immodest make others modest, the unclean make others clean? How can he make peace who hates it? If anyone has soiled hands, how can he cleanse the spots from one contaminated? For it is written, 'If the blind lead the blind, both shall fall into the pit.' Accordingly, first correct yourselves, so that without reproach you can then correct those under your care. If, indeed, you wish to be the friends of God, do generously what you see is pleasing to Him.

"See to it that the affairs of Holy Church, especially, are maintained in their rights, and that simoniacal heresy in no way takes root among you. Take care lest purchasers and venders alike, struck by the lash of the Lord, be disgracefully driven through narrow ways into utter confusion. Keep the Church in all its orders entirely free from the secular power; have given to God faithfully one-tenth of the fruits of the earth, neither selling them, nor withholding. Whoever lays violent hands on a bishop, let him be considered excommunicated. Whoever shall have seized monks, or priests, or nuns, and their servants, or pilgrims, or traders, and shall have despoiled them, let him be accursed. Let thieves and burners of houses and their accomplices be excommunicated from the Church and accursed. Therefore, we must consider especially, as Gregory says, how great will be his punishment who steals from another, if he incurs the damnation of hell who does not distribute alms from his own possessions. For so it happened to the rich man in the Gospel, who was punished not for stealing anything from another, but because, having received wealth, he used it badly.

"By these evils, therefore, as I have said, dearest brethren, you have seen the world disordered for a long time, and to such a degree that in some places in your provinces, as has been reported to us (perhaps due to your weakness in administering justice), one scarcely dares to travel for fear of being kidnapped by thieves at night or highwaymen by day, by force or by craft, at home or out of doors. Wherefore, it is well to enforce anew the Truce, commonly so-called, which was long ago established by our holy fathers, and which I most earnestly entreat each one of you to have observed in his diocese. But if any one, led on by pride or ambition, infringes this injunction voluntarily, let him be anathema in virtue of the authority of God and by the sanction of the decrees of this council."

When these and many other things were well disposed of, all those present, priests and people alike, gave thanks to God and welcomed the advice of the Lord Pope Urban, assuring him, with a promise of fidelity, that these decrees of his would be well kept. . . .

But the Pope added at once that another trouble, not less, but still more grievous than that already spoken of, and even the very worst, was besetting Christianity from another part of the world. He said: "Since, O sons of God, you have promised the Lord to maintain peace more earnestly than heretofore in your midst, and faithfully to sustain the rights of Holy Church, there still remains for you, who are newly aroused by this divine correction, a very necessary work, in which you can show the strength of your good will by a certain further duty, God's concern and your own. For you must hasten to carry aid to your brethren dwelling in the East, who need your help, which they often have asked. For the Turks, a Persian people, have attacked them, as many of you already know, and have advanced as far into the Roman territory as that part of the Mediterranean which is called the Arm of St. George; and, by seizing more and more of the lands of the Christians, they have already often conquered them in battle, have killed and captured many, have destroyed the churches, and have devastated the kingdom of God. If you allow them to continue much longer, they will subjugate God's faithful yet more widely.

"Wherefore, I exhort with earnest prayer—not I, but God—that, as heralds of Christ, you urge men by frequent exhortation, men of all ranks, knights as well as foot-soldiers, rich as well as poor, to hasten to exterminate this vile race from the lands of your brethren, and to aid the Christians in time. I speak to those present; I proclaim it to the absent; moreover, Christ commands it. And if those who set out thither should lose their lives on the way by land, or in crossing the sea, or in fighting the pagans, their sins shall be remitted. This I grant to all who go, through the power vested in me by God. Oh, what a disgrace, if a race so despised, base, and the instrument of demons, should so overcome a people endowed with faith in the all-powerful God, and resplendent with the name of Christ! Oh, what reproaches will be charged against you by the Lord Himself if you have not helped those who are counted, like yourselves, of the Christian faith! Let those who have been accustomed to make private war against the faithful carry on to a successful issue a war against infidels which ought to have been begun ere now. Let those who for a long time have been robbers now become soldiers of Christ. Let those who once fought against brothers and relatives now fight against barbarians, as they ought. Let those who have been hirelings at low wages now labor for an eternal reward. Let those who have been wearing themselves out to the detriment of body and soul now labor for a double glory. On the one hand will be the sad and poor; on the other the joyous and wealthy: here the enemies of the Lord; there His friends. Let no obstacle stand in the way of those who are going, but, after their affairs are settled and expense money is collected, when the winter has ended and spring has come, let them zealously undertake the journey under the guidance of the Lord."

29. Letters of Ivo of Chartres and Ioscerannus of Rome on Lay Investiture (1111–12)

The Letter of Ivo of Chartres to Ioscerannus

To Ioscerannus, by God's grace Archbishop of the primatial see of Lyon, from Daimbert, by the same grace Archbishop of Sens, Ivo,[1] Bishop of Chartres, Walo, Bishop of Paris, John, Bishop of Orleans, and the rest of their fellow-bishops of the province of Sens, all the reverence enjoined by the fathers.

By the prerogative of your primacy, you have invited us to celebrate a council at Anse, in which you have arranged to treat the faith and lay investitures. We take your invitation very seriously, but we are afraid of violating the terms, the ancient terms which our fathers established. For the venerable authority of the fathers never ordained, and antiquity never used to keep the practice, that the bishop of a primatial see invited bishops situated outside his province to a council, except when either the Apostolic See commanded it, or when one of the provincial churches appealed for a hearing to the primatial see for reasons which it had been unable to settle within the province. We do not say this from our own inspiration, but are upheld by apostolic authority and can prove it with incontrovertible decrees. . . . Because we are upheld by these authorities, we will not introduce an unheard-of novelty into our churches, or alter the rights which were of old set up for them.

Because, furthermore, you are planning to treat lay investitures in this council, a matter which some consider to be heresy, you will more likely lay our father's shame open to view, and will expose to derision what should not have been "published in Geth and on the streets of Ascalon,"[2] rather than winning a paternal blessing for yourself by concealing it behind your back. For what the Highest Pontiff, like a father, permitted to happen to himself in order to prevent bloodshed among the people, he was forced to do by necessity, and not because his will approved of it. What proves this is that, as soon as he had escaped the danger, as he himself has written to some of us, he ordered again what he had ordered before, and prohibited

From *Monumenta Germaniae Historica, Libelli de Lite*, vol. 2 (Hannover: Hahn, 1892), pp. 649–57. Translated for this volume by Constantin Fasolt.

1. Quite often, in medieval as in modern politics, letters were written by one person but sent in the name of another person, or in the names of several persons, sometimes without reference to the actual author. Such was the case here. Ivo wrote the letter, but other dissidents joined with him in sending it.

2. Cf. 2 Sam. 1:20.

what he had prohibited, even though under the pressure of danger he may have given rein to some abominable writings of abominable people. Thus Peter cleansed himself from his triple denial by a triple confession, and remained an apostle.[3] Thus Pope Marcellinus was tricked by pagans into burning incense before a temple, but nevertheless was by no means condemned by his brethren, and a few days later even earned the crown of martyrdom. Thus Aaron in the desert, when Moses lingered on the mountain, permitted the people to cast the calf because of their unbearable strife.[4] Even though he was not seduced by them into believing it to be God, or into paying reverence to it in divine service, the stupid people worshiped it. Nevertheless he earned forgiveness for so great a transgression and was, at the Lord's command and by the hand of Moses, raised to the office of high priest.[5] Thus Moses himself, who spoke with the Lord as a friend with a friend, still offended God when the grumbling of the people, who said: "Can he fetch us water out of this rock?"[6] made him become doubtful and argue for the water with the Lord. Thus the teacher of the Gentiles, who declared in public in the synagogues that "circumcision is nothing and Christ shall profit you nothing if you are circumcised,"[7] permitted Timothy to be circumcised in order to avoid offending the Jews, so that he might win them over with his humility.[8] The necessity by which the most exalted, saintly men suffered such weaknesses must be approved, and the dispensation be considered provident, because God thus made good use of our wickedness, in order thereby to teach them to understand themselves, and to learn to ascribe their weaknesses to themselves and the goods conferred upon them to the grace of God. But these things have not been written down in order to be taken as an example for life, but so that posterity might from their forefathers' lapses learn to be afraid of lapsing similarly, and to rise up quickly, should they perhaps have fallen down. If, therefore, the Pope does not yet act with the required severity against the German King, we believe that he is delaying with deliberation, according to the advice of certain teachers who advise that some dangers should be endured so that greater ones can be avoided. . . .

By these words, we believe, we are excused for restraining our tongues from lashing out against the Lord Pope, and for excusing him with the love of children if, in pardoning the German King his investitures, he seems to have acted in any respect against his own sentence or that of his predecessors. For someone who fails to observe the law because he is deceived by some underhandedness, or because necessity forces him to do so, is no

3. John 18:25–27.   4. Exod. 32:4.
5. Lev. 8:12.   6. Num. 20:10.
7. Cf. Gal. 5:2.   8. Acts 16:3.

lawbreaker; that is true only of one who purposely assails the law and does not care to admit his offence. Not only, therefore, do we not accuse his transgression, but, as reason dictates, we even approve it, if, threatened by the slaughter of the people, he wanted out of his fatherly love to stand in the way of so many dangers and suffer considerable injury himself in order to be able with pure love to provide relief against even greater maladies. He is neither the first nor the only one to have mitigated the Lord's precepts in this way, since the mediator of God and men himself, whose life on earth was a school of morals, at first commanded his disciples not to carry "purse or scrip,"[9] because then there was no need for it. But when the time of his passion was imminent, knowing that, moving from one place to another, they would suffer from want of bread, he moderated his command, allowed them to carry "purse and scrip,"[10] and no longer paid attention to the control of greed but rather indulged necessity.

In the same way, when heresies of many kinds were sprouting all over the world, it was ordered with the greatest severity that those who came back from heresy could not become, or remain, clerics, in order that out of their fear of the severity of this sentence Catholics would avoid being seduced by heretics. But when the church suffered extreme damage from the rigor of this decree, the religious made a careful distinction and taught that the judgment be altered. In a brotherly way, they received those who came back from heresy and professed catholic unity, and permitted them to remain in their offices, judging it better to suffer some injury to the bark of the mother tree, which love might heal, than for the church not to gather its branches from whomever it could.

Finally, because some call investiture a heresy, even though heresy is nothing except an error in faith, it must be stressed that, just as the heart's faith makes for justice, and its confession by mouth for salvation,[11] so heresy's error makes for ungodliness, and the profession of such an error, for damnation. Both faith and error proceed from the heart. Investiture, however, about which there is so much commotion, rests solely in the hands of the giver and the receiver; hands can perhaps do good or evil deeds, but can certainly not believe or err in matters of faith. If such investiture were heresy, furthermore, someone who renounces it could not return to it without injury. But we see many respected people in the regions of the Germanies and of Gaul who, having been cleansed of that blemish by some atonement or other, have had their pastoral staffs restored and have received from the hand of the Apostle the investitures that they had surrendered. The Supreme Pontiffs would most certainly not have done so,

9. Luke 10:4.   10. Luke 22:36.
11. Cf. Rom. 10:10.

had they known of any heresy or sin against the Holy Spirit hiding behind such investiture. When therefore measures that are not ordained by eternal law but were established or prohibited for the honor or utility of the church are temporarily abandoned in the same context in which they were invented, that is no damnable violation of what was established, but a praiseworthy and most beneficial dispensation. Many inexpert people pay too little attention to this, and therefore judge too soon, without understanding the difference between spirit mobile and spirit stable. But if any layman should burst forth into the mad belief that, in giving or accepting the staff, he could administer the sacrament or the real content of the ecclesiastical sacrament, we would absolutely judge him to be a heretic, not because he invests with his hands, but because of his diabolical presumption. If we want to call things by their proper names, however, we can say that investiture performed by the hands of laymen is a violation of the right of another and a sacrilegious presumption which should, for the sake of the liberty and the honor of the church, be cut out altogether, provided it can be done without breaking the peace. Where, then, it can be removed without schism, let it be removed. Where it cannot be removed without schism, let it be discreetly protested and its abolition deferred. For such a violation takes nothing away from the ecclesiastical sacraments, since they are, after all, holy and always the same, with whomever they may be, whether with those inside or with those outside.

We are prepared to have rebutted without contumacy what we have written to your Love, if your wisdom can teach us something better than what we have written, provided it is supported by canonical scriptures. Farewell.

Ioscerannus's Response

Ioscerannus, Archbishop of the primatial see of Lyon, salvation to Daimbert, Archbishop of Sens.

Since a little is enough for a wise man, we have decided to approach your Fraternity with a little, and, because sin cannot fail to be present in much talk, we have taken care to avoid making many words and to respond to your lengthy statement as briefly as we could. You have, then, proposed certain things in which you seem to wish partly to label our person with presumptuous pride, partly to detract from the dignity of the church of Lyon, and partly to place an inexpiable blemish on the body of the whole church. . . . I wish you had been serious, Dearest Brother, when you said you had no desire, or would not dare, to violate the ancient boundary stones put up by the fathers. But almost all the Latin-speaking world knows which limits the ancient fathers set up for the churches of Lyon and Sens. No amazement is enough for us [as we read] that you have designated many people as exempt from ecclesiastical judgment, unless, perhaps, you wanted to include all of the bishops in the same immunity. If you were attempting to exempt kings and emperors from pontifical judgment, refer to Emperor Constantine the Great, who can be read to have said the following words at the Council of Nicaea in the presence of Pope Silvester: "You bishops," he said, "are to be judged by the Lord alone." He did not say: "I and you, we are to be judged by the Lord alone." [12] Since he excluded only the bishops, he obviously submitted himself and all kings to ecclesiastical judgment. Do you perhaps blame the most illustrious teacher Ambrose for having excommunicated Emperor Theodosius because of his guilt? Do you bring charges against Gregory VII for having condemned King Henry because of his crimes?

You added that you were afraid that our father's shame might be revealed by our discussion. You were afraid where there was no reason for fear at all. . . . Do you not remember what Christ said to his few disciples? "Be of good cheer," he said, "for I have overcome the world." [13] You preach the victory of the world, therefore, and demolish Christ's victory if you teach that one ought not to be of good cheer. To encourage the timid against the strong, and the idle against the reckless, by asking them to run away from battle, but to be courageous in peace, to be undisturbed by danger, and to exercise their foresight only in safety, is a new and unheard-of kind of philosophy. That captain is detestable who exercises his art to perfection when the weather is fine, but who, during a tempest, abandons the helm and all the rigging. Never fear, Brother, Christ has sown good seed on his field, but do not sow tares on top of it, which grow up and strive to suffocate the good seed. [14] The number of the wicked multiplies, sons of diffidence abound, but Christ has the power to strengthen his own and lay his adversaries low. For what did the apostle say? "I can do all things" he said "through him who strengtheneth me." [15] Was Christ perhaps only in Paul? Can it be that in him alone he could do everything? We believe and confess that he can do everything in each and every one of the faithful. "Lo," he said, "I am with you all days." [16]

You do not seem to argue cogently enough, moreover, in what you say against those who count it among the heresies for laymen to invest with ecclesiastical dignities. For although heretical error resides in the heart, just as the Catholic faith does, we nevertheless recognize a heretic by his heretical works, just as we identify a Catholic by his Catholic works. "By their fruits you shall know them," [17] said the Lord, and "every tree is known

---

12. *Pseudo-Isidorian Decretals*, ed. P. Hinschius (Leipzig, 1863), p. 256.
13. John 16:33.   14. Cf. Matt. 13:25.
15. Phil. 4:13.   16. Matt. 28:20.
17. Matt. 7:16.

by his own fruit." [18] And even though we cannot quite properly call investitures which are physically performed by laymen by the name of heresy, it is nevertheless undoubted heresy to believe and to plead that this is how it should be done. But that, as you say, some were granted the indulgence to accept investiture from the hands of laymen, was written, you will know, as if to soften and extenuate what remains a crime. For what the law makes an exception of in the present, it prohibits in the future. Whence it is clear that every indulgence for past crimes equals a warning and prohibition of future ones. . . .

This we have briefly written in response to Your Love. Should you wish to object anything to this, at close quarters or from a distance, we are prepared to listen and respond. Farewell.

18. Luke 6:44.

30. Concordat of Worms (1122)

The *Privilegium* of Henry V

In the name of the holy and indivisible Trinity, I, Henry by the grace of God Emperor Augustus of the Romans, for the love of God and of the holy Roman church and of the Lord Pope Calixtus, and for the cure of my soul, give up to God and to the holy Apostles of God, Peter and Paul, and to the holy catholic Church all investiture by ring and crozier, and I grant that, in all churches which are in my kingdom or empire, there may be canonical election and free consecration.

I restore to the same Roman church such possessions and regalia of St. Peter as I have which were taken away between the beginning of this conflict and the present day, whether in the time of my father or in my own; and I shall faithfully assist to the end that those which I do not have may be restored.

With the counsel of princes, and by justice, I shall also give back such possessions as I have of all other churches and princes and others, both clergy and laymen, which were lost in this war, and I shall faithfully assist to the end that those which I do not have be given back.

And I give true peace to the Lord Pope Calixtus and to the Roman church and to all who are, or have been, on its side.

And I shall faithfully assist in such matters as the holy Roman church

From *Monumenta Germaniae Historica Constitutiones*, vol. 1, translated by Karl Morrison in *The Investiture Controversy: Issues, Ideals, and Results* (New York: Holt, Rinehart and Winston, 1971), pp. 82–83. © 1971 by Holt, Rinehart and Winston. Reprinted by permission of CBS College Publishing.

asks aid, and I shall do the justice due it in such things as it complains about.

All these things have been enacted with the consent and counsel of the princes whose names are subscribed:

Adalbert, Archbishop of Mainz	Duke Henry
Frederick, Archbishop of Cologne	Duke Frederick
Henry, Bishop of Regensburg	Duke Simon
Otto, Bishop of Bamberg	Duke Bertolf
Bruno, Bishop of Speyer	Margrave Theobald
Herman of Augsburg	Margrave Engelbert
Godebald of Trier	The Palatine Godfrey
Udalrich of Constance	The Count Palatine Otto
Erlholf, Abbot of Fulda	Count Berengar

I, Frederick, Archbishop of Cologne and Archchancellor, have certified this.

The *Privilegium* of Calixtus II (the *Calixtinum*)

I, Calixtus, bishop, servant of the servants of God, grant to you, dear son Henry by the grace of God Emperor Augustus of the Romans, that the elections of bishops and abbots of the German kingdom, which are subject to the kingdom, may take place in your presence, without simony or any sort of violence; and that, if any discord emerges among parties, you may, with the counsel and judgment of the metropolitan and comprovincials, give assent and aid to the sounder party. Let the elect, however, receive the regalia from you by the sceptre and do what he rightly owes to you on their account.

But in other parts of the Empire, let him receive the regalia from you by the sceptre within six months after consecration and do what he rightly owes to you on their account, excepting all things which are to known to belong to the Roman church.

According to what befits my office, I shall give you aid in such things as you shall make complaint about and ask aid.

I give true peace to you and to all who are on your side or have been on it in the time of this dispute.

3

Twelfth-Century Renaissance

The texts in this section complement and extend some themes set forth in the section on the Investiture Controversy, but without explicit reference to institutional life. Much of the vivacity in the intellectual life of the twelfth century was generated by frictions that arose in the eleventh century. For example, Anselm of Canterbury, the earliest writer in this section, played a dramatic role in the English phases of the Investiture Controversy.

European cultural history in the period from 500 to 1500 is punctuated by three so-called "Renaissances." Each of these movements—in the Carolingian era (eighth and ninth centuries), during the twelfth century, and in the fourteenth and fifteenth centuries—occurred in a society that was consolidating itself after a period of acute disorder. Each was characterized by a return to Antiquity for materials and exemplars in the task of consolidation. However, each movement had its own distinctive scope, content, and goal and each followed a singular career. The differences are so marked that some scholars argue that the term "Renaissance" becomes meaningless when applied to all three.

The following documents illustrate some dominant characteristics of the twelfth-century movement, and some tensions within European culture that it both expressed and exacerbated. For example, they illustrate the continued importance of monastic culture, which figured in topic 1 as a primary agent in the reconstitution of Europe after the political disintegration of the Roman Empire. The examples of Anselm of Canterbury and Bernard of Clairvaux point to the central role that monasticism continued to play in the continual refreshment and vitalization of culture. However, these texts also illustrate the expansion of participation in high culture beyond monasteries and royal courts. Though he spent the latter, highly productive years of his life in monasteries, Abelard formed his scholarly apparatus in schools that stood, not in monastic enclosures, but in the world—in cathedrals and in classrooms of secular masters. Secular clergy participated in the making of culture as well as regular (or monastic) clergy, laity as well as clergy, women as well as men. The interplay of secular and religious currents is exemplified by Bernard of Clairvaux's erotic description of his spiritual question. In the third place, the texts illustrate the expansion of areas of interest and genres of literary expression. Political order became a special topic of analysis; a literature of romance, set forth in lyric and in epic poetry, appeared, composed by chivalric bards. Finally, the texts illustrate how the twelfth-century Renaissance both expressed and reinforced class identities. For all of them were written for small, relatively closed elites, and designed to justify and to solidify their exclusive values.

Yet these learned, graceful, and passionate writings also disclose tensions at the heart of the Renaissance. These are to be added to the points of friction exposed during the Investiture Controversy, and to the points of friction identified by movements of reform that arose in the twelfth century. Peter Waldo and Francis of Assisi (documents 40, 43, and 44) were children of the twelfth-century Renaissance.

Another line of stress ran between the elites for and by whom these texts were written and the deep substrata of society. This line is represented by the text (above, document 11) concerning an exchange of female serfs.

There were also strains within elites. These strains are indicated in a number of ways: by allusions to class distinctions, by cynicism regarding the hierarchy and the rituals of the Church (both found in Gottfried of Strassburg), by the evasion or flat betrayal of collective norms by members of the elites, by controversy among the bearers of cultural tradition (most dangerous when it concerned propositions set forth by tradition as fundamental truths), and finally by the hostility between men and women within the elites, sometimes hidden and sometimes overt.

A few words about specific authors represented below may be helpful.

Anselm of Canterbury (1033–1109) was a great prelate of the Church, a founder of scholastic philosophy, and a disseminator of new devotional practices and disciplines (document 31). Born in Aosta, in northern Italy, he heeded a vocation to the monastic life, which he considered a life of learning and contemplation. He traveled to Normandy and entered the monastery of Bec, where he studied under the celebrated Lanfranc. Subsequently, Anselm succeeded Lanfranc as abbot of Bec, holding fast to the theological speculations and devotional practices that formed the heart of his personal religion, even while he administered the vast estates that the monastery held in Normandy and in England. Still later (in 1093),

Anselm also succeeded Lanfranc as archbishop of Canterbury. His accession embroiled him in the English phase of the Investiture Conflict with two kings, William Rufus and Henry I. The English conflict was settled in 1107, at the Synod of Westminster, by an agreement that anticipated the terms of the Concordat of Worms (document 30).

John of Salisbury (ca. 1120–80) came originally from Salisbury in England and died as bishop of Chartres. He was greatly admired by his contemporaries for the quality of his scholarship and his Latinity. He appreciated the classics for their wisdom and beauty, and believed that their study was indispensable for the formation of character and the pursuit of truth. John's educational ideas are found in his *Metalogicon*. He was a loyal servant of the papacy, and spent seven years in exile from England, because he would not bow before King Henry II and his ideas of royal supremacy in ecclesiastical matters. Dedicated to Thomas Becket, the *Policraticus* was written sometime after 1154 while John was secretary to Theobald, archbishop of Canterbury. It ranks among the profoundest treatments of the relationship between individual and community (document 32).

Rogerius was among the leading doctors of Roman law at the University of Bologna in the second half of the twelfth century. The renaissance in legal studies began in Bologna around 1100 with Irnerius, who was probably the first to lecture on the whole of Justinian's *Digest*, who reorganized the *Corpus iuris civilis*, and who provided the standard method of "glossing" or adding interlineal explanations to the texts. Rogerius's *Questions on the Institutes* (document 33) differs in a number of respects from the severe glossatorial style of his contemporaries. He delights in affected elegance that he probably believed was Ciceronian, and indulges in metaphors and words that were never used by either ancient or contemporary authors. Influenced by Ciceronian models fashionable among twelfth-century grammarians, he composed his work as a dialogue in which questions by a pupil are answered by one in authority.

Although no writings of Peter Abelard (1079–1142) are included in this volume, his stature is indicated in several of the texts that are here. Like Anselm, Abelard represents the peripatetic character of scholarly life in the twelfth century. Born into a noble family in Brittany, he studied in various schools in northern France and eventually died at the great monastery of Cluny, in Burgundy. A layman, and largely the student of laymen, Abelard became a master of logic and theology in the cathedral school of Notre Dame, in Paris. A canon of the cathedral, Fulbert, entrusted his niece, Heloise (ca. 1100–63), to Abelard for instruction. Passion, a child, and a secret marriage ensued. Fulbert took his revenge by emasculating Abelard, who then withdrew to a monastery. Heloise was also compelled to enter a convent (about 1118). She became abbess in 1129, and survived Abelard by twenty years. After they were separated, Heloise and Abelard exchanged a number of remarkable letters, one of which is presented here (document 34).

Bernard of Clairvaux (1090–1153) is known as "the last of the Church Fathers." He was born into a noble family in Burgundy, and in early life he followed a wavering career of experimentation in secular and monastic pursuits. Finally, at the age of twenty-two (1112), he converted to the new, and very austere, Cistercian order. During his novitiate at the monastery of Citeaux (1112–15), he practiced mortifications so severe that his health was permanently impaired. In 1115, he was sent out as abbot to found a monastery at Clairvaux. His personal austerity and his brilliant rhetorical skills joined with a fiery zeal for orthodoxy. By his constant preaching, writing, and correspondence, he gained not only moral force but also political power over popes and kings. He was the driving impulse of the rapid and enormous spread of the Cistercian order, which quickly became a conspicuous element in the social fabric of Europe (documents 35–37).

Little is known about the life of Gottfried of Strassburg (flourished 1210). He was a layman, and, though he was not of noble birth, he moved in aristocratic circles. He was superbly educated in pre-Christian classical literature and in theology. He translated great issues in theology into new forms of romantic narrative, using, for example, the language and concepts of mysticism (drawing especially on Bernard of Clairvaux's mysticism) to portray a cult, or religion, of carnal love. He belonged to a generation of great poets, laymen writing in the vernacular, that also included Walther von der Vogelweide (below, p. 376). Gottfried's incomplete epic, *Tristan*, is written on the chivalric theme of nobility through suffering (document 38).

---

31. Anselm, *Prayers and Meditations* (ca. 1100)

Prayer to St. Mary

Mother of the life of my soul,
    nurse of the redeemer of my flesh,
who gave suck to the Saviour of my whole being—
    but what am I saying?

From *The Prayers and Meditations of Saint Anselm*, translated by Benedicta Ward (London: Penguin, 1973), pp. 122–24, 152–55. © 1973 by Benedicta Ward. Reprinted by permission of Penguin Books, Ltd.

My tongue fails me, for my love is not sufficient.
Lady, Lady, I am very anxious to thank you for so much,
but I cannot think of anything worthy to say to you,
and I am ashamed to offer you anything unworthy.
How can I speak worthily
    of the mother of the Creator and Saviour,
      by whose sanctity my sins are purged,
      by whose integrity incorruptibility is given me,
    by whose virginity my soul falls in love with its Lord
      and is married to its God.
What can I worthily tell of the mother of my Lord and God
by whose fruitfulness I am redeemed from captivity,
    by whose child-bearing
I am brought forth from eternal death,
by whose offspring I who was lost am restored,
and led back from my unhappy exile
    to my blessed homeland.

"Blessed among all women,"
    all these things were given to me
    by "the blessed fruit of your womb"
    through his baptism of regeneration,
    some in fact, others in hope;
    yet by sinning I put it all away from me
so that now I have nothing and scarcely any hope.
    What then?
    If they vanished because of my guilt
    surely I will not be ungrateful to her
    by whom so many things came to me?
Stop, lest I add iniquity upon iniquity!
    I give great thanks for what I have had,
    I weep for what I have not,
    I pray so that I may have them again.
For I am sure that since through the Son
    I could receive grace,
I can receive it again through the merits of the mother.
    Therefore, Lady,
    gateway of life, door of salvation,
    way of reconciliation, approach to recovery,
I beg you by the salvation born of your fruitfulness,
    see to it that my sins be pardoned
    and the grace to live well be granted me,

and even to the end keep this your servant
under your protection.

Blessed assurance, safe refuge,
the mother of God is our mother.
The mother of him in whom alone we have hope,
whom alone we fear,
is our mother.
The mother of him who alone saves and condemns
is our mother.

You are blessed and exalted
not for yourself alone but for us too.
What great and loving thing is this
that I see coming to us through you?
Seeing it I rejoice, and hardly dare to speak of it.
For if you, Lady, are his mother,
surely then your sons are his brothers?
But who are the brothers and of whom?
Shall I speak out of the rejoicing of my heart,
or shall I be silent in case it is too high for me to mention?
But if I believe and love
why should I not confess it with praise?
So let me speak not out of pride but with thanksgiving.

For he was born of a mother to take our nature,
and to make us, by restoring our life, sons of his mother.
He invites us to confess ourselves his brethren.
So our judge is our brother,
The Saviour of the world is our brother,
and finally our God through Mary is our brother.
With what confidence then ought we to hope,
and thus consoled how can we fear,
when our salvation or damnation hangs on the will
of a good brother and a devoted mother?
With what affection should we love
this brother and this mother,
with what familiarity should we commit ourselves to them,
with what security may we flee to them!
For our good brother forgives us when we sin,
and turns away from us what our errors deserve,
he gives us what in penitence we ask.

The good mother prays and beseeches for us,
    she asks and pleads that he may hear us favourably
She pleads with the son on behalf of the sons,
    the only-begotten for the adopted,
    the lord for the servants.
The good son hears the mother on behalf of his brothers,
the only-begotten for those he has adopted,
    the lord for those he has set free.

Prayer to St. Paul

O St. Paul, where is he that was called
    the nurse of the faithful, caressing his sons?
Who is that affectionate mother who declares everywhere
    that she is in labour for her sons?
    Sweet nurse, sweet mother,
who are the sons you are in labour with, and nurse,
but those whom by teaching the faith of Christ
    you bear and instruct?
    Or who is a Christian after your teaching
who is not born into the faith and established in it by you?
    And if in that blessed faith we are born
    and nursed by other apostles also,
    it is most of all by you,
for you have laboured and done more than them all in this;
so if they are our mothers, you are our greatest mother.

So then, St. Paul, your son is this dead man.
Mother, this dead man is certainly your son.
Dear mother, recognize your son
    by the voice of his confession;
    he recognizes his mother by her loving compassion.
Recognize your son by his confession of Christianity;
    he recognizes his mother by the sweetness of goodness.
O mother, you who again give birth to your sons,
    offer your dead son again, to be raised up by him
    who by his death gives life to his servants.
O mother, offer your son to him
    who by his death, which was not owing,
    called back his condemned ones
    from the death that was their due;
that he may call back to him the life he has lost.

By baptism he was led out of death;
by barrenness and corruption he is led back into death.
    O mother, well known for your love,
    your son knows the heart of a mother's goodness.
    Show him to God,
you who have brought him back to life
    and cared for him living.
Pray to him for your son, who is his servant;
pray to him for his servant, who is your son.

And you, Jesus, are you not also a mother?
    Are you not the mother who, like a hen,
    gathers her chickens under her wings?
Truly, Lord, you are a mother;
    for both they who are in labour
    and they who are brought forth
    are accepted by you.
You have died more than they, that they may labour to bear.
    It is by your death that they have been born,
    for if you had not been in labour,
    you could not have borne death;
and if you had not died, you would not have brought forth.
    For, longing to bear sons into life,
    you tasted of death,
    and by dying you begot them.
You did this in your own self,
    your servants by your commands and help.
    You as the author, they as the ministers.
    So you, Lord God, are the great mother.

    Then both of you are mothers.
    Even if you are fathers, you are also mothers.
For you have brought it about that those born to death
    should be reborn to life—
    you by your own act, you by his power.
Therefore you are fathers by your effect
    and mothers by your affection.
Fathers by your authority, mothers by your kindness.
Fathers by your teaching, mothers by your mercy.
Then you, Lord, are a mother,
    and you, Paul, are a mother too.
If in quantity of affection you are unequal,
    yet in quality you are not unalike.

Though in the greatness of your kindness
    you are not co-equal,
    yet in will you are of one heart.
Although you have not equal fullness of mercy,
    yet in intention you are not unequal.

Why should I be silent about what you have said?
Why should I conceal what you have revealed?
Why should I hide what you have done?
    You have revealed yourselves as mothers;
    I know myself to be a son.
    I give thanks that you brought me forth as a son
    when you made me a Christian:
    you, Lord, by yourself, you, Paul, through him;
    you by the doctrine you made,
    you by the doctrine breathed into you.
    You by the grace you have granted to me,
    you by the grace you accepted from him.
    Paul, my mother, Christ bore you also;
so place your dead son at the feet of Christ, your mother,
    because he also is Christ's son.
Rather, throw him into the heart of Christ's goodness,
    for Christ is even more his mother.
    Pray that he will give life to a dead son,
    who is not so much yours as his.
St. Paul, pray for your son, because you are his mother,
    that the Lord, who is his mother too,
    may give life to his son.
Do, mother of my soul,
    what the mother of my flesh would do.
At least, if I may hope, I may pray as much as I can;
    nor cease until I obtain what I can.
Certainly, if you will, you need not despair;
    and if you pray, you are able to obtain.
Ask then, that this dead soul which you brought to life,
    may be restored to life,
nor cease until he is given back to you, living.

    And you, my soul, dead in yourself,
    run under the wings of Jesus your mother
    and lament your griefs under his feathers.
    Ask that your wounds may be healed
    and that, comforted, you may live again.

32. John of Salisbury, *Policraticus* (1150s)

<u>Book 4</u>

On the Difference between a Prince and a Tyrant
and of What Is Meant by a Prince

Between a tyrant and a prince there is this single or chief difference, that
the latter obeys the law and rules the people by its dictates, accounting
himself as but their servant. It is by virtue of the law that he makes good
his claim to the foremost and chief place in the management of the affairs
of the commonwealth and in the bearing of its burdens; and his elevation
over others consists in this, that whereas private men are held responsible
only for their private affairs, on the prince fall the burdens of the whole
community. Wherefore deservedly there is conferred on him, and gathered
together in his hands, the power of all his subjects, to the end that he may
be sufficient unto himself in seeking and bringing about the advantage of
each individually, and of all; and to the end that the state of the human
commonwealth may be ordered in the best possible manner, seeing that
each and all are members one of another. Wherein we indeed but follow
nature, the best guide of life; for nature has gathered together all the senses
of her microcosm or little world, which is man, into the head, and has subjected all the members in obedience to it in such wise that they will all
function properly so long as they follow the guidance of the head, and the
head remains sane. Therefore the prince stands on a pinnacle which is exalted and made splendid with all the great and high privileges which he
deems necessary for himself. And rightly so, because nothing is more advantageous to the people than that the needs of the prince should be fully
satisfied; since it is impossible that his will should be found opposed to
justice. Therefore, according to the usual definition, the prince is the public power, and a kind of likeness on earth of the divine majesty. Beyond
doubt a large share of the divine power is shown to be in princes by the fact
that at their nod men bow their necks and for the most part offer up their
heads to the axe to be struck off, and, as by a divine impulse, the prince is
feared by each of those over whom he is set as an object of fear. And this I
do not think could be, except as a result of the will of God. For all power is
from the Lord God, and has been with Him always, and is from everlasting. The power which the prince has is therefore from God, for the power

From *The Statesman's Book of John of Salisbury*, translated by John Dickinson, bk. 4,
chaps. 1–12; bk. 5, chap. 2 (New York: Russell & Russell, © 1963), pp. 3–60, 64–66.
Originally published by Alfred A. Knopf, 1927. Reprinted by permission of Prentice-Hall,
Inc., Englewood Cliffs, N.J.

of God is never lost, nor severed from Him, but He merely exercises it through a subordinate hand, making all things teach His mercy or justice. "Who, therefore, resists the ruling power, resists the ordinance of God," [1] in whose hand is the authority of conferring that power, and when He so desires, of withdrawing it again, or diminishing it. For it is not the ruler's own act when his will is turned to cruelty against his subjects, but it is rather the dispensation of God for His good pleasure to punish or chasten them. Thus during the Hunnish persecution, Attila, on being asked by the reverend bishop of a certain city who he was, replied, "I am Attila, the scourge of God." Whereupon it is written that the bishop adored him as representing the divine majesty. "Welcome," he said, "is the minister of God," and "Blessed is he that cometh in the name of the Lord," and with sighs and groans he unfastened the barred doors of the church, and admitted the persecutor through whom he attained straightway to the palm of martyrdom. For he dared not shut out the scourge of God, knowing that His beloved Son was scourged, and that the power of this scourge which had come upon himself was as nought except it came from God. If good men thus regard power as worthy of veneration even when it comes as a plague upon the elect, who should not venerate that power which is instituted by God for the punishment of evil-doers and for the reward of good men, and which is promptest in devotion and obedience to the laws? To quote the words of the Emperor, "it is indeed a saying worthy of the majesty of royalty that the prince acknowledges himself bound by the Laws." [2] For the authority of the prince depends upon the authority of justice and law; and truly it is a greater thing than imperial power for the prince to place his government under the laws, so as to deem himself entitled to do nought which is at variance with the equity of justice.

What the Law Is; and That Although the Prince Is Not Bound by the Law, He Is Nevertheless the Servant of the Law and of Equity, and Bears the Public Person, and Sheds Blood Blamelessly

Princes should not deem that it detracts from their princely dignity to believe that the enactments of their own justice are not to be preferred to the justice of God, whose justice is an everlasting justice, and His law is equity. Now equity, as the learned jurists define it, is a certain fitness of things which compares all things rationally, and seeks to apply like rules of right and wrong to like cases, being impartially disposed toward all persons, and allotting to each that which belongs to him. Of this equity the interpreter is the law, to which the will and intention of equity and justice are known. Therefore Crisippus asserted that the power of the law extends over all

1. Rom. 13:2.   2. Justin, *Cod.*, I. 14 §4.

things, both divine and human, and that it accordingly presides over all goods and ills, and is the ruler and guide of material things as well as of human beings. To which Papinian, a man most learned in the law, and Demosthenes, the great orator, seem to assent, subjecting all men to its obedience because all law is, as it were, a discovery, and a gift from God, a precept of wise men, the corrector of excesses of the will, the bond which knits together the fabric of the state, and the banisher of crime;[3] and it is therefore fitting that all men should live according to it who lead their lives in a corporate political body. All are accordingly bound by the necessity of keeping the law, unless perchance there is any who can be thought to have been given the license of wrong-doing. However, it is said that the prince is absolved from the obligations of the law; but this is not true in the sense that it is lawful for him to do unjust acts, but only in the sense that his character should be such as to cause him to practice equity not through fear of the penalties of the law but through love of justice; and should also be such as to cause him from the same motive to promote the advantage of the commonwealth, and in all things to prefer the good of others before his own private will. Who, indeed, in the respect of public matters can properly speak of the will of the prince at all, since therein he may not lawfully have any will of his own apart from that which the law or equity enjoins, or the calculation of the common interest requires? For in these matters his will is to have the force of a judgment; and most properly that which pleases him therein has the force of law, because his decision may not be at variance with the intention of equity. "From thy countenance," says the Lord, "let my judgment go forth, let thine eyes look upon equity,"[4] for the uncorrupted judge is one whose decision, from assiduous contemplation of equity, is the very likeness thereof. The prince accordingly is the minister of the common interest and the bond-servant of equity, and he bears the public person in the sense that he punishes the wrongs and injuries of all, and all crimes, with even-handed equity. His rod and staff also, administered with wise moderation, restore irregularities and false departures to the straight path of equity, so that deservedly may the Spirit congratulate the power of the prince with the words, "Thy rod and thy staff, they have comforted me."[5] His shield, too, is strong, but it is a shield for the protection of the weak, and one which wards off powerfully the darts of the wicked from the innocent. Those who derive the greatest advantage from his performance of the duties of his office are those who can do least for themselves, and his power is chiefly exercised against those who desire to do harm. Therefore not without reason he bears a sword, wherewith he sheds blood blamelessly, without becoming thereby a man of blood, and

3. *Dig.*, I. 3 §§1–2.   4. Ps. 17:2.
5. Ps. 23:4.

frequently puts men to death without incurring the name or guilt of homicide. For if we believe the great Augustine, David was called a man of blood not because of his wars, but because of Uria. And Samuel is nowhere described as a man of blood or a homicide, although he slew Agag, the fat king of Amalech. Truly the sword of princely power is as the sword of a dove, which contends without gall, smites without wrath, and when it fights, yet conceives no bitterness at all. For as the law pursues guilt without any hatred of persons, so the prince most justly punishes offenders from no motive of wrath but at the behest, and in accordance with the decision, of the passionless law. For although we see that the prince has lictors of his own, we must yet think of him as in reality himself the sole or chief lictor, to whom is granted by the law the privilege of striking by a subordinate hand. If we adopt the opinion of the Stoics, who diligently trace down the reason for particular words, "lictor" means "legis ictor," or "hammer of the law," because the duty of his office is to strike those who the law adjudges shall be struck. Wherefore anciently, when the sword hung over the head of the convicted criminal, the command was wont to be given to the officials by whose hand the judge punishes evil-doers, "Execute the sentence of the law," or "Obey the law," to the end that the misery of the victim might be mitigated by the calm reasonableness of the words.

That the Prince Is the Minister of the Priests and Inferior to Them; and of What Amounts to Faithful Performance of the Prince's Ministry

This sword, then, the prince receives from the hand of the Church, although she herself has no sword of blood at all. Nevertheless she has this sword, but she uses it by the hand of the prince, upon whom she confers the power of bodily coercion, retaining to herself authority over spiritual things in the person of the pontiffs. The prince is, then, as it were, a minister of the priestly power, and one who exercises that side of the sacred offices which seems unworthy of the hands of the priesthood. For every office existing under, and concerned with the execution of, the sacred laws is really a religious office, but that is inferior which consists in punishing crimes, and which therefore seems to be typified in the person of the hangman. Wherefore Constantine, most faithful emperor of the Romans, when he had convoked the council of priests at Nicaea, neither dared to take the chief place for himself nor even to sit among the presbyters, but chose the hindmost seat. Moreover, the decrees which he heard approved by them he reverenced as if he had seen them emanate from the judgment-seat of the divine majesty. Even the rolls of petitions containing accusations against priests which they brought to him in a steady stream he took and placed in his bosom without opening them. And after recalling them to charity and harmony, he said that it was not permissible for him, as a man, and one who was subject to the judgment of priests, to examine cases touching gods, who cannot be judged save by God alone. And the petitions which he had received he put into the fire without even looking at them, fearing to give publicity to accusations and censures against the fathers, and thereby incur the curse of Cham, the undutiful son, who did not hide his father's shame. Wherefore he said, as is narrated in the writings of Nicholas the Roman pontiff, "Verily if with mine own eyes I had seen a priest of God, or any of those who wear the monastic garb, sinning, I would spread my cloak and hide him, that he might not be seen of any." Also Theodosius, the great emperor, for a merited fault, though not so grave a one, was suspended by the priest of Milan from the exercise of his regal powers and from the insignia of his imperial office, and patiently and solemnly he performed the penance for homicide which was laid upon him. Again, according to the testimony of the teacher of the gentiles, greater is he who blesses man than he who is blessed;[6] and so he in whose hands is the authority to confer a dignity excels in honor and the privileges of honor him upon whom the dignity itself is conferred. Further, by the reasoning of the law it is his right to refuse who has the power to grant, and he who can lawfully bestow can lawfully take away.[7] Did not Samuel pass sentence of deposition against Saul by reason of his disobedience, and supersede him on the pinnacle of kingly rule with the lowly son of Ysai?[8] But if one who has been appointed prince has performed duly and faithfully the ministry which he has undertaken, as great honor and reverence are to be shown to him as the head excels in honor all the members of the body. Now he performs his ministry faithfully when he is mindful of his true status, and remembers that he bears the person of the *universitas* of those subject to him; and when he is fully conscious that he owes his life not to himself and his own private ends, but to others, and allots it to them accordingly, with duly ordered charity and affection. Therefore he owes the whole of himself to God, most of himself to his country, much to his relatives and friends, very little to foreigners, but still somewhat. He has duties to the very wise and the very foolish, to little children and to the aged. Supervision over these classes of persons is common to all in authority, both those who have care over spiritual things and those who exercise temporal jurisdiction. Wherefore Melchisedech, the earliest whom the Scripture introduces as both king and priest (to say nought at present concerning the mystery wherein he prefigures Christ, who was born in heaven without a mother and on earth without a father); of him, I say, we read that he had neither father nor

6. Heb. 7:7.   7. *Dig.*, I. 17 §3.
8. I.e., Jesse.

mother, not because he was in fact without either, but because in the eyes of reason the kingly power and the priestly power are not born of flesh and blood, since in bestowing either, regard for ancestry ought not to prevail over merits and virtues, but only the wholesome wishes[9] of faithful subjects should prevail; and when anyone has ascended to the supreme exercise of either power, he ought wholly to forget the affections of flesh and blood, and do only that which is demanded by the safety and welfare of his subjects. And so let him be both father and husband to his subjects, or, if he has known some affection more tender still, let him employ that; let him desire to be loved rather than feared, and show himself to them as such a man that they will out of devotion prefer his life to their own, and regard his preservation and safety as a kind of public life; and then all things will prosper well for him, and a small bodyguard will, in case of need, prevail by their loyalty against innumerable adversaries. For love is strong as death; and the wedge[10] which is held together by strands of love is not easily broken.

When the Dorians were about to fight against the Athenians they consulted the oracles regarding the outcome of the battle. The reply was that they would be victorious if they did not kill the king of the Athenians. When they went to war their soldiers were therefore enjoined above all else to care for the safety of the king. At that time the king of the Athenians was Codrus, who, learning of the response of the god and the precautions of the enemy, laid aside his royal garb and entered the camp of the enemy bearing faggots on his back. Men tried to bar his way and a disturbance arose in the course of which he was killed by a soldier whom he had struck with his pruning-hook. When the king's body was recognized, the Dorians returned home without fighting a battle. Thus the Athenians were delivered from the war by the valor of their leader, who offered himself up to death for the safety of his country. Likewise Licurgus in his reign established decrees which confirmed the people in obedience to their princes, and the princes in just principles of government; he abolished the use of gold and silver, which are the material of all wickedness; he gave to the senate guardianship over the laws and to the people the power of recruiting the senate; he decreed that virgins should be given in marriage without a dowry to the end that men might make choice of wives and not of money; he desired the greatest honor to be bestowed upon old men in proportion to their age; and verily nowhere else on earth does old age enjoy a more honored station. Then, in order to give perpetuity to his laws, he bound the city by an oath to change nothing of his laws until he should return again. He thereupon set out for Crete and lived there in perpetual exile; and when he died, he

9. *Vota*.   10. I.e., a military formation.

ordered his bones to be thrown into the sea for fear that if they should be taken back to Lacedaemon, they might regard themselves as absolved from the obligation of their oath in the matter of changing the laws.

These examples I employ the more willingly because I find that the Apostle Paul also used them in preaching to the Athenians. That excellent preacher sought to win entrance for Jesus Christ and Him crucified into their minds by showing from the example of many gentiles that deliverance had come through the ignominy of a cross. And he argued that this was not wont to happen save by the blood of just men and of those who bear the magistracy of a people. Carrying forward this line of thought, there could be found none sufficient to deliver all nations, to wit both Jews and gentiles, save One to whom all nations were given for His inheritance, and all the earth foreordained to be His possession. But this, he asserted, could be none other than the Son of the all-powerful Father, since none except God holds sway over all nations and all lands. While he preached in this manner the ignominy of the cross to the end that the folly of the gentiles might gradually be removed, he little by little bore upward the word of faith and the tongue of his preaching till it rose to the word of God, and God's wisdom, and finally to the very throne of the divine majesty, and then, lest the virtue of the gospel, because it has revealed itself under the infirmity of the flesh, might be held cheap by the obstinacy of the Jews and the folly of the gentiles, he explained to them the works of the Crucified One, which were further confirmed by the testimony of fame; since it was agreed among all that they could be done by none save God. But since fame frequently speaks untruth on opposite sides, fame itself was confirmed by the fact that His disciples were doing marvellous works; for at the shadow of a disciple those who were sick of any infirmity were healed. Why should I continue? The subtlety of Aristotle, the refinements of Crisippus, the snares of all the philosophers He confuted by rising from the dead.

How the Decii, Roman generals, devoted themselves to death for their armies, is a celebrated tale. Julius Caesar also said, "A general who does not labor to be dear to his soldiers' hearts does not know how to furnish them with weapons, does not know that a general's humaneness to his troops takes the place of a host against the enemy." He never said to his soldiers, "Go thither," but always "Follow me"; he said this because toil which is shared by the leader always seems to the soldier to be less hard. We have also his authority for the opinion that bodily pleasure is to be avoided; for he said that if in war men's bodies are wounded with swords, in peace they are no less wounded with pleasures. He had perceived, conqueror of nations as he was, that pleasure cannot in any way be so easily conquered as by avoiding it, since he himself who had subdued many nations had been snared in the toils of Venus by a shameless woman.

That It Is Established by Authority of the Divine Law That the Prince Is Subject to the Law and to Justice

But why do I thus resort to begging instances from the history of the gentiles, although they are at hand in countless numbers, seeing that men can be moved to deeds more directly by laws than by examples? That you may not, then, be of opinion that the prince is wholly absolved from the laws, hear the law which is enjoined upon princes by the Great King who is terrible over all the earth and who takes away the breath of princes: [11] "When thou art come," He says, "into the land which the Lord thy God shall give to thee, and shalt possess it and shalt dwell therein and shalt say, 'I will set over me a king such as all the nations that are round about me have over them'; thou shalt appoint him king over thee whom the Lord thy God shall choose from the number of thy brethren. Thou mayst not set over thee for thy king a man of another nation, who is not thy brother. And when he is made thy king, he shall not multiply the number of his horses, nor lead back the people into Egypt, made proud by the number of his horsemen; for the Lord hath enjoined upon thee that no more shalt thou return by that way. He shall not have many wives to turn away his heart, nor a great weight of silver and gold. And it shall be when he sitteth upon the throne of his kingdom that he shall write him a copy of this law of the Deuteronomy in a book, taken from the copy which is in the hands of the priests of the tribe of Levi, and he shall keep it with him and read therein all the days of his life, that he may learn to fear the Lord his God and to keep His words and the rites of His worship which are prescribed in the law. And his heart shall not be lifted up in pride above his brethren, nor incline to the right hand nor to the left, to the end that his reign and his son's reign may be long over Israel." Need I ask whether one whom this law binds is restrained by no law? Surely this law is divine and cannot be broken with impunity. Every word thereof is a thunderclap in the ears of princes if they would be wise. I say nought concerning election, and the form thereof which is prescribed for the creation of a prince; rather attend with me for a little to the rule or formula of living which is enjoined upon him.

When there has been appointed, it is written, a man who professes himself a brother of the whole people in the practice of religion and in affection and charity, he shall not multiply unto himself horses, by the number whereof he may become a burden unto his subjects. For to multiply horses is to collect, from vainglory or some other error, more than need requires. Now "much" and "little," if we follow the prince of the Peripatetics, signify diminution or excess of the legitimate quantity of specific kinds of

---

11. Deut. 17:14 ff.

things. Will it then be lawful to multiply dogs, or rapacious birds, or fierce beasts, or any other monsters of nature, when even the number of horses, which are a military necessity and serve all the useful purposes of life, is thus strictly limited in advance to a lawful quantity? Concerning actors and mimes, buffoons and harlots, panders and other like human monsters, which the prince ought rather to exterminate entirely than to foster, there needed no mention to be made in the law; which indeed not only excludes all such abominations from the court of the prince, but totally banishes them from among the people of God. Under the name of horses is to be understood all things needful for the use of a household, and all its necessary equipment; of which a legitimate quantity is that which necessity or utility reasonably requires, understanding, however, that the useful is identified with the honorable, and that the refined comfort of living is limited to honorable things. For philosophers have long ago agreed that no opinion is more pernicious than the opinion of those who distinguish the useful from the honorable; and that the truest and most useful view is that the honorable and the useful are convertible terms.[12] Plato, as is told in the histories of the gentiles, when he saw Dionysius the tyrant of Sicily surrounded by his bodyguards, asked him, "What harm have you done that you should need to have so many guards?" This in no wise behooves a prince who by the faithful performance of his duties so wins for himself the affection of all that for his sake every subject will expose his own head to imminent dangers in the same manner that by the promptings of nature the members of the body are wont to expose themselves for the protection of the head. And skin for skin, and all that a man has, he will put forward for the protection of his life.

The next commandment is, "He shall not lead back the people into Egypt, made proud by the number of his horsemen." Truly every precaution must be taken, and great diligence used, by all who are set in high place not to corrupt their inferiors by their example,[13] nor by their abuse of things, nor by following the way of pride and luxury to lead back the people into the darkness of confusion. For it often comes to pass that subjects imitate the vices of their superiors, because the people desire to be like their magistrates, and everyone will eagerly follow the appetites which he observes in another who occupies a distinguished station. There is a celebrated passage of the excellent versifier setting forth the opinion and words of the great Theodosius:

> If thou dost bid and decree that aught is to be commonly observed,
> First obey thy decree thyself; then the people will be more observant of that
>   which is just

12. Cicero, *De Officiis* iii, 3 §11.
13. Cf. Jonas of Orleans, *De Inst. Reg.* c. 3 (D'Achéry, *Spicilegium*, 1:324).

And not refuse to bear it when they see the author thereof himself
Obey his own command. The world is shaped
To the model of its king, nor are edicts as effective
To influence the feelings of men as is the ruler's way of life.
The fickle people changes ever with its prince.[14]

But the means of single individuals are of course never so great as the resources of the whole body. The individual draws from his own coffers, the ruling power drains the public chest or exhausts the treasury; and when this finally fails, then he has recourse to the means of private individuals. But private persons must be content with their own. And when this is exhausted, he who but now thirsted after the splendor of the rich and powerful, falls into poverty and disgrace, and blushes at the blackness of his confusion. Therefore by the decree of the Lacedaemonians, a frugal use of the public funds was enjoined upon their rulers, although they were permitted to use according to the common laws their own inherited property and what they chanced to obtain by good fortune.

That the Prince Should Be Chaste and Avoid Avarice

The law adds: "He shall not have many wives to turn away his heart." It was at one time permitted among the people of God that for the sake of propagating the race and increasing the number of the chosen people, each man might have several wives. The patriarchs come to mind as an example of this privilege, as when Sara used her right, to wit to the body of Abraham, in the womb of another, receiving from her husband a son Ismael through the service of her handmaiden. Jacob also, after a double marriage with two sisters, took unto himself their fertile handmaidens. And yet kings are now bound by the restraint of a perpetual prohibition, and are forbidden the embraces of several wives; and though in the case of other men it may have been lawful for several women to be the wife of one man, yet in the case of kings the rule always prevails of one wife for one husband. Shall it be lawful for him to fornicate or commit adultery or defilement with several when not even for the sake of multiplying the race or begetting an heir may he have to do with more than one wife? How shall the ruling power punish immorality and adultery or fornication in others if he is guilty of the same crimes?[15] Let no one bring forward the example of David by way of objection, who perchance in this 'as in so many other respects, enjoyed a special privilege; though for myself I should readily allow that herein he, too, sinned. Clearly his weakness for women drew him

---

14. Claud., *IV. Consul. Hon.*, 296–302. This passage is quoted in the same connection by George Buchanan, *De Jure Regni apud Scotos*, c. xxxvii.

15. Cf. Hincmar of Rheims, *De Ordine Palatii* c. vi.: "Qualiter alios corrigere poterit qui proprios mores ne iniqui sint non corrigit?"

into adultery by the way of treachery and homicide, nor will I labor to excuse a man who, when accused and condemned by the word of the prophet, confessed out of his own mouth that he was a man of death. You have the case of one king sinning like other kings; and would that they would repent as he repented, and confess their fault even as he confessed, and, making satisfaction as he did, return again into the way of life! Even the wisdom of Solomon was infatuated with the love of women.

The next commandment is that he shall not have a great weight of silver and gold. Let them go to, and, against the commandment of God, heap up for themselves a treasure of silver and gold, seeking gain from falsehood; and let them wring abundance from the poverty of others, riches from rapine, and found their own private prosperity on the calamity of many. But someone brings forward the wealth of Solomon as an objection. Granted; I do not say the prince should not be wealthy, but that he should not be avaricious. Were not gold and silver cheap in the time of Solomon? They would not have been by any means so cheap if an immense mass of them, exceeding use, had been hoarded up for himself by a covetous king. By burying them in the ground, he could have effectually withdrawn them from use to the end that they might become dearer. In Petronius, Trimalchio tells a story of a craftsman who made vases of glass of such hardness that they could not be broken more easily than if of gold or silver. When he had once made a vessel of this kind of the purest glass, and worthy, as he thought, of Caesar alone, he went to Caesar with his gift, and was admitted. The beauty of the present was praised, the skill of the artificer was commended, and the devotion of the giver was accepted. But the craftsman, to turn the admiration of the onlookers into wonder, and to win for himself in fuller measure, as he expected, the favor of the emperor, asked Caesar to hand him the vessel, and taking it, hurled it violently to the pavement with such force that the most solid and hardest substance of bronze would not have remained unbroken. At this Caesar was not more astounded than terrified. But the craftsman picked up the vessel from the ground, and it was not broken, but only dented, as if the appearance of glass had but covered the substance of bronze. Then, taking his little hammer from his bosom, he mended the fault skilfully and neatly, and, like a dented vase of bronze, repaired it with repeated blows. When he had completed this, he thought that he had Jupiter's own heaven in his grasp, because he supposed that he had merited the friendship of Caesar and the admiration of all. But it fell out quite otherwise. For Caesar inquired whether any other know this composition of glass vessels. When he replied in the negative, the emperor ordered him to be beheaded at once, saying that if this process should come into common knowledge gold and silver would become as cheap as mud. Whether the story is true or not is doubtful, and there are diverse opinions regarding the act of Caesar. But I for my part, without presuming to pass judgment on the view of wiser men, consider that the devotion of a most able craftsman was ill requited, and that it is a barren prospect for the human race when an excellent art is wiped out in order that money and the material of money, which is the fuel of avarice, the food of death, and the cause of battles and quarrels, may be held in high value, which it would have in any event without effort on the part of the man, since without value there could be no money, which is but the measure of value.

> "Price is the thing now prized; it is a man's census-rating which brings him honors,
> Which brings him friends; the poor man is everywhere trampled on." [16]

To far better advantage have certain peoples sought to banish utterly from their public business this subject-matter of disputes and litigation, this cause of hatred, to the end that the cause being removed the resulting ill-will and its consequences might disappear; such is the enactment of Licurgus among the Lacedaemonians, and such, in ancient Greece, which now is a part of Italy, was the teaching of Pitagoras of Samos, who by the durability and goodness of his constitutions is traditionally reported to have well served all Italy. Would that gold along with silver might become cheap, since the only really valid kind of value is that of the things whose usefulness is recommended by nature, the best guide of life. Then the poor man will not be trampled on, nor the rich man honored solely on account of his money, but each will be held dear or cheap on the strength only of his own endowments. Further, some things derive their value from themselves intrinsically, other things from the opinion of others. Thus bread and victuals, which consist of necessary foodstuffs or clothing, are regarded as valuable everywhere throughout the earth by the dictates of nature. Things which please the senses are naturally valued by all. Why should I elaborate? The things which derive their value from nature are not only everywhere the same, but are held in esteem among all peoples; those which depend upon opinion are uncertain; and as they come with fancy, so they disappear when the fancy passes. The emperor therefore had no need to fear that the material of commercial dealings would become lacking, since buying and selling are common even among those peoples who are not acquainted with the use of money. I know that Solomon was a man of such wisdom that he at least would never have feared lest gold and silver might become cheap for his posterity, whose nature he saw was of a hungry kind, and thirsted chiefly after nothing so much as money. Wherefore, through

16. Ovid, *Fasti* i 217–18.

inspired wisdom, that excellent king despised utterly this rust, and by his example invited those who came after him to share his contempt for money. Of course it is advantageous for a king to be wealthy provided he looks upon his wealth as belonging to the people. He will therefore not regard as his own the wealth of which he has the custody for the account of others, nor will he treat as private the property of the fisc, which is acknowledged to be public. Nor is this any ground for wonder since he is not even his own man, but belongs wholly to his subjects.

That He Should Have the Law of God Ever before His Mind and Eyes, and Should Be Learned in Letters, and Should Be Guided by the Counsel of Men of Letters

"And it shall be when he sitteth upon the throne of his kingdom that he shall write him a copy of this law of the Deuteronomy in a book." Observe that the prince must not be ignorant of the law, and, though he enjoys many privileges, he is not permitted, on the pretext that his duties are military, to be ignorant of the law of God. He shall therefore write the law of the Deuteronomy, that is to say the second law, in the book of his heart; it being understood that the first law is that which is embodied in the letter; the second, that which the mystical insight learns from the first. For the first could be inscribed on tablets of stone; but the second is imprinted only on the purer intelligence of the mind. And rightly is the Deuteronomy inscribed in a book in the sense that the prince turns over in his mind the meaning of this law so that its letter never recedes from before his eyes. And thus he holds the letter firm, without permitting it in any wise to vary from the purity of the inner meaning. For the letter killeth, but the spirit giveth life, and it rests in his hands to give a mediating interpretation of human law and equity which must be at once necessary and general.

"Taken from the copy," says the scripture, "which is in the hands of the priests of the tribe of Levi." And rightly so. Every censure imposed by law is vain if it does not bear the stamp of the divine law; and a statute or ordinance of the prince is a thing of nought if not in conformity with the teaching of the Church. This did not escape the notice of that most Christian prince,[17] who required of his laws that they should not disdain to imitate the sacred canons. And not only are men enjoined to take priests as models for imitation, but the prince is expressly sent to the tribe of Levi to borrow of them. For lawful priests are to be hearkened to in such fashion that the just man shall close his ear utterly to reprobates and all who speak evil against them. But who are priests of the tribe of Levi? Those, namely, who without the motive of ambition, without affection of flesh and blood, have been

17. I.e., Justinian.

introduced into the Church by the law. And not the law of the letter, which mortifieth, but the law of the spirit, which in holiness of mind, cleanness of body, purity of faith and works of charity, giveth life. And as the old law of the shadow, which presented all things figuratively, foreordained to the priesthood the members of a special family of flesh and blood; so after the shadows ceased, and the Truth was revealed, and justice looked forth from heaven, those who were commended by the merit of their life and the fragrance of their good reputation, and whom the united will of the faithful or the diligent foresight of prelates caused to be set apart for the work of the ministry, were enrolled by the spirit into the tribe of Levi, and were instituted lawful priests.

It is added: "He shall keep it with him and read therein all the days of his life." Observe how great should be the diligence of the prince in keeping the law of God. He is enjoined always to have it, read it, and turn it over in his mind, even as the King of kings, born of woman, born under the law, fulfilled the whole justice of the law, though He was subject to it not of necessity but of His own free will; because His will was embodied in the law, and on the law of God He meditated day and night. But it may be thought that in this respect He is not a model for imitation, seeing that He embraced not the glory of kings but the poverty of the faithful, and, putting on servile form, sought on earth no place to lay His head; and, when asked by His judge, confessed that His kingdom was not of this world. If so, other examples may be found of famous kings whose memory is blessed. From the tents of Israel let David, Ezechias and Josias come forth, and the others who thought that the glory of their kingship consisted in this alone, that seeking the glory of God they subjected themselves and their subjects to the bonds of the divine law. And lest perchance these examples appear too remote, and the less to be followed because we seem to have departed somewhat from their law and ritual and religious worship and profession of faith (though our faith and theirs are in fact the same, with only this difference, that what they looked forward to in expectation of the future, we now in great measure enjoy and worship as fulfilled, casting aside the shadows of figures since the Truth has risen from the earth and stands revealed in the sight of the gentiles); yet, as I say, lest their examples be scorned as alien and profane, our own Constantine, Theodosius, Justinian, Leo and other most Christian princes, afford instruction for the Christian prince. For they took especial pains to the end that the most sacred laws, which are binding upon the lives of all, should be known and kept by all, and that none should be ignorant thereof, save in cases where the damage due to the error was compensated by some public advantage or where the edge of the law's severity was mitigated by compassion for age or for the weakness of sex. Their deeds are so many incentives to virtue; their words so many lessons in morals. Finally, their life, with its record of vices subdued and made captive, is like an arch of triumph consecrated to posterity, which they erected and inscribed with the list of their splendid virtues, declaring in every part with devout humility that not our hands, but the hand of God, wrought all these our wondrous works. Constantine, for founding and endowing the Roman church, to say nought of his other excellent deeds, is honored with perpetual benediction. What manner of men Justinian and Leo were is clear from the fact that by disclosing and proclaiming the most sacred laws, they sought to consecrate the whole world as a temple of justice. What shall I say of Theodosius, whom these emperors regarded as a model of virtue, and whom the Church of God has revered not only as an emperor but as a high priest, because of his character, venerable for piety and justice, and his patient humility toward priests, holding himself in low esteem beside them? How patiently he who had himself given laws bore the sentence of the priest of Milan! And, lest you should falsely conceive that that sentence was the light one of a weak and cowardly presbyter accustomed to show complacency toward princes, know that the emperor was suspended from the exercise of his royal rights, was excluded from the church, and was compelled to fulfil a solemn penance. What was it that subjected him to such a necessity? Nought save his own will, which was wholly subjected to the justice of God, and obedient in all respects to His law. And unless you hold in contempt that which is written with the levity of a poet, you will find briefly in Claudius Claudian, in the instructions which the emperor wrote for his son, how high a place he attained in the sanctuary of morals.

To return to the words of the law which I have set forth, when I revolve them in my own mind, each and every one of them seems weighty and strikes upon the mind as if impregnated with the spirit of discernment. "He shall keep the law beside him," it is written, taking care that when he needs to have it, he may not have it against him to his own damnation. For men of might will suffer mighty torments. And it is added, "And he shall read it." It is of little profit to have the law in one's wallet if it is not faithfully treasured in the soul. Therefore it is to be read all the days of his life. From which it is crystal clear how necessary is a knowledge of letters to princes who are thus commanded to turn over the law of God in daily reading. And perchance you will not often find that priests are bidden to read the law daily. But the prince is to read it daily, and all the days of his life; because the day on which he does not read the law is for him a day not of life but of death. But plainly he will hardly be able to do this if he is illiterate. Wherefore in the letter which I remember that the king of the Romans sent to the king of the Franks, urging him to have his children educated in liberal studies,[18] he added tastefully to his other arguments that an illiterate king is like an ass who wears a crown. If, nevertheless, out of consideration for other distinguished virtues, it should chance that the prince is illiterate, it is needful that he take counsel of men of letters if his affairs are to prosper rightly. Therefore let him have at his side men like the prophet Nathan, and the priest Sadoch, and the faithful sons of the prophets, who will not suffer him to turn aside from the law of God; and since his own eyes do not bring it before his mind, let these men, the scholars, make a way for it with their tongues into the opening of his ears. Thus let the mind of the prince read through the medium of the priest's tongue, and whatever of excellence he sees in their lives, let him revere it as the law of the Lord. For the life and tongue of priests are like a book of life before the face of peoples. Perchance this is what is meant when he is bidden to take a copy of the law from the priests of the tribe of Levi; namely, that in accordance with their preaching should the ruling power guide the government of the magistracy committed to him. Nor is he altogether destitute of reading who, although he does not read himself, yet hears faithfully what is read to him by others. But if he does neither, how shall he, thus scorning the precept, fulfil faithfully what the precept enjoins? For the attainment of wisdom is the union and concourse of all desirable things. Did not Tholomeus think that something was still lacking to the sum of his happiness until, summoning seventy interpreters, although he was a gentile, he had communicated the law of God to the Greeks? It makes no difference whether the interpreters were enclosed in the same room and conferred therein together, or whether they prophesied separately, so long as it is established that the king, anxious in pursuit of the truth, caused the law of God to be translated into Greek. In the Attic Nights I remember to have read when the notable traits and habits of Philip of Macedon were treated, that among other things his love of letters colored as it were the business of war and the triumphs of victory, the liberality of his table, the offices of humanity and whatever he did or said gracefully or elegantly. He recognized that in this quality he excelled others, and was anxious to transmit it as the basis of his inheritance to the only son who he hoped would be the heir of his kingdom and good fortune. For this reason he thought fit to write his famous letter to Aristotle, who he hoped would become the teacher of the newly born Alexander. It is substantially in the following words: "Philip sends greetings to Aristotle. Know that a son has been born to me, for which I give thanks to the Gods not more because he has been born than because his birth has chanced in your life-time. For I hope that it will come to pass that, edu-

18. Conrad III to Louis VII.

cated and trained by you, he will grow up worthy of ourselves and of taking over such great affairs." [19] I do not remember that the Roman emperors or commanders, so long as their commonwealth flourished, were illiterate. And I do not know how it chances, but since the merit of letters has languished among princes, the strength of their military arms has become enfeebled and the princely power itself has been as it were cut off at the root. But no wonder, since without wisdom no government can be strong enough to endure or even to exist. Socrates, who was pronounced by the oracle of Apollo to be the wisest of men, and who without contradiction excelled incomparably, not only in reputation for wisdom but also in virtue, those who are called the seven sages, asserted that commonwealths would only be happy if they were governed by philosophers or their rulers at least became students and lovers of wisdom. And (if you hold the authority of Socrates of small account), "Through me," says Wisdom, "kings reign and the establishers of laws decree that which is just; I love them that love me, and they that watch for me in the morning shall find me; with me are wealth and glory, proud riches and justice; better is my fruit than gold and precious stones, my increase than choice silver; I walk in the ways of justice, in the midst of the paths of judgment, that I may enrich them that love me and that I may fill their treasuries." [20] And again, "Counsel is mine and equity, mine is prudence, mine is fortitude." [21] And elsewhere, "Receive my instruction and not money, choose knowledge rather than gold. For wisdom is better than all the most precious riches, and every object of desire is not to be compared with it." [22] While the gentiles thought that nothing should be done without the command of divinities, yet one they worshipped as the god of gods and prince of them all, namely wisdom, as being in authority over all else. Wherefore the ancient philosophers thought fit that the likeness of wisdom should be depicted before the doors of all temples and that these words should be inscribed thereon:

> I am begotten by experience, born of memory;
> "Sophia" the Greeks call me, you "Sapientia." [23]

And these words likewise: "I hate foolish men and idle works and philosophic commonplaces." And surely the fiction was aptly conceived, although they did not know the Truth in its fulness; yet they closely approached thereto, regarding wisdom as the guide and head of all things rightly done, since it truly boasts that in every nation and people from the beginning it has held the primacy, treading under foot by its own inherent

19. Aulus Gellius, ix, 3.   20. Prov. 8:15, 21.
21. Prov. 8:14.   22. Prov. 8:10–11.
23. Quoted from Afranius by Gellius, xiii, 8.

power the necks of the haughty and the proud. Solomon also confesses that he had loved it beyond his own salvation and above all fair things, and that in its company all good things had been added unto him.

That He Should Be Taught the Fear of God, and Should Be Humble, and So Maintain His Humility That the Authority of the Prince May Not Be Diminished; and That Some Precepts Are Flexible, Others Inflexible

The next commandment is that he shall learn to fear the Lord his God, and to keep God's words which are prescribed in the law. The law itself adds the reason for keeping its precepts,—"To the end that he may learn," it says. For the diligent reader of the law is a pupil, not a master; he does not twist the law captive to his own inclination, but accommodates his inclinations to its intention and purity. But what does such a pupil learn? Above all, to fear the Lord his God. Rightly so, because it is wisdom which institutes and strengthens the government of a prince; and the beginning of wisdom is fear of the Lord. He therefore who does not begin with the first step of fear aspires in vain to the pinnacle of legitimate princely rule. I say legitimate; for of certain rulers who are cast down while they are exalted, and are worthy of a yet more miserable fate, it is written: "They have reigned, and not by me; princes have arisen and I knew it not"; [24] and elsewhere, "They that handle the law have not known wisdom." [25] Therefore let the prince fear God, and by prompt humility of mind and pious display of works show himself His servant. For a lord is the lord of a servant. And the prince is the Lord's servant, and performs his service by serving faithfully his fellow-servants, namely his subjects. But let him know also that his Lord is God, to whom is to be shown not alone fear of His majesty, but also pious love. For He is also a father, and one to whom as a result of His merits no creature of His can deny affection and love. "If I am Lord," He says, "where is my fear? If I am father, where is my love?" [26] Also the words of the law are to be kept, which, commencing with the first timid step of fear, mounts upward through the virtues as upon a rising stair with happy ascent. "Love of Him," He says, "is the guardian of His laws" [27] because all wisdom is fear of God. Further: "Who fears God will do good works, and who is faithful unto justice will apprehend her, and she will come forth to meet him as an honored mother." [28]

What are the words which are to be kept with such diligence? First of all the precepts of the law, so that through the prince no jot or tittle of the law

24. *Hos.* 8:4.

26. Macc. 1:6.

28. Eccles. 15:1, 2.

25. Jer. 2:8.

27. Wis. 6:19.

shall fall to earth, because he shall make no exception in favor of his own hands or the hands of his subjects.

Now there are certain precepts of the law which have a perpetual necessity, having the force of law among all nations and which absolutely cannot be broken with impunity. Before the law, under the law, and still under the new covenant of grace, there is one law which is binding upon all men alike: "What thou wouldst not should be done unto thee, do not unto another"; and "what thou wouldst should be done unto thee, do that unto others." Let the whitewashers of rulers now come forward, and let them whisper, or if this is too little, let them trumpet abroad that the prince is not subject to the law, and that whatsoever is his will and pleasure, not merely in establishing law according to the model of equity, but absolutely and free from all restrictions, has the force of law. Let them thus, if they so desire and dare, make of their king, whom they except from the obligations of the law, a very outlaw, and still I will maintain not merely in the teeth of their denials but in the teeth of all the world, that kings are bound by this law. For He who neither deceives nor is deceived says, "By what judgment ye judge, ye shall yourselves be judged." [29] And surely the heaviest judgment that could be passed upon these rulers would be to have their own good measure, pressed down, shaken together, and running over, poured back into their own bosoms. And not only do I withdraw from the hands of rulers the power of dispensing with the law, but in my opinion those laws which carry a perpetual injunction or prohibition are not subject at all to their pleasure. In the case of those rules which are flexible, I admit a power of dispensing with verbal strictness; but only provided that the purpose of the law is preserved in its integrity by a compensating concession made to propriety or public utility.

"And his heart shall not be lifted up," it is written, "in haughtiness above his brethren." This commandment, which is especially needful, is several times repeated, because humility never sufficiently commends itself to princes, and it is very difficult for success in ascending the ladder of honor not to produce inflation in the mind of a man without prudence. But God sets Himself against the proud beyond all others, and bestows His grace upon the humble. Therefore the prudent king prays that pride may not set its foot in his path because those that work iniquity have tripped thereon and have been driven forth and could not stand fast. Let him therefore not be haughty above his brethren; but remembering that they are his brethren, show brotherly affection to all his subjects. It is an admonition of prudence to princes to cultivate humility as well as discretion and charity,

29. Matt. 7:2.

since without these qualities it is altogether impossible for the government of a prince to endure. Whoever therefore loves the height of his own elevation should with the greatest diligence maintain the utmost humility in his life and manners. For whoever falls away from the works of humility, falls from the pinnacle of his honors with all his inflated weight. It is an everlasting and abiding rule that he who humbles himself shall be exalted, and, vice versa, he who exalts himself shall be brought low. Pride made Tarquin the last king of the Romans, and put in his place magistrates who were more useful because of their humility. What man of pride have you ever read of whose reign was longer? History is filled with those who fell because of their pride. But he should not avoid pride to the point of falling into contempt; abjectness is to be avoided as much as haughtiness. Wherefore the Roman law cautions those who administer justice to make themselves easy of access but not to bring themselves into contempt; and the provision is added to the commissions of governors of provinces that they shall not admit provincials to undue familiarity, because association on an equal footing tends to produce contempt for a man's dignity. Let him therefore in public preserve respect for the majesty of the people and at home observe the fit measure of his private station.

This is the precept contained in the writings of the ancient philosophers. A father and son once came to Athens to see and make the acquaintance of the philosopher Taurus. The son was governor of the province of Crete, but the father was a private citizen. Taurus quietly rose to greet them as they approached, and sat down again after their mutual salutation. A single chair which stood nearby was brought, and was placed while others were sent for. Taurus invited the father of the governor to sit down. But he declined, saying, "Rather let him be seated who is a magistrate of the Roman people." "Without prejudice to our decision," said Taurus to him, "do you sit down while we examine which is the more proper, whether you should rather be seated because you are his father, or he because he bears a magistracy of the Roman people." When the father had taken the seat and another chair was placed for the son, Taurus discussed the question before those who had gathered about, weighing with the greatest care the respective claims of fairness, justice, public station, and official duty. The substance of his words was this. In public places and functions, the rights of fathers as compared with those of sons who hold public office and power become dormant. But when, outside the sphere of public affairs, it is a question of sitting, walking, or reclining at a friendly banquet in private life, then as between a son who is a magistrate and a father who is a private citizen, public honors cease and the claims of nature and birth revive. "Your coming to me," said Taurus, "and our talking together at this present time and discussing the question of duties, is a private act. Therefore you as a father are entitled to the same precedence and respect as it is proper for you to enjoy in your own home."

I think that magistrates generally should be urged that in the splendor of their public dignity they should be mindful of their condition as private men, and at the same time should so regard their private station as not to bring disgrace upon the honor of their public office; each should maintain the honor conferred on him without derogating from the dignity of others, and should so value his private dignity as not to bring insult or harm upon the public power.

That the Prince Should Effect a Reconciliation of Justice with Mercy, and Should So Temper and Combine the Two as to Promote the Advantage of the Commonwealth

It should hold true of the prince, as it should hold true of all men, that no one should seek his own interest but that of others. Yet the measure of the affection with which he should embrace his subjects like brethren in the arms of charity must be kept within the bounds of moderation. For his love of his brethren should not prevent him from correcting their errors with proper medicine; he acknowledges the ties of flesh and blood to the end that he may subdue these to the rule of the spirit. It is the practice of physicians when they cannot heal a disease with poultices and mild medicines to apply stronger remedies such as fire or steel. But they never employ these unless they despair of restoring health by milder means, and so the ruling power when it cannot avail by mild measures to heal the vices of its subjects, rightly resorts, though with grief, to the infliction of sharp punishments, and with pious cruelty vents its rage against wrong-doers to the end that good men may be preserved uninjured. But who was ever strong enough to amputate the members of his own body without grief and pain? Therefore the prince grieves when called upon to inflict the punishment which guilt demands, and yet administers it with reluctant right hand. For the prince has no left hand, and in subjecting to pain the members of the body of which he is the head, he obeys the law in sadness and with groans. Philip once heard that a certain Phicias, who was a good fighting man, had become alienated from him because in his poverty he found difficulty in supporting his three daughters and yet received no aid from the king. When his friends advised him accordingly to beware of the man, "What," said Philip, "if a part of my body were sick, would I cut it off rather than seek to heal it?" Then he sought out this Phicias privately in a friendly way, and provided him with sufficient money which he accepted for the necessities of his private difficulties. And thereby the king made this man better disposed toward him and more faithful than he had been before he supposed himself offended. Accordingly, as Lucius says: "A prince should have an old man's habit of mind, who follows moderate counsels, and should play the part of a physician, who heals diseases sometimes by reducing the diet of the overfed, and again by increasing that of the undernourished, who allays pain at times by cautery, and at other times by poultices." In addition, he should be affable of speech, and generous in conferring benefits, and in his manners he should preserve the dignity of his authority unimpaired. A pleasant address and a gracious tongue will win for him the reputation of benignity. Kindness will compel the most faithful and constant love from even the sternest, and will increase and confirm the love which it has produced. And the reverence of subjects is the fit reward of dignity of manners.

Excellently did Trajan, the best of the pagan emperors, answer his friends when they reproached him with making himself too common toward all men and more so, they thought, than was becoming for an emperor; for he said that he desired to be toward private citizens such an emperor as he had desired to have over him when he was a private citizen himself. And in accordance with this principle, acting on the report of the younger Pliny who at that time with other judges was designated to persecute the Church, he recalled the sword of persecution from the slaughter of the martyrs and moderated his edict. And perchance he would have dealt more gently still with the faithful, had not the laws and examples of his predecessors, and the advice of men who were considered wise counsellors, and the authority of his judges, all urged him to destroy a sect regarded by public opinion [30] as superstitious, and as enemies of true religion. I do not unreservedly and in all respects commend the judgment of a man who knew not Christ, yet I do extenuate the fault of him who broke loose from the pressure of others and followed the instinct of his own natural piety toward kindness and pity, a man whose nature it was to be merciful toward all, though stern toward the few whom it would be sinful to spare; so that in the course of his whole reign only one of the senators or nobles of the city was condemned, although a great number could have been found who had offended grievously against him. And this man was condemned by the senate without the knowledge of Trajan himself. For it was his habit to say that a man is insane who, having inflamed eyes, prefers to dig them out rather than to cure them. So again he said that the nails, if they are too sharp, should be trimmed and not plucked out. For if a cithern player and other performers on stringed instruments can by diligence find a way to correct the fault of a string which is out of tune and bring it again into accord with the other strings, and so out of discord make the sweetest harmony, not by

---

30. "Opinio publica"—the expression is noteworthy.

breaking the strings but by making them tense or slack in due proportions; with how much care should the prince moderate his acts, now with the strictness of justice, and now with the leniency of mercy, to the end that he may make his subjects all be of one mind in one house, and thus as it were out of discordant dispositions bring to pass one great perfect harmony in the service of peace and in the works of charity? This, however, is certain, that it is safer for the cords to be relaxed than to be stretched too tautly. For the tension of slack cords can be corrected by the skill of the artificer so that they will again give forth the proper sweetness of tone; but a string that has once been broken, no artificer can repair. Further, if a sound is asked of them which they do not have, they are stretched in vain, and more often come speedily to nought than to what is improperly asked. As the ethical writer says:

> The true prince is slow to punish, swift to reward,
> And grieves whenever he is compelled to be severe.[31]

For while justice is one thing and godliness another, still both are so necessary to the prince that whoever without them attains, not necessarily to princely power, but even to any magistracy whatever, mocks himself in vain but will surely provoke against himself the mockery and scorn and hatred of others. "Let not kindness and truth," saith the Lord, "forsake thee, bind them about thy neck, and write them on the tablet of thy heart; so shalt thou find favor and obedience in the sight of God and men."[32] For kindness deserves favor, justice deserves obedience. The favor and love of one's subjects, which are brought to pass by divine favor, are the most effective instrument of all accomplishments. But love without obedience is of no avail, because when the spur of justice ceases, then the people relax into unlawful courses. Therefore he must ceaselessly meditate wisdom, that by its aid he may do justice, without the law of mercy being ever absent from his tongue; and so temper mercy with the strictness of justice that his tongue speaks nought save judgment. For his office transmutes his justice into judgment continually and of necessity because he may never lawfully repose therefrom without thereby divesting himself of the honor that has been conferred on him. For the honor of a king delights in judgment and represses the faults of offenders with tranquil moderation of mind.

The moderation of magistrates is said to have been the subject of a book written by Plutarch, entitled Archigramaton; and he is also said by word and example to have instructed the magistrates of his own city in forbear-

---

31. Ovid, *Pont.* i 2, lines 123–24.   32. Prov. 3:3, 4.

ance and the practice of justice. Another story is told of him to the effect that he had a slave, a worthless and stubborn fellow, but well trained in liberal studies, and much practised in philosophic disputations. It happened that for some fault, I know not what, Plutarch ordered him to have his tunic taken off and be flogged. He had already begun to be struck sharply with the lash, but still denied the fault, saying that he had done nothing wrong, that he had committed no offence, and insisted that for his many faithful services he did not deserve to be thus beaten. Finally, when he found it all to no avail, he commenced to cry aloud, and in the midst of the flogging broke out, not into complaints and groans, but into words of serious reproach; Plutarch was not acting, he said, as befitted a philosopher; it was disgraceful to give way to anger, especially for a man who had often discoursed on the wrongfulness of anger and had written a fine book on forbearance. He added that it was shameful for him now to contradict his own doctrine by his acts, and, lapsing into inconsistency, to fly off into a rage and punish an innocent man with many blows. At this Plutarch, speaking gently and slowly and with the greatest seriousness, asked the man, "Do I seem to you to be angry for the simple reason that you are receiving a flogging? Is it a sign of anger on my part if you are getting from me that which is your due? Can you perceive from my face or voice or complexion, or even from my words, that I am in the grip of anger? I do not believe that my eyes look fierce or my face passionate, I am not shouting immoderately, nor am I hot or red or perspiring, I am speaking no words for a man to be ashamed of, or any that I ought to repent, nor am I trembling with rage or gesticulating. These, if you do not know it, are the usual signs of anger." And then turning to the man who was administering the blows, he said: "While I and this man dispute, go on with your work; and, without sharing my anger, pound out his slavish obstinacy, and teach him to repent of his wrong-doing instead of thus disputing." Thus Plutarch. Wherein remains much matter of instruction for all who are in high place.

What the Meaning Is of Inclining to the Right Hand or the Left, Which Is Forbidden to the Prince

The next commandment is, "He shall not incline to the right hand nor to the left." To incline to the right hand signifies to insist too enthusiastically on the virtues themselves. To incline to the right is to exceed the bounds of moderation in the works of virtue, the essence of which is moderation. For truly all enthusiasm is the foe of salvation and all excess is a fault; nothing is worse than the immoderate practice of good works. Wherefore the heathen author says:

"The wise man will get the name of mad, the just man of being unjust,
If he pursue virtue itself beyond the measure of what is sufficient." [33]

And the philosopher warns us to avoid excess; for if a man depart from this caution and moderation, he will in his lack of caution forsake the path of virtue itself. Solomon, too, says, "Be not too just." [34] What excess can then be of any profit, if justice herself, the queen of the virtues, is hurtful in excess? And elsewhere to the same effect: "Excessive humility is the high degree of pride." To incline to the left means to slip or deviate from the way of virtue down the precipices of the vices. Therefore one turns aside to the left who is too ready to punish his subjects, and take revenge on them for their faults; on the other hand, he deviates to the right who is too indulgent to offenders out of excess of kindness. Both roads lead away from the true path; but that which inclines toward the left is the more harmful.

Of the Advantage Which Princes May Draw from the Practice of Justice

But is there any advantage in thus keeping the law? The language of the prophet supplies it forthwith,—to the end "that his reign, and the reign of his son, may be long over Israel." Behold, the reward of so difficult a task is the transmission of hereditary kingship from father to son over a long period. For the virtue of the parents will prolong the succession of the children, while the good fortune of later generations will be cut off at the root by the wickedness of their predecessors. For it is certain from the testimony of the Holy Spirit that the unjust shall perish together, and the heirs of the ungodly shall be cut off. [35] But the salvation of the just is from God, who protects them in the time of their tribulation. But since the eternity of time as a whole, however great it is, runs out by the minutest moments, and within the whole nought save an extremely brief moment ever subsists, what can be long therein, since all these moments together, if they might be collected into one, would still not fill the place of a point in comparison with the true eternity, because after all there can be no comparison of things finite with infinite? In the opinion of many, there is a proportion or ratio, though a small one, between the center and the periphery or circumference; but between time and eternity there can be none. What then can be long within that which as a whole is short? Or what blessedness in time will seem long to the faithful and everlasting soul if it must yet lack a still further measure of time? My own opinion, speaking, however, without

33. Hor., *Epist.* i. 6 ll. 15, 16.   34. Eccles. 7:17.
35. Ps. 37:38–39.

prejudice to better, is that in the passage in question "a long reign" means a reign for the life-time of the unfailing soul who will be crowned with the glory of eternal blessedness for a kingdom well administered. For since it is certain that God will reward the works of each and all in overflowing mercy and in the fulness of justice, whom will He look upon with a more searching eye than those who either train all men to justice, or else on the other hand have drawn others down with them to destruction and death? And even as the mighty shall suffer mighty torments, so likewise they shall rejoice more fully in the rewards of justice if they have rightly employed their power; and in the life to come will surpass their subjects in glory, in proportion as they have surpassed them in virtue because of the greater opportunity which they have to sin. "It was within his power to transgress," says the Scripture, "and he transgressed not; to do ill, and he did not; therefore his good works are established in the Lord." [36] For it is imputed as justice to princes that they merely refrain from wrong-doing; and their plentiful opportunity to sin is for them a subject-matter of merit. To turn away from evil is a great thing in princes, even though they do no great good, provided they do not ruin their subjects by tolerating and indulging evil. Is it not a great thing that a continuance of the visible happiness which they enjoy here on earth is promised to them provided they shall have acted rightly? Some say that it is impossible both to prosper in this life after the way of the world and also to attain eternal joy with Christ; and the opinion is a true one if among the prizes of worldly success you include pandering to the vices. And yet it is truly within the power of kings to prosper here and at one and the same time pluck both the sweetest flowers of the world and the most precious fruits of eternity. For what happier fortune is there than if princes are translated from riches to riches, from delights to delights, from glory to glory, from things temporal to things eternal?

Of Another Reward of Princes

Nor do I disregard the promise which is made prima facie by the letter of the law when it promises a long reign to the father and holds out the prospect of succeeding him to his children, who are to be heirs, not merely of his temporal kingdom, but also of eternal blessedness. For I know that the law was speaking to a carnal people, who having as yet a heart of stone and being uncircumcised of mind if not of the flesh, were still for the most part ignorant of eternal life, and set chief store by having the good things of the earth either given or promised them for their bodily subsistence. And so to the carnally minded a carnal promise was given, and a long duration of time was promised to those who had not yet conceived the hope of eternal

36. Eccles. 31:10, 11.

blessedness; and the prospect of a temporal kingdom with succession from father to son was held out to men who as yet did not seek an eternal one. And so, temporally, the father is succeeded by the son, if the latter imitates the father's justice. "Remove ungodliness," says Solomon, "from the face of a king, and his throne shall be established in justice." [37] For if ungodliness departs from his countenance, that is to say from his will, all his acts of rulership will be guided aright by the metwand of equity and by the practice of justice. Whence the saying that, "A king that sitteth on the throne of judgment putteth all evil to flight by his look." [38] Lo, how great a privilege do princes enjoy, for whom the glory of reigning is thus made perpetual in their flesh and blood, to say nought of eternal blessedness! God glories that He has found a man after His own heart, and when He has exalted him to the pinnacle of kingly power, promises to him kingship everlasting in the line of his sons who shall succeed him. "Of the fruit of thy body," he says, "will I set upon thy throne"; and "If thy children keep my commandments which I have given, and my testimonies which I shall teach them through myself or my deputies, they and their children shall sit upon thy throne"; [39] and "I will make his seed to endure forever and his throne as the day of heaven. But if his children forsake my law and walk not in mine ordinances, if they profane my decrees and keep not my commandments, then will I visit their iniquities with a rod," [40] thus signifying that kingly power shall be transferred from one family to another, and that those heirs after the flesh who are seen to be of carnal breed shall be destroyed, and the succession transferred to those who are found to be the heirs of faith and justice. And herein the truth of the promise endures, and the words which have issued from the mouth of the Most High remain in force, to the effect, namely, that to the seed of just kings the succession of the faithful remains everlastingly. It also, I think, holds perpetually true to the letter that parents will be succeeded by their children if these shall have faithfully imitated them in following the commandments of the Lord (to say nought at present concerning Christ, who, being of the seed of David according to the flesh, is King of kings and Lord of all who rule). So that even if, all things being rightly ordered and remaining so, there seems to be no care or any task at all left for a ruler to perform, still, it is a settled fact that those who have once taken a prince to rule over them shall never be without a successor of his seed, although for no other reason than to preserve the honor and renown of his blood. And this is shown by examples drawn from the books of history. For it is told how, when the great Alexander had reached the farthest shore of Ocean, he made ready to vanquish the isle of the Bragmanni.

---

37. Prov. 25:5.   38. Prov. 20:8.
39. Ps. 132:11 ff.   40. Ps. 89:29.

They despatched to him thereupon a letter couched in these terms: "We have heard, most unconquered king, of your battles, and that the good fortune of victory has everywhere followed them. But wherewith will a man be satisfied who is not satisfied with the whole world? We have no riches, whereof the desire might entitle you to attack us; all our goods are common to all. Food is our only wealth, and instead of having ornaments of gold, our raiment is poor and scanty. Our women are not decked out to please; devotion to ornaments they despise as rather a fault than a merit. They know not how to increase their beauty or to pretend to more than that wherewith they were born. Caves serve us for two purposes, for a shelter in life and for a tomb in death. We have a king not for the sake of administering justice but to maintain and preserve his nobility. For what room can there be for administering punishment where no injustice is ever committed?" These words convinced Alexander that it would be no victory to disturb their perpetual peace, and he dismissed them to their own quiet. And perchance had he attacked them in war, he might little enough have prevailed against an innocent people, because not easily is innocence vanquished, and the truth, standing firm in its own strength, ever triumphs over evil, albeit completely armed.

But, since there is nought which men more desire than to have their sons succeed them in their possessions, even as men foreseeing that death is an incident of their mortal state seek to prolong their own existence in the heirs of their body, therefore this promise is given to princes as the greatest incentive to the practice of justice. For somehow it happens that those who are without anxiety for themselves, are always solicitous for the welfare of their children. Herein is an inversion of the proper order of affection in that the love which is due before all else to one's fatherland and parents should be thus poured out by a father upon his children until love of children wholly drains dry his heart, and shuts out all other affections. The children in turn repay their parents as the latter deserve, bestowing on their own children the affection which they received from their parents; although the proper order of affection demands a different order, which was wisely expressed by the most learned of the poets. For after the fall of Troy he places the aged Anchises upon the shoulders of his dutiful son, he gives to Ascanius the right hand of his father Aeneas, while Creusa, the wife, clings to her husband, tracking the footsteps of the others because of the weakness of her sex. To all his fellow-countrymen the poet gave as a leader a man who was famous at once for his feats of arms and for his sense of duty. For a leader of another kind would have availed not, since kingdoms cannot be won without prowess or retained without justice. But today all are actuated by the single motive of making their children, no matter what the character of the latter may be, resplendent with riches and honors rather than with virtues. They even neglect and forget that the burden and responsibility of the common weal rests upon them. After the expulsion of Tarquin the Proud, who was the last king to reign in the City, Brutus, the first who held the office of consul, learned that his sons were concerned in a plot to bring back the kings into the City. He forthwith caused them to be dragged into the forum, and in the midst of a public assembly ordered them to be flogged with rods and afterwards beheaded, to show publicly that he was the father of the whole people and had adopted the people in place of his own children. And although of course I look upon parricide with the utmost horror, still I cannot refrain from approving the loyalty and faithfulness of this consul, who preferred to jeopardize the safety of his own children rather than that of the people. Whether he did rightly, let wiser men decide. For I know that the question has been a battleground of oratorical commonplace, and that declaimers have often enough toiled and sweated over it on both sides, laboring either to excuse the parricide on the ground of fidelity to public duty, or on the other hand to prove that the merit of fidelity to the public was effaced by the infamy of the crime. But if you press me to state an opinion, I will give you the answer which I find was given to Gneius Dolabella by the Areopagites in the case of the woman of Smyrna. For when he governed the province of Asia as proconsul, a certain woman of Smyrna was brought before him, who confessed that she had murdered her husband and son by secretly giving them poison, because they had foully and treacherously slain a son of hers by another marriage, a fine blameless youth. She asserted that her act was lawful by the indulgence of the laws themselves, and that besides she did not know the law, and that she was but punishing an atrocious outrage against herself, her flesh and blood, and the whole commonwealth. The law was separate from the case, since the facts were admitted, and only a question of law remained. Therefore, when Dolabella referred the matter to his council, there was none who in such a doubtful case as it seemed to be was willing either to go the length of absolving the manifest poisoning and parricide, or on the other hand to condemn the just vengeance which had befallen godless wretches who were parricides themselves. The matter was accordingly referred to the council of the Areopagus at Athens, as being graver and more experienced judges. But after they had heard the case, they adjourned it, and ordered the prosecutors and the accused woman to appear before them a hundred years from that day. Thus they neither absolved the poisoning, which was illegal under the law, nor punished the woman who had committed the crime, but who in the opinion of many could have been justly acquitted. This story is told in the ninth book of the work of Valerius Maximus entitled "Memorable Words and Deeds." I will readily agree that both Brutus and the woman transgressed, because "The remedy exceeded due measure and followed too far the course of the disease,"[41] and, although the crimes were great, still it would have been better had they been avenged without resorting to another crime by way of punishment. Wherefore even the poet who lauds Brutus, bears witness also to his unhappy plight; for Virgil says in the sixth book:

> The father in the name of fair liberty will cite to punishment his sons who are kindling new wars,—unhappy father none the less, it matters not how later ages will tell the story of his deed.[42]

But in the following line he seeks to excuse the ill-hap of the parricide, and at the same time blame it, by attributing it to the vanity of vainglory:

> Love of country will prevail with him, and boundless desire of praise.

There is, however, no need for anxiety that the example given by Brutus of preferring the people to one's own children will be followed to excess, since generally a man prefers even the vices of his children to the safety of the commonwealth, although it is certain that the safety of the people ought to be placed before all children. In the Book of Kings it is related how a vow was made to keep a fast day at the peril of him who should break his vow by taking food before night. Jonathan, the son of King Saul, tasted some honey which he had touched with his scepter, that is to say, with his spear; and the king, moved by fatherly affection, is blamed for having spared his son contrary to the obligation of his vow; to which transgression the defeat of the people of Israel on that day was thought to have been due. Heli also, although it is written of him that he was blameless in his own conduct, yet pardoned the vices of his sons; and in consequence when his chair was overturned, he fell and broke his neck and so died. To say nought of others, how greatly, I ask, did He love and seek the general welfare of mankind who did not spare His own Son, but gave Him for our sake, to the end that He might bear the chains and stripes and cross which we had merited, and be condemned to a shameful death, though Himself blameless and innocent? Search the history of the kings of Israel, and you will find that the reason wherefor the people besought God to give them a king was that he might go before the face of the people, and fight their battles, and, after the likeness of the gentiles, bear the burdens of the whole people. And yet a king was not truly needed, had not Israel after the likeness of the gentiles walked crookedly and showed themselves not content to have God for their king. For had they themselves practised justice and walked faithfully in the commandments of the Lord, God would freely and without price have humbled their enemies and stretched out His hand over their

41. Lucan, *Phars.* ii. 143, 144.   42. *Aeneid* vi. 820–23.

tribulations, so that by the wonted help of God one might have vanquished a thousand, and two put to flight ten thousand.

Well do I remember to have heard it said by my host at Placentia, a man of the noblest birth and blood, who had the prudence of this world in the fear of God, that it is well known from frequent experience in the city-states of Italy that so long as they love peace and practise justice and abstain from falsehood and perjury, they enjoy liberty and peace in such fulness that there is nought whatsoever that can in the least degree disturb their repose. But when they fall into deceptions, and by the devious byways of injustice are divided against themselves, then straightway the Lord brings down upon them either the arrogance of Rome or the fury of the Germans, or some other scourge; and His hand remains heavy upon them until of their own free accord they return from their iniquity by the way of repentance; by which remedy alone the storm wholly ceases from among them. He added that the good deserts of the people bring to an end every instance of princely rule or else cause it to be of the mildest character; while on the contrary it is certain that it is because of the sins of the people that God permits a hypocrite to reign over them; and it is impossible that the reign of a ruler should be long who bears himself too haughtily and exults in the humiliation of the people and in his own elevation. But he said that long was the rule of the man who through consciousness of his humility was ever dissatisfied with himself, and reigned as though unwillingly. This was told me by my host of Placentia; and it impressed me as worthy of belief.

Something to the same effect is found in the writings of old times. For Helius, having brilliantly filled the office of prefect of Rome, was advanced from senator to emperor. The Senate then besought him to confer the title of Augustus on his son Caesar; but he replied, "It should be enough that I myself have reigned against my will and without deserving it. For the office of prince is not due to blood, but to merit; and there is no advantage in the rule of one who is born a king without being a king by merit. Nor can there be doubt that he sins against parental affection who crushes his little ones under a burden which they cannot bear. This is to suffocate one's children, not to advance them. They are first to be nourished and trained in the virtues; and when they have become so proficient therein that they prove themselves to excel in virtue those whom they are to excel in public honors, then let them ascend the throne, if they are invited to do so, and let them never lose the good wishes of their fellow-citizens. For who doubts that those are to be preferred above others who besides being enriched as it were with the privilege of natural worth are also inspired to virtue by the example of their ancestors, and by reason of this inspire in others a confidence in their future goodness?" Such were his words. And surely he expressed aptly the privilege of a prince, whose sons succeed him without the raising of any question and in continuance of the original grant from God unless their princely power is subverted as a punishment of iniquity.

For What Reasons the Kingship or Princely Power Is Transferred

A familiar passage of Divine Wisdom teaches that kingship shall be transferred from family to family because of injustices and injuries and contumelies and diverse deceits.[43]

Is it not evident after how short a space of time the throne of the first king among the people of God was overturned? Because of their faults Saul, and Jonathan, and the others of the king's sons, met destruction on the hill-tops to the end that his throne might be established who was chosen from following the ewes that gave suck. Run through the sequence of all the histories and you will see in brief the successions of kings, and how they were cut off by God, like threads in the warp of a web. And the more illustrious the kings, so much the more speedily, if their pride rebels against God, is their seed trampled under foot. There is no wisdom, no prudence, no counsel which can prevail against God, and certainly no courage. If He rises up and pursues, it is vain to have recourse to, or beg aid of, sacraments or the protection of fortresses, because there is none who can escape His hand. Who was greater than Alexander in Greece? And yet we read that he was succeeded not by his own son but by the son of a dancing girl. Who does not know the list of emperors of the house of Caesar? Few or none of them left his heritage to his own son, and all of them in brief, after various perils and many murders of their own flesh and blood, were blotted out as if in a moment by diverse deaths, generally of a shameful kind; and descending into the lower world, they were succeeded by enemies or strangers.

What, I ask, so swiftly subverted and transferred such mighty kingdoms? Surely the indignation of God, provoked by manifold injustices against Him. Injustice, the Stoics think, is a frame of mind which banishes equity from the realm of the habits. That the soul is "deprived" of justice is signified by the use of the privative particle. Now the principal element of justice is not to do harm, and to prevent, out of a duty of humanity, those who seek to do harm. When you do harm, you fall into injustice. And when you put no obstacle in the way of those who seek to do harm, you then serve and aid injustice.

Contumely is when an outward act results from mental passion to the

43. Eccle. 10:8.

manifest hurt of another. And it serves iniquity because it arrogantly rises up against one to whom reverence is due, either because of his rank, or office, or some bond of natural connection.

Deceit, according to the definition of Aquilius, is when one thing is done and another pretended; and is clearly wrong whenever committed with the intention of harming. Deceit differs greatly from contumely, since the latter acts openly and even proudly, while the former acts fraudulently and, as it were, from ambush.

These are the things which, when they occur, overturn the thrones of all rulers because the glory of princes is perpetuated by their opposites. Deceit is the mask of weakness and the image of timidity, and is opposed directly to courage. Contumely is repressed by prudence, which continually repeats "Why should dust and ashes be proud over dust and ashes?" Injury is forbidden by temperance, which is unwilling to inflict on another what it would not wish to suffer from another. And injustice is excluded by justice, which in all things does to others that which it desires to have others do to it. These are the four virtues which philosophers call cardinal, because they are thought to flow like primary rivulets from the original source of honor and right living, and to beget from themselves the streams of all other good things. These are perchance the four rivers which emerge from the delicious paradise of God to water all the earth to the end that it may bear desirable fruit in its own good season. Would that to me from the fountain of life—I speak of the divine grace,—there might penetrate these rivers of plenty, watering the earth of my barrenness, that by increasing fruit of good works I might at least have strength to ward off the blow of the impending axe which for my sins is laid to my root as to the root of an unfruitful tree! The tree which is planted beside those waters does not wither; but the tree which they moisten not at the root, decays and perishes as dust which the wind blows from the face of the earth. In this respect I think no exception is made of leaders nor of rulers, because the glory of kings will be transferred if they are found to be guilty of injustice or injury or contumely, or deceit; for so the mouth of the Lord hath spoken. But with due respect for the opinion of wiser men, my own opinion is that it is not inappropriate that He speaks of the different vices by a plurality of names, and in this plurality has prudently inserted a certain diversity. For He says, as was mentioned above, that kingship shall be transferred from family to family, because of injustice and injuries and contumelies and diverse deceits. The word "diverse," which is added at the end, is to be understood, I think, as referring to all in common, and understood so broadly as to refer not merely to different species of vices, but also to embrace the various kinds of persons and all the modes in which these vices are committed by anyone. For the prince is responsible for all, and seems to be himself the doer of all things, since, having the power to correct all, he is deservedly regarded as a participant in the things which he omits or refuses to correct. For being, as we said above, the public power, he draws from the strength of all, and, in order that his own strength may not fail, he should accordingly take care to preserve the soundness of all the members. For as many offices and stations of duty as there are in the administration of a prince's government, so many are the members as it were of the prince's body. Therefore, in preserving each office in unimpaired integrity of strength and purity of reputation, he is preserving as it were the health and reputation of his own members. But when through the negligence or concealment of the prince as regards the members there is loss of strength or good reputation, then diseases and blemishes come upon his own members. Nor does the well-being of the head long continue when sickness attacks the members.

Here ends the Fourth Book

Here Begins the Fifth Book (and herein of the commonwealth and its members, and especially of the administration of justice)

What a Commonwealth Is, According to Plutarch, and What Fills Therein the Place of the Soul and the Members

The above-mentioned letter is followed by the different headings of this political constitution, set forth in a little treatise entitled "The Instruction of Trajan," which I mean to insert in part in the present work, but in such wise as to follow rather the general trend of the ideas than the actual sequence of the words. The prince is first of all to make a thorough survey of himself, and diligently study the condition of the whole body of the commonwealth of which he is the representative, and in whose place he stands. A commonwealth, according to Plutarch, is a certain body which is endowed with life by the benefit of divine favor, which acts at the prompting of the highest equity, and is ruled by what may be called the moderating power of reason. Those things which establish and implant in us the practice of religion, and transmit to us the worship of God (here I do not follow Plutarch, who says "of the Gods") fill the place of the soul in the body of the commonwealth. And therefore those who preside over the practice of religion should be looked up to and venerated as the soul of the body. For who doubts that the ministers of God's holiness are His representatives? Furthermore, since the soul is, as it were, the prince of the body, and has rulership over the whole thereof, so those whom our author calls the prefects of religion preside over the entire body. Augustus Caesar was to such a degree subject to the priestly power of the pontiffs that in order to set himself free from this subjection and have no one at all over him, he caused

himself to be created a pontiff of Vesta, and thereafter had himself promoted to be one of the gods during his own life-time. The place of the head
in the body of the commonwealth is filled by the prince, who is subject
only to God and to those who exercise His office and represent Him on
earth, even as in the human body the head is quickened and governed by
the soul. The place of the heart is filled by the Senate, from which proceeds the initiation of good works and ill. The duties of eyes, ears, and
tongue are claimed by the judges and the governors of provinces. Officials
and soldiers correspond to the hands. Those who always attend upon the
prince are likened to the sides. Financial officers and keepers [44] (I speak
now not of those who are in charge of the prisons, but of those who are
keepers of the privy chest) may be compared with the stomach and intes-
tines, which, if they become congested through excessive avidity, and retain too tenaciously their accumulations, generate innumerable and incurable diseases, so that through their ailment the whole body is threatened
with destruction. The husbandmen correspond to the feet, which always
cleave to the soil, and need the more especially the care and foresight of the
head, since while they walk upon the earth doing service with their bodies,
they meet the more often with stones of stumbling, and therefore deserve
aid and protection all the more justly since it is they who raise, sustain, and
move forward the weight of the entire body. Take away the support of the
feet from the strongest body, and it cannot move forward by its own power,
but must creep painfully and shamefully on its hands, or else be moved by
means of brute animals. Our author after his fashion lays down many
things of this kind, which he elaborates at great pains and with a treatment
which is rather diffuse, all tending to complete the conception of the commonwealth for the instruction of magistrates; but to follow him verbatim
into these details would belong to that servile kind of interpretation which
seeks rather to expound the surface than the sinews of an author. And because much that he has to say concerning ceremonies and the worship of
the gods, wherein he thought that a religious prince should be deeply in-
doctrinated, is treated from the standpoint of superstition, I shall omit the
things which pertain to the cult of idolatry, and briefly summarize the
meaning of the man insofar as he sought to shape the prince and the offices
of the commonwealth to the practice of justice.

44. This word, while not a translation, serves to reproduce the effect of the double meaning of "*commentarienses*."

33. Rogerius, *Questions on the Institutes* (ca. 1160)

Justice and Law

These Institutes are the laws [*leges*] which Justinian urged us to receive and make the object of enthusiastic study. Because of the instruction they give to men in the conduct of their lives, these laws are meant to be read in advance of others which have been written down; and for this reason, they claim as peculiarly their own, by virtue of a certain preeminence, the title common to all such writings [*Institutes* or *Principles of Instruction*]—especially since they spring from the fountainhead of justice and law [*ius*]. Because they do so, we should, in this introduction entitled "Justice and Law," look first of all at some of their universal qualities, fulfilling the expectations raised by our chapter heading, in order to get to know as best we can what law and justice are, and what they effect, by defining them on the one hand, and considering their precepts on the other. "Now justice is a constant and perpetual will [*voluntas*] allotting each person his right [*ius*]." ROGERIUS: Please explain why the word "will" is used in the definition of justice—and the other terms, as well. Do you mean to say that justice is the will? JURISPRUDENCE: No, justice is not the will; but in setting out to define justice for men, Justinian first uses the word "will" because men observe justice by, above all else, an exercise of the will. Furthermore, because justice is limitless in capacity and able to give each his right, that which men have in rather great supply, namely, will, is central in the concept of justice. Because of their similar extent, and because will is the means by which justice is observed, justice is thus rightly called "will." And indeed, those two words "constant" and "perpetual" are added in praise of justice. In fact, they can even constitute a defining quality of justice, for justice used to be considered variable and inconstant in legal cases, since in one case it shields and defends through its protection, while in another—even at the same time—it rebuffs and condemns the same man. As a result, it was judged guilty of deceit and fickleness, subject to change at different times, and was said not to be "perpetual" but variable (at one moment it gives, at the next it takes away). But this diversity (if there is any) is a function not of justice but of human affairs; and that changeableness, a function of circumstances. Indeed, by these very examples justice is rather shown to be constant and perpetual: for it is on your side when you pursue a just cause; against you, when you pursue an unjust

From Rogerius, *Super institutis*, in *Studies in the Glossators of the Roman Law*, edited by E. Kantorowicz (Cambridge: Cambridge University Press, 1938), pp. 271–75. Translated for this volume by Donald T. Jacques.

cause; and it awards you something while you live righteously, and takes it away after you go astray. If this were not the case, then justice would be termed, with greater truth, lying or fickle. And so, to remove such suspicions and to honor justice itself—or even for the sake of a clear definition—justice is said to be "constant and perpetual." That which follows, namely, "allotting each man his right," is also included for the sake of the definition which distinguishes justice from the other virtues on the strength of its unlimited capacity. ROGERIUS: Is the above-mentioned definition of justice that of its essence? JURISPRUDENCE: Yes. ROGERIUS: Specify, then, what in the definition are the general characteristics, and what the particular. JURISPRUDENCE: This whole phrase, "a constant and perpetual will," is put there for the general class, which is virtue. In fact, because virtue is "a quality of heart or of a well-ordered mind," that is what "a constant and perpetual will" means in this definition. And the phrase "allotting each man his right" is added to serve as a particular characteristic which distinguishes justice from the other virtues. Once these points are understood, that question as to why one's right, which is not justice, nonetheless is used in defining it, becomes rather silly. ROGERIUS: Since justice is a virtue "allotting each man his right," no one can be called just [iustus], because no one can allot each his right. JURISPRUDENCE: Even though no one has the power to render each his right in actual fact, in intention of will and mind—of which, as we said, justice consists—this is possible for just about anyone you please. Hence, that man is correctly called just who is of such intent and purpose that, if he could, he would allot every man his right; for this man bestows upon each his right even if not in deed, yet at least in mind, which is the greater seat of all the virtues. With this in view, the legislator used the word "will" for the general term in his description of justice; and through this definition, just as one comes to know what justice is, so, too, he comes to know who is just. No doubt, in the same way that justice is "a constant and perpetual will," that is, virtue "allotting each his right," so is that man just who has such a will, even if he does not bring it to fruition. Next we must ask, What is jurisprudence? Now, that is "the knowledge of things divine and human, the science of the just and the unjust." ROGERIUS: I do not see why jurisprudence is described here. JURISPRUDENCE: The reason is this: Just as justice has to do with law [ius], from which it derives its name, so too does jurisprudence, although in a different way. For justice is related to the law as its source and origin, since law comes to be through it, whereas jurisprudence is related to the law as its teacher or instructress, since one comes to learn about and understand the law through it. Next follows: What are the precepts of law [ius]? These are "to live honorably, to injure no one, to allot each his right." ROGERIUS: Please tell me what these individual precepts mean. JURISPRUDENCE: The first one, "to live honorably," considered by itself, pertains to love of God, to reverential regard for Him, and to the honor of the community, which is best maintained if all are subject to one tribunal. The purpose of this precept is the warding off of those vices which do greater harm to the offenders. Since these offenses are infrequent, it is no wonder that they are easier to bear; hence, they are guarded against by a single precept. However, the other two, "to injure no one" and "to allot each his right," deal with duties toward fellow citizens, and with preventing the violation of relationships established by nature between all men. Their purpose is the warding off of those crimes which are committed against a neighbor. Indeed, because these are more common and more harmful, it was judged that they be guarded against by two precepts. Now a man transgresses on the one hand, by doing what is forbidden, and on the other, by neglecting what is lawful. And so, the precept "to injure no one" exists, in particular, to do away with crimes which are actually committed, such as theft, homicide, and fratricide. But for the banishment of those offenses which arise through omission, such as when a person is derelict in paying debts, giving true testimony, and pronouncing just decisions, there is the precept "to allot each his right." It is to be noted in this regard, that in the distribution of justice, "allotting each his right" performs exactly the same function that we have now seen these three precepts perform. For that man fully allots to each his right who lives honorably, reveres God Himself, obeys the community and its magistrates, and abstains from the sordidness of wanton behavior. And likewise, he renders each his right by the very fact of not injuring his neighbor in actual deed, nor hurting him through negligence. ROGERIUS: In my opinion, the precept "to live honorably" suffices for love of God and neighbor, and makes the other two appear superfluous, since no one can live honorably unless he also allots his neighbor his right and refrains from injuring him. In the same way, one or the other of the precepts, "to injure no one" and "to allot each his right," would suffice for the duties towards a neighbor, because if anyone really did not want to injure someone else, he would allot him his rights, and vice versa. And so, since the first precept implies the two which follow; and since the latter two are in accord one with the other; all of them really say the same thing. JURISPRUDENCE: I admit that, but superfluous things do no harm so long as it is certain that they are useful and reasonable. ROGERIUS: How so? JURISPRUDENCE: So that his desire to preserve what is just and his more fervent wish to suppress what is unjust might be more fully known, the legislator preferred to set forth in three precepts what he could have set forth in one. He also thought it right and more appropriate to distinguish here the individual cases by individual designations. I also think that in this instance the odd number itself, in which God

takes pleasure, has significance. For all the precepts of law, if taken together, are one: namely, "to live honorably"; taken by themselves, they are
three. ROGERIUS: I doubt whether justice always allots each his right,
since I see it giving someone now what is his, now what belongs to another, now what belongs to no one. For example: Justice allots to me what
belongs to another if it is owed to me; justice allots to me birds, too, which
belong to no one, when I hunt them. JURISPRUDENCE: This may be
true, yet never is anything allotted to you except what is yours. For by
"yours" is meant not just that over which you have actual control, but
everything for which you have a just claim to retention or recovery, or that
which you are legitimately permitted to take, such as birds. For birds, although they, in fact, belong to no one, can be said to belong to anyone who
captures them, since the power to catch them has been granted by God to
all individuals in common. Therefore, something is called "yours" not
only if it is yours in fact, but also if only by designation, as in the case of
something owed to you; and something which is owed to someone else is
similarly believed to be "someone else's" [alienum], although it is so only
by designation, and not in fact. This is how someone is said to owe "someone else's" money [aes alienum = "debt"]; how someone is believed to
"have" that for which he may sue. In this way a person appears "not to
have" that for which he is bound by a suit to another. ROGERIUS: Since
law [ius] and justice now take away what people have, now grant what they
possess, I wonder why in the distribution of these things they were said to
"allot" rather than to "take away" or to "allow"? JURISPRUDENCE: This
word "allot" is taken here in a liberal sense. For whether it gives something
to you, i.e., makes it yours, or allows you to retain it—even though it could
take it away if it wanted to—rightly is it said to "allot" it to you, for it
offers retention of the thing. Even when it takes away, it appears to allot,
for either it takes away in order to set you free (and thus grants freedom to
you, and the thing to another), or, to restrain you (and thus presents you
with a penalty, and the other with vindication). Hence, in this case more
than in others, law and justice appear to allot. Therefore, whether they
give, or allow, or take away, they are said to allot things which are yours,
and so, correctly, what is "his," to a guilty party, when they present him
with a penalty, as also to a good man, what is "his," when they allot him a
reward. ROGERIUS: Since the discussion here concerns law [ius], why is
its definition not put under this chapter heading? JURISPRUDENCE: Because through its precepts, which we have now suitably set forth, one can
better come to an understanding of law, than through its definition.

34. Letter of Heloise to Abelard (1130s)

Your superior wisdom knows better than our humble learning of the many serious treatises which the holy Fathers compiled for the instruction or exhortation or even the consolation of holy women, and of the care with which these were composed. And so in the precarious early days of our conversion long ago I was not a little surprised and troubled by your forgetfulness, when neither reverence for God nor our mutual love nor the example of the holy Fathers made you think of trying to comfort me, wavering and exhausted as I was by prolonged grief, either by word when I was with you or by letter when we had parted. Yet you must know that you are bound to me by an obligation which is all the greater for the further close tie of the marriage sacrament uniting us, and are the deeper in my debt because of the love I have always borne you, as everyone knows, a love which is beyond all bounds.

You know, beloved, as the whole world knows, how much I have lost in you, how at one wretched stroke of fortune that supreme act of flagrant treachery robbed me of my very self in robbing me of you; and how my sorrow for my loss is nothing compared with what I feel for the manner in which I lost you. Surely the greater the cause for grief the greater the need for the help of consolation, and this no one can bring but you; you are the sole cause of my sorrow, and you alone can grant me the grace of consolation. You alone have the power to make me sad, to bring me happiness or comfort; you alone have so great a debt to repay me, particularly now when I have carried out all your orders so implicitly that when I was powerless to oppose you in anything, I found strength at your command to destroy myself. I did more, strange to say—my love rose to such heights of madness that it robbed itself of what it most desired beyond hope of recovery, when immediately at your bidding I changed my clothing along with my mind, in order to prove you the sole possessor of my body and my will alike. God knows I never sought anything in you except yourself; I wanted simply you, nothing of yours. I looked for no marriage-bond, no marriage portion, and it was not my own pleasures and wishes I sought to gratify, as you well know, but yours. The name of wife may seem more sacred or more binding, but sweeter for me will always be the word mistress, or, if you will permit me, that of concubine or whore. I believed that the more I humbled myself on your account, the more gratitude I should win from you, and also the less damage I should do to the brightness of your reputation.

You yourself on your own account did not altogether forget this in the

From *The Letters of Abelard and Heloise*, translated by Betty Radice (Harmondsworth: Penguin, 1974), pp. 112–18. Reprinted by permission of Penguin Books, Ltd.

letter of consolation I have spoken of which you wrote to a friend; there you thought fit to set out some of the reasons I gave in trying to dissuade you from binding us together in an ill-starred marriage. But you kept silent about most of my arguments for preferring love to wedlock and freedom to chains. God is my witness that if Augustus, Emperor of the whole world, thought fit to honour me with marriage and conferred all the earth on me to possess for ever, it would be dearer and more honourable to me to be called not his Empress but your whore.

For a man's worth does not rest on his wealth or power; these depend on fortune, but worth on his merits. And a woman should realize that if she marries a rich man more readily than a poor one, and desires her husband more for his possessions than for himself, she is offering herself for sale. Certainly any woman who comes to marry through desires of this kind deserves wages, not gratitude, for clearly her mind is on the man's property, not himself, and she would be ready to prostitute herself to a richer man, if she could. This is evident from the argument put forward in the dialogue of Aeschines Socraticus[1] by the learned Aspasia to Xenophon and his wife. When she had expounded it in an effort to bring about a reconciliation between them, she ended with these words: "Unless you come to believe that there is no better man nor worthier woman on earth you will always still be looking for what you judge the best thing of all—to be the husband of the best of wives and the wife of the best of husbands."

These are saintly words which are more than philosophic; indeed, they deserve the name of wisdom, not philosophy. It is a holy error and a blessed delusion between man and wife, when perfect love can keep the ties of marriage unbroken not so much through bodily continence as chastity of spirit. But what error permitted other women, plain truth permitted me, and what they thought of their husbands, the world in general believed, or rather, knew to be true of yourself; so that my love for you was the more genuine for being further removed from error. What king or philosopher could match your fame? What district, town or village did not long to see you? When you appeared in public, who did not hurry to catch a glimpse of you, or crane his neck and strain his eyes to follow your departure? Every wife, every young girl desired you in absence and was on fire in your presence; queens and great ladies envied me my joys and my bed.

You had besides, I admit, two special gifts whereby to win at once the heart of any woman—your gifts for composing verse and song, in which we know other philosophers have rarely been successful. This was for you

---

1. Aeschines Socraticus, a pupil of Socrates, wrote several dialogues of which fragments survive. This is however no proof that Heloise knew Greek, as the passage was well known in the Middle Ages from Cicero's translation of it in *De inventione* 1.31.

no more than a diversion, a recreation from the labours of your philosophic work, but you left many love-songs and verses which won wide popularity for the charm of their words and tunes and kept your name continually on everyone's lips. The beauty of the airs ensured that even the unlettered did not forget you; more than anything this made women sigh for love of you. And as most of these songs told of our love, they soon made me widely known and roused the envy of many women against me. For your manhood was adorned by every grace of mind and body, and among the women who envied me then, could there be one now who does not feel compelled by my misfortune to sympathize with my loss of such joys? Who is there who was once my enemy, whether man or woman, who is not moved now by the compassion which is my due? Wholly guilty though I am, I am also, as you know, wholly innocent. It is not the deed but the intention of the doer which makes the crime, and justice should weigh not what was done but the spirit in which it is done. What my intention towards you has always been, you alone who have known it can judge. I submit all to your scrutiny, yield to your testimony in all things.

Tell me one thing, if you can. Why, after our entry into religion, which was your decision alone, have I been so neglected and forgotten by you that I have neither a word from you when you are here to give me strength nor the consolation of a letter in absence? Tell me, I say, if you can—or I will tell you what I think and indeed the world suspects. It was desire, not affection which bound you to me, the flame of lust rather than love. So when the end came to what you desired, any show of feeling you used to make went with it. This is not merely my own opinion, beloved, it is everyone's. There is nothing personal or private about it; it is the general view which is widely held. I only wish that it *were* mine alone, and that the love you professed could find someone to defend it and so comfort me in my grief for a while. I wish I could think of some explanation which would excuse you and somehow cover up the way you hold me cheap.

I beg you then to listen to what I ask—you will see that it is a small favour which you can easily grant. While I am denied your presence, give me at least through your words—of which you have enough and to spare— some sweet semblance of yourself. It is no use my hoping for generosity in deeds if you are grudging in words. Up to now I had thought I deserved much of you, seeing that I carried out everything for your sake and con- tinue up to the present moment in complete obedience to you. It was not any sense of vocation which brought me as a young girl to accept the aus- terities of the cloister, but your bidding alone, and if I deserve no gratitude from you, you may judge for yourself how my labours are in vain. I can expect no reward for this from God, for it is certain that I have done nothing as yet for love of him. When you hurried towards God I followed you, indeed, I went first to take the veil—perhaps you were thinking how Lot's wife turned back when you made me put on the religious habit and take my vows before you gave yourself to God. Your lack of trust in me over this one thing, I confess, overwhelmed me with grief and shame. I would have had no hesitation, God knows, in following you or going ahead at your bidding to the flames of Hell. My heart was not in me but with you, and now, even more, if it is not with you it is nowhere; truly, without you it cannot exist. See that it fares well with you, I beg, as it will if it finds you kind, if you give grace in return for grace, small for great, words for deeds. If only your love had less confidence in me, my dear, so that you would be more concerned on my behalf! But as it is, the more I have made you feel secure in me, the more I have to bear with your neglect.

Remember, I implore you, what I have done, and think how much you owe me. While I enjoyed with you the pleasures of the flesh, many were uncertain whether I was prompted by love or lust; but now the end is proof of the beginning. I have finally denied myself every pleasure in obedience to your will, kept nothing for myself except to prove that now, even more, I am yours. Consider then your injustice, if when I deserve more you give me less, or rather, nothing at all, especially when it is a small thing I ask of you and one you could so easily grant. And so, in the name of God to whom you have dedicated yourself, I beg you to restore your presence to me in the way you can—by writing me some word of comfort, so that in this at least I may find increased strength and readiness to serve God. When in the past you sought me out for sinful pleasures your letters came to me thick and fast, and your many songs put your Heloise on everyone's lips, so that every street and house echoed with my name. Is it not far better now to summon me to God than it was then to satisfy our lust? I beg you, think what you owe me, give ear to my pleas, and I will finish a long letter with a brief ending: farewell, my only love.

35. Bernard of Clairvaux, *On Women, Marriage, and Celibacy* (1130s to 1140s)

On the Song of Songs, Sermon 38:4–5

3.4. However, in a beautiful way he calls her, not beautiful in every regard, but beautiful among women, making a distinction, namely, to the end that she may thereby be all the more fully subdued, and that she may know what is lacking to her. For I think that carnal and worldly souls are called

From Sermons 38 and 66, *Super Cantica*, in *Sermones super Cantica Canticorum*, vol. 2 (Rome: Editiones Cistercienses, 1958), pp. 16–18, 178–83. Translated for this volume by Donald T. Jacques.

by the noun "women" here, having nothing virile in them, displaying nothing strong or constant in their deeds, but all slack, all effeminate and soft in how they live and act. A spiritual soul is already beautiful because she walks not according to the flesh but according to the spirit. Yet, by the fact that she still lives in the body, she still falls far short of perfect beauty. Correspondingly, she is not beautiful in every regard, but beautiful among women (that is, among earthly souls and those which are not, like herself, spiritual), not among the angelic beatitudes, not among the Virtues, Powers, Dominions. Just as a certain Father [Noah] once was found and said to be just in his generation (that is, more "just" than all those of his own time and his own generation); and Tamar is held to have been justified by virtue of Judah (that is, more than Judah); and in the Gospel, the Publican is said to have gone down from the temple justified, but justified in comparison with the Pharisee; and likewise as that great man, John, was once mightily praised because, indeed, he had no superior, that is to say, no superior among those born of women, not, however, among the choirs of the blessed and celestial spirits. So too, the bride now is said to be beautiful, but still, for the time being, among women, and not among heavenly beatitudes.

3.5. Let her cease, thenceforth, as long as she is on earth, to investigate too curiously the things that are in heaven, lest by chance while she surveys the [heavenly] majesty she be overwhelmed by the [heavenly] glory. Let her cease, I say, as long as her converse is among women, to inquire into things which reside in the presence of those powers that are on high, things manifest to their sight alone, permitted to their sight alone, as the things of heaven are for the inhabitants of heaven. "Wondrous is that vision," he says, "performed for your sake, O my bride, the vision which you ask to be revealed to you; but you are not now strong enough to look upon the midday wondrous brightness wherein I dwell. For you have said: *Show me where you pasture your flocks, where you make them lie down at noon*. But in fact, to be led into the clouds, to penetrate into the fullness of light, to burst upon the depths of brightness and to dwell in inaccessible light, is neither for this time, nor for this body. That is reserved for you in the last days, when I will exhibit you to myself glorious, having neither spot nor wrinkle nor anything of the kind. Do you not know that as long as you live in this body you are wandering from the light? How do you who are not yet all-beautiful, think yourself worthy to look upon the All of beauty? How, then, do you ask to see me in my splendor, you who still do not know yourself? For if you know yourself more fully, you would doubtless know that while weighed down with a body which is corrupted, you can in no way raise up your eyes and fix them upon that radiance which the angels yearn to gaze upon. It will be, when I appear, that you will be all-beautiful, just as I am all-beautiful; and being very like to me, you will see me as I am.

Then will you hear: *You are all-beautiful, my darling, and there is no blemish in you.* But now, though already alike in part (yet in part unlike), be content in part to understand. Watch yourself: seek not things too far above you, nor investigate those beyond your might. Otherwise, *if you do not know yourself, O beautiful one among women*—for I, too, call you beautiful, but among women, that is, in part; however, when that comes which is perfect, then the partial will be superseded. *If,* therefore, *you do not know yourself. . . .*" But the things that follow [in the Scriptural text] have [already] been spoken of, and there is no need to speak of them again. I had promised that I would, in a useful way, examine a twofold lack of knowledge. If I appear in any way to have fallen short of that promise, forgive me, as I meant well: the will is within my grasp, but I find no way to perfect it—except to the extent that in his kindness, the bridegroom of the Church will deign for your edification to grant it, Jesus Christ our Lord, who is blessed forever. Amen.

On the Song of Songs, Sermon 66:1–7

1.1. *Catch for us the little foxes that spoil the vines.* Behold, I turn now to those foxes. They are the ones that leave the way and take the grapes. They are not content to desert the way unless they can also make the vineyard a desert, compounding their wickedness. It is not enough for them to be heretics unless they can also be hypocrites, so that sin's sinfulness may be beyond measure. These are they who come in sheep's clothing to fleece the sheep and rob the rams. Does it not seem to you that both things happen when congregations are found to be stripped of their faith, and priests of their congregations? Who are these robbers? They are sheep in appearance, foxes in cunning, wolves in conduct and cruelty. They are the ones who wish to seem, not to be, good; not to seem, but to be, evil. They are evil and wish to seem good, lest they alone be evil. They are afraid to seem evil, lest they be too little evil. For indeed, malice always does less harm in the open, and a good man is never deceived except through the feigning of good. And so, therefore, to do evil to the good they work hard to appear good; they do not wish to appear evil, so that they be allowed to work their mischief all the more. For it is not the practice among them to cultivate virtues, but to color their vices, as if with a certain tincture of virtue. They even bestow the title of religion upon the impiety of superstition! Innocence they define merely as not openly doing injury, thereby claiming for themselves only the color of innocence. As a cover for their turpitude, they have embellished themselves with the vow of continence. Furthermore, they think that turpitude should be imputed only to wives, since the only cause that excuses turpitude in intercourse rests with the wife. Bumpkins they are, and ignorant fellows—and altogether contemptible; but I say to you, they are not to be dealt with negligently: *For they increase in Godlessness, and their words spread like canker.*

2. Moreover, the Holy Spirit has not neglected these people—the Holy Spirit who once so manifestly prophesied concerning them, when the Apostle said: *moreover, the Spirit manifestly says that in the last times certain men will depart from the faith, heeding the spirits of error and the teachings of devils that utter falsehood in pretense, that have their consciences seared with a hot iron; that prohibit marriage [and command] abstinence from foods which God has created to be received with thanksgiving.* These are indeed the ones—they are the ones of whom he was speaking! They prohibit marriage; they abstain from foods which God has created, about which we will see later. Now, however, see whether this is not properly a sport of devils, and not of men, as the Spirit had predicted. Ask them the author of their sect: they will name no man. What heresy has not had its own heresiarch from among men? The Manichaeans had Manes as their founder and teacher; the Sabellians, Sabellius; the Arians, Arius; the Eunomians, Eunomius; the Nestorians, Nestorius. So all the other plagues of this sort: each is known to have had a man as its particular master, from whom it derived both its origin and its name. By what name or title will you call them? For not from a man does their heresy spring, nor through a man did they receive it. It could not be that they got it through the revelation of Jesus Christ, but rather, no doubt, just as the Holy Spirit predicted, through the plotting and deceit of devils, uttering lies in pretense and prohibiting marriage.

1.3. In pretense, plainly, and with fox-like trickery do they utter this, pretending that they are saying it out of a love of chastity, whereas they have invented it rather for the sake of fostering and multiplying turpitude. Nevertheless, the matter is so obvious that I wonder how any Christian can ever have been persuaded—except of the fact that these people are so bestial that they do not realize how he who condemns marriage gives free rein to every manner of impurity; or, at any rate, of the fact that they are so full of wickedness and absorbed with diabolical malice, that, realizing it, they dissemble, and delight in the ruin of men.

2. Take honorable marriage and the pure marriage bed from the Church: do you not then fill it with concubine-keepers, incestuous, promiscuous, and effeminate people, with male homosexuals and, in short, with every sort of the impure? Make your choice, then, which it is to be: either all these human monstrosities are to be saved, or the number of those to be saved is to be reduced to the continent few. How small is the number in the one case; how plentiful in the other! Neither of these suits the Savior. What? Will turpitude be crowned? Nothing befits the Author of moral honor less.

Will all be condemned except for the small handful of the continent? This is not what it is to be the Savior. Rare is continence on earth; and not for so little a gain did that [divine] plenitude empty itself out upon the earth. And how have we all received a portion of that plenitude if it granted a partaking of itself to the continent alone? They have nothing to say in reply to this. But I believe that they have nothing to say to the following, either: if there is a place in heaven for moral honor, there may be no partnership between the honorable and the base man, just as there is no association of light with the darkness; indeed, no place awaits the impure man in the place of salvation. If anyone thinks otherwise, the voice of the Apostle will confute him, asserting without any ambiguity: *For those who do such things will not possess the Kingdom of God.* From what hollow will this insidious little fox come out? I think that it has been caught in a hole in which it made, as it were, two doorways: one by which to enter, the second by which to exit, for such is its custom. See then how his escape has been closed off on both sides. If he only puts the continent in the company of heaven, the greatest part of salvation is lost; if he places all the filth equally together with the continent, that which is morally honorable perishes. But more justly does the fox, itself, perish, able to exit neither this way nor that, shut up forever and caught in the pit of his own making.

2.4. Certain people, however, dissenting from others, say that marriage can be contracted only between virgins. But I do not see what rationale they could offer for this distinction—except that they strive among themselves, each according to his own taste, to rival one other in tearing with viperous teeth the sacraments of the Church, as it were the viscera of their mother. For as to their reported allegation concerning the first married couple [Adam and Eve]—namely, that they were virgins—why does that prejudice the freedom of matrimony so that it may not also be contracted between non-virgins? But they whisper that they have found something or other in the Gospel which they vainly think supports their foolishness— that, I believe, which the Lord said when he had given witness concerning the Genesis: *And God created man in His image and likeness, male and female He created them.* Later he added: *Therefore, what God has joined together, let no man put asunder.* "These," they say, "God has joined together, because both were virgins, and it was not licit for them to be separated; otherwise, however, the coupling will not be presumed to be of God."—"Who told you that they were joined by God because they were virgins? For Scripture does not say this."—"Were they not virgins?" he says.—"They were, but it is not the same to say that virgins were coupled and that they were coupled because they were virgins, yet you will find not even this explicitly stated—that they were virgins—even though they were. The difference between the sexes—not virginity—was expressed when it was said: *male and female He created them*. Quite rightly: for marital coupling requires, not corporal purity, but sexual capacity. In establishing marital coupling, then, the Holy Spirit did well in speaking explicitly about sex, but being silent about virginity; and he did not give the insidious little foxes the opportunity to hunt for a word—which they surely would have been glad to do, although this, too, in vain. For what if he had said: 'Virgins he created them'? Would you really, on that account, have straightway carried the point that virgins alone were permitted to be married? And how could you have revelled in the sole occurrence of that word? How could you have reviled second or third marriages? How could you have railed at the Catholic Church for being so much the more willing to join pimps and prostitutes together the more confident it is that they thereby pass from vice to moral honor? Perhaps you would also rebuke God for telling the Prophet [Osee = Hosea] to marry a fornicator; but now, too, you lack the chance, and you like being a heretic for nothing. Indeed, the testimony which you have usurped has been found potent to destroy your error, to destroy it utterly, doing nothing for you but altogether much against you.

2.5. And hear, now, what entirely either confounds or corrects you, and at once grinds away and shatters your heresy. *A woman, as long as her husband is alive, is bound to her husband; but if her husband dies, she is freed from the law of her husband: let her marry whomever she wishes, only in the Lord*. Paul is the one who permits a widow to marry whomever she wishes: and do you, on the contrary, teach that no one except a virgin should marry—and then should marry only a virgin, so that she herself may not even marry whomever she wishes? Why do you shorten the hand of the Lord? Why do you restrict the generous blessing of marriage? Why do you claim as belonging to a virgin what pertains to sex? Paul would not allow this unless it were permitted. But I say too little when I say that he 'allows' it: he also wishes it. *I want*, he says, *the younger ones to marry*—and there is no doubt that he speaks of widows. What could be more obvious? Therefore, what he allows because it is permitted, he also wishes because it is expedient. Does the heretic forbid what is permitted and what is expedient? He will persuade us of nothing as a result of this prohibition—except of the fact that he is a heretic."

3.6. It remains for us to criticize them a bit concerning the rest of the Apostle's prophecy. These people, in fact, abstain as he foretold, from foods which God created to be received with thanksgiving, thereby proving again that they are heretics—not because they abstain, but because they abstain in heretical fashion. For I, too, abstain now and then; but my abstinence is satisfaction for sins, not superstition for impiety. Are we to find fault with Paul, because he chastises his body and reduces it to servitude? I will abstain from wine because in wine there is licentiousness; or, if I am sick, I will use a little, in keeping with the Apostle's counsel. I will abstain from meats, lest while they overly nourish my flesh, they also, at the same time, nourish the vices of the flesh. Even bread will I strive to consume in moderation, lest it weary me to stand for prayer with a heavy stomach; lest the Prophet, too, reproach me because I ate my bread in surfeit. But I will train myself to have my fill not even of plain water, lest distention of the stomach prove a step toward the titillation of sensual desire. The heretic does otherwise: in fact, he shudders at milk and anything made from it, and ultimately, everything which is produced through intercourse. That is a right and Christian practice, if indeed the foods are abstained from, not because they arise from intercourse, but lest they provoke it.

3.7. But what does [the heretic] wish for himself, by avoiding so generally everything that is begotten through intercourse? That observation of foods so markedly expressed makes me suspicious. But still, if you defend this to us, quoting from a rule of the physicians, we do not find fault with the care of the flesh (no one ever hated such care, if only it was not excessive); if, from the discipline of those who practice abstinence, that is, from the school of spiritual physicians, we likewise applaud the virtue by which you tame the flesh and bridle lust. But if you make a prescription for God's beneficence drawing upon the madness of a Manichaean, so that what He created and gave to be received wih thanksgiving, you, being not only an ungrateful, but also a rash, critic, determine to be unclean, and abstain from it as if from an evil—then I clearly will not join in praise of your abstinence, but I will curse your blasphemy: rather, I would call you impure for thinking anything impure. *All things are pure to the pure*, says that supreme assessor of things, and nothing is impure except to the one who thinks it impure: *To the impure, however, and to the unfaithful, nothing is pure, but the mind and conscience of these men is polluted.* Woe to you who have spat out the foods which God has created, judging them impure and unworthy to pass into your bodies, because for this reason the body of Christ, which is the Church, has spat you out, as polluted and impure.

36. Bernard of Clairvaux, *Letters* (1130s to 1140s)

Letter 116

To the Virgin Sophia

Bernard, Abbot of Clairvaux, to the virgin Sophia that she may never sully her virginity, but attain its reward.

From *The Letters of Saint Bernard*, edited and translated by Bruno Scott James (London: Burns, Oates, 1953), pp. 174–77, 181–82, 207, 267–68, 315–17, 346, 460, 494. Some footnotes deleted.

"Vain are the winning ways, beauty is a snare; it is the woman who fears the Lord that will achieve renown." I rejoice with you, my daughter, in the glory of your virtue whereby, you tell me, you have cast away the false glory of the world. It is well to be rid of it, and you deserve praise for not having been deceived in a matter concerning which many people, wise enough in other respects, are exceedingly foolish. What is the glory of the world but the flower of grass, a mere vapour that passes away! Whatever its degree, there is more anxiety in it than joy. When you are advancing claims, protecting yourself, envying others, suspecting all, ever wanting what you have not got, never satisfied with what you have but always wanting more, what rest can there be in your glory? If there should be any, the pleasure of it soon goes, never to return, and only anxiety is left. Moreover you can see how many for all their efforts never attain it and how few ever learn to despise it, because what is a necessity for many is a virtue for few. I say for few, and this is especially so of the nobility: "Not many noble, but the base things of the world hath God chosen." Hence you are indeed blessed amongst others of your rank, because while they are contending for worldly glory you, by your very contempt for it, are exalted much more gloriously and by a far truer glory. You are far more distinguished and honourable for being one of so few than for being one of a great family. For what you have been able to do by the grace of God is yours, but what you have by your birth is the gift of your ancestors. And what is yours is all the more precious for being so rare. Moral vigour amongst men is "a rare bird on earth" [1] but it is even more so among refined and noble women. "Who will find a vigorous woman?" the Scriptures ask, but it is much harder to find one who is also of high birth. God is not at all a respecter of persons and yet, I don't know why it is, virtue is far more pleasing in the nobility. Perhaps because it is more evident. It is not easy to know whether the baser sort lack the glory of the world by their own choice or by force of circumstances. I certainly praise anyone who is virtuous through necessity, but I praise far more her who is virtuous by the free choice of her will.

2. Let other women who know no better contend amongst themselves for the tawdry and fleeting glory of short-lived and deceitful things, but do you strive to set your heart upon what can never fail. Do you, I say, strive for that "eternal weight of glory which our present momentary and light tribulation worketh for us above measure exceedingly." And if those daughters of Belial who "put on airs, walk with heads high, and with mincing steps" got up and adorned like a temple, abuse you, answer them: "My kingdom is not of this world"; answer them: "My time has not yet come, but your time is always ready"; answer them: "My life is hid with Christ in God. When Christ shall appear, who is my life, then I also shall appear

1. Horace, Sat. 2.26.

with him in glory." Although, if one must glory, you too can do so quite simply and quite safely, but only in the Lord. I will not mention the crown which the Lord has prepared for you in eternity. I will say nothing of the promises he has given you, that as a happy bride you will be admitted to contemplate face to face the glory of the Bridegroom, that "he will bring you into his presence glorious, without spot or wrinkle or any such thing," that he will receive you into his eternal embraces, that his "left hand will pillow your head, and his right hand embrace you." I will pass over in silence the special place reserved for virgins amongst the sons and daughters of the kingdom. I will not mention the new song which you will sing as a virgin amongst virgins, but with special and most sweet tones all your own, rejoicing in it yourself and giving joy to the whole city of God, whilst you sing and dance and follow the Lamb whithersoever he goeth. "The eye has not seen, nor the ear heard, neither has it entered into the heart of man to conceive" what the Lord has prepared for you and for what you must prepare yourself.

3. So I will pass over what is promised to you in the future and concern myself solely with the present, with what you have already, with the "first fruits of the spirit," the gifts of the Bridegroom, the pledges of betrothal, the "abundant blessings with which he has met you on the way," he whom you await to follow you and complete what is lacking. May he come out into the open to be seen by his bride in all his beauty and admired by the angels in all his glory. If the daughters of Babylon have anything like this, let them bring it forth, "whose only glory is their shame." They are clothed in purple and fine linen, but their souls are in rags. Their bodies glitter with jewels, but their lives are foul with vanity. You, on the contrary, whilst your body is clothed in rags, shine gloriously within, but in the sight of heaven, not of the world. What is within delights because he is within you who is delighted, for you cannot have any doubt that "Christ dwells in your heart": "All the splendour of the king's daughter is within." Rejoice and be exceeding glad, O daughter of Sion, shout for joy, O daughter of Jerusalem, for the King has greatly desired thy beauty "if confession and beauty are thy clothing and light is a garment thou dost wrap about thee" since "confession and beauty wait on his presence." On whose presence? On his who is "beautiful above the sons of men" and "on whom the angels desire to look."

4. You hear to whom it is you are pleasing? Love what enables you to please him, love confession if you would desire beauty. Beauty is the handmaid of confession. "Confession and beauty are thy clothing" and "Confession and beauty wait on his presence." In truth where there is confession, there too is beauty. If there are sins, they are washed away in confession; if there are good works, they are commended by confession. The confession

of what you have done amiss is "a sacrifice to God of a contrite heart"; the confession of God's mercies to you is "a sacrifice of praise." What an excellent ornament of the soul is confession! It cleans the sinner of his sin and renders the righteous man more unsullied. Without confession the righteous man is insensible, the sinner dead: "Confession perisheth from the dead." Confession therefore is the life of a sinner and the glory of a righteous man. It is necessary for the sinner and becoming to the righteous: "Praise becometh the upright." Silk, purple, and paint have their beauty, but they do not impart it. They show their own beauty when applied to the body, but they do not make the body beautiful. When the body is taken away, they take their beauty with them. The comeliness which goes on with clothes, comes off with clothes, it belongs to the clothes and not the clothed.

5. Therefore do not emulate evil-doers and those who borrow their beauty elsewhere when they have lost their own. They prove themselves destitute of any proper or natural beauty who go to such pains and such expense to make up after the fashion of the world that passes away so as to be admired by the foolish people who see them. Consider it wholly beneath you to borrow your appearance from the furs of animals and the work of worms, let what you have be sufficient for you. The true and proper beauty of anything needs no help from other sources. The ornaments of a queen have no beauty like to the blushes of natural modesty which colour the cheeks of a virgin. Nor is the mark of self-discipline a whit less becoming. Self-discipline composes the whole bearing of a maid's body and the temper of her mind. It bows her head, smoothes her brow, composes her face, binds her eyes, controls her laughter, bridles her tongue, calms her anger, and governs her steps. Such are the pearls which adorn the vesture of a virgin. What glory can be preferred to virginity thus adorned? The glory of angels? An angel has virginity, but he has no body. Without doubt he is more happy, if less strong in this respect. Excellent and most desirable is the adornment which even angels might envy!

6. There remains another thing concerning the same subject. Without any doubt the more your adornment is your own the safer it is. You see women burdened rather than adorned with ornaments of gold, silver and precious stones, and all the raiment of a court. You see them dragging long trains of most precious material behind them, stirring up clouds of dust as they go. Do not let this trouble you. They leave it all behind them when they die, but you will take your holiness with you. What they carry about does not belong to them. When they die they will not be able to take a thing with them, none of all their worldly glory will go down with them to the grave. These things of theirs belong to the world and the world will send the wearers naked away and keep all their vanities to seduce others equally

vain. But your adornments are not like this. They remain securely yours, secure because yours. You cannot be deprived of them by violence nor lose them to guile. Against them the cunning of the thief and the cruelty of the madman are of no avail. They are not corrupted by moth and they do not wear out with age, nor are they spent with use. They survive death, for they belong to the soul and not the body. They do not die with the body, but leave the body in company with the soul. Even those who kill the body are powerless against the soul.

Letter 119

To Ermengarde, Formerly Countess of Brittany

To his beloved daughter in Christ, once a distinguished countess, but now a humble handmaid of Christ, the respectful affection of a holy love, from Bernard, Abbot of Clairvaux.

I wish I could find words to express what I feel towards you! If you could but read in my heart how great an affection for you the finger of God has there inscribed, then you would surely see how no tongue could express and no pen describe what the spirit of God has been able to inscribe there. Absent from you in body, I am always present to you in spirit and, although neither of us can come to the other, yet you have it within your power, not yet indeed to know me, but at any rate to guess something of what I feel. Do not ever suppose that your affection for me is greater than mine for you, and so believe yourself superior to me inasmuch as you think your love surpasses mine. Search your heart and you will find mine there too and ascribe to me at least as great an affection for you as you find there for me. But your modesty is so great that you are more likely to believe that he who has moved you to esteem me and choose me as your spiritual counsellor has also moved me with a like feeling of affectionate concern for you. It is for you to see that you have me always by you; for my part, I confess, I am never without you and never leave you. I wanted to scribble these few brief lines to you from the road while travelling, and I hope, if God wills, to write to you more fully when I have the leisure.

Letter 139

To the Empress of Rome

When I reconciled the Milanese I did not forget your instructions. Even if you had not mentioned it, I would have borne in mind the interests of yourself and your kingdom, as I always and everywhere do, so far as I am able. They were not received back into the favour of the lord Pope and the unity of the Church until they had openly defied and denied Conrad, received our lord Lothair as their master and king, and with all the world acknowledged him as the august Emperor of Rome; until with their hands upon the Gospels they had promised, according to the wish and command of the lord Pope, that they would make full satisfaction for the injuries they have inflicted in the past. I give thanks to the divine goodness who has thus laid your enemies at your feet without any of the risks of war or human bloodshed; and I beg that when the time comes for them to seek through the lord Pope, as their mediator in this matter, to be received into your favour, they may experience that leniency which I myself know so well, so that they may not regret having followed good advice and may render you due service and honour. It is not fitting that the faithful servants who have worked so hard for your interests should be put to shame. But put to shame they would be if you were found to be inexorable and were to disappoint the hopes of forgiveness which they have held out to the Milanese.

Letter 198

To Matilda, Queen of England

To his dear daughter in Christ, Matilda, by the grace of God Queen of the English, that she may reign for ever with the angels, from Brother Bernard, styled Abbot of Clairvaux.

I gladly take this opportunity of affectionately greeting in the Lord your Majesty and not only gladly but also faithfully suggesting certain things which I know to concern your own salvation and the glory of your kingdom. If you fear God and if you wish at all to harken to my counsel, do everything you possibly can to prevent that man from occupying the see of York any longer. I have heard all about his life and the manner of his election from religious men who are utterly trustworthy. This is the cause of God and I entrust it to you. It is for you to see that my trust is not betrayed. I commend to you all who are labouring in the cause that you may see they do not suffer from the wrath of the king nor any hurt whatsoever, for they are doing a good work. Further, if you could arrange that the king should abjure before his bishops and princes the sacrilegious intrusion on the liberty of the chapter, so that it alone should have the decision to which it alone is entitled, know that it would be greatly to the honour of God, the well-being and security of the king and his friends, and to the profit of the whole realm.

Letter 238

To the Bishops and Cardinals in Curia

To the lords and reverend fathers, the Bishops and Cardinals in Curia, from the child of their holiness.

No one has any doubt that it belongs especially to you to remove scandals from the Kingdom of God, to cut back the growing thorns, to calm quarrels. For this is what Moses commanded when he went up the mountain, saying: "Wait here till we come back to you. You have Aaron and Hur with you; to them refer all matters of dispute." I speak of that Moses who came through water, and "not by water only, but by water and blood." [2] And therefore he is greater than Moses because he came through blood. And because by Aaron and Hur the zeal and authority of the Roman Church are signified, I do well to refer to her, not questions about the faith, but wounds to the faith, injuries to Christ, insults and dishonours to the Fathers, the scandals of the present generation and the dangers of those to come. The faith of the simple is being held up to scorn, the secrets of God are being reft open, the most sacred matters are being recklessly discussed, and the Fathers are being derided because they held that such matters are better allowed to rest than solved. Hence it comes about that, contrary to the law of God, the Paschal Lamb is either boiled or eaten raw, with bestial mouth and manners. And what is left over is not burned with fire, but trodden under foot. [3] So mere human ingenuity is taking on itself to solve everything, and leave nothing to faith. It is trying for things above itself, prying into things too strong for it, rushing into divine things, and profaning rather than revealing what is holy. Things closed and sealed, it is not opening but tearing asunder, and what it is not able to force open, that it considers to be of no account and not worthy of belief.

2. Read, if you please, that book of Peter Abelard which he calls a book of Theology. You have it to hand since, as he boasts, it is read eagerly by many in the Curia. See what sort of things he says there about the Holy Trinity, about the generation of the Son, about the procession of the Holy Spirit, and much else that is very strange indeed to Catholic ears and minds. Read that other book which they call the *Book of Sentences*, [4] and

2. "This is he that came by water and blood, Jesus Christ; not by water only but by water and blood" (1 John 5:6).

3. "No part must be eaten raw, or boiled, it must be roasted over the fire . . . whatever is left over, you must put in the fire and burn it" (Exod. 12:9).

4. Abelard denied that he had ever written a book with this name and implied that St. Bernard could not distinguish between Peter Lombard and himself. But Bernard was familiar with the works of Peter Lombard, and also his *Book of Sentences* was not published when this letter was written. Undoubtedly he is referring here to Abelard's book *Sic et Non*, which

also the one entitled *Know Thyself*, and see how they too run riot with a whole crop of sacrileges and errors. See what he thinks about the soul of Christ, about the person of Christ, about his descent into hell, about the Sacrament of the Altar, about the power of binding and loosing, about original sin, about the sins of human weakness, about the sins of ignorance, about sinful action, and about sinful intention. And if you then consider that I am rightly disturbed, do you also bestir yourselves and, so as not to bestir yourselves in vain, act according to the position you hold, according to the dignity in which you are supreme, according to the power you have received, and let him who has scanned the heavens go down even into hell, and let the works of darkness that have braved the light be shown up by the light, so that while he who sins in public is publicly rebuked, others, who speak evil in their hearts and write it in their books, may restrain themselves from putting darkness for light, and disputing on divine matters at the crossroads. Thus shall the mouth that mutters wickedness be closed.

Letter 273

To the Queen of Jerusalem

To the most illustrious Queen of Jerusalem, Melisande, that she may find favour with the Lord, from Bernard, styled Abbot of Clairvaux.

Were I only to regard the glory of your kingdom, your power, and your noble lineage, my writing to you amidst all the many cares and occupations of your royal court might seem rather inappropriate. All these things are seen by the eyes of men, and those who have not got them envy those who have and call them happy. But what happiness is there in possessing what will "soon fade like the grass and wither away like the green leaf"? These things are good, but they are transient and changeable, passing and perishable, because they are the goods only of the body. And of the body and its goods it has been said: "Mortal things are but grass, the glory of them is but grass in flower." So, when writing to you, I must not hold in too much awe those things of which we know "the comeliness to be vain, and the beauty a snare." Receive, therefore, what I have to say in a few words, for although I have many things to say to you, I will do so briefly because of your many affairs and mine. Receive a brief but useful word of advice from a distant land, as a small seed which will bear a great harvest in time. Receive advice from a friend who is seeking your honour and not his own ends. No one can give you more loyal advice than one who loves you and not your

---

starts: "Here begin sentences taken from the Holy Scriptures which seem opposed to each other. . . ."

possessions. The king, your husband, being dead, and the young king still unfit to discharge the affairs of a kingdom and fulfil the duty of a king, the eyes of all will be upon you, and on you alone the whole burden of the kingdom will rest. You must set your hand to great things and, although a woman, you must act as a man by doing all you have to do "in a spirit prudent and strong." You must arrange all things prudently and discreetly, so that all may judge you from your actions to be a king rather than a queen and so that the Gentiles may have no occasion for saying: Where is the king of Jerusalem? But you will say: Such things are beyond my power; they are the duties of a man and I am only a woman, weak in body, changeable of heart, not far-seeing in counsel nor accustomed to business. I know, my daughter, I know that these are great matters, but I also know that although the raging of the sea is great, the Lord is great in heaven. These are great affairs, but great too is our Lord, and great his power.

Letter 390

To Hildegard of Bingen

To his beloved daughter in Christ, Hildegard, whatever the prayers of a sinner can avail, from Brother Bernard, styled Abbot of Clairvaux.

That others should believe me a better person than I know myself to be, is due more to human stupidity than any special merits of my own. I hasten to reply to your sweet and kindly letter, although the multitude of my affairs obliges me to do so more briefly than I could wish. I congratulate you on the grace of God that is in you and admonish you to regard it as a gift and respond to it with all humility and devotion in the sure knowledge that "God flouts the scornful, and gives the humble man his grace." This is what I beg and implore you to do. How could I presume to teach or advise you who are favoured with hidden knowledge and in whom "the influence of Christ's anointing still lives so that you have no need of teaching," for you are said to be able to search the secrets of heaven and to discern by the light of the Holy Spirit things that are beyond the knowledge of man. It is rather for me to beg that you may not forget me before God, or those who are united to me in spiritual fellowship. I am sure that when your spirit is united to God you could help and benefit us much, for "when a just man prays fervently, there is great virtue in his prayer." We pray without ceasing for you that you may be strengthened in all good, instructed in interior things, and guided to what endures, so that those who put their trust in God may not fall by losing faith in you, but may rather derive strength, so as to make ever greater progress in good, from the sight of your own progress in the graces which you are known to have received from God.

Letter 425

To the Abbess of Faverney

From Bernard, styled Abbot of Clairvaux, to A ——, Abbess of Faverney, the title of modesty and virtue.

These good brothers, who came to me for spiritual counsel, have given me not a little pleasure by telling me of your excellent zeal in restoring the property over which, by the grace of God, you preside. But I advise and beg you to take as much trouble in reforming manners as you do in repairing buildings. It is most important that you should give your best attention not only to the convent but also to the "Maison-Dieu" hospice which these brothers serve under your guidance, so that it may be protected from the oppression and rapacity of your agents and vassals. I understand that, on the evil advice of these men, you have taken away the property with which your predecessors had endowed this place, and I beg you to return it. For just as it is your business to suppress or correct the misdeeds of others, so it is your duty to increase and multiply, not merely to preserve firm and unshaken, what has been done well. It seems that a priest who is living in the house still keeps his possessions outside being obliged by you either to give them up or leave the house. Farewell, and, believe me, I am ready and willing to serve you in every way I can for the sake of the good I have heard about you.

37. Bernard of Clairvaux, *Advice to Pope Eugenius III* (1145–53), *De consideratione* (selections)

Book 1

The Malice of Our Days

9.12. But what can you do? If you suddenly devote yourself completely to this philosophy, although it is not customary for a pope to do so, you will indeed annoy many people. You will be like a person who abandons the footsteps of his ancestors, and this will be seen as an affront to them. You will be censured with the common saying, "Everyone wonders about a person who behaves differently." It will seem that you only want attention. You cannot suddenly correct every error at once or reduce excesses to moderation. There will be an opportunity at the proper time for you to pursue this little by little, according to the wisdom given you by God (2 Pet 3:15). In

From Bernard of Clairvaux, *Five Books on Consideration: Advice to a Pope*, translated by John D. Anderson and Elizabeth T. Kennan (Kalamazoo, Mich.: Cistercian Publications, 1976), pp. 42–45, 56–61, 110–18.

the meantime, do what you can to utilize other people's evil for good. If we look for examples of good Roman Pontiffs and not just recent ones, we will discover some who found leisure in the midst of the most important affairs. When Rome was besieged and the barbarian sword threatened the necks of its citizens, did fear stop blessed Pope Gregory from writing about wisdom in leisure? At that very time, as his preface reveals, he wrote his commentary on the very obscure final section of Ezekiel (Homily on Ezekiel 2: preface; *PL* 76:934). And he did this carefully and elegantly.

10.13. But let that be; a different custom has developed. The times and the habits of men are different now. Dangers are no longer imminent, they are present. Fraud, deceit and violence run rampant in our land. False accusers are many; a defender is rare. Everywhere the powerful oppress the poor. We cannot abandon the downtrodden; we cannot refuse judgment to those who suffer injustice (Ps 102:6; 145:7). If cases are not tried and litigants heard, how can judgment be passed?

Advocates

Let cases be tried, but in a suitable manner. The way which is frequently followed now is completely detestable. It would hardly suit civil courts, let alone ecclesiastical. I am astonished that you, a man of piety, can bear to listen to lawyers dispute and argue in a way which tends more to subvert the truth than to reveal it. Reform this corrupt tradition; cut off their lying tongues and shut their deceitful mouths (Ps 11:4). These men have taught their tongues to speak lies (Jer 9:5). They are fluent against justice. They are schooled in falsehood. They are wise in order to do evil; they are eloquent to assail truth. These it is who instruct those by whom they should have been taught, who introduce not facts but their own fabrications, who heap up calumny of their own invention against innocent people, who destroy the simplicity of truth, who obstruct the ways of justice. Nothing reveals the truth so readily as a simple straightforward presentation. Therefore, let it be your custom to become involved in only those cases where it is absolutely necessary (and this will not be every case) and decide them carefully but briefly, and to avoid frustrating and contrived delays. The case of a widow requires your attention, likewise the case of a poor man and of one who has no means to pay. You can distribute many cases to others for judgment and many you can judge unworthy of a hearing. What need is there to hear those whose sins are manifest before the trial?

The Ambitious

Some people are so impudent that, even when their case openly abounds with the itch of ambition, they are not embarrassed to demand a hearing. They flaunt themselves before the public conscience in a trial where they provide sufficient evidence to condemn themselves. There has been no one to restrain their hard-headedness and therefore they have multiplied and become even more set in their ways. I do not understand why, but the guilty are not shamed by the consciences of other guilty men; where all are filthy, the stench of one is hardly noticed. For example, are the greedy embarrassed before their own kind, the unclean before others like them, or the profligate before other profligates? The Church is filled with ambitious men; in our age she shudders at the calculated strivings of ambition no more than a den of thieves shudders at the spoils taken from travellers (Mt 21:13).

Book 2

Why He Has Been Elected to the Supreme Pontificate

6.9. We cannot ignore the fact that you have been elected to the supreme position, but, indeed, it must earnestly be asked, "for what purpose?" Not, in my opinion, to rule. For the Prophet, when he was raised to a similar position, heard, "So that you can root up and destroy, plunder and put to flight, build and plant" (Jer 1:10). Which of these rings of arrogance? Spiritual labor is better expressed by the metaphor of a sweating peasant. And, therefore, we will understand ourselves better if we realize that a ministry has been imposed upon us rather than a dominion bestowed. "I am not greater than the Prophet; even if I am equal in power, still there is no comparison of merits." Say this to yourself and teach yourself, you who teach others. Think of yourself as one of the Prophets. Is this not enough for you? Indeed it is too much. But by the grace of God you are what you are (1 Cor 15:10). What is that? Be what the Prophet was. Or should you be more than the Prophet? If you are wise you will be content with the measure which God has apportioned you (cf. 2 Cor 10:13). For anything more than this comes from the evil one (Mt 5:37). Learn by the example of the Prophet to preside not so much in order to command as to do what the time requires. Learn that you need a hoe, not a sceptre, to do the work of the Prophet. Indeed, he did not rise up to reign, but to root out. Do you think that you also can find work to be done in the field of your Lord? Much indeed. Certainly the Prophets could not correct everything. They left something for their sons, the Apostles, to do; and they, your parents, have left something for you. But you cannot do everything. For you will leave something to your successor, and he to others, and they to others until the end of time. Still around the eleventh hour the workers are scolded for their idleness and sent into the vineyard (Mt 20:6–7). Your predecessors, the Apostles, heard that "The harvest indeed is great, but the laborers are few"

(Mt 9:37). Claim your inheritance from your fathers. For "if a son, then you are also an heir" (Gal 4:7). To prove you are an heir, be watchful in your responsibilities; do not become sluggish and idle lest it also be said to you, "Why do you stand here the whole day idle?" (Mt 20:6).

6.10. It is hardly fitting for you to be found relaxing in luxury or wallowing in pomp. Your inheritance does not include any of these things. But what does it include? If you were content with its meaning you would realize that you are to inherit responsibility and labor rather than glory and wealth. Does the throne flatter you? It is a watchtower; from it you oversee everything, exercising not dominion, but ministry through the office of your episcopacy. Why should you not be placed on high where you can see everything, you who have been appointed watchman over all? In fact, this prospect calls forth not leisure but readiness for war. And when is it suitable to boast, where it is not even possible to relax? There is no place for leisure where responsibility for all the churches unremittingly presses upon you (2 Cor 11:28). But what else did the holy Apostle leave to you? He says, "What I have I give to you" (Acts 3:6). What is that? I am sure of one thing: it is neither gold nor silver; for he himself says, "I do not have silver and gold" (Acts 3:6). If you happen to have these, use them not for your own pleasure, but to meet the needs of the time. Thus you will be using them as if you were not using them (1 Cor 7:31). These things are neither good nor bad when you consider the good of the soul, but the use of them is good, the abuse bad, solicitude for them is worse, and using them for profit is shameful. You may claim these things on some other ground but not by apostolic right. For the Apostle could not give you what he did not have. What he had he gave: responsibility for the churches, as I have said. Did he give dominion? Listen to him, "Not lording it over your charge but making yourself a pattern for the flock" (1 Pt 5:3). You should not think he was prompted to say this only by humility and not by truth, for the Lord says in the Gospel, "The kings of the nations lord it over them and those who have power over them are called benefactors" (Lk 22:25). And he adds, "But you are not like this" (Lk 22:26). It is clear: dominion is forbidden for Apostles.

6.11. Therefore, go ahead and dare to usurp the apostolic office as a lord, or as pope usurp dominion. Clearly, you are forbidden to do either. If you want to have both of these at the same time, you will lose both. Moreover, you should not think that you are excluded from those about whom God complains, "They have reigned but not by me; princes have arisen but I did not recognize them" (Hos 8:4). Now if it pleases you to reign without God, you have glory, but not before God (Rom 4:2). But if we believe this to be forbidden, let us listen to the decree which says, "Let the one who is greater among you become lesser, and let the one who is foremost become as a servant" (Lk 22:26). This is the precedent established by the Apostles: dominion is forbidden, ministry is imposed. This is confirmed by the example of the Lawgiver himself who adds, "But I am among you as one who serves" (Lk 22:27). Who would think himself without glory if he possessed that title which the Lord of glory first applied to himself? Paul rightly glories in it saying, "They are servants of Christ and so am I" (2 Cor 11:23). And he adds, "I speak as a fool: I am more. In many more labors, in prison more frequently, in beatings beyond measure, and often in danger of death" (2 Cor 11:23). O wondrous ministry! What sovereignty is more glorious than this? If it is necessary to glory, the example of the saints is set before you, the glory of the Apostles is proposed to you. Does this glory seem insignificant to you? Who can make me equal to the saints in glory (Ecclus 45:2)? The Prophet cries out, "But to me your friends, God, are made exceedingly honorable; their sovereignty is made exceedingly strong" (Ps 138:17). The Apostle exclaims, "Far be it from me to glory except in the cross of our Lord Jesus Christ" (Gal 6:14).

6.12. I wish that you would glory always in this highest form of glory which the Apostles and Prophets chose for themselves and have passed on to you. Acknowledge your inheritance in the cross of Christ, in a multitude of labors. Happy the man who can say, "I have labored more than all" (1 Cor 15:10). This is glory, but there is nothing vain in it, nothing weak, nothing boastful. If the labor is terrifying, let the reward be an enticement. "For each one will be rewarded according to his labor" (1 Cor 3:8). Even if the Apostle has labored more than all, nevertheless he has not completed the entire task. There is still a place for you.

An Exhortation to Responsibility and Humility

Go out into the field of your Lord and consider how even today it abounds in thorns and thistles in fulfillment of the ancient curse (Gen 3:18). Go out, I say, into the world, for the field is the world (Mt 13:38) and it is entrusted to you. Go out into it not as a lord, but as a steward, to oversee and to manage that for which you must render an account (cf. Lk 16:1 ff.). Go out, I should have said, with footsteps of careful responsibility and responsible care. For those who were ordered to go into the whole world (Mk 16:15) did not circle the world physically, but provided for it mentally. And so, lift up the eyes of your consideration and see whether the lands are not more like fields dried for the fire than white for the harvest (Jn 4:35). How many of the trees which you thought were fruitful, when closely inspected, will turn out to be brambles instead? In fact, they are not even brambles; they are old and decrepit trees which actually bear no fruit except perhaps acorns or husks for swine to eat. How long will they occupy the land? If you go out and see them, will you not be ashamed that your axe is lying idle, that you received the sickle of the Apostles in vain?

Book 4

The Behavior of the Clergy and the Roman People

2.2. First of all, these clergy should be very well ordered, for they especially set the example for clergy throughout the whole Church. Furthermore, every offense which is perpetrated in your presence is more disgraceful for you. It is important for the glory of your holiness that those whom you have in your sight be ordered and organized in such a way that they be a model and mirror of all honor and order. They above all others should be prompt in fulfilling their duties, worthy to administer the sacraments, concerned for the people's instruction, careful to maintain themselves in all purity.

What shall I say about the people? They are the Roman people. I cannot express my feelings about the people of your diocese more briefly or more forcefully. What has been so well known to the ages as the arrogance and the obstinacy of the Romans? They are a people unaccustomed to peace, given to tumult; people rough and intractable even today and unable to be subdued except when they no longer have the means to resist. Behold your affliction: its care rests with you; it is not right for you to neglect it. Perhaps you laugh at me, persuaded that it is incurable. Do not despair: care is required of you, not a cure. You have heard, "Take care of him" (Lk 10:35) and not "Cure," or "Heal him." Indeed, someone has said, "It is not always possible for the doctor to heal the sick" (Ovid, *Epistola ex Ponto* 1:3:17). But even better, I offer you something from one of your own. Paul says, "I have labored more than all" (1 Cor 15:10). He does not say, "I have achieved more than all," or, "I have produced greater results than all," but very scrupulously he avoids an arrogant word. Moreover, the man whom God taught knew that each one would receive according to his labor (1 Cor 3:8), not according to his results. And, therefore, he thought man should glory in his labors rather than in his achievements, just as you have him saying elsewhere, "In many more labors" (2 Cor 11:23). And so, I say, you do your part and God will take care of his satisfactorily without your worry and anxiety. Plant, water, be concerned, and you have done your part. To be sure, God, not you, will give the growth when he wishes (1 Cor 3:6–7). Whenever he does not wish it, it costs you nothing, as Scripture says, "God will reward the labors of his saints" (Wis 10:17). The labor is secure, for no failure can vitiate it. And I have said this without prejudice to divine power and goodness. I know the hardened heart of this people, but "God is able to raise up children to Abraham out of these stones" (Mt 3:9). Who knows but he may return and forgive (Jn 3:9), relent and heal them? (Is 6:10). But it is not my intention to tell God what he should do; would that I could convince you of what you ought to do and how you ought to do it!

2.3. But the course of my argument has become rough and uncertain. For as soon as I rise to say what I am thinking I can anticipate what will happen: anything I say will be decried as an innovation. Indeed, I know that it was once customary, and from this state it could fall into disuse; but to revive it would not be an innovation. For will anyone deny that a thing is customary which is known not only to have been done once, but to have been repeated over a long period of time? I could state what this is but there would be no point. Why? Because it will not please the satraps (1 Sam 29:6) who favor majesty more than truth. There were those before you who devoted themselves completely to feeding their sheep, glorying in the work and in the name of shepherd, counting nothing unworthy of them except what they thought was a hindrance to the safety of the sheep. They were not self-seeking (1 Cor 13:5) but unsparing, unsparing of their care, their wealth, and themselves. Whence one of them says, "I will gladly be spent for your souls" (2 Cor 12:15). And as if they had said, "We did not come to be served, but to serve" (cf. Mt 20:28), they presented the Gospel without charge as often as was necessary (1 Cor 9:18). The only profit they sought from their subjects, their only glory, their only desire was in some way to be able to prepare them as perfect people for the Lord (Lk 1:17). They devoted every effort to this, even in great suffering of heart and body, in labor and hardship, in hunger and thirst, in cold and nakedness (2 Cor 11:27).

2.4. Where, I ask, is this custom now? A very different one has sprung up; interests have changed drastically and I only wish it were not for the worse! Nevertheless, I admit care and anxiety, rivalry and worry persist: they are transferred, not diminished. I bear witness to you that you do not withhold your wealth any more than your predecessors. However, the difference lies in your perverse expenditures. What a great abuse! Few look to the mouth of the lawgiver, all look to his hands. But not without reason: they carry out all the papal business. Whom can you name from all this great City who received you as Pope without a reward or the hope of one? When they offer service, then especially do they wish to rule. They promise to be loyal so they can better harm the faithful. Because of this you will have no deliberation from which they think they should be excluded, no secret into which they will not intrude. If the doorkeeper makes anyone of them delay outside your door, even for a short time, I would not want to be in his place. And now from a few examples judge whether I am at least somewhat acquainted with the practices of this people. Above all they are wise to do evil (Jer 4:22), but they do not know how to do good. They are detested on earth and in heaven, they are hostile toward both; irreverent toward God, disrespectful toward holy things, quarrelsome among themselves, envious of their neighbors, discourteous to strangers. Loving no one, no one loves them; and since they strive to be feared by everyone, they must fear everyone. There are men who do not endure subjection, who do not know how to command; they are unfaithful to superiors, insupportable to inferiors. These are brazen in asking, shameless in denying. These are insistent to receive, restless until they do, ungrateful when they have. They have taught their tongues to say grand things, although their deeds are paltry. They are most generous in their promises, but most sparing in their gifts; they are fawning in flattery and biting in slander; they are blatant liars and wicked traitors. We have proceeded this far thinking you should be fully and clearly warned about such people inasmuch as they are among those things which are around you.

2.5. Now let us return to the order of the work. How is it that those who say to you, "Well done, well done" (Ps 39:16), are bought with the spoils of the churches? The life of the poor is sown in the streets of the rich. Silver glistens in the mud; people run to it from every direction and it is picked up not by the man who is more in need but by the stronger, or by the one who happens to run faster. Nevertheless, this custom, or rather this sickness, did not begin with you; I only wish it would end with you! But let us go on to the rest. In the midst of all this, you, the shepherd, go forth adorned with gold and surrounded by colorful array (Ps 44:10). What do the sheep receive? If I dare say it: this is more a pasture for demons than for sheep. Doubtless Peter engaged in the same practice, and Paul amused himself thus! You see the entire zeal of the Church burn solely to protect its dignity. Everything is given to honor, little or nothing to sanctity. If, when circumstances require, you should try to act a little more humbly and to present yourself as more approachable, they say, "Heaven forbid! It is not fitting; it does not suit the times; it is unbecoming to your majesty; remember the position you hold." Pleasing God is their very last concern. There is no hesitation for the loss of salvation, except that they confuse what is exalted with what is helpful to salvation, and whatever smells of glory, this they call just. All that is humble is felt to be shameful among the courtiers such that you can more easily find someone who wishes to be humble than someone who wishes to appear so. Fear of the Lord is thought simple-mindedness, not to say foolishness. They condemn as a hypocrite the circumspect man and the man who is the friend of his own conscience. Moreover, they say he is useless who loves quiet and who sometimes gives himself leisure.

Let Him Give the Example

3.6. What are you doing about this? Are you as yet on your guard against those who have surrounded you with the snares of death? (Ps 17:6). I implore you, endure a little more and bear with me. Rather, forgive me not so much for saying these things indiscreetly as for saying them timidly. I am jealous of you with a jealousy that is good (cf. 2 Cor 11:2), and would that it were as useful as it is vehement. I know where you dwell (Rev 2:13); unbelievers and subversive men are with you. They are wolves, not sheep; but still you are the shepherd of such men. It is useful for you to consider how you might find a way—if this is possible—to convert them, so they do not subvert you. Why do we doubt that they can be changed back into the sheep from which they were turned into wolves? Here, indeed, I do not spare you, in order that God may spare you. Either deny openly that you are the shepherd of this people or show it by your actions. You will not deny it unless you deny you are the heir of him whose throne you hold. This is Peter, who is known never to have gone in procession adorned with either jewels or silks, covered with gold, carried on a white horse, attended by a knight or surrounded by clamoring servants. But without these trappings, he believed it was enough to be able to fulfill the Lord's command, "If you love me, feed my sheep" (cf. Jn 21:15). In this finery, you are the successor not of Peter, but of Constantine. I suggest that these things must be allowed for the time being, but are not to be assumed as a right. Rather, I urge you on to those things to which I know you have an obligation. You are the heir of the Shepherd and even if you are arrayed in purple and gold, there is no reason for you to abhor your pastoral responsibilities: there is no reason for you to be ashamed of the Gospel (Rom 1:16). If you but preach the Gospel willingly you will have glory even among the Apostles. To preach the Gospel is to feed. Do the work of an evangelist and you have fulfilled the office of shepherd (cf. 2 Tim 4:5).

3.7. "You instruct me to feed dragons and scorpions, not sheep," you reply. Therefore, I say, attack them all the more, but with the word, not the sword. Why should you try to usurp the sword anew which you were once commanded to sheathe? (Jn 18:11). Nevertheless, the person who denies that the sword is yours seems to me not to listen to the Lord when he says, "Sheathe your sword" (ibid.). Therefore, this sword also is yours and is to be drawn from its sheath at your command, although not by your hand. Otherwise, if that sword in no way belonged to you, the Lord would not have answered, "That is enough" (Lk 22:38), but, "That is too much," when the Apostles said, "Behold here are two swords" (ibid.). Both swords, that is, the spiritual and the material, belong to the Church; however, the latter is to be drawn for the Church and the former by the Church. The spiritual sword should be drawn by the hand of the priest; the material sword by the hand of the knight, but clearly at the bidding of the priest and at the command of the emperor. But more of this elsewhere. Now, take the sword which has been entrusted to you to strike with, and for their salvation wound, if not everyone, if not even many, at least whomever you can.

38. Gottfried of Strassburg, *Tristan* (ca. 1210)

The Ordeal

I say quite openly that no nettle has so sharp a sting as a sour neighbour, nor is there a peril so great as a false house-mate. This is what I call false: the man who shows his friend the face of a friend and is his enemy at heart. Such comradeship is terrible, for all the time he has honey in his mouth, but venom on his sting! Such venomous spite puffs up ill fortune for his friend in all that he sees or hears, and one cannot keep anything safe from him. On the other hand, when a man lays his snares for his enemy openly I do not account it falseness. As long as he remains an overt foe he does not do too much harm. But when he feigns friendship for a man, let his friend be on his guard!

This is what Melot and Marjodoc did. With deceit in their hearts they often sought Tristan's company, and, the one like the other, offered him their devoted friendship with cunning and dissembling. But Tristan had been amply warned, and he warned Isolde in turn. "Now, queen of my heart," he said, "guard yourself and me in what you say and do. We are beset by great dangers. There are two poisonous snakes in the guise of doves who with their suave flattery never leave our sides—be on the alert for them, dear Queen! For when one's house-mates are faced like doves and tailed like the serpent-brood, one should cross oneself before the hailstorm and say a prayer against sudden death! Dearest lady, lovely Isolde, be much on your guard against Melot the Snake and Marjodoc the Cur!" Indeed, that is what they were—the one a snake, the other a cur, who were always laying their traps for the two lovers, whatever they did, wherever they went, like cur and snake. Morning and night they treacherously worked upon Mark with schemes and accusations till he began to waver in his love again and suspect the lovers once more and lay traps and make trial of their intimacy.

One day, on the advice of his false counsellors, Mark had himself bled, and Tristan and Isolde, too. They had no suspicion that any sort of trouble was being prepared for them and were entirely off their guard. Thus the King's intimate circle lay pleasurably at ease in their room.

From Gottfried of Strassburg, *Tristan*, translated by A. T. Hatto (Harmondsworth: Penguin, 1960), pp. 240–48. All footnotes deleted.

On the evening of the following day, when the household had dispersed and Mark had gone to bed, there was no one in the chamber but Mark, Isolde, Tristan, Melot, Brangane, and one young lady-in-waiting, as had been planned beforehand. Moreover, the light of the candles had been masked behind some tapestries to dim their brightness. When the bell for matins sounded, Mark silently dressed himself, absorbed in his thoughts as he was, and told Melot to get up and go to matins with him. When Mark had left his bed, Melot took some flour and sprinkled it on the floor so that if anyone should step to or away from the bed his coming or going could be traced. This done, they both went to church, where their observance had little concern with prayer.

Meanwhile, Brangane had at once seen the stratagem from the flour. She crept along to Tristan, warned him, and lay down again.

This trap was mortal pain for Tristan. His desire for the woman was at its height and his heart yearned in his body as to how he could get to her. He acted in keeping with the saying that passion should be without eyes, and love know no fear when it is in deadly earnest. "Alas," he thought, "God in Heaven, what shall I do in face of this cursed trap? This gamble is for high stakes!" He stood up in his bed and looked all about him to see by what means he could get there. Now there was light enough for him to see the flour at once, but he judged the two positions too far apart for a leap; yet on the other hand he dared not walk there. He was nevertheless impelled to commit himself to the more promising alternative. He placed his feet together and ran hard at his mark. Loveblind Tristan made his gallant charge too far beyond his strength; he leapt on to the bed, yet lost his gamble, for his vein opened and this caused him much suffering and trouble in the outcome. His blood stained the bed and its linen, as is the way with blood, dyeing it here, there, and everywhere. He lay there for the briefest space, till silks and gold brocades, bed and linen, were altogether soiled. He leapt back to his bed as he had come and lay in anxious thought till the bright day dawned.

Mark was soon back and gazing down at the floor. He examined his trap and found no trace. But when he went along and studied the bed, he saw blood everywhere. This caused him grave disquiet.

"How now, your Majesty," asked Mark, "what is the meaning of this? How did this blood get here?"

"My vein opened, and it bled from it. It has only just stopped bleeding!"

Then, as if in fun, he turned to examine Tristan. "Up you get, lord Tristan!" he said, and threw back the coverlet and found blood here as there.

At this Mark fell silent and said not a word. He left Tristan lying there and turned away. His thoughts and all his mind grew heavy with it. He pondered and pondered, like a man for whom no pleasant day has dawned. Indeed, he had chased and all but caught up with his mortal sorrow, yet he had no other knowledge of their secret and the true state of affairs than he was able to see from the blood. But this evidence was slender. Thus he was now yoked again to the doubts and suspicions which he had utterly renounced. Having found the floor before the bed untrodden, he imagined that he was free of misdemeanour from his nephew. But again, finding the Queen and his bed all bloody, he was at once assailed by dark thoughts and ill humour, as always happens to waverers. Amid these doubts he did not know what to do. He believed one thing, he believed another. He did not know what he wanted or what he should believe. He had just found Love's guilty traces in his bed, though not before it, and was thus told the truth and denied it. With these two, truth and untruth, he was deceived. He suspected both alternatives, yet both eluded him. He neither wished the two of them guilty, nor wished them free of guilt. This was a cause of lively grief to that waverer.

Mark, lost man that he was, was now weighed down more than ever before by pondering on how he might find a way out and compose his doubts, how he might throw off his load of uncertainty and wean the court from the suspicions with which it was so busy concerning his wife and nephew. He summoned his great nobles, to whom he looked for loyalty, and acquainted them with his troubles. He told them how the rumour had sprung up at court, and that he was much afraid for his marriage and his honour, and he declared that in view of how the allegation against them had been made public and noised about the land, he felt no inclination to show favour to the Queen or to be on terms of intimacy with her till she had publicly vindicated her innocence and conjugal fidelity towards him, and that he was seeking their general advice as to how he could eliminate all doubt concerning her delinquency, one way or the other, in a manner consonant with his honour.

His kinsmen and vassals advised him forthwith to hold a council at London in England and make known his troubles to the clergy, to those shrewd prelates so learned in canon law.

The council was promptly called to meet in London after Whitsun week when May was drawing to a close. A great number of clergy and laymen arrived on the appointed day in answer to the royal summons. And now Mark and Isolde arrived, both weighed down with sorrow and fear—Isolde in great fear of losing her life and her honour, Mark in great sorrow that through his wife Isolde he might cripple his happiness and noble reputation.

When Mark had taken his seat at the council he complained to his great nobles of the vexation to which this slander was subjecting him and begged them earnestly for the sake of God and of their honour, if they had the skill, to devise some remedy whereby he could exact satisfaction and justice for this delict and settle the issue in one sense or another. Many aired their views on this topic, some well, others ill, one man this way, another that.

Then one of the great lords present at the council rose to his feet, a man well fitted by sagacity and age to offer good advice, the Bishop of the Thames, who was old and distinguished in appearance and as grey as he was wise.

"My lord King, hear me," said the bishop, leaning over his crook. "You have summoned us, the nobles of England, into your presence to hear our loyal advice, in dire need of it as you are. I am one of the great nobles, too, Sire. I have my place among them, and am of an age that I may well act on my own responsibility, and say what I have to say. Let each man speak for himself. Your majesty, I will tell you my mind, and if it meets with your approval and pleases you, be persuaded by me and follow my advice.

"My lady Isolde and lord Tristan are suspected of serious transgressions, yet judging by what I have heard, they have not been proved guilty by any sort of evidence. How can you allay this evil suspicion with evil? How can you sentence your nephew and your wife to forfeit their honour or their lives, seeing that they have not been caught in any misdemeanour and very likely never will be? Somebody makes this allegation against Tristan; but he does not attest it on Tristan, as by rights he ought to do. Or someone spreads rumours about Isolde; but that someone cannot prove them. Nevertheless, since the court so strongly suspects that they have misconducted themselves, you must deny the Queen community of bed and board till such time as she can prove her innocence before you and the realm, which knows of this report and busies itself with it daily. For alas, true or false, people's ears are eager for such rumours. Whatever is made common gossip when someone impugns a reputation, whether there be truth or falsehood behind it, it excites our baser feelings. However the matter stands here, whether it be true or not, reports and allegations have been gossiped about to such a point that you have taken offence and the court is scandalized.

"Now this is my advice, Sire: that since madam the Queen has had this fault imputed to her, you summon her here into the presence of us all, so that your indictment and her reply may be heard in such terms as shall please the court."

"I will do so, my lord," answered the King. "What you have said by way of advice appears to me appropriate and acceptable." Isolde was sent for, and she came into the Palace to the council. When she had taken her seat, the grey, wise Bishop of the Thames did as the King had bidden him.

He rose and said: "Lady Isolde, noble Queen, take no offence at what I say—my lord the King has ordered me to be his spokesman and I must obey his command. Now may God be my witness that, if there is anything that will compromise your honour and rob you of your spotless reputation, I shall bring it to light most reluctantly. Would that I might be spared it! My good and gracious Queen, your lord and consort commands me to indict you in respect of a public allegation. Neither he nor I knows whether perhaps someone is paying back a grudge; but your name has been linked with his nephew Tristan's both at court and in the country. If God so will, you shall be innocent and free of this fault, madam. Yet the King views it with suspicion because the court declares it to be so. My lord himself has found nothing but good in you. It is from rumours fostered by the court that he brings suspicion to bear on you, not from any evidence; and he indicts you so that kinsmen and vassals can hear the case and discover whether, with our joint advice, he can perhaps root out this slander. Now I think it would be wise if you were to speak and account to him for this suspicion, in the presence of us all."

Since it was for her to speak, Isolde, the sharp-witted Queen rose in person, and said: "My lord Bishop, you Barons here, and the Court! You shall all know this for a fact: whenever I am called upon to answer for my lord's dishonour and for myself, I shall most assuredly answer, now and at all times. You lords, I am well aware that this gross misbehaviour has been imputed to me for the past year, at court and in the country. But it is well known to you all that there is none so blessed by heaven as to be able to live to everybody's liking all the time, and not have vices attributed to him. And so I am not surprised that I too am the victim of such talk. There was no chance that I should be passed over and not be accused of improper conduct, for I am far from home and can never ask here for my friends and relations. Unfortunately, there is scarcely a soul in this place who will feel disgraced with me—rich or poor, you are each one of you very ready to believe in my depravity! If I knew what to do or what remedy there were for it, so that I could persuade you all of my innocence in accordance with my lord's honour, I would gladly do so. Now what do you advise me to do? Whatever procedure you subject me to, I gladly accept it so that your suspicions may be set aside, yet more, by far, in order to vindicate my lord's honour and mine."

"I am content to leave it there, your Highness," answered the King. "If I am to have satisfaction from you as you have proposed to us, give us your surety. Step forward at once and bind yourself to the ordeal of the red-hot iron, as we shall instruct you here." The Queen complied. She promised to submit to their judgement in six weeks' time in Carleon in accordance with the terms laid down for her. Then the King, his peers, and indeed the whole council withdrew.

Isolde, however, remained alone with her fears and her sorrows—fears and sorrows that gave her little peace. She feared for her honour and she was harassed by the secret anxiety that she would have to whitewash her falseness. With these two cares she did not know what to do: she confided them to Christ, the Merciful, who is helpful when one is in trouble. With prayer and fasting she commended all her anguish most urgently to Him. Meanwhile she had propounded to her secret self a ruse which presumed very far upon her Maker's courtesy. She wrote and sent a letter to Tristan which told him to come to Carleon early on the appointed day when he could seize his chance, as she was about to land, and to watch out for her on the shore.

This was duly done. Tristan repaired there in pilgrim's garb. He had stained and blistered his face and disfigured his body and clothes. When Mark and Isolde arrived and made land there, the Queen saw him and recognized him at once. And when the ship put to shore she commanded that, if the pilgrim were hale and strong enough, they were to ask him in God's name to carry her across from the ship's gangway to the harbour; for at such a time, she said, she was averse to being carried by a knight. Accordingly, they all called out, "Come here, good man, and carry my lady ashore!" He did as he was bidden, he took his lady the Queen in his arms and carried her back to land. Isolde lost no time in whispering to him that when he reached the shore he was to tumble headlong to the ground with her, whatever might become of him.

This Tristan duly did. When he came to the shore and stepped on to dry land the wayfarer dropped to the ground, falling as if by accident, so that the fall brought him to rest lying in the Queen's lap and arms. Without a moment's delay a crowd of attendants ran up with sticks and staves and were about to set upon him. "No, no, stop!" said Isolde. "The pilgrim has every excuse—he is feeble and infirm, and fell accidentally!" They now thanked her and warmly commended her, and praised her in their hearts for not punishing the poor man harshly. "Would it be surprising if this pilgrim wanted to frolic with me?" asked Isolde with a smile. They set this down in her favour as a mark of her virtue and breeding, and many spoke highly in praise of her. Mark observed the whole incident and heard various things that were said. "I do not know how it will end," continued Isolde. "You have all clearly seen that I cannot lawfully maintain that no man other than Mark found his way into my arms or had his couch in my lap." With much banter about this bold rogue they set out towards Carleon.

There were many barons, priests, and knights and a great crowd of commoners there. The bishops and prelates who were saying mass and sanctifying the proceedings quickly dispatched their business. The iron was laid in the fire. The good Queen Isolde had given away her silver, her gold, her jewellery, and all the clothes and palfreys she had, to win God's favour, so that He might overlook her very real trespasses and restore her to her honour.

Meanwhile Isolde had arrived at the minster and had heard mass with deep devotion. The wise, good lady's worship was most pious: she wore a rough hair-shirt next her skin and above it a short woollen robe which failed to reach to her slender ankles by more than an hand's breadth. Her sleeves were folded back right to the elbow; her arms and feet were bare. Many eyes observed her, many hearts felt sorrow and pity for her. Her garment and her figure attracted much attention. And now the reliquary was brought, on which she was to swear. She was ordered forthwith to make known to God and the world how guilty she was of the sins that were alleged against her. Isolde had surrendered her life and honour utterly to God's mercy. She stretched out her hand to take the oath upon the relics with fearful heart, as well she might, and rendered up heart and hand to the grace of God, for Him to keep and preserve.

Now there were a number present who were so very unmannerly as to wish to phrase the Queen's oath in a way that aimed at her downfall. That bitter-gall, Marjodoc the Steward, plotted her ruin in many devious ways, but there were no few who treated her courteously and gave things a favourable turn for her. Thus they wrangled from side to side as to what her oath should be. One man wished her ill, another well, as people do in such matters.

"My lord King," said the Queen, "my oath must be worded to your pleasure and satisfaction, whatever any of them says. Therefore see for yourself whether, in my acts and utterances, I frame my oath to your liking. These people give too much advice. Hear the oath which I mean to swear: 'That no man in the world had carnal knowledge of me or lay in my arms or beside me but you, always excepting the poor pilgrim whom, with your own eyes, you saw lying in my arms.' I can offer no purgation concerning him. So help me God and all the Saints that be, to a happy and auspicious outcome to this judgement! If I have not said enough, Sire, I will modify my oath one way or another as you instruct me."

"I think this will suffice, ma'am, so far as I can see," answered the King. "Now take the iron in your hand and, within the terms that you have named to us, may God help you in your need!"

"Amen!" said fair Isolde. In the name of God she laid hold of the iron, carried it, and was not burned.

Thus it was made manifest and confirmed to all the world that Christ in His great virtue is pliant as a windblown sleeve. He falls into place and clings, whichever way you try Him, closely and smoothly, as He is bound to do. He is at the beck of every heart for honest deeds or fraud. Be it deadly earnest or a game, He is just as you would have Him. This was amply revealed in the facile Queen. She was saved by her guile and by the doctored oath that went flying up to God, with the result that she redeemed her honour and was again much beloved of her lord Mark, and was praised, lauded, and esteemed among the people. Whenever the King observed that her heart was set on anything, he sanctioned it at once. He accorded her honour and rich gifts. His heart and mind were centred only upon her, wholly and without guile.

His doubts and suspicions had been set aside once more.

4
Authority, Conflict, and Repression

The Mendicant Orders and the Attack against Heresy

Writing to the Corinthians, Paul stated what would become an unassailable truth for medieval men and women: "there must be also heresies, that they which are approved may be made manifest among you" (1 Cor. 11:19). Indeed, heresy was of great importance in early Christianity in prodding churchmen to define their teachings, while they were led to condemn dissident beliefs and practices. Heresy was an obstinate refusal to give up one's private convictions when they conflicted with the teachings of the Church. In the words of the English theologian Robert Grosseteste (ca. 1175–1253), "a heresy is an opinion chosen by human perception contrary to holy Scripture, publicly avowed and obstinately defended."

The spread of heresy in the twelfth century presented a greater threat to religious unity than it had for centuries. Not content with self-abnegation, heretics were now religious enthusiasts, who employed preaching and sought popular support among laymen, to spread their own beliefs concerning pastoral care, the social implications of the Gospel, and the relationship between Church and society. Many heretics insisted that poverty was necessary to the ideal Christian life and to salvation—an idea rooted in the fundamental teachings of Christianity as well as being a basic tenet of monasticism. No monk was allowed to own any property; everything belonged to the community as a whole. Yet, the wealth and what was perceived as the luxurious style of life of the monastic orders as well as of the secular clergy were an affront to innumerable religious enthusiasts, whose zeal for poverty, chastity, preaching, and the communal life led them to reject the entire structure of the established Church.

The most extreme of the religious enthusiasts were the Cathars. Their name derives from the Greek word *katharoi*, meaning the pure. They were also called Albigensians after the southern French town Albi. They were a western branch of the Bogomils, a dualist sect which originated in Bulgaria in the tenth century. A description of their beliefs is provided in a confession made in Milan sometime between 1176 and 1190 by Bonacursus, a convert from the Cathars (document 39). The Waldensians or the Poor Men of Lyon accepted the fundamental teachings of Christianity, but insisted that the Church had lost its authority, since it no longer adhered to those teachings. The leader of this heresy was Peter Waldo (d. 1217), who began his career as a prosperous merchant and usurer in Lyon. An account of the origins of the Waldensians, based on firsthand testimony from those who knew Peter Waldo, is offered by Stephen of Bourbon, a Dominican inquisitor of the early thirteenth century (document 40). Inquisitorial procedure and practice are detailed by the Dominican Bernard Gui (ca. 1261–1331), in his *The Conduct of the Inquisition of Heretical Depravity* (document 45) completed in 1323–1324. This work is based on the author's extensive experience as an inquisitor in the diocese of Toulouse. An able administrator and prolific writer, Bernard Gui is regarded as one of the most notable medieval inquisitors.

Zeal for religious perfection also animated the two great orders of mendicant friars, the Order of Friars Preachers (Dominicans) and the Order of Friars Minor (Franciscans). Their zeal was, however, employed by the papacy in the struggle against heresy. An account of the founding of the Order of Friars Preachers by Dominic and his confrontation with the Cathars is vividly presented by Jordan of Saxony (document 41), who succeeded Dominic as second master of the order in 1221. Jordan's historical testimony is extremely valuable, since Dominic himself wrote almost nothing. Dominic's first regulations for his order were revised after his death in 1228. These were later codified (document 42) by Raymond of Peñafort, a distinguished canon lawyer, who served as master-general of the order from 1238 to 1240.

The story of the conversion of Francis of Assisi (1182–1226) from a gay and carefree life to one devoted to "Lady Poverty" is graphically told by Thomas of Celano, who joined Francis and his companions around 1215. It was Pope Gregory IX who commissioned Thomas to write the first biography (document 44) of Francis for the purpose of commemorating his elevation to sainthood in 1228. The ideals of what eventually became the most popular and largest religious order in Europe are contained in Francis's *Rule* (document 43), which was approved by Pope Honorius III in 1223. Francis's *Testament* (document 43), composed near the end of his life, was revered by his followers for its expression of spirituality.

39. Bonacursus, *Description of Cathars* (1176–1190)

<u>1176–90</u>

An Exposure of the Heresy of the Cathars, Made before the People of Milan by Bonacursus, Who Formerly Was One of Their Masters

In the name of our Lord Jesus Christ.

Our Lord Jesus Christ, who always and everywhere protects and guides His Church and confirms and preserves the Catholic faith, desiring in His holy mercy to make public and expose the error of those who are called Cathars, compassionately illumined a certain teacher among them, Bonacursus by name, by the grace of His Holy Spirit and restored him by grace to the bosom of Holy Mother Church, for which we give boundless praise to God and all the saints. Their heresy is, indeed, not only terrifying but is, truly, too frightful and execrable to speak of or hear about. For some of them say that God created all the elements, others say that the devil created these elements; but their common opinion is that the devil divided the elements. They state also that the same devil made Adam from dust of the earth and with very great force imprisoned in him a certain angel of light, of whom they think it was said in the Gospel, "A certain man went down from Jerusalem to Jericho," and so on. They say that the devil made Eve, with whom he lay, and from this union Cain was born. On discovering this, Adam came to know Eve and she bore Abel, whom Cain killed; and of the latter's blood, they declare dogs are born, and are, for that reason, so faithful to men. The union of Adam and Eve was, in their words, the forbidden fruit. They put forward another error, which is that all things that have been made—in the air, in the sea, and on the earth, such as men and animate and inanimate things—were made by the devil. From the daughters of Eve and demons were born giants, who learned from the demons, their fathers, that the devil had created all things. Hence, the devil, sorrowing at their knowledge thereof, said, "It repenteth me that I have made man"; and Noah, because he had not that knowledge, was delivered from the flood and was told by the devil, as they say, to "Go into the ark." They say that Enoch was translated by the same devil.

Again, they assert that whatever things were done or said by Abraham, Isaac, or Jacob were said and done by a demon. They also aver that it was the devil who appeared to Moses in the bush and spoke to him. Moreover,

From *Heresies of the High Middle Ages*, translated and edited by Walter Wakefield and A. P. Evans (New York: Columbia University Press, 1969), pp. 171–73. Footnotes deleted. © 1969 by Columbia University Press. Reprinted by permission of the publisher.

the miracles performed by Moses in Pharaoh's presence, the fact that the children of Israel passed through the Red Sea and were led into the Promised Land, God's speaking to Moses, and the Law which God gave to him—all these, they say and believe were the work of this same devil, their master. In regard to the utterances of the holy prophets, they affirm that some of the prophecies were disclosed by the Spirit of God, others by a wicked spirit; hence the Apostle: "Prove all things; hold fast that which is good." They condemn David for adultery and murder; they say Elijah was carried off in a chariot by the devil. They assert that the angel sent to Zacharias by God was an angel of the devil. They also condemn John [the Baptist] himself, than whom none is greater, according to the word of the Lord. Why? Because the Lord says in the Gospel, "He that is the lesser in the kingdom of God is greater than he," and because he [John] doubted Christ by saying: "Art thou he that art to come, or look we for another?" Mary, the mother of our Lord, they believe to have been born of woman alone, not of man. Of Christ, they declare that He did not have a living body, that He did not eat, or drink, or do anything else as men do, but that it only seemed that he did. They say that the thief on the left hand is in hell. They do not believe that the body of Christ rose again or was taken into heaven, nor in the resurrection of the flesh, nor that Christ descended into hell. They do not think the Son equal to the Father, for He said, "The Father is greater than I." They say that the Cross is the sign of the beast of which one reads in the Apocalypse and is an abomination in a holy place. They assert that the Blessed Sylvester was the Antichrist of whom one reads in the Epistle: "The son of perdition," is he "who is lifted up above all that is called God." From that day, they say, the Church was lost. They believe that in matrimony no one can attain salvation.

They condemn all the doctors—that is, they damn Ambrose, Gregory, Augustine, Jerome and the others all together. If anyone shall have eaten meat, eggs, or cheese, or anything of an animal nature, [they believe] he consumed damnation for himself. They think that the Holy Spirit can in no way be received in the baptism of water, nor do they believe that any visible substance can by any means be changed into the body of Christ. They believe, also, that anyone who takes an oath will be damned, and they think that no one can be saved except by a certain imposition of hands which they call baptism and the renewal of the Holy Spirit. They hold that the devil himself is the sun, Eve the moon; and each month, they say, they commit adultery, like a man with some harlot. All the stars they believe to be demons. Finally, they say that no one can attain salvation outside of their sect. Lo, such is the heresy of the Cathars, from which God keep all Catholics. Amen.

40. Peter Waldo, *Accounts of His Conversion and Translation of Scripture* (1173–1184)

1173

In the course of the same year (that is, 1173) of our Lord's incarnation, there was at Lyons in Gaul a certain citizen named Waldes, who had amassed a great fortune through the wicked practice of lending at interest. One Sunday he had been attracted by the crowd gathered around a minstrel and had been touched by the latter's words. Wishing to talk to him more fully, he took him to his home, for the minstrel was at a place in his narrative in which Alexis had come peacefully to a happy end in his father's house.

On the following morning, the said citizen hastened to the school of theology to seek counsel for his soul's welfare and, when he had been instructed in the many ways of attaining to God, asked the master which was the most sure and perfect way of all. The master replied to him in the words of the Lord: "If thou wilt be perfect, go sell what thou hast," and so on. Waldes came to his wife and offered her the choice of keeping for herself all his property in either movable goods or real estate, that is, in lands, waters, woods, meadows, houses, rents, vineyards, mills, and ovens. Though greatly saddened by the necessity, she chose the real estate. From his movable goods, he made restitution to those from whom he had profited unjustly; another considerable portion of his wealth he bestowed upon his two small daughters, whom without their mother's knowledge he confided to the order of Fontevrault; but the greatest part he disbursed for the needs of the poor.

Now, a very severe famine was then raging throughout all Gaul and Germany. Wherefore Waldes, the citizen mentioned above, on three days a week from Pentecost to St. Peter in Chains gave bountifully of bread, vegetables, and meat to all who came to him. On the feast of the Assumption of the Blessed Virgin, as he was in the streets distributing an appreciable sum of money among the poor, he cried out, "No man can serve two masters, God and mammon." Then all the citizens hurried to him, supposing that he had lost his senses, but he climbed to a commanding spot and addressed them thus: "My friends and fellow townsmen! Indeed, I am not, as you think, insane, but I have taken vengeance on my enemies who held me in

From *Heresies of the High Middle Ages*, translated and edited by Walter Wakefield and A. P. Evans (New York: Columbia University Press, 1969), pp. 200–203, 208–11. Footnotes deleted. © 1969 by Columbia University Press. Reprinted by permission of the publisher.

bondage to them, so that I was always more anxious about money than about God and served the creature more than the Creator. I know that a great many find fault with me for having done this publicly. But I did it for myself and also for you: for myself, so that they who may henceforth see me in possession of money may think I am mad; in part also for you, so that you may learn to fix your hope in God and to trust not in riches."

As he was leaving the church on the following day, he asked a certain citizen, one of his former associates, to give him food for the love of God. The latter took him to his home and said, "As long as I live I will give you the necessities of life." His wife, on learning of this incident, was no little saddened. Like one beside herself, she rushed into the presence of the archbishop of the city to complain that her husband had begged his bread from another rather than from her. This situation moved all who were present to tears, including the archbishop himself. At the archbishop's bidding, the citizen brought his guest [Waldes] with him into his presence, whereupon the woman, clinging to her husband's garments, cried, "Is it not better, O my husband, that I, rather than strangers, should atone for my sins through alms to you?" And from that time forth, by command of the archbishop, he was not permitted in that city to take food with others than his wife.

1177

Waldes, the citizen of Lyons whom we have already mentioned, having taken a vow to the God of heaven henceforth and throughout his life never to possess either gold or silver or to take thought for the morrow, began to gather associates in his way of life. They followed his example in giving their all to the poor and became devotees of voluntary poverty. Little by little, both publicly and privately, they began to declaim against their own sins and those of others.

Stephen of Bourbon on Waldenses

1173–84 (written after 1249)

Now, the Waldenses are so named from the founder of this heresy, who was named Waldes. They are also called the Poor of Lyons because it was in that city that they entered upon their life of poverty. They also refer to themselves as the Poor in Spirit because of what the Lord said, "Blessed are the poor in spirit." Verily, they are poor in spirit—in spiritual blessings and in the Holy Spirit.

The sect began in this way, according to what I have heard from several persons who observed its earliest members and from a certain priest,

named Bernard Ydros, in the city of Lyons, who was himself quite respected and well-to-do and a friend of our brethren [the Dominicans].
When he was a young man and a scribe, he was employed by Waldes to
write in the vernacular the first books possessed by those people, while a
certain grammarian, Stephen of Anse by name—whom I often encountered—translated and dictated them to him. Stephen, a prebendary of the
cathedral of Lyons, subsequently came to a sudden death by falling from
the upper story of a house which he was building.

There was in that city a rich man named Waldes, who was not well educated, but on hearing the Gospels was anxious to learn more precisely what
was in them. He made a contract with these priests, the one to translate
them into the vernacular and the other to write them down at his dictation.
This they did, not only for many books of the Bible but also for many passages from the Fathers, grouped by topics, which are called Sentences.
When this citizen had pored over these texts and learned them by heart, he
resolved to devote himself to evangelical perfection, just as the apostles
had pursued it. Selling all his possessions, in contempt of the world he
broadcast his money to the poor and presumptuously arrogated to himself
the office of the apostles. Preaching in the streets and the broad ways the
Gospels and those things that he had learned by heart, he drew to himself
many men and women that they might do the same, and he strengthened
them in the Gospel. He also sent out persons even of the basest occupations
to preach in the nearby villages. Men and women alike, stupid and unedu-
cated, they wandered through the villages, entered homes, preached in the
squares and even in the churches, and induced others to do likewise.

Now, when they had spread error and scandal everywhere as a result of
their rashness and ignorance, they were summoned before the archbishop
of Lyons, whose name was John, and were forbidden by him to concern
themselves with expounding the Scriptures or with preaching. They, in
turn, fell back on the reply made by the apostles. Their leader, assuming
the role of Peter, replied with his words to the chief priests: "We ought to
obey God, rather than men"—the God who had commanded the apostles to
"Preach the gospel to every creature." He asserted this as though the Lord
had said to them what He said to the apostles; the latter, however, did not
presume to preach until they had been clothed with power from on high,
until they had been illuminated by the best and fullest knowledge, and had
received the gift of tongues. But these persons, that is to say, Waldes and
his fellows, fell first into disobedience by their presumption and their usurpation of the apostolic office, then into contumacy, and finally under the
sentence of excommunication. After they were driven out of these parts
and were summoned to the council which was held in Rome before the
Lateran Council, they remained obdurate and were finally judged to be

schismatics. Thereafter, since they mingled in Provence and Lombardy with other heretics whose errors they imbibed and propagated, they have been adjudged by the Church most hostile, infectious, and dangerous heretics, who wander everywhere, assuming the appearance but not the reality of holiness and sincerity. The more dangerous the more they lie hidden from sight, they conceal themselves under various disguises and occupations. Once there was captured a leader of their sect who carried with him the trappings of various crafts by which he could transform himself like Proteus. If he were sought in one disguise and realized the fact, he would change to another. Sometimes he wore the garb and marks of a pilgrim, at others he bore the staff and irons of a penitent, at still other times he pretended to be a cobbler or a barber or a harvester, and so on. Others do the same. This sect began about the year of our Lord 1170, in the episcopacy of John, called "of the Fair Hands," archbishop of Lyons.

41. Jordan of Saxony, *On the Beginnings of the Order of Preachers* (ca. 1200–1228)

Prologue

To all the brethren of the Order of Preachers, sons of grace that they are and co-heirs of glory, brother Jordan, their useless servant, wishes health and joy in their holy profession.

Many of the brethren have been asking about the founding of the Order of Preachers, which God's providence has raised up as a remedy for the perils of these latter days, and how it all began; they want to know who the first brethren of our Order were and what they were like, how they increased in number and how they were made "strong in grace." Prompted by such queries, I have for some time now been questioning the brethren who were involved in the very beginnings of the Order, who were able to watch and listen to the venerable servant of Christ, Master Dominic, the first founder of this Order, its first Master and its first member, whose mind communed devoutly with God and the angels even while he was living in this mortal flesh, surrounded by sinners; he kept God's commandments and zealously followed the counsels, serving his eternal Maker in every way he knew how to and was able to, and the innocence and heavenly purity of his way of life shone like a beacon in the grim darkness of this world.

Now that I have gone systematically through all this material, I have

From *Jordan of Saxony, On the Beginnings of the Order of Preachers*, Dominican Sources, translated and edited by Simon Tugwell, O.P. (Chicago: Parable Press, 1982), pp. 1–14, 24–31. Some footnotes deleted.

decided to write it down, so that the sons who are to be born to the Order in the future will not be ignorant of how it began, and will not be frustrated in their desire to find out about it, when there is no longer anyone there, because of the passage of time, to give them any reliable information. I know that I was not one of the very first brethren, but I have lived with some of them, and I was acquainted with the blessed Dominic both before and after I joined the Order, and indeed I knew him quite intimately, because I went to confession to him and it was at his wish that I became a deacon, and it was only four years after the founding of the Order that I received the habit. So, as I say, I have decided to write down both what I observed and heard for myself, and what I have learned from the earliest brethren, about the beginings of the Order and about the life and miracles of our blessed father, Dominic, and also about some of the other brethren, as they occur to my mind.

So, my dearest brothers and children in Christ, please accept this book, which has been put together as best I can, to encourage and inspire you, and receive it with devotion, and, when you read about the friars' first fervour of charity, strive eagerly to imitate it.

Chapter 1

There lived in Spain a venerable man named Diego, the bishop of Osma, who was renowned for his knowledge of the bible and for the worldly respectability of his birth, but who was particularly distinguished for the remarkable integrity of his character and behaviour. His love was so totally given to God that he renounced himself and sought only what belongs to Jesus Christ, turning his mind and will especially to finding some way of winning many souls for Christ. He was determined that his Master should receive back his talent with generous interest. So he sought out, wherever he could, men who were commended by integrity of life and character and, by any means at his disposal, he tried to draw such men to himself and to give them benefices in the church which he ruled.

If any of his subjects were sluggish in their desire for holiness, being more interested in worldly things, he urged them in words and inspired them by his example to adopt a more commendable pattern of behaviour and a more serious form of religious life. As part of this programme, he did his best, by means of frequent exhortations and unceasing encouragement, to persuade his canons to agree to follow the Rule of St. Augustine and to live as canons regular, and, as a result of his efforts, he succeeded in winning their minds to his purpose, though some of them resisted him.

During his time there lived a young man called Dominic, who was born in the same diocese, in a small town called Caleruega. From his earliest years Dominic had been brought up with loving care by his family, especially a certain archpriest who was an uncle of his. The earliest education they procured for him was in the practices of the church, so that, as one whom God had foreseen as a "vessel of election," he would absorb in childhood, like the proverbial "new-made pot," an odour of sanctity which he would never thereafter lose.

Afterwards he was sent to Palencia to be formed in the liberal arts, because there was a thriving arts faculty there at this time. When he thought he had learned enough of the arts, he abandoned them and fled to the study of theology, as if he was afraid to waste his limited time on less fruitful study. He began to develop a passionate appetite for God's words, finding them "sweeter than honey to his mouth."

He spent four years in these sacred studies, and throughout the whole period his eagerness to imbibe the streams of holy scripture was so intense and so unremitting that he spent whole nights almost without sleep, so untiring was his desire to study; and the truth which his ears received he stored away in the deepest recesses of his mind and guarded in his retentive memory. His natural abilities made it easy for him to take things in, and his love and piety fertilized whatever he learned, so that it brought forth fruit in the form of saving works. The verdict of Truth himself pronounces him blessed: as he said in the gospel, "Blessed are those who hear the word of God and keep it." There are two ways of keeping the word of God: one is to retain the word in our memories, once we have heard it, the other is to put it into practice and display it in action. There is no doubt that the second way is better, just as it is better to keep seed by planting it in the earth than by hoarding it in a box. Now this fortunate servant of God, Dominic, was adept at keeping God's word in both ways: his memory was a kind of "barn" for God, which God "filled to overflowing" with crops of every kind, and his external behaviour and actions broadcast publicly the treasure that lay hidden in his holy breast.

Because he accepted the Lord's commandments so warmly, and because his will welcomed the voice of his Lover with such loyalty and pleasure, the God of all knowledge gave him an increase of grace, so that he became capable of receiving more than the milk of beginners, and was able to penetrate the mysteries of difficult theological questions with the humble understanding of his heart, and to swallow easily enough the testing promotion to more solid food.

He was of a good disposition from the time he was a baby, and his remarkable childhood promised that great things could be expected from him when he grew up. He did not join in with other children's games, nor did he associate himself with those who "walk frivolously"; like quiet Jacob, he avoided the wanderings of Esau, preferring to remain in the lap of his mother, the church, and the homely tents of sanctity and repose. Looking at him, you would have said that he was young and old at once; his lack of years proclaimed him a child, but the maturity of his way of life and the stability of his character were more suggestive of old age. He spurned the enticements of a dissolute world, to walk in the way of innocence. To the end of his life he preserved the glory of virginity intact for the Lord, who loves purity.

While he was still a child, God, for whom the future is no secret, granted a sign that remarkable things were to be hoped from him. His mother saw him in a vision, with the moon on his forehead, signifying that he would one day be given to the world as a light for the nations, to give light to those who sit in darkness and in the shadow of death. In the outcome, this was proved to be a true prediction.

While he was a student at Palencia, there was a severe famine throughout almost the whole of Spain. He was deeply moved by the plight of the poor, and resolved, in the warmth of his compassion, to do something which would both accord with the Lord's counsels and do as much as possible to remedy the needs of the poor who were dying. So he sold the books which he possessed, although he needed them very much, and established an almonry where the poor could be fed. In this way "open-handed he gave to the poor." His exemplary kindness so moved some of the other theologians and masters that they too began to give more lavish alms, seeing their own sluggish parsimony shown up by the young man's generosity.

While the man of God was "planning his pilgrimage in his heart" like this and progressing from strength to strength, daily surpassing himself in goodness, as everyone could see, because his innocence of life shone out like the morning star in the midst of the clouds, making everybody marvel at him, his fame reached the bishop of Osma, who carefully enquired into the truth of what was being said about him, and then had him sent for, to make him a canon regular in his church.

He at once became conspicuous like a brilliant constellation among his fellow canons. He was the lowliest of them all in his humility of heart, but he was their leader in holiness. For all of them he was "a fragrance of life leading them on to life" and "incense on a summer's day." The brethren were amazed that he attained to such an unusual height of religious perfection so quickly and they appointed him subprior, so that his superior position would attract everybody's attention and they would all be led on by his example. Like "a fruitful olive-tree," like "a cypress which rears itself up to heaven," he haunted the church by day and by night, devoting himself ceaselessly to prayer. Claiming for himself the leisure for contemplation, he hardly ever showed himself outside the confines of the monastery. God had given him a special grace to weep for sinners and for the afflicted and oppressed; he bore their distress in the inmost shrine of his compassion, and the warm sympathy he felt for them in his heart spilled over in the tears which flowed from his eyes.

It was his very frequent practice to spend the night at his prayers, praying to his Father, "with his door shut." During these prayers, he sometimes felt such groaning in his heart that he could not stop himself from bursting out loudly, so that even at a distance people could hear him roaring and crying. He had a special prayer which he often made to God, that God would grant him true charity, which would be effective in caring for and winning the salvation of men; he thought he would only really be a member of Christ's Body when he could spend himself utterly with all his strength in the winning of souls, just as the Lord Jesus Christ, the Saviour of us all, gave himself up entirely for our salvation.

He read and loved a book entitled "Conferences of the Fathers," which deals with the vices and with the whole matter of spiritual perfection, and in this book he strove to explore the ways of salvation and to follow them with all the power of his mind. With the help of grace, this book brought him to the highest purity of conscience and to considerable enlightenment in contemplation and to a veritable peak of perfection.

Chapter 2

While Dominic was being cosseted like this in the embrace of the beautiful Rachel, Leah began impatiently to claim him for herself, wanting him to come in to her so that she could silence the people who criticized her for her bleary eyes by showing how fertile she could be in bearing children.

King Alfonso of Castile was wanting at this time to arrange a marriage between his son, Fernando, and a noble lady from the Marches. For this reason, he approached the bishop of Osma to ask if he would act as his agent in the matter. The bishop accepted the commission, and quickly gathered together a respectable entourage, such as the holiness of his position required, and set off, taking the man of God, Dominic, the subprior of his church, with him.

In time they came to Toulouse. When the bishop learned that the people in that neighbourhood had been heretics for some time, he was sincerely upset and sorry for all the many souls who were being so wretchedly deceived. During the night which they spent in lodgings in Toulouse, the subprior argued powerfully and passionately with their host, who was a heretic, and at last brought him back to the faith, by the help of the Spirit of God, because the heretic was unable to withstand "the wisdom and Spirit which was addressing him."

After that, they left Toulouse and went to their destination, where the girl was, arriving there at last after a great many difficulties. They explained why they had come and obtained the girl's consent, and then returned quickly to the king. The bishop told him of their success and of the girl's reply.

The king accordingly decided to send him back again, with a more splendid entourage, to fetch the girl with all due honour, so that she could be married to his son. So the bishop undertook the difficult journey for a second time.

When he reached the Marches, though, he found that the girl had died in the meantime. However, the journey was not wasted, because God was planning to make use of it for something far more profitable. As we can see from what happened afterwards, he was taking the opportunity of this journey to arrange the beginnings of a much more wonderful marriage, between God and souls, in which souls throughout the church would be joined to everlasting salvation and recalled in various ways from various kinds of sin and error.

The bishop sent a messenger back to the king, and then made use of the occasion to hurry off with his clergy to the papal court. As soon as he came into the presence of pope Innocent, he begged to be allowed to resign his see, if possible. Over and over again he pleaded his own incompetence and argued that the enormous dignity of the job was beyond his powers; he also opened his mind to the pope about a purpose he had conceived of devoting all his energies to the conversion of the Saracens, should the pope allow his resignation. But the pope refused, and would not even accept his suggestion that he might be permitted to go and preach to the Saracens while remaining a bishop. This was, of course, due to a hidden purpose of God, who had destined the energies of this great man for a rich harvest of salvation in another direction.

On his way back home, the bishop visited Citeaux, and when he saw the way of life of all God's servants there, he was drawn by the excellence of their religious observance and put on the monastic habit. Then he hurried on to return to Spain, taking with him some monks from whose teaching he could learn their pattern of life. He had no inkling of the obstacle which was going to prevent him, by God's providence, from hurrying home as he intended.

Chapter 3

Pope Innocent had recently sent twelve Cistercian abbots and one papal legate to preach the faith against the Albigensian heretics, and these men were holding a council with the archbishops and bishops and other prelates of the region, to discuss the best way of carrying out their commission effectively. During their meeting the bishop of Osma happened to pass through Montpellier, where the council was being held. They received him with honour, and, since they knew that he was a holy, judicious and just man, and that he was zealous for the faith, they asked for his advice.

He was a prudent man, and he had some understanding of the ways of God, so he enquired about the practices and behaviour of the heretics. Learning how the heretics were enticing people into their faithless party by arguing and preaching and by a feigned example of holiness, and seeing how this contrasted with the missionaries' enormous supply of provisions and horses and clothing, he said, "No, brethren, I do not think that you are setting about things in the right way. In my opinion you will never be able to bring these people back to the faith just by talking to them, because they are much more inclined to be swayed by example. Look how the heretics urge their ways on the simple people by displaying an outward show of holiness, by feigning an example of evangelical austerity and asceticism. If the example you give is the opposite of all this, you will build little and perhaps destroy what is already there, without ever convincing them. Use a nail to drive out a nail. Chase off their feigned holiness with true religious life. The imposing appearance of the false apostles can only be shown up for what it is by manifest humility. Paul found himself obliged to play the fool and list his genuine virtues and show off all the hardships and hazards of his life, in order to rebut the conceit of people who were boasting of the meritoriousness of their lives."

They asked him, "So what do you advise us to do, good father?" He replied, "Do what you see me doing." At once the Spirit of the Lord came upon him, and he summoned his companions and told them to return to Osma with his horses and goods and all the various kinds of provisions that he had brought with him. He only kept a few of his clergy with him. His intention, he told them, was to stay on in that country to spread the faith.

One of those whom he kept behind was Dominic, his subprior, for whom he had a high regard and a warm affection. This Dominic was the first founder and the first member of the Order of Preachers, and from that time onward he was no longer called "subprior," but "brother Dominic." And "Dominic" indeed he was, because he was "kept by the Lord" in innocence of sin, and because he "kept the Lord's will" with all his might.

The abbots listened to the bishop's advice, and, inspired by his example, they agreed to adopt a similar policy themselves. They sent back to their monasteries everything that they had brought with them, except for the books which they would need for the celebration of the Office and for study and, should the opportunity arise, for purposes of debate. They accepted the bishop as their superior and as the head of the whole enterprise, and set off on foot and without provisions to proclaim the faith in voluntary poverty.

When the heretics saw this, they launched a counter-offensive of more insistent preaching.

Frequent debates were held, at Pamiers, Lavaur, Montréal and Fanjeaux. Judges were appointed to pronounce on the outcome of these debates, and, on the days fixed for them, rulers and knights and women and the ordinary people assembled, all wanting to listen to the arguments over the faith.

On one occasion a famous debate was held at Fanjeaux, for which a large crowd of believers and unbelievers was assembled. Several of the believers had composed tracts containing arguments and authorities to support the faith. When these were all examined, the one which was considered best and was most generally approved of was one by the blessed Dominic, so this was the one chosen to be submitted to the three judges who had been appointed, with the agreement of all the parties concerned, to decide the debate. The heretics too had written a tract, which was also to be submitted. Whichever side submitted the book which the judges ruled to be more reasonable, the faith of that side was to be considered the winner.

There was a long verbal tussle, but the judges still could not agree on a verdict in favour of either party. Eventually they had the idea of throwing both books into the fire. Should either of them chance not to be burned, that one was to be regarded as undoubtedly containing the true faith.

A big fire was lit, and both the books were thrown in. The heretics' book burned up immediately, but the other one, the one written by the man of God, Dominic, not merely remained unharmed by the flames, it actually leaped a long way out of the fire in the sight of them all. They threw it in again, and it jumped out again. When the same thing happened a third time, this plainly proved both the truth of the faith and the holiness of the book's author.

The character of the man of God, bishop Diego, was so radiantly attractive that he won the affection even of unbelievers and he touched the hearts of everyone with whom he came into contact, so that the heretics said of him that it was impossible for such a man not to be predestined for eternal life. They surmised that perhaps he had been sent to that part of the world precisely in order to learn the doctrine of the true faith from them!

At a place called Prouille, between Fanjeaux and Montréal, he established a monastery to receive certain noble women whose parents had been forced by poverty to entrust them to the heretics to be educated and brought up. To this day the handmaids of Christ there offer acceptable service to their Maker, leading vigorously holy lives, in outstanding innocence and purity; a life such as theirs is conducive to salvation for those who lead it, an example to others, a joy to the angels, and pleasing to God.

Bishop Diego exercised his ministry of preaching for two years, but at the end of this time he decided to return to Spain, to avoid incurring the charge of neglecting his own church if he stayed away any longer. After visiting his church, he intended to come back, bringing some money with him to finish building his monastery for sisters; he also wanted, with the pope's permission, to ordain some men in that region who would be suitable as preachers, whose job it would be to keep hammering away at the errors of the heretics and tirelessly to support the truth of the faith.

He left brother Dominic in charge of the spiritual government of those who remained behind, because he knew him to be a man genuinely full of the Spirit. In temporal affairs, William Claret of Pamiers was to be in charge, it being understood that he was to give an account to brother Dominic of everything that he did.

So the bishop took leave of the brethren and set off on foot. After passing through Castile, he arrived at Osma. But a few days later he fell ill and finished his life in this world in great sanctity, winning a glorious reward for the good and hard work he had done, and going to his grave in prosperity to enter into "a wealthy rest."

It is said that after his death he also won renown for working miracles, and it would not be surprising if he were powerful in this way in the presence of God, since even while he was among men in this weak and miserable dwelling place of ours his life was characterised by remarkable evidence of God's favours and by the resplendent beauty of his virtues.

When the news of the death of the man of God reached the missionaries who had stayed on in the Toulouse district, they all went back to their homes. Brother Dominic was the only one who carried on preaching the whole time. Some people did join him, but they were not bound to him by any promise of obedience.

Amongst those who joined him were William Claret, whom we have already met, and a Spaniard called brother Dominic, who was later the prior of Madrid in Spain.

Chapter 4

After the death of the bishop of Osma, a crusade against the Albigensians began to be preached in France. Pope Innocent was angry that the unremitting rebelliousness of the heretics could not be tamed by any love for the truth, so he decided that, if they could not be pierced by the sword of the Spirit, which is the word of God, at least they should feel the power of the material sword brought against them.

While he was still alive, bishop Diego had forewarned them, in a kind of prophetic imprecation, that they would be punished by the full rigour of the secular arm. Once, when he had plainly and publicly exposed the errors and rebelliousness of the heretics in the presence of many of the nobility, and they mockingly defended the heretics who were ruining them, offering pleas in their favour which were quite sacrilegious, the bishop angrily lifted his hands to heaven and said, "Lord, stretch forth your hand and punish them" (those who heard this realised afterwards that what he said was inspired by the Spirit) "so that they may at last be brought to understand the truth, if only by being harassed in this way."

While the crusaders were in the land, brother Dominic continued to stay there up to the time of the death of the count de Montfort, constantly preaching the word of God. And how much violence he endured there from wicked men! How much plotting of theirs he defeated! On one occasion they even threatened him with death, and he replied, quite calmly, "I am not worthy of the glory of martyrdom; I have not yet merited such a death." On another occasion, when he was passing by a place where he suspected that perhaps they were lying in wait for him, he went on his way singing cheerfully. When the heretics heard about this, they were astonished at his imperturbable firmness and asked him, "Do you have no fear of death? What would you have done if we had taken you prisoner?" He said, "I should have asked you not to strike me down quickly and kill me all at once, but to prolong my martyrdom by mutilating my limbs one by one, and then to display the mangled bits of my body before my eyes, and then to gouge out my eyes and either leave what remained of my body wallowing in its own blood or finish me off completely; a slow martyrdom like that would win me a much finer crown." The enemies of truth were astounded to hear him talk like this. They stopped plotting against him and "lying in wait for the just man's life," because they realised that if they killed him they would be doing him a favour rather than harming him. For his part, brother Dominic, with all his energy and with passionate zeal, set himself to win all the souls he could for Christ. His heart was full of an extraordinary, almost incredible, yearning for the salvation of everyone.

He certainly did not lack the greatest form of charity that a man can have, the charity to lay down his life for his friends. Once, when he was urging one of the unbelievers, with loving encouragement, to return to the faithful embrace of mother church, the man explained that his association with the unbelievers was prompted by his worldly needs, because the heretics gave him necessary funds, which he could not obtain in any other way. Brother Dominic was so moved by sympathy that he decided immediately to sell himself and relieve the poverty of this endangered soul with the price of himself. And he would really have done it, had not the Lord, "whose riches are for all," made other arrangements for meeting the man's needs.

The servant of God, Dominic, made such progress in virtue and in his reputation that the heretics became jealous. As he grew in goodness, they looked more and more askance at him. Their bleary eyes could not stand the brilliance of his light. So they made mock of him and followed him around, teasing him in various ways, bringing forth evil from the evil treasure in their hearts.

But, while unbelievers mocked, the faithful were filled with holy joy because of him. All the Catholics felt such respect for him that even the hearts of the nobility were touched by the charm of his holiness and the attractiveness of his character. And the archbishops and other prelates in the area considered him worthy of the highest honour.

Count de Montfort, who was particularly devoted to him, gave an important castle called Casseneuil to him, with his men's consent, and to all those who were accompanying him and helping in the mission of salvation which he had begun. In addition, brother Dominic held the church of Fanjeaux and certain other properties, from which he could provide for the needs of himself and his associates. (The Order of Preachers had not yet been founded, and they had done no more than discuss such a foundation, although brother Dominic was already applying himself with all his might to the job of preaching; nor were they yet observing the constitution that was later promulgated about not accepting properties and not keeping properties which had been accepted previously.)

In this way, about ten years passed from the death of the bishop of Osma up to the Lateran Council, and all this time brother Dominic remained more or less alone.

Chapter 5

At the time when the bishops were beginning to go to Rome for the Lateran Council, two upright and suitable men from Toulouse gave themselves to Christ's servant, Dominic. One of them was Peter Selhan, who was later the prior of Limoges, the other was brother Thomas, a very attractive and eloquent man. Brother Peter made over to brother Dominic and his companions some tall, noble houses which he possessed in Toulouse near the Châteaux Narbonne, and it was in these houses that the brethren now first began to live in Toulouse, and from that time onwards all those who were with brother Dominic began to humble themselves more and more profoundly and to adopt the manner of religious.

Bishop Fulk of Toulouse, of happy memory, was very fond of brother Dominic, who was "beloved of God and men," because he saw the brethren's religious way of life and the grace they had, and their fervour in preaching, and he rejoiced at the appearance of this new light. So, with the consent of his whole Chapter, he granted them a sixth of all the tithes of his diocese, to enable them to obtain what they needed in the way of books and food.

Brother Dominic joined the bishop to go with him to the Lateran Council, to present with him a joint petition to pope Innocent to confirm for brother Dominic and his companions an Order which would be and would be called an Order of Preachers, and also to confirm the revenues already mentioned which had been assigned to the brethren, whether by the Count or by the bishop.

The bishop of the see of Rome listened to their petition, and then told brother Dominic to return to his brethren and, after full discussion with them, to choose, with their unanimous agreement, some approved Rule. When all this was done, brother Dominic was to return to the pope to receive confirmation of all that he had asked.

After the council they accordingly returned to Toulouse. The brethren were informed of what the pope had said, and the preachers-to-be quickly chose the Rule of St. Augustine, who was himself an outstanding preacher; in addition, they adopted certain stricter observances in connection with diet, fasting, bedding and woollen clothing. And, to ensure that no worldly responsibilities and worries would hinder their job of preaching, they decided and decreed that they would not own properties, but would only accept revenues with which to provide for the food they needed.

The bishop also assigned some churches to them: one within the city, one in Pamiers and a third between Sorèze and Puylaurens, namely the church of St. Mary de Lescure. In each of these they were to establish a community and priory. They were given their first church in the city of Toulouse in the summer of 1216, a church which had been founded in honour of St. Romanus. In the other two churches, as it turned out, no friar was ever to live, but at this church of St. Romanus a cloister was soon built, with cells above it suitable for studying and sleeping in.

At that time the brethren numbered sixteen.

In the meantime, pope Innocent was taken out of the world, and Honorius was made his successor. Brother Dominic soon went to see him, and obtained full confirmation of the Order, in terms appropriate to its purpose and his ideas about its organization, and everything else which he had wanted to obtain.

Chapter 6

In 1217 the people of Toulouse determined to revolt against Count de Montfort, an event which we reckon the man of God, Dominic, had foreseen in spirit some time in advance. He had seen a vision of a tall, beautiful tree, in whose branches a large number of birds were living. Then the tree was felled, and the birds which were sitting on it all took to flight. Filled with the Spirit of God, brother Dominic realized that the great and exalted prince, the Count de Montfort, patron of many people, was soon to meet his death.

Invoking the Holy Spirit, brother Dominic called the brethren together and told them that he had decided to send them out, few as they were, into all the world; he did not want them all to go on living there together for much longer.

The announcement of this sudden dispersal amazed them, but their confidence in the evident authority which his sanctity gave him made them more prepared to agree to what he said, because they were hopeful that it would all lead to a satisfactory outcome.

He also gave it as his opinion that they should elect one of the brethren as their abbot, to have authority to rule the others as their superior and head, though he retained to himself the right to discipline such an abbot. Brother Matthew was canonically elected, and he was the first and last in the Order to be called "abbot," because afterwards, as a mark of humility, the brethren preferred to have their superior called "Master of the Order," not "abbot."

So four brethren were sent to Spain, brothers Peter of Madrid, Gomez, Miguel de Ucero and Dominic. These last two were later sent by Master Dominic from Rome to Bologna, after they had returned to him from Spain, and there they remained. They had not been able to realize their desire for a fruitful mission in Spain, though the other two made good progress there and sowed the seed of God's word.

This brother Dominic of whom we are speaking was a man of outstanding humility; he lacked knowledge, but was splendid in virtue, and it will be worth recalling briefly an episode from his life.

Some people who were perhaps resentful of him once formed a conspiracy against him: a shameless instrument of Satan, an obstacle to chastity, a brand of vice, a prostitute, in short, was sent to him on the pretext of going to confession. She said, "I am in terrible agony, I am all incredibly on fire, and the man I love does not even know me, and if he did, he would probably take no notice of me. But I love him, and there is nothing I can do to calm my heart. Please advise me. Help me, before I perish. I know you can help me." The prostitute went on trying to seduce the innocent man with cunning, poisonous words like these, and she was not to be put off by any of his godly advice. So he then inquired who the person was who had brought her into such a parlous condition. She revealed that it was he himself who was the object of her passion.

"Go now," he said, "and come back later. I will prepare somewhere where we can meet properly." Then he went into his room and built two fires, with only a narrow space between them.

When the prostitute came in, he stretched himself out in between the two fires and bid her come to him. "Look," he said, "Here is a suitable place for such a sin. Come and make love, if you want to."

She was terrified at the sight of the man throwing himself so fearlessly right in among the flames. She screamed and fled, full of remorse. But he got up unharmed, triumphant over the material fire and the fire of lust.

A party of friars was also sent to Paris: brother Matthew, who had been elected abbot, with brother Bertrand, who was later provincial of Provence, a man of great holiness and ruthless self-discipline, in that he mortified his flesh savagely and had taken to heart in many ways the example of his master, Dominic, whose travelling companion he had sometimes been. These two men were sent to Paris with letters from the pope, to make the Order known there. With them went two brethren who were to study there, brother John of Navarre and brother Laurence the Englishman.

Before they reached Paris, a great deal of what was to happen to the friars there was revealed by the Lord to brother Laurence, about the houses they would live in and where they were going to be, and about the number of novices they were going to receive. He told them about all this, and events proved him right.

A second, separate party was also sent to Paris, consisting of brother Mames, Master Dominic's half-brother, and brother Miguel of Spain. They took with them a Norman laybrother called Oderic.

All these men were sent to Paris, but the last three travelled faster and arrived first, reaching Paris on September 12. The others arrived three weeks later. They rented a house near the hospice of our Lady, not far from the gate of the bishop of Paris' residence.

In 1218 the brethren were given the house of St. Jacques, though they were not yet given absolute possession of it. It was given them by Master John, the dean of St. Quentin, and by the University of Paris, at the request of pope Honorius. They moved in to live there on August 6.

In the same year, some young, simple friars were sent to Orléans. They were small seeds, as it were, but the much richer growth which came later all started with them.

Near the beginning of 1218 Master Dominic sent some friars from Rome to Bologna, namely brothers John of Navarre and Bertrand. Later he sent brother Christian too, together with a laybrother. During their time in Bologna they endured the most appalling poverty.

Chapter 10

In Bologna Master Dominic was now approaching the end of his earthly pilgrimage, and was seriously ill. He called twelve of the more sensible brethren to his sick-bed and exhorted them to be eager in their practice of the religious life and zealous in its support, and to persevere in the way of holiness, and he advised them to avoid keeping dubious company with women, particularly young women, because they are a real temptation, all too liable to ensnare souls which are not yet completely purified. "Look at me," he said, "God's mercy has preserved me to this day in bodily virginity, but I confess that I have not escaped from the imperfection of being more excited by the conversation of young women than being talked at by old women."

Before his death he also told the brethren confidently that he would be more useful to them after his death than he had been during his lifetime. He knew well to whom he had entrusted the treasure of his work and of his fruitful life, and he had no doubt that a crown of righteousness was stored up for him, whose possession would make him a far more powerful intercessor, in as much as it would give him far more certain access to "the Lord's mighty deeds."

As his illness became more and more oppressive, he suffered from fevers and from dysentery, until at last his soul was freed from the flesh to return to the Lord from whom it came, exchanging this dingy dwelling place for the everlasting comfort of a heavenly home.

That same day, at the very hour of his death, brother Guala, the prior of Brescia and later bishop of the same city, had lain down and dozed off in the place where the brethren's bell-tower was in Brescia, and he saw a shining opening made in heaven, and through it a golden ladder came down. Jesus Christ was holding the top of it on one side and his glorious mother was holding the other side. At the bottom of the ladder he saw a friar, whose face he could not recognise, because it was covered with his hood, which is the normal way for our dead brethren to be buried. This friar was seated on a chair. Then Christ the Lord and his mother began to draw the ladder back up, until the person sitting at the bottom of it was brought up to their own level. He was then received into heaven, and the radiant opening in the sky was shut, and nothing more was seen. The brother who saw this vision went to Bologna, where he soon discovered that the servant of Christ, Dominic, had died on the very day and at the very time of the vision, as we learned from his own account.

We must now turn briefly to the distinguished funeral of the blessed Dominic. At the time of his death, the venerable bishop of Ostia (who was at the time papal legate in Lombardy; now he is pope of the see of Rome, under the name of Gregory) happened by God's providence to be in Bologna, and because of his presence there were many other important men and senior churchmen there too. The bishop had known Master Dominic intimately and loved him warmly, knowing that he was a good and holy man, and so he came to the convent as soon as he learned of his death. He personally performed the burial service, in the presence of a large number of people. The happy death of the blessed man and the manifest holiness which they all knew him to have had in his life on earth and the garment of immortality which their consciences assured them he had received were a veritable sermon in the hearts of everyone present on contempt for the world, because the funeral gave them an incentive to realise how surely we can win our heavenly home and our place of eternal rest by despising this present life and how certain we are of a death which is "precious" if we adopt an inglorious, poor way of life in this world.

Among the common people, a great feeling of devotion and reverence sprang up, and many of them came along, who had been troubled by all kinds of diseases, and they stayed there for days and nights on end telling everyone that they had been entirely cured, and they brought mementos of their cures, fixing on the tomb wax images of eyes, hands, feet and other parts of the body, depending on the nature of their infirmities and the kind of help they had received in their bodies or their affairs.

But while this was going on, there was scarcely anyone among the brethren to respond to this divine grace with the gratitude it deserved. Many of them were of the opinion that these miracles should not be broadcast, for fear that it would look as if they were trying to make money out of them, under the guise of piety. But in guarding their own reputation like this, because of a rather mindless scruple of holiness, they failed to consider how the church as a whole might have benefited, and they buried the glory of God.

All the same it is a fact that even in his life on earth Master Dominic did on occasion perform dazzling miracles and acts of supernatural power. Many such have been reported to me, but I have not written them down because of discrepancies in the different accounts of them. If I were to give an uncertain account of what happened, it would only give the reader an unclear impression. However I do want to mention some of these miracles, of which we have more definite knowledge.

Once when he was in Rome, a young relative of cardinal Stephen of Fossanova was thrown from the horse he was riding, because he was playing about rather foolishly so that the horse suddenly bolted. He had a dreadful fall, and people wept as they saw him carried away. They thought he was as good as dead; at best he was only half-alive, and perhaps he was already quite dead. Amid the growing clamour of grief and mourning, Master Dominic arrived with that good and fervent man, brother Tancred, later prior of Rome, who told me all this. Brother Tancred said to him, "You cannot ignore this. Don't you see them all weeping? Why do you not pray to the Lord? What has happened to your love of your neighbour? What has happened to your deep trust in God?"

Moved by the brother's words and overwhelmed by his feeling of compassion, Master Dominic had the young man taken into a private room, and
there, by the power of his prayers, he coaxed him back to life and produced
him alive and well in the sight of them all.

I learned about another miracle from brother Bertrand, who has already
been mentioned above as one of the friars sent to Paris. Once he was travelling with Master Dominic when a great storm blew up over their heads.
The ground was already beginning to be flooded by the great downpour of
rain, but Master Dominic drove back the waters before them by making the
sign of the cross, so that, as they continued on their way, they could see the
rain still pouring down only a yard or so away from them, but not a single
drop of water touched them; not even the hem of their clothes got wet.

Several other stories of cures have come to my knowledge, which are
further evidence of his sanctity, though I have not written them down here.

Far more impressive and splendid than all his miracles, though, were the
exceptional integrity of his character and the extraordinary energy of divine zeal which carried him along; these proved beyond all doubt that he
was a vessel of honour and grace, adorned with every kind of "precious
stone." His mind was always steady and calm, except when he was stirred
by a feeling of compassion and mercy; and, since a happy heart makes for
a cheerful face, the tranquil composure of the inner man was revealed outwardly by the kindliness and cheerfulness of his expression. He never allowed himself to become angry. In every reasonable purpose which his
mind conceived, in accordance with God's will, he maintained such constancy that he hardly ever, if ever, consented to change any plan which he
had formulated with due deliberation. And though, as has been said, his
face was always radiant with a cheerfulness which revealed the good conscience he bore within him, "the light of his face never fell to the ground." [1]
By his cheerfulness he easily won the love of everybody. Without difficulty
he found his way into people's hearts as soon as they saw him.

Wherever he went, whether he was on the road with his companions or
in some house, with his host and the rest of the household, or among important people and rulers and prelates, he always overflowed with inspiring
words. He had an abundant supply of edifying stories, with which he directed people's minds to the love of Christ and to contempt for the world.
Everywhere, in word and in deed, he showed himself to be a man of the
gospel.

During the daytime nobody was more sociable and happy with his

1. Job 29:24. As the gloss and Hugh of St. Cher make clear, this signifies that even
though he was always cheerful, he never descended to petty worldly concerns (as might have
been expected).

brethren and companions, but at night nobody was more thoroughly dedicated to keeping vigil and to prayer. "Tears waited for him at night, but joy in the morning." The day he gave to his neighbours, the night he gave to God, knowing that "by day the Lord sends his mercy, and by night he gives songs of praise."

He used to weep plenteously and frequently, and "his tears were his bread by day and by night," by day especially when he celebrated his daily Mass, and by night especially when he kept watch in his uniquely unwearying vigils.

It was his very frequent habit to spend the whole night in church, so that he hardly ever seemed to have any fixed bed of his own to sleep in. He used to pray and keep vigil at night to the very limit of what he could force his frail body to endure. When at last weariness overtook him and his spirit succumbed, so that he had to sleep for a while, he rested briefly before the altar or absolutely anywhere, sometimes even leaning his head against a stone, like the patriarch Jacob. But then he would soon be awake again, rallying his spirit to resume his fervent prayer.

Everybody was enfolded in the wide embrace of his charity, and since he loved everyone, everyone loved him. He made it his own business to rejoice with those who were rejoicing and to weep with those who wept. He was full of affection and gave himself utterly to caring for his neighbours and to showing sympathy for the unfortunate.

Another thing which made him so attractive to everybody was his straightforwardness; there was never a hint of guile or duplicity in anything he said or did.

He was a true lover of poverty, and he always wore cheap clothes. He confined himself to a very modest allowance of food and drink, avoiding all luxuries. He was quite content with very simple food, so firm was his bodily self-control, and he drank wine so austerely diluted that, though it satisfied his bodily needs, it never blunted his fine, sensitive spirit.

Who could ever hope to imitate the virtues of this man? We can however admire them, and weigh up the slackness of our own generation against his example. To be able to do what he did requires more than human strength, it presupposes a particular grace, which he alone had, unless perhaps God in his merciful kindness deigns to bring anyone else to a similar peak of holiness. But who is there who would be ready for such a gift? But still, brethren, let us follow in our father's footsteps to the best of our ability, and let us also give thanks to our Redeemer, who has granted to his servants such a remarkable man to lead us along the path we are walking, giving us new birth through him into the clear light of this way of life. And let us entreat the Father of mercies that we may be directed by the Spirit who leads God's children, so that, following the path marked out by our fathers, we may attain to that same goal of eternal happiness and everlasting bliss to which he has already happily come, and that we may never turn aside from the right way.

42. Raymond of Peñafort, *Constitutions of the Dominican Order* (ca. 1238–40)

From the Introduction

. . . On this, however, let the superior have in his convent with his brothers the power of dispensing, whenever it shall seem to him expedient, especially in those things which will seem to hinder study or preaching or the harvest of souls, since it is recognized that our order was established from the beginning especially for preaching and the safety of souls, and our study ought to be principally directed to this, so that we may be useful to the souls of our neighbors. Let the priors avail themselves of dispensations as the other brothers. . . .

12. Concerning Preachers

. . . No one is to be appointed to the office of preaching outside the cloister or the company of brethren who is less than twenty-five years old. In fact, those who are suited, when they have to go out to preach will be given companions by the prior according as he judges it advantageous to their behavior and character. When, after receiving a blessing, these go out, just as men who desire to achieve their own salvation and that of others, let them everywhere conduct themselves religiously and honorably as men of the Gospel, following in the footsteps of their Savior, speaking profitably with God and about God with themselves and with their neighbor. They will avoid the intimacy of questionable friendship.

Let them not take part in pleading cases unless on business of the faith. When our brothers enter the diocese of any bishop to preach, they shall first, if possible, visit the bishop so that according to his counsel they may bring to the people the fruit they intend to bring; and as long as they are in his diocese, they shall not meddle in those things which are irregular and themselves be faithfully obedient.

Let no one, indeed, dare to preach in the diocese of any bishop who has forbidden him to preach, unless he has letters from the supreme pontiff. Moreover, let our brothers beware, lest in raising their voices too high they

From Marshall Baldwin, *Christianity through the Thirteenth Century* (New York: Harper & Row, 1970), pp. 364–67. All footnotes deleted.

scandalize the religious and clergy by their preaching; but let them take care of those things which they see ought to be corrected in themselves by imploring the fathers to correct them separately. The companion given to a preacher must obey him as his prior in all things. We order that our brothers do not suggest in their preachings that money be given or taken for the house or for any particular person.

13. Concerning the Brothers on a Journey

Those going to fulfil a mission of preaching or those who travel for other purposes shall not receive or carry gold, silver, money or gifts except food and the necessary clothing and books. If anyone receives anything of the above-mentioned things let him hold it to present freely to his superior on his return. The brethren are not to receive little presents from women, nor give them, especially confessors. Likewise, brothers are not to be stewards of the possessions or money of others, nor receive deposits of things from outside except of books or ecclesiastical robes.

Preachers or travelers when they are en route must say their office as they know how and can, and be content with the office of those whom they are visiting at any time. Brothers are to take with them official travel letters and correct faults in the convents where they visit. . . .

14. Concerning Students

Inasmuch as particular prudence must be observed toward students, let them have a special brother without whose permission they are not to write essays or hear lectures. He must correct those things which deserve correction which he has observed in them, and if it exceeds his powers, he should refer [it] to the superior.

They are not to study the books of the pagan philosophers even if they look at them for a short time; they must not learn the secular sciences of the arts which are called liberal, unless at sometime the master of the order or the general chapter wishes to order otherwise, but the young men as well as the others may read only theological books. Indeed, they must be so intent in study that day and night, at home, on the road, they read something or meditate and strive to retain as much as they can by heart.

If he has some [brothers] suited to teaching who can in a short time be capable of lecturing, the provincial prior should be sure to send them for study to the places where a studium [school] is well established. . . . Three brothers are to be sent from a province to the studium at Paris. Five provinces [with later changes and omissions] are to see to it that in some suitable convent there is a *studium generale (et solempne)* and to this any provincial prior should have the power to send two brothers suited to study.

We decree that each province shall be required to provide its brothers sent to the studium with at least three books of theology, namely the bible, the histories, and the sentences. They must study carefully in them and pay as much attention to the text as to the glosses. Likewise, no one is to have books written concerning the affairs of the house save for the common good. To no one must be conceded the definite use of books and no one must be disturbed if they are taken by anyone or assigned to the custody of anyone. On Sundays and feast days they are to refrain from writing essays. . . .

With regard to those who are studying, the superior must so arrange that they are not easily kept or prevented from study because of duty or anything else. A place must be established according as it shall seem appropriate to the master of students where, after the discussion or vespers or at some time when he is unoccupied they may convene in his presence for raising questions or points of dispute. And when one is asking or making a suggestion, let the others be silent so as not to hinder the speaker. If anyone gives offense in questioning, objecting, or replying ungraciously or in a confused or clamorous or rude manner, he is to be immediately disciplined by whoever among them is presiding.

Let cells be assigned to those for whom the master of students thinks it expedient. But if anyone is found unproductive in his study, let his cell be given to another, and let him be set to work in other duties. In the cells, moreover, they can write, read, pray, sleep, and even stay awake at night if they desire on account of study. Moreover, no one may become a public doctor or debate unless with the license of the provincial prior and the diffinitors [elected representatives] of the provincial chapter. None of our brothers may read in the psalms or prophecies any literal meaning except that which the saints approve and confirm.

43. Francis of Assisi, *Rule* (1223) and *Testament* (1226)

Rule

In the Name of the Lord Begins the Life of the Friars Minor [1]

The Rule and life of the Friars Minor is this, namely, to observe the Holy Gospel of our Lord Jesus Christ by living in obedience, without property,

From *St. Francis of Assisi's Writings and Early Biographies: English Omnibus Sources for the Life of Saint Francis*, edited by Marion A. Habig (Chicago: Franciscan Herald Press, 1972), pp. 57–70. Some footnotes deleted.
   1. These words of the papal bull are prefaced to the rule: "Honorius Bishop, servant of the servants of God. To our beloved sons Brother Francis and the other brothers of the Order of Friars Minor, health and apostolic benediction. The Apostolic See is accustomed to comply

and in chastity. Brother Francis promises obedience and reverence to his holiness Pope Honorius and his lawfully elected successors and to the Church of Rome. The other friars are bound to obey Brother Francis and his successors.

Of Those Who Wish to Take Up This Life and How They Are to Be Received

If anyone wants to profess our Rule and comes to the friars, they must send him to their provincial minister, because he alone, to the exclusion of others, has permission to receive friars into the Order. The ministers must carefully examine all candidates on the Catholic faith and the sacraments of the Church. If they believe all that the Catholic faith teaches and are prepared to profess it loyally, holding by it steadfastly to the end of their lives, and if they are not married; or if they are married and their wives have already entered a convent or after taking a vow of chastity have by the authority of the bishop of the diocese been granted this permission; and the wives are of such an age that no suspicion can arise concerning them: let the ministers tell them what the holy Gospel says (Mt. 19:21), that they should go and sell all that belongs to them and endeavour to give it to the poor. If they cannot do this, their good will is sufficient.

The friars and their ministers must be careful not to become involved in the temporal affairs of newcomers to the Order, so that they may dispose of their goods freely, as God inspires them. If they ask for advice, the ministers may refer them to some God-fearing persons who can advise them how to distribute their property to the poor.

When this has been done, the ministers should clothe the candidates with the habit of probation, namely, two tunics without a hood, a cord and trousers, and a caperon reaching to the cord, unless the ministers themselves at any time decide that something else is more suitable. After the year of the novitiate, they should be received to obedience, promising to live always according to this life and Rule. It is absolutely forbidden to leave the Order, as his holiness the Pope has laid down. For the Gospel tells us, *No one, having put his hand to the plough and looking back, is fit for the kingdom of God* (Lk. 9:62).

The friars who have already vowed obedience may have one tunic with a hood and those who wish may have another without a hood. Those who are forced by necessity may wear shoes. All the friars are to wear poor clothes

---

with the pious wishes and to bestow a benevolent regard on the laudable desires of petitioners. Wherefore, beloved children in the Lord, moved by your pious prayers, We, in virtue of the Apostolic authority, confirm, and by these letters present, sanction with our protection, the Rule of your Order, approved by Pope Innocent, our Predecessor of happy memory. Which Rule is as follows."

and they can use pieces of sackcloth and other material to mend them, with God's blessing.

I warn all the friars and exhort them not to condemn or look down on people whom they see wearing soft or gaudy clothes and enjoying luxuries in food or drink; each one should rather condemn and despise himself.

Of the Divine Office and Fasting, and How the Friars Are to Travel about the World

The clerics are to recite the Divine Office according to the rite of the Roman Curia, except the psalter; and so they may have breviaries. The lay brothers are to say twenty-four *Our Fathers* for Matins and five for Lauds; for Prime, Terce, Sext, and None, for each of these, they are to say seven; for Vespers twelve and for Compline seven. They should also say some prayers for the dead.

All the friars are to fast from the feast of All Saints until Christmas. Those who voluntarily fast for forty days after Epiphany have God's blessing, because this is the period our Lord sanctified by his holy fast (cf. Mt. 4:2). However, those who do not wish to do so, should not be forced to it. All the friars are bound to keep the Lenten fast before Easter, but they are not bound to fast at other times, except on Fridays. However, in case of manifest necessity, they are not obliged to corporal fasting.

And this is my advice, my counsel, and my earnest plea to my friars in our Lord Jesus Christ that, when they travel about the world, they should not be quarrelsome or take part in disputes with words (cf. 2 Tim. 2:14) or criticize others; but they should be gentle, peaceful, and unassuming, courteous and humble, speaking respectfully to everyone, as is expected of them. They are forbidden to ride on horseback, unless they are forced to it by manifest necessity or sickness. *Whatever house* they *enter*, they should *first say, "Peace to this house"* (Lk. 10:5), and in the words of the Gospel they *may eat what is set before* them (Lk. 10:8).

The Friars Are Forbidden to Accept Money

I strictly forbid all the friars to accept money in any form, either personally or through an intermediary. The ministers and superiors, however, are bound to provide carefully for the needs of the sick and the clothing of the other friars, by having recourse to spiritual friends, while taking into account differences of place, season, or severe climate, as seems best to them in the circumstances. This does not dispense them from the prohibition of receiving money in any form.

The Manner of Working

The friars to whom God has given the grace of working should work in a spirit of faith and devotion and avoid idleness, which is the enemy of the soul, without however extinguishing the spirit of prayer and devotion, to which every temporal consideration must be subordinate. As wages for their labour they may accept anything necessary for their temporal needs, for themselves or their brethren, except money in any form. And they should accept it humbly as is expected of those who serve God and strive after the highest poverty.

That the Friars Are to Appropriate Nothing for Themselves; On Seeking Alms; and On the Sick Friars

The friars are to appropriate nothing for themselves, neither a house, nor a place, nor anything else. As *strangers and pilgrims* (1 Pet. 2:11) in this world, who serve God in poverty and humility, they should beg alms trustingly. And there is no reason why they should be ashamed, because God made himself poor for us in this world. This is the pinnacle of the most exalted poverty, and it is this, my dearest brothers, that has made you heirs and kings of the kingdom of heaven, poor in temporal things, but rich in virtue. This should be your portion, because it leads to the land of the living. And to this poverty, my beloved brothers, you must cling with all your heart, and wish never to have anything else under heaven, for the sake of our Lord Jesus Christ.

Wherever the friars meet one another, they should show that they are members of the same family. And they should have no hesitation in making known their needs to one another. For if a mother loves and cares for her child in the flesh, a friar should certainly love and care for his spiritual brother all the more tenderly. If a friar falls ill, the others are bound to look after him as they would like to be looked after themselves.

Of the Penance to Be Imposed on Friars Who Fall into Sin

If any of the friars, at the instigation of the enemy, fall into mortal sin, they must have recourse as soon as possible, without delay, to their provincial ministers, if it is a sin for which recourse to them has been prescribed for the friars. If the ministers are priests, they should impose a moderate penance on such friars; if they are not priests, they should see that a penance is imposed by some priest of the Order, as seems best to them before God. They must be careful not to be angry or upset because a friar has fallen into sin, because anger or annoyance in themselves or in others makes it difficult to be charitable.

The Election of the Minister General of the Order and the Pentecost Chapter

The friars are always bound to have a member of the Order as Minister General, who is the servant of the whole fraternity, and they are strictly bound to obey him. At his death the provincial ministers and the custodes are to elect a successor at the Pentecost Chapter, at which the provincial ministers are bound to assemble in the place designated by the Minister General. This chapter should be held once every three years, or at a longer or shorter interval, if the Minister General has so ordained.

If at any time it becomes clear to all the provincial ministers and custodes that the Minister General is incapable of serving the friars and can be of no benefit to them, they who have the power to elect must elect someone else as Minister General.

After the Pentecost Chapter, the provincial ministers and custodes may summon their subjects to a chapter in their own territory once in the same year, if they wish and it seems worthwhile.

Of Preachers

The friars are forbidden to preach in any diocese, if the bishop objects to it. No friar should dare to preach to the people unless he has been examined and approved by the Minister General of the Order and has received from him the commission to preach.

Moreover, I advise and admonish the friars that in their preaching, their words should be examined and chaste. They should aim only at the advantage and spiritual good of their listeners, telling them briefly about vice and virtue, punishment and glory, because our Lord himself kept his words short on earth.

On Admonishing and Correcting the Friars

The ministers, who are the servants of the other friars, must visit their subjects and admonish them, correcting them humbly and charitably, without commanding them anything that is against their conscience or our Rule. The subjects, however, should remember that they have renounced their own wills for God's sake. And so I strictly command them to obey their ministers in everything that they have promised God and is not against their conscience and our Rule. The friars who are convinced that they cannot observe the Rule spiritually, wherever they may be, can and must have recourse to their ministers. The ministers, for their part, are bound to receive them kindly and charitably, and be so sympathetic towards them that the friars can speak and deal with them as employers with their servants. That is the way it ought to be; the ministers should be the servants of all the friars.

With all my heart, I beg the friars in our Lord Jesus Christ to be on their guard against pride, boasting, envy, and greed, against the cares and anxieties of this world, against detraction and complaining. Those who are illiterate should not be anxious to study. They should realize instead that the only thing they should desire is to have the spirit of God at work within them, while they pray to him unceasingly with a heart free from self-interest. They must be humble, too, and patient in persecution or illness, loving those who persecute us by blaming us or bringing charges against us, as our Lord tells us, *Love your enemies, pray for those who persecute and calumniate you* (Mt. 5:44). *Blessed are those who suffer persecution for justice' sake, for theirs is the kingdom of heaven* (Mt. 5:10). *He who has persevered to the end will be saved* (Mt. 10:22).

The Friars Are Forbidden to Enter the Monasteries of Nuns

I strictly forbid all the friars to have suspicious relationships or conversations with women. No one may enter the monasteries of nuns, except those who have received special permission from the Apostolic See. They are forbidden to be sponsors of men or women lest scandal arise amongst or concerning the friars.

Of Those Who Wish to Go among the Saracens and Other Unbelievers

If any of the friars is inspired by God to go among the Saracens or other unbelievers, he must ask permission from his provincial minister. The ministers, for their part, are to give permission only to those whom they see are fit to be sent.

The ministers, too, are bound to ask the Pope for one of the cardinals of the holy Roman Church to be governor, protector, and corrector of this fraternity, so that we may be utterly subject and submissive to the Church. And so, firmly established in the Catholic faith, we may live always according to the poverty, and the humility, and the Gospel of our Lord Jesus Christ, as we have solemnly promised.[2]

Testament (1226)

This is how God inspired me, Brother Francis, to embark upon a life of penance. When I was in sin, the sight of lepers nauseated me beyond measure; but then God himself led me into their company, and I had pity on them. When I had once become acquainted with them, what had previously nauseated me became a source of spiritual and physical consolation for me. After that I did not wait long before leaving the world.

2. The following words of the papal bull bring the rule to a close: "To no one, therefore, be it allowed to infringe on this page of our confirmation or to oppose it with rash temerity. But if any one shall have presumed to attempt this, be it known to him that he will incur the indignation of Almighty God and of his holy Apostles Peter and Paul. Given at the Lateran on the 29th of November, in the 8th year of Our pontificate."

And God inspired me with such faith in his churches that I used to pray with all simplicity, saying, "We adore you, Lord Jesus Christ, here and in all your churches in the whole world, and we bless you, because by your holy cross you have redeemed the world."

God inspired me, too, and still inspires me with such great faith in priests who live according to the laws of the holy Church of Rome, because of their dignity, that if they persecuted me, I should still be ready to turn to them for aid. And if I were as wise as Solomon and met the poorest priests of the world, I would still refuse to preach against their will in the parishes in which they live. I am determined to reverence, love and honour priests and all others as my superiors. I refuse to consider their sins, because I can see the Son of God in them and they are better than I. I do this because in this world I cannot see the most high Son of God with my own eyes, except for his most holy Body and Blood which they receive and they alone administer to others.

Above everything else, I want this most holy Sacrament to be honoured and venerated and reserved in places which are richly ornamented. Whenever I find his most holy name or writings containing his words in an improper place, I make a point of picking them up, and I ask that they be picked up and put aside in a suitable place. We should honour and venerate theologians, too, and the ministers of God's word, because it is they who give us spirit and life.

When God gave me some friars, there was no one to tell me what I should do; but the Most High himself made it clear to me that I must live the life of the Gospel. I had this written down briefly and simply and his holiness the Pope confirmed it for me. Those who embraced this life gave everything they had to the poor. They were satisfied with one habit which was patched inside and outside, and a cord, and trousers. We refused to have anything more.

Those of us who were clerics said the Office like other clerics, while the lay brothers said the *Our Father*, and we were only too glad to find shelter in abandoned churches. We made no claim to learning and we were submissive to everyone. I worked with my own hands and I am still determined to work; and with all my heart I want all the other friars to be busy with some kind of work that can be carried on without scandal. Those who do not know how to work should learn, not because they want to get something for their efforts, but to give good example and to avoid idleness. When we receive no recompense for our work, we can turn to God's table and beg alms from door to door. God revealed a form of greeting to me, telling me that we should say, "God give you peace."

The friars must be very careful not to accept churches or poor dwellings for themselves, or anything else built for them, unless they are in harmony with the poverty which we have promised in the Rule; and they should occupy these places only as strangers and pilgrims.

In virtue of obedience, I strictly forbid the friars, wherever they may be, to petition the Roman Curia, either personally or through an intermediary, for a papal brief, whether it concerns a church or any other place, or even in order to preach, or because they are being persecuted. If they are not welcome somewhere, they should flee to another country where they can lead a life of penance, with God's blessing.

I am determined to obey the Minister General of the Order and the guardian whom he sees fit to give me. I want to be a captive in his hands so that I cannot travel about or do anything against his command or desire, because he is my superior. Although I am ill and not much use, I always want to have a cleric with me who will say the Office for me, as is prescribed in the Rule.

All the other friars, too, are bound to obey their guardians in the same way, and say the Office according to the Rule. If any of them refuse to say the Office according to the Rule and want to change it, or if they are not true to the Catholic faith, the other friars are bound in virtue of obedience to bring them before the custos nearest the place where they find them. The custos must keep any such friar as a prisoner day and night so that he cannot escape from his hands until he personally hands him over to his minister. The minister, then, is strictly bound by obedience to place him in the care of friars who will guard him day and night like a prisoner until they present him before his lordship the Bishop of Ostia,[3] who is the superior, protector, and corrector of the whole Order.

The friars should not say, this is another Rule. For this is a reminder, admonition, exhortation, and my testament which I, Brother Francis, worthless as I am, leave to you, my brothers, that we may observe in a more Catholic way the Rule we have promised to God. The Minister General and all the other ministers and custodes are bound in virtue of obedience not to add anything to these words or subtract from them. They should always have this writing with them as well as the Rule and at the chapters they hold, when the Rule is read, they should read these words also.

In virtue of obedience, I strictly forbid any of my friars, clerics or lay brothers, to interpret the Rule or these words, saying, "This is what they mean." God inspired me to write the Rule and these words plainly and simply, and so you too must understand them plainly and simply, and live by them, doing good to the last.

And may whoever observes all this be filled in heaven with the blessing

3. Cardinal Ugolino at this time.

of the most high Father, and on earth with that of his beloved Son, together with the Holy Spirit, the comforter, and all the powers of heaven and all the saints. And I, Brother Francis, your poor worthless servant, add my share internally and externally to that most holy blessing. Amen.

44. Thomas of Celano, *Life of Saint Francis* (1182–1228)

Book 1

To the Praise and Glory of Almighty God, the Father, Son, and Holy Spirit. Amen.
Here begins the life of our most blessed father Francis.

How Francis Lived in the World before His Conversion

1. In the city of Assisi, which lies at the edge of the Spoleto valley, *there was a man* by the name of Francis, who from his earliest years was brought up by his parents proud of spirit, in accordance with the vanity of the world; and imitating their wretched life and habits for a long time, he became even more vain and proud. For this very evil custom has grown up everywhere among those who are considered Christians in name, and this pernicious teaching has become so established and prescribed, as though by public law, that people seek to educate their children from the cradle on very negligently and dissolutely. For, indeed, when they first begin to speak or stammer, children, just hardly born, are taught by signs and words to do certain wicked and detestable things; and when they come to be weaned, they are forced not only to speak but also to do certain things full of lust and wantonness. Impelled by a fear that is natural to their age, none of them dares to conduct himself in an upright manner, for if he were to do so he would be subjected to severe punishments. Therefore, a secular poet says well: "Because we have grown up amid the practices of our parents, we therefore pursue all evil things from our childhood on." This testimony is true, for so much the more injurious to their children are the desires of the parents, the more successfully they work out. But when the children have progressed a little in age, they always sink into worse deeds, following their own impulses. For from a corrupt root a corrupt tree will grow, and what has once become wickedly depraved can hardly ever be brought into harmony with the norms of uprightness. But when they begin to enter the portals of adolescence, how do you think they will turn out? Then, in-

From *St. Francis of Assisi's Writings and Early Biographies: English Omnibus Sources for the Life of Saint Francis*, edited by Marion A. Habig (Chicago: Franciscan Herald Press, 1972), pp. 229–31, 288–92, 308–11, 325–30, 335–41, 376–78. All footnotes deleted.

deed, tossed about amid every kind of debauchery, they give themselves over completely to shameful practices, in as much as they are permitted to do as they please. For once they have become the slaves of sin by a voluntary servitude, they give over all their members to be instruments of wickedness; and showing forth in themselves nothing of the Christian religion either in their lives or in their conduct, they take refuge under the mere name of Christianity. These miserable people very often pretend that they have done even worse things than they have actually done, lest they seem more despicable the more innocent they are.

2. These are the wretched circumstances among which the man whom we venerate today as a saint, for he is truly a saint, lived in his youth; and almost up to the twenty-fifth year of his age, he squandered and wasted his time miserably. Indeed, he outdid all his contemporaries in vanities and he came to be a promoter of evil and was more abundantly zealous for all kinds of foolishness. He was the admiration of all and strove to outdo the rest in the pomp of vainglory, in jokes, in strange doings, in idle and useless talk, in songs, in soft and flowing garments, for he was very rich, not however avaricious but prodigal, not a hoarder of money but a squanderer of his possessions, a cautious business man but a very unreliable steward. On the other hand, he was a very kindly person, easy and affable, even making himself foolish because of it; for because of these qualities many ran after him, doers of evil and promoters of crime. And thus overwhelmed by a host of evil companions, proud and high-minded, he walked about the streets of Babylon until the *Lord looked down from heaven* and for his own name's sake removed his *wrath far off* and for his praise bridled Francis lest he should perish. *The hand of the Lord* therefore came *upon him* and a change was wrought by the right hand of the Most High, that through him an assurance might be granted to sinners that they had been restored to grace and that he might become an example to all of conversion to God.

Of the Clarity and Constancy of Francis' Mind, and of His Preaching before Pope Honorius; and How He Committed Himself and His Brothers to the Lord Hugo, Bishop of Ostia

71. The man of God Francis had been taught not to seek his own, but to seek especially what in his eyes would be helpful toward the salvation of others; but above everything else he desired *to depart and to be with Christ*. Therefore, his greatest concern was to be free from everything of this world, lest the serenity of his mind be disturbed even for an hour by the taint of anything that was mere dust. He made himself insensible to all external noise, and, bridling his external senses with all his strength and repressing the movements of his nature, he occupied himself with God alone.

In the clefts of the rock he would build his nest and *in the hollow places of the wall* his dwelling. With fruitful devotion he frequented only heavenly dwellings, and he who had totally emptied himself remained so much the longer in the wounds of the Savior. He therefore frequently chose solitary places so that he could direct his mind completely to God; yet he was not slothful about entering into the affairs of his neighbors, when he saw the time was opportune, and he willingly took care of things pertaining to their salvation. For his safest haven was prayer; not prayer of a single moment, or idle or presumptuous prayer, but prayer of long duration, full of devotion, serene in humility. If he began late, he would scarcely finish before morning. Walking, sitting, eating, or drinking, he was always intent upon prayer. He would go alone to pray at night in churches abandoned and located in deserted places, where, under the protection of divine grace, he overcame many fears and many disturbances of mind.

72. He fought hand to hand with the devil, for in such places the devil not only struck at him with temptations but discouraged him by ruining and destroying things. But the most valiant soldier of God, knowing that his Lord can do all things everywhere, did not give in to fright, but said within his heart: "You can no more rattle the weapons of your wickedness against me here, O evil one, than if we were in public before all the people." Indeed, he was extremely steadfast, and he paid no attention to anything except what pertained to the Lord. For when he so very often preached the word of God to thousands of people, he was as sure of himself as though he were speaking with a familiar companion. He looked upon the greatest multitude of people as one person and he preached to one as he would to a multitude. Out of the purity of his mind he provided for himself security in preaching a sermon and, without thinking about it beforehand, he spoke wonderful things to all and things not heard before. When he did give some time to meditation before a sermon, he at times forgot what he had meditated upon when the people had come together, and he knew nothing else to say. Without embarrassment he would confess to the people that he had thought of many things but could remember nothing at all of them; and suddenly he would be filled with such great eloquence that he would move the souls of the hearers to admiration. At times, however, knowing nothing to say, he would give a blessing and dismiss the people feeling that from this alone they had received a great sermon.

73. But when at one time he had come to Rome because the interests of his order demanded it, he longed greatly to speak before Pope Honorius and the venerable cardinals. When the lord Hugo, the glorious bishop of Ostia, who venerated the holy man of God with a special affection, understood this, he was filled with both fear and joy, admiring the fervor of the holy man but conscious of his simple purity. But confident of the mercy of

the Almighty, which in the time of need never fails those who trust in it, the bishop brought Francis before the lord pope and the reverend cardinals; and standing before such great princes, after receiving their permission and blessing, he began to speak fearlessly. Indeed, he spoke with such great fervor of spirit, that, not being able to contain himself for joy, when he spoke the words with his mouth, he moved his feet as though he were dancing, not indeed lustfully, but as one burning with the fire of divine love, not provoking laughter, but drawing forth tears of grief. For many of them were *pierced to the heart* in admiration of divine grace and of such great constancy in man. But the venerable lord bishop of Ostia was kept in suspense by fear and he prayed with all his strength to the Lord that the simplicity of the blessed man would not be despised, since the glory of the saint would reflect upon himself as would his disgrace, in as much as he had been placed over Francis' family as a father.

74. For St. Francis had clung to him as a son to his father and as an only son to his mother, sleeping and resting securely upon the bosom of his kindness. In truth, the bishop held the place and did the work of a shepherd, but he left the name of shepherd to the holy man. The blessed father provided what provisions were necessary, but the kindly lord bishop carried them into effect. O how many, above all when these things were first taking place, were plotting to destroy the new Order that had been planted! O how many were trying to choke off this new *chosen vineyard* that the hand of the Lord had so kindly planted in the world! How many there were who were trying to steal and consume its first and purest fruits! But they were all *slain by the sword* of the reverend father and lord who *brought* them to *nothing*. For he was a river of eloquence, a wall of the Church, a champion of truth, and a lover of the humble. Blessed that day, therefore, and memorable, on which the holy man of God committed himself to such a venerable lord. For once when that lord was exercising the office of legate for the holy see, as he often did, in Tuscany, Blessed Francis, who as yet did not have many brothers but wanted to go to France, came to Florence where the aforementioned bishop was staying at the time. As yet they were not joined in that extraordinary familiarity, but only the fame of Francis' blessed life joined them in mutual affection and charity.

75. For the rest, because it was blessed Francis' custom upon entering any city or country to go to the bishops or priests, hearing of the presence of so great a bishop, he presented himself to his clemency with great reverence. When the lord bishop saw him, he received him with humble devotion, as he always did those who professed holy religion, those particularly who loved the noble insignia of blessed poverty and holy simplicity. And because he was solicitous in providing for the wants of the poor and in han-

dling their business with special care, he diligently asked Francis the reason for his coming and listened to his proposal with great kindness. When he saw that Francis despised all earthly things more than the rest and that he was alight with that fire that Jesus had sent upon earth, his soul was from that moment knit with the soul of Francis and he devoutly asked his prayers and most graciously offered his protection to him in all things. Then he admonished Francis not to finish the journey he had begun but to give himself solicitously to the care of and watchfulness over those whom the Lord had committed to him. But St. Francis, seeing such a venerable lord conducting himself so kindly, giving such warm affection and such efficacious advice, rejoiced with a very great joy; and then, *falling at his feet*, he handed himself over and entrusted himself and his brothers to him with a devout mind.

Concerning Francis' Spirit of Charity and Compassion Toward the Poor; and How He Treated a Sheep and Some Lambs

76. The father of the poor, the poor Francis, conforming himself to the poor in all things, was grieved when he saw some one poorer than himself, not because he longed for vainglory, but only from a feeling of compassion. And, though he was content with a tunic that was quite poor and rough, he very frequently longed to divide it with some poor person. But that this very rich poor man, drawn on by a great feeling of affection, might be able to help the poor in some way, he would ask the rich of this world, when the weather was cold, to give him a mantle or some furs. And when, out of devotion, they willingly did what the most blessed father asked of them, he would say to them: "I will accept this from you with the understanding that you do not expect ever to have it back again." And when he met the first poor man, he would clothe him with what he had received with joy and gladness. He bore it very ill if he saw a poor person reproached or if he heard a curse hurled upon any creature by anyone.

Once it happened that a certain brother uttered a word of invective against a certain poor man who had asked for an alms, saying to him: "See, perhaps you are a rich man and pretending to be poor." Hearing this, the father of the poor, St. Francis, was greatly saddened, and he severely rebuked the brother who had said such a thing and commanded him to strip himself before the poor man and, kissing his feet, beg pardon of him. For, he was accustomed to say: "Who curses a poor man does an injury to Christ, whose noble image he wears, the image of him who made himself poor for us in this world." Frequently, therefore, when he found the poor burdened down with wood or other things, he offered his own shoulders to help them, though his shoulders were very weak.

Book 2

Concerning the Vision of the Man in the Likeness of a Crucified Seraph

94. Two years before Francis gave his soul back to heaven, while he was living in the hermitage which was called Alverna, after the place on which it stood, he saw *in the vision of God* a man standing above him, like a seraph with six wings, his hands extended and his feet joined together and fixed to a cross. Two of the wings were extended above his head, two were extended as if for flight, and two were wrapped around the whole body. When the blessed servant of the Most High saw these things, he was filled with the greatest wonder, but he could not understand what this vision should mean. Still, he was filled with happiness and he rejoiced very greatly because of the kind and gracious look with which he saw himself regarded by the seraph, whose beauty was beyond estimation; but the fact that the seraph was fixed to a cross and the sharpness of his suffering filled Francis with fear. And so he arose, if I may so speak, sorrowful and joyful, and joy and grief were in him alternately. Solicitously he thought what this vision could mean, and his soul was in great anxiety to find its meaning. And while he was thus unable to come to any understanding of it and the strangeness of the vision perplexed his heart, the marks of the nails began to appear in his hands and feet, just as he had seen them a little before in the crucified man above him.

95. His hands and feet seemed to be pierced through the middle by nails, with the heads of the nails appearing in the inner side of the hands and on the upper sides of the feet and their pointed ends on the opposite sides. The marks in the hands were round on the inner side, but on the outer side they were elongated; and some small pieces of flesh took on the appearance of the ends of the nails, bent and driven back and rising above the rest of the flesh. In the same way the marks of the nails were impressed upon the feet and raised in a similar way above the rest of the flesh. Furthermore, his right side was as though it had been pierced by a lance and had a wound in it that frequently bled so that his tunic and trousers were very often covered with his sacred blood. Alas, how few indeed merited to see the wound in his side while this crucified servant of the crucified Lord lived! But happy was Elias who, while the saint lived, merited to see this wound; and no less happy was Rufino who touched the wound with his own hands. For when this Brother Rufino once put his hand upon the bosom of this most holy man to rub him, his hand fell down to the right side of Francis, as it can happen; and it happened to touch the precious wound. The holy man of God was not a little grieved at this touch, and pushing his hand away, he cried out to the Lord to forgive Rufino. For he made every effort

to hide this wound from those outside the order, and he hid it with such great care from those close to him that even the brothers who were always at his side and his most devoted followers did not know of this wound for a long time. And though the servant and friend of the Most High saw himself adorned with so many and such great pearls, as with the most precious gems, and endowed in a wonderful manner above the glory and honor of all other men, he did not become vain in heart nor did he seek to please anyone out of thirst for vainglory; but, lest human favor should steal any of the grace given him, he strove in every way he could to hide it.

96. It was Francis' custom to reveal his great secret but rarely or to no one at all, for he feared that his revealing it to anyone might have the appearance of a special affection for him, in the way in which special friends act, and that he would thereby suffer some loss in the grace that was given him. He therefore carried about in his heart and frequently had on his lips this saying of the prophet: *Thy words have I hidden in my heart, that I may not sin against thee.* Francis had given a sign to his brothers and sons who lived with him, that whenever any lay people would come and he wanted to refrain from speaking with them, he would recite the aforementioned verse and immediately they were to dismiss with courtesy those who had come to him. For he had experienced that it is a great evil to make known all things to every one, and that he cannot be a spiritual man whose secrets are not more perfect and more numerous than the things that can be read on his face and completely understood by men. For he had found some who outwardly agreed with him but inwardly disagreed with him, who applauded him to his face, but ridiculed him behind his back, who acquired credit for themselves, but made the upright suspect to him. For wickedness often tries to blacken purity, and because of a lie that is familiar to many, the truth spoken by a few is not believed.

The Sorrowing of the Brothers and Their Joy When They Saw Francis Bearing the Marks of the Cross; and Of the Wings of the Seraphim

112. There was therefore a concourse of many people *praising God and saying:* "Praised and blessed be you, our Lord, God, who have entrusted so precious a treasure to us who are unworthy! Praise and glory be to you, ineffable Trinity." The whole city of Assisi rushed in a body and the whole region hastened to see the wonderful things of God which the Lord of Majesty had made manifest in his holy servant. Every one sang a canticle of joy, as their heartfelt gladness prompted them; and all blessed the omnipotence of the Savior for the fulfillment of their desire. However, Francis' sons were filled with sorrow at being deprived of so great a father and they showed the pious affection of their hearts by tears and sighs.

But an unheard of joy tempered their grief and the newness of a miracle threw their minds into great amazement. Their mourning was turned to song and their weeping to jubilation. For they had never heard or read in the Scriptures what was set before their eyes, what they could hardly be persuaded to believe if it had not been proved to them by such evident testimony. For in truth there appeared in him a true image of the cross and of the passion of the *lamb without blemish* who washed away the sins of the world, for he seemed as though he had been recently taken down from the cross, his hands and feet were pierced as though by nails and his side wounded as though by a lance.

They saw his flesh, which before had been dark, now gleaming with a dazzling whiteness and giving promise of the rewards of the blessed resurrection by reason of its beauty. They saw, finally, that his face was like the face of an angel, as though he were living and not dead; and the rest of his members had taken on the softness and pliability of an innocent child's members. His sinews were not contracted, as they generally are in the dead; his skin had not become hard; his members were not rigid, but they could be turned this way and that, however one wished.

113. And because he glowed with such wondrous beauty before all who looked upon him and his flesh had become even more white, it was wonderful to see in the middle of his hands and feet, not indeed the holes made by the nails, but the nails themselves formed out of his flesh and retaining the blackness of iron, and his right side was red with blood. These signs of martyrdom did not arouse horror in the minds of those who looked upon them, but they gave his body much beauty and grace, just as little black stones do when they are set in a white pavement.

His brothers and sons came hurriedly, and weeping, they kissed the hands and feet of their beloved father who was leaving them, and also his right side, in the wound of which was presented a remarkable memorial of him who in pouring forth both *blood and water* from that same place reconciled the world to his Father. Not only those who were permitted to kiss the sacred stigmata of Jesus Christ which St. Francis bore on his body, but even those who were permitted only to see them, thought they had been granted a very great gift. For who, seeing this thing, would give himself to weeping rather than to joy? Or if he wept, would he not do so rather from joy than from sorrow? Whose breast is so much like iron that it would not be moved to sighs? Whose heart so much like stone that it would not be broken to compunction, that it would not be fired to love of God, that it would not be strengthened to good will? Who is so dull, so unfeeling, that he would not realize in truth that as this saint was honored upon earth with so singular a gift, so would he also be magnified in heaven by an ineffable glory?

114. Singular gift and mark of special love, that a soldier should be adorned with the same arms of glory that were suitable for the son of the King by reason of their most excellent dignity! O miracle worthy of admirable and unceasing reverence, which represents to the eyes of faith that mystery in which the blood of the *lamb without blemish* flowed from five outlets to wash away the sins of the world! O sublime splendor of the living cross that gives life to the dead, the burden of which presses so gently and pricks so delicately that by it dead flesh is made to live and the weak spirit is made strong! He loved you much, whom you adorned so very gloriously. Glory and blessing be *to the only wise God* who renews *signs* and works *new miracles* that he might console the minds of the weak with new revelations and that by means of a wonderful work in things visible their hearts might be caught up to a love of things invisible. O wonderful and lovable disposition of God, which, that no suspicion might arise concerning this new miracle, first mercifully displayed in him who *descended from heaven* what a little later was to be wonderfully wrought in him who dwelt upon earth! And indeed the true Father of mercies wanted to show how great a reward he is worthy of who tried to love him with all his heart, namely, to be placed in the highest order of celestial spirits and indeed in the order nearest to himself.

We can without a doubt attain this reward, if, after the manner of the seraphim, we extend two wings above our head, that is, if we have, after the example of the blessed Francis, a pure intention in all our works and if our actions are upright, and if, directing these to God, we strive tirelessly to please him alone in all our works. These two wings must be joined together to cover the head, because the Father of lights will by no means accept either the uprightness of a work without purity of intention or vice versa, for he says: *If thy eye be sound, thy whole body will be full of light. But if thy eye be evil, thy whole body will be full of darkness.* The eye is not sound if it does not see what is to be seen, lacking the knowledge of truth, or if it looks upon what it should not see, not having a pure intention. In the first case, simple reasoning will show that the eye is not sound, but blind; in the second, that it is evil. The feathers of these wings are love of the Father, who saves us in his mercy, and fear of the Lord, who judges us terribly. These feathers must raise the souls of the elect from earthly things by repressing evil impulses and properly ordering chaste affections. With two wings for flying one is to extend a twofold charity to one's neighbor, namely, by refreshing his soul with the word of God and by sustaining his body with earthly help. These two wings, however, are rarely joined together, for both can hardly be fulfilled by anyone. The feathers of these wings are the various works which must be shown to one's neighbor to advise and help him. Lastly, with two wings the body that is bare of merits must be covered, and this is properly done when as often as sin has intervened it is again clothed with innocence through contrition and confession. The feathers of these wings are the many various affections which are born of hatred for sin and hunger for justice.

115. These things the most blessed father Francis fulfilled most perfectly; he bore the image and form of a seraph and, persevering upon the cross, merited to rise to the ranks of the heavenly spirits. For he was always on the cross, fleeing no labor or suffering, if only he could fulfill the will of the Lord in himself and concerning himself.

The brothers, moreover, who lived with him knew how his daily and continuous talk was of Jesus and how sweet and tender his conversation was, how kind and filled with love his talk with them. His mouth spoke *out of the abundance of* his *heart*, and the fountain of enlightened love that filled his whole being bubbled forth outwardly. Indeed, he was always occupied with Jesus; Jesus he bore in his heart, Jesus in his mouth, Jesus in his ears, Jesus in his eyes, Jesus in his hands, Jesus in the rest of his members. O how often, when he sat down to eat, hearing or speaking or thinking of Jesus, he forgot bodily food, as we read of the holy one: "Seeing, he did not see, and hearing he did not hear." Indeed, many times, as he went along the way meditating on and singing of Jesus, he would forget his journey and invite all the elements to praise Jesus. And because he always bore and preserved *Christ Jesus and him crucified* in his heart with a wonderful love, he was marked in a most glorious way above all others with the seal of him whom in a rapture of mind he contemplated sitting in inexpressible and incomprehensible glory at the right hand of the Father, with whom he, the co-equal and most high Son of the Most High, lives and reigns, conquers and governs in union with the Holy Spirit, God eternally glorious through all ages forever. Amen.

Concerning the Grief of the Ladies at St. Damian's; and How St. Francis Was Buried with Praise and Glory

116. Francis' brothers and sons, therefore, who gathered together with a great multitude of people from the cities nearby and rejoiced to be present at such great solemnities, spent the whole night in which the holy father had died singing the praises of God, so much so that, because of the charm of the jubilation and the brightness of the lights, it seemed to be a wake of the angels. But when morning had come, a great multitude from the city of Assisi assembled with all the clergy, and, taking the sacred body from the place where Francis had died, they carried it amid great honor to the city, with hymns and praises and sounding trumpets. They all took up branches of olive trees and of other trees, and, carrying out the obsequies with solemnity, they discharged the duties of praise with many lights and with loud

voices. When, with the sons carrying their father, and the flock following their shepherd who was hastening to meet the Shepherd of all, they came to the place where he had himself first planted the religion and order of holy virgins and poor ladies, they placed him in the church of St. Damian, where these same daughters whom he had won for the Lord dwelt; there they paused and the little window through which the handmaids of Christ were accustomed to receive at the appointed time the sacrament of the body of the Lord was opened. The coffin was opened, in which lay hidden the treasure of supercelestial virtues and in which he was being borne by a few who was accustomed to bear many. And behold, the Lady Clare, who was truly illustrious by the holiness of her merits and was the first mother of the rest since she was the very first plant of this holy Order, came with the rest of her daughters to see their father who would no longer speak to them or return to them but was hastening elsewhere.

121. At his tomb, too, new miracles are constantly occurring, and, the number of petitions greatly increasing, great benefits for body and for soul are sought at that same place. Sight is given to the blind, hearing is restored to the deaf, the ability to walk is given to the lame, the mute speak, he who has the gout leaps, the leper is healed, he who suffers from a swelling has it reduced, and those who suffer diverse and various infirmities obtain health, so that his dead body heals living bodies just as his living body had raised up dead souls.

The Roman pontiff, the highest of all bishops, the leader of the Christians, the lord of the world, the pastor of the Church, the anointed of the Lord, the vicar of Christ, heard and understood all this. He rejoiced and was happy, he danced with joy and was glad, when he saw the Church of God renewed in his own day by new mysteries but ancient wonders, and that in his own son, whom he bore in his holy womb, cherished in his bosom, nursed with his words, and nourished with the food of salvation. The rest of the guardians of the Church too heard it, the shepherds of the flock, the defenders of the faith, *the friends of the bridegroom*, those who are at his side, the hinges of the world, the venerable cardinals. They congratulated the Church, they rejoiced with the pope, they glorified the Savior, who with the highest and ineffable wisdom, the highest and incomprehensible grace, the highest and immeasurable goodness chooses the foolish and base things of this world that he might thus draw the strong things to himself. The whole world heard and applauded, and the entire realm that was subject to the Catholic faith superabounded in joy and overflowed with holy consolation.

122. But there was a sudden change in things and new dangers arose meanwhile in the world. Suddenly the joy of peace was disturbed and the torch of envy was lighted and the Church was torn by domestic and civil

war. The Romans, a rebellious and ferocious race of men, raged against their neighbors, as was their custom, and, being rash, they stretched *forth their hands against* the *holy places*. The distinguished Pope Gregory tried to curb their growing wickedness, to repress their savagery, to temper their violence; and, like a tower of great strength, he protected the Church of Christ. Many dangers assailed her, destruction became more frequent, and in the rest of the world *the necks of sinners* were raised against God. What then? Measuring the future by his very great experience and weighing the present circumstances, he abandoned the city to the rebels, so that he might free the world from rebellions and defend it. He came therefore to the city of Rieti, where he was received with honor, as was befitting. From there he went to Spoleto where he was honored with great respect by all. He remained there a few days, and, after the affairs of the Church had been provided for, he kindly visited, in the company of the venerable cardinals, the Poor Ladies of Christ, who were dead and buried to the world. The holy life of these Poor Ladies, their highest poverty, and their glorious way of life moved him and the others to tears, stirred them to contempt of the world, and kindled in them a desire for the life of retirement. O lovable humility, nurse of all graces! The prince of the world, the successor of the prince of the apostles, visits these poor women, comes to them lowly and humble in their seclusion; and, though this humility is worthy of just approbation, it was nevertheless an unusual example and one that had not been seen for many ages past.

123. Then he hastened on, hastened to Assisi, where a glorious treasure awaited him, that through it the universal suffering and imminent tribulation might be extinguished. At his approach, the whole region rejoiced, the city was filled with exultation, the great throng of people celebrated their happiness, and the already bright day was further illuminated by brighter lights. Every one went out to meet him and solemn watches were kept by all. The pious fraternity of Poor Brothers went out to meet him, and they all sang sweet songs to Christ the Lord. The vicar of Christ arrived at the place and going first to the grave of St. Francis, he greeted it reverently and eagerly. He sighed deeply, struck his breast, shed tears, and bowed his venerable head with great devotion. While he was there a solemn discussion was held concerning the canonization of the holy man, and the noble assembly of cardinals met often concerning this business. From all sides many came together who had been freed from their illnesses through the holy man of God, and from every side a very great number of miracles gave forth their luster: these were approved, verified, heard, accepted. Meanwhile, the urgency of the affairs of his office pressed upon the pope, a new emergency threatened, and the holy father went to Perugia that by a superabounding and singular grace he might return again to Assisi in the

interests of this very great business. Then they met again at Perugia, and a sacred assembly of cardinals was held concerning this matter in the room of the lord pope. They were all in agreement and they spoke unanimously; they read the miracles and regarded them with great reverence, and they commended the life and conduct of the blessed father with the highest praises.

124. "The most holy life of this most holy man," they said, "needs no attestation of miracles; *what we have seen with our eyes, what our hands have handled*, we have proved with the light of truth." They were all transported with joy, they rejoiced, they wept, and indeed in those tears there was a great blessing. They immediately appointed the happy day on which they would fill the whole world with saving happiness. The solemn day came, a day to be held in reverence by every age, a day that shed its sublime rapture not only upon the earth but even upon the heavenly mansions. Bishops came together, abbots arrived, prelates of the Church were present from even the most remote parts of the world; a king too was present, and a noble multitude of counts and princes. They then escorted the lord of all the world and entered the city of Assisi with him amid great pomp. He reached the place prepared for so solemn an event and the whole multitude of glorious cardinals, bishops, and abbots gathered around the blessed pope. A most distinguished gathering of priests and clerics was there; a happy and sacred company of religious men was there; the more bashful habit of the sacred veil was there too; a great crowd of all the people was there and an almost innumerable multitude of both sexes. They hurried there from all sides, and every age came to the concourse of people with the greatest eagerness. *The small and great* were *there*, the servant and they who were free of a master.

125. The supreme pontiff was there, the spouse of the Church of Christ, surrounded by a variety of his great children and with a crown of glory on his head, *an ornament of honor*. He stood there adorned with the pontifical robes and clad in holy vestments ornamented with *jewels set in gold and graven by the work of a lapidary*. The anointed of the Lord stood there, resplendent in *magnificence and glory in gilded clothing*; and covered with engraven jewels sparkling with the radiance of spring, he caught the attention of all. Cardinals and bishops stood around him; decked with splendid necklaces and clad in garments as white as snow they showed forth the image of super-celestial beauties and displayed the joy of the glorified. All the people stood in expectation of *the voice of mirth, the voice of gladness*, a new voice, a voice full of all sweetness, a voice of praise, a voice of constant blessing. First Pope Gregory preached to all the people, and with a sweetly flowing and sonorous voice he spoke the praises of God. He also praised the holy father Francis in a noble eulogy, and recalling and speak-

ing of the purity of his life, he was bathed in tears. His sermon had this text: *He shone in his days as the morning star in the midst of a cloud, and as the moon at the full. And as the sun when it shineth, so did he shine in the temple of God*. When the *faithful saying and worthy of all acceptation* was completed, one of the lord pope's subdeacons, Octavian by name, read the miracles of the saint before all in a very loud voice, and the lord Raynerius, a cardinal deacon, a man of penetrating intellect and renowned for his piety and life, spoke about them with holy words and with an abundance of tears. The Shepherd of the Church was carried away with joy, and sighing from the very depths of his being and sobbing, he shed torrents of tears. So too the other prelates of the church poured out floods of tears, and their sacred vestments were moistened with their abundance. All the people too wept, and with the suspense of their longing expectation, they became wearied.

126. Then the happy pope spoke with a loud voice, and extending his hands to heaven, he said: "To the praise and glory of Almighty God, the Father, Son, and Holy Spirit, and of the glorious Virgin Mary and of the blessed apostles Peter and Paul, and to the honor of the glorious Roman Church, at the advice of our brothers and of the other prelates, we decree that the most blessed father Francis, whom the Lord has glorified in heaven and whom we venerate on earth, shall be enrolled in the catalogue of saints and that his feast shall be celebrated on the day of his death." At this decree, the venerable cardinals began to sing in a loud voice along with the pope the *Te Deum Laudamus*. Then there was raised a clamor among the many people praising God; the earth resounded with their mighty voices, the air was filled with their rejoicings, and the ground was moistened with their tears. New songs were sung, and the servants of God gave expression to their joy in melody of spirit. Sweet sounding organs were heard there and spiritual hymns were sung with well modulated voices. There a very sweet odor was breathed, and a more joyous melody that stirred the emotions resounded there. The day was bright and colored with more splendid rays than usual. There were green olive branches there and fresh branches of other trees. Brightly glittering festive attire adorned all the people, and the blessing of peace filled the minds of those who had come there with joy. Then the happy Pope Gregory descended from his lofty throne, and going by way of the lower steps, he entered the sanctuary to offer *the vows and voluntary oblations*; he kissed with his happy lips the tomb that contained the body that was sacred and consecrated to God. He offered and multiplied his prayers and celebrated the sacred mysteries. A *ring of his brethren* stood about him, praising, adoring, and blessing Almighty God who had done *great things in all the earth*. All the people increased the praises of

God and they paid due thanksgiving to St. Francis in honor of the most holy Trinity. Amen.

These things took place in the city of Assisi in the second year of the pontificate of the lord pope Gregory on the seventeenth day of the calends of the month of August.

Book 3

Of the Parable Francis Spoke before the Pope

16. At the time when Francis presented himself along with his followers before Pope Innocent to ask for a rule of life, the pope, a man endowed with the greatest discretion, seeing that his proposed way of life was beyond his powers, said to him: "Pray, son, to Christ, that he may show us his will through you, so that, knowing his will, we may more securely give assent to your pious desires." The holy man agreed to the command of the supreme shepherd and hastened confidently to Christ; he prayed earnestly and devoutly exhorted his companions to pray to God. But why should we speak at length? He obtained an answer by prayer and reported the news of salvation to his sons. The familiar talk of Christ is made known in parables. "Francis," he said, "speak thus to the pope. A certain woman who was poor but very beautiful lived in a certain desert. A certain king loved her because of her very great beauty; he gladly married her and begot very handsome sons by her. When they had grown to adulthood and been brought up nobly, their mother said to them: 'Do not be ashamed, my loved ones, in that you are poor, for you are all sons of that king. Go gladly to his court and ask him for whatever you need.' Hearing this they were in admiration and rejoiced, and buoyed up by the assurance of their royal origin, they regarded want as riches, knowing that they would be heirs. They boldly presented themselves to the king and they did not fear the face of him whose likeness they bore. Recognizing his own likeness in them, the king wondered and asked whose sons they were. When they said they were the sons of that poor woman living in the desert, the king embraced them and said: 'You are my sons and heirs; fear not. For if strangers are fed at my table, it is all the more just that I see to it that those be fed to whom my entire heritage is reserved by right.' The king then ordered the woman to send all the sons he had begotten to the court to be provided for." The saint was made happy and glad by the parable and reported the holy message to the pope.

17. This woman was Francis, because he was fruitful in many sons, not because of any softness in his actions. The desert was the world, untilled

and barren at that time in the teaching of virtues. The handsome and numerous progeny of sons was the great multitude of brothers adorned with
every virtue. The king was the Son of God, to whom they bore a resem-
blance by their holy poverty. And they received nourishment at the table of
the king, despising all shame over their meanness; for, content with imitating Christ and living by alms, they knew they would be happy amid the
reproaches of the world.

The lord pope wondered at the parable proposed to him and recognized
without doubting that Christ had spoken in man. He recalled a certain vision he had had a few days before, which, he affirmed, under the guidance
of the Holy Spirit, would be fulfilled in this man. He had seen in his sleep
the Lateran basilica about to fall to ruin, when a certain religious, small
and despised, propped it up by putting his own back under it lest it fall.
"Surely," he said, "this is that man who, by his works and by the teaching
of Christ, will give support to the Church." For this reason the lord pope
readily gave in to the petition of Francis. Therefore, filled with love of God
he always showed a special love toward the servant of Christ. And therefore
he quickly granted what had been asked, and he promised to grant even
greater things than these. Francis, therefore, by reason of the authority
granted him, began to scatter the seeds of virtue, going about *the towns
and villages* preaching fervently.

45. Bernard Gui, *Manual of the Inquisitor* (1323–1324)

General Instruction

. . . It is very difficult to seize heretics if they do not confess their error
openly, but conceal it, or if there is no certain and sufficient testimony
against them. In that case the inquisitor is troubled on all sides. For, on one
side, his conscience troubles him if someone is punished who has neither
confessed nor been convicted. But if, on the other, people of whose falsity,
cunning, and malice he has repeatedly been informed escape with the cleverness of foxes to do more damage to the faith, his heart is even more
troubled, because as a result they are only strengthened, multiply, and acquire still more cunning. On yet another side, it scandalizes faithful laymen
if an inquisition is undertaken against someone and then abandoned in
frustration, as it were. When they see that learned men are duped by un-

From Bernard Gui, *Practica inquisitionis heretice provitatis*, in Guillaume Mollat, editor,
Manuel de l'inquisiteur, Les classiques de l'histoire de France du Moyen Age, VIII, IX
(Paris, 1926–27), vol. 1: 6–9, 178–82; vol. 2: 123–43. Translated for this volume by Con-
stantin Fasolt.

educated, base people, their faith weakens a little. They believe that we are able at any moment to explain the faith so lucidly and clearly that no one could withstand us without our being able instantly to refute him so clearly that even the laymen could understand why. This is why it is not profitable to dispute the faith in front of laymen with heretics as clever as this.

One should also point out that the same medicine does not heal all illnesses, because each illness has its own specific medicine. In the same way no unvarying method of interrogation, investigation, and examination should be used for every one of the heretics of the different sects. A method unique and specific to each must rather be used for individuals as well as for groups of people. Like a prudent doctor of souls, the inquisitor should consider the quality, condition, status, illness, and place of the people whom, or about whom, he is investigating. He should proceed cautiously in inquiring into and examining these matters, should not put, or persist in putting, all of the following questions in the same way and the same order to all people, and in the case of some people he should not be satisfied with having asked these particular questions, not even all of them, but should bridle the heretic's cunning with the harness of his discretion so that, with God's help, he can act the midwife and drag the winding snake from a bottomless bilge of errors.

A single, infallible rule can really not be given in these matters, or else the sons of darkness will have time to become familiar with the procedure, foresee it, avoid it the more easily, like a trap, and even manage to take precautions against it. A knowledgeable inquisitor will therefore carefully take his cue from the answers of the deponents, from the statements of the accusers, from what experience has taught him, from his own good judgment, or from the following questions or interrogations, whichever God may provide.

In order to familiarize the reader briefly with the method of examining the five sects, i.e., the Manichaeans, the Waldensians, also known as the Poor of Lyons, the pseudo-Apostles, those who are popularly known as the Beguines, and Jewish converts to Christianity who return to the vomit of Judaism, as well as fortune-tellers, magicians, and those who pray to demons, pests which gravely interfere with the purity of the faith, we shall on the following pages methodically add certain observations, first describing the general substance of each sect's error, then adding the proper method of examination. This will become clear in the following. . . .

How to Avoid the Cunning of the Beguines

. . . One must, therefore, safeguard oneself in one's investigation against the malice and the astuteness of such people. They must in all circumstances be forced to swear, simply and absolutely, without any conditions or reservations, that they will say the full truth, and nothing but the truth, about themselves as well as about their accomplices, believers, favorers, hosts, and defenders, according to the meaning of the inquisitor's questions, without bad faith or deceit, regardless whether they are confessing on their own or responding to the inquisitor's questions, about themselves or others, in the affirmative or the negative, and all of this for the entire length of the inquisition. Otherwise they shall automatically bring perjury and the penalty thereof upon themselves.

One must avoid accepting an oath from them which is accompanied by any conditions or reservations, or by a protestation like the one mentioned above. One must explain to them that, contrary to what they say they believe, it does not amount to offending God, and that God is in fact not offended, if a judge seeks the truth in order to discover error and heresy, and that they must stand by the judgment of the inquisitor in this matter, and not their false opinion.

Contrary to what they say, it really has nothing to do with wounding, or inflicting damage or injury on, a neighbor, but rather with helping him to his good and the salvation of his soul, when people who are infected by, and embroiled in, errors are denounced so that they can be corrected, turned back from their error to the way of truth, and better themselves, lest they become even more corrupt and infect and corrupt others with their errors.

But if they pertinaciously refuse to swear without said conditions and reservations, if, that is to say, they have not precisely sworn to say the full truth and nothing but the truth in the trial in which they are being charged, as has already been explained, they should first be admonished according to the rule of canon law. Someone who has been admonished and still refuses to swear shall be sentenced to excommunication in writing, unless he immediately swears the desired oath precisely, or at least swears at the hour, the day, or the time which the investigating judge may, out of his kindness or equity, have thought fit to give him as a last chance, even though legally he is obliged to swear precisely, simply, immediately, and without any delay. When the sentence of excommunication has been ordered, formulated, and issued, it shall be entered in the proceedings.

When someone has incurred a sentence of excommunication and has pertinaciously borne it with a hardened heart for several days, he shall be called back to trial and be asked if he considers himself excommunicated and bound by said sentence. If he answers that he does not consider himself excommunicated and bound by said sentence, he proves *ipso facto* that he obviously scorns the keys of the Church. This is a definite case of error and heresy, and someone who pertinaciously perseveres in this belief must be considered a heretic. Both the question and his response shall be entered in the proceedings, and one should go on to prosecute him as the law demands, admonish him canonically, and warn him one last time to abandon and abjure such error and heresy. Otherwise he will from that time on be judged a heretic, will be condemned, and as such will be relinquished to the judgment of a secular court.

Note also that, in order to prove his malice, to make his error more obvious, and to justify the process against him, another, new sentence of excommunication may be issued in writing against him for contumacy in matters of faith, inasmuch as he pertinaciously refuses to swear simply and precisely, to answer questions concerning the faith and to abjure an express heretical error, thus manifestly dodging obedience, no less than one who has been summoned for some other reason and contumaciously absents himself. He shall be informed in writing that another sentence has been issued against him. Because, furthermore, he has been excommunicated for contumacy in matters of faith, he must and can be legally condemned as a heretic as soon as he has endured said sentence for more than one year with a stubborn heart.

Note, moreover, that, if anybody is willing to testify, one may proceed to hear witnesses against such a person, and that, in order to draw out the truth, he may be starved, imprisoned, or chained, and that, on the advice of experts, he may also be questioned, to the degree which the nature of the affair and the condition of his person may require.

On the Inquisitors' Sermon in General

When the confessions and depositions about heresy, harboring heretics, favoring heretics, regarding themselves or others, or whatever else may be within the competence of the inquisition, have been received from the confessors; when the defense of the dead and the living has been stated and been brought to a conclusion; when all statements of confession or defense have also been carefully and faithfully examined; and when advice has been sought and obtained from prelates and lawyers, then the inquisitors will proceed with the necessary solemnity to pronounce the sermon in which thanks are given, penances enjoined, and sentences issued according to the merits and demerits of everyone.

At a suitable time before the sermon, however, the inquisitors will seek advice from the aforementioned persons. First, a brief summary of offenses shall be compiled, in which the substance of everybody's confession concerning his own offense shall be completely dealt with, without mentioning any names, in order to ensure that the counsellors' decision on the penance to be imposed for every offense will be free of any personal regard. It is true that their advice would be more to the point if everything were recounted in detail. This procedure should therefore be followed where and when counsellors to whom these things can be revealed without any risk can be found. The risk of calumny would then also be smaller. But, because of the just mentioned danger, this has from the beginning not been the habit of the inquisition. A fully detailed account of everybody's confession, however, is given to the bishop or his vicar beforehand, in the presence of a few experts, secretaries, and jurors.

For one or two days before the sermon, furthermore, and in the presence of a notary and several witnesses, the inquisitor will read to everyone individually and separately a vernacular version of the summary of his offenses. He will likewise read it in the public sermon, addressing the person concerned and saying: "You such and such, from such and such a place, as is proved by your confession, have done such and such."

Likewise, on the day before the sermon, the inquisitor himself or his representative, whichever may seem better, will order each and everyone to appear the following day in the place where the public sermon will be given, where they will receive their penance or hear their sentence, according to the nature of their offense. On the following day he will begin with the sermon early in the morning.

The following order applies to what should be done in the general sermon of inquisitors for heresy in the regions of Toulouse and Carcassone:

First of all, a sermon shall be given, which, considering how much is to be done, should be brief. Then the customary indulgence shall be granted.

Second, the oath of the officers of the royal court, of the consuls, and of others present with temporal jurisdiction shall be received.

Third, crosses shall be taken off those to whom that grace is due.

Fourth, the men and women for whom it is judged expedient shall be led out of the prison, and crosses and pilgrimages shall be imposed on them.

Fifth, the offenses of those on whom penances or sentences are to be imposed shall be recounted and read in the vernacular in the following order: first, of those on whom discretionary penances are to be imposed, like going on pilgrimage, bearing the cross, and living according to certain general rules; then those who are to be immured simply; then those who must do penance for bearing false testimony and be immured; then, if there are any, the priests and clerics who are to be deposed and immured; then the dead of whom it must be made known that they would have had to be immured had they been alive; then those who died without repenting of their heresy, whose bodies are to be exhumed; then fugitives who are to be condemned as heretics; then heretics who relapsed into a heresy which they had abjured in a trial, who are to be relinquished to the secular arm, first the laymen, then the clerics, if there are any; then the perfect heretics, who refuse to turn away from heresy and to return to the unity of the Church, whether they are Manichaeans, Waldensians, or belong to the heretical sect of those who call themselves Beguines or the Poor of Christ, keep themselves separate from the community of the others, and weaken the power of Pope and Church; finally those who had confessed heresy in a previous trial and later revoked their confession, or whom witnesses overwhelmingly convicted of heresy and who still refuse to admit the truth even though they are unable to defend themselves against it, or clear themselves of it, in a trial, who are to be relinquished to the secular court as impenitent heretics.

Sixth, when the offenses have been recounted and before penances are to be imposed, penitents shall abjure their heresy and swear an oath to obey the orders of the Church and the inquisitors. Then they shall be absolved from the sentences of excommunication which have been promulgated by the law against such people in general, and which they are known in fact to have incurred because of their heretical offenses.

Seventh, the sentences shall be first read in Latin and then briefly explained in the vernacular, in the same order in which the offenses were read, if that is convenient to do. The number of people on whom penances, punishments, or sentences are to be imposed, however, is occasionally so great that such an order cannot very well be observed, but must be altered in some respects and within reasonable limits. It depends on the discretion of the judge to decide which order seems the most fitting and expedient to be observed.

A convenient order in which to enjoin or issue penances and sentences in the sermon could thus be the following:

First, discretionary penances are enjoined;

Second, the sentence or penance of those to be immured may have its place;

Third, the sentence of the deceased of whom it was to be made known that, if alive, they would have had to be immured, so that, if necessary, the testator's heresy can be used to prevent the heirs from gaining access to his goods, notwithstanding that he died before any sentence of heresy was pronounced against him during his lifetime, since he died too soon;

Fourth, the sentence of condemnation of all such deceased as are known to have favored heretics during their lives, but who have neither confessed it in a trial nor been judicially absolved of the sentence of excommunication which canon law imposes on them, who are to be exhumed simply without their bones being burned;

Sixth, the sentence of fugitives who are to be condemned as heretics;

Seventh, the sentence of those who relapsed into a heresy which they abjured in a previous trial, who are to be relinquished to the secular court, or arm, first laymen, then clerics, if any must be condemned;

Eighth, the sentence of condemnation of perfect heretics, who refuse to turn from heresy and come back to the unity of the Church;

Ninth, the sentence of those who lawfully confessed their heresy in trial previously and later revoked their lawful confession, or who have been convicted by witnesses but refuse to confess the truth about their heresy;

Tenth, the sentence of excommunication may be pronounced against people whose processes have not yet been brought to the point of definitive sentencing, but who are contumacious in matters of faith and are fugitive because of their heresy;

Finally, the sentence is issued to demolish houses because people became heretics, or were received into a condemned sect of heretics, in them, or for other just reasons; if it seems more expedient, it is sometimes also proper to pronounce a sentence of this kind immediately after the sentence of the people who became heretics, or were received into a condemned sect of heretics, in such houses.

Form of the Oath to Be Sworn by the Sénéchal and the Royal Officers with Their Hands Placed upon the Gospels

We, Sénéchal so and so, Viguier of Toulouse so and so, Judge Ordinary so and so (and similarly for all of the other officials present) swear on the Holy Gospels of God that we shall keep our faith towards our Lord Jesus Christ and the Holy Roman Church, ensure that it is kept by others, and defend it against everybody to the best of our ability.

Likewise, we shall pursue and capture, or have captured, heretics and their believers, favorers, hosts, and defenders, as well as fugitives by reason of heresy, whenever we can, and shall accuse and denounce them to the Church and the inquisitors if we find out wherever they, or anyone of them, may be.

Likewise, we shall confer no bailiwicks, judicatures, other administrative districts, or other public offices on anyone of these pestiferous people, nor on anyone who is suspected, or defamed, of being a heretic, nor shall we permit anyone whom the law or the inquisitors have prohibited from exercising public offices because of heresy or any other reason to use or to hold public offices.

Likewise we shall not knowingly receive or maintain any one of these people in our family, company, service, or in our counsel. And if we should perhaps unwittingly have done otherwise, we shall expel them altogether as soon as the inquisitors or other trustworthy people shall have informed us of this.

In these as well as in other matters which pertain to the office of the inquisition we shall obey God and the Roman Church and its inquisitors. So help us God and these Holy Gospels of God.

What to Do about Heretics Who Repent at the Moment of Punishment

If it happens, as has already more than once been the case, that someone has been relinquished and handed over to the secular arm and court, was received by that court, has been led to the place of execution, and then says and asserts that he wants to do penance and to renounce his errors, then such a person must be kept alive and given back to the inquisitors. Unless he has perhaps relapsed again, the inquisitors must receive him, so as to put equity above rigor in this matter and avoid scandalizing those of little faith by the Church's denial of the sacrament of penance to someone seeking it. The office of the inquisition is known to have done something like this several times already.

In such a case the inquisitors must, however, exercise the greatest caution and carefully observe whether the conversion is true or simulated, since those who are converted on the point of death may well be suspected of having only acted out of fear of punishment. Let them be tested, to show whether they walk in darkness or in light, lest they act the wolf in sheep's clothing.

Whether or not they are honest can be reliably determined by the following methods and trials: they are, if they promptly and voluntarily denounce and reveal all their accomplices to the inquisitors; likewise, if they persecute their sect in signs, words, and actions, and humbly confess their old errors one by one and execrate and abjure them all in the same way. All of this can be evidently ascertained by examining them and reading their confession, which should be taken down in writing.

After such people have been received and have confessed in trial, they must with their own mouths revoke and execrate all the errors they held before, abjure each individual error as well as the whole of their heresy in public trial, confess the Catholic faith, and promise and swear whatever else is customary in the case of people received back from heresy. Finally, they shall be incarcerated forever in order to do penance, with the power to mitigate the sentence being reserved, as is the custom.

Even though it is not common law to save them and receive them into penance after their sentence has been issued, as it has just been described, the office of the inquisition has nevertheless observed this procedure previously in several similar cases. Because it has the greatest privileges, and seeks the salvation of souls and the purity of the faith above all else, it is also the first to receive heretics into penance who wish to be converted and return to the unity of the Church. Through their confessions, moreover, accomplices and more errors are often discovered, the truth is found thereby and error revealed, and the office prospers.

But if such conversion seems more likely to be feigned or simulated to the inquisitors, the aforesaid procedures shall be stopped so that the sentence which has been issued may take effect.

Commerce Confronts the Usury Prohibition

Medieval commerce reached its peak between 1100 and 1300. The primary impetus to commercial activity was the agricultural prosperity and the steady growth of population. By the beginning of the twelfth century, commercial activity was absorbing increasing numbers of the urban population. This development was especially true of Italy, where urban centers dominated the landscape and commercial activity dominated the urban centers from the tenth century onward. Commerce was rarely a local affair; led by the Genoese and Venetians, Italian merchants and merchandise were found throughout the Mediterranean and Europe. The expansion of commerce was aided by the increasing use of coinage, by the development of new forms of economic arrangements for the mobilization, transfer, and safekeeping of capital, by the revival of Roman law which sanctified contracts and private ownership of property, and by a corps of professional notaries who transformed oral agreements into written contracts and professional jurists who arbitrated the disputes that inevitably arose.

The first of the readings below illustrates the diversity of arrangements—simple loans, partnerships, letters of exchange, and deposit contracts—used by Genoese merchants (document 46). Partnerships or *commenda* facilitated overseas commerce, which demanded more capital for a longer period than a single individual possessed, by allowing two or more persons to join together in a common venture. Letters of exchange provided the means to effect monetary payments and transfers at a distance with little or no exchange of coin. Unlike straight loans and deposit contracts, which were often denounced by churchmen as usurious, partnerships and exchange contracts were generally held to be licit.

Other readings in this section illustrate the nature of the prohibition against usury. The classic definition of usury came from the pen of the

Church Father, Bishop Ambrose of Milan: "whatever is added to the principal is usury." This definition referred only to loans, and thus usury came to mean anything given or accepted beyond the principal of a loan. Usury was prohibited by both the Old and New Testaments and considered an evil, because it was a sin against charity and brotherhood. Christ's oft-quoted command, "Lend freely and hope for nothing in return" (Lk 6:35), condemned the very intention to profit from a loan. The revival of the Aristotelian notion that money is artificially made by men and not by nature and that to profit from a loan is unnatural contributed a powerful weapon to the war against usury.

However, the war raged because evasion of the prohibition against usury was endemic. A classic struggle between ideology and practice ensued. Papal decrees, conciliar legislation, sermons, theological and legal opinions and tracts, and manuals for the instruction of confessors roundly denounced usury and demanded that usurers make restitution of their illicit gain. Some followed this injunction (document 47). But as economic organization and credit arrangements became increasingly complex, evasion of the prohibition became easier, while at the same time it became more and more difficult to tell—apart from simple money-lending—whether or not a commercial activity was usurious. The readings below shed considerable light on this problem. The influential, yet ambiguous, decretal *Naviganti*, promulgated by Gregory IX in 1234, treats the morality of the sea loan and the widespread practice of discounting (document 48). The Franciscan theologian, Peter John Olivi (d. 1298), lays bare the distinctions between usury (*usura*) and legitimate compensation (*interesse*) and between juridically sterile money (*pecunia*) and economically fertile capital (*capitale*) (document 50). Olivi hailed from southern France, studied at the University of Paris, taught in Franciscan convent schools, was a prolific writer, and is generally regarded as a theologian of towering intellect. The occasional character of Olivi's quodlibetal disputations can be contrasted with Thomas Aquinas's (1225–1274) systematic treatment of usury in his *Summa theologiae*. Thomas became a Dominican friar in 1245 and the first Dominican to teach theology at the University of Paris (1256). Between 1265 and 1274 he composed the *Summa theologiae*, from which the selection below (document 51) is taken. Another selection (document 49), the decree *Ex gravi* enacted by the council of Vienne (1311–12), reveals the difficulties of enforcing the prohibition against usury.

46. Contracts: Loan, Partnership, Letter of Exchange, and Deposit (ca. 1100–1200)

1. The Business Unit: A Loan, 1192.

Alberto Balbo of Saint Peter of Arena agrees that he will give to Gandulf of Raalvengo [both small towns near Genoa] £12 1/2 in Genoese money, which Gandulf lent out of love, on or before the first of next March under the penalty of paying double should he fail to pay by then. At the store of the Fornarii 28 January 1192. Witnesses Otto of Langasco, Jordan Ricerio, Henry Porco.

2. The Business Unit: A Commenda, 1086.

Ogerio Aragano and Ogerio Aguzzino witnesses. I, Alberto Ceclieto, have received in form of *commenda* from you, Bellobruno of Castello, £100 in Genoese money, which I shall take to Alexandria for the purpose of trading, and from there, should I wish, to Ceuta, [Morocco] and I am to return to Genoa without any other change in my route. I am to send either to you or your designated agent the capital and the profit from this venture, and after the capital has been deducted, I am to keep one quarter of the profit.

I swear on the Holy Gospels to keep safe, watch over, and increase the *commenda*, etc., and to turn over and give to you or to your designated representative the capital and profit of the venture in good faith and with no deceit; and furthermore not to spend more than two shillings for expenses during the whole voyage.

Done at Genoa in the castle, at the house of Bellobruno, in the year 1086, in the third indiction and the ninth day before the end of September.

3. The Business Unit: Partnership, 1191.

In the house of Ingo Longo, 11 October 1191. Witnesses Fredenzo Ontardo, William Rava.

Lanfranco Lizano in partnership with Isoberto agrees to carry £152 of the money of Isoberto and £76 of his own to Septa [Ceuta], and from there wherever he shall think best for the purpose of trading in good faith. On his return to Genoa Isoberto promises to give to Lanfranco or his designated

From Thomas C. Mendenhall, Basil D. Henning, A. S. Foord, eds., *Ideas and Institutions in European History, 800–1715* (New York: Holt, Rinehart and Winston, 1964), pp. 93–95. © 1964 by Holt, Rinehart and Winston. Reprinted by permission of CBS College Publishing.

agent his share of whatever profit God may give together with his capital. When each has got his capital back, the profit is to be divided equally. Lanfranco may send the money back to Genoa to Isoberto, should it seem best, provided there are witnesses.

5. The Business Instrument: Letter of Exchange, Genoa, 1202.

I, John Ascherio, in my own name and in the name of my partnership, agree that I have received and have in my possession from you, Rondano of Rondani of Placentia, on your behalf and on behalf of your partners a certain sum of Genoese money. I yield my right to claim that I do not have said money or that it was not given to me, as well as all my other legal rights. In return for this money I promise by way of exchange to pay to you or your designated agent, either myself or through my designated agent, £ two hundred in the money of Provins [one of the Champagne fair towns] at the next fair of Troyes [Champagne] as payment in full. If the said fair should not be held, I shall pay at the time that it should have been held. Done at Genoa in front of the House of the Canons of St. Laurent where lived the late Aimus [a spice merchant] on 23 June 1202, in the late afternoon.

Deposit Contract

[Genoa,] November 7, 1200

I, Oberto, banker, of Pollanexi, acknowledge that I have received from you, Maria, wife of Rolando Generificio, £50 Genoese in *accomendacio*, which belong to your husband, the aforesaid Rolando. I am to keep them in the bank and to employ [them] in trade in Genoa as long as it shall be your pleasure; and I promise to give you the profit according to what seems to me ought to come to you. Moreover, I promise to return and to restore the aforesaid £50 or just as much instead of them, myself or through my messenger, to you or to your husband or to your accredited messenger, within eight days after you tell me and make the request, and similarly [to give you] the profit; otherwise the penalty of the double and the seizure of my goods as security. Done in the house of the late Baldovino de Arato. Witnesses: Rufo de Arato and Aimerico, cooper. In the year of the Nativity of the Lord 1200, third indiction, the seventh day of November.

47. Restitution of Usury (1220–1221)

Lucca, March 13, 1220

Ugolino and Arduino, brothers, [sons] of the late Ildebrandino, feeling weighed down by usuries which Genovese, [recently] deceased, had extracted from them, therefore appealed to the Supreme Pontiff, [asking] that Filippo, priest [and] rector of the church of S. Pietro Somaldi, must not bury him before they are satisfied in regard to the usuries which they had asked him to return. This was done in Lucca, in the court of S. Pietro Somaldi, in the portico, in the presence of Gaiascone, [son] of the late Orlando Guasone, and of Guido, [son] of the late Orlandino. 1220, the third [day] before the Ides of March.

[I], Benedetto, judge and notary of the lord emperor, took part in this entire [transaction], and I wrote this as a record.

Siena, September 27, 1221

On the same day. I, Aringhiero d'Altavilla, promise you, Magister Pietro, rector of the Church of S. Pietro delle Scale, and I swear on the holy Gospels of God that if I escape from this illness I shall be and remain [obedient] to the order of the lord bishop of Siena in regard to the usuries which I have collected up to this day, satisfying whoever proves to me his legal [claims] in regard to them and making restitution of these [usuries] as he [the bishop] shall charge me. And in regard to the excommunication laid upon me in the case of the money of Boncompagno, late of the monastery, I shall likewise be [obedient] to his order, so far as it concerns my part.

And I, Mezzolombardo d'Altavilla, in his behalf promise you and swear that if said Aringhiero dies from this illness, I shall remain [obedient] to and shall observe, in regard to the aforesaid, the order of the lord bishop, according to the form and content mentioned above. In the presence of Tornampuglia, [son] of Salsidone, Rustichino, [son] of Sinibaldo, Bartolo of Leonessa, and many others invited.

From Robert Lopez and Irving Raymond, *Medieval Trade in the Mediterranean World* (New York: Columbia University Press, 1955), pp. 159–60. © 1955 by Columbia University Press. Reprinted by permission of the publisher.

48. Decretal of Gregory IX, *Naviganti* (1234)

Gregory IX. To Brother R.

If anyone who lends a certain amount of money to someone sailing or

From *Corpus iuris canonici*, ed. E. Friedberg (Leipzig, 1879–81), p. 816. Translated for this volume by Julius Kirshner.

traveling to market is expected to get back more than the principal, because he has taken on the risk, he must be considered a usurer. Conversely, someone who pays ten shillings in order that the equivalent measures of grain, wine, or oil will be handed over to him at some other time shall not be considered a usurer, even if they then turn out to be worth more, so long as there is a reasonable doubt whether they were going to be worth more or less at the time of settlement. By reason of the same doubt even someone is excused who sells cloth, wine, oil, or other goods so that after a certain amount of time he gets back more for them than they were worth initially, if he was not intending to sell them at the time of the contract.

49. Decree 29, On Usury, of Vienne (1311–12)

Reliable sources inform us that certain communities in violation of the law, both human and divine, approve the practice of usury. By their statutes confirmed by oath they not only permit the exaction and payment of usury, but deliberately compel debtors to pay it. They also try by heavy statutory penalties and various other means and threats to prevent recovery by individuals who demand repayment of excessive interest. For our part, we want to put an end to these abuses and so we decree, with the approval of the council, that all civil officials of these communities, that is, magistrates, rulers, consuls, judges, lawyers and other similar officials, who in future make, write, or draw up statutes of this kind or knowingly decide that usury may be paid or in case of it having been paid may not be freely and fully restored when its return is demanded, incur the sentence of excommunication. They shall incur the same sentence if they do not within three months remove such statutes from the books of those communities (if they have the power to do so), or if they presume in any way to observe the said statutes or customs to the same effect. Moreover, since money-lenders frequently conclude loan-contracts in an occult or fraudulent manner, which makes it difficult to convict them on a charge of usury, we decree that they should be forced by ecclesiastical censure to produce their books on such occasions.

Finally, if anyone falls into the error of believing and affirming that it is not a sin to practise usury, we decree that he be punished as a heretic, and we strictly command the ordinaries of the localities and the inquisitors to proceed against those suspected of such errors in the same way as they would proceed against those accused publicly or suspected of heresy.

From H. J. Schroeder, O.P., *Disciplinary Decrees of the General Councils* (St. Louis: B. Herder, 1937), p. 401.

50. Peter John Olivi, *On Usury and Credit* (ca. 1290)

Quodlibets, 1, Question 17

THE QUESTION IS whether that contract is usurious by which one person hands over to another one hundred pounds to be spent on his own personal needs. He gives them, I say, with the agreement that, just as a similar one hundred pounds will earn more or suffer loss with your average merchant engaged in legitimate enterprise, so will those pounds earn or lose money for the giver.

THIS SEEMS TO BE USURIOUS for the following reasons:

IN THE FIRST PLACE, because such a pact appears to have arisen from a fraudulent intent to obtain usury.

IN THE SECOND PLACE, because money alone, by itself, is not lucrative, nor does it have a value beyond itself, but it becomes lucrative through the activity of merchants in their business dealings; yet, such is not the case here.

IN THE THIRD PLACE, because that money was handed over either as a loan, or as a deposit, or as capital, so that on behalf of the giver it may be allotted for purchases or business.

If as a loan, then it is clearly usury, because a loan passes wholly into the ownership of the borrower; thus, profit or loss should accrue only to him.

If, on the other hand, as a deposit, then, too, the money itself alone should be returned without any profit—or it should even be the person who preserved such a deposit who should be remunerated. And yet, from the form of the case mentioned, it is clear that the money was not handed over as a deposit, nor as capital, because then it would be in the agreement that he was obligated to allot the money faithfully in mercantile dealings only.

IN THE FOURTH PLACE, because if it is lucrative in any way, this is only because he assumes the risk for it, as if he were delivering capital to a merchant. But that this does not remove the baseness of usury is proved by Gregory's decretal on usury, "Naviganti," where he says that a person delivering a certain sum of money to someone undertaking a maritime venture or going to a market who expects to get back something beyond his principal because he is assuming the risk, is to be deemed a usurer.

IN THE FIFTH PLACE, this contract is, at any rate, unlawful, because every contract which goes directly against the good of charity and brotherhood is unlawful. But that is what this contract does, because, insofar as it

From Amleto Spicciani, "Gli scritti sul capitali di Fra Pietro di Giovanni Olivi," *Studi Francescani* 73 (1976): 225–316. Translated for this volume by Donald T. Jacques.

is a contract arising from compulsion, each one of the parties is forced to wish for loss to the other, because neither can profit unless the other loses; and when one loses, the other profits, and vice versa.

And furthermore, I declare that the ensuing profit could not lawfully be retained because, if the root is infected, so too are the branches; and, if the foundation is unjust, so too are the fruits of the edifice set upon it.

ON THE OTHER HAND, the contract appears not to be usurious because the contract of gamblers is like this, and yet it is not usurious.

SO TOO, there is like judgment in like matters. But if a merchant to whom money was delivered for doing business does no business with it, no less will he who delivered the money derive profit from it, approximating the gain of those faithfully transacting business; therefore, the money handed over became gainful not from the activity of any businessman, but only from itself.

LIKEWISE, everyone is owner of himself and his own as regards every contract or exchange, when no right or law stands in the way. But such a manner of agreeing or contracting is not prohibited by law; therefore it is permitted.

IN THE SAME WAY, what I in no way deliver or intend to give over as a loan, but by some other means and agreement, does not have the status of a loan, because such things derive their principal status from the intention of the givers and the receivers—especially when it is clearly expressed in the outward form of the delivery, as in the aforementioned case. But if it is not a loan by explicit statement or interpretation of outward form, then there can be no usury therein. The rest follows from this.

I SAY IN REPLY that the case is quite uncertain, and for that reason different people have different opinions about it. Nevertheless, what gives me pause is the third reason of the first part given above; for that reason appears to make a strong case that money thus handed over can only have the status of a loan.

CERTAIN PEOPLE HOLD, however, that, in a case where he who hands over the money was, either on his own or through another, going to transact business or purchase some profitable things, but only out of piety and the need and importunate entreaty of a friend, delivers the money to him, wanting nothing from it but the profit which would probably have accrued to him (and it is for this reason alone that he contracts the agreement with him in the aforesaid form: not forever, but for some reasonable length of time), there is nothing unlawful here, because he gives him not just money simple in nature, but also his capital; therefore, he can and ought rightly be held under obligation on the ground that it is capital.

And in support of these is FIRST, what was said in the preceding question: namely, that the man who retains a loan beyond the time allowed is under obligation as if it were capital to the owner who would have used the money, so that in view of this, it takes on, thereafter, the nature of capital, even if no one transacts business with it.

SECOND, is a certain sense of equity and piety, because it is a just and pious thing to help a friend in need; and it is not unjust if the capital nature of the money, which was already his explicitly in intent—and almost in fact—were preserved for him without loss.

THIRD, is that which is said in the decretal "Naviganti": namely, that "he who sells cloths or grain or other merchandise so as to receive for them at a fixed point in time more than they would be worth at that moment—provided, however, that at the time of the contract he was not about to sell them," is not considered a usurer if it is truly believed that at the predetermined time of payment, they would be worth so much. Note that it says here: "If at the time of the contract he was not about to sell them." This condition is added for the following reason alone: because if at that time he was going to sell them, then he could not have considered them as something to be sold at the predetermined future time. Therefore, because they are of a saleable nature for that future time, for this reason he sells them lawfully according to the value believed to be likely for that future time. And so in a similar fashion, because his money already has the nature of capital, he can demand of it its "capitality" in the aforesaid case.

If, in fact, he were to do this—the situation involving necessity, piety and the importunate entreaty of his friend aside—then by this very thing is he proven to prefer to use the money for a usurious loan, rather than as genuine capital in profitable business dealings; and, therefore, from that time on, he is in no way acquitted of blame for a usurious contract.

FOURTH, is that if a king or community were forcibly to take from their merchants money which had been designated for business dealings, they would be obligated to them for some likely amount of gain, just as in the case of capital. They would not be liable, however, if the merchants had not intended to use the money for business.

FIFTH, is that if someone were to lend money to another for a certain time because he believes that he will not pay at that time, and thus, that he would be held liable for compensation for probable profit, there is no doubt that such a person would be a usurer, and that whatever he received thence beyond the principal would be usury—because it is clear that he did not hand over the money in good faith as a simple and gratuitous loan, but rather as a loan at usury; and for that reason, a transaction for a predetermined term period cannot justifiably give the money the nature of capital. So then will it be in the case set forth, if the principal intent of the lender lies in the handing over of the money because he prefers to make a profit this way, rather than through commerce.

THE REPLIES TO THE FIRST THREE reasons of the first part, in light of the preceding, are obvious.

REGARDING THE FOURTH, I should say that the situation is different in that case, because the creditor simply hands over the money purely as a loan; and therefore, given the very nature of a loan, the person to whom the loan is made and who then is going to use it in transactions as his own, assumes the risk. It is apparent from this that the creditor assumed the risk solely for the fraudulent purpose of usury.

REGARDING THE FIFTH, I must say that in this case there is nothing contrary to the good of charity or brotherhood; rather, this is a very useful thing for a friend, and it is a work of piety as well as equity. And, indeed, a friend ought rightly to wish that the other gain from it a probable profit; nor should that one wish for more. And so, their just desires are not at variance, but in harmony.

As to the addition that profit which derives from an evil root is unjust—it is true insofar as the root is evil; it is not true, however, insofar as the root is good; otherwise the harvest planted without your knowledge in your field from stolen wheat would be evil, and because of the stolen seed, you would be obligated to discard the whole thing. A merchant, too, who sells his merchandise at about its true value would be obligated to restore the entire profit—yes, the whole thing, because there had been many sins in his act of selling.

CONCERNING THE FIRST POINT of the second part, I must also say that that contract, however it comes to be, is not like the gambling contract, because that contract has only to do with money handed over or to be handed over.

Indeed, a gambling contract is chiefly concerned with the game itself and the victory in the game; and so, there is no usury in a gambling contract because it is not in the nature of a loan. Furthermore, if the game is licit and takes place under proper supervision, it can be carried on lawfully; and given only that it is illicit, but that it is fully voluntary on both sides, and that no ordinance or civil custom observed as civil law prohibits it, there is no need to give back the profit therefrom.

But if the game has been played without fraud, there should still be laid upon it the penitence due for sin, and such penitence as would act as medicine against the disease of unseemly desire that readily attends the game.

NOW THE SECOND ARGUMENT makes a good point—but for that case alone which was considered in the main reply [the case of the friend in need]. And, following this, the proof itself can be taken up to corroborate the aforesaid reply.

CONCERNING THE THIRD POINT, I must say that no man is owner of himself or of his own in those things which are against God; nor is he owner of a thing which he has alienated from himself, to the extent that there is an owner in this case. Even if he intends to alienate the thing from himself, as happens in a loan, then he cannot make a contract concerning it as his own property, since it has already been presupposed to have been alienated.

CONCERNING THE FOURTH, I have to say that when a deed stemming from a proper desire contradicts its estimated intention (such as a deed evil and vicious in itself), then such a desire does not simply remove the wickedness of the deed. Hence, one who steals with the intent of contributing alms, truly commits an act of theft.

If, therefore, a contract for profit over and above a loan is, of itself, usurious, then no intention of a second contract makes it otherwise—unless the nature and form of the contract, in itself, is actually changed.

On Usurious Contracts, Case

If, indeed, the case were put (one which often applies among businessmen in certain lands) wherein the creditor assumes the risk, so that when capital is lost in business dealings or otherwise (there being no one to blame) it is the creditor's loss; yet his profit is fixed and certain, because the businessman to whom he delivered that capital purchased the entire future profit to be derived from it for such a price as the probability of future profit allows one reasonably to estimate before the fact—then CERTAIN PEOPLE consider it usury on four counts:

THE FIRST is because he who sells what does not exist in something of his by virtue of a cause as if it did so exist, or was likely to arise from it, perpetrates the same inequity as is found in a contract for usury (as is demonstrated in the first question on usury): namely, that in that instance there is sold what does not exist, as if it did; or, that what is not his is sold as if it were his; but the aforementioned profit does not arise by virtue of a cause from the aforesaid capital, but rather from the labor and activity of the businessman.

THE SECOND is because that capital seems in this case to be handed over fraudulently, as if in the nature of a loan for profit, rather than as capital to be employed in business ventures on behalf of the creditor; for it is clear that thereafter no profit from the subsequent dealings is gained for the creditor, but rather for the merchant venturer or businessman. Therefore, it is not, by nature, capital for commerce with regard to the initial creditor, but only in regard to the businessman. It has only, then, in regard to the first, the nature of a proffered loan.

THE THIRD is because the profit or price, which is given by the businessman to the creditor, is given to him undoubtedly in return for the employ of that capital in business ventures. Moreover, it is well established that at the time of its delivery, the capital has no value beyond itself; or at least it does not have the value of that profit or price, because that cannot be taken from mercantile ventures which are only going to be financed with it. Furthermore, who would doubt that the profit which, before all the transactions to be carried on using the capital, is given by the businessman to the creditor, does not arise from any mercantile activity of his? It appears, then, that the profit is altogether usurious.

THE FOURTH is because, given that the businessman who bought the future profit of the capital which was delivered to him does no business with it, then he will be obligated to return all the capital without loss—and beyond this, the entire price for the purchase of the future profit. If, then, this is usurious, usury can occur[1] in the form of the aforementioned contract.

BUT OTHERS THINK that there is no usury in the aforesaid contract—unless, by chance, it arose from some particular fraudulent intention to exact usury, so that the capital had not actually, in fact, been handed over as capital, but rather as a loan—and for usurious profit. In addition, that otherwise there would not be usury present, they show FIRST from three coincidental points:

The first of these is the risk attached to the capital itself which, in all mercantile ventures to be financed with the capital (and even when it is idle), the creditor, not the businessman, assumes—unless, as a result of his own blameworthy negligence or ill-doing, he should lose it. Moreover, it is clear that capital ought to be profitable for the one who assumes all the risks.

The second is the appreciable value of the probability, or of the probable hope, of profit to be drawn from that capital through business dealings. For since this probability has some worth to which some temporary price can be set, it can lawfully be sold at that price.

The third is that, since that probability is sold at a lesser price than the profit from the use of the capital at that time would be believed to be or be worth, it is agreed that in the selling of the capital it is always thought probable that the buyer would, in the end, profit or have more than he gave in buying it. Therefore, the creditor assumes the risk for the capital, as for the principal and final profit of the capital; hence, there is no usury at all involved here.

SECOND, they demonstrate this from a similar or equivalent case. Given that he who is himself about to employ his own capital in business ventures sells to another the probability of future profit therefrom, on the

---

1. Read: *incidere* for *intercidere*.

agreement that he use it as faithfully as if he himself had not sold it—all agree that in such a sale there is no usury, since it cannot be considered a loan. But this case does not differ from the first as regards the risk attached to the capital or the sale of probable gain, but only as regards mercantile activity which is mediated or not mediated; therefore, there is no more usury in the first instance than in the second.

THIRD, they demonstrate this because, as will be touched upon below, in the case of capital offered or detained by virtue of force, one can demand compensation for probable profit without the sin of usury; for the owner of the capital is truly considered to have suffered damages to such an extent at the hands of the one forcibly detaining or demanding his capital, because truly and not falsely was he to employ it in merchant ventures. Therefore, the aforementioned compensation for probable profit was, in a certain way, contained causally, and, as it were, seminally, in the capital, insofar as it was capital; for otherwise it could not be lawfully demanded. But in the above-mentioned case, nothing is sold except the aforementioned compensation as causally contained in the capital insofar as it is capital—that is, insofar as it is ordained and destined truly and not falsely to be used in business dealings. Hence, there is no sin of usury here.

FOURTH, they demonstrate this from a similar contract involving leases. For suppose that someone hands over his horse to another on the agreement that he have him on lease for a year for use either in battles or for transport; and that, at length, the man to whom the horse was thus handed over purchases the total future profit of the annual rental of the horse: indeed, just as this can legally be purchased, so in the same way, too, the probable profit from the capital can legally be bought.

FOLLOWING THEIR POSITION, therefore:

IN REPLY TO THE FIRST ARGUMENT I must say that in this instance there is no selling of what does not exist, or of what is not his own as if his own, or of the same thing twice, because capital, insofar as it is capital—that is, insofar as it is destined for lucrative business dealings—takes on a certain lucrative nature beyond that of mere money of the same amount which is not so destined for mercantile dealings. And so, the aforementioned capital, insofar as that is what it is, can be sold beyond the cost of simple money. For just as the value of the simple money belongs to the creditor, so, too, does the value of the aforesaid capital. From this it is clear that there is sold, in this instance, that which was his own, and he sells a value which differs from the first.

IN REPLY TO THE SECOND I must say that the aforementioned capital, after the aforesaid contract, truly has the nature of capital in respect to the initial creditor (despite the fact that, thereafter, its final profit does not accrue to him) because the money is still ventured totally at his peril, just as if he were acquiring the entire final profit for himself alone; and that such is the case, I demonstrate using an incontrovertible example:

Suppose that someone, under firm oath and instrument, gives to another the whole future profit from his capital, which he himself, by himself, is going to venture very faithfully and under oath for the profit of that other person. As a result, does the capital truly belong to the very one venturing and giving away his only profit? It is certainly so. Then, obviously, it is not essential that the man who owns the capital always acquire the profit; or, for the sake of those who like to argue, this proposition can be made clear by saying: this capital is this man's or that man's, because both the final cause and the cause of possession and ownership can be designated by the genitive case. First, one can say that the capital belongs to this one for whom it acquires profit, that is, to whose advantage it is ordained as to a final cause; and, second, one can say that it belongs only to that one by virtue of whose ownership and authority and peril it is ventured—and, in this way, it belongs only to the initial creditor.

Again, still other replies can be given, because the final profit from the capital can be taken up and considered in two ways:

First, insofar as it is presupposed to be contained in the capital itself by virtue of causality and probability. Second, insofar as it originates and exists, by virtue of finality, in itself. According to the first, the final profit accrues to the initial creditor—and for this reason, the profit, as if already accrued and his own, is sold by the creditor and bought by another. According to the second, it turns out that it belongs to the buyer himself—like the case of a man who sells a chest which he is going to make, for such a person sells it as his own property and his product; yet, when, in effect, it exists, it is not his, but the buyer's.

IN REPLY TO THE FOURTH, I have to say that it is a different matter if that were to be done with the consent or knowledge of the initial creditor; for then he would appear by this very act to be delivering that money not as capital—that is, not for commerce—but rather as a loan subject to usury. However, when this is done without the consent and knowledge of the creditor, then no charge can be laid against him as a result; but instead from this comes proof for the case at hand, because given that he who received a person's capital for commerce so that he may earn profit through his dealings for the initial creditor ceases, at length, to venture that capital without the consent of the creditor, it is agreed that he will be obligated to pay the creditor not only the capital, but also the probable profit—yet only as much as the probable profit would be worth when the capital is at risk (insofar as it has a value when the capital is not at risk).

51. Thomas Aquinas, *On Usury* (ca. 1270)

Question 78. The Sin of Usury

Our next task is to examine the sin of usury, which arises in the course of lending. There are four points of inquiry here:

1. is it a sin to make a charge for lending money, which is what usury is?
2. is one entitled to take anything by way of compensation for a loan?
3. is one bound to restore any gains one has lawfully made out of the profits of lending?
4. is one entitled to borrow money subject to the payment of interest?

article 1. is it a sin to make a charge for lending money?

The First Point: 1. Making a charge for lending money would not seem to be a sin. For nobody can commit a sin by doing what Christ did. Yet *Luke* reports the Lord as identifying himself with the saying, *And at my coming I should have collected it*, i.e. money lent, *with interest*. It is, therefore, not a sin to make a charge for lending money.

2. According to the *Psalm*, *The commandment of the Lord is pure*, and this is because it forbids sin. Yet the law of God allows for lending at interest, as is clear from *Deuteronomy*, *You shall not lend upon interest to your brother, interest on money, interest on victuals, interest on anything that is lent for interest. To a foreigner you may lend upon interest*. Even more, a reward is promised for the observance of the law, *You shall lend upon interest to many nations, but you shall not borrow*. It is, therefore, not a sin to make a charge for lending.

3. It is the laws of the land that determine what is just in human affairs. But such laws allow the taking of interest on loans, which would, therefore, not seem to be illicit.

4. It is not a sin to fail to live up to the counsels of perfection.[1] Yet one of the counsels mentioned by *Luke* is this, *Lend, expecting nothing in return*. It is, therefore, not a sin to accept a return from lending money.

5. It would not seem to be sinful in itself to make a charge for something one is not bound to do. But not everybody who has money is always bound

From St. Thomas Aquinas, *Summa Theologica*, 2a.2ae. 78, translated and edited by Marcus Lefebure, O.P. (New York: Blackfriars, McGraw-Hill, 1975), pp. 233, 235, 237, 239, 241, 243, 245, 247, 249, 251, 253. Some footnotes deleted. Reprinted by permission of the publisher.

1. The terms "counsel" and "precept" are both technical terms, and, as such, distinct in meaning. This distinction is explained in 1a.2ae. 108,4: precept implies necessity, whereas a counsel is left to the discretion of the person to whom it is communicated.

to lend it to his neighbour. It is, therefore, sometimes permissible to make a charge for lending money.

6. Silver remains silver whether it is in the form of coinage or of silver plate. Yet one is entitled to receive money for the latter, and one is, therefore, also entitled to receive money for silver in the form of coinage. Making a charge for a loan is not, therefore, sinful in itself.

7. Anyone is entitled to take anything that the owner thereof voluntarily hands over to him. But somebody who borrows money voluntarily hands over the usury for it. The lender is, therefore, entitled to take it.

ON THE OTHER HAND, there is what *Exodus* says, *If you lend money to any of my people with you who is poor, you shall not be to him as a creditor, and you shall not exact interest from him.*[2]

REPLY: Making a charge for lending money is unjust in itself, for one party sells the other something non-existent, and this obviously sets up an inequality which is contrary to justice. To understand this, one has to realize that there are some things the use of which consists in their being consumed, in the way in which we consume wine by using it for drinking and consume corn by using it for eating. We should not, therefore, reckon the use of such things apart from the things themselves. For, instead, when we grant to someone the use by that very fact we grant also the thing, and for this reason to lend things of this kind is to transfer the ownership, so that somebody who wanted to sell wine and the use of wine separately would be selling the same thing twice over or be selling something non-existent. And this would obviously be to commit the sin of injustice. By the same token, however, somebody commits an injustice if he lends corn or wine and asks for a twofold recompense—not merely the restoration of some equivalent but also a charge for its use, which is what usury strictly is.

There are, however, other things the use of which does not consist in their being consumed, so that, for instance, the use of a house is its being lived in, not its being used up. It follows that in such cases the two aspects can be dealt with separately, as in the case where somebody transfers the ownership of a house to another whilst reserving the use of it to himself for a stated time, or where on the contrary somebody allows another to use the house but retains the ownership for himself. And this is the reason why one is fully entitled to make a charge for the use of a house and then to ask for its return in due course, as in the case of renting and letting.

Now money, however, according to Aristotle,[3] was invented chiefly for

2. Exod. 22:25.
3. *Ethics* V, 5. 1133a20. *Politics* I, 9.1257a35.

exchanges to be made, so that the prime and proper use of money is its use and disbursement in the way of ordinary transactions. It follows that it is in principle wrong to make a charge for money lent, which is what usury consists in. Similarly a man is just as much bound to restore money earned in this way as he is to make restitution for any other ill-gotten gains.

Hence: 1. The interest referred to here is to be taken metaphorically to mean that natural increase of spiritual goods which God expects of us in so far as he wants us to be always making more of the gifts we have received from him. And this is for our good and not for his.

2. The Jews were forbidden to lend upon interest *to their brothers*, that is to say, to their fellow Jews. What we are meant to understand by this is that lending upon interest to any man is wrong in itself, in so far as we ought to treat every man as our brother and neighbour, especially in the epoch of the Gospel to which we are all called. This is why the *Psalm* speaks quite simply about the man *who does not put out his money at interest*,[4] and *Ezekiel* likewise about the man who *takes no interest or increase*.[5] And the fact that they took interest from foreigners shows not that they were entitled to do so as of right but only that they were allowed to do so in order to avoid the greater evil of taking interest from their fellow Jews, God's own people, out of sheer greed, to which they were prone, as *Isaiah* points out.[6] And when they are promised as it were by way of reward that they will *lend to many nations*, this is to be taken to refer to the simple capacity to lend, as it is in the passage of *Sirach* which declares, *It is not because of wickedness that many have refused to lend*,[7] that is to say, to lend without interest. What the Jews were promised, therefore, was such wealth as would enable them to lend it to others.

3. The civil law leaves certain sins unpunished to accommodate imperfect men who would be severely disadvantaged if all sins were strictly prohibited by suitable sanctions. Human law, therefore, allows the taking of interest, not because it deems this to be just but because to do otherwise would impose undue restrictions on many people. This is why Roman law itself provides, *Goods meant for consumption are neither in reason nor by civil law appropriate subjects of usufruct*; and also, *The Senate neither did nor could make such things subject to usufruct, but it did make provision for quasi-usufruct*,[8] which amounted to allowing lending at interest. Similarly Aristotle, following natural reason, said that *making a profit out of lending money is absolutely contrary to nature*.[9]

4. A man is not always bound to make a loan to another, and it is to this

4. Ps. 15 (14):5.   5. Ezek. 18:17.
6. Isa. 56:11.   7. Ecclus. 29:7.
8. *Institutiones* II, 4, 2. K 1, 13b. §2. *Digesta* VII, 5, 1 & 2.
9. *Politics* I, 10. 1258b7. *lect.* 8.

extent that lending is included amongst the counsels. Yet a man is prohibited by way of precept from making a profit out of such a loan. An alternative way of interpreting the injunction is to see it as a counsel in comparison with the sayings of the Pharisees, who allowed the making of a charge for loans in certain cases, in the same sort of way as the love of one's enemies is a counsel. Yet another possibility is that the expectation talked about is not the expectation of profit but the expectations we have of men. For we should make loans and indeed do any good deed not because we expect anything of men, but because of what we expect of God.

5. Anyone who is not bound to make a loan is entitled to receive compensation for what he has done, but no more than that. But the balance of justice is restored if a man receives back what he has lent, with the result that if he demands more for the enjoyment of a thing the use of which consists in its consumption and in that alone, he is making a charge for something non-existent. The demand is, therefore, unjustified.

6. Silver plate is not primarily meant for consumption, so that it is legitimate to sell the right to use it to another whilst retaining ownership for oneself. The primary use of silver coin, however, is its disbursement in commercial transactions. It is, therefore, not legitimate both to make a charge for its use and to expect the money lent to be restored.

We ought, however, to note that silver plate can also be used for bartering, and it would in such a case not be legitimate to make a separate charge for its use. In a similar sort of way silver coinage can also have a secondary use: specially minted coins could, for instance, be lent for exhibition or as security. A man would in such a case be entitled to make a separate charge for its use.

7. A man who pays interest on a loan cannot be said to be acting quite voluntarily, but under some pressure, in so far as he needs to borrow money which the lender who has it is not prepared to lend without making a charge for it.

article 2. is one entitled to seek any other compensation for lending money?

THE SECOND POINT:[10] 1. A man would seem to be entitled to seek some other sort of compensation for lending money. For everyone is entitled to look after his own interests. But a man sometimes incurs a loss by lending money, and he is therefore entitled to seek or even to ask for some compensation over and above the return of the money lent.

2. Everyone, as Aristotle says, is under a debt of honour *to make some*

10. Cf. *De malo* XIII, 4 ad 13. *De regimine Judaeorum* 5.

return for any favour he may have been shown.[11] But a person who lends money to somebody in need is doing him a favour, so that a debt of gratitude is set up. It follows that the recipient of the favour is under a moral obligation to make some sort of return therefor. Nor does it seem to be wrong to bind oneself by promise to do something that by natural law one is bound to do. It would not, therefore, seem to be wrong for somebody who lends another money to put on a legal footing the duty to make some return.

3. *Gifts can be made by the tongue and in the form of service* as well as *by hand*, according to a gloss[12] on *Isaiah, Blessed is he who shakes his hands free of gifts.*[13] But one is entitled to accept services and even praise from a borrower, from which it would seem to follow that one is also entitled to accept other forms of gift.

4. One loan would seem to be related to another loan in the same sort of way as one gift is related to another gift. But one is entitled to receive money in return for giving money, so that one is also entitled to accept a loan from a borrower in return for making him a loan.

5. When one lends money, one transfers the possession of it so that one parts with it much more completely than in entrusting it to a merchant or to a craftsman. But one is entitled to make a profit out of entrusting money to a merchant or to a craftsman, so that one is also entitled to make a profit out of lending money.

6. Somebody who lends money is entitled to take a pledge for it, and to sell the right to use the thing pledged; a case in point would be giving a field or a habitable house in pledge. One is, therefore, entitled to make some profit out of lending money.

7. People sometimes charge somebody to whom they have previously lent money more for their goods, or buy goods more cheaply from such a person; or else they increase their price when payment is delayed or give a discount for prompt payment. In all these cases there seems to be some sort of recompense for lending money which does not seem to be obviously illicit. One would seem, therefore, to be entitled to expect or even to ask for some compensation for lending money.

ON THE OTHER HAND, *Ezekiel* includes among the marks of the just man that *he takes no interest or increase.*[14]

REPLY: According to Aristotle[15] anything the price of which can be measured in money terms is deemed to be money. Therefore just as anyone

11. *Ethics* V, 5.1133a4. *lect.* 8.
12. *Interlinear.* IV, 61a. Cf. Gregory, *Hom. in Evang.* 4. *PL* 76:1092.
13. Isa. 33:15.   14. Ezek. 18:17.
15. *Ethics* IV, 1. 119b26.

who, whether by explicit or tacit agreement, accepts money in return for lending money or any other commodity the use of which consists in its consumption is acting contrary to justice, as we have explained,[16] so anyone who, whether by explicit or tacit agreement accepts anything the price of which can be measured in money terms, commits a similar sin. Yet if one accepts anything that is equivalent to money in this way, not in response to a demand or out of an expressed or tacit sense of obligation, but as a gift, there is no sin; the reason for this is that one would have been entitled to accept a gift before making the loan and one is not worse off through lending. A lender is, however, entitled to seek the sort of compensation that cannot be measured in terms of money—things like benevolence and love towards the lender.

Hence: 1. Somebody who makes a loan is within his rights to settle terms of compensation for the loss of any advantage which he is entitled to enjoy, for this does not amount to selling the use of money, but is a question of avoiding loss. And it can happen that the borrower avoids a greater loss thereby than that incurred by the lender, in which case the borrower finances the other's loss out of his own advantage. One is, however, not entitled to make a contract to secure compensation for the loss that consists in not being able to use the money lent in order to make a profit, because one should not sell something which one has not yet got and which one may be prevented in many ways from getting.

2. There are two grounds for compensating somebody for benefits received. The first is an obligation of justice which can rise out of a precise contract. And the measure of this obligation is the extent of the benefit which the beneficiary has received, so that the person who has borrowed the money or any commodity the use of which consists in the consumption is not bound to return more than he has been lent. In fact it would be unjust for him to be obliged to do so. The other ground for making compensation for a benefit received is the obligation of friendship, and here what really counts is the spirit in which the benefit is conferred rather than its quantity. But a legal obligation is hardly an appropriate sanction for such a debt, since it introduces a note of necessity that tends to stifle any spontaneous return.

3. A lender who expects or asks, as if, by a binding agreement, tacit or expressed, to be compensated with a gift of either services or some suitable speech, is in the same position as if he expected or asked for a gift in the hand, since both of these things can be measured in money terms, as is clear from the case of those who make a living out of the work they do with their hands or their speech. A person is, however, entitled to accept, and even to ask for, and to expect some service or the expression of some senti-

16. Art. 1.

ment, provided it is motivated by good will and not by a feeling of obligation, since good will cannot be measured in terms of money.

4. One is entitled neither to sell money for more money than the quantity that has been lent and has to be repaid, nor to expect or ask for anything other than feelings of good will which cannot be reduced to money value, and which as a result can prompt the borrower to offer a loan spontaneously in return. Now the obligation to lend in return at some future time is repugnant, for such an obligation can have a pecuniary price, consequently it is lawful for the lender to borrow something else at the same time, but it is unlawful for him to bind the borrower to grant him a loan at some future time.

5. Somebody who lends money hands over the possession of it to the borrower, and with it the attendant risks and the obligation to make complete restitution, from which it follows that the lender is not entitled to ask for more. Somebody, on the other hand, who entrusts his money to a merchant or a craftsman in a sort of partnership does not hand over the ownership, and so it is still at his risk that the merchant trades or the craftsman works. The lender is, therefore, entitled to ask for a part of the profit of the undertaking in so far as it is also his own.

6. If a borrower secures the loan with the pledge of something the use of which can be assessed in money terms, the lender must offset this use-value against the sum to be repaid. Otherwise wanting to have the use of the thing in question for nothing is tantamount to taking money for the loan, which constitutes usury. The only exception to this would be where it is the sort of thing that friends give each other free, for instance, the loan of a book.

7. If a seller wants to charge more than the just price for his goods in return for allowing a postponement of payment, he is quite obviously committing usury, since this sort of postponement is in the nature of a loan. For asking more than the just price in respect of such a postponement amounts to making a charge for a loan, which is what usury consists in. By the same token, if a buyer wants to buy something for less than its just price in return for paying for it before delivery, there is also a sin of usury, for this sort of allowance in respect of advance payment is also in the nature of a loan, the charge for which is the reduction in the just price. If, on the other hand, a seller is willing to take a lower price in order to have the cash in hand, he is not committing usury.

article 3. is one bound to restore any gains one has made out of the profits of lending?

THE THIRD POINT: [17] 1. A man would seem to be bound to restore any gains he has made out of the interest on a loan. For St. Paul says, *If the root is holy, so are the branches.*[18] By the same token, if the root is infected, so are the branches. But in the case in question the root of the transactions is profit made out of lending, with the result that any gain made therefrom is also profit made from lending. A man is, therefore, bound to make restitution of all such gains.

2. One of the *Decretals* on usury provides, *Possessions which have been procured with the profits made from lending at interest must be sold and the proceeds of the sale restored to those from whom the interest was extorted.*[19] By the same reasoning anything else that has been gained with the profits of lending ought to be restored.

3. Anything a man has bought out of the proceeds of lending is of its nature part of the money he has lent. He has, therefore, no greater right to whatever he has acquired than to the money. But he is obliged to restore the money he has made out of lending, and he is therefore also obliged to restore anything he has acquired with it.

ON THE OTHER HAND, anyone is entitled to hold on to whatever he has acquired legitimately. But it is sometimes possible to make a legitimate acquisition with the proceeds of lending, in which case one is entitled to hold on to it.

REPLY: We have already seen[20] that there are some things the use of which consists in their being consumed and which cannot, therefore, be the subject of usufruct in law.[21] It follows that a lender who has extorted such things as money, corn or wine by way of interest on a loan is bound to restore only what he has actually received from the borrower, since anything that has been made out of such a commodity is the fruit, not of this thing itself, but of human industry. This reasoning does not, however, apply where holding on to the thing on the part of the lender results in the borrower at interest suffering some loss in his possessions; in such a case the lender is bound to recompense the borrower for the latter's loss.

There are, however, other things the use of which does not consist in

17. Cf. *Quodl.* III, 7, 2. *De regimine Judaeorum* I.
18. Rom. 11:16.
19. *Decretals of Gregory IX*, V, 19, 5. RF 11, 813.
20. Art. 1.
21. *Institutiones*, II, 4.2 K 1, 13b. Cf. *Digesta*, VII, 5. 1 & 2.

their being consumed, and such things—like houses or fields—are the subject of usufruct. It follows that if somebody has extorted another's house or field or such like from a borrower by way of interest, he is bound to restore not only the house or the field but also all the fruits thereof, because they are the fruits of things of which another is the owner and which therefore belong to that other.

Hence: 1. The metaphor of the root can be taken to mean the material in question, thus the money gained by way of usury, or it can refer to an active cause, in so far as it provides nourishment. And the two cases are not the same.

2. Any goods that have been bought with the usury on a loan belong not to the borrower who has paid the interest, but to the direct purchaser of them. The borrower who has paid the interest does, however, have a certain right over such goods, as he does over other goods in the possession of the usurer. And so there is no precept that such goods be assigned to those who have paid interest, since they may be worth more than the interest paid. What is prescribed, however, is that the goods be sold and that out of the proceeds the borrower be repaid the sum he gave in interest.

3. The reason why anything that has been acquired with money charged as interest belongs to the purchaser is not so much that he has used the money paid to him by way of interest as a means, but rather that he has drawn upon his own industry as his principal resource. He therefore has more right to anything acquired with money charged as interest than to that money itself.

article 4. is one entitled to borrow money subject to the payment of interest?

THE FOURTH POINT:[22] 1. One would not seem to be entitled to borrow money subject to the payment of interest. According to Paul, *Not only those who do such things deserve to die, but also those who approve those who practise them.*[23] But a person who borrows money subject to the payment of interest does approve the lender in his sin, and provides him with an opportunity to commit a sin. He is, therefore, committing a sin himself.

2. Nobody ought to give another the occasion of sinning for the sake of any temporal advantage whatever, for this is what active scandal, which is always a sin,[24] consists in. But this is just what somebody who asks a regular money-lender to make him a loan is doing. There is, therefore, no excuse for him, whatever temporal advantage he secures.

22. Cf. III *Sent.* 37, 1, 6.   23. Rom. 1:32.

24. 2a2ae. 43, 2. The distinction between "active" and "passive" scandal, giving and taking scandal; the former consists in somebody occasioning another's spiritual downfall through a sinful act; the latter in that other suffering the fall.

3. A man would sometimes seem to be under as much pressure to deposit money with a money-lender as to take a loan from him. Yet it would seem to be wrong to deposit money with a money-lender—as wrong as it is to entrust a sword to a madman, or a virgin to a lecher, or food to a glutton. By the same token it is not right to accept a loan from a money-lender.

ON THE OTHER HAND, according to Aristotle,[25] somebody who suffers harm does not sin, which is why justice is not a mean between two vices, as he also says in another place.[26] But a money-lender commits a sin in so far as he inflicts an injustice on the person who borrows at interest; from which it follows that a person who borrows at interest does not sin.

REPLY: Whilst one is in no way entitled to induce another man to sin, one is entitled to turn another's sin to good, since God himself draws some good out of all evil and so turns all sins to some good, as the *Enchiridion* says.[27] And Augustine expresses a similar opinion elsewhere in answering somebody who swore by false gods, something that was manifestly sinful in so far as it involved showing the reverence due to God alone; he says, *Somebody who for good purposes and not for bad, relies upon the oath of a person who has sworn by false gods is not associating himself with the sin of swearing by demons but with the integrity that has made him keep faith.*[28] He would, however, be sinning if he were to induce another to swear by false gods.

Applying this to the case in question, then, it is never right to induce another to lend at interest, although it is permissible to accept a loan from somebody who is prepared to make such a loan and so is already in this business, if the object is the doing of some good in the shape of relieving one's own or another's need. In the same sort of way a man who falls among thieves is entitled to declare his possessions to his captors even though they sin by seizing them, if this is done in order to save his life, following the example of the ten men who said to Ishmael, *Do not kill us, for we have treasure hidden in the fields.*[29]

Hence: 1. Somebody who borrows money subject to the payment of interest does not approve the sin of usury but uses it. And what he likes is not the taking of interest but the lending, which in itself is good.

2. Somebody who borrows money subject to the payment of interest gives the lender an opportunity not so much to charge interest but to lend; it is the lender himself who out of his own evil heart makes this an occasion

25. *Ethics* V, 10. 1138a35. *lect.* 17.   26. *Ethics* V, 5. 1133b33. *lect.* 10.
27. Augustine, *Enchiridion* 11. PL 40:236.
28. *Epist. XLVII ad Publicolam.* PL 33:184.
29. Jer. 41:8.

of sin. It is, therefore, a case of the lender allowing himself to stumble and not of the borrower positively providing a stumbling-block. Not that a prospective borrower should therefore refrain from asking for a loan if he needs to do so, since allowing oneself to stumble in this way springs, not from weakness or ignorance, but from a deliberately evil intention.

3. If somebody entrusts his money to a money-lender who could not go on lending money at interest without this money or entrusts it to him so that the latter can make even grosser profits out of lending, he is giving the other an occasion to sin, so that he is an accomplice in his sin. If, on the other hand, he entrusts his money for safe-keeping to a lender who has other means to lend money at interest, he is not committing a sin, but is using the sinner for good.

Control of Learning

The authors of a leading textbook have characterized the thirteenth century in the following way:

> The thirteenth century was an age of outstanding achievement in many diverse areas of human activity—in religious organization, law, philosophy, architecture, art, and literature. The century opened with the pontificate of Innocent III (1198–1216), who is commonly regarded as the greatest of all the medieval popes, both in ability and in achievement. Under him and his immediate successors, the medieval church reached the apex of its spiritual, intellectual, and temporal power. The papal monarchy perfected its organization and expanded its authority over both ecclesiastical and secular affairs. The integration, development, and application of the canon law continued steadily, culminating in the *Decretals* of Pope Gregory IX (1234). As the ardor of the old monastic orders cooled with the passage of time, vigorous, fresh spiritual leadership was provided by new "mendicant," or begging, orders.[1]

We present this statement as a starting point for discussion and debate. The appraisal of the thirteenth century as an age of serene and monumental greatness is a common one. It is also well defended. And yet, even those who espouse this view admit that the thirteenth century witnessed a bitter struggle against the spiritual and temporal authority of the Church and the papacy. The century was marked by heresy and its sup-

---

1. Brian Tierney and Sidney Painter, *Western Europe in the Middle Ages, 300–1475* (New York: Knopf, 1983), p. 345.

pression as well as by a mutually destructive struggle between a monarchic papacy and the emperors and the kings of England and France. Ever finer legal definitions meant that the categories of those on the border, or beyond the pale, of social acceptability multiplied. Thus, the age was also marked by increasing social and legal hostility to usurers, Jews, homosexuals, and foreigners. Although no theologian was sent to the stake in this century for his teachings, tolerance for theological innovation decidedly narrowed. Above all else, the thirteenth century was an age of unprecedented legislation, codification, and institutional conformity, when all sorts of beliefs and activities became subject to scrutiny, regulation, and, perhaps, repression. Innovation and repression were two sides of the same coin.

The university as we know it today was a creation of the Middle Ages. Bologna was renowned for law, Salerno for medicine, Paris, Oxford, and Cambridge for the liberal arts and theology. Their origins can be traced back to the informal communities of students and teachers that spontaneously appear in the twelfth century. Formal recognition of the right to confer a degree or teaching license transformed these communities into *studia generalia*, a term used for institutions of higher learning throughout the latter Middle Ages. The Latin term *universitas* referred only to guilds or corporate associations of teachers or students. Formal recognition was granted to the school of law at Bologna by the Emperor Frederick I Barbarossa in 1158. The masters at Bologna, unlike those at Paris, were not clerics, but customarily citizens of the town. They were elected to teach by students, generally foreigners, who formed their own guilds for mutual protection. Students' resentment over what they considered excessive fees, rents, and prices charged by masters, landlords, and shopkeepers, coupled with the citizens' resentment over violent student behavior, resulted in continual conflict between town and gown. Despite the violent tenor of life at Bologna and at other Italian universities, students from all parts of Europe flocked there to study with the leading jurisprudents.

Students had also flocked to Paris in the twelfth century to hear the lectures of such masters as Anselm of Laon, Peter Abelard, and Alan of Lille. Yet the masters' control over students was rarely questioned at the University of Paris, as it was at Bologna. Indeed, the University of Paris was formed by a community of masters attracted by the scholarly distinction of the cathedral school of Notre Dame. By the end of the twelfth century, many of the masters had moved to the left bank of the Seine and organized themselves into a corporate association separate from the cathedral. In 1200, King Philip II Augustus recognized the clerical privileges of the masters and their students, guaranteeing them exemption and immunity from the civil and criminal jurisdiction of local magistrates, and confirming that, as clerics, they were subject to their own elected officials and to the bishop of Paris. Soon after, the university obtained papal sanction as a corporate association. In 1215, the papal legate Robert de Courçon promulgated regulations concerning comportment and instruction for the masters in arts and in theology (document 52).

There were four faculties: arts, medicine, canon law, and theology. The faculty of arts, the largest of the faculties and the stepping stone to the others, was organized into four nations (*nationes*) initially reflecting the origins of both masters and students: French, Picard, Norman, and English (English-German). Members of the French nation, for example, were not only of French origin, but also came from southern and eastern Europe and from Asia Minor. The sometimes violent tenor of university life is illustrated in the proclamation of 1269 against criminous clerks (document 53).

The general method of instruction was the lecture or commentary and gloss on a specific text, followed by a review and discussion. The lectures were either "ordinary," normally given in the morning by masters in the faculty, or "extraordinary," normally given in the late afternoon or on a feast day by bachelors and guest masters (document 56). There were also disputations that involved the presentation, explanation, and proving of a specific proposition and the answering of objections raised against it. Reference to the Bible, Church Fathers, Aristotle, and other authorities was standard. This method was employed by Thomas Aquinas in the *Summa theologica* (document 54). There were also public disputations, where a master was asked to resolve, by primarily relying upon reason rather than authority, random questions concerning issues of contemporary interest. This kind of disputation is illustrated above in Peter John Olivi's quodlibetal disputation on usury and capital (document 50).

The burning issue of the day was the conflict between Aristotle and Christian doctrine. Beginning in the twelfth century the entire corpus of Aristotle's work gradually became available in Latin translation. The reception of Aristotle was part of an enormous intellectual task: absorbing the heritage of philosophy, medicine, astrology, and natural science not only of ancient Greece but also of Judaism and Islam. The challenge facing theologians was not a simple conflict between this heritage and Christian doctrine. For the masters of arts, Aristotle's method of rational inquiry served as a model that placed a premium on relentless questioning of one's predecessors. The search for truth now meant freedom from authority and dogmatism; the collision between truth grounded on rational inquiry and truth grounded on revelation was inevitable. The challenge posed by the reception of Aristotle and the new professional ethos of the masters in arts was great. Theologians of many conflicting positions, including Aquinas, accepted this challenge, and were determined to make theology a science based upon reason as well as revelation (document 54). Meanwhile, the papacy wielded its authority to repress university masters whose teachings were considered incompatible with the faith (document 55). Missionary activity was yet another way to combat not only the religion of, but also the dread ideas imported from, Islam. The Spanish theologian Raymond Lull (ca. 1235–1315) in 1298–99 urged the University of Paris to contribute to this missionary effort by adding the study of oriental languages to its curriculum (document 57). Christians were to defeat the infidel by using his own weapons against him.

---

52. Gregory IX, *Papal Regulations for the University of Paris*, 13 April 1231

Gregory, bishop, servant of the servants of God, to his cherished sons, the masters and scholars of Paris, greeting and apostolic benediction. Paris, parent of sciences, like another Cariath Sepher, city of letters, shines clear, great indeed but raising still greater hopes in teachers and pupils, where, as it were in wisdom's special workshop, veins of silver have their beginning and there is a proper place for forging gold, from which those prudent in mystic eloquence stamp golden earrings vermiculated with silver, fabricate necklaces adorned with precious stones, nay fit and decorate the spouse of Christ with priceless jewels. There iron is mined, whose earthy fragility is solidified by firmness, and from which is made the breastplate of faith, sword of the spirit, and other armor of Christian soldiery, potent against the powers aerial. And the ore dissolved by heat is turned to copper, because while stony hearts flame with the fervor of the Holy Spirit, they take fire and are made to herald praises of Christ in sounding preaching. Wherefore there is not doubt that he would gravely displease God and men who in the said city should strive in any way to disturb such signal grace or who should not openly oppose those disturbing it with all his might and main. Hence, since concerning dissension arisen there by instigation of the devil, greatly disturbing the university, we have diligently considered questions brought before us, by the advice of our brethren we have decided that they should be quieted by moderate provision rather than judicial sentence.

Concerning the state therefore of schools and scholars we decree that these things are to be observed: namely, that every chancellor of Paris to be named henceforth shall swear in the presence of the bishop or by his man-

From *University Records and Life in the Middle Ages*, edited and translated by Lynn Thorndyke (New York: Columbia University Press, 1944), pp. 35–38. © 1944 by Columbia University Press. Reprinted by permission of the publisher.

date in the Paris chapter, to which shall be summoned and present two masters on behalf of the university of scholars. He shall swear in good faith on his conscience, at the time and place according to the state of the city and honor and respect of the faculties, that he will not bestow the licentiate to teach theology or decretals except to the worthy nor admit the unworthy, ratification by persons and nations being abolished. But before he shall license anyone, within three months from the time of the petty license, in the presence of all masters of theology in the city and other respectable and learned men by whom the truth can be learned, he shall make diligent inquiry as to the life, knowledge, facility, and also the promise and hope of success and other points which are required in such cases, and, having made such inquiry, according to what seems proper and expedient he shall give or deny according to his conscience the license asked for. The masters, moreover, of theology and decretals, when they begin to lecture, shall publicly take oath that they will furnish faithful testimony on the aforesaid points. The chancellor shall also swear that he will in no wise reveal the advice of the masters to their hurt, maintaining in their integrity the Parisian rules, liberty and law which obtain in incepting.[1]

Concerning the medical men and artists and others the chancellor promises to examine the masters in good faith, to repel the unworthy and admit only the deserving.

But because, where there is no order, horror easily creeps in, we have conceded to you the function of making due constitutions or ordinances as to the method and hour of lectures and disputations, as to the costume to be worn, as to funerals of the dead, and also, concerning the bachelors, who should lecture and at what hour and on what subject, as to rentals of lodgings or even their prohibition, and of duly punishing rebels against those constitutions or ordinances by expulsion from your society. And if it chance that the rental of lodgings is taken from you or that—which God forbid—injury or enormous excess be inflicted on you or any of you, such as death or mutilation of a limb, unless, after due complaint has been lodged, satisfaction is given within fifteen days, it shall be permitted you to suspend lectures until condign satisfaction is given. And if any of you shall have been unjustly imprisoned, it shall be right for you, unless the injury ceases when complaint is made, to stop lectures immediately, if it shall seem expedient.

We order, moreover, that the bishop of Paris so punish the excesses of delinquents that the honor of the scholars is preserved and crimes do not remain unpunished; but because of delinquents the innocent shall not suffer, nay, if probable suspicion shall arise against anyone, after honorable

---

1. Inception was the final process of becoming a master, entering the university or scholastic guild, and beginning to teach.

detention on furnishing suitable bail he shall be dismissed and exactions of the jailers cease. But if he has committed a crime which calls for imprisonment, the bishop shall retain the culprit in prison, it being utterly forbidden to the chancellor to have a prison of his own. We further prohibit that a scholar henceforth be arrested for debt, since this is forbidden by the canons and lawful sanctions. But neither the bishop nor his official nor the chancellor shall require a fine for raising an excommunication or any other censure, nor shall the chancellor demand from licentiates an oath or obedience or other pledge, nor shall he receive any emolument or promise for conceding the license, abiding by the terms of his oath named above.

Furthermore, the summer vacation shall henceforth not exceed a month, and in vacation time the bachelors may continue their lectures if they wish. Moreover, we expressly enjoin that scholars shall not go about town armed, and that the university shall not defend disturbers of the peace and of studies. And those who pretend to be scholars but do not attend classes or have any master shall by no means enjoy the privileges of scholars.

We further order that masters of arts always give one ordinary reading of Priscian and one other afterwards, and those books on nature which were prohibited in provincial council for certain cause they shall not use at Paris until these shall have been examined and purged from all suspicion of errors. Moreover, the masters and scholars of theology shall strive to exercise themselves praiseworthily in the faculty which they profess and not show themselves philosophers but endeavor to know God, nor speak in the vernacular nor confound the Hebrew popular language with the Azotic, but dispute in the schools concerning those questions only which can be settled by theological works and the treatises of the holy fathers.

Furthermore, concerning the goods of scholars who die intestate or do not commit the care of their affairs to others, we have decided to provide thus, namely, that the bishop and one of the masters whom the university shall ordain for this, receiving all the goods of the defunct and depositing them in a safe and fit place, shall set a day by which his death can have been announced in his native place and those upon whom the succession to his goods devolves can come to Paris or delegate an appropriate messenger; and if they come or send, the goods shall be restored to them with a security which has been determined. But if no one appears, then the bishop and master shall use the goods for the soul of the defunct as they shall see fit, unless it chance that the heirs for some just cause cannot come, in which case the disposition shall be deferred to a suitable time.

But since the masters and scholars who suffered injury and damage from the breaking of the oath made to them by the city of Paris have departed from the university, they seem to have pled not so much their own case as the common cause. We, with the general need and utility of the church in view, will and order that henceforth the privileges shall be shown to the masters and scholars by our dearest son in Christ, the illustrious king of France, and fines inflicted on their malefactors, so that they may lawfully study at Paris without any further delay or return of infamy or irregularity of notation. To no man then be it licit to infringe or with rash daring to contradict this page of our provision, constitution and inhibition. If anyone shall presume to attempt this, let him know that he will incur the wrath of almighty God and of the blessed apostles Peter and Paul. Given at the Lateran on the Ides of April, the fifth year of our pontificate.

53. Conflict between Town and Gown at Paris (1269)

Proclamation of the Official of the Episcopal Court of Paris against Clerks and Scholars Who Go about Paris Armed by Day and Night and Commit Crimes; January 11, 1269

The official of the court of Paris to all the rectors of churches, masters and scholars residing in the city and suburb of Paris, to whom the present letters may come, greeting in the Lord. A frequent and continual complaint has gone the rounds that there are in Paris some clerks and scholars, likewise their servants, trusting in the folly of the same clerks, unmindful of their salvation, not having God before their eyes, who, under pretense of leading the scholastic life, more and more often perpetrate unlawful and criminal acts, relying on their arms: namely, that by day and night they atrociously wound or kill many persons, rape women, oppress virgins, break into inns, also repeatedly committing robberies and many other enormities hateful to God. And since they attempt these and other crimes relying on their arms, we, having in mind the decree of the supreme pontiff in which it is warned that clerks bearing arms will be excommunicated, also having in mind that our predecessors sometimes excommunicated those who went about thus, and in view of the fact that this is so notorious and manifest that it cannot be concealed by any evasion and that their proclamation was not revoked, wishing to meet so great evils and to provide for the peace and tranquillity of students and others who wish to live at peace, at the instance of many good men and by their advice do excommunicate in writing clerks and scholars and their servants who go about Paris by day or night armed, unless by permission of the reverend bishop of Paris or ourself. We also excommunicate in writing those who rape women, break into inns, oppress virgins, likewise all those who have banded together for this purpose. No less do we excommunicate all those who have known anything

From *University Records and Life in the Middle Ages*, edited and translated by Lynn Thorndyke (New York: Columbia University Press, 1944), pp. 78–80. © 1944 by Columbia University Press. Reprinted by permission of the publisher.

about the aforesaid, unless within seven days from the time of their information, after the proclamation issued against the aforesaid has come to their notice, they shall have revealed what they know to the said reverend bishop or ourselves and have submitted to fitting emendation. Nevertheless we specially reserve to the lord bishop or ourselves the right to absolve clerks excommunicated for the aforesaid reasons.

But inasmuch as some clerks and scholars and their servants have borne arms in Paris, coming there from their parts or returning to their parts, and likewise certain others, knowing that clerks, scholars and their servants have borne arms in Paris, fear that for the said reasons they have incurred the said penalty of excommunication, we do declare herewith that it neither is nor was our intention that those clerks, scholars and their servants should be liable to the said sentence who, coming to Paris for study and bearing arms on the way, on first entering the city bear the same to their lodgings, nor, further, those, wishing to return home or setting out on useful and honest business more than one day's journey from the city of Paris, who have borne such arms going and returning while they were outside the city. We further declare that in the clause in which it is said, "We excommunicate all those who have known anything about the aforesaid," etc., we do not understand that word, *aforesaid*, to refer to all and each of the aforesaid but to the clauses immediately preceding, namely, concerning those who rape women, break into inns, oppress virgins and those who band together for these ends. Moreover, you shall so observe the present mandate that you cannot be charged with or punished for disobedience. Given in the year 1268 [1] A.D., the Friday following Epiphany.

1. According to the medieval calendar.

54. Thomas Aquinas, *On Christian Theology* (1270)

Question 1. On What Sort of Teaching Christian Theology Is and What It Covers

In order to keep our efforts within definite bounds we must first investigate this holy teaching and find out what it is like and how far it goes. Here there are ten points of inquiry:

1. about the need for this teaching;
2. whether it be science;
3. whether it be single or several;

From St. Thomas Aquinas, *Summa Theologica*, Ia.I. 1, translated and edited by Marcus Lefebure, O.P. (New York: Blackfriars, McGraw-Hill, 1975), pp. 240–57. Some footnotes deleted. Reprinted by permission of the publisher.

4. whether it be theoretical or practical;
5. how it compares with other sciences;
6. whether it be wisdom;
7. what is its subject;
8. whether it sets out to prove anything;
9. whether it should employ metaphorical or symbolical language;
10. whether its sacred writings are to be interpreted in several senses.

article 1. is another teaching required apart from philosophical studies?

THE FIRST POINT: 1. Any other teaching beyond that of science and philosophy seems needless. For man ought not to venture into realms beyond his reason; according to *Ecclesiasticus, Be not curious about things far above thee.*[1] Now the things lying within range of reason yield well enough to scientific and philosophical treatment. Additional teaching, therefore, seems superfluous.

2. Besides, we can be educated only about what is real; for nothing can be known for certain save what is true, and what is true is identical with what really is. Yet the philosophical sciences deal with all parts of reality, even with God; hence Aristotle refers to one department of philosophy as theology or the divine science.[2] That being the case, no need arises for another kind of education to be admitted or entertained.

ON THE OTHER HAND the second epistle to Timothy says, All Scripture inspired of God is profitable to teach, to reprove, to correct, to instruct in righteousness.[3] Divinely inspired Scripture, however, is no part of the branches of philosophy traced by reasoning. Accordingly it is expedient to have another body of sure knowledge inspired by God.

REPLY: It should be urged that human well-being called for schooling in what God has revealed, in addition to the philosophical researches pursued by human reasoning.

Above all because God destines us for an end beyond the grasp of reason; according to Isaiah, Eye hath not seen, O God, without thee what thou hast prepared for them that love thee.[4] Now we have to recognize an end before we can stretch out and exert ourselves for it. Hence the necessity for our welfare that divine truths surpassing reason should be signified to us through divine revelation.

1. Ecclus. 3:22.
2. *Metaphysics* VI, 1. 1026a19. I. 2, 983a10.
3. 2 Tim. 3:16. 4. Isa. 64:4.

We also stood in need of being instructed by divine revelation even in religious matters the human reason is able to investigate. For the rational truth about God would have appeared only to few, and even so after a long time and mixed with many mistakes; whereas on knowing this depends our whole welfare, which is in God. In these circumstances, then, it was to prosper the salvation of human beings, and the more widely and less anxiously, that they were provided for by divine revelation about divine things.

These then are the grounds of holding a holy teaching which has come to us through revelation beyond the discoveries of the rational sciences.

Hence: 1. Admittedly the reason should not pry into things too high for human knowledge, nevertheless when they are revealed by God they should be welcomed by faith: indeed the passage in *Ecclesiasticus* goes on, *Many things are shown thee above the understanding of men.*[5] And on them Christian teaching rests.

2. The diversification of the sciences is brought about by the diversity of aspects under which things can be known. Both an astronomer and a physical scientist may demonstrate the same conclusion, for instance that the earth is spherical; the first, however, works in a mathematical medium prescinding from material qualities, while for the second his medium is the observation of material bodies through the senses. Accordingly there is nothing to stop the same things from being treated by the philosophical sciences when they can be looked at in the light of natural reason and by another science when they are looked at in the light of divine revelation. Consequently the theology of holy teaching differs in kind from that theology which is ranked as a part of philosophy.

article 2. is Christian theology a science?

THE SECOND POINT: 1. Christian theology does not look like science. For every science advances from self-evident principles. Yet Christian theology advances from the articles of faith and these are not self-evident, since not everybody grants them; *for not all have faith*, says the second epistle to the Thessalonians.[6] Consequently it is not a science.

2. Besides, a science is not concerned with individual cases. Sacred doctrine, however, deals with individual events and people, for instance the doings of Abraham, Isaac, Jacob and the like. Therefore sacred doctrine is not a science.

ON THE OTHER HAND. Augustine says that *this science alone is credited with begetting, nourishing, protecting, and making robust the healthiest*

---

5. Ecclus. 3:25.   6. 2 Thess. 3:2.

faith.[7] These functions belong to no science other than holy teaching. Therefore it is a science.

REPLY: Christian theology should be pronounced to be a science. Yet bear in mind that sciences are of two kinds: some work from premises recognized in the innate light of intelligence, for instance arithmetic, geometry, and sciences of the same sort; while others work from premises recognized in the light of a higher science, for instance optics starts out from principles marked out by geometry and harmony from principles indicated by arithmetic.

In this second manner is Christian theology a science, for it flows from founts recognized in the light of a higher science, namely God's very own which he shares with the blessed. Hence as harmony credits its principles which are taken from arithmetic so Christian theology takes on faith its principles revealed by God.

Hence: 1. Let us repeat that the premises of any science, no matter what, are either evident in themselves or can be resolved back into what a higher science recognizes. Such, as we have observed, are the principles of Christian theology.

2. Sacred doctrine sets out individual cases, not as being preoccupied with them, but in order both to introduce them as examples for our own lives, as is the wont of moral sciences, and to proclaim the authority of the men through whom divine revelation has come down to us, which revelation is the basis of sacred Scripture or doctrine.

article 3. is Christian theology a single science?

THE THIRD POINT: 1. The holy teaching would not appear to form one science. For, according to Aristotle, *a science has unity by treating of one class of subject-matter.*[8] Now here the Creator and creatures are both treated of, yet they cannot be grouped together within the same class of subject-matter. Therefore holy teaching is not just one science.

ON THE OTHER HAND holy Scripture refers to it as being one; thus the *Wisdom of Solomon, he gave to him the science of holy things.*[9]

REPLY: Holy teaching should be declared a single science. For you gauge the unity of a faculty and its training by its object, and this should be taken precisely according to the formal interest engaged and not according to what is materially involved; for instance the object of the sense of sight is a

7. *De Trinitate* XIV, 7. *PL* 42:1037.   8. *Posterior Analytics* I, 28. 87a38.
9. Wis. 10:10.

thing as having colour, a formal quality exhibited by men, donkeys, and stones in common. Now since holy Scripture looks at things in that they are divinely revealed, as already noted,[10] all things whatsoever that can be divinely revealed share in the same formal objective meaning. On that account they are included under holy teaching as under a single science.

Hence: 1. Holy teaching does not pronounce on God and creatures as though they were counterbalancing, but on God as principal and on creatures in relation to him, who is their origin and end. Hence its unity as science is not hampered.

2. Nothing debars the distinct subject-matters which diversify the lower and more particular faculties and trainings from being treated in common by a higher and more general faculty and training; this is because the latter envisages an object in a wider formal scene. Take for instance the central internal sense; visual and audible phenomena are both included in its object, namely a thing the senses can perceive, and while gathering in all the objects of the five external senses it yet remains a single unified faculty. Likewise different classes of object separately treated by the diverse philosophical sciences can be combined by Christian theology which keeps its unity when all of them are brought into the same focus and pictured in the field of divine revelation: thus in effect it is like an imprint on us of God's own knowledge, which is the single and simple vision of everything.

article 4. is Christian theology a practical science?

THE FOURTH POINT: 1. Christian theology appears to be a practical science. For Aristotle says that *a practical science is that which ends in action*.[11] But Christian theology is for action, according to St. James, *Be ye doers of the word and not hearers only*.[12] Therefore Christian theology is a practical science.

2. Moreover, sacred doctrine is divided into the Old Law and the New Law. Now law is part of moral science, which is a practical science. Therefore sacred doctrine is a practical science.

ON THE OTHER HAND, every practical science is concerned with what men can do and make, thus ethics is about human acts and architecture about building. Christian theology, however, is about God, who makes men and is not made by them. It is therefore more contemplative than practical.

REPLY: As already remarked,[13] the holy teaching while remaining single nevertheless embraces things belonging to the different philosophical sci-

10. Ia. I, 2.
12. James 1:22.

11. *Meta.* II, 1. 993b21.
13. Ia. I, 3.

ences because of the one formal meaning which is its interest in all manner of things, namely the truth they bear in the light of God. Whereas some among the philosophical sciences are theoretical and others are practical, sacred doctrine takes over both functions, in this being like the single knowledge whereby God knows himself and the things he makes.

All the same it is more theoretical than practical, since it is mainly concerned with the divine things which are, rather than with things men do; it deals with human acts only in so far as they prepare men for that achieved knowledge of God on which their eternal bliss reposes.

This leaves the way open for the answer to the difficulties.

article 5. is Christian theology more valuable than the other sciences?

THE FIFTH POINT: 1. It would seem that Christian theology is not more valuable than the other sciences. For certainty is part of a science's value. Now the other sciences, the premises of which are indubitable, look more assured and certain than Christian theology, of which the premises, namely the articles of faith, are open to doubt. Accordingly these other sciences seem more valuable.

2. Again, a lower science draws on a higher, like the musician on the arithmetician. Holy teaching, however, draws on philosophical learning; for St. Jerome allows that *the ancient writers so filled their books with the theories and verdicts of philosophers that at first you are at a loss which to admire more, their secular erudition or their skill in the Scriptures.*[14] Holy teaching, then, has a lower standing than other sciences.

ON THE OTHER HAND the book of *Proverbs* describes the other sciences as its maidservants: *She hath sent her handmaids to invite to the tower.*[15]

REPLY: Having noticed that this science is theoretical in one respect and practical in another we now go on to observe how it ranks above all the other sciences, theoretical and practical alike.

Among the theoretical sciences one is reckoned more important than another, first because of the certitude it brings, and next because of the worth of its subject. On both counts sacred doctrine surpasses the others. As to certitude, because theirs comes from the natural light of human reason which can make mistakes, whereas sacred doctrine's is held in the light of divine knowledge which cannot falter. As to worth of subject, because their

14. *Epistola ad Magnum Oratorem Urbis Romae*, Ep. 70. *PL* 22:668.
15. Prov. 9:3.

business is only with things set under reason, whereas sacred science leads to heights the reason cannot climb.

Then among the practical sciences, that stands higher which has the further purpose, for instance statesmanship commands military skill because the efficiency of the fighting services subserves the good of the commonwealth. Now in so far as sacred doctrine is a practical science, its aim is eternal happiness, and this is the final end governing the ends of all the practical sciences.

Hence it is clear that from every standpoint sacred doctrine excels all other sciences.

Hence: 1. There is nothing to stop a thing that is objectively more certain by its nature from being subjectively less certain to us because of the disability of our minds, which, as Aristotle notes, *blink at the most evident things like bats in the sunshine.*[16] Doubt about the articles of faith which falls to the lot of some is not because the reality is at all uncertain but because the human understanding is feeble. Nevertheless, as Aristotle also points out, the slenderest acquaintance we can form with heavenly things is more desirable than a thorough grasp of mundane matters.[17]

2. Holy teaching can borrow from the other sciences, not from any need to beg from them, but for the greater clarification of the things it conveys. For it takes its principles directly from God through revelation, not from the other sciences. On that account it does not rely on them as though they were in control, for their rôle is subsidiary and ancillary; so an architect makes use of tradesmen as a statesman employs soldiers. That it turns to them so is not from any lack or insufficiency within itself, but because our understanding is wanting, which is the more readily guided into the world above reason, set forth in holy teaching, through the world of natural reason from which the other sciences take their course.

article 6. is this teaching wisdom?

THE SIXTH POINT: 1. Apparently it is not wisdom. For no teaching which assumes its principles from elsewhere deserves the name of wisdom, since, as Aristotle remarks, *the office of the wise is to govern others, not to be governed by them.*[18] Now the principles of this teaching are suppositions from another place, as noted earlier on.[19] Therefore it is not wisdom.

2. Further, one charge on wisdom is to prove the premises of the other

16. *Meta.* II, 1. 993b10.   17. *De Partibus Animalium* I, 5. 644b31.
18. *Meta.* I, 2. 982a18.
19. Ia. I, 2, that holy teaching derives from God's own knowledge and the knowledge of the blessed in heaven.

sciences; that is why Aristotle calls it *the chief of the sciences*.[20] But theological teaching does not prove the premises of the other sciences, and therefore it is not wisdom.

3. Besides, this teaching is acquired by study. Wisdom, however, is received from the outpouring of the Spirit, and as such is numbered among the seven Gifts of the Holy Spirit, set forth by Isaiah.[21] This teaching, then, is not wisdom.

ON THE OTHER HAND *Deuteronomy* says early on, before setting down the ten commandments, *This is our wisdom and understanding in the presence of the people*.[22]

REPLY: Holy teaching should be declared to be wisdom highest above all human wisdoms, not indeed in some special department but unconditionally.

To govern and judge belongs to the wise person, and since judgment in the light of the higher cause also holds judgment in the light of lower causes, that person is called wise about any matter who there maturely considers the highest cause. Take architecture for example: you apply the terms "wise" and "master-builder" to the artist who plans the whole structure, and not the artisans under him who cut the stones and mix the mortar; hence the reference in the first epistle to the Corinthians, *As a wise architect I have laid the foundations*.[23] Then again, take the scene of human living by and large, and you call that person wise because he directs human acts to their due end for good and all; hence *Proverbs* say, *Wisdom is prudence to a man*.[24] That person, therefore, who considers maturely and without qualification the first and final cause of the entire universe, namely God, is to be called supremely wise; hence wisdom appears in St. Augustine as knowledge of divine things.[25]

Now holy teaching goes to God most personally as deepest origin and highest end, and that not only because of what can be gathered about him from creatures (which philosophers have recognized, according to the epistle to the Romans, *What was known of God is manifest in them*)[26] but also because of what he alone knows about himself and yet discloses for others to share. Consequently holy teaching is called wisdom in the highest degree.

Hence: 1. Holy teaching assumes its principles from no human science,

---

20. *Ethics* VI, 7. 1141a16. "The most finished of the forms of knowledge." Aristotle is comparing philosophic and practical wisdom.

21. Isa. 2:2. 22. Deut. 4:6.

23. 1 Cor. 3:10. 24. Prov. 10:23.

25. *De Trinitate* 12, 14. *PL* 42:1009. 26. Rom. 1:19.

but from divine science, by which as by supreme wisdom all our knowledge is governed.

2. The premises of other sciences are either self-evident, in which case they cannot be proved, or they are proved through some natural evidence in some other science. What is peculiar to this science's knowledge is that it is about truth which comes through revelation, not through natural reasoning. On this account establishing the premises of other sciences is none of its business, though it may well be critical of them. For whatsoever is encountered in the other sciences which is incompatible with its truth should be completely condemned as false: accordingly the second epistle to the Corinthians alludes to the pulling down of ramparts, destroying counsels, and every height that rears itself against the knowledge of God.[27]

3. Since having a formed judgment characterizes the wise person, so there are two kinds of wisdom according to the two ways of passing judgment. This may be arrived at from a bent that way, as when a person who possesses the habit of a virtue rightly commits himself to what should be done in consonance with it, because he is already in sympathy with it; hence Aristotle remarks that the virtuous man himself sets the measure and standard for human acts.[28] Alternatively the judgment may be arrived at through a cognitive process, as when a person soundly instructed in moral science can appreciate the activity of virtues he does not himself possess.

The first way of judging divine things belongs to that wisdom which is classed among the Gifts of the Holy Ghost; so St. Paul says, *The spiritual man judges all things*,[29] and Dionysius speaks about *Hierotheus being taught by the experience of undergoing things, not only by learning about them*.[30] The second way of judging is taken by sacred doctrine to the extent that it can be gained by study; even so the premises are held from revelation.

article 7. is God the subject of this science?

THE SEVENTH POINT: 1. God would not seem to be the subject of this science. For, according to Aristotle, every science should begin by presupposing what its subject is. This science, however, does not start by making the assumption of defining God; as St. John Damascene remarks, *In God we cannot say what he is*. It follows that God is not the subject of this science.

2. Besides, all matters about which a science reaches settled conclusions enter into its subject. Now sacred Scripture goes as far about many things other than God, for instance about creatures and human conduct. Therefore its subject is not purely God.

27. 2 Cor. 10:4–5.   28. *Ethics* X, 5. 1176a17.
29. 1 Cor. 2:15.
30. *De Divinis Nominibus* II, 9. *PG* 3:648.

ON THE OTHER HAND, what a science discusses is its subject. In this case the discussion is about God; for it is called theology, as it were, talk about God. Therefore he is the subject of this science.

REPLY: That God is the subject of this science should be maintained. For a subject is to a science as an object is to a psychological power or training. Now that properly is designated the object which expresses the special term why anything is related to the power or training in question; thus a man or a stone is related to eyesight in that both are coloured, so being coloured is the proper object of the sense of sight. Now all things are dealt with in holy teaching in terms of God, either because they are God himself or because they are relative to him as their origin and end. Therefore God is truly the object of this science.

This also is clear from the fact that the first principles of this science are the articles of faith, and faith is about God. Now the subject of a science's first principles and of its entire development is identical, since the whole of a science is virtually contained in its principles.

Some writers, however, preoccupied with the things treated of by sacred doctrine rather than with the formal interest engaged, have indicated its subject-matter otherwise, apportioning it between the reality and its symbols, or regarding it as the works of redemption, or the whole Christ, namely head and members. All these indeed are dwelt on by this science, yet as held in their relationship to God.

Hence: 1. Though we cannot know what God is, nevertheless this teaching employs an effect of his, of nature or of grace, in place of a definition, and by this means discusses truths about him. Some of the philosophical sciences adopt a similar method, of grounding the argument on the effect, not on the definition, of the cause when demonstrating something about a cause through its effect.

2. All other things that are settled in Holy Scripture are embraced in God, not that they are parts of him—such as essential components or accidents—but because they are somehow related to him.

article 8. is this teaching probative?

THE EIGHTH POINT: 1. This teaching does not seem to be probative. For St. Ambrose says, *Away with arguments where faith is at stake.*[31] Now faith is the principal quest of this teaching, according to St. John: *These things are written that you may believe.*[32] Therefore it is not probative.

2. Again, were it to advance arguments, they would be either from

31. *De fide Catholica* I, 13. *PL* 16:570.   32. John 20:31.

authority or from the evidence of reason. If from authority, then the process would be unbefitting the dignity of this teaching, for, according to Boëthius,[33] authority is the weakest ground of proof. If from the evidence of reason, then the process would not correspond with its purpose, for according to St. Gregory, *Faith has no merit where the reason presents actual proof from experience.*[34] Well then, holy teaching does not attempt proofs.

ON THE OTHER HAND the epistle to Titus requires of a bishop that he should *embrace the faithful word which is according to doctrine that he may be able to exhort in sound doctrine and convince the gainsayers.*[35]

REPLY: As the other sciences do not argue to prove their premises, but work from them to bring out other things in their field of inquiry, so this teaching does not argue to establish its premises, which are the articles of faith, but advances from them to make something known, as when St. Paul adduces the resurrection of Christ to prove the resurrection of us all.[36]

Then bear in mind that among the philosophical sciences subordinate sciences neither prove their premises nor controvert those who deny them; these functions they leave to a superior science. The supreme science among them, namely metaphysics, contests the denial of its principles with an opponent who will grant something; if nothing, then debate is impossible, though his reasonings may be demolished.

So sacred Scripture, which has no superior science over it, disputes the denial of its principles; it argues on the basis of those truths held by revelation which an opponent admits, as when, debating with heretics, it appeals to received authoritative texts of Christian theology, and uses one article against those who reject another. If, however, an opponent believes nothing of what has been divinely revealed, then no way lies open for making the articles of faith reasonably credible; all that can be done is to solve the difficulties against faith he may bring up. For since faith rests on unfailing truth, and the contrary of truth cannot really be demonstrated, it is clear that alleged proofs against faith are not demonstrations, but charges that can be refuted.

Hence: 1. Though arguments of human reason reach no position to prove the things of faith, nevertheless, as noted above, holy teaching does work from the articles of faith to infer other things.

2. Argument from authority is the method most appropriate to this

33. *In Topicis Ciceronis* I. *PL* 64:1166. *De differentia Topicorum* 3. *PL* 64:1199. Boëthius (c. 480–525), a main bridge between classical and early scholastic philosophy.

34. *In Evang.* II, 26. *PL* 76:1197.   35. Titus 1:9.

36. 1 Cor. 15:12.

teaching in that its premises are held through revelation; consequently it has to accept the authority of those to whom revelation was made. Nor does this derogate from its dignity, for though weakest when based on what human beings have disclosed, the argument from authority is most forcible when based on what God has disclosed.

All the same holy teaching also uses human reasoning, not indeed to prove the faith, for that would take away from the merit of believing, but to make manifest some implications of its message. Since grace does not scrap nature but brings it to perfection, so also natural reason should assist faith as the natural loving bent of the will yields to charity. St. Paul speaks of *bringing into captivity every understanding unto the service of Christ.*[37] Hence holy teaching uses the authority of philosophers who have been able to perceive the truth by natural reasoning, for instance when St. Paul quotes the saying of Aratus, *As some of your poets have said, we are of the race of God.*[38]

Yet holy teaching employs such authorities only in order to provide as it were extraneous arguments from probability. Its own proper authorities are those of canonical Scripture, and these it applies with convincing force. It has other proper authorities, the doctors of the Church, and these it looks to as its own, but for arguments that carry no more than probability.

For our faith rests on the revelation made to the Prophets and Apostles who wrote the canonical books, not on a revelation, if such there be, made to any other teacher. In this sense St. Augustine wrote to St. Jerome; *Only to those books or writings which are called canonical have I learnt to pay such honour that I firmly believe that none of their authors have erred in composing them. Other authors, however, I read to such effect that, no matter what holiness and learning they display, I do not hold what they say to be true because those were their sentiments.*

37. 2 Cor. 10:5.   38. Acts 17:28.

55. Orthodoxy Enforced at Paris (1272)

Statute of the Faculty of Arts Against Artists Treating Theological Questions and That No One Shall Dare to Determine Against the Faith Questions Which Touch the Faith As Well As Philosophy

To each and all the sons of holy mother church who now and in the future shall see the present page, the masters of logical science or professors of

From *University Records and Life in the Middle Ages*, edited and translated by Lynn Thorndyke (New York: Columbia University Press, 1944), pp. 85–88. © 1944 by Columbia University Press. Reprinted by permission of the publisher.

natural science at Paris, each and all, who hold and observe the statute and ordinance of the venerable father Symon by divine permission cardinal priest of the title of St. Cecilia, legate of the apostolic see, made after separate deliberation of the nations, and who adhere expressly and entirely to the opinion of the seven judges appointed by the same legate in the same statute, greeting in the Saviour of all. All should know that we masters, each and all, from the preceding abundant and considered advice and deliberation of good men concerning this, wishing with all our power to avoid present and future dangers which by occasion of this sort might in the future befall our faculty, by common consent, no one of us contradicting, on the Friday preceding the Sunday on which is sung *Rejoice Jerusalem*, the masters one and all being convoked for this purpose in the church of Ste. Geneviève at Paris, decree and ordain that no master or bachelor of our faculty should presume to determine or even to dispute any purely theological question, as concerning the Trinity and incarnation and similar matters, since this would be transgressing the limits assigned him, for the Philosopher says that it is utterly improper for a non-geometer to dispute with a geometer. But if anyone shall have so presumed, unless within three days after he has been warned or required by us he shall have been willing to revoke publicly his presumption in the classes or public disputation where he first disputed the said question, henceforth he shall be forever deprived of our society.

We decree further and ordain that, if anyone shall have disputed at Paris any question which seems to touch both faith and philosophy, if he shall have determined it contrary to the faith, henceforth he shall forever be deprived of our society as a heretic, unless he shall have been at pains humbly and devoutly to revoke his error and his heresy, within three days after our warning, in full congregation or elsewhere where it shall seem to us expedient. Adding further that, if any master or bachelor of our faculty reads or disputes any difficult passages or any questions which seem to undermine the faith, he shall refute the arguments or text so far as they are against the faith or concede that they are absolutely false and entirely erroneous, and he shall not presume to dispute or lecture further upon this sort of difficulties, either in the text or in authorities, but shall pass over them entirely as erroneous. But if anyone shall be rebellious in this, he shall be punished by a penalty which in the judgment of our faculty suits his fault and is due. Moreover, in order that all these may be inviolably observed, we masters, one and all, have sworn on our personal security in the hand of the rector of our faculty and we all have spontaneously agreed to be so bound. In memory of which we have caused this same statute to be inscribed and so ordered in the register of our faculty in the same words. Moreover, every rector henceforth to be created in the faculty shall swear that he will cause all the bachelors about to incept in our faculty to bind themselves to this same thing, swearing on their personal security in his hand. Given at Paris the year of the Lord 1271, the first day of April.[1]

1. As Easter fell at that time after the first of April, the year is 1272 according to our reckoning.

56. Teaching Obligations in the Faculty of Arts, Paris (ca. 1280)

These are the articles which bachelors about to incept in arts are required to swear to, when they come before the rector pledging faith in person. First, it should be said to them: You are to deliver ordinary lectures in the round cope or in the pallium. You will dispute at the hour set and you will discuss your questions for forty days continuously after you have incepted. You are to carry on for fifteen (forty?) days in the said costume. You shall not have shoes with pointed toes or ornaments or openings, nor are you to wear a surcoat slashed on the sides, nor shall you have a mitre on your head so long as you lecture or dispute in the round cope. You will attend the meetings, obey the commands of the rector and proctor in things lawful and honorable. You shall not permit dances to go on before your house nor anything unseemly to occur at your opening lecture under penalty of degradation from being a master. You shall not reveal the secrets of the university. You are to be present at the burial of students on feast days when you know of them; on other days, when you shall be asked, you shall in the aforesaid costume read or cause to be read the Psalter at the death of a master of the faculty. You will observe and defend the accustomed freedom of examination of Ste. Geneviève. You will promise to incept under the master under whom you were licentiated, or with his consent under another, so that you have adequately sought his consent or would gladly have done so if you could, and so that you intend no guile or fraud towards your master under whom you gained the licentiate with respect to your inception. Also, you will observe the order or ordinance as to the method of giving ordinary lectures and of disputing. Also, you will stand with the secular masters and defend their status, statutes, and privileges all your lifetime, to whatever position you may come. Also, so long as you shall teach in arts, you will dispute no purely theological question, for example, concerning the Trinity and incarnation. And if you chance to discuss any question which has to do with the faith and philosophy, you will settle it in favor of the faith and

From *University Records and Life in the Middle Ages*, edited and translated by Lynn Thorndyke (New York: Columbia University Press, 1944), pp. 103–5. Some footnotes deleted. © 1944 by Columbia University Press. Reprinted by permission of the publisher.

answer the arguments contrary to the faith as it shall seem to you they should be answered.

Also, you shall swear without any fraud that you have fulfilled the requirements in arts at Paris according to the custom hitherto observed, or in some university where there are at least twelve teachers. Also, that you will observe the ordinance recently passed as to the method of announcing general meetings to the dean of the canon law faculty and the dean of the medical faculty. Also, you shall swear that, if you shall have known that a nation is going to rise against a nation or a province against a province or a person against a person, you will reveal it to the nation against which there is to be made an insurrection of a person or province. Also, you shall swear that you will not incept while you see another bachelor incepting, but you will wait until he has given his lecture and finished his discussion before you begin. Also, that you will observe the ordinance of the masters as to bachelors examined on the island by masters not of the faculty. Also, you shall swear to, and to the best of your ability, obtain freedom of the university from debt. Also, you shall swear that you will incept in your own cope, not one borrowed or hired, if you put two solidi or more in the purse. Also, you shall swear that you have heard lectures for six years in arts. Also, you shall swear that you will lecture for two years continuously unless a reasonable excuse shall occur. Also, you shall swear to defend the particular liberties of the faculty and the honorable customs of the faculty and the privileges of the whole university, to whatever position you may come.

57. Raymond Lull, *On the Study of Oriental Languages* (1298–99)

Faithful to God is he and burning with supreme charity who in the knowledge and enjoyment of supreme wisdom and love directing the ignorant, illuminating the blind, leading back the dead to the way of life, fears not perils of his own adversity and bodily death for the testament of God. Who shall tell his glory and great splendor? Who shall number the generations of infidels who today know not God? Who shall estimate how many from the blindness of error slip into the shadows of hell? Alas! the devout Christian people of the faithful justly laments so great evils. O fount of science supernal, that at Paris hast intoxicated with marvelous doctrine so many professors of so great authority, extend thy torrents to the lands of the infidels, and irrigate the totally arid hearts of the erring with dew celestial,

From *University Records and Life in the Middle Ages*, edited and translated by Lynn Thorndyke (New York: Columbia University Press, 1944), pp. 125–27. © 1944 by Columbia University Press. Reprinted by permission of the publisher.

and drive away darkness, open to them the rays of light eternal. Ah, when shall all nations walk in thy light and every man walking in the splendor of thy sun see the salvation of God? With desire have I, Raymond Lull, desired this which is supremely desirable for all faithful Christians and obtainable by those whose intellects the supreme wisdom has divinely illuminated. Happy is that university which bears so many defenders of the faith, and happy that city whose soldiers armed with the wisdom and devotion of Christ can subdue barbarous nations to the supreme king. When shall all the earth adore Thee, God, hymn and bless Thy name, and every tribe and tongue serve Thee?

Consider this, reverend fathers and sirs, with intellects and wills whose object is the highest truth and highest goodness. Since just as God is intelligible and lovable because supremely true and supremely good, so He is everywhere and much, because immense, and present at all times, because eternal. O how happy were the apostles and martyrs, since their sound has gone forth into all the earth and their words to the ends of the world preaching Jesus Christ! O how precious their death in the sight of the Lord, who recalled many from death unto life! O would that there were now many repairers of their ways, since it would be indeed glorious and necessary for the whole Christian people. Because as I know, since I speak from experience, there are many philosophers of the Arabs who strive to pervert Christians to the perfidy of Mahomet and the sons of unbelievers pester us saying, Where is their God? And further, the Jews and Saracens to the best of their ability try to bring the Tartars into their sects. And if it happens, which God forbid, that the Tartars become Jews or Saracens or constitute a sect by themselves, it is to be feared that this will result in incomparable detriment to all Christendom, just as happened from the sect of Mahomet at whose foundation the Saracens invaded us and about a third part of Christendom was lost. Innumerable is that generation of Tartars, in a short time indeed it has subjugated many kingdoms and principalities by warlike hand.

You, reverend fathers and masters, see peril threaten the entire church of God, and unless your wisdom and devotion, by which all Christendom is sustained, opposes the shield of salvation to the perfidy of the Saracens, and if it neglects to restrain the impetuous torrent of Tartars—I will not say more—but think what may happen! And strange it is that there are more adversaries of God than defenders, and more men vituperate than praise Him; and God was made man for men and died that they might live; and many, too, have now declined from the unity of the church, like the Greeks and many other schismatics. Consider how great Evil is returned for good to God and how great opprobrium by those who were created to praise God, and how great persecution threatens us faithful, and what question we must answer to God at the last judgment, when He requires from us the death of those who should have enjoyed life eternal from our preaching and example.

Here the prick of conscience stings me and compels me to come to you, whose high discretion and wisdom it behooves to act in such a matter, so pious, so meritorious, in a service so grateful to God and useful to the entire world, namely, that here at Paris, where the fountain of divine wisdom rises, where the light of truth shines on Christian peoples, there should be founded study of Arabic, Tartar and Greek, that we, having learned the languages of the adversaries of God and ourselves, by preaching to and teaching them may overcome their errors in the sword of truth and render the people acceptable unto God and convert enemies into friends. If this be done and it please God that it so be, Christendom will receive the greatest exaltation and extension. And of this so inestimable thing you will be the foundation, and thou, university of Paris, will by no means be least among thy doctors, for from thee will come light to all peoples, and thou wilt offer testimony to the truth, and masters and disciples will flock to thee, and all shall hear all sciences from thee. What of good will the Greeks and Arabs have in their volumes that will not be known to thee, when thou shalt understand their tongues without an interpreter? Who will estimate how great praise, how great honor to God, how great compassion of charity towards poor sinners, and how great good would result in and from this place? And this can easily be done, if you direct your prayers to the illustrious king of France, that he, who is noblest among the kings of earth, see fit to bestow his well-merited alms on this noblest of all undertakings, namely, to found and endow the said study or studies. And he will listen to you, I believe, after he has understood the importance of this undertaking.

Papal Monarchy and Its Critics

The growth of papal government has been one theme running throughout the documents in this collection. Resistance to, or defiance of, papal authority has been another. This subtopic under the heading "Authority, Conflict, and Repression," deals chiefly with papal assertions and popular defiance during the reign of Pope Innocent III (1198–1216).

Innocent, the child of a noble Roman family, studied in two of the major universities of his time. He studied law at Bologna and theology in Paris. His lineage, education, and innate intelligence were recognized when the College of Cardinals elected him as pope at the relatively early age of thirty-seven. While he vigorously and persistently asserted the absolute dominance of the papacy over the Church and its circumstantial dominance over individual secular kingdoms, Innocent also pursued Church reform. His concern for the spiritual purification of the Church was expressed most prophetically in the encouragement that he gave Francis of Assisi. The Fourth Lateran Council (1215) was the culmination of his efforts to establish the papacy's juridical and moral headship of Christendom.

Still, despite Innocent's abilities and labors, many of his greater enterprises were frustrated. The texts below indicate his vain attempts to salvage whatever papal dignity he could from the catastrophe of the Fourth Crusade, his futile assertion of suzerainty over England, and the somber outlook of the Fourth Lateran Council (documents 58–61).

The verses of Walther von der Vogelweide (ca. 1170–ca. 1230) record the hostility of a German *samurai* and troubadour toward the political program that Innocent imposed (document 62). Writing in the vernacular (Middle High German) for an aristocratic, military elite, Walther meandered from court to court as a mercenary knight. The Emperor Frederick II, embroiled (after Innocent III's death) in a ferocious war with the papacy, found him a loyal servant.

The positions set forth by Pope and Troubadour in the following documents illuminate Innocent's ironic failures, episodes in the continuing critique of the papacy that led to movements of protest and reform from the eleventh century onward through the Reformation.

58. Letter of Innocent III to the Crusaders (1203)

To the Marquis of Montferrat and Counts Baldwin of Flanders, Louis of Blois, and Hugh of St. Paul, that they should cross the sea to help the Holy Land. Given in Ferentinum, in the sixth year of Innocent's pontificate (1203).

Since you had marched out of Egypt strong in hand and with an outstretched arm to offer yourselves in sacrifice to the Lord, we were grieved not a little, and are still grieving now, that Pharaoh pursues you in flight, or rather, that you are following Pharaoh, who under some pretense of necessity and a covering of piety is striving with the yoke of sin to subject you to the ancient slavery. We were grieved, we said, and are grieving now, for

From *Patrologiae cursus completus,* Latin Series 215, edited by J. P. Migne (Paris, 1890), pp. 104–7. Translated for this volume by Constantin Fasolt.

ourselves as well as for you and the entire Christian people. For ourselves, because we used to believe that we would reap in exultation what we sowed in tears when we explained the word of God through our legates and letters to you and to others often, not without some bitterness in our heart, and with no small distress for our body, urging men who cultivate their Christian name to avenge the injury of Jesus Christ; but, without warning, an enemy of our harvest has sown tares on top and spoiled the seed so that the wheat seems to have turned into tares.

And for you we grieve, because you had cleansed yourselves of the old yeast and were already trusted to have put off the old man and his acts entirely; but then a little yeast—oh how I wish it were a little—infected all the dough again, and you no longer keep your garments white but have put the old mantle on, so to speak, taking your hand from the plow, and looking back with the wife of Lot, so that according to the Apostle you are no longer seen fit for the kingdom of God. And for the Christian people we were grieved, and are still grieving now, because they are the more humiliated by those who they had hoped would the more exalt them. For when the many who had preceded you to relieve the Holy Land heard that you had not embarked, they despaired of your further voyage and returned to their own affairs. The Saracens, doubtful of your approach, and certain of their retreat, took courage against the Christians. We do not wish to relate how with the force of sin the Saracens prevailed over them, since that has almost everywhere been published.

But we rejoice that, after you received our letters and recognized the error of your excess, you have devotedly and humbly fulfilled the apostolic order and, your oath having been sworn and acknowledged, have received the benefit of absolution, and obliged yourselves, my sons—you counts and you two Gallic barons, and your successors—to satisfy our orders concerning the sentence of excommunication which you incurred through letter patent at Zara. If only your repentance were so true, that is, that thus you would repent your deeds, that from now on you would refrain from similar ones. For one who still does what he has repented of doing is not a penitent but an impostor, and a penitent who goes back to his sin is like a dog returning to his vomit. A sin committed once, moreover, is lighter than one committed once and then repeated.

None of you should therefore blindly fall for the delusion that he may occupy or plunder the land of the Greeks as though it were not quite so subject to the Apostolic See, and that, because his brother was deposed and even blinded, the Emperor of Constantinople usurped the empire. Indeed, however great a wrong the emperor and the men within his jurisdiction may have done in this or other matters, it still is not for you to judge their crimes, nor have you taken up the cross's sign in order to take vengeance for this injury, but rather to avenge the shame of the Crucified whom you have specially been assigned to serve.

We admonish Your Nobility, therefore, we urge you attentively, and by apostolic writings order and command you not to deceive yourselves, or to allow yourselves to be deceived by others, to do under a pretense of piety what—far be it—will redound to the damnation of your souls, but rather to desist from frivolous opportunities and feigned necessities, to sail to the aid of the Holy Land, and to avenge the injury of the cross, taking from the spoils of the enemies only what the time you may have wasted in Romania may perhaps make it necessary to extort from those who are your brothers. For otherwise, because we neither can nor must, we do not offer you the grace of remission at all. And we want you to memorize the tenor of our prohibition, and warn you not to go against it lightly, by which we forbid you, under threat of excommunication, to try to invade or harm the lands of Christians, unless they wickedly obstruct your course, or if another just and necessary cause should perhaps occur which would, on the advice of our legate, enable you to do otherwise. In order to prevent the Doge's and the Venetian people's guilt from being added to your punishment, moreover, we want and we command that you will have our letter, which we saw fit to have addressed to them, and which is known to be still in your hands, transferred to them, so that they cannot make excuses for their sins.

59. Letter of Innocent III to the People of Metz (1199)

Since by the apostolic office enjoined on us we have become, as the Apostle says, "debtors to the wise and to the unwise,"[1] we must for the salvation of all be zealous to retrieve the wicked from their vices and nurture the good in their virtues. Still greater discretion is called for when vices creep in covertly, under the guise of virtues, and when the angel of Satan changes himself into an angel of pretended light.

Our venerable brother, the Bishop of Metz, has sensibly informed us by his letters that both in the diocese and the city of Metz, no small number of laymen and women, drawn, as it were, by a desire for the Scriptures, have had the Gospels, the Letters of Paul, the Psalter, the Morals of Job, and many other books translated into French for them. These laymen and women find so much pleasure in devoting themselves to these translations—would that it were discreetly too!—that they dare to regurgitate such things among themselves in secret meetings and to preach to one an-

From *Patrologiae cursus completus,* Latin Series 214, edited by J. P. Migne (Paris, 1890), pp. 695-8. Translated for this volume by Constantin Fasolt.

1. Rom. 1:14.

other. They also scorn the company of those who do not involve themselves with similar matters, and they regard as strangers those who do not apply their ears and minds to this. When some of their parish priests wished to rebuke them for it, they resisted them to their faces and tried to draw reasons from the Scriptures that they ought not in any way to be prohibited from doing so. Some of them also sniff at the simplemindedness of their priests, and when the priests propound the word of salvation to them, they mutter to themselves that they have it better in their booklets, and that they can talk about it more intelligently.

Although the desire to understand the divine Scriptures and to encourage enthusiasm for them deserves not censure, but rather praise, such people nevertheless deserve to be criticized for holding their meetings in secret, usurping the office of preaching, making fun of the priests' simplemindedness, and scorning the company of those not interested in such things.

For God, the true light that illuminates every man who comes into this world, hates the works of darkness so much that, when he was about to send his apostles to the whole world to preach the Gospel to all creatures, he told them outright: "What I tell you in the darkness, that speak in the light; and what you hear in the ear, that preach upon the housetops." [2] Thereby he clearly announced that the Gospel should not be preached in secret meetings, as heretics do, but publicly proclaimed in the churches according to Catholic custom. By the testimony of the Truth "everyone that does evil hates the light, and comes not to the light, that his works may not be reproved. But he that does truth, comes to the light, that his works may be made manifest, because they are done in God." [3] When the high priest questioned Jesus about his disciples and his doctrine, he replied therefore: "I have spoken openly to the world, I have always taught in the synagogue, and in the temple, whither all the Jews resort, and in secret I have spoken nothing." [4]

If someone should go on to object that "what is holy should not be given to dogs, nor pearls be cast before swine," [5] according to the Lord's precept, since Christ himself did not say to all, but only to the apostles, that "to you it is given to know the mystery of the kingdom of God; but to the rest only in parables," [6] he should understand that dogs and swine are not those who thankfully receive what is holy and gladly accept the pearls, but those who tear apart what is holy and spurn the pearls, such as those who do not venerate the words of the Gospel and the sacraments of the Church like Catho-

2. Matt. 10:27.   3. John 3:20–21.
4. John 18:20.   5. Matt. 7:6.
6. Luke 8:10.

lics, but rather abhor them like heretics who forever carp and blaspheme, and of whom the Apostle Paul teaches that after a first and second admonition they are to be shunned.[7]

The hidden sacraments of the faith are to be expounded not to all at large, as they cannot be understood by all at large, but only to those able to take them in with faithful understanding. That is why the Apostle says to the more simpleminded: "As unto little ones in Christ, I gave you milk to drink, not meat."[8] Solid food, as he said to others, is for adults: "We speak wisdom among the perfect. But among you I have decided I know nothing, save Jesus Christ, and him crucified."[9] For such is the depth of divine Scripture that not only the simpleminded and illiterate, but even the wise and learned are not fully competent to search out its meaning. Hence the verse in Scripture: "For many have failed in their search."[10] For this reason it has long ago been rightly established in the divine law that any beast that touched the mountain should be stoned,[11] namely in order that nobody simpleminded and untaught should presume to reach the sublimity of holy Scripture or preach it to others. For it is written: "Seek not the things that are too high for thee."[12] This is why the Apostle says: "Not to be more wise than it behooves to be wise, but to be wise unto sobriety."[13] Just as there are many parts of the body, but not all parts have the same function, so there are many orders in the Church, but not all have the same office, for according to the Apostle, "the Lord gave some apostles, some prophets, and some doctors,"[14] and so on. Because the order of doctors is, so to speak, outstanding in the Church, it is thus not right for just anyone to usurp the office of preaching. For according to the Apostle, "how shall they preach unless they be sent?"[15] And the very Truth instructed the apostles: "Pray the Lord of the harvest, that he send laborers into his harvest."[16]

But suppose somebody should cunningly reply that, even if men like that are not sent visibly by man, they are sent invisibly by God, because an invisible mission is worth much more than a visible, and a divine far better than a human, whence we read that John the Baptist was sent not by man but by God, as the Evangelist bears witness: "There was a man, sent from God, whose name was John,"[17] then one definitely can and should base one's reply on the principle that, as that inner mission is hidden, it is not

7. Titus 3:10.   8. 2 Cor. 3:1–2.
9. 2 Cor. 2:6,2.   10. Ps. 63:7, Douai (64:6, King James).
11. Exod. 19:13, where the Israelites and their cattle are commanded, on pain of death, to stay away from Mount Sinai while the Lord speaks to Moses.
12. Ecclus. 3:22.   13. Rom. 12:3.
14. Eph. 4:11; "doctors" in the sense of teachers.
15. Rom. 10:15.   16. Luke 10:2.
17. John 1:6.

enough for anyone merely to make the bare assertion that he is sent by God, because any heretic would assert the same. In addition, he must confirm his invisible mission by working a miracle or by a special testimony of Scripture. This is why, when the Lord wished to send Moses to Egypt to the sons of Israel, he gave him the power to change a rod into a serpent and the serpent back into a rod as a sign, so that he would be believed to have been sent by him.[18] John the Baptist, on the other hand, produced a special testimony for his mission from Scripture, when he answered the priests and Levites sent to ask who he was and why he had assumed the office of baptizing: "I am the voice of one crying in the wilderness: Make straight the way of the Lord, as said the prophet Isaiah."[19] When someone has not been sent by man, he should therefore not be believed, if he says he is sent by God, unless he produces a special testimony about himself from the Scriptures or works an obvious miracle. For the Evangelist testifies even of those who we read were sent by God that "they went forth and preached everywhere, the Lord working with them and confirming the word with signs that followed."[20]

Even though knowledge is highly necessary for priests to teach, as according to the word of the prophet "the priest's lips keep knowledge, and they seek the law at his mouth,"[21] simpleminded priests are nevertheless not to be spoken ill of, not even by scholars, because the priestly ministry in them should be honored. This is why the Lord commanded in the Law: "Thou shall not revile the gods,"[22] meaning the priests, who are called by the name of gods because of the eminence of their order and the dignity of their office. In the same sense he says elsewhere of the servant who wished to remain with his lord, that "the lord should bring him unto the gods."[23] Since a servant should according to the word of the Apostle "stand or fall to his own lord,"[24] a priest should really be chastised in the spirit of mildness by the bishop to whose correction he is subject, and not reviled in the spirit of pride by the people for whose correction he is appointed. For by the Lord's precept father and mother must not be cursed but be honored instead[25]—which must be understood much more strongly of a spiritual than of a bodily father.

18. Exod. 4:1–5, 30–31.   19. John 1:23; Isa. 40:3.
20. Mark 16:20.   21. Mal. 2:7.
22. Exod. 22:28. In Hebrew, the same plural form, elohim, normally refers either to pagan gods or to the God of Israel. However, in this passage and a few others, it was often interpreted to mean not "God" but "judges," and Innocent means to improve on this interpretation.
23. Cf. Exod. 21:6, concerning the servant who does not wish the emancipation he is entitled to after six years of servitude.
24. Rom. 14:4; i.e., only his master has the right to judge him.
25. Exod. 20:12, 21:17, etc.

Let no one defend the audacity of his presumption with the examples of the ass, of which we read that it rebuked the prophet,[26] or of the Lord, who said: "Which of you shall convict me of sin?"[27] and: "If I have spoken evil, bear witness of the evil."[28] It is one thing to rebuke your brother in private for offending against you, which everyone is expressly required to do by the rule of Gospel.[29] This is the context in which Balaam may be understood to have been rebuked by his ass. It is something else to reprehend your father in public, even if he is at fault, and especially to call him a fool, rather than simpleminded, which expressly no one may do by the truth of the Gospel. For "whosoever shall say: Thou fool, even to his brother, shall be in danger of hell."[30] Again, it is one thing for a superior of his own free will and confident of his innocence to permit his inferiors to accuse him. This is the context in which the Lord's word above should be understood. It is another thing for an inferior to stand up to his superior brazenly, with a mind less to rebuke than to defame, although he rather has the duty to obey. If it should happen to be necessary to remove the priest from the charge of his flock for uselessness or unworthiness, it should be handled regularly, before the bishop, whose office is recognized to include the appointment as well as the suspension of priests.

Their attitude of scorning everyone else as though they alone were just, proceeds from a sort of Pharisaic pride and should be scorned by all, because we read about the many saints who have been there from the very beginning of the Church to the present that they neither were like that nor attached themselves to such men, and because it may be that such men, more of whom we read have now arisen, unless they are content to be taught rather than to teach, will belong to those to whom the Lord says: "Be not many masters."[31]

For these reasons, children, as we love you with the affection of a father, we insistently ask, warn, and urge everyone of you in the Lord not to fall into the pit of error under the cloak of truth, nor into the trap of vices in the guise of virtues, and we enjoin you for the remission of your sins to recall your tongues and your minds from the offenses we have reprobated above, and to observe the Catholic faith and the rule of the Church, so that it will not befall you to be encircled by the treachery of words, or even to encircle others. Unless you humbly and devoutly accept our fatherly correction and admonition, we will pour the wine on after the oil,[32] and apply ecclesi-

26. Num. 22:28–30.   27. John 8:46.
28. John 18:23.   29. Matt. 18:15.
30. Cf. Matt. 5:22. Innocent infers that it is all the more damnable to call one's father, and especially one's priest or spiritual father, a fool.
31. James 3:1; i.e., let there not be more than a few teachers among you.
32. An allusion, perhaps, to Luke 10:34, allegorized by Innocent so that wine becomes the harsher medicine, as it often symbolizes in the Bible the punishment of the sinner.

astical severity, so that those who would not obey willingly may learn to give in even against their will.

Given at the Lateran [July 12, 1199].

60. Innocent III Annulling *Magna Carta* (1215)

Innocent, bishop, servant of the servants of God, to all the faithful of Christ who will see this document, greeting and apostolic benediction.

Although our well-beloved son in Christ, John illustrious king of the English, grievously offended God and the Church—in consequence of which we excommunicated him and put his kingdom under ecclesiastical interdict—yet, by the merciful inspiration of Him who desireth not the death of a sinner but rather that he should turn from his wickedness and live, the king at length returned to his senses, and humbly made to God and the Church such complete amends that he not only paid compensation for losses and restored property wrongfully seized, but also conferred full liberty on the English church; and further, on the relaxation of the two sentences, he yielded his kingdom of England and of Ireland to St. Peter and the Roman Church, and received it from us again as fief under an annual payment of one thousand marks, having sworn an oath of fealty to us, as is clearly stated in his privilege furnished with a golden seal; and desiring still further to please Almighty God, he reverently assumed the badge of the life-giving Cross, intending to go to the relief of the Holy Land—a project for which he was splendidly preparing. But the enemy of the human race, who always hates good impulses, by his cunning wiles stirred up against him the barons of England so that, with a wicked inconsistency, the men who supported him when injuring the Church rebelled against him when he turned from his sin and made amends to the Church. A matter of dispute had arisen between them: several days had been fixed for the parties to discuss a settlement: meanwhile, formal envoys had been sent to us: with them we conferred diligently, and after full deliberation we sent letters by them to the archbishop and the English bishops, charging and commanding them to devote earnest attention and effective effort to restoring a genuine and full agreement between the two sides; by apostolic authority they were to denounce as void any leagues and conspiracies which might have been formed after the outbreak of trouble between the kingdom and

From *The Letters of Pope Innocent III (1198–1216) Concerning England and Wales*, edited and translated by Christopher R. Cheney and Mary G. Cheney (Oxford: Clarendon Press, 1967), pp. 212–16. All footnotes deleted. Reprinted by permission of Oxford University Press.

the priesthood: they were to prohibit, under sentence of excommunication, any attempt to form such leagues in future: and they were prudently to admonish the magnates and nobles of England, and strongly to enjoin on them, to strive to conciliate the king by manifest proofs of loyalty and submission; and then, if they should decide to make a demand of him, to implore it respectfully and not arrogantly, maintaining his royal honour and rendering the customary services which they and their predecessors paid to him and his predecessors (since the king ought not to lose these services without a judicial decision), that in this way they might the more easily gain their object. For we in our letters, and equally through the archbishop and bishops, have asked and advised the king, enjoining it on him as he hopes to have his sins remitted, to treat these magnates and nobles kindly and to hear their just petitions graciously, so that they too might recognise with gladness how by divine grace he had had a change of heart, and that thereby they and their heirs should serve him and his heirs readily and loyally; and we also asked him to grant them full safeconduct for the outward and homeward journey and the time between, so that if they could not arrive at agreement the dispute might be decided in his court by their peers according to the laws and customs of the kingdom. But before the envoys bearing this wise and just mandate had reached England, the barons threw over their oath of fealty; and though, even if the king had wrongfully oppressed them, they should not have proceeded against him by constituting themselves both judges and executors of the judgement in their own suit, yet, openly conspiring as vassals against their lord and as knights against their king, they leagued themselves with his acknowledged enemies as well as with others, and dared to make war on him, occupying and devastating his territory and even seizing the city of London, the capital of the kingdom, which had been treacherously surrendered to them. Meantime the aforesaid envoys returned to England and the king offered, in accordance with the terms of our mandate, to grant the barons full justice. This they altogether rejected and began to stretch forth their hands to deeds still worse. So the king, appealing to our tribunal, offered to grant them justice before us to whom the decision of this suit belonged by reason of our lordship: but this they utterly rejected. Then he offered that four discreet men chosen by him and four more chosen by themselves should, together with us, end the dispute, and he promised that, first in his reforms, he would repeal all abuses introduced into England in his reign: but this also they contemptuously refused. Finally, the king declared to them that, since the lordship of the kingdom belonged to the Roman Church, he neither could nor should, without our special mandate, make any change in it to our prejudice: and so he again appealed to our tribunal, placing under apostolic protection both himself and his kingdom with all his honour and rights. But making no progress by any method, he asked the archbishop and the bishops to execute our mandate, to defend the rights of the Roman Church, and to protect himself in accordance with the form of the privilege granted to Crusades. When the archbishop and bishops would not take any action, seeing himself bereft of almost all counsel and help, he did not dare to refuse what the barons had dared to demand. And so by such violence and fear as might affect the most courageous of men he was forced to accept an agreement which is not only shameful and demeaning but also illegal and unjust, thereby lessening unduly and impairing his royal rights and dignity.

But because the Lord has said to us by the prophet Jeremiah, "I have set thee over the nations and over the kingdoms, to root out, and to destroy, to build and to plant," and also by Isaiah, "Loose the bands of wickedness, undo the heavy burdens," we refuse to ignore such shameless presumption, for thereby the apostolic See would be dishonored, the king's rights injured, the English nation shamed, and the whole plan for a Crusade seriously endangered; and as this danger would be imminent if concessions, thus extorted from a great prince who has taken the cross, were not cancelled by our authority, even though he himself should prefer them to be upheld, on behalf of Almighty God, Father, Son, and Holy Spirit, and by the authority of SS Peter and Paul His apostles, and by our own authority, acting on the general advice of our brethren, we utterly reject and condemn this settlement, and under threat of excommunication we order that the king should not dare to observe it and that the barons and their associates should not require it to be observed: the charter, with all undertakings and guarantees whether confirming it or resulting from it, we declare to be null, and void of all validity for ever. Wherefore, let no man deem it lawful to infringe this document of our annulment and prohibition, or presume to oppose it. If anyone should presume to do so, let him know that he will incur the anger of Almighty God and of SS Peter and Paul His apostles.

Anagni, the 24th of August, in the eighteenth year of our Pontificate.

61. Eyewitness Account of the Fourth Lateran Council (1215)

1. Unequal to the task of writing to Your Sincerity about all of the things which seem so remarkably worthy of being admired in Rome, I merely inform you that "eye has not seen, nor ear heard, neither are believed to have

From S. Kuttner and A. Garcia y Garcia, "A New Eyewitness Account of the Fourth Lateran Council," in *Traditio* 20 (1964): 123–29. Translated for this volume by Constantin Fasolt.

entered the heart of man"[1] so many kinds of languages, so many trains of venerable persons as have at present gathered "from every nation under heaven"[2] at the Apostolic See. "Parthians and Medes and Elamites are dwelling with them in Jerusalem,"[3] and so on. Hoping, however, that one day the "proper hour to talk with you about these things will finally arrive for my narrations,"[4] I have for now presented Your Kindness with what you desired to hear most, namely the council's solemnity, and what was done in it and instituted, in the order in which I saw them: "For what has fallen on ears excites the mind less quickly than what faithful eyes have seen."[5]

2. On St. Martin's day, then, the council was begun.[6] At the break of dawn, the lord pope first of all celebrated mass in the church of the Savior which is known as the Church of Constantine.[7] Only cardinals, archbishops, and bishops were admitted. When mass had been said, and when the bishops and abbots, who, unlike the bishops, wore no mitres, had been placed on the proper seats, many thousand, even ten times a hundred thousand clerics and people were let into the interior of the same church. When so many had entered that in spite of the church's tremendous size hardly any room was left, the lord pope, a man more discerning than men and truly filled with the spirit of wisdom and understanding, standing with his cardinals and ministers in an elevated position, began to sing the hymn "Come Creator." When the hymn had solemnly been sung to the end in a manner worthy of God, and not without tears flowing for spiritual joy, the lord pope added the following collect: "Our actions, we beg you, Lord" and so on. . . .[8] Because no one was able to calm the tumult of the people, I could unfortunately only understand very little of his sermon. But I did not cease to search for it as best I could, until I obtained a copy and committed it to writing. Among other things in this sermon he most of all urged the recovery of the Holy Land. Then the patriarch of Jerusalem gave a sermon to the same effect. The lord pope also asserted in his sermon that, if the princes would take thought for the Holy Land, he would personally assume the task; if not, he promised to pay in addition for the preparation of ships for pilgrims leaving from Rome. These and similar matters were dealt with in the Lateran church on the first day of the council.

3. On the following day, in the larger palace, a thorough and protracted debate revolved around the establishment of a patriarch at Constantinople, something which has never before been permitted to the Roman church.[9]

1. 1 Cor. 2:9; Isa. 64:4.   2. Acts 2:5.
3. Acts 2:9.   4. Ovid, *Metamorphoses* 5.499–500.
5. Horace, *Ars Poetica* 180–81.   6. Wednesday, 11 November 1215.
7. I.e., the Lateran.

8. Some text is missing, presumably dealing with Innocent's opening sermon.

9. Thomas Morosini, whose death in 1211 had left the patriarchal see of Constantinople vacant until this time, had already been appointed by the pope as Latin patriarch.

4. On the third day, the lord pope tried to sort out the quarrel between the bishops of Compostella and Toledo about who should have the primacy, which has continued thus far, and thence to arrive at a reasonable settlement.

5. For several days afterwards the count of Toulouse [10] was dealt with. Because heretics had at one time stayed on his land, he had been accused of heresy. As a result he lost his castles and a great part of his land through the efforts of the king of France, [11] and was indeed thoroughly ruined by yet other crusaders who had been sent against him. But because at one time the count was present at the council with his wife (who is the sister of the wife of Lord Frederick our king), took up the cross, and is going to remain overseas forever, the lord pope allotted forty marks [12] for his support to him from all the income God had conferred upon him. To the countess he awarded whatever land beyond the Jordan the count had held from the king of France. It is said that he intended to use a sentence of excommunication to force the King of France to leave her in peace. The count of Montfort, [13] however, will hold the rest of the land from the hands of the lord pope and St. Peter. . . . [14] Here I must pass over many other matters whose truth I could not ascertain because I only heard rumors about them, which usually add falsehoods to the truth, thrive on their changeability, and gain in strength as they make the rounds.

6. Who would not have wished to participate in the extraordinary glory of the first Sunday after St. Martin's? [15] The highest pontiff was conducted with the greatest honors to the consecration of the church of St. Mary which is called the Church of the Flowing Oil. [16] The greatest Roman noblemen, swathed in silk and purple, preceded him to the accompaniment of drum and chorus, strings and organ, and the resounding harmonies of trumpets, and an infinite multitude of clerics and people followed. Roman boys, raising olive branches, met the lord pope with shouts and, as is their custom, kept saying *Kyrieleyson* and *Christeleyson* without interruption. Right away, at the other end of the bridge across which one approaches the church, uncounted lanterns, suspended on ropes throughout the streets and

10. Raymond VI, count of Toulouse from 1194 to 1222. As the text suggests, it was during his rule that the war on the Cathar heretics in his territories was begun. In the end it led not only to the suppression of the Cathars but also to the downfall of Raymond's powerful house and a considerable increase in the power of the French monarchy.

11. Philip Augustus was actually too busy battling the English during those years to be able to participate in the crusade which Innocent III had proclaimed after his legate in Toulouse, Peter of Castelnau, had been murdered in 1208.

12. Four hundred marks is the correct figure.

13. Simon of Montfort, count of Leicester, died 1218. He was the principal figure in the war against Toulouse, and won the main victory over Raymond VI in 1213 near Muret.

14. The text, which should here be giving an account of Pope Innocent's decision concerning the son of Count Raymond, is mutilated.

15. 15 November 1215.   16. S. Maria in Trastevere.

alleys, strove to make the brightness of that day succumb to the brilliance of their own light. The number of banners and pieces of purple cloth, which were unfolded on the houses and the high towers of the Romans, cannot be estimated at all. But since my account should rather turn from these matters to the solemnity of said church's dedication itself, and I am not capable of expounding it in order, I shall only add very briefly that almost that entire day was taken up with the consecration of the church. For it was only towards evening that, with no less solemnity, the Romans led the lord pope back to his palace.

7. On the eighth day after St. Martin's,[17] I saw a crowd of people like sand on the shores of the sea gathering from all parts of the world at the church of St. Peter and Paul[18] to celebrate the anniversary of its dedication. Because the people moving through the streets and alleys created such a huge crush, the lord pope barely gained access to the church of St. Peter.

8. On the following Friday[19] the council met again in solemn session. The bishop of Palermo first read a letter from King Frederick and then spoke on his behalf.[20] Afterwards some prudent men of Milan, ambassadors of the former emperor Otto, urgently requested that a letter from Otto should be admitted.[21] In response, many of the archbishops, bishops, abbots, and clerics, or more prelates than can be counted, protested, especially the marquis of Montferrat, who maintained that for three reasons the legates should not be heard. First, because they had perjured themselves. Second, because they favored heretics. Third, because they had asked him to assist themselves and Lord Otto with an agreement not to abandon them for any reason, not even excommunication by the lord pope. He further maintained that Lord Otto himself must not be absolved for seven reasons: First, because a sworn pledge was no longer sufficient to absolve Lord Otto since he had already once committed perjury. Second, because he could not do satisfaction for the damages inflicted on the Roman church. Third, because he had attacked King Frederick and occupied the lands which he holds of the Roman church, and still keeps them occupied. Fourth, because

17. 18 November 1215.   18. St. Peter's Cathedral.
19. 20 November 1215.

20. Frederick II, king of Sicily, of the house of Hohenstaufen, had been elected emperor by the German princes in 1212. Innocent III had decided to support him in the contest for the Empire carried out by the houses of the Welfs and the Hohenstaufen, when his original choice, Otto IV, the Welf whom he had crowned emperor in 1209, continued the policy of increasing imperial power in Italy, a policy to which Innocent was understandably opposed. The purpose of the embassy of the archbishop of Palermo was now to win Innocent III's approval to Frederick II's succession to the Empire.

21. The ambassadors of the Welf party were attempting to obtain absolution for Otto IV from his longstanding excommunication. In that case, not only his deposition by the German princes in 1211, but also the election of Frederick II, could have been challenged.

he had captured the bishop of Münster. Fifth, because he had destroyed the monastery of Quedlinburg and erected a castle there. Sixth, because he had disdainfully said that King Frederick, even though the princes of the Empire had elected him Emperor, was only a king of priests. Seventh, because he had offered the regalia to the bishop of Bremen, who had been excommunicated and deposed.

9. Finally the lord pope quieted the marquis and the others who were protesting against Lord Otto, and said that the holy council had been organized so that both the guilty and the innocent, the rich as well as the poor could be heard there, adding that, if the devil could repent, even he should certainly be received. Then he began to take stock of the arguments of the marquis in Latin, which he speaks with extraordinary power and fluency. When he had finished, silence was ordered, and the letter of former emperor Lord Otto was read. It began with the following greeting: "To the venerable Lords Cardinals, Archbishops, Bishops, Prelates, and to the whole council, salvation in the Lord and a demonstration of his good will from Otto, by God's grace Emperor of the Romans and forever Augustus." In the remainder of the letter he devoutly asked them to plead with the lord pope for his absolution since he repented of his sins, and was willing to obey orders. His ambassadors would stand as his sureties.

10. When the letter had been read to the end and carefully listened to, the person who had recited it rebutted every one of the points proposed by the marquis. To the first point, namely that the ambassadors had perjured themselves, he replied that it was not true, and that they would prove it at once. He similarly replied that it was not true that they favored heretics, but that on the contrary, wherever heretics were known to be among them, they punished them and expelled them from their company or had a procession of the entire city and the bishop with the cross to the houses of those who let heretics stay in them, banished them,[22] and destroyed their houses. And those who put up heretics as guests had to pay ten pounds. To the third point he replied by saying that they wanted to admit the marquis to their community on whichever conditions he preferred, but reserving all reverence due to the apostolic see. The points raised against Lord Otto he rebutted as follows: first, with regard to the charge that Otto had perjured himself: "Holy Father, either you consider it a fact that he perjured himself, or you do not." When the pope replied that he did, he answered: "In that case, Holy Father, he repents of having perjured himself. He asks for forgiveness and offers to do satisfaction. Therefore he should be received." To the second point, that he could not do satisfaction for the damages, he replied that the people of Milan, Piacenza, and other allied cities were pre-

22. *Exterminarent.*

pared to guarantee by oath, faith, and hostages that they would do satisfaction for all damages which the emperor had inflicted on the Roman church. To that the pope replied that, even if all of these cities were extremely wealthy, they would still never be able to repair the damage inflicted on the Roman church by Otto. To the charge that Otto had destroyed the cloister of Quedlinburg, the emissary replied that he had not destroyed the cloister but built a castle on the mountain above the cloister because he was afraid his enemies would occupy it, and that neither the church nor the nuns had suffered any ill as a result. Even though he could not excuse Otto from all blame on the other points, he nevertheless asked that he be forgiven and granted the grace of absolution for these as well as the preceding matters. This is how and what was done during the second solemn session of the council.

11. The third solemn session of the council took place on St. Andrew's day.[23] When mass had been celebrated very early in the morning, and all the bishops were placed on their seats, the lord pope ascended to the elevated place with his cardinals and ministers, and had the faith of the Holy Trinity and each article of the faith recited. When they had been read, everybody was loudly asked: "Do you believe this in every respect?" Everybody answered: "We believe it." Then all heretics were condemned, and the opinions of some in particular, namely of Joachim of Fiore and Amaury of Paris, were reproved.[24] When the corresponding decrees had been read, everybody was asked again: "Do you reprove the opinions of Joachim and Amaury?" And even more fiercely they shouted: "We reprove them."

12. Afterwards, the question of the holy cross and the crusaders' expedition was dealt with. A state of peace was most firmly enacted and put into effect. On this occasion all the barons of England and everyone assisting them with advice or aid against their king, who had taken up the cross, were uncompromisingly struck with excommunication.[25] The lord pope also explained how much power the king has, in his person as well as in his

23. Monday, 30 November 1215.

24. Joachim of Fiore, born ca. 1130, died 1202, developed a philosophy of history according to which an age of the spirit and an unwritten Gospel were to follow on what he saw as the Old-Testamentarian age of the Father and the New-Testamentarian age of the Son. Even though his ideas on the Trinity were condemned at the Lateran Council, his hopes for an age of perfection soon to begin proved extremely influential in the later Middle Ages, especially among spiritual Franciscans.

Very little is known about Amaury of Paris, better known as Amaury of Bène, except that he seems to have taught a form of pantheism and developed a doctrine of the progressive manifestation of the Trinity which superficially resembled the views of Joachim of Fiore.

25. The context is King John's submission to Innocent III, after years of resistance, and Innocent's resulting decision to support John against the barons who were responsible for Magna Charta.

belongings, to render support for the Holy Land; how he had acted like a very special son of the Roman church in making his land pay an annual tribute of one thousand marks sterling for the benefit of the church; how he had accepted the land from the hand of the pope according to feudal law, and how large a claim to honor he had thereby conferred upon the apostolic see. But because it is said that the kingdom of England is subject to the imperial power, and in order to protect the princes of the empire from losing their rights in this matter forever, Siegfried, archbishop of the holy see of Mainz, rose before the others and tried to assert and to prove that legally the said kingdom belonged to the emperor of the Romans and the princes of Germany. The lord pope, having thought about it, imposed silence upon him by raising his hand in order to make him stop with the speech he had begun, and said this against him: "Listen to me now, and I shall listen to you later." And thus the archbishop behaved like a prompt son of obedience, as was only proper and necessary, and did not in the least continue against the will of the father and lord. He did, however, stand up three times in order to give an answer to the pope on this account.

Because the lord pope's praise and defense of the king of England led, it seems to me, to the belief that he was reinstituting the former emperor Otto, the lord pope added the following words: "No one may doubt that we accept the validity of what the princes of Germany and the Empire have done with regard to King Frederick of Sicily, and that we even want to favor and promote him in every respect and will complete our task."

13. Then the constitutions of the lord pope were read.[26] When they had been read to the end, and it was already past the ninth hour of the day, he showed to all a large part of the wood of the holy cross which had been brought from Constantinople. When everybody had venerated it on their knees, the pope began the "We praise you God." When all had finished singing solemnly, the pope added this collect: "Omnipotent, eternal God, make us devoutly bear your will always" and so on, blessed everyone with the wood of the holy cross, and absolved and concluded the council. These things were done before an infinite multitude of Catholic men on the final day of the feast, when the council had solemnly met in the Lateran church on only the three aforesaid days.

14. On the day after the council had been brought to an end,[27] many bishops and other prelates left with papal permission. A great number of bishops, however, especially from Germany, stayed at the curia during all

26. This brief mention should not obscure the fact that the body of canons published at the fourth Lateran council is among the most important pieces of medieval ecclesiastical legislation. Among other things, it required every Christian to confess to, and receive communion from, his parish priest at least once a year.

27. 1 December 1215.

of Advent, and some even up to Lent, in order to take care of special business. What was done and treated in the curia during the time intervening between the beginning of the council and mid-Lent, I have not allowed my pen to write down, in order to avoid perhaps boring the reader with tedious details. "And he who saw them testifieth of these things and wrote them down, and we know that his testimony is true." [28]

62. Walther von der Vogelweide Criticizes the Papacy

From the "Song of Discontent" (1213–1214)

We all complain, yet do not know what troubles us: the pope himself, our father, has led us into this confusion. For after all he does now walk ahead of us quite like a father; we follow him and never step outside his tracks. But pay attention, world, to what displeases me in this: if he is greedy, all are greedy along with him; if he lies, all lie his lies along with him; if he is treacherous, they do his treacheries along with him. Now let us see who could twist that around on me. And thus the younger Judas brings as much disrepute upon himself as did that older one.

You bishops and you noble clergymen are being led astray. Look how the pope is using the devil's ropes to fetter you. If you should say to us he has Saint Peter's keys, then please explain to us why he eradicates Saint Peter's teaching from the book. At our baptism we were commanded that we should never either buy or sell the gifts of God; now he is being taught to do the opposite from the black book the Moor of Hell has given him, and with your help he fills his chests.[1] You cardinals, you can cover your chancel with a roof, but our holy altar of God stands under a leaky roof.

The see of Rome has only now been really put in order, as once before it was put into order by Gerbert, that sorcerer.[2] But that one only brought his own life to ruin; now this one wants to ruin both himself and all of Christendom. All tongues must cry to God for help and call on him to ask how long he wants to stay asleep. They work against his works; they falsify his word; his chamberlain is stealing from him his celestial treasure; his propitiator murders here and plunders there; his shepherd has become for him a wolf among his sheep.

I say! How like a Christian the pope is laughing now when he says to his Romans:[3] "This is what I have done" (what he is saying there he should

28. John 21.45, 19.35.

From *Die Politischen Lieder Walthers von der Vogelweide*, ed. Friedrich Maurer (Tübingen: Max Niemeyer Verlag, 1954), pp. 91–93. Translated for this volume by Constantin Fasolt.

1. The translation of the last phrase is disputed.

2. Gerbert of Aurillac, Pope Sylvester II (999–1003).

3. The German "Walhen", here translated as "Romans", originally referred to "Gae-

have never even thought), "I brought two Alemans under one crown.[4] Let them disturb and burn and devastate the realm. Meanwhile we keep filling our chests. I have led them to my money box, all of their goods are mine. German silver is traveling into my Roman shrine. You clergymen, eat chicken and drink wine and let the German laymen fast and grow lean."

Tell us, Lord Money Box, has the pope sent you here that you can make him rich and make us Germans poor and put us into debt? Whenever a full measure reaches him in the Lateran he plays a dirty trick, as he has done before; tells us again how much the realm continues to be troubled, until all parishes have made the measure full again. I fancy little of that silver ever goes to help the land of God, for hands of clergymen rarely divide great treasure. Lord Money Box, you have been sent here to do harm: to seek among the German people foolish men and women.

If any heart is not turned inside out during these times in which the pope himself increases unbelief, in such a heart there dwells a blessed spirit and true love of God. Now you can see what is the work of clergymen and what their teaching is. Once both their teaching and their works were pure. Now all of them are equal once again, but in a different way, for now we see that they are doing wrong and saying wrong who should instruct us by their good example. That is good reason for us speechless laymen[5] to lose hope.

---

lics"—a meaning preserved in the contemporary "Welsh"—but was then applied to Frenchmen and Italians and carries a strong overtone of hostility to foreigners.

4. The reference is to the two Hohenstaufen kings, Philip of Swabia (1198–1208) and Frederick (1212–1250), whom Pope Innocent III supported during the turmoil following upon the disputed double election of a "Guelf" and a "Ghibelline" king of Germany in 1198, and whose troubles enabled him to exercise an increasing measure of control over the affairs of the empire.

5. The original "tumbe leien" connotes silence, lack of education, and "dumbness." The line is a perfect expression of the sense of despondency and impotent wrath felt by laymen who perceived the clergy as corrupt but could not speak their language.

5
The Babylonian Captivity and the Great Schism

Storm Over the Papacy

The documents concerning the investiture controversy (above, documents 20–30) identified several areas of tension within European society including one between popes and kings, another between kings and their subjects (notably bishops), and a third between popes and "territorial" or "national" churches. Antecedents of these points of friction can be traced back to the Christianization of Europe, and indeed they are foreshadowed in the earliest texts in this collection. During the fourteenth and fifteenth centuries, they were brought to a great climax by a series of four events, or movements, that shook the institutional fabric of Europe: the conflict between Pope Boniface VIII (1294–1303) and King Philip IV of France (1285–1314); the Babylonian Captivity of the Papacy (1305–77); the Great Schism (1378–1415); and the Conciliar Movement (1415–39).

The conflict between Pope Boniface VIII and King Philip IV of France began in 1296, when the pope (by the bull *Clericis Laicos*, document 63) forbade clergy to pay taxes to secular princes without explicit approval by the pope. Philip IV responded with force to this challenge to his authority. A reconciliation was patched together in 1297. However, in 1301, the combative Boniface renewed hostilities, challenging the king's authority to punish recalcitrant bishops and withdrawing his earlier concessions to Philip. Sticking to the principles of canon law (in which he was a master) and buoyed up by the successes of his jubilee year (1300), Boniface was in no mood to compromise. In 1302, he issued the bull *Unam sanctam* (document 63), asserting the pope's absolute headship over all Christians, and he prepared the ultimate attack: an excommunication of Philip. Philip struck first. He had his councillors prepare against Boniface charges of unnatural sexual practices, witchcraft, murder, and other offences, and sent a special detachment to seize the pope (document 64). Philip's henchmen captured Boniface at Anagni, beat and mocked him, and left him near death (1303).

The Babylonian Captivity of the papacy, a phrase coined by Petrarch, followed from Philip IV's attempt, not merely to remove Boniface VIII from the scene, but also to capture the papacy itself. After the brief pontificate of Benedict XI (1303–4), Philip secured the election of the archbishop of Bordeaux as Pope Clement V (1305–14). Heeding his master's voice, Clement moved the seat of papal government from Rome to Avignon, where it remained for seventy-two years. During that time, the French composition of the papal court and the dominant influence of the French kings in papal diplomacy made the impartiality of Avignonese popes suspect in many parts of Europe.

Among the conflicts that damaged the credit of the popes during the Babylonian Captivity, that between Pope John XXII (1316–34) and the Emperor Louis IV of Germany (1314–47) was one of the most divisive. A divided election in 1314 pitted Louis against Frederick of Austria. Seeking to extend his own sphere of influence, Pope John XXII declared (in 1317) that the imperial throne was vacant, since Louis and Frederick had not appealed their dispute to him for judgment. A heated controversy between the pope and Louis ensued; it moved to a new level in 1323. In that year, the pope, ruling on a dispute within the Franciscan order, declared that the rule of absolute poverty taught by Francis of Assisi and upheld by one faction in the order, was heretical. The adherents of absolute poverty immediately rejected John XXII as heretical himself and took refuge with Louis IV. Sustained by them, Louis issued the Sachsenhausen decree (1324, document 65), appealing to a Church council against a heretical pope and declaring that his own imperial title and rights were independent of the pope. He found many adherents, including the Parisian master, Marsiglio of Padua (ca. 1290–ca. 1343). Marsiglio wrote his treatise, *The Defender of Peace* (1324, document 66), to demolish all basis for the coercive jurisdiction over secular government that popes had long claimed and that John XXII was determined to impose. Expelled from the University of Paris and excommunicated by the pope (1326–27), he joined Louis IV and was present at his secular coronation in Rome (1328), over which city Louis appointed him ecclesiastical vicar.

63. Boniface VIII, *Clericis Laicos* (1296) and *Unam Sanctam* (1302)

Clericis Laicos

Boniface Bishop, servant of the servants of God, for the perpetual record of the matter. That laymen have been very hostile to the clergy antiquity relates; and it is clearly proved by the experiences of the present time. For not content with what is their own the laity strive for what is forbidden and loose the reins for things unlawful. Nor do they prudently realize that power over clerks or ecclesiastical persons or goods is forbidden them: they impose heavy burdens on the prelates of the churches and ecclesiastical persons regular and secular, and tax them, and impose collections: they exact and demand from the same the half, tithe, or twentieth, or any other portion or proportion of their revenues or goods; and in many ways they try to bring them into slavery, and subject them to their authority. And, we regret to say, some prelates of the churches and ecclesiastical persons, fearing where there should be no fear, seeking a temporary peace, fearing more to offend the temporal majesty than the eternal, acquiesce in such abuses, not so much rashly as improvidently, without obtaining authority or license from the Apostolic See. We therefore, desirous of preventing such wicked actions, decree, with apostolic authority and on the advice of our brethren, that any prelates and ecclesiastical persons, religious or secular, of whatsoever orders, condition or standing, who shall pay or promise or agree to pay to lay persons collections or taxes for the tithe, twentieth, or hundredth of their own rents, or goods, or those of the churches, or any other portion, proportion, or quantity of the same rents, or goods, at their own estimate or at the actual value, under the name of aid, loan, relief, subsidy, or gift, or by any other title, manner, or pretext demanded, without the authority of the same see:

And also whatsoever emperors, kings, or princes, dukes, earls, or barons, powers, captains, or officials, or rectors, by whatsoever names they are called, of cities, castles, or any places whatsoever, wheresoever situate, and all others of whatsoever rank, eminence or state, who shall impose, exact, or receive the things aforesaid, or arrest, seize, or presume to take possession of things anywhere deposited in holy buildings, or to command them to be arrested, seized, or taken, or receive them when taken, seized, or arrested, and also all who knowingly give aid, counsel, or support,

From *Documents of the Christian Church*, translated by H. Bettenson (New York: Oxford University Press, 1943), pp. 159–61. Reprinted by permission of Oxford University Press.

openly or secretly, in the things aforesaid, by this same should incur sentence of excommunication. Universities, too, which may have been to blame in these matters, we subject to ecclesiastical interdict.

The prelates and ecclesiastical persons above mentioned we strictly command, in virtue of their obedience, and on pain of deposition, that they in no wise acquiesce in such things without express leave of the said see, and that they pay nothing under pretext of any obligation, promise, and acknowledgment whatsoever, made in the past, or in existence before this time, and before such constitution, prohibition, or order come to their notice, and that the seculars aforesaid do not in any wise receive it; and if the clergy do pay, or the laymen receive, let them fall under sentence of excommunication by the very deed.

Moreover, let no one be absolved from the aforesaid sentences of excommunications and interdict, save at the moment of death, without authority and special leave of the Apostolic See, since it is part of our intention that such a terrible abuse of secular powers should not be carried on under any pretense whatever, any privileges whatsoever notwithstanding, in whatsoever tenors, forms or modes, or arrangement of words, conceded to emperors, kings and the others aforesaid; and we will that aid be given by no one, and by no persons in any respect in contravention of these provisions.

Let it then be lawful to none at all to infringe this page of our constitution, prohibition, or order, or to gainsay it by any rash attempt; and if anyone presume to attempt this, let him know that he will incur the indignation of Almighty God, and of his blessed apostles Peter and Paul.

Given at Rome in St. Peter's on the 25th of February in the second year of our Pontificate.

Unam Sanctam

We are obliged by the faith to believe and hold—and we do firmly believe and sincerely confess—that there is one Holy Catholic and Apostolic Church, and that outside this Church there is neither salvation nor remission of sins. . . . In which Church there is one Lord, one faith, one baptism.[1] At the time of the flood there was one ark of Noah, symbolizing the one Church; this was completed in one cubit[2] and had one, namely Noah, as helmsman and captain; outside which all things on earth, we read, were destroyed. . . . Of this one and only Church there is one body and one head—not two heads, like a monster—namely Christ, and Christ's vicar is

---

1. Eph. 4:5.   2. Gen. 6:16.

Peter, and Peter's successor, for the Lord said to Peter himself, "Feed My sheep."[3] "My sheep" He said in general, not these or those sheep; wherefore He is understood to have committed them all to him. Therefore, if the Greeks or others say that they were not committed to Peter and his successors, they necessarily confess that they are not of Christ's sheep, for the Lord says in John, "There is one fold and one shepherd."[4]

And we learn from the words of the Gospel that in this Church and in her power are two swords, the spiritual and the temporal. For when the apostles said, "Behold, here" (that is, in the church, since it was the apostles who spoke) "are two swords"—the Lord did not reply, "It is too much," but "It is enough." Truly he who denies that the temporal sword is in the power of Peter, misunderstands the words of the Lord, "Put up thy sword into the sheath."[5] Both are in the power of the Church, the spiritual sword and the material. But the latter is to be used for the Church, the former by her; the former by the priest, the latter by kings and captains but at the will and by the permission of the priest. The one sword, then, should be under the other, and temporal authority subject to spiritual. For when the apostle says "there is no power but of God, and the powers that be are ordained of God"[6] they would not be so ordained were not one sword made subject to the other. . . .

Thus, concerning the Church and her power, is the prophecy of Jeremiah fulfilled, "See, I have this day set thee over the nations and over the kingdoms," etc.[7] If, therefore, the earthly power err, it shall be judged by the spiritual power; and if a lesser power err, it shall be judged by a greater. But if the supreme power err, it can only be judged by God, not by man; for the testimony of the apostle is "The spiritual man judgeth all things, yet he himself is judged of no man."[8] For this authority, although given to a man and exercised by a man, is not human, but rather divine, given at God's mouth to Peter and established on a rock for him and his successors in Him whom he confessed, the Lord saying to Peter himself, "Whatsoever thou shalt bind," etc.[9] Whoever therefore resists this power thus ordained of God, resists the ordinance of God. . . . Furthermore we declare, state, define and pronounce that it is altogether necessary to salvation for every human creature to be subject to the Roman pontiff.

---

3. John 21:17.
4. John 10:16. "Fold" translates the Vulgate "ovile"; the Greek is ποίμνη, "flock."
5. Luke 22:38.   6. John 18:11.
7. Jer. 1:10.   8. 1 Cor. 2:15.
9. Matt. 16:19.

64. The General Assembly of Paris, June (1303)

In the name of the Lord, Amen. In the year of the Lord 1303, in the first indiction, on the thirteenth of June, in the eighth year of Lord Pope Boniface's pontificate. May all know by the tenor of the present public instrument that, in the presence of the Most Serene Prince, Lord Philip, by God's grace illustrious king of the French; the reverend fathers in Christ archbishops and bishops; the religious men abbots and priors; as well as the noblemen counts, barons; and many other people ecclesiastical and secular, as written below, and in the presence of ourselves, the undersigned notaries public, specially called and requested for this purpose, as is contained in the subscriptions written below:

The magnificent and noble men, Lords Louis of Evreux, son of the king of the French, Gui of Saint-Pol, and John of Dreux, counts, and William of Plaisians, Lord of Vézénobres, knight, spoke.[1] They were moved, they said, by the fervor of faith, induced by a feeling of sincere devotion and the zeal of charity, out of the deepest compassion for their mother, the sacrosanct Roman and universal Church. That Church, they said, is being dangerously drawn down by the presidency of said Lord Boniface and is suffering monstrous disfigurement and privation. They were grieved, they said, by the danger for the Christian faith, on which the salvation of souls depends and which, alas, is miserably wasting away and perishing at this time. They directed fervent prayers, they said, for the health of the government of the Church and all of Christendom, for the good state, the repair, and the exaltation of the catholic faith. Above all they stated that it would highly benefit the Church, the foundation of the faith, and the salvation of souls if none but a true and legitimate pastor presides truly and legitimately over the Lord's flock of sheep, if all error, scandal, iniquity, and injustice were repelled from the Church, the spouse of Christ, who has no spots or wrinkles, and if through the favor of divine mercy salvation, peace, and

From Georges Picot, *Documents relatifs aux états généraux et assemblées réunis sous Philippe le Bel* (Paris, 1901), pp. 34–53. Translated for this volume by Constantin Fasolt.

1. The individuals here mentioned as playing the leading part before the general assembly belonged to Philip IV's closest circle of advisers. Louis of Evreux, brother of Philip IV and son of King Philip III, and Gui of Saint-Pol, butler of France, were great nobles who regularly participated in the king's most important acts. William of Plaisians, like William Nogaret, mentioned below, is one of the men who owed their paramount influence in Philip IV's government not to their noble status, which was nominal, but their expertise in Roman law and public administration. As can be seen in this document, he played the part of the protagonist in the proceedings against Boniface, even though the final decision in policy-making most likely remained with Philip IV.

tranquillity were obtained for the whole world, which, they said, the perverse acts, abominable deeds, and pernicious examples of said Lord Boniface cause to be ridden by wars and darkness. The aforementioned lords therefore said and asserted in the presence of said lord king, the archbishops, bishops, and other prelates, as well as ecclesiastical persons, who had assembled to act for themselves and their churches, and of the barons, counts, and other noblemen, whose names are written below, that said Lord Boniface was caught in, and publicly and notoriously defamed on account of, the crime of heresy and various other horrible and abominable crimes. The said William submitted the case and raised the charges, and all of them, physically touching the holy Gospels of God, swore they believed each and every aforesaid thing to be true and to be able to prove it. The same William of Plaisians then added an oath to the effect that he thought he was able to prove aforesaid things, and that he would prosecute his affair against said Lord Boniface in a general council or other place, where, when, and before whom the law should require it, to its proper end. They urgently requested the said lord king, in his capacity as fighter for the faith and defender of the Church, to lend his support, and to do so effectively, to the convocation and congregation of said general council, insofar as it concerned him, for the sake of declaring the truth, in praise of the divine name, for the increase and exaltation of the catholic faith, and the honor and good state of the universal Church and the entire Christian people, since in such and all similar matters his royal house had out of the fervor of faith and zeal for justice always shown itself to be a guide of truth. He urgently requested the same of the archbishops, bishops, and the other above-mentioned prelates, and effectively pressed his case with them, and the counts and knights also requested the same prelates urgently and several times, to lend their support, and to do so effectively, in their role as columns of the Church and the faith, in legitimate ways and means, according to the establishments of the holy fathers and the canonical sanctions, to the convocation and congregation of the said council, so that it would be held. The same prelates, however, having heard and fully understood the said charges, submissions, and requests, believing that this affair was not merely arduous, but arduous in the highest degree, and that it required the mature counsel of deliberation, retired from that place.

On the following Friday, the fourteenth of June, in the presence of the said lord king and of the undersigned lords archbishops, bishops, abbots, priors, and witnesses, and in the presence of ourselves, the undersigned notaries public, specially called and requested for this purpose, the said William of Plaisians, knight, said, submitted, charged, asserted, and read what is more fully contained in a certain document which he held in his hands, as follows:

"I, William of Plaisians, knight, say, submit, and assert that Boniface, who presently presides over the apostolic see, is a perfect heretic in and because of heresies, monstrous acts, and perverse dogmas to be declared below, which I believe to be true and to be able to prove, or which are in themselves sufficient to prove him to be a perfect heretic, at the proper time and place, and before whom this can and should be done by law. I swear this on these holy Gospels of God, which I am now touching.

"First, that he does not believe in the immortality or incorruptibility of rational souls, but thinks that a rational soul is destroyed with the body.

"Likewise, that he believes there is no eternal life, nor that human beings can obtain ultimate relief, but that the whole and the parts of consolation and happiness are to be found in this world. In consequence he asserts that to enjoy one's body and any of its delights whatever is no sin. Drawing on the superabundance of such yeast he has not blushed to say and preach in public that he would rather be a dog, a donkey, or whatever brute animal, than a Frenchman. He would not have said that, had he believed that Frenchmen have a soul which can merit eternal beatitude. He has taught this to many people, who acknowledged it at the moment of death.

"Likewise, that these are matters of public report against him.

"Likewise, that he does not faithfully believe that the body of Christ is in the host over which a faithful and properly ordained priest, representing the Church, has said the words instituted by Christ. He therefore pays no, or only very little, reverence to the host, when it is elevated by the priest, does not stand up for it, even turns his back on it, and lets himself be honored more highly, and the place where he is seated be decorated more beautifully, than the altar on which the host is consecrated.

"Likewise, that he is publicly defamed on this account.

"Likewise, he is reported to say that fornication is no sin any more than the rubbing of hands. This is a matter of public talk and report.

"Likewise he has said more than once that he would bring down himself, the whole world, and the whole Church in order to humble the king and the French, if it could not be done in any other way. And when some bystanders said to him that God would prevent it, he even answered: 'May God not prevent it.' When good men who had heard this replied that he should not say so, because the Church of God and all Christians would be greatly scandalized, he answered: 'I do not care whatever scandals may come, so long at least as the French and their pride are destroyed, for of necessity scandals must come.'

"Likewise, he recalled and even approved a certain book composed by Master Arnold of Villa-Nova, doctor, which contains, or smacks of, heresy, was reproved, condemned, and burned by the bishop of Paris and the masters of the Faculty of Theology in Paris, and had similarly been publicly reproved, condemned, and burned by Boniface in a full consistory of cardinals, but was later rewritten with the same error.[2]

"Likewise, he had silver likenesses of himself set up in churches in order to perpetuate his most damnable memory, and thus induced people to idolatry.

"Likewise, he has a private demon, on whose advice he relies in every respect. Once he said, therefore, that, even if all people in the world were on one side, and he on the other, they could not deceive him, neither in law nor in fact, which would be impossible if he did not employ the art of demons. And on this account he is publicly defamed.

"Likewise, he is a soothsayer and consults male and female fortune-tellers. On this account he is publicly defamed.

"Likewise, he has preached in public that the Roman pope cannot commit simony, which is heresy. This crime has been reproved in the Old Testament as well as the New, and in the holy general councils. Thus, with the services of a certain usurer called Simon, he publicly trades in the greater prelacies, parsonages, dignities, and ecclesiastical benefices, to which a sacred order is specially and necessarily attached, and in absolutions and dispensations, in the same way in which profane things are usually traded in the markets where commodities are for sale. This is a matter of public report against him.

"Likewise, contrary to the special disposition made by Christ for his own sons when he said: 'I leave you peace,' he impedes peace among Christians with all his might and strives to sow discords and wars. When it was once said in front of him that certain parties honestly wished to come to a certain amicable agreement with each other, he prevented peace by forbidding the other party to agree to peace. And when the first party humbly begged him to allow the other party to come to an agreement, he said he would not do so, and that, if the son of God, or the Apostle Peter should descend on earth and order him to do so, he would say: 'I don't believe you.'

"Likewise, in the custom of perfect heretics, who say that they alone have the true faith and are the Church, but assert that those who are the real cultivators of the orthodox faith are Patarenes, because they disagree with their errors, it is said that he believes and publicly states that each and every member of the French nation is a Patarene, because the French nation, a nation notoriously most Christian, does not follow his errors in the faith.[3]

"Likewise, he labors under the crime of sodomy and has male concu-

---

2. Arnold of Villanova (c. 1240–1311), doctor of medicine from Barcelona, had written a book paraphrasing the prophecies of Daniel and predicting the end of the world. It had been condemned in Paris in 1299 and by Boniface VIII a year later, but, when he was given the chance, Arnold defended himself sufficiently well that Boniface reconsidered.

3. *Patarenes*, the term which was in the eleventh century applied to radical supporters of

bines with him. And on this account he is publicly defamed among the most common people.

"Likewise, he had several murders, even of clerics, committed in his presence, at his orders, and rejoiced in their death. And, if in the beginning they were not beaten to death by his ministers, he ordered them so often to strike them, saying: 'Hit, hit, *dali, dali,*' that many died as a result. . . .

"Likewise, striving to destroy the faith, he has of old conceived a hatred against the kingdom of France, in abomination of the faith, because that is where there is, and has been, the splendor of faith, and a great mainstay and example for Christendom. And even before he held the apostolic see he is found to have said that, if he were pope, he would rather overturn all of Christendom than not destroy the nation, which he calls 'the pride,' of the French.

"Likewise he is defamed for answering the ambassadors of the king of England, when they petitioned for a tithe of the kingdom of England in the name of their king, that he would not give them the tithe except on the condition that they would use it to make war against the king of France. And beyond this he is said to have given large quantities of money to certain people to make them impede peace between the said two kings, and he himself impeded it as best he could with ambassadors, letters, and in whichever other ways he could, even giving presents. He is also said to have instructed Frederick, who holds the island of Sicily, that, if he wanted to betray King Charles and break, rather than maintain, the peace which he had made and sworn to keep with Charles, he would move with him against the said king and kill all the French; that in order to accomplish this he would also give him money, aid, counsel, and help; and that for doing this he would give and grant him the said kingdoms.[4] He also confirmed the king of Germany as emperor-to-be, and publicly preached that he had done this in order to destroy the nation, which he calls 'the pride,' of the French, because they said that they were not subject to anyone temporally. He said that they were lying through their teeth in this matter and declared that anyone, even an angel descending from heaven, who denied that all the kings of the world were subject to him and the king of Germany, should be anathema. Earlier, however, he had often publicly said (although by submitting it I do not mean to endorse the truth of what he said) that said king was a

---

the reform papacy, had by the thirteenth and fourteenth centuries come to be regularly applied to Cathars, or even any kind of heretic.

4. Frederick II, king of Sicily from 1296 to 1337, of the house of Aragon, fought constantly over possession of Sicily and southern Italy with Charles II, king of Naples from 1285 to 1309 and son of Charles of Anjou, who had taken southern Italy and Sicily from the Hohenstaufen. As a result of the bloody uprising of 1282, known as the Sicilian Vespers, Frederick's father, Peter III of Aragon, had taken Sicily from the Anjou. French memories of that event were clearly still strong.

traitor of his lord, that he had treacherously murdered him, that he was not worthy of being called or nominated king, and that he was not duly elected. He also dissolved the agreement of this king of Germany with the king of France for the good of peace whereby the right of each was saved and whatever was found to have been occupied on either side was on either side returned to its proper state. And he is said to have enjoined the procurators of the king of Germany by oath not to observe the peace, thus battling the good of peace and striving to sow tares among Christians.[5]

"Likewise, he is publicly defamed because the Holy Land has been lost and has come to the enemies of God and the faith through his fault, and because he works hard to hold out against it, and denies a subsidy to the Christians who defended it, and removed the subsidy established and allotted by the highest pontiffs, in order to use up the treasures and the money of the Church, which, since they are the patrimony of Jesus Christ, should rather be turned to the purposes of the Holy Land, by spending them on the persecution of faithful Christians and friends of the Church, and on the enrichment of his relatives. . . .

"Likewise, he is publicly defamed because he treated his predecessor Celestine, a man of holy memory, who led a holy life, inhumanly, put him in prison, and had him quickly and secretly killed there, perhaps because he was aware that Celestine could not resign, so that Boniface had no legitimate access to the apostolic see, and about this there is public talk and report in the whole world. He also threw many learned men, who were living according to a monastic rule, and who had debated the question 'whether Celestine could resign,' into prison, and let them die there.[6]

"Likewise, because he called religious persons who were living according to a monastic rule back to the world, without reasonable cause and to the scandal of many.

"Likewise, he is defamed because he said that he would shortly make all Frenchmen martyrs or apostates.

"Likewise, he is publicly defamed because he does not seek the salvation of souls, but their perdition."

5. Albert I (1298–1308), son of Rudolf of Habsburg, was elected and crowned king of Germany in 1298. His predecessor, Adolf of Nassau (1292–98) had been deposed by the electors and was soon thereafter killed in battle by his successor. Boniface had long refused to recognize Albert, especially since Albert had formed an alliance with Philip IV. Under the extreme pressures of 1303, however, Boniface changed course and recognized Albert in return for Albert's willingness to give up his understanding with Philip IV.

6. The pontificate of Pope Celestine V (1294), a saintly hermit who was elected at more than eighty years of age, was marked by much political confusion. He resigned under pressure after a few months in office and was succeeded by Boniface VIII. The French, who had drawn considerable advantage from their influence over Celestine, as well as the spiritual Franciscans, used the unusual circumstance that Celestine had resigned as a tool to attack the legitimacy of Boniface's pontificate.

When these points had been submitted and read to the end, the same William protested, said, swore, called for review, appealed, and subjected himself, reading from a written document, as follows:

"I, the said William of Plaisians, protest that I submit and say the said things, neither out of any special hatred of Boniface, since I have no hatred for him, but only for his said misdeeds, nor in order to injure or slander him or anyone else, but only out of my zeal for the faith and my devotion to the holy Church of God and the holy Roman see, saying that, because of what I have seen and what I have heard about his deeds from trustworthy men, and because of likely conjectures and probable presumptions following from the said and many other points, to be declared in their proper place and time, I swear, touching the holy Gospels of God with my hand, that I believe him to be a perfect heretic, and that I also believe that of the said and other things such can be proved against him as will suffice to judge him a heretic according to the statutes of the holy fathers.

"I also swear that I will prosecute the said matters against him as best I can, in a general council to be congregated in a place safe and secure for me, for the honor of God and the exaltation of the Christian faith, always reserving the right, honor, and state of the holy apostolic see in every respect. Therefore I urgently and reverently request you, lord king, whom the defense of holy mother Church and the Catholic faith concerns, and for which you will render account in your final examination, as well as you, lords prelate, who are columns of the faith, and who should be the judges of said things together with other reverend fathers, Catholic prelates of the holy Church, to be congregated in general council, to procure, and make an effective effort towards, the congregation of a general council in a proper and secure place at an opportune time, before which said matters can be submitted, processed, and proved, as has been said, against the same Boniface. I also urgently request you, lord king, to request and effectively induce the same prelates whom it concerns, present or absent, anywhere on earth, to strive manfully, and faithfully to request others, so that the said council will congregate for the said purposes in the said manner. And because I have probable cause to suspect Boniface while this matter is pending, in order to ensure that, shaken up and excited by the said things, he will not proceed in any way while this matter is pending, or attempt to proceed, against me, my adherents, procurators, adjutants, friends, and servants, my goods and theirs, by these writings, before you, lord king, lords prelate, and before you notaries public here present, I call for review[7] and appeal to the said sacred general council-to-be-convoked, to the Catho-

7. In Roman law, the terminology of which informs much of the present document, the technical term *provocatio*, here translated as "call for review," originally stood for the appeal of a citizen from the criminal judgment brought against him by a magistrate to the popular assemblies. The difference between *appellatio* ("appeal") and *provocatio* is slight, but the

lic pope-to-be, and to the holy apostolic see, and to him and to those to whom I can and must best do so by law, urgently petitioning you once, twice, and thrice to have letters of dismissal[8] and of witness made out to me from you, subjecting myself, my adherents, favorers, reputation, friends, and procurators, and all of those who want to adhere to me in the future, as well as my and their goods, to the protection and custody of the holy apostles Peter and Paul, the said sacred council-to-be-congregated, the holy Roman see, and the Catholic pope-to-be. Nevertheless I adhere to the warrant, and wish to adhere to the appeal and appeals, process and processes, made on this account by the nobleman Lord William of Nogaret, knight, to the extent that they are found to have been lawfully made with all due formalities, without withdrawing the present appeal."

When this had been read and performed, the said lord king answered, requested the said prelates, called for review, appealed, and made requests, calls for review, and appeals, as is more fully contained in the document attached below, which was there read to him, the prelates, and others, as written below, present and listening, as follows:

"We, Philip, by God's grace king of the French, have heard and understood the submissions and charges made by you, William of Plaisians, knight, and those previously made by our beloved and faithful Knight William of Nogaret, against Boniface, now presiding over the government of the Roman Church. We would gladly cover the shame of any father with our own mantle. Nevertheless, because of our fervor for the catholic faith, and the outstanding devotion we have for the sacrosanct Roman and universal Church, our mother and that of all the faithful, the spouse of Christ, following in the footsteps of our progenitors (who for the exaltation and the defense of ecclesiastical liberty and faith had no doubts at all about shedding their own blood), desiring to look after the interests of the faith and the state of the Church, in order to avoid the costs of a general scandal, we are unable under the pressure of conscience any longer to pass over said matters with closed eyes and pretended ignorance. Since Boniface's reputation has more and more often been vehemently and prominently burdened by frequently repeated complaints on these accounts, driven home by trustworthy men of great authority, since, when our faith is being destroyed, our own negligence, that of anybody else, and especially that of the kings and princes of the earth, who we know have received the power conferred upon

---

connotation of "appeal to a popular assembly" is probably more strongly present in the latter than the former.

8. *Apostoli*, here translated as "letters of dismissal," is also a technical term of Roman law, which refers to the written report by a judicial official about an appeal to a higher court. The appealing party had to present such a "letter of dismissal" to the court to which it was appealing, in this case the general council as well as the other institutions mentioned, for the appeal to be considered properly documented.

us by the Lord in order to exalt and augment the faith, must be reproved, we assent to your requests in this respect, out of reverence for the divine name, reserving in all respects due honor and reverence to the sacrosanct Roman Church. We are prepared, and gladly offer ourselves, to the extent to which it falls within our purview, to lend our support, and to do so effectively, to the convocation and congregation of the said council, so that in the said matters the truth may shine forth and all error recede, so that the state of the universal Church and of all Christendom, the faith, and the interests of the Holy Land may be taken thought for, and so that impending scandals and dangers may be countered. And we urgently request you archbishops, bishops, and other prelates here present, as sons of the Church and pillars of faith, called by the Lord to exercise your part of the solicitude for the exaltation, augmentation, and conservation of the faith, and we beseech you by the bowels of Jesus Christ's mercy to devote every effort, as is fitting, to the convocation and congregation of the council, at which we are planning to be present in person, and to work in fitting ways and means effectively towards it.

"There is need to ensure, however, that the said Boniface, who has already several times angrily and unlawfully threatened to proceed against us, will not, in trying to prevent his works of darkness, if there are any, from coming to light, directly or indirectly impede the convocation and congregation of the council, or, if he should fail in this endeavor, that he will not proceed against us, our state, churches, prelates, barons, and other faithful, vassals, and subjects, our lands or theirs, our kingdom and the kingdom's state, in any respect, abusing the spiritual sword, by excommunication, interdict, suspension, or in any other way, with the effect that our position in the same council would no longer be quite sound. We therefore call for review and appeal in writing, for ourselves and our adherents, and those wishing to adhere to us, to said general council, which we urgently petition be convoked, and to the true and legitimate supreme pontiff-to-be, and to others to whom one should be required to appeal, without withdrawing the appeal registered by said William of Nogaret, to which we adhered then and still adhere, urgently requesting testimonial letters of dismissal from you prelates and notaries, and expressly protesting our right to alter these calls for review and appeals where, when, and before whom we may consider it expedient."

The said things thus having been done and concluded, the undersigned archbishops, bishops, abbots, and priors answered, called for review, appealed, subjected themselves, and protested, and made answers, calls for review, appeals, subjections, and protestations as is more fully contained in a certain document which was there publicly and earnestly read, as follows:

"We, archbishops of Nicosia, Reims, Sens, Narbonne, and Tours; bishops of Laon, Beauvais, Châlons, Auxerre, Meaux, Nevers, Chartres,

Orléans, Amiens, Térouanne, Senlis, Angers, Avranches, Coutances, Évreux, Lisieux, Séez, Clermont, Limoges, Le Puy, and Mâcon; abbots of Cluny, Prémontré, Marmoutiers of Tours, St. Denis in France, Compiègne, St. Victor, Ste. Geneviève of Paris, St. Martin of Laon, Figeac, and Beaulieu in the Limousin; Brother Hugh, visitor of the houses of the order of the Militia of the Temple, and the priors of St. John of Jerusalem in France and St. Martin of the Fields of Paris, have heard what was said, submitted, and charged by you, the said lords counts and William, yesterday and today, against Pope Boniface VIII. Induced by what you so said, submitted, asserted, and swore, by your requests and other legitimate causes, forced by a certain necessity, as it were, observing that the interests of faith, that is, of Christ, are concerned in these matters, we, who have been called, though through no merits of our own, to exercise a part of the solicitude for the defense and exaltation of the faith and for the government of souls, desire to oppose the dangers which are imminent, considering the convocation and congregation of said council useful and altogether necessary for the said and other reasons, so that Lord Boniface's innocence may shine forth—as, witness our conscience, we desire—or that a council will discuss, establish, and act upon the charges raised against him according to what canonical sanctions demand.

"We answer you, lord king, and you, lords counts and William, that, reserving in every respect the honor and reverence due the sacrosanct Roman Church, we assent to your requests in this respect, concerning the convocation of the council. We are prepared to lend our support, and to do so effectively, to the convocation and congregation of the said council according to the establishments of the holy fathers and canonical and legitimate sanctions, not intending in any way to take sides in this affair, or to adhere to anyone taking sides.

"There is need to ensure, however, that Lord Boniface, moved or angered by these events, which we have reason to fear he will be, because of likely conjectures and the many threats he made to proceed against us, will not in any way proceed or start proceedings against us, our churches, parish priests, and subjects, by his own or whatever other authority, by excommunication, suspension, interdict, deposition, deprivation, or whichever other way, and under whichever pretext, to the impediment or disturbance of the said council, so that we would not be able to sit in this council and judge together, and do everything else which pertains to the office of a prelate. We also must ensure that our own state as well as that of our adherents and of those wishing to adhere to us will remain secure in every respect. We therefore call for review and appeal in writing for ourselves, our churches, parish priests, and our subjects, and for our adherents or those wishing to adhere to us on this account, to the said council-to-be-congregated, to the true and legitimate supreme pontiff-to-be, and to whomever the law should require appeal, and we urgently petition for letters of dismissal, subjecting ourselves, our churches, parish priests, subjects, and adherents, our and their states and rights, and our and their goods, to the divine protection of the said council and of the true and legitimate supreme pontiff-to-be. And we protest our right to alter this appeal where, when, and before whom we may consider it expedient."

Done in Paris at the Louvre, in the chamber of the said lord king, in the said year, indiction, month, and pontificate, on Thursday and Friday, in the presence of the noblemen lords of Angers, Boulogne, Dammartin, and the other above-named Counts; Matthew of Trye, Peter, lord of Chambley, Peter, lord of Wirmes, Hugh of Boville, knights; Masters Stephen, archdeacon of Bruges, Nicholas, archdeacon in the church of Reims, William, treasurer of Angers, Peter of Belle Perche, Reginald called Barbou, and John of Montigny; and several others, clerics as well as laymen, specially called and asked to be witnesses of these events.

And I, Evenus Phyli of St. Nicas, cleric, notary public by apostolic authority, was present at all the said events which occurred on the said Friday only, have here subscribed, and, having been so asked, have attached my usual sign.

And I, Geoffrey of Plessis, cleric, notary public by apostolic authority, was present at each and everyone of the said events occurring on the said days, as written above, and, having been so asked, have subscribed and have attached my customary sign.

And I, Giles of Remine, cleric, notary public by apostolic authority, was present at each and everyone of the said events occurring on the said days, and, having been so called and asked, have subscribed and attached my customary sign.

65. Ludwig the Bavarian's Appeal to a General Council (1324)

Sachsenhausen, 22 May 1324

We, Ludwig, by God's grace king of the Romans forever Augustus, submit against John XXII, who calls himself pope, that he is an enemy of peace and intends to raise discords and scandals, not merely, as is notorious, in Italy, but also in Germany, by rousing the prelates and agitating the princes with frequent messengers and letters, persuading them that they must make

From *Monumenta Germaniae Historica, Legum Sectio IV. Constitutiones et Acta Publica Imperatorum et Regum, Tomus V* (Hannover-Leipzig: Hahn, 1909–13), pp. 722–44. Translated for this volume by Constantin Fasolt.

war on the Holy Empire and ourselves, and rebel with all their might. That he sows discords and plants tares among the faithful of Christ is manifest. For he reportedly says in public that, whenever there is discord among the kings and princes of the world, the pope is truly pope, is feared as the pope ought to be, and that everyone fears him and does whatever is desired. Thus he manifestly convicts himself of thirst for the shedding of Christian blood. Above all, however, he reportedly says that the discord among the princes, the noblemen, and the people of Germany amounts to salvation and peace for the Roman pontiffs and the Church. When, therefore, killings, murders, wounds, wars, and the shedding of, alas, innocent blood multiplied in Germany because of disputed elections, he never sent a single letter or any messenger to prevent the said dangers and evils, even though he had many tax exactors and collectors in the region for his own purposes, whom he could have so instructed without any burden for himself, had he so wished or cared about it in any way.[1] Thus he revealed that he acts against the doctrine, the life, and the examples of Christ, whose vicar he falsely pretends to be.

Likewise, he is at the same time a thoroughly malicious plaintiff and the judge, and thus completely subverts judgment. It is publicly and notoriously known that malice has blinded him so much that, with one of the keys in his hands going completely astray,[2] he condemned guiltless, pious, innocent, just, and faithful Catholics in all of Lombardy and in various parts of Italy as Patarenes and heretics, as has become thoroughly notorious everywhere. If his wicked and iniquitous sentence contained any truth, there would be far more heretics and favorers of heretics than other people, since he wrongly and iniquitously pronounces the Empire's faithful and loyal members Patarenes without discrimination, for no other reason than that they are faithful to the Empire, without realizing that Peter's privilege only continues where judgment is given with Peter's equity.[3] That one of his keys is going astray is obvious because he [John] makes members of Christ into members of the devil and judges them as such, and he condemns and

1. Uncertain what effect the dual election of 1314 would have on papal interests in Italy, John XXII waited until Ludwig IV had gained a decisive military victory over his opponent in 1322 before taking a decided stand against him. In the meantime, John's position was that the Empire was vacant, and that therefore he had the right to act as its representative.

2. According to contemporary doctrine, the power of the pope consisted in his control over two "keys": the key of power and the key of knowledge.

3. The term *Patarenes*, which had been used in the eleventh century to describe the Milanese supporters of radical church reform, and was mostly applied to Cathars in the thirteenth, came to be seen as almost synonymous with "heretic" in the fourteenth century. John XXII did in fact depose the imperial officials loyal to Ludwig IV and started proceedings for heresy against them if they did not obtain papal approbation, thus using the Inquisition to suppress the Ghibelline party in Italy.

punishes true Catholics as though they were true heretics. He takes on the haughtiness of the Pharisees in believing that he can absolve whom God binds, and bind whom God absolves, and thus he acts against God, Catholic faith, Sacred Scripture, truth, and justice.

Likewise, he changes and alters the statutes and canons of the holy fathers as he likes, even if they declare a truth of the faith, and he quite openly contradicts them, even though antiquity, for which the decrees of the fathers enjoined reverence, should survive without its roots being torn out, and even though such declarations are completely immutable.

Likewise, he forces men into desperation thereby and plunges them into error in many ways, even though apostolic authority condemns both the erring and those causing their error.

Likewise, he does not ponder that whatever liberty or honor the Church has today, Constantine most magnificently conferred on Pope St. Silvester, who was living hidden in a cave at that time.[4] This successor of Silvester, as he calls himself, however, gives a bad return to the emperor for the said benefits, and even tries to ruin the holy Empire by good or evil and to destroy in any way its faithful and devoted liegemen, as appears from the process recently started against the holy Empire, ourselves, and our justice. In this matter he notoriously abuses the plenitude of power, which is only given for the edification of the Church. And since he can and must judge only according to justice, he acts maliciously and unlawfully in perverting legal procedure and basing his processes on notorious matters which are not only notorious, but manifestly false, as appears clearly from his processes.

Likewise, it appears evident that no party at all was cited to appear in court in the said process, which should rather be called an excess. We were neither present nor contumaciously absent, nor were we cited in any way, as legal procedure requires.[5] Sacred Scripture testifies that it is not the custom of the Roman pontiffs to condemn anyone before the accused is in the presence of the accusers and takes the stand to defend himself in order to

4. This is a reference to the famous eighth-century forgery known as the *Donation of Constantine*, according to which Emperor Constantine, when moving the capital of the Roman Empire to Constantinople, left all power in the western part of the Empire to Pope Sylvester and his successors. Although it was usually employed to shore up claims for papal primacy, the *Donation* could also be interpreted in the opposite sense, as this passage makes clear.

5. When Ludwig's military victory of 1322 enabled him to lend active support to the Visconti, dukes of Milan, in 1323, against whom John XXII had started a crusade even though Duke Giangaleazzo had willingly resigned his title of imperial vicar, the Pope charged Ludwig IV with favoring heretics and contested the validity of his election. John threatened to excommunicate and depose Ludwig if he did not resign his office within three months. The charges were published in Avignon in October 1323, but not sent to Ludwig.

clear himself of the crimes, and divine law does not judge a man unless it has heard and learned from himself what he has done. He, however, completely subverts divine and human laws. In brief, even the tenor itself of the pronouncement which is said to have been made declares his sentence to be void for lack of a judge, as we shall make most manifest, and as will be made most manifest, in its place and time, before whom and where we must do so.

Likewise, his intention evidently appears corrupt in that he aims for the ruin of the Holy Empire, ourselves, the princes, and its devoted liegemen, even though it is an established fact that the Roman Empire has been prepared by God to provide for the Gospel, to spread it, and to remove the catholic faith from all harmful attacks. And thus he is a notorious subverter and destroyer of the holy Gospel.

Likewise, it is an established fact that by these and his other harmful processes, which can more truthfully be called excesses, he aims for the ruin of the Holy Empire, ourselves, the Empire's prince electors, the other princes, the Empire's loyal members, its liberty and dignity, and at the destruction of the Empire's unwavering customs, which are observed by us as law without a doubt, and which have been so observed of old.

Likewise, he is partial in conferring archbishoprics, bishoprics, and abbacies on thoroughly unworthy candidates, regardless of their age and their manner of life, so long as they are rebels and enemies of the Empire, however much they may be born to be the Empire's vassals. No one who supports the Empire has any chance of being promoted by him, unless perhaps he feigns a desire to favor his [John's] iniquitous will against the Empire, however worthy and qualified, however experienced and learned, however good and holy in their manner of life such a person may otherwise be. Thus he has acted, and continues to act, in contempt of God, to the damage of the churches, the danger of souls, notoriously to the prejudice of the Holy Empire, and to the notable prejudice of our own justice and right, and that of the Empire's subjects and devoted liegemen.

Likewise, it appears evident from the process which he is said to have recently started, if what should rather be considered an excess can be called a process at all, that he aims at the ruin and destruction of the Holy Empire, a striking prejudice of our justice and right, a perpetual burden and prejudice for the Empire's prince electors, and the destruction and annullment of the Empire's approved and reasonable customs, prescribed and observed from time immemorial in the Empire's acts and processes. This is evident from each and everyone of the chapters written below.

First, because someone elected by a majority of the electors, that is, by four of them, is considered to have been elected to the Empire in concord. But even though we were not only elected by a majority of the prince electors, but even by two parts of them, as is notorious, this reckless lover of falsity and enemy of truth and justice is reportedly telling the lie that our election occurred in discord. This conflicts with the approved customs of the Empire, is to the prejudice of the Empire's prince electors and the prejudice and burden of the Holy Empire, and is a manifest scandal for ourselves and all the faithful of Christ, especially in Germany.[6]

Likewise, even though an approved custom of the Empire, which is observed as law by us, manifestly establishes that someone elected at the place appointed for the election of the king of the Romans and emperor-to-be, namely in the town of Frankfurt, by all of the electors, or their majority, or even a minority so long as the election is brought about by at least two of the electors there present on the day fixed for the election by the person competent to do so, that someone elected in this manner is to be considered elected in true concord, that the Empire's subjects and vassals must obey him as king, and that the crown must be offered him in Aachen whenever he wishes. If some vassals and faithful members of the Empire do not obey him, they ipso facto are to be deprived of everything they hold of the Empire. That evildoer, however, malevolently aiming at the ruin of the Holy Empire and the Empire's prince electors, the destruction and subversion of our justice and right and the Empire's approved customs and liberties, falsely and mendaciously says that our election, which was not only brought about by a majority, but even by two parts of the electors, in Frankfurt, the place destined for this purpose of old, and on the day fixed for the election by one who had the right to do so, was performed in discord, that because we were so elected we cannot serve, have not served legitimately, were unable to demand, and are unable to receive, homage, oaths of fealty, and other imperial rights. It is an established fact, however, that this is false in every respect, altogether alien to the truth, and against the aforesaid approved customs of the Empire.

Likewise, since after this election we were crowned and anointed in the place destined of old for the coronation and anointing of elected kings of the Romans and emperors-to-be, namely in the town of Aachen, the elect, according to the said approved customs which are observed as law, is from

6. The arithmetic of this election needs explanation. The right to elect the king of Germany had traditionally been exercised by a group of seven princes. But at the time of Ludwig's election the right of only five of them was undisputed. Four princes competed for the right to the remaining two votes, and all of them did in fact vote. A total of nine votes was therefore cast on this occasion. Five went to Ludwig, and four to his opponent, Frederick of Austria, with the disputed votes split equally between them. By this reckoning Ludwig had a majority of only one vote, far from the two-thirds that he claimed. Since voting by simple majority had not yet been unequivocally recognized as binding, Ludwig's claim was only slightly better than Frederick's.

that moment on and by the said election true king of the Romans right away, must be obeyed as the true king by the Empire's subjects and vassals, homage and oaths of fealty must be offered him, and the rights of Empire must be awarded him. That malicious subverter of canons and violator of rights and the said customs, however, aiming only at the ruin of the Holy Empire and the Empire's liberties and dignities, and at the ruin and annullment of the Empire's prince electors, all of the Empire's subjects, and the whole of Germany, reportedly falsely asserts in the process, if what should rather be named an excess can at all be called a process, that even though we have thus been elected, anointed, and crowned king, the Empire is still vacant, and he asserts that, when the Empire is thus vacant, its government belongs to him. It is an established fact that this is quite false and altogether alien to any truth, as anyone who inspects what has been said above can see.

And he maintains that we had no right to bestow, and therefore only bestowed de facto, the markgravate of Brandenburg, which he calls the markgravate of Magdeburg. But it was vacant and had devolved to the Empire, so that we conferred it with great counsel on our firstborn son. He also maintains that we had no right to do many other things which we did and which are known to concern the government of this kingdom and Empire.[7] It is an established fact that this is totally unjust, reckless, iniquitous, asserted with great falsity, emanated from an abyss of supreme malice, against God, justice, the Empire's rights and ours, the aforesaid approved customs, the Holy Empire's liberty, dignity, and utility, the rights and liberties of the Empire's prince electors, of the other princes, the whole of Germany, and all of the Empire's subjects and vassals, to the prejudice and burden of our said son, Markgrave of Brandenburg, against his justice and rights, and that of others who are harmed by these processes in any way. . . .

Likewise, he persecutes the Empire's supporters and the Holy Empire itself in various parts and provinces of the world, and has favored and still favors the party battling them, as is notorious in the whole world, calling them dearest sons of the Church and trying with all his might to subdue the Empire's devoted and faithful liegemen and to let them be devoured by the jaws of their enemies, so much so that he boasts that shortly not one of all the Empire's supporters and adherents will remain whom he could not destroy and confound, so that no supporters, adherents, and faithful liegemen of the Empire will be left—far be it. By the oath which we have sworn at

7. The markgravate of Brandenburg, carrying one of the electoral voices in the Empire, was a major power in Germany. The house which had ruled it since the twelfth century failed to produce an heir in 1320. After his victory of 1322, Ludwig managed to win it for his son. Even though he had to make considerable concessions to the princes in return, the acquisition of Brandenburg amounted to a major expansion of Ludwig's slender power base.

our coronation we are held and obliged manfully to resist and oppose this impiety and cruelty, so that his blood-drenched hands and cruel heart, which thirsts for Christian blood, may not be able to complete and fulfill what they have thought, planned, and begun to do in the aforesaid respects. . . .

It was not enough for him to lay hands upon, and subvert the rights of, the temporal empire, and so wickedly to rage against our crown and the Empire's faithful members, but that he did rise up against Lord Jesus Christ himself, the king of kings, lord of lords, prince of the kings of the earth, against his most holy mother, who lived in observance of poverty according to the same vows and in the same state as her son, and against the holy college of apostles by denigrating their lives, deeds, and evangelical doctrine of deepest poverty, by which their exemplary perfection of the exterior life is secured as by an immovable foundation, in full and perfect contempt of the world. This foundation he not only tries to subvert with his evil life, which is alien to any contempt of the world, but in public and solemn sermons and various assertions he even affirms heretical dogma and venomous doctrine by asserting that Christ and the apostles had temporal goods in common in the same way as other colleges do.[8] This statement is notoriously heretical, profane, and against the sacred text of the Gospel. For the holy prophets preach in countless sayings that deepest poverty of Christ, which was principally restored by seraphic Francis. And every syllable of the sacred Gospel concerning Christ's birth, life, and death, and the sayings of the holy doctors, disciples of the apostles themselves, all proclaim to the present time that Christ and the apostles lived in said deepest poverty, which consists in having nothing in this world according to civil law. . . .

And it has been truthfully related to us by trustworthy men that this one, being one with Christ and the apostles, collided with those who disseminated evangelical poverty by the rule of the Friars Minor, and stated before many great and most trustworthy men of the aforesaid order that for a long time, maybe forty years or thereabouts, he had harbored a plan to destroy and abolish the rule of St. Francis, if God would give him the power, since it existed only in fantasy and could not be observed, and to give the Order of the Friars Minor another rule, by which they could possess goods in common, as other religious orders do. . . .

It is thus clear as day that he wanted to define it as, and intends it to be, heretical to say that Christ and the apostles owned nothing in common ac-

---

8. Ludwig had only recently become aware of the struggle pitting the Franciscans against John XXII. The work of Franciscan theologians, who were opposed to John, rather than devoted to Ludwig, supplied him with a new source of arguments against the pope.

cording to civil and worldly law. As has been shown above,[9] he openly says like an impudent heretic that the Gospel of Christ, the holy apostles, the ancient teachers of Sacred Scripture, and the definitions by the aforesaid highest pontiffs contain falseness and are full of lies, like a blasphemer and sacrilegious person. In the general chapter celebrated in Perugia, the corporation of the Friars Minor frankly recognized that this is heretical and mad, and it expressly issued a sentence asserting that it neither was nor is heretical, but sound, catholic, true to the faith, and defined as catholic by the holy fathers supreme pontiffs to say that Christ and the apostles had nothing in common. It declared the contrary reproved and as such bound by a sentence of excommunication and anathema. . . .

And in the aforesaid letter[10] the general chapter stood firm on this foundation. For what the supreme pontiffs and vicars of God have once defined with the key of knowledge as a truth of the faith cannot be called into doubt by any successor, nor can the contrary be affirmed of what has been defined, or else he who does so must be considered a manifest heretic. The reason and foundation of this truth is that the catholic faith is only about truth eternal and immutable. What has thus once been defined as true of the faith itself or of morals is eternally true and cannot be changed by anyone. It is different with what is established by the key of power. For what it was expedient to do at one time is often expedient to prohibit at another. But it is an established fact that the aforesaid pontiffs and general councils most openly defined the contrary with the key of knowledge, and issued a sentence of condemnation for the book and the sayings of the masters and those who assert that poverty and manner of life are not evangelical and apostolic, strictly prohibiting anyone by apostolic letters from presuming pertinaciously to maintain any of the aforesaid opinions or in any way to defend them. . . .

And thus it appears most manifestly that according to either constitution he is convicted of being a manifest heretic.[11]

We, Ludwig, by God's grace King of the Romans forever Augustus, protest[12] that we neither submit nor say these things out of hatred for him who

9. The reference is to John XXII's constitution *Cum inter nonnullos* of November 1323, which condemned the doctrine of Christ's and the apostles' utter poverty as heretical. It was directed against the declarations made by the Franciscan general chapter of June 1322, which met in Perugia and is mentioned below.

10. This refers to the documents spread by the general chapter of Perugia in order to win support for the Franciscan cause against the pope.

11. The two constitutions are *Cum inter nonnullos*, mentioned in n. 9 above, and John's decision of 1322 to prohibit the Franciscans from circumventing their own doctrine of poverty by holding property in the name of the Holy See. Ludwig refers to the latter in his remarks about Pope John's plans to give the Franciscans another rule.

12. The remainder of this document is copied almost verbatim from the charges raised by

calls himself Pope John XXII. We have no hatred for him, but only for his injustice and his evil deeds. We do not act out of a desire to injure or to slander him, but only out of the zeal of faith and the devotion which we have for the holy Church of God, whose defender, patron, and advocate we are. We perceive it as being dangerously drawn down under the said lord's presidency and to be suffering monstrous disfigurement and privation. We act out of the deepest compassion for it, and for the sake of the holy catholic faith, which, alas, is altogether languishing under him. We thus hope to relieve the Holy Empire, its princes, vassals, and loyal members, which and whom we are obliged by oath to defend and to protect, at whose ruin he aims, and in order to care for our justice and that of our men, which he has unjustly begun to oppress and plans to oppress with all his might. But we say it because of what we have heard and perceived about himself and his deeds, and because of what is quite obvious from likely and probable inferences and the evidence of his own deeds, and from many other points to be declared in their place and time. We have sworn on the holy Gospels of God, touching the book, that we believe each and every one of these things to be true, and that of these things such can be proved against him as are sufficient according to the statutes of the holy fathers to judge him a heretic. We also swear that we will prosecute matters against him with all our powers in a general council, to be congregated in a place safe and secure, to the honor of God, the exaltation of the Christian faith, and, God permitting, the conservation and augmentation of the holy Church of God, the Holy Empire, its princes, loyal members, and vassals. With God's favor, we are planning to be present at this council in person, subjecting the Holy Empire, the princes, ourselves, our subjects, vassals, loyal followers, our adherents and those wishing to adhere to us now or in future, the goods of the Holy Empire, theirs and ours, the dignities and states of the Holy Empire, ours and theirs, to the protection of God, his apostles St. Peter and St. Paul, said sacred council-to-be-congregated, the holy Church, the apostolic see, and the apostolic, catholic, and legitimate supreme pontiff-to-be.

We would gladly cover the shame of the father with our own mantle. Nevertheless, out of favor for the catholic faith and the devotion we are obliged to have for the holy Roman Church, our mother, desiring to look after the interests of the faith and the state of the Church, in order to avoid the cost of a general scandal, we are unable under the pressure of conscience to pass over said matters and his other wickednesses with closed eyes and pretended ignorance. Since his reputation has been vehemently and notably burdened by frequently repeated complaints on these accounts,

---

William of Plaisians against Boniface VIII on 13 June 1303, and from the appeal to the general council registered by Philip IV on the following day.

more and more often driven home by trustworthy men, we petition that said general council be congregated for said purposes, and urgently repeat our petition. There is need to ensure, however, that John, who has already angrily and unlawfully begun to proceed against us and the Holy Empire, is proceeding, it is said, without observing any legal procedure at all, and threatens to proceed even more relentlessly, will not, in trying to prevent his works of darkness from coming to light, directly or indirectly impede the convocation and congregation of the general council, or, if he should fail in this endeavor, that he will not proceed in fact against the Holy Empire, ourselves, our state, the rights of the Empire, our own, their lands and ours, the churches, prelates, ecclesiastical and worldly princes, barons, our other faithful, vassals, and subjects, our lands and theirs, the Holy Empire itself, and its state, abusing the spiritual sword in any respect, by excommunication, interdict, suspension, deprivation, transfers, or by ordaining anything else, with the effect that in the council the position of the Holy Empire, our own, that of our princes, and of its subjects would no longer be quite sound. We therefore call for review and appeal in writing for ourselves, our adherents, and those now or in the future wishing to adhere to us, of whatsoever state or condition they may be, ecclesiastical or worldly, to said general council, which we urgently and with repeated urgency petition be convoked at a place safe for us and ours, to the true and legitimate supreme pontiff-to-be, the holy Church our mother, the apostolic see, and others to whom one should be required to appeal. We renew the appeals we made elsewhere, and urgently request once, and urgently request again, testimonial letters of dismissal from you, our ecclesiastical and worldly princes and notaries public, here present. We expressly protest our right to alter aforesaid calls for review, appeals, and protestations where, when, how, and before whom we may consider it expedient, are obliged to by law, and must for the protection and security of the Holy Empire, ourselves, and each and everyone of the aforesaid persons.

This appeal was executed and published in the year of the Lord 1324.

66. Marsiglio of Padua, *The Defender of Peace* (1324)

Discourse Two

On the Canonic Scriptures, the Commands, Counsels, and Examples of Christ and of the Saints and Approved Doctors Who Expounded

From Marsilius of Padua, *The Defender of Peace*, translated by Alan Gewirth (New York: Columbia University Press, 1956), 2:113–26, 156–63. Some footnotes deleted. © 1956 by Columbia University Press. Reprinted by permission of the publisher.

the Evangelic Law, Whereby It Is Clearly Demonstrated That the Roman or Any Other Bishop or Priest, or Clergyman, Can by Virtue of the Words of Scripture Claim or Ascribe to Himself No Coercive Rulership or Contentious Jurisdiction, Let Alone the Supreme Jurisdiction Over Any Clergyman or Layman; and That, by Christ's Counsel and Example, They Ought to Refuse Such Rulership, Especially in Communities of the Faithful, if It Is Offered to Them or Bestowed on Them by Someone Having the Authority to Do So; and Again, That All Bishops, and Generally All Persons Now Called Clergymen, Must Be Subject to the Coercive Judgment or Rulership of Him Who Governs by the Authority of the Human Legislator, Especially Where This Legislator Is Christian.

We now wish from the opposite side to adduce the truths of the holy Scripture in both its literal and its mystical sense, in accordance with the interpretations of the saints and the expositions of other approved doctors of the Christian faith, which explicitly command or counsel that neither the Roman bishop called pope, nor any other bishop or priest, or deacon, has or ought to have any rulership or coercive judgment or jurisdiction over any priest or non-priest, ruler, community, group, or individual of whatever condition; understanding by "coercive judgment" that which we said in Chapter II of this discourse to be the third sense of "judge" or "judgment."

The more clearly to carry out this aim, we must not overlook that in this inquiry it is not asked what power and authority is or was had in this world by Christ, who was true God and true man, nor what or how much of this power he was able to bestow on St. Peter and the other apostles and their successors, the bishops or priests; for Christian believers have no doubts on these points. But we wish to and ought to inquire what power and authority, to be exercised in this world, Christ wanted to bestow and in fact [*de facto*] did bestow on them, and from what he excluded and prohibited them by counsel or command. For we are bound to believe that they had from Christ only such power and authority as we can prove to have been given to them through the words of Scripture, no other. For it is certain to all the Christian believers that Christ, who was true God and true man, was able to bestow, not only on the apostles but also on any other men, coercive authority or jurisdiction over all rulers or governments and over all the other individuals in this world; and even more perhaps, as for example the power to create things, to destroy or repair heaven and earth and the things therein, and even to be in complete command of angels; but these powers Christ neither bestowed nor determined to bestow on them. Hence Augustine, in the tenth sermon *On the Words of the Lord in Matthew*, wrote the following: " 'Learn of me' not how to make a world, not how to create all visible and invisible things, nor how to do miracles in the world and revive the dead; but: 'because I am meek and humble of heart.'" [1]

Therefore for the present purpose it suffices to show, and I shall first show, that Christ himself came into the world not to dominate men, nor to judge them by judgment in the third sense, nor to wield temporal rule, but rather to be subject as regards the status of the present life; and moreover, that he wanted to and did exclude himself, his apostles and disciples, and their successors, the bishops or priests, from all such coercive authority or worldly rule, both by his example and by his words of counsel or command. I shall also show that the leading apostles, as Christ's true imitators, did this same thing and taught their successors to do likewise; and moreover, that both Christ and the apostles wanted to be and were continuously subject in property and in person to the coercive jurisdiction of secular rulers, and that they taught and commanded all others, to whom they preached or wrote the law of truth, to do likewise, under pain of eternal damnation. Then I shall write a chapter on the power or authority of the keys which Christ gave to the apostles and their successors in office, bishops and priests, so that it may be clear what is the nature, quality, and extent of such power, both of the Roman bishop and of the others. For ignorance on this point has hitherto been and still is the source of many questions and damnable controversies among the Christian faithful, as was mentioned in the first chapter of this discourse.

And so in pursuit of these aims we wish to show that Christ, in his purposes or intentions, words, and deeds, wished to exclude and did exclude himself and the apostles from every office of rulership, contentious jurisdiction, government, or coercive judgment in this world. This is first shown clearly beyond any doubt by the passage in the eighteenth chapter of the gospel of John. For when Christ was brought before Pontius Pilate, vicar of the Roman ruler in Judaea, and accused of having called himself king of the Jews, Pontius asked him whether he had said this, or whether he did call himself a king, and Christ's reply included these words, among others: "My kingdom is not of this world," that is, I have not come to reign by temporal rule or dominion, in the way in which worldly kings reign. And proof of this was given by Christ himself through an evident sign when he said: "If my kingdom were of this world, my servants would certainly fight, that I should not be delivered to the Jews," as if to argue as follows: If I had come into this world to reign by worldly or coercive rule, I would have ministers for this rule, namely, men to fight and to coerce transgressors, as the other kings have; but I do not have such ministers, as you can clearly see. Hence the interlinear gloss: "It is clear that no one defends

---

1. St. Augustine, *Sermo LXIX* on Matthew 11:28–29 (*PL* 38: 441).

him." And this is what Christ reiterates: "But now my kingdom is not from hence,"[2] that is, the kingdom about which I have come to teach.

Expounding these evangelic truths, the saints and doctors write as follows, and first St. Augustine:

> If he had answered Pilate's question directly, he would have seemed to be answering not the Jews but only the Gentiles who thought this of him. But after answering Pilate, he answered the Jews and the Gentiles more opportunely and fitly, as if to say: Hear ye, Jews and Gentiles, I do not impede your rule in this world. What more do you want? Through faith approach ye the kingdom which is not of this world. For what is his kingdom but those who believe in him?[3]

This, then, is the kingdom concerning which he came to teach and order, a kingdom which consists in the acts whereby the eternal kingdom is attained, that is, the acts of faith and the other theological virtues; not, however, by coercing anyone thereto, as will be made clear below. For when there are two coercive dominions in respect of the same multitude, and neither is subordinated to the other, they impede one another, as was shown in Chapter XVII of Discourse I. But Christ had not come to impede such dominion, as Augustine said. Hence on the passage in the same chapter of John: "Thy own nation and the chief priests have delivered thee up to me. What hast thou done?"[4] Augustine wrote: "He sufficiently shows that the act is looked upon as a crime, as if to say: If you deny you are a king, what then have you done to be delivered up to me; as if it would not be strange if he who called himself king were delivered up to the judge to be punished."[5] So, then, Augustine thought that it would be nothing strange if Christ had been punished, had he called himself secular king, especially before those who did not know he was God; and that he denied he would be a king of such a kingdom or with such authority, namely, to coerce transgressors of the law. Hence on the words in the same chapter of John: "Sayest thou this thing of thyself, or did others tell it thee of me?"[6] Theophylact wrote: "Christ spoke to Pilate as if to say: If you say this on your own, show the signs of my rebellion, but if you have heard it from others, then make the ordinary inquiry."[7] But if the opinion of our adversaries were correct, Christ should never have said what Theophylact states, namely, that Pilate should make the ordinary inquiry about him; indeed,

---

2. John 18:36, and *Glossa interlinearis, ad loc.*
3. See Thomas Aquinas, *Catena aurea* (XII, 442).
4. John 18:35.
5. See Thomas Aquinas, *Catena aurea* (XII, 442).
6. John 18:34.
7. See Thomas Aquinas, *Catena aurea* (XII, 442).

were they correct, he should rather have said that it did not pertain to Pilate to make this inquiry, inasmuch as he, Christ, of right [*de jure*] was not and did not wish to be subject to him in jurisdiction or coercive judgment.

6. Again, on the words, "my kingdom is not from hence," Chrysostom says: "He does not deprive the world of his providence and leadership, but he shows that his kingdom is not human or corruptible." [8] But every kingdom which is coercive over anyone in this world is human and corruptible. Moreover, on the words in the same chapter of John: "Thou sayest that I am a king," [9] Augustine wrote: "He spoke in this manner not because he feared to admit that he was king, but so that he might neither deny he was a king nor affirm that he was such a king whose kingdom is thought to be of this world. For he said, 'Thou sayest,' as if to say: You, a carnal man, speak carnally," [10] that is, about carnal rule over contentious and carnal temporal acts, taking "temporal" in its third sense; for the Apostle called such acts "carnal" in the first epistle to the Corinthians, Chapter 3. [11]

From the above it appears, therefore, that Christ came into the world to dispose not about carnal or temporal rule or coercive judgment, but about the spiritual or heavenly kingdom; for almost always it was only about this latter that he spoke and preached, as is plain from the gospel in both its literal and its mystical sense. And hence we most often read that he said: "Like is the kingdom of heaven," etc., but very rarely did he speak of the earthly kingdom, and if he did, he taught that it should be spurned. For he promised that in the heavenly kingdom he would give rewards and punishments according to the merits or demerits of the agents, but never did he promise to do such things in this world, but rather he does the contrary of what the rulers of this world do. For he most often afflicts or permits the affliction of the just and the doers of good, and thus he leads them to the reward of his kingdom. [12] For "all that have pleased God passed through many tribulations," as it is written in the eighth chapter of Judith. [13] But the rulers of this world, the judges of the worldly kingdom, do and ought to do the contrary, maintaining justice; for when they distribute rewards in this world to those who observe the laws, and punishments to perpetrators of evil, they act rightly; whereas if they did the contrary they would sin against human and divine law.

Let us return to the principal question through what Christ showed by deed or example. For in the sixth chapter of John we read that "when Jesus

8. See ibid.   9. John 18:37.

10. See Thomas Aquinas, *Catena aurea* (XII, 442).

11. 1 Cor. 3:1–3.

12. Cf. Augustine, *De civitate Dei* I. viii; ix; xx. ii; and Augustinus Triumphus, *Summa de ecclesiastica potestate* (Augsburg, 1473) qu.6. a. 1.

13. Jth. 8:23.

therefore knew that they would come to take him by force and make him king, he fled again into the mountain, himself alone." [14] Whereon the interlinear gloss: "From this he descended to care for the multitude, teaching men to avoid the good fortunes of this world and to pray for strength to withstand them." [15] It is certain, therefore, that Christ avoided rulership, or else he would have taught us nothing by his example. This view is supported by the expositions of St. Augustine, who wrote that "the Christian faithful are his kingdom, which is now cultivated, now redeemed, by the blood of Christ. But his kingdom will be manifest when the clarity of his saints will be revealed after the judgment made by him. But the disciples and the crowds, believing in him, thought he had come to reign." [16] So, then, the saints never understood, by Christ's kingdom in this world, temporal dominion or judgment over contentious acts and its execution by coercive power against transgressors of the laws in this world; but by his kingdom and governance in this world they understood, rather, the teaching of the faith, and governance in accordance with it toward the heavenly kingdom. This "kingdom," says Augustine,[17] will indeed be "manifest after his judgment" in the other world. He repeatedly states that to think Christ then reigned as the crowds thought was to "ravish him," that is, to have a wrong assumption and opinion of him. Whereon Chrysostom also: "And the prophet," that is, Christ, "was now among them, and they wanted to enthrone him as king," that is, because he had fed them. "But Christ fled, teaching us to despise worldly honors." [18]

Moreover, the same is shown very evidently by Christ's words and example in the following passage of the twelfth chapter of Luke: "And one of the multitude said to him, Master, speak to my brother, that he divide the inheritance with me. But he," that is, Christ, "said to him, Man, who hath appointed me judge or divider over you?" [19] As if to say: I did not come to exercise this office, nor was I sent for this, that is, to settle civil disputes through judgment; but this, however, is undoubtedly the most proper function of secular rulers or judges. Now this passage from the gospel contains and demonstrates our proposition much more clearly than do the glosses of the saints, because the latter assume that the literal meaning, such as we have said, is manifest, and have devoted themselves more to the allegorical or mystical meaning. Nevertheless, we shall now quote from the glosses for a stronger confirmation of our proposition, and so that we may not be accused of expounding Scripture rashly. These words of Christ, then, are expounded by St. Ambrose as follows: "Well does he who descended for

---

14. John 6:15.   15. *Glossa interlinearis, ad. loc.*
16. See Thomas Aquinas, *Catena aurea* (XII, 330).
17. Ibid.   18. Ibid.
19. Luke 12:13–14.

the sake of the divine avoid the earthly, and does not deign to be judge over disputes and appraiser of wealth, being the judge of the living and the dead and the appraiser of their merits." And a little below he adds: "Hence not undeservedly is this brother rebuffed, who wanted the dispenser of the heavenly to concern himself with the corruptible." [20] See, then, what Ambrose thinks about Christ's office in this world; for he says that "well does he avoid the earthly," that is, the judgment of contentious acts, "who descended for the sake of the divine," that is, to teach and minister the spiritual; in this he designated Christ's office and that of his successors, namely, to dispense the heavenly or spiritual; that spiritual of which Ambrose spoke in his gloss on the first epistle to the Corinthians, Chapter 9, which we quoted in Chapter II of this discourse under the third meaning of this word "spiritual."

It now remains to show that not only did Christ himself refuse rulership or coercive judgment in this world, whereby he furnished an example for his apostles and disciples and their successors to do likewise, but also he taught by words and showed by example that all men, both priests and non-priests, should be subject in property and in person to the coercive judgment of the rulers of this world. By his word and example, then, Christ showed this first with respect to property, by what is written in the twenty-second chapter of Matthew. For when the Jews asked him: "Tell us therefore, what dost thou think? Is it lawful to give tribute to Caesar, or not?" Christ, after looking at the coin and its inscription, replied: "Render therefore to Caesar the things that are Caesar's, and to God the things that are God's." [21] Whereon the interlinear gloss says, "that is, tribute and money." [22] And on the words: "Whose image and inscription is this?" [23] Ambrose wrote as follows: "Just as Caesar demanded the imprinting of his image, so too does God demand that the soul be stamped with the light of his countenance." [24] Note, therefore, what it was that Christ came into the world to demand. Furthermore, Chrysostom writes as follows: "When you hear: 'Render to Caesar the things that are Caesar's,' know that he means only those things which are not harmful to piety, for if they were, the tribute would be not to Caesar but to the devil." [25] So, then, we ought to be subject to Caesar in all things, so long only as they are not contrary to piety, that is, to divine worship or commandment. Therefore, Christ wanted us to be subject in property to the secular ruler. This too was plainly the doctrine of St.

20. See Thomas Aquinas, *Catena aurea* (XII, 145).

21. Matt. 22:17, 20–21.   22. *Glossa interlinearis, ad. loc.*

23. Matt. 22:20.

24. *Glossa ordinaria, ad loc.* See Thomas Aquinas, *Catena aurea* (XI, 410), where an earlier form of this gloss is cited from Jerome, with no mention of Ambrose.

25. See Thomas Aquinas, *Catena aurea* (XI, 253).

Ambrose, based upon this doctrine of Christ, for in his epistle against Valentinian, entitled *To the People*, he wrote: "We pay to Caesar the things that are Caesar's, and to God the things that are God's. That the tribute is Caesar's is not denied." [26]

The same is again shown from the seventeenth chapter of Matthew, where it is written as follows: "They that received the didrachmas came to Peter, and said, Doth not your master pay the didrachmas?" and then, a little below, is written what Christ said to Peter: "But that we may not scandalize them, go to the sea and cast in a hook, and that fish which shalt first come up, take: and when thou hast opened its mouth, thou shalt find a piece of money: take that, and give it to them for me and thee." [27] Nor did the Lord say only, "Give it to them," but he said, "Give it to them for me and thee." And Jerome on this passage says: "Our Lord was in flesh and in spirit the son of a king, whether we consider him to have been generated from the seed of David or the word of the Almighty Father. Therefore, being the son of kings, he did not owe tribute." And below he adds: "Therefore, although he was exempt, yet he had to fulfill all the demands of justice, because he had assumed the humility of the flesh." [28] Moreover, Origen on the words of Christ: "That we may not scandalize them," spoke more to the point and in greater conformity to the meaning of the evangelist, as follows: "It is to be understood," that is, from Christ's words, "that while men sometimes appear who through injustice seize our earthly goods, the kings of this earth send men to exact from us what is theirs. And by his example the Lord prohibits the doing of any offense, even to such men, either so that they may no longer sin, or so that they may be saved. For the son of God, who did no servile work, gave the tribute money, having the guise of a servant which he assumed for the sake of man." [29]

How, then, is it possible, on the strength of the words of the evangelic Scripture, that the bishops and priests be exempt from this tribute, and from the jurisdiction of rulers generally, unless by the rulers' own gratuitous grant, when Christ and Peter, setting an example for others, paid such tribute? And although Christ, being of royal stock in flesh, was perhaps not obliged to do this, yet Peter, not being of royal stock, had no such reason to be exempt, just as he wanted none. But if Christ had thought it improper for his successors in the priestly office to pay tribute and for their temporal goods to be subject to the secular rulers, then without setting a bad example, that is, without subjecting the priesthood to the jurisdiction of secu-

26. St. Ambrose, *Sermo contra Auxentium de basilicis tradendis* cap. xxxv (*PL* 16: 1061).

27. Matt. 17:23, 26.

28. See Thomas Aquinas, *Catena aurea* (XI, 209).

29. See ibid.

lar rulers, he could have ordained otherwise and have made some arrangement about those tax collectors, such as removing from them the intention of asking for such tribute, or in some other appropriate way. But he did not think it proper to do so, rather he wanted to pay; and from among the apostles, as the one who was to pay with him the tribute, he chose Peter, despite the fact that Peter was to be the foremost teacher and pastor of the church, as will be said in Chapter XVI of this discourse, in order that by such an example none of the others would refuse to do likewise.

The passage of Scripture which we quoted above from the seventeenth chapter of Matthew is interpreted in the way we have said by St. Ambrose in the epistle entitled *On Handing Over the Basilica*, where he writes as follows: "He," that is, the emperor, "demands tribute, it is not denied. The fields of the church pay tribute." And a little further on he says, more to the point: "We pay to Caesar the things that are Caesar's, and to God the things that are God's. The tribute is Caesar's, it is not denied." [30] Expressing more fully this which we have called the meaning of the above-quoted passage of Scripture, St. Bernard in an epistle to the archbishop of Sens wrote as follows: "This is what is done by these men," namely, those who suggested that subjects rebel against their superiors. "But Christ ordered and acted otherwise. 'Render,' he said, 'to Caesar the things that are Caesar's, and to God the things that are God's.' What he spoke by word of mouth, he soon took care to carry out in deed. The institutor of Caesar did not hesitate to pay the tax to Caesar. For he thus gave you the example that you should do likewise. How, then, could he deny the reverence due to the priests of God, when he took care to show it even for the secular powers?" [31]

And we must note what Bernard said, that Christ, in taking care to pay the tax to the secular powers, showed "due," and therefore not coerced, "reverence." For everyone owes such tax and tribute to the rulers, as we shall show in the following chapter from the words of the Apostle in the thirteenth chapter of the epistle to the Romans, and the glosses thereon of the saints and doctors; although perhaps not every tax is owed everywhere by everyone, such as the entry tax [32] which was not owed by the inhabitants, although the custodians or collectors sometimes wrongly demanded and exacted it from simple inhabitants or natives, such as were the apostles. And therefore, in agreement with Origen, who I believed grasped the meaning of the evangelist on this point better than did Jerome, I say that it

30. St. Ambrose, *Sermo contra Auxentium* cap. xxxiii (*PL* 16: 1060–61).

31. St. Bernard, *De moribus et officio episcoporum* cap. viii (*PL* 182: 829).

32. This is the *pedagium*, a tax paid to the ruler of a territory by those who come into the territory from outside. See the many references in Du Cange, *Glossarium mediae et infiniae Latinitatis*, s.v. *pedagium*.

seemed customary and was perhaps commonly established in states, especially in Judaea, that entry taxes were not to be paid by inhabitants or natives, but only by aliens. And hence Christ said to Peter: "Of whom do the kings of the earth receive tribute?" etc.,[33] by "tribute" meaning that entry tax which the tax collectors were demanding. For Christ did not deny that the children of the earth, that is, natives, owe "tribute," taking the word as a common name for every tax; on the contrary, he later said of it, excepting no one: "Render to Caesar the things that are Caesar's"; and this was also expressed by the Apostle in agreement with Christ, when he said, in the thirteenth chapter of the epistle to the Romans: "For this cause also you pay tribute," that is, to rulers, "for they are the ministers of God."[34] By "children," therefore, Christ meant the children of kingdoms, that is, persons born or raised therein, and not the children of kings by blood; otherwise his words would not seem to have been pertinent, for very often he spoke in the plural both for himself and for Peter, who was certainly not the child of kings as those discussed by Jerome. Moreover, if Christ was of David's stock in flesh, so too were very many other Jews, although not perhaps Peter. Again, the tribute was not then being exacted by David or by anyone of his blood; why, therefore, should Christ have said, "The kings of the land . . . then the children are free,"[35] saying nothing about the heavenly king? But it is certain that neither Christ nor Peter was a child of Caesar, either in flesh or in spirit. Moreover, why should Christ have asked the above question? For everyone certainly knows that the children of kings by blood do not pay tribute to their parents. Jerome's exposition, therefore, does not seem to have been as much in agreement with Scripture as was Origen's. But the above words of Scripture show that Christ wanted to pay even undue tribute in certain places and at certain times, and to teach the Apostle and his successors to do likewise, rather than to fight over such things. For this was the justice of counsel and not of command which Christ, in the humility of the flesh which he had assumed, wanted to fulfill and to teach others to fulfill. And the Apostle, like Christ, also taught that this should be done. Hence, in the first epistle to the Corinthians, Chapter 6: "Why do ye not rather take wrong? why do ye not rather suffer yourselves to be defrauded?"[36] than to quarrel with one another, as he had said before.

Moreover, not only with respect to property did Christ show that he was subject to the coercive jurisdiction of the secular ruler, but also with re-

---

33. Matt. 17:24.   34. Rom. 13:6.

35. Matt. 17:24–25. The complete text, required to make sense of the fragment quoted by Marsiglio, is as follows: "The kings of the earth, of whom do they receive tribute or custom? Of their own children, or of strangers? And he said: Of strangers. Jesus said to him: Then the children are free."

36. 1 Cor. 6:7.

spect to his own person, than which no greater jurisdiction could be had by the ruler over him or over anyone else, for which reason it is called "capital jurisdiction" [*merum imperium*] by the Roman legislator.[37] That Christ was thus subject can be clearly shown from the twenty-seventh chapter of Matthew; for there it is written that Christ allowed himself to be seized and brought before Pilate, who was the vicar of the Roman emperor, and he suffered himself to be judged and given the extreme penalty by Pilate as judge, although he perhaps indicated that he was suffering an unjust punishment. But it is certain that he could have undergone such judgment and punishment at the hands of priests, had he so desired, and had he deemed it improper for his successors to be subject to the secular rulers and to be judged by them.

But since this view is borne out at great length in the nineteenth chapter of John, I shall here adduce what is written there. When Christ had been brought before Pilate, vicar of Caesar, to be judged, and was accused of having called himself king of the Jews and son of God, he was asked by Pilate: "Whence art thou?" But having no reply from Jesus, Pilate spoke to him the following words, which are quite pertinent to our subject; here is the passage: "Pilate therefore saith to him, Speakest thou not to me? Knowest thou not that I have power to crucify thee, and I have power to release thee? Jesus answered: Thou shouldst not have any power against me, unless it were given thee from above."[38] See, then, Jesus did not deny that Pilate had the power to judge him and to execute his judgment against him; nor did he say: This does not pertain to you of right [*de jure*] but you do this only in fact [*de facto*]. But Christ added that Pilate had this power "from above." How from above? Augustine answers: "Let us therefore learn what he," that is, Christ, "said, and what he taught the Apostle," that is, Paul, in the epistle to the Romans, Chapter 13.[39] What, then, did Christ say? What did he teach the Apostle? "That there is no power," that is, authority of jurisdiction, "except from God," whatever be the case with respect to the act of him who badly uses the power. "And that he who from malice hands over an innocent man to the power to be killed, sins more than does the power itself if it kills the man from fear of another's greater power. But God had certainly given to him," that is, Pilate, "power in such manner that he was under the power of Caesar."[40]

The coercive judicial power of Pilate over the person of Christ, therefore, was from God, as Christ openly avowed, and Augustine plainly

---

37. For this untranslatable phrase, see *Corp. jur. civ.*, *Digest* II. i. 3: "Capital jurisdiction is to have the power of the sword to punish criminal men, which jurisdiction is also called power."

38. John 19:9–11.   39. Rom. 13:1–7.

40. See Thomas Aquinas, *Catena aurea* (XII, 445).

showed, and Bernard clearly said in his epistle to the archbishop of Sens: "For," as he wrote, "Christ avows that the Roman ruler's power over him is ordained of heaven," [41] speaking of Pilate's power and with reference to this passage of Scripture. If, then, the coercive judiciary power of Pilate over Christ was from God, how much more so over Christ's temporal or carnal goods, if he had possessed or owned any? And if over Christ's person and temporal goods, how much more over the persons and temporal goods of all the apostles, and of their successors, all the bishops or priests?

Not only was this shown by Christ's words, but it was confirmed by the consummation of the deed. For the capital sentence was pronounced upon Christ by the same Pilate, sitting in the judgment seat, and by his authority that sentence was executed. Hence in the same chapter of John this passage is found: "Now when Pilate had heard these words, he brought Jesus forth, and sat down in the judgment seat"; and a little below is added: "Then therefore he delivered him," that is, Jesus, "to them to be crucified." [42] Such was the Apostle's view regarding Christ, when he said in the third chapter of the epistle to the Galatians: "But when the fulness of the time was come, God sent his son, made of a woman, made under the law," [43] and therefore also under the judge whose function it was to judge and command in accordance with the law, but who was not, however, a bishop or a priest.

Not only did Christ wish to exclude himself from secular rulership or coercive judicial power, but he also excluded it from his apostles, both among themselves and with respect to others. Hence in the twentieth chapter of Matthew and the twenty-second chapter of Luke this passage is found: "And there was also a strife among them," that is, the apostles, "which of them should seem to be the greater. And he," Christ, "said to them, The kings of the Gentiles lord it over them, and they that have power over them are called beneficent." (But in Matthew this clause is written as follows: "And they that are the greater exercise power upon them.") "But you not so: but he that is the greater among you, let him become as the younger; and he that is the leader, as he that serveth." [44] "But whosoever will be the greater among you, let him be your minister. And he that will be first among you shall be your servant: even as the Son of man is not come to be ministered unto, but to minister," [45] that is, to be a servant in the temporal realm, not to lord it or rule, for in spiritual ministry he was first, and not a servant among the apostles. Whereon Origen comments: " 'You know that the princes of the Gentiles lord it over them,' that is, they are not content merely to rule their subjects, but try to exercise violent lordship over

---

41. St. Bernard, *De moribus et officio episcoporum* cap. ix (*PL* 182: 832).
42. John 19:13, 16.   43. Actually Gal. 4:4.
44. Luke 22:24–27.   45. Matt. 20:25–28.

them," that is, by coercive force if necessary. "But those of you who are mine will not be so; for just as all carnal things are based upon necessity, but spiritual things upon the will, so too should the rulership of those who are spiritual rulers," prelates, "be based upon love and not upon fear."[46] And Chrysostom writes, among other remarks, these pertinent words:

> The rulers of the world exist in order to lord it over their subjects, to cast them into slavery and to despoil them [namely, if they deserve it] and to use them even unto death for their [that is, the rulers'] own advantage and glory. But the rulers [that is, prelates] of the church are appointed in order to serve their subjects and to minister to them whatever they have received from Christ, so that they neglect their own advantage and seek to benefit their subjects, and do not refuse to die for their salvation. To desire the leadership of the church is neither just nor useful. For what wise man is there who wants to subject himself of his own accord to such servitude and peril, as to be responsible for the whole church? Only he perhaps who does not fear the judgment of God and abuses his ecclesiastic leadership for secular purposes, so as to change it into secular leadership.[47]

Why, then, do priests have to interfere with coercive secular judgments? for their duty is not to exercise temporal lordship, but rather to serve, by the example and command of Christ. Hence Jerome: "Finally he," that is, Christ, "sets forth his own example, so that if they," the apostles, "do not respect his words they may at least be ashamed of their deeds,"[48] that is, wielding temporal lordship. Hence Origen on the words: "And to give his life a redemption for many,"[49] wrote as follows:

> The rulers of the church should therefore imitate Christ, who was approachable, and spoke to women, and placed his hands upon the children, and washed the feet of his disciples, so that they might do the same for their brethren. But we are such [he is speaking of the prelates of his day] that we seem to exceed even the worldly rulers in pride, either misunderstanding or despising the commandment of Christ, and we demand fierce, powerful armies, just as do kings.[50]

46. See Thomas Aquinas, *Catena aurea* (XI, 234).

47. Ibid. Here again it will be noted how Marsiglio's interpolation ("if they deserve it") falsifies the meaning of Chrysostom by blurring the latter's condemnation of secular rulers.

48. Ibid. Marsiglio's misinterpretation of Jerome's meaning necessitates a mistranslation of this passage. What Jerome says is that the apostles "may at least be shamed to deeds" (*erubescant ad opera*), i.e., deeds such as Christ wanted them to perform, not the "wielding temporal lordship" with which Marsiglio taxes them.

49. Matt. 20:28.

50. See Thomas Aquinas, *Catena aurea* (XI, 234).

But since to do these things is to despise or be ignorant of Christ's commandment, the prelates must first be warned about it, which is what we shall do in this treatise, by showing what authority belongs to them; then, if they disregard this, they must be compelled and forced by the secular rulers to correct their ways, lest they corrupt the morals of others. These, then, are the comments made on the passage in Matthew. On Luke, Basil writes: "It is fitting that those who preside should offer bodily service, following the example of the Lord who washed the feet of his disciples." [51]

Christ, then, said: "The kings of the Gentiles lord it over them. But you," that is, the apostles, "not so." So Christ, king of kings and lord of lords, did not give them the power to exercise the secular judgments of rulers, nor coercive power over anyone, but he clearly prohibited this to them, when he said: "But you not so." And the same must consequently be held with respect to all the successors of the apostles, the bishops or priests. This too is what St. Bernard clearly wrote to Eugene, *On Consideration*, Book II, Chapter IV, discussing the above words of Christ: "The kings of the Gentiles lord it over them," etc. For Bernard wrote, among other things:

> What the apostle [Peter] has, this did he give, namely, the guardianship, as I have said, of the churches. But not lordship? Hear him. "Neither as lording it over the clergy," he says, "but being made a pattern of the flock." And lest you think he spoke only from humility, but not with truth, the voice of the Lord is in the gospel: "The kings of the Gentiles lord it over them, and they that have power over them are called beneficent." And he adds: "But you not so." It is quite plain, then, that lordship is forbidden to the apostles. Go, then, if you dare, and usurp either the apostolate if you are a lord or lordship if you are an apostle. You are plainly forbidden to have both. If you wish to have both at once, you shall lose both. In any case, do not think you are excepted from the number of those about whom God complains in these words: "They have reigned, but not by me: they have been princes, and I knew not." [52]

And so from the evangelic truths which we have adduced, and the interpretations of them made by the saints and other approved teachers, it should be clearly apparent to all that both in word and in deed Christ excluded and wished to exclude himself from all worldly rulership or governance, judgment, or coercive power, and that he wished to be subject to the secular rulers and powers in coercive jurisdiction.

51. Ibid. (XII, 229).

52. St. Bernard, *De consideratione* II. vi (*PL* 182: 748). The first citation is from 1 Pet. 5:3, the last from Hos. 8:4.

On the Division of Human Acts, and How They Are Related to Human Law and the Judge of This World

Every coercive judgment is concerned with human voluntary acts in accordance with some law or custom, and with these acts insofar as they are ordered either toward the end to be attained in this world, that is, sufficiency of worldly life, or toward the end to be attained in the future world, which we call eternal life or glory. Hence, in order to make clearer the distinction between those who judge or ought to judge with regard to each of these ends, and between the laws in accordance with which, the judgments by which, and the manners in which they must respectively judge, let us discuss the differences between the acts themselves. For the determination of these points will be of no little help toward the solution of the earlier questions.

Let us say, therefore, that of human acts arising from knowledge and desire, some arise without any control by the mind, and others arise through the control of the human mind. Of the first kind are cognitions, desires, affections, and pleasures which arise from us and in us without any control or command being given about them by the intellect or the appetite; such are the cognitions and emotions which we have when we are aroused from sleep, or which arise in us in other ways without any control by our mind. But these acts are followed by cognitions, feelings, and emotions which are concerned with continuing the prior acts, or with investigating and understanding some of them, as in the action which proceeds through recollection; and these are and are called "controls" or "commands" of the mind, because they are done or elicited by our control, or because certain other acts are elicited by them, such as pursuits and avoidances.[53]

But between controlled and uncontrolled acts there is this difference arising from what we have said, that over uncontrolled acts we do not have complete freedom or control as to whether or not they shall be done, but

53. For a possible source of this distinction between "uncontrolled" and "controlled" acts, see Thomas Aquinas, *Summa theologica* II. 1. qu.8. *init*. Marsiglio's interpretation of the distinction, however, is not entirely the same as Thomas's. Thomas first distinguishes between "voluntary" and "involuntary" acts, and then distinguishes between two kinds of voluntary acts, the "elicited," which are acts immediately of the will itself (like willing and choosing), and the "controlled," which are acts of other powers moved by the will. Marsiglio, on the other hand, identifies controlled, elicited, and voluntary acts, and then divides these into "immanent" and "transient" acts (see para. 3). It should be noted that the term here translated "controlled" is *imperatus*; the English term is used in order to avoid confusion with the important term *praeceptum*, which, following William of Moerbeke, who used *praecipere* to translate Aristotle's ἐπιτάττειν, is translated "command" or "commanded."

over controlled acts we do have this power, according to the Christian religion.[54] And I have said that we do not have complete power over the former kind of acts, because it is not in our power wholly to prohibit their occurrence, although by acts of the second kind, which are called "controls," and by what follows from them, we may so dispose the soul that it will not easily perform or receive acts of the first kind, that is, when each of us has become accustomed to commanding himself to desire or think about the opposites of these acts.

Of controlled acts some are and are called "immanent," and others "transient." Immanent acts are controlled cognitions, emotions, and the corresponding habits made by the human mind; they are called "immanent" because they do not cross over into any subject other than the agent himself. Transient acts, on the other hand, are all pursuits of things desired, and the omissions thereof, in the manner of privations, and the motions produced by some of the body's external organs, especially of those which are moved in respect of place. Again, of transient acts some exist and are done without harm or injury to any individual group or community other than the agent; such are all the kinds of productive activity, and also the giving of money, pilgrimages, castigation of one's own body by scourging or beating or any other way, and other similar acts. Other transient acts, however, exist and are done with the opposite circumstances, that is, with harm or injury to someone other than the agent; such are flogging, theft, robbery, bearing false witness, and many others of various manners and kinds.

Now of all these acts which arise from the human mind, especially the controlled ones, there have been discovered certain standards or measures or habits whereby they arise and are done properly and correctly for the attainment of the sufficient life both in this world and in the next. Of these habits or standards there are some in accordance with which the acts of the human mind, both immanent and transient, are guided and regulated in their being done or omitted without any reward or punishment being given to the doer or omitter by someone else through coercive force; such are most of the operative disciplines, both those of action and those of production. But there are other standards in accordance with which such acts are commanded to be done or omitted with reward or punishment being given to the doers or omitters by someone else through coercive force. Of these coercive standards, again, there are some in accordance with which their observers or transgressors are rewarded or punished in and for the status of

---

54. This reference to religion may indicate some skepticism as to whether such freedom is rationally demonstrable.

the present life; such are all human civil laws and customs. But there are other coercive standards in accordance with which doers are rewarded or punished in and for the status of the future life only; such are divine laws for the most part, which are called by the common name "religions," [55] among which, as we said in Chapter VI of Discourse I, only that of the Christians contains the truth and the sufficiency of what must be hoped for the future world.

For the sufficient life or living of this world, therefore, there has been laid down a standard of controlled transient human acts which can be done for the benefit or harm, right or wrong, of someone other than the agent; a standard which commands and coerces transgressors by pain or punishment for the status of the present world alone. This standard we called by the common name "human law" in Chapter X of Discourse I; its final necessity and efficient cause we indicated in Chapters XI, XII, and XIII of Discourse I.

On the other hand, for the life or living in this world, but for the status of the future world, a law has been given and laid down by Christ. This law is a standard of controlled human acts, both immanent and transient, which are in the active power of our mind, according as they can be done or omitted rightly or wrongly in this world, but for the status or end of the future world. [56] This law is coercive and distributes punishments or rewards, but inflicts these in the future world, not in the present one, in accordance with the merits or demerits of those who observe or transgress it in the present life.

But since these coercive laws, both the divine and the human, lack a soul and a judicial and executive moving principle, they needed to have some animate subject or principle which should command and regulate or judge human acts in accordance with these laws, and which should also execute the judgments and coerce their transgressors. This subject or principle is called a "judge," in what we called the third sense of this term in Chapter II of this discourse. Hence in Book IV of the *Ethics*, the treatise on justice, it is said that "the judge is like an animate justice." [57] It is necessary, then, to have a judge in accordance with human laws, a judge of the kind we have said, having the authority to judge, by a judgment in the third sense, about contentious human acts, to execute the judgments, and to punish by coercive force anyone who transgresses the law. For this judge "is the minister of God," and "a revenger to execute wrath upon him that

55. *Sectae.*
56. Reading, with Scholz, comma after *seculi.*
57. Aristotle, *Nicomachean Ethics* V. 4. 1132a 22.

doeth evil," as the Apostle said in the epistle to the Romans, Chapter 13;[58] he has been sent by God for this purpose, as it is said in the first epistle of Peter, Chapter 2.[59]

And the Apostle said: "him that doeth evil," whoever he be, understanding this to apply to all men without differentiation. Consequently, since priests or bishops and generally all ministers of temples, who are called by the common name "clergyman," can do evil by way of commission or omission, and since some (would that it were not most) of them do sometimes in fact harm and wrong other persons, they too are subject to the revenge or jurisdiction of the judges to whom belongs coercive power to punish transgressors of human laws. This was also clearly stated by the Apostle in the epistle to the Romans, Chapter 13: "Let every soul," he said, "be subject to the higher powers," namely, "to kings, princes, and tribunes," according to the exposition of the saints.[60] For the same proper matter must undergo the action of the same agent which is naturally endowed and ordained to act upon it for the end for which it is apt, as is clear from the second book of the *Physics*. For as it is there written, "each thing is acted upon as it is naturally endowed to be acted upon,"[61] and conversely. But the transgressor of the law is the matter or subject upon which the judge or ruler is naturally endowed and ordained to act by bringing it to justice in order to effect due equality or proportion for the purpose of maintaining peace or tranquillity and the living together or association of men, and finally for the sake of the sufficiency of human life. Consequently, wherever such matter or subject is found in a province subject to a judge, this judge must bring him to justice. Since, therefore, the priest can be such proper or essential matter, that is, a transgressor of human law, he must be subject to the judgment of this judge. For to be a priest or nonpriest is accidental to the transgressor in his relation to the judge, just as to be a farmer or house-builder; in the same way, to be musical or unmusical is accidental to the healthy or the sick man in his relation to the physician.

58. Rom. 13:4.   59. 1 Pet. 2:14.

60. In Peter Lombard, *Collectanea* (*PL* 191: 1503).

61. See Aristotle, *Physics* II. 8. 199a 9. Marsiglio's text reads: *Sic agitur unumquodque sicut natum est agi*. This is a misquotation of William of Moerbeke's translation of this passage, which reads: *Ergo sicut agitur, sic aptum natum est: et sicut aptum natum est, sic agitur unumquodque* (in Thomas Aquinas, *Opera omnia*, ed. Leonine [Rome, 1884], II, 92). Aristotle's Greek is as follows: Οὐκοῦν ὡς πράττεται, οὕτω πέφυκε, καὶ ὡς πέφυκεν, οὕτω πράττεται ἔκυστον. Moreover, Marsiglio misinterprets the passage, which is rendered as follows in the Oxford translation of R. P. Hardie and R. K. Gaye: "Now surely as in intelligent action, so in nature; and as it is in nature, so it is in each action." However, Marsiglio's misinterpretation is also found in Thomas Aquinas's commentary on the passage; see p. 93 of his commmentary in the edition cited in this note.

For that which is essential is not removed or varied by that which is accidental; otherwise there would be infinite species of judges and physicians.[62]

Therefore, any priest or bishop who transgresses human law must be brought to justice and punished by the judge who has coercive power over transgressors of human law in this world. But this judge is the secular ruler as such, not the priest or bishop, as was demonstrated in Chapters XV and XVII of Discourse I, and in Chapters IV and V of this discourse. Therefore, all priests or bishops who transgress human law must be punished by the ruler. And not only must the priest or other minister of the temple be punished for a transgression as the layman is, but he must be punished all the more in proportion as he sins more gravely and unseemingly, since he whose duty it is to be better acquainted with the commands of what must be done and avoided, has greater knowledge and ability to choose; and again, since the sin of the person whose duty it is to teach is more shameful than the sin of the person whose duty it is to be taught. But such is the relation of the priest's sin to that of the non-priest. Therefore, the priest sins more gravely, and should be punished more.

Nor must the objection be sustained which holds that injuries by word of mouth, or to property or person, and other deeds prohibited by human law, are spiritual actions when inflicted on someone by a priest, and that it does not therefore pertain to the secular ruler to take revenge on the priest for such acts. For such deeds as are prohibited by law, like adultery, beating, homicide, theft, robbery, insult, libel, treason, fraud, heresy, and other similar acts committed by the priest, are carnal and temporal, as is very well known by experience, and as we showed above in Chapter II of this discourse by the words of the Apostle in the first epistle to the Corinthians, Chapters 3 and 9, and in the epistle to the Romans, Chapter 15. And so much the more must these actions be adjudged carnal and temporal, in proportion as the priest or bishop sins by them more gravely and shamefully than do the persons whom he must recall from such actions, for by his vicious example he gives them an opportunity and an excuse for doing wrong.

Therefore, like laymen, every priest or bishop is and ought to be subject to the jurisdiction of the rulers in those matters whose observance is commanded by the human law. The priest neither is himself exempt from the coercive judgment of rulers, nor can he exempt anyone else from it by his own authority. This I demonstrate, in addition to what was said in Chapter XVII of Discourse I, by deducing from its contradictory, the greatest evil. For if the Roman bishop or any other priest were thus exempt, so that he

62. This point is reminiscent of Aristotle's doctrine that the accidental attributes of a thing are infinite in number. Cf. *Metaphysics* IV. 4. 1007a 14 ff.; VI. 2. 1026b 6 ff.

would not be subject to the coercive judgment of rulers but would himself be such a coercive judge without the authorization of the human legislator and could separate all ministers of temples, who are called by the common name of "clergymen," from the jurisdiction of rulers, and could subject them to himself, as is done by the Roman pontiffs in modern times, then it would necessarily follow that the jurisdiction of secular rulers would be almost completely annulled. This I believe would be a grave evil of serious import to all rulers and communities; for "the Christian religion deprives no one of his right," as we showed in Chapter V of this discourse from the words of Ambrose on the passage in the epistle to Titus, Chapter 3: "Warn them to be subject to the princes and powers."

The consequence of this evil I show as follows: In divine law one finds that for the priest or bishop to have a wife is not prohibited but rather allowed, especially if he have not more than one, as it is said in the first epistle to Timothy, Chapter 3.[63] But that which is decreed by the human law or constitution can be revoked by the same authority, as such. Therefore, the Roman bishop who makes himself legislator, or who uses his plenitude of power (if one grant that he has this), can allow all priests, deacons, and subdeacons to have wives, and not only them, but also other persons not ordained in the priesthood or diaconate or otherwise consecrated, who are called "clergy of the simple tonsure"; indeed, he can grant such permission even more fittingly to these latter, as Boniface VIII is seen in fact to have done, in order to increase his secular power. For all who had taken one virgin wife, and who were willing, he enrolled by his ordinances which are called "decretals";[64] and not stopping there, these bishops have similarly exempted from human civil laws, duly made, certain laymen who are called "jolly friars" in Italy and Beguins elsewhere; on the same ground they have dealt and can deal at their pleasure with the Knights Templars, the Hospitallers, and many other such orders, like that of Altopascio and so on.[65] But if all such persons are thus exempted from the jurisdiction of rulers in accordance with these decretals, which also grant certain immunities from public or civil burdens to those who are thus exempted, then it seems very likely that the majority of men will slip into these orders, especially since both literate and illiterate persons are accepted indiscrimi-

63. 1 Tim. 3:2, 12.

64. *Corp. jur. can., Sext. Lib.* III. Tit. 2 cap. 1 (*De clericis coniugatis*). This declares that married "clerks" who bear the tonsure and clerical garbs are not to be tried or condemned by the secular tribunal.

65. The "jolly friars" or Frati Gaudenti were the Knights of the Virgin founded in Bologna in 1261. The Beguins were associations of pious persons. The Knights Templars and Hospitallers were likewise lay orders, dating from the twelfth century. The canons or knights of Altopascio maintained hospitals for pilgrims (spreading from a township near Lucca).

nately. For everyone is prone to pursue his own advantage and to avoid what is disadvantageous. But with the greater number or majority of men slipping into clerical orders, the jurisdiction and coercive power of rulers will become ineffective, and the number of those who have to bear the public burdens will be reduced to almost nothing; which is the gravest evil, and destructive of the polity. For he who enjoys civil honors and advantages, like peace and the protection of the human legislator, must not be exempt from the civil burdens and jurisdiction without the determination of the same legislator. Hence the Apostle said, in the epistle to the Romans, Chapter 13: And for this very reason "pay ye tribute." [66]

To avoid this eventuality it must be granted, in accordance with the truth, that the ruler by authority of the legislator has jurisdiction over all bishops or priests and clergymen, lest the polity be destroyed by having an unordered multiplicity of governments, as was shown in Chapter XVII of Discourse I; and the ruler must determine, in the province subject to him, the definite number of clergymen, as also of the persons in every other part of the polity, lest by their undue increase they be able to resist the ruler's coercive power, or otherwise disturb the polity, or deprive the city or state of its welfare by their insolence and their freedom from necessary tasks, as we showed from the *Politics*, Book V, Chapter 1, in Chapter XV of Discourse I.

Thus, therefore, it is the human law and judge, in the third sense, which have to regulate transient human acts which affect the advantage or disadvantage, right or wrong, of someone other than the agent. To this coercive jurisdiction all men, lay and clergy, must be subject. But there are also certain other judges according to human laws, who have been called judges in the first or the second sense, such as the teachers of these laws; but these judges have no coercive authority, and there is nothing to prevent that in any one community there be many of them, even when they are not subordinate to one another.

The Great Schism

Catherine of Siena was one of the greatest figures in the later history of the Babylonian Captivity. The twenty-third child of a Sienese dyer, Catherine (1347–80) is known as an ascetic, mystic, and reformer. She had the first of her many visions at the age of seven. As a young woman, she entered (1365) the Dominican order as a tertiary (tertiaries were

66. See Rom. 13:6.

laypeople who formed a branch of a religious order but who remained in the world pursuing the ordinary activities of secular life). She quickly achieved a wide reputation for sanctity and extreme asceticism. Although she never learned to read or write, she left an imposing literary monument in the form of about 350 letters addressed to popes, princes, and other great personages; these letters she dictated to relays of secretaries, drawn from her most devoted followers. Powerful in thought, commanding in language, and often as dazzling in defiance of logical sequence as St. Paul, she called for an end of civic factionalism, for Church reform (including the return of the papacy to Rome), for a crusade against the infidel, and for other cherished ideals (document 67). Catherine was canonized in 1461, declared patron saint of Italy in 1939, and proclaimed a doctor of the Church by Pope Paul VI, the only woman yet elevated to the rank of such authorities as Augustine of Hippo, Jerome, Bernard of Clairvaux, and Thomas Aquinas.

The Babylonian Captivity and the numerous cracks that it opened in the fabric of Christendom prepared for the Great Schism. In 1377, heeding Catherine of Siena's impetuous exhortations, Pope Gregory XI returned the papal court to Rome. His prompt death (1378), and the election of the archbishop of Bari, an Italian, as Pope Urban VI, eventually led to a split in the College of Cardinals (document 68). The Italian faction remained with Urban in Rome. The French faction rejected Urban, whom they had elected and acknowledged as true pope, and elected Bishop Robert of Geneva as Pope Clement VII. Clement and his supporters cheerfully returned to Avignon. Catherine of Siena accepted the sadistic Urban as true pope, demanded from his bloodstained hands the same reforms that she had sought from Gregory XI, and urgently sought the reunion of the Church under his rule. But the schism between the Roman and the Avignonese papacy divided the religious loyalties of Europe, and naturally gave renewed vigor to the idea that the Church was superior to the pope, and that it could act against delinquent popes through councils. However, the attempt of the Council of Pisa (1409) to depose both the Roman and the Avignonese claimants complicated the situation by establishing a Pisan line of claimants. Between 1409 and 1415, there were three lines of rivals for the papal title.

Nicholas of Clémanges (ca. 1360–1437) provides a striking witness to the crosscurrents in the Conciliar Epoch (document 69). Born to a poor bourgeois family in Clémanges, Nicholas Poillevillain obtained his master of arts and bachelor of theology degrees at the University of Paris, where he began to teach in 1381. On several occasions, he was chosen to represent the University of Paris in debates provoked by the Great Schism; but the alternations in his later career reveal the difficulties to which his conflicting loyalties to the pope and to France exposed him in those troubled years. Intellectually as well as chronologically, his life and thought blended characteristics of the age that was passing, the medieval period, with those of the age that had not yet come, the age of the Renaissance and Reformation. Like many works in his large and varied literary production, the treatise *On the Ruin and the Repair of the Church* (probably 1400/1401) deals with Church reform. His doctrines made him a favorite not only in his own time with conciliar reformers (like Pierre d'Ailly) but also in the sixteenth century with Protestants. That may explain why his writings were put on the *Index of Forbidden Books* by Pope Paul IV in 1559.

The conciliar epoch eventually resolved the question of who was true pope. But, between the Council of Constance (1415) and the Council of Ferrara-Florence (1439), serious divisions had grown yet more acute. The conciliar epoch reunited the Church hierarchy and reestablished the dominance of the popes over councils. However, it also engendered lasting religious struggles, such as the Hussite wars in Bohemia. Leading to the Pragmatic Sanction of Bourges (1436), and numerous concordats between the papacy and German princes, it confirmed the existence of "national" churches, presided over by their kings, anticipating the moment when Henry VIII had himself proclaimed the "head of the Church in England." Finally, the conciliar epoch failed to achieve the reformation of the Church, leaving the task of protest and reform to later generations.

---

67. Letters of Catherine of Siena to Popes Gregory XI and Urban VI

To Gregory XI (ca. 1375)

Most holy and sweet father, your unworthy, lowly daughter Catherine in sweet Christ Jesus implores you by His precious blood: I want to see you a forceful man, fearless and without earthly love for yourself or for any being related to you by blood. When I consider [this question] I can see, in the sweet presence of God, that nothing so hinders your good and holy wishes or tends to tarnish the honor of God and work against the exaltation and reformation of the holy church more than this. Thus my soul's desire, in inestimable love, is that God in His infinite mercy strip you of all [worldly] passion and all indifference of the heart and make another man of you—

From *Le Lettere de S. Caterina da Siena*, edited by Piero Misciattelli (Florence: Casa Editrice Marzocco, 1939), 3:83–85, 221–28. Translated for this volume by Lydia G. Cochrane.

that is, a man re-formed in fiery and most ardent desire. In no other way can you fulfill God's will and his servants' desires. *Oimé* [alas], *oimé*, dearest *Babbo* [father], pardon me for my presumption in what I have said to you and say to you now: it is the sweet first truth that compels me to speak. His will, father, is this, and this is what He asks of you: He demands that you do away with the enormous number of iniquities committed by those who are pastured and fed in the garden of the holy church. He says that animals should not feed on the food of men. Since He has given you authority and you have accepted it, you must use your virtue [*virtù*] and your power. If you are not willing to use them, you should have refused what you took on; it would have been better for the honor of God and the salvation of your soul.

Furthermore, His will is this, and this He demands of you: He wants you to pacify all Tuscany, with which you are quarreling, drawing whatever [concessions] you can from all of your sinful children who have rebelled against you, as much as possible without warfare, but still chastising them as a father should when his son has offended him. Moreover, the sweet goodness of God demands that you give full authority to those who ask [your leave] to arrange for the holy voyage [to Avignon to the gathering of the Knights of Rhodes]. This may seem impossible to you, but it is possible to the sweet goodness of God, who ordained it and wills it. Take care, as you hold life dear, not to neglect this matter, and do not mock the operation of the Holy Spirit: [these acts] are demanded of you and you are perfectly able to do them. If you want justice, you can wield justice. You can have peace if you cleanse it of perverse pomp and worldly delights, insisting only on the honor of God and what is due the holy church. You also have the authority to give peace to those who ask for it. Therefore, since you are not poor but rich, and since you hold in your hands the keys to heaven and since its gates are open to those for whom you open them and closed to those for whom you close them, God would rebuke you if you failed to do this. If I were you, I would fear lest divine judgment come down upon me. Therefore I beg you most sweetly by Christ crucified to be obedient to the will of God, for I know that all that you want and desire is to do His will. Then this harsh judgment will not fall upon you: "Accursed may you be, for you have not put to good use the time and the strength that were given to you." I believe, father, by God's goodness—and I also take hope from your Holiness—that you will act to prevent this judgment from falling upon you.

I will say no more. Forgive me, forgive me: my great love for your salvation and my great grief when I see it threatened make me speak as I do. I would have liked to tell you this in person to unburden my conscience fully. Whenever it pleases your Holiness that I come to you, I will come will-

ingly. Do not make me have to appeal to you in the name of Christ crucified. There is no one else to whom I can appeal, for there is no one
greater on earth. May you remain in the holy and sweet love of God. Humbly I beg your blessing. Sweet Jesus, Jesus love.

To Urban VI (ca. 1378)

Most holy and dearest Father in sweet Jesus Christ, I, Catherine, servant
and slave of the servants of Jesus Christ, write to you in His precious blood
in the desire to see you firmly founded in true and perfect charity, so that,
like a good shepherd, you will dedicate your life to your little sheep. And
truly, most holy father, only one who is ready to die for the love of God and
the salvation of souls can be founded in charity, because such a man is free
of self-love and free of himself. For anyone who is wrapped up in self-love
is not ready to give his life. Not only is he unwilling to give his life, he is
also unwilling to suffer the least small bother, because he is constantly
afraid for himself, fearing to lose his bodily life and the consolations attached to it. Everything he does is imperfect and corrupt, because the love
[*affetto*] that underlies his every act is corrupt. And such a man, be he
pastor or subordinate, acts with little forcefulness. The shepherd who is
founded in true charity does not do this: all his works are good and perfect,
because his love is united with and conjoined to the perfection of divine
charity. Such a man fears neither the demon nor his fellow man, but only
his Creator. He takes no heed of the distractions of this world and cares
little for opprobrium, mockery, or villainy, nor for scandal or the mutter-
ings of his subordinates. They may be scandalized and start muttering
when their superior rebukes them, but like a truly forceful man, robed in
the strength of charity, he pays no attention to them.

   He takes care, however, to feed the fire of holy desire and to guard the
pearl of justice which, joined with mercy, he carries in his shining bosom.
If justice were without mercy, it would be shrouded in the shadows of
cruelty and would be injustice more than justice. But mercy without justice
would be for a subordinate like putting ointment on a wound that needs
cauterization by fire: when an uncauterized wound is salved it will fester
rather than heal. But when the two are united, justice gives life to the prelate in whom it shines and health to a member of the clergy, unless he is
already of the devil's minions and refuses all correction. However, even if a
subordinate resists correction a thousand times, the prelate must not tire of
rebuking him. His virtue will be no less if the wicked refuse its fruit. This
is how pure and sincere charity acts when it dwells in the soul [of a man]
who has no thought for himself for his own sake, but only for God's sake,
and who seeks God for the glory and praise of His name, since he sees that

He is worthy of being loved for His infinite goodness. Nor does he seek his neighbor for his own sake but for God's in a desire to serve his neighbor in ways that he cannot serve God. Because he sees clearly and recognizes that although He is our God He has no need of us, he does his utmost to serve his fellow man, and particularly the subordinates who have been entrusted to his command. And [such a man] does not shrink from providing for the health of their bodies and the salvation of their souls just because they have proven ungrateful, either by their threats or by their flattery. But in truth and arrayed in the nuptial garment [of charity], he follows the teaching of the humble and immaculate lamb, the sweet, good shepherd, who, like a lover, went gladly to an opprobrious death on the most holy cross. The ineffable love that the soul has conceived for Christ crucified can do all this.

Most holy Father, God has placed you as a shepherd over all his sheep of the Christian religion. He has placed you as cellarer [*celleraio*] to administer the blood of Christ crucified, whose vicar you are. He has placed you in an age in which there is more wickedness among the clergy than during long ages past, both within the body of the holy church and in the universal body of all the Christian religion. This is why it is absolutely necessary that you be firmly founded in perfect charity and [hold fast to] the pearl of justice, in the way I have said. If you do so you will lose all caring for this world and for evil's miserable devotees and all their infamy. Then, like a true knight and a just shepherd, you will chastise with virility, uprooting vice and planting virtue, and preparing yourself to lay down your life if need be. Oh, sweetest Father, the world can take no more! There is so much vice abroad, particularly among those who have been placed in the garden of the holy church like sweet-smelling flowers to spread the perfume of virtue. We can see that they are so overflowing with miserable and wicked vices that they stink up the entire world. *Oimé!* Where is heart's charity and perfect honesty? Their honesty is supposed to lead the unchaste to chastity, but the very opposite is true, and often the chaste and the pure first taste incontinence through their filthy habits. *Oimé!* Where is charity's generous care of souls and its distributions to the poor, for the works of the church, for their needs? You know very well that they are doing just the opposite. Oh, miserable me! It grieves me to say it: your children are nourishing themselves on what they receive through the blood of Christ; they are not ashamed to play the swindler with the very hands you have sanctified and anointed—you, the vicar of Christ—without speaking of the other miserable things they do. *Oimé!* Where is profound humility—the humility that they confuse with the arrogance of their own sensuality? By arrogance, combined with great avarice, they commit simony, buying benefices with gifts, with flattery, or money, or with dissolute and vain adornments, not [behaving] like members of the clergy, but worse than laymen.

Oimé, my sweet *Babbo*, put a stop to this! Bring comfort to the yearning desires of the servants of God, who die of grief and cannot die. They burn with desire to see you lift your hand to chastise like a true shepherd, not with your words alone, but with your love, the pearl of justice shining in you, accompanied by mercy, and [to see you], without servile fear, truly chastise those who are feeding at the breast of this sweet bride.

But in all truth, most holy father, I cannot see how this can be done properly unless you totally reform the garden of your bride with good and virtuous plants. Take care to choose a company of men in whom you find virtue, holy men and unafraid of death. And do not look to their importance, but [make sure] they are shepherds who will govern their flock with solicitude. Then [choose] a company of good cardinals who will be true pillars for you and, with divine aid, will help you bear the weight of your many labors. Oh! how happy my soul will be then, when I see the bride of Christ come back into her own and when I see feeding at her breast men who look to the glory and praise of the name of God rather than to their personal gain, and who partake of the soul's food at the table of the cross. When this happens I have no doubt that the laity will mend their ways: they will do so necessarily when they are constrained by [the clergy's] holy teaching and honest life. This is not something to sleep on, but something to strive for all you possibly can until death, with forcefulness and neglecting nothing, for the glory and praise of God's name.

Next I beg of you, and I compel you by the love of Christ crucified, not to delay, by love of that Blood the minister of which you are, in receiving with mercy the little sheep who have strayed from the fold (through my sins, I do believe) and in breaking their hard-heartedness with your benignity and holiness. Do them that service—that is, bring them back to the fold. And if they fail to ask this in true and perfect humility, [I beg] your Holiness to make up for their imperfection. Accept from a sick man what he is capable of giving. *Oimé, oimé!* Have mercy on the many souls who are perishing! And do not look too closely into how scandal came to this city [Florence], where the very demons of hell have been working against the peace and tranquillity of both souls and bodies. Divine goodness saw to it that no great evil has come of this great evil. Your children have reached a peace and even ask you for the oil of mercy. One might suppose that it seems to you, most holy father, that they did not ask it with agreeable manners and heartfelt contrition for the fault they committed, as they should have done and as your Holiness would like them to have done. *Oimé!* Do not give up hope, for they will come to be better children than the others.

Oimé, Babbo mine, how I would like not to stay here any longer! Afterward do with me what you will. Be merciful and do me this favor—to me, the lowest of the low, knocking at your door. My dearest father, do not deny me these crumbs that I ask of you for your children so that, once peace is made, you can raise the standard of the most holy cross. As you can plainly see, the infidels have arrived on our shores to challenge you. I put my hope in the sweet goodness of God: may He fill you with the fire of His charity. Then you will know how many souls have been lost and what deep love you owe them, and you will yearn to free them from the hands of the Devil and will seek to heal the mystical body of the holy Church and the universal body of the Christian religion. And in particular you will seek to reconcile your children and bring them back to obedience, with benignity and with as much of the rod of justice as they can properly bear and no more. I am certain that without the virtue of charity, this cannot be done. This is why I told you that I wanted to see you founded in true and perfect charity. Not that I think that you are not in charity, but (since we are all pilgrims and wayfarers in this life) because we can always grow more perfect in charity. This is why I said that I wanted you to have perfect charity—that is, I want you to nourish it continually with the fire of holy desire, like a good shepherd, so that it can bear fruit among your clergy. This is what I pray you will do; and I will continue to work until I die, in my prayers and with all means at my disposal, for the honor of God and for your peace and that of your children.

I will say no more. Remain in the holy and sweet love of God. Forgive my presumption, most holy father. Love and grief are my excuses before your Holiness. Humbly I ask your blessing. Sweet Jesus, Jesus love.

68. Manifesto of the Cardinals against Urban VI (1378)

Be it known to all the faithful that, after Gregory XI's death on 27th March last, officials of the city of Rome conferred with the Cardinals, both in secret and in public, as is the custom when important business has to be decided upon. These conferences dealt with the procedure and attitude to be adopted by the cardinals. As it was reported by some witnesses, the officials compelled the cardinals to elect a Roman or at least an Italian to ensure that the curia remained at Rome. The then Archbishop of Bari was present at one of these conferences, as he himself has publicly confessed, although he advised that the cardinals should be treated gently. Some credible witnesses testify that this same archbishop had frequently recommended himself to the officials, in the church of S. Maria Nuova, before the entry into the conclave. Immediately after Gregory's death the city officials were desirous to guard all gates and bridges, including those which

From Walter Ullmann, *The Origins of the Great Schism* (London: Burns and Oates, 1948), pp. 69–75. All footnotes deleted.

had traditionally been guarded by the officials of the Vatican. Indeed, they guarded these localities safely night and day. It was everywhere thought at the time that they did so to prevent the cardinals leaving for any place to perform the election. During the ten days that elapsed between Gregory's death and the beginning of the conclave, the city officials approached the cardinals several times in the company of a great number of citizens, in order to beg them to elect a Roman or at least an Italian pope; they added that the cardinals should declare publicly before the whole people that they would comply with the wishes of the population: in order to avoid grave perils and dangers, the cardinals should comply with the wishes of the people. At the same time individual citizens were sent to the private quarters of the cardinals to submit this request personally. All members of the nobility were to leave the city within three days. The request of the cardinals that at least the Counts of Nola and Fondi should be permitted to stay in Rome, since they were officials of the curia, was flatly rejected. The cardinals sent for the officials and made it clear to them that they had erroneous conceptions of the cardinals; moreover, the requests of the officials were simply threats and intimidations, and an election thus influenced would be null and void. If they tried to keep the curia in Rome by such measures, they themselves would be the cause of losing it for ever. The cardinals put two requests to the officials. Firstly, they should send back the great numbers of country folk who had streamed into the city recently; they should give orders to the people to abstain from public meetings which inflamed the passions of the people. Secondly, they should detail a suitable captain and an adequate number of citizens, to guard the Borgho of St. Peter; the expenses would be met by the cardinals; care should be taken that the people could not advance up to the palace.

The officials complied with this request and appointed one *banderensis* [district governor] as captain, who selected four citizens as constables. They all swore solemnly to protect the cardinals effectively and efficiently and to preserve them from all violence. But actually these officials kept none of their promises.

Thus, when the cardinals were about to go into the conclave they had difficulty in entering the palace, because the square in front of it was thronged with people, many of whom were armed. Moreover, a huge crowd entered the palace together with the cardinals, and the doors had to be kept open throughout the night, because the crowd would not allow them to be shut. The whole palace was surrounded by armed men, so that nobody could go in or out without the mob's permission. All left the palace, except the senator and a few individuals, and the cardinals requested him to lock the doors so as to prevent anyone getting in. The district governors and officials, however, pressed to be admitted into the conclave. They repeated their request, when it was made clear to them that their entry into the conclave would be quite unusual, especially at such a late hour. Fearing that the doors might be broken open and that they themselves would be in grave danger, the cardinals permitted the entry of the governors. As soon as they had entered, they repeated the request that a Roman or at least an Italian be elected, otherwise the cardinals would be in great peril. The cardinals had heard from trustworthy persons that there were some prelates in the city, partly Romans, partly Italians, who incited the population and promised them money in case of their election. At the time of Gregory's death there were sixteen cardinals at Rome, of whom twelve were ultramontane, and only four Italian. The ultramontane cardinals had a two-thirds majority and, as soon as the vacancy had occurred, had decided to elect one of the College and a non-Italian, until they had been subjected to the pressure to be described later. The Italians, though desirous to elect one of the College, suggested one of their own nationality. After the entry into the conclave there was no change of mind until the next morning, when they all said mass according to tradition—all this regardless of the fact that the Romans, in contradiction to the old custom, refused to allow the bricking up of the door of the conclave. Only after the cardinals had gone to bed was it possible for the guards to put a beam across the door of the conclave. The crowd, however, occupied the palace, particularly that part which lay under the conclave, and caused great noise throughout the night, clashing their arms and shouting all the time: "Romano lo volemo o Italiano [we want a Roman or an Italian]." Some are reported to have heard the cry, "Moriantur [let them die]." All this commotion continued until next morning, so that the cardinals could find little sleep. Tired out by their continued shouting, the crowds abstained for a little while, but the clamouring started again while the cardinals were saying their masses, so that one could hardly hear or understand the words of the mass. Just when the cardinals were about to begin the election, the bells of the capitol and of St. Peter's began to ring, as if to summon the people, and immediately afterwards the cries, "Romano lo volemo o al manco Italiano [we want a Roman or at least an Italian]," became more furious than ever before. The cardinals were advised by some of the guards (some of whom were ultramontane, and some Romans) immediately to elect a Roman or an Italian, if they wanted to safeguard their own lives. For this reason the ultramontane cardinals condescended to the election of an Italian, only in order to escape the danger of death, as they then declared—in no other circumstances would they have agreed to it. Moreover, some of the Italian cardinals declared that, if they happened to be elected, they would not accept the election, because of the obvious pressure. Since they all were anxious to escape danger, they hastily nominated the Archbishop of Bari without any discussion of his merits.

They immediately elected him pope, as he was well known to them and, they trusted, greatly experienced in the business and customs of the curia, though later experience plainly proved the belief erroneous. Some cardinals added that they elected him as true pope, but they did so only out of fear for their lives. An exception to this was an Italian cardinal who said that, because of the notorious intimidation, he would not give his vote for anyone, unless he were in a position to do so freely. An ultramontane cardinal declared that he had first voted for an Italian cardinal, but later in fear of death had cast his vote for the Archbishop of Bari. Another ultramontane cardinal though voting for the archbishop, did so protesting that the election was null and void, whilst a third ultramontane cardinal had declared before a notary and prior to the conclave that if he were to elect an Italian, he would do so only under pressure. Moreover, some cardinals said amongst themselves that they had the firm intention to go to a safe place as soon as possible, and to re-elect him [*sic!*] there anew. In the meanwhile the crowd made unmistakable signs that they were preparing to break open the conclave, and the cardinals did not dare to announce the result of the election to the masses, which had become seriously enraged. Instead, they sent out three cardinals, who told and promised the people that they would be comforted on the next day at the third hour with news of a Roman or an Italian pope. The cardinals asked the mob to withdraw. Only a few did so, whilst the great majority remained and even prevented food being brought to the cardinals for their lunch. They did not allow anyone to go in or out of the palace. In the meantime the cardinals had sent for some prelates, amongst whom was the Archbishop of Bari, the newly elected pope. When he arrived, he saw the disorderly state of the crowd and heard cries; as it was thought at the time, he had forebodings of his election, to which he tacitly agreed, and he quietened the crowd, so that the cardinals could receive their food. The crowd was somewhat calmer, though it still remained in the palace armed. Then the cardinals had their meal, after which all, except three cardinals, went to the palace chapel. After they had gathered there, an Italian cardinal said that the fury of the people had now abated and that they could now proceed to a re-election. But one of the ultramontane cardinals maintained the opposite view and said that the danger was now greater than before. Nevertheless, without informing the three absent cardinals, they proceeded to a re-election, but while still engaged in it, the crowd, incited by some officials, broke into the conclave with very great rage clamouring: "Per lo clavellato de Dio Romano lo volemo [By the nails of God, we want a Roman]," and smashed the whole conclave in pieces. The cardinals, hardly knowing if they were dead or alive, withdrew into a secret chapel of the palace, but its door was forced and smashed. In surged the armed crowd and surrounded the cardinals. They believed that all, or at least the ultramontane cardinals, would have been slain, if one of them had not had the idea of announcing to the people that they had elected the Cardinal of St. Peter, who was alleged to have resisted election: they begged the people to induce him to accept. As soon as the crowd heard this, they rushed to the reluctant Cardinal of St. Peter and elevated him twice upon a throne. The cardinals took advantage of this scene: they slipped away as well as they could and hastened on foot to their private dwellings, some of them without hats or coats. Towards the evening some cardinals fled disguised into the castle of St. Angelo, others betook themselves outside the city, and others again remained in their own homes. Next morning, when the crowd had become quiet, the Archbishop of Bari, who had stayed behind in the Vatican, in spite of three demands made by the cardinals that he should leave the palace, sent for those staying in the castle or in their private quarters in order to avoid placing their lives in greater danger. First they all failed to comply with this request, but later they became tired of refusing, and the cardinals who were in the castle sent a note [*cedulla*] to the Archbishop of Bari, in which they agreed to his enthronement. Those who spent the night in their dwellings came to the palace. But he was displeased with the absence of the cardinals in the castle and again sent word to them that they should come to avoid still greater danger and trouble. Although still doubting the gravity of the threatened trouble, they went to the palace, because all their possessions and the members of their households were dispersed throughout the city; furthermore, the food situation in the castle was precarious, and the castle itself was not a particularly safe place. He was enthroned in the usual manner. Shortly after this ceremony those who had fled outside the city also returned, with a bad grace, but fearing that if they did not come, the Romans might suspect them of impugning the election, and might take reprisals against them. Then he was crowned by all cardinals.

From this time onwards the cardinals treated him as pope and paid homage to him, but never in the intention that he should be true pope. In consistories and in all ecclesiastical functions he acted as pope. Yet all this was within the city of Rome where the cardinals, especially the ultramontanes, never felt themselves secure. They believed that if they had cast any doubt on the election, they would all have been killed, since they were still under duress. For this very reason they did not even dare to confer with each other and to discuss this matter whilst in Rome. Since he did not want to leave the city in their company, nor to permit them to remove their residences from Rome, they were forced to withdraw one by one to Anagni, while he, almost alone went to Tivoli without a single cardinal.

69. Nicholas of Clémanges, *On the Ruin and the Repair of the Church* (ca. 1400)

As I picked up the Book of Holy Eloquence yesterday and began to read the first letter of Peter, which I first came across, I fell upon the words where the Apostle says: "The time is come that judgment must begin on the house of God."[1] These I did not skim as quickly as the other parts of the letter, but, checking my impulse to go on reading for a moment, compelled my mind, which had been shaken as if by a kind of sudden dread, to dwell on these words and to fasten them deeply and permanently in itself. In this context, the pressures and calamities which the Church is now enduring, and those even greater ones which, unless I am completely mistaken, it is still going to suffer, occurred to my quite horrified and upset mind.

At the same time the reasons why so many ills are well-deserved occurred to me. For all pollution with earthly desires must be struck from the ministers of the Church, whose dowry and possession should consist of Christ; and it befits those who treat, make, and confer celestial sacraments and the worthiest prize of human redemption upon others to be chaste, alien from all filth, and the wantonness of flesh; and they whose lot it is to represent as vicars the most pious judge should themselves be pious, as, who represent the justest, just, the humblest, humble, and who ought to be the agents and the mediators of peace and harmony between God and men, harmonious and pacific; and it is becoming, finally, for those who are set up as mirrors and ought to provide others with a pattern and an exemplar of life, to shine with all the light of virtue. If, instead by these and other virtues with which they ought to be adorned, they are contaminated by the welter of all vices, what wonder after all if many adversities happen to them, or if God, turned away from them because of the enormity of their misdeeds, should say in the words of the Psalmist: "I have hated the Church of evildoers."[2] So as to list in glancing a few of these ministers' vices, for which they rightfully deserve to be afflicted and punished by an irate God, let us begin with cupidity, which is the touchstone and root of all evils.

From Nicholas de Clémanges, *De ruina ecclesiae* in *Le traité de la ruine de l'église de Nicolas de Clémanges* (Paris, 1936), chaps. 1–4, 9–12, 20–21, 25, 37, 46–48. Translated for this volume by Constantin Fasolt.

1. 1 Pet. 4:17.   2. Ps. 26:5.

On the Cause of the Original Foundation and Endowment of Churches and Monasteries

There is no one, I believe, who has not heard enough about, and keeps in mind, how much the ministers of the Church of Christ, most famous men and proved in every virtue, who should be honored with deserved praise at every time, despised terrestrial affluence, how much they neither cared nor labored for temporal advantages, more than satisfied with only food and clothing and what pertains to them. "Having food and raiment," said the Apostle, "therewith we are content."[3] How liberally they cared to spend their private property, if a rather ample one perhaps had fallen to their lot from somewhere else, in order to alleviate the hunger of the poor. These most devout men, who carried only meditation on celestial matters in their hearts, assuredly were afraid that, if they were to set their feelings more abundantly on the embrace of transitory things, their hearts would as much more be called away from spiritual contemplation, to which they had completely devoted themselves, and as much less be carried towards God, as they would be bent on caring and thinking about inferior things, although imbued with words of heaven. "One cannot serve God and Mammon at the same time."[4] But divine grace brought it about that, the more they spurned temporal pride or glory, the more abundantly it flowed to them from everywhere, just like a shadow runs away from its pursuer, but always follows like a tireless companion, wherever one may run away.

For secular people, princes as well as other wealthy men, who saw the holy and straightforward conduct of the men of God, from which the fire of divine love had smelted all earthly dross, strove everywhere to heap most ample goods upon them, although against their will, in order that, absolved from every care, they would be able to exert the fervor of devotion more freely without interruption, esteeming themselves fortunate if they had contributed any of their wealth to uses of such kind, or if these devout and god-deserving men deigned to accept from them such wealth, and, for the expiation of their sins, to intercede with divine clemency.

The Church was thus augmented and adorned by many splendid gifts and magnificent wealth, thus monasteries were founded, convents instituted, chapters and colleges set up, thus came into existence bishops' sees and parishes, thus temples, thus most beautiful cathedrals were constructed, with vast expenditures and wondrous effort, at the cost of princes and the people. Thus, finally, all ranks, and everyone of the professions, and of the soldiers of the Church grew into most abundant wealth, which those origi-

3. 1 Tim. 6:8.   4. Matt. 6:24; Luke 16:13.

nal fathers, who had obtained it through their virtues, did not consume for profane purposes, as most of them are doing now, but either spent on alms and hospitality and other works of charity and piety, or turned, if anyone was still left over for such works and for their frugal table, to the construction of new cells, if other brothers, inspired by heaven, had perhaps arrived out of desire for religion, or to provide such other things as had to be provided. They had no other treasure than good works, but that was very large and densely packed. No drink was taken from a silver vessel, nor from a golden one, but from pottery and earthenware. No show of great horses and decorated bridles, no crowd of clowns walking in front, no retinue of youths with curled and well-kempt hair, dressed in striped habits bearing images of monsters, with wide sleeves flowing to the ground, almost according to barbarian style.

With such inhabitants the world was blessed, cities and country full of people whom no, or scarcely any, plagues carried away, stables were full of cattle, farm animals teeming with young, trees full of fruit, crops rich in grain since heaven's temperate climate, too, was bent on making the earth fertile for every proper shoot. And the earth, subjected to no curse, but by the intervention of such things endowed with copious blessings, produced all goods almost spontaneously. People lived long, and enjoyed prosperous health. There was no rebellion at home, no fear abroad, all was peaceful, safe, and calm. There flourished in the people of that age charity, innocence, faith, piety, justice, honest friendship, and hardly any harm or calumny happened to neighbors, since in the holy ways and healthy doctrine of their pastors examples of every kind of good were shining to be emulated by the flock. For so large was the power of such men with God, out of the soundness of their lives, that through their intercession the world obtained most copious goods, and felt few adversities.

How Insolence Arose in the Church from Affluence in Temporal Goods

But when, as usually is the custom, little by little from wealth and affluence in secondary things, inconstancy and insolence entered the Church, when religion started slowly to grow cold, virtue to grow faint, discipline to be relaxed, charity to be diminished, humility to be abolished, and poverty, just like frugality, to be accounted a shame, then avarice began to grow, so that the wherewithal might be available for pomp and luxury, and, not content with its domain for long, began not merely to solicit others' property, but to rob and to attack, oppress the lower people and despoil them, right or wrong. And since we have now entered on this most extensive field, I want to talk a little more extensively about this execrable pest, which has consumed the Church so much already that there is very little left to be consumed. But we can best begin by quoting the prophetic oracle, and with the holy Prophet Jeremiah, who says most truly of our ministers today: "From the least of them even unto the greatest of them every one is given to covetousness; and from the prophet even unto the priest every one dealeth falsely."[5] For how can we say enough of their insatiable avarice, which seems to overwhelm the greed of any layman merchant, and which indeed provokes and stimulates all secular people, whether princes or simple folk, to every injustice, malice, fraud, or robbery, since simple-minded little sheep imitate the examples of their pastors, and think that what they see them do is allowed to them as well. But, to go on with our inspection of the origin and progress of this wicked pest from the top of the head to the bottom of the feet, when, as I already had begun to say, from opulence an eagerness for temporal things had begun to occupy the minds of God's servants, they could no longer equally serve two such opposed lords as God and Mammon.[6] In consequence they had to take away as much attention from the one as they devoted to the service of the other. The more they fixed their hearts on temporal gain, however, the more they began to thirst for it, the more to be immersed in it, and the further thus to turn away from celestial love.

For we know wealth's nature to be such that the more one has of it, the more one is wont to be inflamed with the desire forever to increase it. This is how it therefore slowly happened that the spirit was extinguished in their hearts, that charity grew cold, devotion became lukewarm, God was forgotten, and that they longed only to snatch up temporal fruits and to measure their advantages in dignities and other benefits. Today, when pastoral responsibilities are taken up, and when the care of souls is undertaken, there is no mention whatsoever of divine service, salvation of the subject flock, or of edification; one only asks about the richness and the size of revenues. One does not ask what the value of a benefice is for a *man*, for one who properly performs the ceremonies in the Church, but what it returns in annual profit to its *owner*, who may be idling far away, perhaps remaining there forever. Who nowadays makes application for a benefice— for none is given, regardless of merit, without an urgent and persistent application—who, I say, is the petitioner who has found out which saint is being worshipped in the Church that he is seeking to obtain, which gifts of saints there are, which shrines, which relics? Who asks about the nature of the people over whom he wishes to be put in charge, about their morals or their vices? Who wants a monastery, and questions the observance of the rule in it, the tenor of religion, the cult of ceremonies, and the subjects'

5. Jer. 6:13.   6. Matt. 6:24; Luke 16:13.

discipline? Who weighs the power of his shoulders, if he be strong enough to bear the burden under which he seeks to place himself? Who considers his perils or those of his subjects? Who preaches or brings the Gospel to them? Who shows in deed or word the way by which they reach salvation? Which prelate does not, on the contrary, today despoil his subjects everywhere, whichever way he can? Who among them pities dearth, is compassionate with poverty, provides relief for indigence, and does not on the contrary increase their indigence by right or wrong? So as to demonstrate that this is really how things are, from the very summit of the Church down to its humblest members, we shall, if there is no objection, first inspect the head, from which the rest depends.

On the Three Vices from Which the Other Evils Arose in the Church

When an overflowing abundance of worldly things and immense avarice had entered the hearts of ecclesiastical men with blind ambition, and when the virtues of the fathers had been put behind, this was the consequence, that they began to be elated by the pride of glory and of domination, and to be weakened by effeminate luxury, and therefore had to satisfy three lords, without a doubt most violent exactors: Luxury, which demanded the delights of wine, sleep, banquets, music, games, effeminate procurers, and prostitutes; Pride, which required lofty houses, castles, citadels, palaces, sumptuous and abundant furniture, and the ceremonious display of the most expensive clothes and private horses; and Cupidity, which diligently stored enormous treasures to carry out the things just mentioned, or, if they had been sufficiently procured from other sources, at least feasted the eyes with the delight of vainly looking at the figure of their coin. Without a doubt, to execute the mandates of these insatiable lords and to perfect their golden needs, the age of Saturn, as in the fables, would hardly seem to be enough, if at this time it were to come back to the world. Because, therefore, to do what these three grasping harpies were demanding, no office of the Church, howevermuch the best and filled with revenues, is known to have sufficient wealth, subsidiary means have been contrived, so that they might be satisfied from other sources.

On the Exorbitances Introduced into the Church
by the Supreme Pontiffs

For when the supreme pontiffs (in order finally to turn to them, who saw by how much they surpassed the rest in primacy and authority, and raised themselves, by reason of such primacy and highest power, but mostly out of lust of domination, that much above the others) determined that the profits of the Roman bishopric and that St. Peter's patrimony, which is most ample over all kingdoms, although it has already been somewhat attenuated by their sloth, would not suffice in any way for the eminence of their state, which they decreed to raise to a lofty height above the emperors and kings of all nations, they attacked the sheep of others, their wool and copious milk.

On the Abolition of Elections and the Reservation of Benefices

They, in fact, attribute to themselves the rights and the bestowal of every vacant church, wherever in the world Christian religion spreads, of all the prelacies and other dignities, which used to happen by election. They decree about elections, which once were instituted by the holy fathers with so much vigilance and usefulness, that they are fruitless and invalid, in order to be able thus to fill their pouches even more, and to assemble for the employment of their Treasury from every province dedicated to the name of Christ an endless heap of gold and silver in zealous enterprise. . . .

On the Institution of Collectors and the Evils Inflicted by Them

In order to exact all of these burdens and to have them transported to that which I should call the Treasury, or rather the Charybdis, they set up their collectors in all the provinces, men, that is to say, whom they knew to be the most effective in extorting money, either through whatever industry, or by diligence, or by the harshness of their character, men who would not spare anyone at all, exempt no one, but even coax gold out of rocks. They would also grant them the authority to strike anyone, even prelates, with anathema, and to banish them from the communion of the faithful, if they did not take care to satisfy demands for money within a fixed number of days. It is, however, better to pass over how many evils these collectors did, and how much they oppressed poor churches and poor people, for fear of never finding an exit from that topic. Hence come so many grievances of the unhappy ministers of the Church, whom we have heard, and see groaning under an unbearable yoke, even perishing from hunger. Hence those suspensions of divine services, those interdicts from entering the temples, those most oppressive anathemas, heaped so often one upon the other, which used to be inflicted by the fathers only very rarely, and only for most horrible crimes, since man is after all by them excluded from the association of the faithful and reduced to Satan's power. But nowadays they have been so much cheapened that they are randomly imposed for every slightest fault, and often even none at all. And thus they are not only feared no longer, but have even come to be exceedingly despised. Hence afterwards so many churches thoroughly in ruins, so many monasteries destroyed, in so many places sacred buildings overthrown and levelled with the ground, while what used to be expended on restoring and repairing them is being spent on paying up so many taxes. And furthermore, as has been gathered from to whom the thing has really happened, in most churches sacrosanct relics, crosses, chalices, caskets, and other precious ornaments had to be sold to render all this tribute. Who does not know that funerals, that solemn obsequies and burials were denied so many abbots and so many other prelates, unless they were perhaps interred in fields or gardens, or in some other profane place in secret, because, when they departed from the Treasury, they were exposed to penury. We see that priests are being forced by shortage of their own possessions to leave their villages, their places, and their benefices, so as to keep on looking for the food to still their hunger, and to serve laymen in profane functions. So long as they were fat and fruitful, the churches carried these burdens for a while, but, since all of them have been exhausted by their long experience of being swindled, they really cannot bear them any longer.

On the Lawsuits of the Roman Curia

Aside from these, I must pass over many other things if I want to emerge from this abyss, that is, how much fraud is happening in the Roman Curia—for this is how they used to call it, although it is quite far away from Rome—how much deceit, and calumny, how many treacherous attacks upon the rights of innocents performed by those who have been bribed to stir up suits, how many judgments can be had there for a price, how great the strength of gold there is to upset justice. How rarely does a poor man carry home the verdict he desired for his trial, if he has met a wealthy adversary, although so very few obtain a benefice at all without a trial and adversary, regardless on which title they may base their claim.

On the Rules and Institutions of the Chancellery

For what are all of these new rules and constitutions published by each pontiff, and prescribed to be observed, besides the ancient laws and sanctions of the fathers, if not some captious snares providing most abundant matter for lawsuits which those quibbling curial officials and sophistical perverters of the laws use as a thousand methods to do damage, in order to provoke unending suits against the law and truth, so that hardly anyone is to be found who, even if he showed a title clearer than the sun, has obtained a benefice without dispute.

On the Prosperity of the Roman Curia

For they affirm that thus their Curia is flourishing and blessed, if it is able to exult at the demented roar arising on all sides from many cases, lawsuits, protests, and disputes, but, on the other hand, that it is useless, deserted, and destitute when it is void of lawsuits, when it enjoys peace, when rights are peacefully surrendered to their owners. Today, therefore, it makes no difference at all, or only very little, on which condition someone holds his benefice, whether he enters by the proper door like a true shepherd, or whether he deceitfully breaks in from elsewhere like a thief.[7] If, therefore, some intelligent investigator could by a clear criterion make out the numbers of both kinds, I have no doubt it would be found that in the Church more thieves are now about than are true pastors, so that Christ's sentence would already be fulfilled in which he told the money changers whom he had cast out of his house: "My house shall be the house of prayer; but ye have made it a den of thieves."[8]

On the Vices of Prelates

But look, while I have not been paying attention, I went beyond the limits of the Roman Curia's very own, and have descended to those vices which are also shared by prelates among others. But since the topic has come up, I want to give a more detailed, yet brief account of it. To start with, it must seem to no one either strange or wonderful if our prelates stay up late to rake together money from all over with the greatest effort; if meager, frail, and drained of sap, they concentrate on fattening themselves off their sheeps' wool and milk, whose pastors they became at such great cost. For, as the proverb has it, gnats who are worn out by leanness bite more viciously. Also all animals who are deprived of food bear down more eagerly upon their prey. For even though, before they undertook the pastoral care, they might have been extremely well-to-do, since, as a rule, the indigent are not admitted to this kind of work, nevertheless, the ministry conferred on them required that their money-chests be emptied of at least the greatest portion, wherefore they, on their part, alike proceed with utmost industry, not undeservedly, to follow the example of a wise farmer and gather with increase the seeds tossed from an ample yield, or in the manner of most watchful merchants attentively display their wares for sale to all who need them, so that they can accordingly recover their diminished wealth and zealously augment it. If any cleric should be thrown in prison at their court

---

7. Cf. John 10:1.   8. Matt. 21:13.

for theft, for murder, rape, or sacrilege, or any other monstrous crime, and be sentenced to feed on bitter bread and water, he will be subject to the penalty, and like a culprit suffer for his deeds, until he pays in due proportion a tax, or money which he obtained from his relations. But as soon as he does that, he is allowed to walk away a free man, like an innocent. By money every misconduct, every error, all the crimes, even capital ones, can be reduced and wiped away. What shall I say, moreover, about the practice of their jurisdiction, which is directed with such violence, and so tyrannically, that people nowadays will rather choose to undergo the judgment of most savage tyrants than of the Church?

On the Promoters of Episcopal Jurisdiction and Their Abuses

It is impossible to say how many evil deeds those heinous criminal investigators who are called promoters everywhere commit. They often call to court for nothing the simple, hapless countryfolk, who in their huts lead harmless lives, quite unaware of urban trickery. They diligently fabricate claims and crimes against them, harry, detain, and threaten them, and by such means force them to settle, and reach a compromise with them. If they refuse to do so, they excessively harass them with frequent summons, repeated every day. And if just once, prevented by some reason, they fail to show in court, they are punished with anathema for rebellion and contumacy. But if they persevere in being there on the appointed day, however many times they have been called, they will impede their hearings before the judges' benches, try to procure delays and, by subterfuge, adjournments and judicial orders, which are quite easily obtained in ecclesiastical courts, so that, worn out by either constant tedium or by the constant sacrifice of their own time, they will be forced to enter an agreement to buy off future harassment and expenditure of money. Thus it happens that from a slight offense, or even none at all, that from a trivial debt a mound of infinite expenses grows, before one is allowed to go away, free and acquitted by the court. . . .

On the Perpetual Absence of Prelates from Their Churches

I now come back to our bishops, who have been reared on every slipperiness from the beginning of their youth and introduce these pests (not to refer to them as ministers) into the Church.[9] Among their deeds there are some memorable ones. This one I must not fail to mention, namely, that many of them, who have obtained the pastoral mitre, and have been hold-

9. The author has been discussing episcopal appointments of unworthy priests.

ing it for many, many years, have never entered their cities, seen their churches, visited their places or dioceses, never recognized the faces of their flock, heard their voices, or felt their wounds, unless perhaps through foreign mercenaries they themselves brought on those wounds by whipping them and skinning them. Therefore they are no bishops, if only in an empty word, because what that word really means has nothing much to do with them. For "bishop" means a watchman, or an overseer. "I have made thee a watchman unto the house of Israel" said the Prophet.[10] But these assuredly do not oversee any sheep at all, watch nothing, and look out for nothing. They exercise the care of their own bodies, feed themselves and not their sheep, not thinking it especially important if any accident should happen to the sheep, if they should die, consumed by illness or starvation, so long at any rate as they themselves can profit from their death. . . .

Comparison of the Customs of Our Contemporaries with Those of the Fathers of Old

Now go and compare this manner of life, these customs, and this kind of conduct with the fathers' original discipline, with our ancestors' charity, their continence, sobriety, and strict austerity. Unless you are blinder than a mole, you will see that they are as far apart as weld and gold, for after having bit by bit been sliding from the golden head of that enormous statue which Nebuchadnezzar saw in a dream, through silver, brass, and iron down to an ever worse condition, we have at last in these our days, to which the dregs of centuries have sunk, come to the section of the feet of mud and clay.[11] . . .

That the Schism Was the Beginning of the Church's Desolation

This schism is indeed quite similar to the one which, after King Solomon's death, God's vengeance brought into existence between Juda and Israel, Roboam and Jeroboam. For just as in the division of that kingdom ten tribes of Israel's sons passed over to the party of Jeroboam, who was a foreigner and usurped the scepter, and hardly two tribes, on the other hand, remained for Roboam, so also in this schism of the Church of twelve parts of the catholic people, if it were divided into twelve parts, barely two parts have followed the true pontiff, and all the rest the pseudo-pontiff, who intruded on the see by force, sedition, and a tumult of the people.[12] In brief,

---

10. Ezek. 3:17.   11. Cf. Dan. 2:31–45.

12. Nicholas of Clémanges is here giving expression to his conviction that the Avignonese pope Benedict XIII, who was appointed in 1394, deposed in 1409, and died in 1423, represented the true papacy.

just as that schism lasted through a succession of many times and many kings, accompanied by infinite disasters, down to Jerusalem's destruction and the captivity of the people, who were hunted by the Babylonian king, so there is reason to be thoroughly afraid that this pestiferous division will continue in the Church, which has been shaken by so many daily evils, until at last it will be robbed and captured by some Babylonian or Mahometan prince, whoever he will be. Some men, indeed, who were some while ago, it is believed, divinely instigated to predict much about this schism and, because of it, the Church's future desolation, these men are now supposing that a most horrible oppression and unimaginable devastation will originate for the whole Church out of this schism through the violence of the earthly Empire, many of the rights of which the Church has taken for itself. The Church, which had devoured the goods of others, will vomit what has not been properly digested, will be denuded of terrestrial possessions, and will lament that many sons of fornication, whom it has brought into existence, in part because of the relentless pressure of the princes, in part through most improper trade, will be oppressed by death, flight, exile, hunger, and captivity. Perhaps this persecution will bear down on our necks more speedily than most believe. For, if we have not been blinded, we already see its great foundations being laid, of which no one who has a little understanding would not be able to perceive that more and more they daily rise above the ground, and any moment now will burst into broad daylight.

That the Church Must be Crushed Because of Its Abominations and Great Madness

So great a flood of evils must assuredly be crushed and utterly destroyed by God's most righteous judgment. It has grown to such insanity in all abominations that it does not seem possible in any other way to chasten it, or to restore it to its former innocence. Countless signs, admonishments, threats, reproaches, disasters, words, and plagues have gone before which called upon it to return to sanity, so that it would not imminently suffer punishment. But nothing was achieved by all of that, since on the contrary it was all worn away without effect. "The founder melteth in vain," the Prophet said, "for their wickednesses are not plucked away." [13] For, with a face set obdurately against God, they scorned all signs, and with ever more rapid impetus, like an unbridled horse, ran for their lusts.

---

13. Jer. 6:29. The Latin text omits the "not."

Whether the Church Will Flourish and Bear Fruit. A Reform of Morals in Every State of the Church Is Announced

What method is thus left to you, oh Christ, if you dispose to free your Church from all this filth into which its silver and its gold have turned, except to throw all of the slag which cannot be again turned into gold or silver by any smelter's art, or any purgatory fire, out of the furnace of the Church, and to put metals shining with unsullied splendor into it once again. And if, besides, you wish to bring your barren vineyard, which is sealed off by wayward vines and thorny undergrowth which suffocates the shoots, back to its natural condition, what better way to do so than tear out the roots of useless plants which make it unproductive, which sprout again if they are merely cut off with a sickle, to lease the vineyard to other workers, and plant it again with new and fertile shoots. For, as you yourself have testified, "grapes are not gathered of thorns, or figs of thistles," but you established that a "tree that bringeth not forth good fruit is hewn down and cast into the fire." [14] Whoever thinks the Church's troubles and its pains are ending with these ills which we already suffer, therefore deceives himself. These are only feeble presages of pains, and just a pleasant overture for that which is to follow. But it has long been time to steer towards the harbor, because the storm is bearing down on us already, and to take thought for our salvation in these dangers, or else so great a force of gales will shake the mangled boat of Peter with more violent blows of whirling wind than at any other time, as to submerge on the high seas ourselves along with those who will go under in deserved shipwreck.

The Author's Devout Prayer for the Salutary Fruit of Reformation

At the conclusion of this little work, which is already being stretched out to a rather long extent, we pray to you, most gentle Jesus, suppliantly for one thing only: that, regardless what your judgments on the Church will be— for great ones there will be without a doubt—you will not issue them with the severity of vengeance according to the measure of the Church's sins, and not make retribution as the degree of its iniquities, which merit boundless anger, demands, but in proportion to your clemency's inexplicable mildness, and, in exacting punishment, that you will deign to treat it with a piety which it has not deserved. Thus cut away what is injurious and in excess, so that you will not simultaneously destroy even the little which is not wholly without use. In such a manner, therefore, exercise your power that you will not annihilate it totally; in such a manner castigate that you

---

14. Matt. 7:16.

will not extinguish it; at least, so that it will not be like Sodom or Gomorrah, spare it a little seed, mindful of your most sacred word, by which you promised it would be with you all days until the consummation of the world. Thanks be to God.

Black Death and Social Dislocations

One sudden, catastrophic event permanently transformed all aspects of life—including Church order—at the middle of the fourteenth century. A combination of plague strains, the Black Death devastated Europe from 1347 to 1351, killed an estimated 25 to 45 percent of Europe's population, and effected or accelerated political, social, and economic change. Originating in Asia, the plague first appeared in Europe in October 1347 at the Sicilian port of Messina. It traveled up the Italian peninsula, reached Florence in the winter of 1348, and left in its wake about 50,000 Florentines dead. The Florentine chronicler Matteo Villani, a close and pessimistic observer of his times, provides a detailed description of a city devastated by the Black Death (document 70). His brother Giovanni died in 1348 and Matteo himself fell victim to the plague when it recurred in 1363. The ravages wrought by the plague in France are related by the French Carmelite, Jean de Venette, in his chronicle (document 71).

The first shock wave of the Black Death depopulated vast regions of Europe. Population growth that had lasted from 1000 to 1300 gave way to chronic population loss that lasted for more than a century. Periodic recurrences of the plague prevented Europe from reaching its preplague population until the sixteenth century. The adverse effects of plague were reinforced by continual war in France, civil strife in Spain and Germany, and the havoc caused by marauding bands of discharged soldiers. Yet, given the chronic condition of overpopulation that had cramped Europe in the early fourteenth century, resulting in a decline of economic growth and standard of living, many modern historians—from a distance of 600 years—have been led to view the Black Death as a blessing in disguise. There was a rise in the standard of living as the wages of workers, especially skilled craftsmen, soared during and after 1348, while prices for shelter, food, and clothing remained relatively stable. The promise of a high standard of living and civic privileges offered by towns to attract peasants contributed to the abandonment of rural villages and manors (document 72). In the absence of traditionally high food prices and cheap labor, rural lords were now forced to offer peasants attractive wages, better terms of land tenure, and commutation of their obligations. Attempts to limit the wages of workers and to reintroduce manorial obligations threatened the relatively higher standard of living that workers and peasants enjoyed after 1348, and thus provoked a violent reaction. In 1358 the peasantry in northern France, aided by townsmen, took up arms against their lords. In 1378 the workers in Florence's wool industry rose up against their masters. And in 1381 the peasants in eastern England revolted against their rulers (document 73). If these uprisings did little to alter basic economic and social relationships, they remain symptomatic of the unsettled political and social conditions characterizing the postplague period.

Although the long-term effects of the Black Death upon religious institutions and conduct are difficult to measure, there is no question that churches, monasteries, confraternities, and hospitals everywhere benefited from an unprecedented number of pious legacies. At the same time, the revenues of Europe's greatest landlord, the Church, declined. Further, the death toll among the monastic and mendicant orders was disproportionately higher than among the laity. The plague swept away 83 of the 130 Dominicans attached to the convent of Santa Maria Novella in Florence. At Montpellier only seven of the town's 140 Dominicans survived. And it has been estimated that in England the monastic population plummeted about 50 percent. Attracting able and educated recruits to minister to the spiritual needs of the laity as well as to administer the Church became one of the most pressing problems of the day. Reverberations of this catastrophe—moral, psychological, and institutional—were part of the call for reform that was so persistent an aspect of the Babylonian Captivity and the Great Schism.

---

70. Matteo Villani, *Description of Plague in Florence* (1348)

On the Unprecedented Death

We can read in the Holy Scriptures that when sin had corrupted every branch of human flesh, God sent the Flood over the earth, in his mercy sparing mankind in eight souls—Noah, his three sons, and their wives—in the Ark, and all the rest he submerged in the Deluge. Afterward, as men multiplied through the ages, there were a good many particular floods, deaths, corruptions and pestilences, famines, and many other ills, which

From *Matteo Villani, Cronica*, edited by F. G. Dragomanni (Florence, 1846). Translated for this volume by Lydia G. Cochrane.

God permitted to come upon men because of their sins. One of the worst of these epidemics came during the reigns of the emperors Marcus Aurelius and Antoninus or Lucius Aurelius Commodus, around the year of Christ 171. It began in Egyptian Babylonia, and it struck many parts of the world. When Lucius Commodus[1] returned from Asia with his Roman legions, it appears that he fought with particular ferocity against the men of the provinces through which they passed because they were infected and in Rome [the disease] wiped out a great many of the city's inhabitants. The other [epidemic] occurred in the age of the emperor Gallus Hostilianus and his son Bolussenus,[2] who occupied the Empire and bitterly persecuted the Christians. It began around the year of Christ 254, and, returning intermittently, it lasted around fifteen years, bringing incredible illnesses of various sorts to many parts of the world. As far as can be found in written records, however, there has been no more widespread judgment by mortal illness from the universal Deluge to the present, nor one that embraced more of the universe, than the one that has occurred in our own day. According to the opinion of many scholars, [if we] calculate the population living at the time of this recent mortality and compare it to the number of people living at the time of the universal Deluge, [we can see that] a great many more died in our own age than at that earlier date. Since the author of the chronicle entitled *The Chronicle of Giovanni Villani*, citizen of Florence (to whom I was closely related by both blood and affection)[3] rendered up his soul to God in that recent death, I took it into my mind, after experiencing many serious misfortunes and acquiring much more knowledge of the world's calamities than of the prosperity he wrote about, to consider the varied and calamitous events of our time as the begining of a new age and epoch, setting down each year's noteworthy events, as far as my feeble intelligence permits, as a way of making the most faithful possible record for future times.

How Long the Plague Lasted in Each Land

Having decided to begin my history with an account of the extermination of humankind, and realizing that we need to consider its ages and manners of being—its quality and its quantity—my mind reels as I prepare to write of the sentence that divine justice, in its infinite mercy, meted out to

1. Emperor from A.D. 180 to 192.

2. Whether owing to misinformation or scribal error, Villani probably meant the Emperor Gallienus (253–68) and his son Cornelius Valerianus.

3. Giovanni Villani (ca. 1276–1348) was Matteo's brother. Matteo's chronicle was a continuation of Giovanni's chronicle of Florence which achieved an instant success.

men, deserving of final judgment by the corruption of sin. But on thinking that this account might be useful for the salvation of nations who will come after us, I take heart and begin in this manner.

In the year of Christ's Incarnation for our salvation 1346, a conjunction of three large planets was visible in the sign of Aquarius; and according to the astrologists, Saturn was dominant in this conjunction. From this they predicted great and grave events to come in the world. But a similar conjunction had occurred and been documented many times in the past; so the influence it may have had over other particular events did not seem to be the cause of this one, but rather divine judgment decreed by the absolute will of God. There arose, in the year mentioned, and in the parts of the Orient that lie closest to Cathay and northern India and in the ports and other provinces surrounding the coastal ones, a pestilence [that struck] men of all conditions and ages and both sexes. They began to spit blood and to die, some immediately, some within two or three days, though a good many took longer to die. And it happened that those who served these sick people, catching that sickness or infected with that same corruption, immediately became sick and died in a similar manner. Most of them had a swelling in the groin, many had swellings in their armpits, right and left, and others had swellings in other parts of their bodies; in almost every instance some singular swelling was evident in the infected body. This pestilence came intermittently, and passing from one nation to the next, before the end of one year, it had struck all of that third part of the world that is called Asia. Toward the end of this time, it reached the nations of the Great Sea [the Mediterranean], the shores of the Tyrrhenian Sea, Syria and Turkey, down into Egypt and to the shores of the Red Sea and, to the North, to Russia and Greece, Armenia, and the other nearby countries.

During that time, Italian galleys were departing from the Great Sea and from Syria and from Rumania to flee death and carry their merchandise to Italy. But they could not escape having a great many [of their crews] die at sea of that same sickness. When they arrived in Sicily, they had concourse with the natives there and left their sick among them, after which the pestilence immediately began among the Sicilians. Then, when these galleys came to Pisa and then to Genoa, this deadly sickness took hold in those places, through contact with those men; but it was not widespread. Then, in accordance with the time God had ordained for each land, Sicily was totally enveloped by this mortal pestilence. Next, the ports of Africa and its eastern provinces, and then the shores of our own Tyrrhenian Sea. And moving little by little westward, it reached Sardinia and Corsica and the other islands of this sea. On the other side, which is called Europe, it reached in like manner the nearby lands to the West, attacking the south more fiercely than the northern parts.

In the year of Christ 1348 [the plague] had infected all of Italy except
the city of Milan and some cities near the Alps, which divide Italy from
Germany, where it had little hold. And in this same year it began to pass
over the mountains and spread into Provence, Savoy, the Dauphiné, and
Burgundy, in the ports of Marseille and Aigues-Mortes, in Catalonia, on
the island of Majorca, and in Spain and in Grenada. By 1349[4] it had extended all the way west to the shores of the Oceanic Sea of Europe, to the
shores of Africa, Ireland, the island of England and Scotland and the other
islands of the West, and all the lands between with an almost equal deadly
force—except for Brabant, where it did little harm. In 1350 it crushed the
Alamans, the Hungarians, the Frisians, the Danes, the Goths, the Vandals,
and the other peoples of the northern nations. In the lands where it took
hold, it lasted five successive months or five moons: we have this on the
sure reports from many countries.

Since this pestilent infection seemed to spread by sight or by touch, it
happened that when a man, woman, or child was found to be sick with
these swellings, many abandoned them, and enormous numbers of people
died who would have survived if their needs had been taken care of. An
inhuman cruelty arose, beginning among the infidels, mothers and fathers
abandoning their children and the children their mothers and fathers, or
brothers or other kin—a cruel and astonishing thing, quite foreign to human nature and detestable to faithful Christians, yet found among them, in
imitation of the barbarous nations. When [the pestilence] arose in our city
of Florence, wiser men condemned the many people who looked out [only]
for themselves and closed themselves up in isolated places, where the air
was healthy, where they had all sorts of good things to live on, and where
there was not the slightest trace of infection. In several places, however,
divine judgment (to which no one can bar his door) struck them down just
like those who took no such precautions. And many others, who resigned
themselves to death so that they could serve their stricken relations and
friends, were sick but lived through it; and a good many people did not
catch the infection at all, while they continued to serve others. This made
people see the error of their ways; and they began to help and serve one
another without fear, so that many recovered, and in recovering were more
secure in serving the others.

In our city, [the pestilence] became widespread at the begining of the
month of April in the year of our Lord 1348, and it lasted until the beginning of the month of September of the same year. And in the city, the *contado*, and the district of Florence three out of five persons or more died, of
both sexes and all ages, among the lowly, the middling, and the great alike,

---

4. The text reads "1339."

because some were more sorely stricken, or because it began sooner, or because they were unaided and suffered more discomfort and distress.

Throughout the entire world, the human race lost like numbers and in like fashion, according to the information we had from many foreign lands and many parts of the world. There were in fact provinces of the Levant where even more died. Doctors in every part of the world had no theory that could explain this pestiferous infirmity, either in natural philosophy, in physic, or in the art of astrology, and they [could devise] no cure for it. A good many of them went around visiting [the sick] to make money and discussed their theories, which they proved to be false and fictitious by their own death. A number of them, conscience-stricken, left wills returning their ill-gotten gains.

We heard from Genoese merchants, trustworthy men, who had received information from those lands, that some time before this pestilence somewhere in upper Asia there either emerged from the earth or fell from the skies a great fire, a fire which spread westward, consuming a vast land and offering no refuge. And a good many people said that the smell of this fire generated the corruptible matter of the general pestilence. But this we cannot ascertain. . . .

71. Jean de Venette, *Description of Famine, War and Plague in France* (1315–1349)

1340

Let anyone who wishes to be reminded of most of the noteworthy events which happened in the kingdom of France from 1340 on read this present work in which I, a friar at Paris, have written them down briefly, in great measure as I have seen and heard them. I shall begin with some hitherto unknown prognostications or prophecies which have come to hand. What they mean is not altogether known. Whether they speak truth or not I do not say but leave to the decision of the reader. This is one such. A priest of the diocese of Tours, freed in A.D. 1309 from the hands of the Saracens, who had held him captive for the space of thirteen years and three months, was saying mass in Bethlehem where the Lord was born. While he was praying for all Christian people in the Secret of the Mass, there appeared to him letters of gold written in this wise:

From *The Chronicle of Jean de Venette*, edited by Richard A. Newhall and translated by Jean Birdsall (New York: Columbia University Press, 1953), pp. 31–34, 48–52. All footnotes deleted. © 1953 by Columbia University Press. Reprinted by permission of the publisher.

In the year of the Lord 1315, on the fifteenth day of the month of March, shall begin so great a famine on earth that the people of low degree shall strive and struggle against the mighty and rich of this world. Also the wreath of the mightiest boxer shall fall to the ground very quickly afterwards. Also its flowers and its branches shall be broken and crushed. Also a noble and free city shall be seized and taken by slaves. Also strangers shall dwell there. Also the Church shall totter and the line of Saint Peter shall be execrated. Also the blood of many shall be poured out on the ground. Also a red cross shall appear and shall be lifted up. Therefore, good Christians, watch.

These are the words of this vision, but what they mean is not known.

Yet you must know that I, at the age of seven or eight, saw this great and mighty famine begin in the very year foretold, 1315. It was so severe in France that most of the population died of hunger and want. And this famine lasted two years and more, for it began in 1315 and ceased in 1318. Then, suddenly, by God's providence, crops became as abundant as they had been scarce and the famine ceased. Furthermore, women began to conceive more abundantly than before and gave birth to fair offspring. If any other items of the vision come to pass they will be noted hereafter.

Another prophecy is even more obscure.

The son reigning in the better part of the world shall be moved against the seed of the lion and shall stand in the field amid the thorns of the region. Then the son of man shall come, carrying wild beasts on his arm, whose kingdom is in the land of the moon, and with a great army he shall cross over the waters and enter the land of the lion who is in need of aid, since the beasts of his region have torn his hide. In that year shall come an eagle from the east, its wings extended in guile, with a great multitude of its eaglets, to the aid of the son of man. In that year castles shall be destroyed, a great terror shall be upon the people, and in the region of the lion there shall be a lily. Among many kings in that day there shall be a deluge of blood, and the lily shall lose its crown, wherewith afterward the son of man shall be crowned. For four years following, wars shall be waged in the world among the faithful; the greater part of the world shall be destroyed; the head of the world shall be brought down to the ground, but the son of man with the eagle shall prevail. Then there shall be peace and plenty throughout the world; then, wonderful sign, the son of man shall cross over to the land of promise, since all things promised of the first cause shall then be fulfilled.

These are the words of this prophecy which, it is said, Master Jean de Murs, a great astronomer in his time, composed. What it means I do not know, and many others share my ignorance. I shall insert another and clearer prophecy in its proper place below. Now, as I promised, I come to some of the noteworthy events, though not to all, which took place in the kingdom of France, and to a few which took place elsewhere, about A.D. 1340 and thereafter. I shall narrate them truthfully, as I saw them or heard about them.

About A.D. 1340, a comet appeared in Gaul between the south and the west. Its tail and rays extended toward the east and north. It is thought that this star was a presage of tribulations and wars to come in the kingdom. For about this time, in the twelfth year of the reign of Philip of Valois, son of Charles of Valois, count of Anjou, who was the brother of King Philip the Fair, Edward, king of England, became convinced that he and none other should reign in France, by reason of his mother Isabelle, daughter of King Philip the Fair. According to him there was no male heir to the French throne closer than he. For this reason he had before renounced his allegiance to Philip of Valois, king of France, although he had long before done homage for the lands which he had held and continued to hold in France. At this time he determined to make war on the kingdom of France and to cross over to France; this on the advice of Robert of Artois and of William, count of Hainaut, whose daughter King Edward had married. So at that time the king of England made alliances with John, duke of Brabant, with William, count of Hainaut, with many Germans, and also with the people of Flanders, who had driven their count, Louis, from the country and had unnaturally set up a certain burgess of Ghent, Jacques van Artevelde by name, a very eloquent man, to rule over them. Philip, king of the French, on learning that King Edward, with a large number of armed men, had embarked for France, sent [Nicholas] Behuchet, a burgess of Tours or Le Mans, with a great multitude of ships and fighting men to meet him at sea and to prevent his making port. At a naval battle begun before Sluys in Flanders near Cadzand, Behuchet, who bore himself bravely, was conquered with his men by the English and put to death. The Flemings who were helping the king of England, English nobles, and others were slain in large numbers by the French. Then the king of England came to Sluys and then, by further seafaring, to Antwerp in the duchy of Brabant.

At this time Philip, king of the French, seeing the Flemings in rebellion against their count and against the kingdom of France, begged the Church to lay an interdict on Flanders. And the Church did so. This interdict was very faithfully and obediently observed by all the clergy—to their great peril, because that Jacques, who was tyrannically ruling over all Flanders, endeavored to kill the clergy who obeyed the interdict. But God, the protector of the obedient, did not permit this.

The king of England with his army traversed Brabant, reached Thiérache, and headed for Guise, plundering, burning, and devastating French territory. Philip, king of the French, with a very large multitude of men-at-arms from Aquitaine, Brittany, and other parts of the kingdom, marched out to meet him as far as Buironfosse in Thiérache near Guise. There was no battle. On the contrary, a truce was arranged, and the king of England returned through Flanders to his own country and the king of France returned to Paris.

Shortly after this, Edward crossed the sea again and was again received by the Flemings. By their counsel, he took the title of king of France and of England and quartered the arms of England with those of France on his shield and elsewhere, to designate his new domain. While he was sojourning in Ghent, his wife, who had come pregnant from England, gave birth to a son, who, by his command, was baptized Lionel. His usurpation of the title of the king of France and of the arms of France was a source of no slight scandal and roused the indignation of the king of France and of many others, churchmen and laymen alike.

The king of England then asked Lewis, duke of Bavaria, at that time excommunicate and schismatic because of his usurpation of the Empire against the will of the Church, to make him his vicar in Hainaut and Cambrai. When he had obtained his request, he marched through Hainaut with the purpose of attacking Cambrai, whose bishop and citizens were bringing aid and comfort to the French king. The men of Cambrai sustained many injuries from the king of England and from the men of Hainaut, but they offered manful resistance. Then the cardinals sent by the pope into France to make peace imposed a truce upon the kings. So the king of England went back to Flanders, where he remained a long time, planning the invasion of France, which he carried out afterward, as shall be told. But first let us speak of some happenings at this time in various places.

Men were now beginning to wear disfiguring costumes. This was especially true of noblemen: knights, squires, and their followers, but it was true in some measure of burgesses and of almost all servants. Garments were short to the point of indecency, which was surprising in a people who had up to this time conducted themselves becomingly. Everyone also began to grow long beards. This fashion which nearly everyone in France, except those of the royal blood, adopted gave rise to no little mockery on the part of the common people. Men thus tricked out were more likely to flee in the face of the enemy, as the event afterwards many times proved.

In the same year Philip of Valois detained his sister, the wife of Robert of Artois, and her children in prison on her husband's account. He had been banished from France and had fled to England, where he remained, assisting the king of England in all the undertakings of his war against the king of the French.

1348

In A.D. 1348, the people of France and of almost the whole world were struck by a blow other than war. For in addition to the famine which I described in the beginning and to the wars which I described in the course of this narrative, pestilence and its attendant tribulations appeared again in various parts of the world. In the month of August, 1348, after Vespers when the sun was beginning to set, a big and very bright star appeared above Paris, toward the west. It did not seem, as stars usually do, to be very high above our hemisphere but rather very near. As the sun set and night came on, this star did not seem to me or to many other friars who were watching it to move from one place. At length, when night had come, this big star, to the amazement of all of us who were watching, broke into many different rays and, as it shed these rays over Paris toward the east, totally disappeared and was completely annihilated. Whether it was a comet or not, whether it was composed of airy exhalations and was finally resolved into vapor, I leave to the decision of astronomers. It is, however, possible that it was a presage of the amazing pestilence to come, which, in fact, followed very shortly in Paris and throughout France and elsewhere, as I shall tell. All this year and the next, the mortality of men and women, of the young even more than of the old, in Paris and in the kingdom of France, and also, it is said, in other parts of the world, was so great that it was almost impossible to bury the dead. People lay ill little more than two or three days and died suddenly, as it were in full health. He who was well one day was dead the next and being carried to his grave. Swellings appeared suddenly in the armpit or in the groin—in many cases both—and they were infallible signs of death. This sickness or pestilence was called an epidemic by the doctors. Nothing like the great numbers who died in the years 1348 and 1349 has been heard of or seen or read of in times past. This plague and disease came from *ymaginatione* or association and contagion, for if a well man visited the sick he only rarely evaded the risk of death. Wherefore in many towns timid priests withdrew, leaving the exercise of their ministry to such of the religious as were more daring. In many places not two out of twenty remained alive. So high was the mortality at the Hôtel-Dieu in Paris that for a long time, more than five hundred dead were carried daily with great devotion in carts to the cemetery of the Holy Innocents in Paris for burial. A very great number of the saintly sisters of the Hôtel-Dieu who, not fearing to die, nursed the sick in all sweetness and humility, with no thought of honor, a number too often renewed by death, rest in peace with Christ, as we may piously believe.

This plague, it is said, began among the unbelievers, came to Italy, and then crossing the Alps reached Avignon, where it attacked several cardinals and took from them their whole household. Then it spread, unforeseen, to France, through Gascony and Spain, little by little, from town to town, from village to village, from house to house, and finally from person to person. It even crossed over to Germany, though it was not so bad there as with us. During the epidemic, God of His accustomed goodness deigned to grant this grace, that however suddenly men died, almost all awaited death joyfully. Nor was there anyone who died without confessing his sins and receiving the holy viaticum. To the even greater benefit of the dying, Pope Clement VI through their confessors mercifully gave and granted absolution from penalty to the dying in many cities and fortified towns. Men died the more willingly for this and left many inheritances and temporal goods to churches and monastic orders, for in many cases they had seen their close heirs and children die before them.

Some said that this pestilence was caused by infection of the air and waters, since there was at this time no famine nor lack of food supplies, but on the contrary great abundance. As a result of this theory of infected water and air as the source of the plague the Jews were suddenly and violently charged with infecting wells and water and corrupting the air. The whole world rose up against them cruelly on this account. In Germany and other parts of the world where Jews lived, they were massacred and slaughtered by Christians, and many thousands were burned everywhere, indiscriminately. The unshaken, if fatuous, constancy of the men and their wives was remarkable. For mothers hurled their children first into the fire that they might not be baptized and then leaped in after them to burn with their husbands and children. It is said that many bad Christians were found who in a like manner put poison into wells. But in truth, such poisonings, granted that they actually were perpetrated, could not have caused so great a plague nor have infected so many people. There were other causes; for example, the will of God and the corrupt humors and evil inherent in air and earth. Perhaps the poisonings, if they actually took place in some localities, reenforced these causes. The plague lasted in France for the greater part of the years 1348 and 1349 and then ceased. Many country villages and many houses in good towns remained empty and deserted. Many houses, including some splendid dwellings, very soon fell into ruins. Even in Paris several houses were thus ruined, though fewer here than elsewhere.

After the cessation of the epidemic, pestilence, or plague, the men and women who survived married each other. There was no sterility among the women, but on the contrary fertility beyond the ordinary. Pregnant women were seen on every side. Many twins were born and even three children at once. But the most surprising fact is that children born after the plague, when they became of an age for teeth, had only twenty or twenty-two teeth, though before that time men commonly had thirty-two in the upper and lower jaws together. What this diminution in the number of teeth signified I wonder greatly, unless it be a new era resulting from the destruction of one human generation by the plague and its replacement by another. But woe is me! the world was not changed for the better but for the worse by this renewal of population. For men were more avaricious and grasping than before, even though they had far greater possessions. They were more covetous and disturbed each other more frequently with suits, brawls, disputes, and pleas. Nor by the mortality resulting from this terrible plague inflicted by God was peace between kings and lords established. On the contrary, the enemies of the king of France and of the Church were stronger and wickeder than before and stirred up wars on sea and on land. Greater evils than before pullulated everywhere in the world. And this fact was very remarkable. Although there was an abundance of all goods, yet everything was twice as dear, whether it were utensils, victuals, or merchandise, hired helpers or peasants and serfs, except for some hereditary domains which remained abundantly stocked with everything. Charity began to cool, and iniquity with ignorance and sin to abound, for few could be found in the good towns and castles who knew how or were willing to instruct children in the rudiments of grammar.

In the same year, 1348, Blessed Yves Hellory of Brittany, priest and confessor of wonderful virtue and grace, was canonized by the Church and Pope Clement VI. The following year his body was raised from the ground by the prelates and the clergy of Brittany, and many signs and wonders were then wrought through him and by God on his account. At that time also the church under his invocation in the street of Saint Jacques of Paris was first begun and the foundations laid. How his virtues and sanctity flourished is clearly declared in the church at Tréguier in Brittany, where his body rests.

1349

In the year 1349, while the plague was still active and spreading from town to town, men in Germany, Flanders, Hainaut, and Lorraine uprose and began a new sect on their own authority. Stripped to the waist, they gathered in large groups and bands and marched in procession through the crossroads and squares of cities and good towns. There they formed circles and beat upon their backs with weighted scourges, rejoicing as they did so in loud voices and singing hymns suitable to their rite and newly composed for it. Thus for thirty-three days they marched through many towns doing their penance and affording a great spectacle to the wondering people.

They flogged their shoulders and arms with scourges tipped with iron points so zealously as to draw blood. But they did not come to Paris nor to any part of France, for they were forbidden to do so by the king of France, who did not want them. He acted on the advice of the masters of theology of the University of Paris, who said that this new sect had been formed contrary to the will of God, to the rites of Holy Mother Church, and to the salvation of all their souls. That indeed this was and is true appeared shortly. For Pope Clement VI was fully informed concerning this fatuous new rite by the masters of Paris through emissaries reverently sent to him and, on the grounds that it had been damnably formed, contrary to law, he forbade the Flagellants under threat of anathema to practise in the future the public penance which they had so presumptuously undertaken. His prohibition was just, for the Flagellants, supported by certain fatuous priests and monks, were enunciating doctrines and opinions which were beyond measure evil, erroneous, and fallacious. For example, they said that their blood thus drawn by the scourge and poured out was mingled with the blood of Christ. Their many errors showed how little they knew of the Catholic faith. Wherefore, as they had begun fatuously of themselves and not of God, so in a short time they were reduced to nothing. On being warned, they desisted and humbly received absolution and penance at the hands of their prelates as the pope's representatives. Many honorable women and devout matrons, it must be added, had done this penance with scourges, marching and singing through towns and churches like the men, but after a little like the others they desisted.

72. Depopulation and Its Effects in Burgundy and Bordeaux (1360s)

1361

We make known to all, now and hereafter, that the inhabitants of our town of Buxeaul in Burgundy have declared to us that they owe us tax, from all alike, and willingly, twice a year, that is, at Saint Rémy and at the beginning of Lent, and they owe us ploughing, certain *corvées* and other dues. It happens that the said inhabitants are for the most part diminished in numbers because of the plague caused by the massacre, which has occurred in parts of this area; for before this massacre, there were 50–60 households

From Georges Duby, *Rural Economy and Country Life in the Medieval West*, translated by Cynthia Postan (Columbia, S.C.: University of South Carolina Press, 1968), pp. 523–25. © 1968 by Edward Arnold, Ltd. Reprinted by permission of the University of South Carolina Press and Edward Arnold, Ltd.

and more in the said town, while now there are no more than about 10. Nevertheless they have paid, and would like to pay, as large a tax as they did before the said massacre; which thing they could neither do nor support, but would have to flee and leave the place, and become poor beggars. They have thus humbly begged us to spare them these things, especially as through wars they have been pillaged and ruined by our enemies, in such a way that little or nothing remains to them, wherefore some of the said inhabitants have left the place and are still leaving from day to day. And thus those who have remained would not be able to pay the said taxes and other dues, unless they are spared by our favour. We, in consideration and regard to the above-mentioned things, and because the said town is much damaged, and a great part of its buildings ruined by inhabitants or beggars leaving them, and also so that those from the said place who have left on account of the heavy burden of the taxes and other above-mentioned dues, may return to live there, we, in our joyful accession in Burgundy, have granted and grant to the said inhabitants, for them, their heirs, and the succeeding inhabitants of the said town, in certain knowledge, full power and special favour, by these present, that the said 2 taxes, paid each year at the time of Saint-Rémy and the beginning of Lent, should be made into one tax, which will in future be paid at the time of Saint-Rémy only, and that the said inhabitants shall not be taxed except according to their means which they have or will have at the time they are taxed, and not in accordance with previous taxes if their means do not run to it. And moreover, in addition to our said favour, we have freed them and do free them forever, and their heirs and succeeding inhabitants of the said town, from the heriot we have over them and their possessions, in case of heriot of inheritance when it is due to us, by nevertheless paying the rents and dues that they owe us each year. We issue a mandate by these letters, to our castellan of Aisy, and to all the Justiciaries and officers of our Duchy of Burgundy, present and hereafter, or to their Lieutenants, and to each of those as it is fitting, which our present Ordinance, grant and favour accomplish and maintain: to allow and suffer the said inhabitants, their heirs and succeeding inhabitants henceforth to enjoy and use in peace these rights; and may the terms of our said Ordinance, favour and grant, not hinder, molest or constrain them; nor cause them to be hindered, molested or constrained in any way; but if anything be done to the contrary, they should report or cause it to be reported in a proper statement without any delay. And so this may be a firm and fixed thing for ever, we have had our seal appended to these letters. This was done in the said town of Buxeaul, the year of grace 1361, in the month of February.

3 February 1365

Let it be known that the honourable lord official of Bordeaux has received the instance, supplication and request of the procuror and syndic of the honourable and discreet lords, dean and chapter of the Church of St. Andrew of Bordeaux, who have reported the following facts. There were tenants who had, and held in fief, at the time they were living certain houses in the place called "St. Julian's" near Bordeaux, for which they were bound to pay annually certain rents, at certain times, contained and specified in the rolls and registers of St. Andrew's church, and furthermore certain fines for recognition of transfer. The tenants are dead and none of their heirs nor any other person, to whom the houses belonged or ought to belong, has come or presented themselves before the lords, dean and chapter, have informed them of their rights, or paid the rents due for these properties, and this during the space of twenty years and more; and the houses have been reduced to—and are still—in the state of deserted and abandoned sites, to the great prejudice and damage of the said church and the lords of the chapter. And the latter have not known the heirs nor the property holders of these tenements, nor known if there were any or not.

And upon this, the procuror and syndic of the lords has prayed, required and supplicated the lord official of Bordeaux to be so good as to award the rents and the arrears of these sites, and this in order that the lords dean and chapter may dispose of them. The official has made proclamations, announcements and public and peremptory callings in the largest church and in the fifteen parochial chapels of Bordeaux, once, twice, thrice and a fourth time additionally, and after three defaults, announcing what follows: if any person or persons exist to whom these sites belong or ought to belong in whole or in part as heirs of the deceased, or who believe themselves to have a right to them through succession, purchase, infeodation, gift, obligation, mortgage, or for any other cause, let them come and appear, at the days and hours fixed by the said public proclamation before the lord official of Bordeaux, at the instance of the procuror and syndic above mentioned, to inform him of their rights, pay to the lords, dean and chapter the rents and relief, arrears, and other rights due for the sites and recognition of them; if not the lord official of Bordeaux will award these sites by default to the lords, dean and chapter and to their church, as being their lords of fief, will authorize them to dispose of them, and will impose a perpetual silence on these suits to the non-appearers despite their absence.

At the days and hours contained and set out in the public announcements, nobody has appeared except the procuror and syndic; and the lord official of Bordeaux has awarded these sites to the lords, dean and chapter and has given to them and drawn up licence and authority to dispose of them to the profit and utility of their church. All these clauses, at the same time as several others, I, the notary below named, have seen and read that they were fully contained in the public announcements given by the lord official on the questions, and especially in a memorandum of the last judgment by default, containing the award of the sites and the sentence, of which the date is as follows: given at Bordeaux, the Wednesday after the feast of the conversion of St. Paul, 29th January of the year of Our Lord indicated below.

Thus, let it be known that the lords of the chapter of St. Andrew's church at Bordeaux — the dean of the said church being absent — have given in fief feudally and by new title of fief, according to the tribunals and customs of the Bordeaux district, both to Arnold de Longueville, of the parish of St. Eulalie of Bordeaux, and to Aliande, his wife, absent, all that piece of ground where there is a site and a half, which is outside the gate of St. Julian. Arnold de Longueville has been invested by the honourable and discreet lord, Master Bertrand Bonaffos, canon of the said St. Andrew's church, and the same Master Bertrand Bonaffos has feudally invested him against 5s. of the current money at Bordeaux as fine for recognition of transfer and 22s. 6d. of the said current money of Bordeaux of annual rent brought to Bordeaux the day of the feast of the Purification of Our Lady, the Virgin.

73. The Peasants' Revolt, England (1381)

Pleas in the Isle of Ely before the justices appointed in the county of Cambridge to punish and chastise insurgents and their misdeeds, on Thursday next before the feast of St. Margaret the Virgin,[1] 5 Richard II.

Inquisition taken there on the said Thursday by the oath of John Baker[2] . . . who say on their oath that Richard de Leycestre of Ely on Saturday next after the feast of Corpus Christi in the 4th year of the Lord the King that now is, of his own will made insurrection, gathering to himself John Buk of Ely and many other evildoers unknown, and went through the whole town of Ely, commanding that all men, of whatsoever estate, should make insurrection and go with him to destroy divers traitors whom he would name to them on behalf of the lord King Richard and the faithful commons; and hereupon he made divers proclamations seditiously and to the prejudice of the lord the King, whereby the people of the same town of Ely and other townships of the isle aforesaid were greatly disturbed and

From *English Economic History. Select Documents*, edited by A. E. Bland, P. A. Brown, R. H. Tawney (London: Bell and Hyman, 1941), pp. 105–10.

1. July 20.   2. And eleven others.

injured. Further they say that the same Richard [de Leycestre] on Sunday following commanded John Shethere of Ely, Elias Glovere, John Dassh, skinner, John Tylneye, wright, and John Redere of Ely, Thomas Litstere of Ely, Richard Swonn of Ely and John Milnere of Ely and many others of the commons there assembled, that they should go with him to the monastery of Ely to stand with him, while he, in the pulpit of the same monastery, should declare to them and all others the matters to be performed on behalf of King Richard and the commons against traitors and other disloyal men, and this under pain of the burning of their houses and the taking off of their heads; and so the same Richard [de Leycestre] was a notorious leader and assembler feloniously, and committed all the aforesaid acts to the prejudice of the crown of the lord the King. Further they say that the same Richard on Monday next following at Ely, as principal leader and insurgent, with the aforesaid men above named and many others unknown of his fellowship, feloniously broke the prison of the lord Bishop of Ely at Ely and feloniously led away divers felons there imprisoned.

And that the same Richard on the said Monday at Ely feloniously adjudged to death Edmund de Walsyngham, one of the justices of the peace of the lord the King in the county of Cambridge, whereby the said Edmund was then feloniously beheaded and his head set on the pillory there, the same being a pernicious example. And that the same Richard was the principal commander and leader in all the felonies, seditions and other misdeeds committed within the isle at the time aforesaid, etc.

And hereupon the aforesaid Richard was taken by the justices aforesaid and afterwards brought before them and charged and diligently examined touching all the felonies and seditions aforesaid, article by article, in what manner he would acquit himself thereof; and he made no answer thereto but proffered a protection of the lord the King granted to him for the security of his person and his possessions to endure for one year according to the form and effect used in the Chancery of the lord the King; and he says that he does not intend to be annoyed or disquieted touching any presentments made against him by the justices, by virtue of the protection aforesaid, etc. And the aforesaid Richard was asked if he would make any other answer to the premises under the peril incumbent, in that the protection aforesaid is insufficient to acquit him of the premises or of any article of the same. And hereupon the same Richard made no further denial of any of the premises presented against him, but said, "I cannot make further answer, and I hold myself convicted." And because it is clear and plain enough to the aforesaid justices that the same Richard is guilty of all the felonies and seditions aforesaid, as has been found before the same justices in lawful manner, therefore by the discretion of the said justices he was drawn and hanged the same day and year, etc., and [it was adjudged] that his lands and tenements, goods and chattels, should be forfeit to the lord the King, as law requires. And order was made to Ralph atte Wyk, escheator of the lord the King, that he should make due execution thereof forthwith for the lord the King, etc. And it is to be known that it was found before the aforesaid justices that the same Richard has a shop in "le Bocherie" in Ely, which is worth yearly beyond reprises 10s., and chattels to the value of 40 marks, which the same Ralph seized forthwith, etc.

Further the aforesaid jurors say that John Buk of Ely was a fellow of the aforesaid Richard Leycestre all the time of the insurrection and tumult at Ely in the accomplishing of all the felonies, treasons and misdeeds, whereof the said Richard was indicted. And specially that the same John, of his malice, at the time when Edmund de Walsyngham was adjudged to death, feloniously came to him and feloniously snatched a purse of Edmund attached to his tunic containing 42 1/2 d., and violently assaulted the said Edmund, dragging him to the place of his beheading, and carried away the said money except 12d. thereof which he gave to John Deye of Willingham, who there feloniously beheaded Edmund, for his labour. And hereupon the aforesaid John Buk was taken and charged touching the premises article by article, in what manner he will make answer thereto or acquit himself. And he says that as to all the matters touching Edmund de Walsyngham whereof he is charged, he came with many others to see the end of the said Edmund and to hear the cause of his death, and not otherwise, and this by the command of divers of the said commons. And he was asked further by whose command he came there and snatched the purse with the money aforesaid from the said Edmund in the form aforesaid, and he said that he believes it was by command of the devil. And he confessed further how and in what manner he dealt with the aforesaid purse with the money aforesaid, as was found above. And to all other presentments made against him he made no further answer. And because it is clear and plain enough, as well by his own acknowledgment as by lawful finding otherwise, that the same John is guilty of all the felonies and treasons aforesaid, therefore by the discretion of the said justices he was drawn and hanged, etc.; and [it was adjudged] that his lands and tenements, goods and chattels, should be forfeit to the lord the King, as law requires. And order was made to Ralph atte Wyk, escheator of the lord the King, that he should make due execution thereof forthwith for the lord the King, etc., because it was found before the aforesaid justices that he has goods and chattels to the value of 20l., which the same Ralph seized forthwith and made further execution, etc.

Ely

Adam Clymme was taken as an insurgent traitorously against his allegiance, and because on Saturday next after the feast of Corpus Christi in the 4th year of the reign of King Richard the second after the Conquest, he traitorously with others made insurrection at Ely, feloniously broke and entered the close of Thomas Somenour and there took and carried away divers rolls, estreats of the green wax of the lord the King and the Bishop of Ely, and other muniments touching the Court of the lord the King, and forthwith caused them to be burned there to the prejudice of the crown of the lord the King.

Further that the same Adam on Sunday and Monday next following caused to be proclaimed there that no man of law or other officer in the execution of duty should escape without beheading.

Further that the same Adam the day and year aforesaid at the time of the insurrection was always wandering armed with arms displayed, bearing a standard, to assemble insurgents, commanding that no man of whatsoever condition he were, free or bond, should obey his lord to do any services or customs, under pain of beheading, otherwise than he should declare to them on behalf of the Great Fellowship. And so he traitorously took upon him royal power. And he came, brought by the sheriff, and was charged before the aforesaid justices touching the premises, in what manner he would acquit himself thereof. And he says that he is not guilty of the premises imputed to him or of any of the premises, and hereof puts himself on the country, etc. And forthwith a jury is made thereon for the lord the King by twelve [good and lawful men] etc., who being chosen hereto, tried and sworn, say on their oath that the aforesaid Adam is guilty of all the articles. By the discretion of the justices the same Adam is drawn and hanged, etc. And it was found there that the same Adam has in the town aforesaid chattels to the value of 32*s.*, which Ralph atte Wyk, escheator of the lord the King, seized forthwith and made further execution for the lord the King, etc.

Cambridge

John Shirle of the county of Nottingham was taken because it was found that he was a vagabond in divers counties the whole time of the disturbance, insurrection and tumult, carrying lies and worthless talk from district to district whereby the peace of the lord the King could be speedily broken and the people disquieted and disturbed; and among other dangerous words, to wit, after the proclamation of the peace of the lord the King made the day and year aforesaid, the assigns[3] of the lord the King being in the town and sitting, he said in a tavern in Bridge Street, Cambridge, where many were assembled to listen to his news and worthless talk, that the stewards of the lord the King, the justices and many other officers and ministers of the King were more worthy to be drawn and hanged and to

3. I.e., the justices assigned.

suffer other lawful pains and torments, than John Balle, chaplain, a traitor and felon lawfully convicted; for he said that he was condemned to death falsely, unjustly and for envy by the said ministers with the King's assent, because he was a true and good man, prophesying things useful to the commons of the realm and telling of wrongs and oppressions done to the people by the King and the ministers aforesaid; and his death shall not go unpunished but within a short space he would well reward both the King and his officers and ministers aforesaid; which sayings and threats redound to the prejudice of the crown of the lord the King and the contempt and manifest disquiet of the people. And hereupon the aforesaid John Shirle was brought forthwith by the sheriff before the aforesaid assigns in Cambridge castle, and was charged touching the premises and diligently examined as well touching his conversation as touching his tarrying and his estate, and the same being acknowledged by him before the aforesaid assigns, his evil behaviour and condition is plainly manifest and clear. And hereupon trustworthy witnesses at that time in his presence, when the aforesaid lies, evil words, threats and worthless talk were spoken by him, were asked for, and they being sworn to speak the truth in this behalf, testify that all the aforesaid words imputed to him were truly spoken by him; and he, again examined, did not deny the premises imputed to him. Therefore by the discretion of the said assigns he was hanged; and order was made to the escheator to enquire diligently of his lands and tenements, goods and chattels, and to make due execution thereof for the lord the King.

Index